Worshipper and Worshipped

'Is it any wonder that he was welcome in every mess, that the men worshipped the ground he trod on . . .'

16th (Irish) Division sentiment

Dedicated to the memory of the Irishmen who were 'over there'.

'Fr Doyle was a good deal amongst us. We couldn't possibly agree with his religious opinions, but we simply worshipped him for other things.'

36th (Ulster) Division sentiment

WORSHIPPER AND WORSHIPPED

Across the Divide – An Irish Padre of the Great War
Fr Willie Doyle Chaplain to the Forces 1915–1917

Carole Hope

Reveille
PRESS

Reveille Press is an imprint of
Tommies Guides Military Booksellers & Publishers

Gemini House
136–140 Old Shoreham Road
Brighton
BN3 7BD

www.tommiesguides.co.uk

First published in Great Britain by
Reveille Press 2013
Second Revised Edition, 2016

For more information please visit
www.reveillepress.com

© 2013 Carole Hope

A catalogue record for this book is available
from the British Library

All rights reserved. Apart from any use under UK copyright
law no part of this publication may be reproduced, stored in a retrieval system, or
transmitted, in any form or by any means, without prior written permission of the
publisher, nor be otherwise circulated in any form of binding or cover other than
that in which it is published and without a similar condition being
imposed on the subsequent publisher.

ISBN 978-1-908336-86-6 (PB)
ISBN 978-1-908336-92-7 (HB)

Cover design by Reveille Press

Printed and bound in Great Britain

Also commemorating my maternal great-uncle, Private (acting Lance Corporal) John Alfred Ebdon, 9th Battalion York & Lancaster Regiment, who perished on 1 October 1917 during the Battle of the Menin Road, whose body was not recovered; his name appears on the memorial to the missing at Tyne Cot, not far from Fr Willie's.

Contents

Acknowledgements 7
About this Biography 10
Chronology of Fr Doyle's Life 17
Glossary 22
Structure of BEF 24
List of Maps 25
Prologue 26
Plate Section .... i–xv

PART 1: Victorian Beginnings – and Contemplating a New Century 29
Chapter 1: Birth and Background: First experience under fire! 30
Chapter 2: Childhood and Youth: Songs, stilts, stunts and sports 44
Chapter 3: Schooldays: General Blue 53
Chapter 4: Novice: Man proposes and God disposes 60
Chapter 5: Colleges: Mr Doyle becomes Fr Doyle 66
Chapter 6: Apprentice Again: Marches and retreats 87
Chapter 7: Missions and Retreats: 'Weary-Wobblers and Whole-Hoggers' 106
Chapter 8: Willie Volunteers: War brewing, war boiling 128
Chapter 9: On the Cusp: Lord Kitchener points his finger 144

PART 2: Industrial Warfare 163
Chapter 10: About Chaplains: Padres, not officers 164
Chapter 11: The Novice Chaplain Arrives: With Faughs and Skins ... 176
Chapter 12: Finding his Feet: Amongst fosses and crassiers 186
Chapter 13: Difficulties and Opportunities: Loose ends 206
Chapter 14: Scribblings from the Front: Loose information 216
Chapter 15: Gas Attack: Gallantry and devotion 240
Chapter 16: Bad Gas Discipline: Mention in Dispatches 258
Chapter 17: Easter Rising: 'Was it needless death after all?' 273
Chapter 18: Trips and Raids: Moving along the line 285
Chapter 19: From Loos to the Somme: Dead man talking 313

Chapter 20: Guillemont and Ginchy: Dead man walking 330
Chapter 21: Not much rest with the Devils: Dawn breaking 358
Chapter 22: Transferred to the 'Dubs': A Catholic chaplain's cheery chat...... 378
Chapter 23: Pork and Beans: And Maconochie rations! 406
Chapter 24: Rehearsing Plumer's Plan: Aided by Gabriel....................... 436
Chapter 25: Approaching the Battle of Messines: 'What Ho! She bumps!'..... 466
Chapter 26: The Battle for the Ridge: Bite and Hold! 490
Chapter 27: Peaceful Days in the Pas de Calais: And a Tale of Two Williams . 524
Chapter 28: Interlude: Bits and Scraps for an Old Man's breakfast 544
Chapter 29: The Start of Another Battle: Third Ypres 556
Chapter 30: Fateful August: Muck, mud and mire................................ 577

PART 3: Finale – but not the End! 597

Chapter 31: The old Armchair: 'Everywhere and Always Faithful' 600
Chapter 32: Lost at Ypres: The Confounding Circumstances of
    Fr Willie's Death.. 615
Chapter 33: Aftermath: 'Cast aside like old shoes'................................ 625
Chapter 34: VC or no VC?: That is a good question!............................. 636
Chapter 35: Mopping Up: 1918-2013.. 663

Appendix A: Major General William Hickie's letter to Brigadier
    General H.F. Kays, dated 18 November 1917 684

Appendix B: Tributes.. 686

Appendix C: The curious case of Fanny Cranbush 697

References... 701
Bibliography 714
Picture Credits & Permissions 724
Index 726

Acknowledgements

'I will already have embarked on the next stage of my life's journey, my journey in faith, travelling in the sure and certain hope that I will, at last, stand before Him who made me, in that place that is forever light.'
Brian William Pearce, Monday 5 April 1948 to Tuesday 19 March 2013

Thanks is an insufficient word to record my debt of gratitude to the late Brian Pearce for reviewing most of my manuscript. He intercepted several 'faux pas' with regard to Roman Catholicism and contributed many useful suggestions, and some blocks of text, on both religious and military issues. He also corrected my grammar, although he had no control over my revisions once he had done his bit! I had planned this thank you to him to follow the dedications to those who are no longer with us. Sadly for those left behind, Brian suddenly departed this world far too early, joining our mutual friend Michael O'Rahilly (9 July 1931 to 28 July 2012) who told me about the Irish involvement in the Great War and who worked tirelessly to raise awareness of that contribution. Thank you to Michael for your inspiration. It was a privilege to know those two gentlemen, Brian and Michael.

Two other personal commemorations: my lovely mum, Joan Cooke (16 July 1930 – 2 November 2009) and my best friend Hazel Atkins (21 August 1957 to 21 May 2004) both of whom would have been very proud of this book no matter what the critics may think!

Very many thanks are also due to the following:

Firstly, to Andrew Tonge for giving me his copy of Professor O'Rahilly's biography; also for sharing his military expertise and his extensive library, and for his persistence in tracking down Frank Laird's *Personal Experiences of the Great War*. But thanks most of all for his unfailing love, support and patience.

Cliché or not, this has been a journey for me and heartfelt thanks to Keith Hope for supporting me at the start and during the early years of the project, and for his continued interest and encouragement, along with that of the rest of our family.

Thank you to Hugh, Alice and Mark Cumisky for welcoming me into their home, for allowing me to photograph and make use of their archive, for their congenial company and for sharing stories of Fr Willie. Without their contribution this biography would have told less than the fullest story possible about Fr Willie's military career.

Very many thanks to Pat Kenny, who is always on call to respond to my queries; for his *Remembering Father William Doyle* website; for being a friend in Dublin, and for helping me to make useful contacts in Ireland. Two of these were Keith and Kate Hammond and thanks to them for welcoming me into their home and sharing stories of Fr Willie.

Thank you to Adrian Field for researching Paul Smith, and for his words of encouragement.

Thank you to Dominiek Dendooven who always extends a friendly welcome at the *In Flanders Fields Museum*, Ieper and for his prompt informative responses to email enquiries. Thanks are also due to Caroline Mullen for welcoming me to Blackrock College archives and taking time out of her busy schedule to look up files and make suggestions. Similarly, I was warmly welcomed by Margaret Doyle, the archivist of Clongowes Wood College, together with Fr Bernard McGuckian, S.J., and their colleagues there. Oliver Murphy at Belvedere College provided a key piece of information which helped me track down Fr Willie's descendants; so many thanks are due to him also.

David Blake, curator at Museum of Army Chaplaincy welcomed me as a visitor at the beginning of this project and has responded quickly to email enquiries since. The staff at the National Archives at Kew were very co-operative in allowing me access to War Office war diaries, at a time when they had been withdrawn from the Reading Room in order to be digitalised. Thanks to staff at the National Library of Ireland for introducing me to the fascinating reference source, Thoms Directory.

Thanks to Jack Sheldon for providing me with information and translation from *Das K.B.9 Infanterie – Regiment 'Wrede'*.

Not forgetting, of course, Ryan Gearing, Reveille Press and the Western Front Association for making this publication possible.

About this Biography

'In looking at his photograph I see the face of a man with a broad, high forehead, the sweetest, kindest smile, a face without guile, the soul of sincerity and kindness. He was born to puzzle the world, and we must place him in a niche among great men.' [1]

Dowanhill Training College Magazine, January 1923, page 47

Fr Willie Doyle's life story has been told before. I started writing this new biography for reasons I don't entirely understand myself; only that Willie Doyle has 'got under my skin'.

This is a story of a remarkable man; a man who would have objected to that adjective. A man who believed that all people he came into contact with - friend or foe, Catholic or Protestant, Irish or otherwise - were human beings in need of spiritual aid. He reached across the divide on many levels; religious, national and social.

Whilst I have been diligent in my research and in checking my references, I make no pretence to this being a work of scholarship. It is simply my telling of the story of a historical character and his interaction with the people and events of his era. An era which spanned two centuries, three monarchs and two vastly different worlds; one man who passed from a gently glowing gas-lit Victorian childhood into a new electric century, before encountering a thunderous epoch where mass production and deployment of munitions was a reality of his adulthood.

Fr Doyle's life as a military chaplain was bound up with the stories of the officers and men he served with, particularly as he was one of those chaplains who insisted in accompanying his flock as far forward as he could get away with. Therefore, I have included detail and experiences of as many of those men of 16th (Irish) Division as I was able, and yet more others who were faced with similar occurences. In reality this could only ever skim the surface but I felt it worth doing, even though received wisdom says that such a resulting 'big' book should not work.

Fr Willie was not an obvious candidate to be found serving in the British army, having been born and brought up in a prosperous Catholic family in County Dublin before entering the Society of Jesus. Despite having an English grandmother,

ABOUT THIS BIOGRAPHY

and both his father and an older brother pursued careers working for Her/His Majestys' governments, Willie was Irish to the core. As a young child Willie was fond of playing soldiers; at seven years old he was the proud owner of a home-made soldier's tunic, complete with battle stripes and cap. But the mock battles he engaged in with his tin soldiers were fought for Ireland, versus the armies of his brother Charlie, who took the cause of Grandmamma's England. Charlie observed:

> *His love to be a soldier even from his babyhood was wonderful – to fight for Ireland.*[2]

Willie Doyle's first biographer, Professor Alfred O'Rahilly, stated:

> *Though he was human and social as well as many-sided in his interests, the central realities of his life were God and his own soul. God was to him no distant creator or far off Judge, He was an ever-present companion whose voice he could not mistake, to whom he always turned ... The latter portion of this memoir recounts Fr. Doyle's experiences as a Military Chaplain. It has been compiled almost entirely from the letters or budgets which he used to send home to be perused by his relatives and intimate friends, without the slightest thought of publication. In including these interesting letters from the Front, it has not been my intention, any more than it was the writers, to make another addition to 'war literature'.*[3]

Professor O'Rahilly may not have written his biography, first published in February 1920, with any intention of contributing to war literature, but that was an unwitting consequence. Many excerpts of Willie's career as a Chaplain to the Forces, taken from O'Rahilly's work, have been included in accounts of the Great War.

Whilst their faith may have been both Willie Doyle's and Alfred O'Rahilly's central reality and therefore the raison d'etre for the first biography, I am drawn as much to the other aspects of Willie's life. Although I have tried to paint a picture of his faith, and the struggles he had with his expression of it, which informed his daily existence, I leave the detailed commentary of Willie's spiritual inner life to Professor O'Rahilly whose book, *Father William Doyle, S.J., A Spiritual Study*, is still available.

Where I quote from O'Rahilly, I have no means of verifying the context; hence

I have used the material sparingly. Professor O'Rahilly often does not give a date, rarely names the correspondent or uses the full text. Moreover, although the biography is chronological to a degree, many of the quotes are grouped thematically and omit large chunks of Fr Doyle's letters written from the Western Front.

The main sources for my biography are some of the personal letters and diaries written by Willie Doyle, of which I would guess there were hundreds of letters alone. I have only used a small proportion of the pre-war material; whereas I have reproduced almost word for word the letters Willie wrote from the Western Front to his father during the war.

Although I have had access to some of the original hand-written documents, most of the material comes from typed transcripts held by Willie's descendants in Ireland. It seems that as Willie's war-time letters arrived, his sister Lena would transcribe them. This facilitated both easier reading for their octogenarian father, Hugh Doyle, and also provided an extra copy to be circulated. Unfortunately, we only have Willie's side of the correspondence.

The bulk of the original hand-written material, spanning all of Willie's adult life, including diaries as well as letters retrieved from friends and family, was given to Professor Alfred O'Rahilly to write his biography. Therefore, some of my quotes are taken either from the O'Rahilly biography, or from another work first published in the 1930's *Merry in God, A Life of Father William Doyle, S.J.*, which was published by Roman Catholic Books and does not acknowledge an author. Some of it has quite obviously been lifted from the O'Rahilly biography, as stated in the Foreword, but there is plenty of other material which O'Rahilly does not cover. The book must have been compiled by Willie's brother, Fr Charles Doyle, S.J., which becomes obvious when reading it, and it is also the belief of the family in Ireland that Charles was the author. Charles includes many anecdotes, particularly from his childhood, which are not covered by O'Rahilly.

Charles Doyle steers clear of judgemental issues in *Merry in God*, although he is clearly, and quite naturally, biased in his high opinion of Willie:

> *This book is intended mainly for young people, or for old people who are young. In simple words it tells of one whose story has already gone forth and gone straight to many hearts in many lands, and won their admiration and affection. It makes little attempt to analyse or explain the spiritual ideals and practices of its hero.*[4]

ABOUT THIS BIOGRAPHY

Reading *Merry in God* I felt the deep, abiding love Charlie and Willie had for each other, from being inseparable childhood companions, to adults who kept in close contact as often as they could manage, even if only by letter. This was confirmed by the brothers' great-nephew, whom I have visited at his home in Ireland.

From an early age Willie exuded an exuberance of spirit which touched all who came into contact with him. His new brother-in-law, Frank Whelan, declared the teenaged Willie to be: *'the nicest schoolboy he had ever met'*.[5] Maybe some of Charlie's memoirs had meat added to the bone from a distance of time, maybe he is over-effusive at times, but my instinct is that they are largely accurate recollections. For example, when Charlie recalls Willie being a gifted and natural teacher at Clongowes Wood College, I think it unlikely that he would have witnessed a lesson in progress. However, I confidently assume that he based his assertion on the testimony of at least one of Willie's former pupils.

Memoirs from those who paid tribute to Willie after his death may be subject to small inaccuracies or ambiguities, through the passing of time playing tricks on the memory. For example, the man who remembers being a schoolboy when Mr Doyle was his Third Line prefect at Clongowes Wood College, states that the boys ranged from ten to fifteen years, when in fact the younger boys would have been First or Second Line.

I have quoted extensively from memoirs of the Great War, several of which were written by Irishmen, and the earlier comment about 'meat and bone' may apply, along with the fact that they would have been unaware of the 'bigger picture' during their service. However, what is indisputable is that the writers were there and their voices are an expression of their times.

The two earlier biographies would not have been written, or certainly not in so much detail, had Willie Doyle's wishes been carried out. After Willie's death during the Third Battle of Ypres, Charles Doyle went to the Jesuit Province at Rathfarnham, County Dublin where Willie had been working before taking up his post as a Chaplain to the Forces. He had been asked to go through Willie's papers and belongings and to take anything he wished. In addition, two of Willie's penitents had already been in touch with Charlie to ask him to retrieve their letters. One wanted them returned and the other requested they be burnt. On a shelf Charlie found several piles of letters, diaries, notebooks and other manuscripts with a note lying on top, on which was written: *'To be burned should anything happen to me'*.[6]

Charlie recovered the penitents' letters to carry out their wishes, but was left with a dilemma as to what to do with the remainder of the papers. Instinctively, he did not wish to burn them, but such was Willie's request. Charlie sought the advice of the Superior of Rathfarnham, Fr J. Brennan, S.J. and they both agreed that much of the documentation might in the future prove to be of great help and comfort to tortured souls. (Indeed, Fr Doyle's engaging personality masked his own deep, inner turmoil, much of which only came to light after his death, as revealed by these personal papers.) With some reluctance they concluded that Willie's wishes should be disregarded and the documents were preserved, later providing a rich source for the O'Rahilly biography.

In his introduction, Professor O'Rahilly relays the struggle Fr Charles Doyle and Fr Brennan had with their consciences on this matter. He also includes some quotes for and against their decision from reviews of the first edition of his book. Ironically, it may be that Willie's wish was eventually granted; his personal papers may have subsequently been burned in an accidental fire.

In addition to the papers that were handed to Alfred O'Rahilly, Charlie kept a small archive of his own which was added to after Willie's death, including some personal letters and prayer cards. I have been fortunate in being allowed access to the family's typed transcripts and some original hand-written documents, but the majority of Willie's original papers appear to have been retained by Professor O'Rahilly, whose belongings were ravaged by a fire at Blackrock College, County Dublin, where he spent the last years of his life in residence. There is a fire-damaged file of his papers in the college archives, amongst which is a letter from Mother Rosario Nesbitt, containing the following comment:

> *Now as to those old notes of yours and the paper, I have them quite safely in Bray, locked up with Fr. W. Doyle's ? letters.*[7]

Mother Rosario's letter was headed Loreto, Balbriggan (even though she refers to Fr Willie's letters being at Bray) and dated 4 August but the year is unclear. The word denoted by a ? is also illegible. Whether the letters were eventually returned by Mother Rosario to Professor O'Rahilly is not known and an enquiry to the former Loreto Convent at Bray, County Wicklow elicited no response.

Whilst there are singed letters addressed to O'Rahilly praising his biography of Fr Doyle in the Blackrock College file, there are no remnants of Willie's documents.

ABOUT THIS BIOGRAPHY

I have been unable to ascertain whether Willie's letters were consumed by the fire, or if they were in the possession of a person or persons unknown prior to the blaze at Blackrock College; but they are not in the possession of the family. I have made extensive enquiries, including at the Jesuit Archives in Dublin, to try and locate the original papers, all to no avail.

A note on my penultimate chapter, which explores the issue of why Fr Doyle was not awarded the Victoria Cross despite being recommended by Major General William Hickie. I hope it is clear that I do not mean any disrespect to those winners of the UK's highest award for gallantry in comparing some of their cases to that of Fr Doyle. I can state most emphatically this was not my intention. I hope the reader understands my reasoning for making a comparison to the three military chaplains who were awarded the Victoria Cross during the Great War, along with that of stretcher-bearer Room whose actions were commended for the same day Fr Doyle died. My rationale for including the case of the medical officer, Noel Chavasse, may not be immediately obvious, but I hope it will become clear as the reader progresses. I should point out that this author is well aware that Noel Chavasse was a very exceptional and brave man.

All my sources are listed in the bibliography at the end of this book. These include British War Office war diaries held at the National Archives at Kew, England; personal testimonies, military histories/memoirs and pertinent academic histories. I have used as wide a variety of sources as possible to back up Willie Doyle's accounts of his military service, and to try and foster in those readers who are not conversant with the Great War some small sense of understanding for the vastness of the subject matter. I am grateful that British Army Officers, such as Lieutenant Colonel S.T. Watson, and his counterpart G.W. Kenny, diligently wrote up, in legible hand-writing, detailed daily diaries of the battalions Willie Doyle was associated with. I have tried to weave together in a coherent fashion the strands of all the resources available to me, which I hope the reader will find as fascinating to read as it was for me to research and write, whilst acknowledging that it was not my intention to attempt a comprehensive account of the war.

My transcription of Willie Doyle's (mainly) handwritten letters from the Western Front is a second copy of what was transcribed by his sister Lena. I have, with the help of the late Brian Pearce, been as diligent in proof-reading as possible and I am sure the same can be said for Lena, but there are bound to be some errors. I have made minimal changes, only correcting obvious spelling mistakes or adding punctuation for extra clarity. I have also included many of the endearments Willie used to start and finish his letters. I have left all quotes from other sources unamended, apart from using 'sic' where appropriate.

Any errors or omissions are mine but unintended, and comments and corrections would be welcomed in the event that there is a future edition of this book. To anyone whose copyright I have unwittingly infringed I offer my sincere apologies.

Finally, I hope that I have been a conduit for Willie Doyle and the other people whose personal testimony I have quoted in this work.

Chronology of Fr Doyle's Life

*'And the angel answering said unto him, I am Gabriel,
that stand in the presence of God; and am sent to speak unto thee,
and to shew thee these glad tidings.'*

Luke 1:19

1873, 3 March: William Joseph Gabriel Doyle born in Dalkey, County Dublin, Ireland

1884 – 1890: attended Ratcliffe College, Leicestershire

1891, 31 March: entered the Jesuit Novitiate of Tullabeg, near Tullamore, County Offaly

1894 – 1898: at Clongowes Wood College, County Kildare, as a teacher and prefect

1898 – 1900: studying philosophy at a Jesuit house of studies at Enghien, near Brussels

1900 – 1901: studying philosophy at St Mary's Hall, Stonyhurst, England

1901 – 1903: at Clongowes Wood College, prefecting

1903 – 1904: at Belvedere College, Dublin, teaching

1904 – 1907: studying theology at Milltown Park, Dublin

1907, 28 July: ordination ceremony, Milltown Park

1907, 29 July: Fr William Doyle, S.J. says his first Mass

1907, 23 September: sets out from Dublin to Tronchiennes, near Ghent, via Paris, Lyons and other places of pilgrimage en route

1907, 10 October to 13 November: Long Retreat at a Jesuit Abbey, Tronchiennes (now Drongen), Belgium

1907 – 1908: Tertianship at Tronchiennes, including pilgrimage in July 1908 to the shrine of Our Lady of Chévremont, near Liege: his stay in Tronchiennes coming to an end after the retreat in July 1908

1908 – 1910: at Belvedere College, teaching

1910: appointed to the mission staff of the Jesuit Province, Dublin

1910 – 1915: gives 140 missions and retreats (as well as special sermons and talks) in Ireland, Scotland and England

1912, November: visits Lourdres and other shrines at Tours, Angers and Lisieux, during a reconnaissance trip to inspect retreat-houses for workingmen in France, Belgium and Holland

1913: Society of Jesus acquires Rathfarnham Castle with intention of opening a retreat house for working men, but did not open its door for this purpose until 11 March 1921. Fr Doyle, S.J. based at Rathfarnham

1914, November: volunteers to be a Military Chaplain

1915, April: organises the first retreat given for working men in Ireland, at the Providence Woollen Mills, Foxford, County Mayo

1915, November: receives appointment letter from the War Office as a chaplain to the 16th (Irish) Division; proceeds to Witley Camp, Surrey and is attached to 8th Battalion Royal Irish Fusiliers

1916, 1 January: moves to Borden Camp, Hampshire

1916, 18–20 February: left Bordon, embarked at Southampton, disembarked at Le Havre

1916, February – March: travelling through France to arrive at 16th (Irish) Division posting in the Loos sector

1916, 23 April: Easter Sunday, in front line trenches where he celebrates Mass for the first time in a trench

1916, 24 April: Easter Rising

1916, 27 April: German gas attack of 16th (Irish) Division's front line trenches in the Hulluch area

1916, 29 April: 2nd German gas attack of 16th (Irish) Division's front line trenches in the Hulluch area

1916, May: awarded 16th (Irish) Division *Parchment of Merit* for work in front line trenches during April gas attacks

1916, June: first leave home

1916, 27 August: left Loos sector to march to Somme sector

1916, 3 September: waiting in Happy Valley and Battle of Guillemont

1916, 9 September: Battle of Ginchy, working in aid post

1916, 15 September: administers last rites for Joseph Carey, shot at dawn at Corbie

1916, 23 September: arrived at Kemmel for new posting south of Ypres

1916, November: returns home on leave

1916, 1 December: transferred to 8th Battalion Royal Dublin Fusiliers

- 1916, 23 December: first met Fr Frank Browne, S.J.
- 1916, Christmas: in billets at Locre Convent
- 1917, 1 January: gazetted in *London Gazette* New Year Honours List - awarded Military Cross
- 1917, 4 January: *London Gazette* - Mentioned in Dispatches
- 1917, February: renews contract as chaplain with Expeditionary Force
- 1917, March: last leave home
- 1917, 31 March: start of journey to Pas de Calais for period of training and recreation
- 1917, 15 April: Easter Sunday, celebrates Mass in church at Nordesques and start of return journey back to Kemmel
- 1917, 7 June: Battle of Messines – recommended (but not granted) for DSO for helping to dig out buried men from collapsed Chinese trench
- 1917, 10 June: visits grave of Major William Redmond at Locre Convent
- 1917, 11 June: march from Clare Camp to Locre bound for Pas de Calais for training
- 1917, 15 July: gives last sermon to packed congregation at St Omer Cathedral
- 1917, 22 July: start of return march
- 1917, 25 July: arrives Watou Camp west of Poperinghe
- 1917, 31 July: in reserve at Brandhoek Camp west of Ypres for opening battle of Third Ypres – the Battle of Pilkem Ridge
- 1917, 1–2 August: in the front line near Frezenberg
- 1917, 2 August: at Erie Camp
- 1917, 3–16 August: working continuously in the front line, administering to the needs of all four battalions of 48th Infantry Brigade, following the transfer of Fr Browne to the Irish Guards, whose replacement failed to take up the new appointment
- 1917, 16 August: Battle of Langemarck – killed in front of the Black Line near the railway
- 1917, August – some time post 16th: recommended (not granted) for Victoria Cross
- 1917, 18 November: Major General William Hickie writes to Brigadier General Horace Kays advising him that he recommended Fr Doyle for the Victoria Cross but – *'Superior authority however has not granted it'*.
- 1917, 24 December: *London Gazette* – Mentioned in Dispatches

Opposite: A map showing the main areas visited by Father Doyle

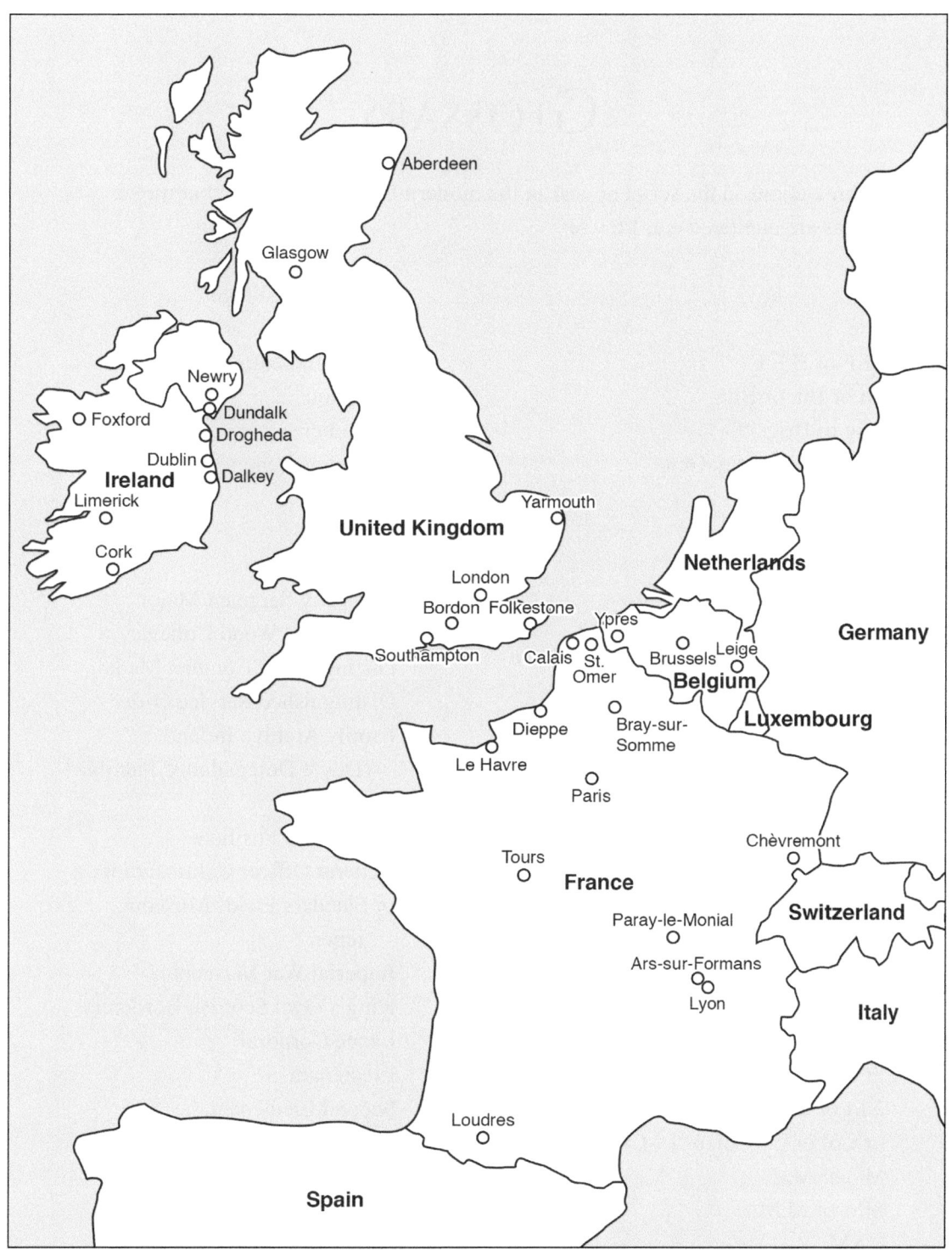

Glossary

Abbreviations in the script appear in the modern format e.g. Lt Col but direct quotes are unaltered e.g. Lt. Col.

BC	Blackrock College
Bde	Brigade
BEF or B.E.F.	British Expeditionary Force
Bn or Bn. or Bttn.	Battalion
Brig or Brig.	Brigadier
Brig Gen or Brig. Gen.	Brigadier General
Capt or Capt.	Captain
Coy	Company
Cpl or Cpl.	Corporal
CSM or C.S.M.	Company Sergeant Major
CWC	Clongowes Wood College
DCM or D.C.M.	Distinguished Conduct Medal
DSO or D.S.O.	Distinguished Service Order
FAI	Family Archive Ireland (Doyle Descendants' Family Archive)
Faughs	Royal Irish Fusiliers
GOC or G.O.C.	General Officer Commanding
IFFM	In Flanders Fields Museum, Ieper
IWM	Imperial War Museum
KOSB or K.O.S.B.	King's Own Scottish Borderers
L/Cpl	Lance Corporal
Lt or Lt. or Lieut.	Lieutenant
2/Lt or 2nd Lt. or 2nd Lt or 2/2	Second Lieutenant
Lt Col or Lt.-Col. or Lt-Col or Lieut.-Colonel	Lieutenant Colonel
MC or M.C.	Military Cross
MM or M.M.	Military Medal
NAM	National Army Museum

GLOSSARY

NCO or N.C.O.	Non-commissioned Officer
OP	Observation Post
PP	Parish Priest(s)
Pte or Pte.	Private
RAMC or R.A.M.C.	Royal Army Medical Corps
Rev or Rev.	Reverend
RDF	Royal Dublin Fusiliers
RIF	Royal Irish Fusiliers
RInnF	Royal Inniskilling Fusiliers
RMO or R.M.O.	Regimental Medical Officer
RPO	Regimental Aid Post
Skins	Royal Inniskilling Fusiliers
The Dubs	Royal Dublin Fusiliers
TNA	The National Archives
VC or V.C.	Victoria Cross

Structure of BEF

The following table shows the typical structure of BEF for much of the war.

Flow from smallest unit of 12 men in a Section through to 200,000 or more in an Army – numbers are approximate and assuming each unit at full strength.

Approximate Number of men	Name of Unit	Commander	Composition of Units
12	Section	Corporal or Lance Corporal	Not applicable – first unit of the structure
48	Platoon	Lieutenant or Second Lieutenant	Four Sections
200	Company	Major or Captain	Four Platoons and Co. Headquarters
1,000	Battalion	Lieutenant Colonel	Four Companies Battalion Headquarters and Specialists
4,000	Infantry Brigade	Brigadier General	Four Infantry Battalions, Machine Gun Company and Trench Mortar Battery
18,000	Division	Major General	Three Infantry Brigades plus a Pioneer Battalion
60,000+	Corps	Lieutenant General	Two or more divisions
200,000+	Army	General	Two or more Corps

List of Maps

Map showing the main areas visited by Father Doyle .... page 21

Schlieffen Plan .... page 136

16th (Irish) Division front line Loos sector 1916 .... page 217

Albert-Bapaume (Guillemont and Ginchy) .... page 331

Leuze Wood .... page 336

Pas de Calais and adjoining areas .... page 447

Trench map, Messines area .... page 455

Battle of Messines .... page 502

Front Line of 31 July 1917 .... page 560

Frezenberg August 1917 .... page 582

Frezenberg trench map (Hooge) .... page 613

Prologue

*'I sought the Lord, and he heard me
(and delivered me from all my fears)'*

Psalm 34.15-22

On Friday 17 August 1917 readers of *The Times* picked up their newspapers, in their clean and dry cosy homes, to see the headline: '*Ypres Battle Resumed*'. The report referred to splendid advances around Langemarck, despite stubborn resistance by the enemy. Whilst it conceded that most enemy counter-attacks had been successful, it had been at great cost to the Germans. According to the *Spectator*'s account: '*strong and promising new blows ... have been struck in the new battle ...*' [1] The London Correspondent of the *The Irish Times* reported: '*All seems to be going well with the British advance and the news today is good.*' The truth of the matter was somewhat different. British army advances were far from impressive and the cost incurred was as heavy as that inflicted on the German army.

Only hours before the publication of the Friday morning newspapers, the drenched, dangerous and filthy existence of the men of 48th Infantry Brigade was compounded by the loss of their chaplain. His name was William Joseph Gabriel Doyle and he died in Flanders fields at the age of forty-four, having already been awarded the Military Cross, leaving in his wake a huge out-pouring of grief.

William had quickly become Willie, but often during the last eighteen months of his life he rejoiced over his middle-name Gabriel and the angel he believed watched over him, until that fateful day in August 1917. A Belfast Orangeman wrote to the *Glasgow Weekly News* shortly after, published on 1st September 1917:

> *Fr. Doyle was a good deal amongst us. We couldn't possibly agree with his religious opinions, but we simply worshipped him for other things. He didn't know the meaning of fear, and he didn't know what bigotry was. He was as ready to risk his life to take a drop of water to a wounded Ulsterman, as to assist men of his own faith and regiment.*

Willie Doyle was dismissive of all personal comforts as well as his own safety and he had a tremendous work ethic. Thus he adapted very well to life as a conscientious hard-working Army Chaplain. During the final days of his life, from 2 August 1917 until his death on 16 August, his workload doubled when he had to take temporary charge of the spiritual needs of two extra battalions, becoming Chaplain for the whole of the 48th Infantry Brigade of the 16th (Irish) Division. He worked almost constantly in the Front Line during that period as the four battalions were rotated, under gas and shell bombardments.

Willie Doyle trusted his God and trusted his luck. On 14 August 1917 he wrote:

I have told you all my escapes, dearest Father, because I think what I have written will give you the same confidence which I feel, that my old armchair up in Heaven is not ready yet, and I do not want you to be uneasy about me. I am all the better for these couple of days' rest, and am quite on my fighting legs again. Leave will be possible very shortly, I think, so I shall only say au revoir in view of an early meeting.[2]

Sadly, whilst Fr Doyle's faith was infinite, his luck was finite and his God claimed him two days later, from the heat of battle whilst trying to render assistance to an injured soldier.

After Willie Doyle lost his life his body vanished. He perished on a bleak, blood-spattered battlefield leaving his flock bereft. His mortal remains commingled with those of countless other men whose bodies were never recovered. He is commemorated by the Commonwealth War Graves Commission on the Memorial to the Missing at Tyne Cot in Belgium.

Major General William Hickie's opinion, expressed three months after Willie's death was: '*I think that his was the most wonderful character that I have ever known.*'[3]

Ultimately, Willie Doyle was a man of God first and a proud Irishman second. He lived during a tumultuous era that shaped and changed his country, and others close by, almost beyond recognition. For Ireland one turbulent era led to another; an era in which Willie would play no part and during which the southern Irish participation in the Great War was to be air brushed from her history. The legend of Saintly Fr Willie also softly, softly slipped away.

This is Willie's story.

PLATE SECTION

Area of final actions, death and possible burial

Medal case of Fr Doyle's War and Victory Medal, Military Cross and Death Plaque – Oak Leaf for Mention in Dispatches is missing

Memorial Window dedicated to Fr Doyle, St Finian's Church, Dromin, County Louth

'The Mikado', Clongowes Wood College, 1898, produced by Willie Doyle

16th (Irish) Division Memorial, Wytschaete

16th (Irish) Division Memorial, Guillemont

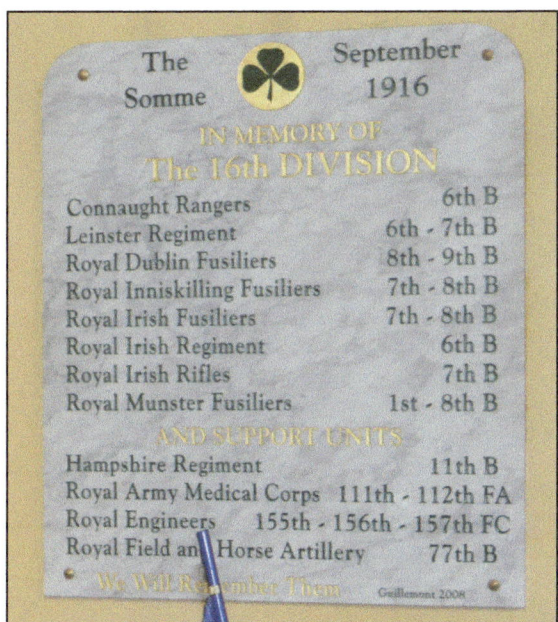

Guillemont Church Memorial to 16th (Irish) Division

Island of Ireland Peace Park, Messines, memorial stones to the three Irish Divisions

Nov. 18th 1917

My dear Kays

Father Doyle was one of the best priests I have ever met — and one of the bravest men who have fought or worked out here. He did his do (and more than his duty) most nobly and has left a memory & a name behind him that will never be forgotten. On the day of his death — August 16th he had worked in the

Hickie letter to Kays (page 1)

front line and even in front of that line and appeared to know no fatigue. (He never knew fear.) He was killed by a shell towards the close of the day & was buried on the Frezenberg Ridge. I hope to be allowed when things settle down and we can get a party there to do it, to move his remains to the Convent

Hickie letter to Kays (page 2)

Garden at Locre and to put them in a grave beside that of Willie Redmond.

He was recommended for the Victoria Cross by his C.O. - by his Brigadier & by myself. Superior authority however has not granted it, and as no other posthumous reward is given, his name will I believe be mentioned in the Commander in Chief's Despatch. If I had known his father's address I would have written to him to congratulate him upon having had such a

Hickie letter to Kays (page 3)

son, and in the name of the Division I would offer him my thanks for the work of the Priest, and in my own name as Commander I would offer my own for the spirit he infused into all he came in contact with – officers & men – and for his very glorious example. I can say without boasting that this is a Division of brave men – and even among these Father Doyle stood out. All goes well. I am prouder than ever of my Commands. I suppose we are half through the War now.
Yours ever W. B. Hickie

Hickie letter to Kays (page 4)

Envelope in which Hickie letter to Kays was sent

Postcards sent by Fr Doyle to his nieces

Joseph Carey, Corbie Communal Cemetery Extension

Michael Byrne, La Laiterie Military Cemetery

Daniel Hayes, La Laiterie Military Cemetery

Interior view of St Omer Cathedral

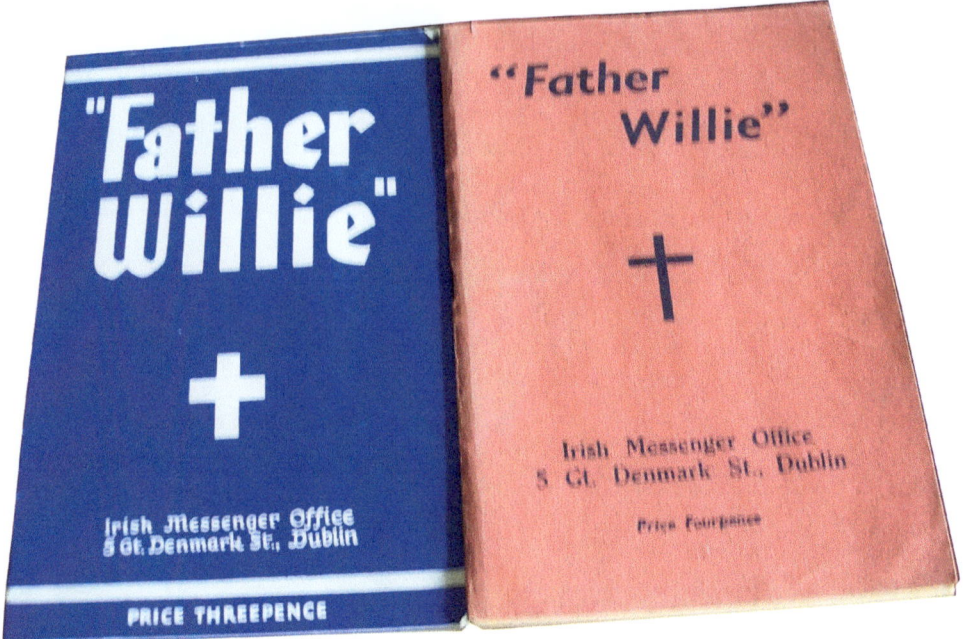

Irish Messenger booklet, cover and inside double page

Major William Redmond's burial party, Locre

Willie Redmond's grave, Locre

Major General William Hickie

Fr Doyle in uniform of Chaplain to the Forces

16th (Irish) Division Parchment of Merit awarded to Fr Doyle

Framed certificate from King George V which accompanied the death plaque

Field where surviving NCOs of 8th RDF dug in 16 August 1917. Car seen on the horizon is on the road which replaced the former railway line

Fr Doyle's name on the Memorial to the Missing at Tyne Cot

PART 1

VICTORIAN BEGINNINGS – AND CONTEMPLATING A NEW CENTURY

CHAPTER 1
BIRTH AND BACKGROUND:
FIRST EXPERIENCE UNDER FIRE!

In the beginning was the Word, and the Word was with God, and the Word was God.

John 1:1

Willie Doyle was born a little over half-way through the reign of Queen Victoria. Dalkey Avenue is where his story begins, at *Melrose,* the home of his family in the town of Dalkey. Imagine the scene, conjure a snapshot of a prosperous Victorian childhood. Picture one of those twee, sparkly Christmas cards, illustrating a cosy detached dwelling, standing in a garden of glistening virgin snow. Maybe a friendly robin surveys the scene approvingly from a wooden fence, or perhaps there are smartly dressed carol singers outside the front door, in their velvet and fur trimmed overcoats and muffs. Or is there an immaculately uniformed postman with bulging mail bag? Possibly one of the bay windows invites a peek into the festive living room, with its log fire, gas lights, piano and brightly festooned Christmas tree. Caricatures maybe, but such images convey an impression of the times for those fortunate few. It was into this kind of snug environment that the subject of this biography was born. He, together with his slightly older brother, left in their writings a flavour of their anglicised home town in County Dublin during the late Nineteenth Century. But, in Willie Doyle's case, much more beyond that; so, let us begin at the beginning.

On Monday 10 March 1873 the following birth announcement appeared in the *Dublin Evening Post:*

Doyle: March 3 at Melrose, Dalkey, the wife of Hugh Doyle Esq., of a son.

Thus the arrival of William Joseph Gabriel Doyle was announced to the world.

BIRTH AND BACKGROUND

Casting a careful eye over the same edition of the newspaper, the reader will come across Dublin company William Wight's advertisement for the import of the celebrated wine, Veuve Cliquot Champagne. Whether the arrival of this particular baby was toasted in champagne in his genteel, middle-class household is not recorded, but it is evident from the personal anecdotes of his brother Charles that Willie was to be the cause of much joy at *Melrose*.

The relationship between the two brothers is encapsulated in this vignette written by Charlie long after Willie's death:

'Fetch this!' shouted a sturdy youngster of twelve, sprawling in an easy-chair on the lawn with his legs dangling over the arm-rests. Whiz! A ball flew across the tennis-court, hotly pursued by a small boy who pounced on it almost before it had touched the ground, and tossed it back to its owner. Again and again was the ball flung hither and thither, and again and again was it retrieved by the human terrier on two swift little legs. But soon the fun of the game began to wear thin. The lad in the chair pocketed his ball and took up a book, and the small boy threw himself panting at his brother's feet.[1]

The lawn and tennis court were to be found in the grounds of the Doyle family home, a detached residence built in 1843, located along Dalkey Avenue, just past the railway line which intersects that road. *Melrose* is a solid rectangular building, modelled on classical lines, with tall chimneys and with a large central porch on its front elevation. The six-bedroomed house stood in its own grounds, well laid back from the road, complete with gardens, greenhouse and the tennis court plus lawn, which was large enough to play croquet and (with caution!) cricket. There was also a coach house and gate-lodge attached to the property. Into this comfortable setting Christina Mary Doyle gave birth to her seventh, and last, child William.

His birth certificate may have said William, but to his family and friends it was Willie (or sometimes Bill or Billie.) As he grew up he was also occasionally referred to by the nickname Sloper, due to a resemblance to Ally Sloper, the hero of a comic paper *The Ups and Downs of Ally Sloper*. They shared the same high forehead, slightly protruding ears and aquiline nose. Or perhaps the comparison was because Willie had the same tendency for getting into scrapes. Whilst the comic paper character of Ally Sloper could be found up to mischief, in such chapters as

Melrose

Wandling: A narrative of wild adventure, Willie also got himself into tight spots, as on one occasion described by Charlie:

There was a short cut to a neighbouring common across a field belonging to the residence opposite Melrose. This was sometimes made use of by the brothers on their stilts. The crossing was not always made without adventure. A fierce dog would sometimes rush out from the house, and though its charges and snaps at the stilts were an amusement to the youngsters perched safely far above, its barking would at times bring on the scene a crabbed old gardener who disliked trespassers, and said so loudly, and in unusual language. One day Willie was making his way across the field, when he noticed a cow, that was grazing not far away, raise its head and stare at the queer-looking object passing by, and then came trotting towards him. Next moment he had slid down one stilt to the ground and was taking to his heels. Whereupon the bull – for it was a bull – with an angry bellow came tearing after him with head down and tail in air. It was a close shave, but Willie just managed to half jump, half fling himself over the paling that bounded the field as the bull crashed into it. Foiled of its prey, the enraged animal knelt down and tore up the ground with its horns as though to show what it would have done had it caught the fugitive, while Willie made faces at it and encouraged its efforts from a safe vantage.[2]

In whatever manner the nickname Sloper was acquired, it was certainly nothing to do with personality and character. Whereas Ally Sloper was flippant, dissipated and selfish, Willie was the complete opposite. He was certainly mischievous and frivolous whilst at play, but his kind nature often lead him to forgo treats in order to help other less fortunate folk. Charlie said that much of his brother's pocket money was spent on the poor of Dalkey Hill, the common land on the high ground beyond the Killiney end of Dalkey Avenue, and also those living on The Flags, round the corner off Cunningham Road.

He was welcomed as 'Master Willie' bearing general gifts of tea and sugar; sometimes with soup, jelly and cod liver oil for the sick and clothing for the absolutely destitute. The services of Sil Doyle (unrelated), the family's handyman and gardener, and other household servants, were sometimes called upon for the execution of his good deeds:

One old woman who lived all alone was very fond of a pinch of snuff, nor did she disdain a whiff from a battered clay pipe when she thought no one was looking! Willie soon discovered these little weaknesses, and saw that a supply of tobacco and snuff were always at hand for her. This old woman was very infirm and could do little to keep her house clean and tidy. Willie noticed its dirty, neglected, condition, and went off and bought lime and a brush, and after some instruction from Sil, he whitewashed the whole house from top to bottom. Then he went down on his knees and scrubbed the floors amid the old lady's mingled protestations and benedictions. No one knew of this except the cook and parlour-maid who lent him their aprons to save his clothes, and kept dinner hot for him until he returned late in the evening.[3]

Willie's innate kind and charitable nature had been inherited as much from his father as his mother. Hugh Doyle was often consulted by the poor of Dalkey about their troubles and difficulties. And it was a long-standing tradition at *Melrose* to distribute provisions and money to the needy of the neighbourhood on Christmas Eve. Although the actual date of joining is unknown, Hugh Doyle was an active volunteer in the St Vincent de Paul Society, a charity which assisted the poor by providing food, clothing, shoes, bedding, fuel and other necessities.

The town in which Willie spent his seemingly idyllic childhood is embedded on a seam of granite eight miles south-east of Dublin city centre, on the coast between Dun Laoghaire (which between 1821 and 1920 was named Kingstown) and Bray Co. Wicklow. To one side Dalkey surveys the Irish Sea and Dalkey Island. On its other flank are steep wooded hills spreading towards Killiney. Its coastal perimeter roads straddle craggy cliffs towering over the ocean, with spectacular views across Killiney Bay. Moving inland up the gorse-crowned hillsides, granite quarries, ancient wells and disused lead mines are to be found. Arbutus trees and shrubs, which favour a rocky habitat and a mild marine climate, proliferate in Dalkey, together with native species from New Zealand, the Cordyline, Griselina and Euonymous, which are also suited to coastal conditions.

Archaeologists believe that Dalkey Island was inhabited from as early as 4000BC. At various times it has been used for military purposes; there is a battery for three 24 pound guns and a Martello tower at its summit. On the mainland there is evidence of settlement around 1800BC on Dalkey Common. Moving through Anno Domini, there has been a community in Dalkey since pre-Norman times. Subsequently, a charter was signed on 8 February 1358 incorporating a Provost and Bailiffs for the town of Dalkey which, during these Middle Ages, was at the extreme southern end of an area known as The Pale, directly under the control of English kings, and which also extended through parts of Counties Kildare, Meath and Louth.

In the fifteenth and sixteenth centuries Dalkey was the main port for Ireland. The deep harbour sheltered trading vessels in Dalkey Sound, the strip of ocean between the coastline and Dalkey Island, where sailing conditions were always favourable. Dalkey hosted regular fairs and markets and seven castles (of which two remain) were erected in the area to secure the merchandise. Tolls levied on trading paid for improvements to the fabric of the town, such as paving.

Subsequently Dalkey suffered a decline in fortunes, when areas closer to Dublin were developed in the seventeenth century and the former port became dilapidated. Early in the nineteenth century the town began to be revitalised when workers moved there to quarry stone from the Common, for the construction of the Kingstown Harbour piers between 1816 and 1859. The quarrymen built stone cabins with thatch or slate roofs to house themselves and their families. Dalkey also attracted wealthy people moving out of Dublin city centre following the capital's loss of status, along with its Parliament, after the Act of Union of 1801.

A railway was constructed, part funicular, part horse-drawn, to transport the huge granite stones that were blasted out of the ground using gunpowder. The highest section of this original railway intersects Dalkey Avenue, a short stroll from the Doyle family home. From here to the quarry face was known as Windmill Flags, after a windmill situated there from 1860 until the turn of the century, which pumped water from the quarry reservoir to a smaller reservoir on Dalkey Hill.

Dalkey Hill and Windmill

The dawning of the Victorian era saw the advent of the passenger railway and Dalkey became a fashionable place for Dubliners and others to move to, or have a holiday residence. The naming of large properties such as *Victoria House* and

Queenstown Castle reflected British Victorian society, whilst the seaside nature of Dalkey is indicated in exotic street names, such as Sorrento Terrace, Seafield Terrace and Island View Parade. The large coastal properties were mainly inhabited by Anglo-Irish Protestants, who formed the majority of the prosperous residents of the town.

By the time of Willie Doyle's birth in 1873, the parish of Dalkey covered some 600 acres. The population of the township was 2,326, plus nine people and one dwelling on Dalkey Island. There were fifty named streets containing 561 dwellings, from tenements to grand seaside villas, and more people subsisted in improvised cabins on Dalkey Hill. Dalkey Avenue cuts a swathe through the woods of Dalkey Hill, ending at the junction of Castle Street and what was to become, a few years later, Barnhill Road. A left turn at this end of Dalkey Avenue heads into mainstream County Dublin. A right turn along Castle Street leads on towards the coastline, with other town roads fanning out en route. Just beyond the east end of Castle Street could be found the Metropolitan Police Station at the junction of Tubbermore Avenue and Sorrento Road. Dalkey was also home to the Loretto Convent and school, both day and boarding, and other educational establishments, including a school on the Common for poorer children, which was maintained by subscription.

Castle Street is the main thoroughfare in which the Doyle family purchased all their basic needs. Indeed, the first port of call at the corner of Dalkey Avenue and Castle Street was a pastry shop *'its windows filled with tempting cakes and sweets.'*[4] Trading further along Castle Street were merchants of general provisions, greengrocers, a baker, a dairy and a poulterer. There was a coal merchant, ironmonger and bootmaker. Fabric and sewing items could be found at the drapers and haberdashers. Craftsman included a builder, mason, carpenter and a chandler. There was also a dispensary physician for those that could afford such luxury; otherwise alternative relief could be obtained from the wine and spirit merchants! Anyone visiting Castle Street on an errand, perhaps to shop or to visit Miss Elizabeth Hynes the postmistress, could take refreshment in the Queens Hotel or the Railway Hotel. A visitor to Dalkey needing longer-term, cheaper accommodation might find room at Miss Gilligan's furnished lodgings, number 28 Castle Street. The first stop for the horse-drawn tram was in Castle Street, for local journeys towards Kingstown two miles away. For longer trips there was a train service from the railway station round the corner in Sorrento Road.

The Reverend Patrick McCabe and the Reverend Pierce O'Donnel served the

Doyle's local Roman Catholic Church of the Assumption, also located in Castle Street. The Protestant Church of Ireland, St Patrick's, was to be found in an exclusively residential area nearer to the coast in Church Road. Both were built around the same time as *Melrose,* although the Church of the Assumption, where the Doyle children were baptised, was a very simple structure for the first fifty years of its existence, after which the original nave was extended. Next to, and opposite it, are the only two remaining castles from the original seven built in the town.

Castle Street, Dalkey

Eugene Doyle and Christina Mary Byrne, both aged 25, had been married in August 1857, their marriage witnessed by John Waters and Angelica Byrne. Eugene, who was always known as Hugh, and his wife were living at *Melrose* when their first child, Frederick Timothy, was born in 1859; John Waters doing duty once again as one of the Godparents. Hugh had rented *Melrose* because it was large enough to accommodate an expanding family. They were a prosperous family, but being Catholics they were familiar with the concept of renting property. Hugh Doyle's grandfather would have been the first Doyle in generations allowed by law to own property, according to the terms of the Second Catholic Relief Act of 1782. Hugh actually owned *Lynton,* the smaller house next door, which he, in turn, rented out to Mr Thomas Smith.

The first of the Doyle children was followed by three brothers and three sisters and Fred was 14 and away at boarding school when his last sibling, Willie, was delivered to the household. The oldest sister, Elizabeth, had just turned 12, Robert was nine, Mary eight, Angelina approaching six and Charles two and a half. These births were registered by Elizabeth Byrne, Willie's English grandmother who lived with the family when he was growing up. Although the Doyles employed a nurse-maid, it must have been a blessing for Christina to have had the support of her mother in bringing up the children. Grandmamma Byrne was more than experienced, having had thirteen children herself and was a devout convert to Catholicism:

> *...she gave her little grandsons many a wise, kind correction, or word of advice; she kept them often in her thoughts and prayers. Sometimes they would awake at night and find grandma kneeling at their bedside, praying for them, or chafing their little feet if she thought they felt cold.*[5]

Christina and Hugh Doyle were equally devout; on arising every morning Hugh was to be found in the Drawing Room saying his prayers. On Sunday mornings after breakfast Hugh would listen as each of his children read aloud from Thomas à Kempis or Challoner's Meditations. Sometimes he joined in the reading in *'... a beautifully modulated voice, and read with much sweetness and reverence'.*[6]

Known as 'The Little Mother' Mrs Doyle was 41 years old when her last child was born. She was totally devoted to her husband, home and family with few outside interests. Charlie reports that she was thoughtful, kind and gentle but also firm and persistent in moulding and bending the will of all other members of the household to her own wise views.

Hugh was reported to be a strikingly handsome man, always impeccably dressed, but tempered by a modest, caring character. He had the courtly manners of mid-Victorian society and always tried to be a Good Samaritan. He was employed as one of two Registrars in the Court of Bankruptcy located in the legal district of Four Courts, Dublin. He worked alongside the Chief Registrar, a deputy Registrar and two Judges, along with sixteen others in the department, just one of whom was a woman; Mrs Fitzpatrick the Court Keeper. Easy access to the railway line enabled Hugh to commute to his job in Dublin city centre from his home on the scenic coastline.

The original Dublin to Kingstown railway line started in 1834. By 1844 passengers could travel from Dalkey into Kingstown, where they would have to change for Dublin and other destinations. The Dalkey line used part of the Dalkey Quarry tramway, a former industrial service for transporting the granite quarried there. The new passenger line was an atmospheric railway (hence the naming of Atmospheric Road running alongside, which is still a thoroughfare of Dalkey). The carriages ran on a 4'8$^{1/2'}$ gauge track driven by air pressure. Vacuum power, provided by an arrangement of pistons working within a large pipe, propelled the carriages from Dalkey to Kingstown; the return journey downhill was made by gravity and momentum alone. If a train stopped short of the station, the passengers would alight to walk and the Third Class passengers were requested to help push the train!

This period was one of railway mania; the Atmospheric Railway was a novel attraction and proved a big talking point. Indeed, *The Illustrated London News* dated 6 January 1844 published an article about this Dalkey phenomenon. Eventually, after ten years, conformity beckoned and the line was converted to the Irish standard gauge (5 feet 3 inches) using steam propelled locomotive engines. The line was also extended and on 2 July 1856 commuters such as Hugh Doyle could travel directly into Dublin's Westland Row (Pearse Station) using the hourly service, whilst others could travel in the opposite direction along the coast to Bray. [FN1]

If, in the summer of 1873, Mr and Mrs Doyle ever took baby Willie on a Sunday outing further along the coast to Bray, on the *Dublin, Wicklow and Wexford Railway*, the Second Class fare would have been 1s 3d (First Class 2s 6d). Hackney Carriages and Cabriolets were still common-place and in March 1873 the fare from Dublin city centre to Dalkey was 4s 6d or 6s 9d return. Venturing further afield, the *City of Dublin Steam Packet Company* had routes to Belfast, Holyhead and Liverpool.

Back in the family home, Christina Doyle, as well as being assisted by her mother and the children's nurse, also oversaw the daily toil of a cook, two maids and a handyman/gardener. The children largely received their secondary education at boarding schools in Ireland and England, although there is a record of Robert being a Day Student at Blackrock College, even though it was predominantly a boarding school. Charlie and Willie eventually became the only children living in the house during term time.

Yet the Doyle household was by no means the wealthiest establishment in Dalkey. The year Willie was born there were thirteen (unnumbered) residences along Dalkey

Avenue and by far the largest was *Summerfield House* with a rateable value of £65, inhabited by Mr and Mrs Keogh, compared to £32 for *Melrose* opposite, and £23 for *Lynton*. When Willie had reached the age of nine in 1882, Dalkey Avenue had expanded up the steep incline towards Killiney and had sixty-seven (numbered) residences, five of which were vacant, and another five building plots. Indeed, although the number of named roads for Dalkey Township had reduced by eight to forty-two, there had been an expansion in building with yet more plots being available in eighteen of the roads and the population had increased by a thousand. Dalkey Avenue was a mixed community and the cheapest rateable value was paid by Michael Murphy at number 61, who had to hand over ten shillings.

Whilst Dalkey itself was home to the shopkeepers, crafts-people and professionals who plied their trade in the town, not forgetting servants and those who subsisted on common land, numerous other residents travelled into Dublin to work. For example, Edward Hamilton, a Medical Doctor, who owned *Clifton House* in Colliemore Road in 1882, was also registered at 120 Stephen's Green, Dublin; two of his neighbours, William Carte, a Surgeon residing at *Atlanta,* and George Patton, a Solicitor at *Iniscae,* both had interests in properties in Dublin. In 1882 more than a dozen highly qualified medical and legal professionals owned properties in Dalkey, alongside Charles Dawson M.P. and Sir Francis William Brady.

Sir Dominic Corrigan, the son of a poor shopkeeper who became a noted physician and leading authority on diseases of the aortic valves, had the villa *Inniscorrig* built on Colliemore Road, which boasted a small boat harbour and fish ponds attached to it. Presumably the young Willie Doyle did not come into contact with a later owner of *Inniscorrig,* Henry Vincent Jackson, in his professional capacity as Justice of the Peace! However, Willie's love of high stilts nearly brought him into the clutches of another long arm of the law:

> *One evening the boys had rather an alarming experience. They had gone out on their giant-stilts up Dalkey Avenue. They noticed in front of them a policeman who was carrying his helmet in his hand and walking somewhat unsteadily. These were the days of the land agitation when policemen went about armed, and this policeman was carrying a sword. They soon caught up with him and were about to pass, when he suddenly wheeled round, drew his sword and rushed at them shouting 'Do you think I'm afraid of you?' Probably his heated brain made him take them for Moonlighters! But the*

youngsters were too quick for him. In an instant they had slid down one stilt, as they had trained themselves to do, and were soon at a safe distance, while the abandoned stilts fell in a shower on the head of the guardian of the peace! Dire vengeance would doubtless have followed this outrageous act, had not two men with a barrel-organ come along to distract the irate constable from the boys. While he was questioning these men and taking down particulars about them in a note-book, the lads stole up quietly and removed their stilts and themselves from the spot.[7]

Willie would have been about nine by now and the essential character of Dalkey's traders had started to change. John Leahy, the provision dealer, had moved from number 15 Castle Street (rateable value £10 10s) to number 19 (rateable value £24) and become J.T.C. Leahy Italian Warehouse! Similarly, the new postmistress, Miss Tomkins, had expanded into the business of a stationer and fancy warehouse. In addition to the pastry shop, another attractive port of call for Willie and Charlie may have been one of the two confectioners in Railway Road, a step or two away from Castle Street. By now the two hotels had competition for refreshments from Higginbotham's Restaurant and added to the long-established craftsmen and traders, there was a tailor, dressmaker and milliner, as well as a plumber and sanitary contractors; these two latter being a sign of the impetus towards modernisation. Dalkey had also acquired its own branch of the Bank of Ireland. Yet progress continued to be mitigated by the age-old problem of poverty:

At the foot of the stone pavement that led to Dalkey Hill an old blind man used to sit selling bootlaces and sugar-sticks. Up this pavement and over the hill Willie and Charlie passed almost daily in summer on their way to Vico bathing-place. Willie would often stop to give a kind word and patronage to the blind man. The conversation always began in the same way. 'Do you sell sugar-sticks?' 'I do.' 'Will you give me a pennyworth?' 'I will.' Never did the same answer fail to come, and always did Willie chuckle and enjoy it.[8]

Workhouses were still common place. On the day Willie was born, the Dublin Evening Post of 10 March 1873 invited tenders from butchers, millers, barm brewers and egg and flour merchants for their products to supply the North Dublin Union workhouse. Five days later, and at the opposite end of the city, a vacancy was advertised for the post of Ward Master at the South Dublin Union. This post carried a salary of £26 per annum, with clothing, first class rations and an apartment.

Willie Doyle's parents were teenagers during the famine years of the 1840's and Willie grew up to a back-drop of agrarian struggle as well as political struggle. The Liberal British Prime Minister, William Gladstone, oversaw the Land Acts of 1870, followed by another four during the 1880's (as well as the first Home Rule Bill of 1885.) Ireland was still a largely agrarian economy, which was also almost completely dependent on the English market for their produce. The *Dublin Evening Post* of 15 March 1873 published a detailed schedule of prices for wheat, oats, bere and barley and stock exchange dealings were given for London and Liverpool markets as well as Dublin.

The Doyle family had no worries about either the workhouse or agricultural prices. Reading Charlie's accounts of the vigour and *joie de vivre* of their childhood it is difficult to believe that Willie's health caused the Doyle family much anxiety. He was a frail and delicate child who suffered from frequent nose bleeds; habitually weak and pale, yet conversely Willie had great reserves of energy. However, the most serious threat to his health as a youngster resulted from an accident rather than sickness:

> *When he was quite a little fellow, his nurse one night placed a lighted candle by the side of his cot to enable herself to sew until he went to sleep. But nurse, too, fell asleep, and the candle overturned and set the bed-clothes on fire. Fortunately, his father, who was sleeping in the next room, was awakened by the smoke and rushed into the nursery. He found the cot on fire, and little Willie fast asleep with his legs curled up, as though he felt the fire creeping towards him. In an instant the child was lifted out of bed, and the mattress and bedclothes thrown out through the window.[9]*

Willie referred to this incident when serving as a Military Chaplain at the Front, declaring it to be his first experience under fire!

Footnote 1: Experiments with Atmospheric Railways were soon abandoned elsewhere owing to the problems of maintaining an adequate vacuum within the train pipe. To allow the piston to pass along the pipe, a slot had to be provided in the top of the pipe, and this was sealed using strong leather straps, which moved aside when the piston passed through, but then fell back into place again, to maintain the vacuum. Unfortunately, the leather had to be well lubricated, using a cream made of animal fats, and the cream proved irresistible to rodents, who ate through the leather straps, and thus caused holes in the seal, which allowed the vacuum to escape.

CHAPTER 2
CHILDHOOD AND YOUTH:
SONGS, STILTS, STUNTS AND SPORTS

Because a friend lived there once
and timing is always awry —

and the train sides
with the small sea
that might as well
be everything

sea that meets and parts
in every gesture —
the one constant.

The road down
crowded with villas
hoarding the outlook
we see through chinks —

another life
till the coast opens
and the island beckons

too perfect and close
to be borne

all that we wanted
boat after boat with no one
to row us out.

Dalkey by Tracy Ryan[1]

Willie and Charlie Doyle were devoted siblings who loved nothing better than messing around in the sea on their doorstep. Willie's devotion to Charlie was particularly constant; where Charlie went, Willie was to be found not far behind. Charlie returned the affection in equal measure, whilst also basking in the advantages of being the slightly older, hero-worshipped, brother. If Charlie wanted something fetched or carried, Willie was at hand to provide the service. Everything was shared with Charlie:

> *... sweets, secrets, sorrows ... Together they learnt their first letters, together they knelt and prayed, together they fished and bathed, and built themselves a wonderful house in the branches of a mighty elm. And when bedtime came, the last 'Good Night!,' conveyed in a mysterious formula, was always to Charlie.*[2]

Until the age of eleven the two boys were educated at home. All the Doyle children learnt early to read and write and both Willie and Charlie developed a love of reading, especially the lighter texts in the *Melrose* library. *The Boys Own Paper* was eagerly received into the house each week, when Charlie was always allowed the first read. They learnt English, arithmetic, French and Latin and their older brothers provided coaching, when they were at home. Fred supervised Willie, whilst Robert coached Charlie. The future nun of the family, Mary (known as Mai) supervised prayers, the catechism and all things religious. A saintly old aunt often lent a hand in the spiritual upbringing of the youngsters and was consulted when they came to make their first confession, hearing: *'what sins they should tell, and how exactly they should tell them!'*[3]

The younger brothers were both musical and often entertained all members of the household, including the lady residing at the gate-lodge, singing and playing instruments on an improvised stage in the coach-house, or within the bay window of the parlour. Willie could read music scores and became proficient on the banjo, piano, accordion and organ. He used to spend many hours practising on the organ in church.

Willie also had a love of plants, which was fostered by Sil, the handyman who looked after the garden, and later by one of his masters at boarding school, Ratcliffe College. As well as being hands-on helping Sil, Willie filled note-books during his time at Ratcliffe with coloured drawings and dried, pressed specimens, labelled both in English and Latin. Back at *Melrose* on vacation he completely stripped the tennis court beyond an encroaching embankment, to lay out a bigger court. He then levelled and replaced all the sods (fashioning the extra sods needed from the spoil of the embankment.) Charlie remembers helping Willie plant a small patch of potatoes at *Melrose*:

> *There was great excitement when the stalks began to appear above the ground, and day by day their growth was watched with increasing interest. At last the time came when Sil announced they were ready for digging out, and a couple of stone of fine new potatoes were carried in triumph to grandmamma, and sold to her at the highest market price, and then quickly consumed by the two brothers!* [4]

Willie Doyle grew into a sturdy frame, in spite of contending with a fragile constitution. He eventually reached his adult height of six feet, with broad shoulders and back and muscular arms and legs. He developed a love of sport and became a powerful swimmer. He was far from molly-coddled as a child and his first experience in deep sea was a sink-or-swim episode deliberately engineered by his father. Living in a coastal environment the family developed a love for the sea and one day, when small boys, Willie and Charlie were taken out for a sail on Dalkey Sound by Hugh Doyle before either of them had learnt to swim. The anchor was dropped and Mr Doyle undressed and went overboard for a swim, instructing his boys to undress also so they could go for a ride on his back. Having done so for twenty or thirty yards they returned to the boat, where Hugh let them slip off his back into the water to learn instantly the art of treading water:

> *How they kept their heads above water and got to the boat and were lifted in, they could never rightly tell. The experience gave them great courage when they started to learn swimming, which they promptly did the next day, in case they got another invitation for a swim on father's back!* [5]

Willie grew to love swimming long distances from the shore in order to feel: *'how big the sea was.'* [6] In fact, he loved all water-based activities. He was a good oarsman and sailor and also enjoyed fishing. Mackerel proliferated in Dalkey Sound and the rocky isles known as the Muglins were famous for fat rock bream, both of which Willie dexterously caught with pieces of red flannel as bait.

Dalkey Coastline

The Doyle children created their own amusements in the main. Occasionally there would be a party or the circus to look forward to, or in summer a gymkhana or picnic outing. At Christmas time, tea would be taken in Dublin as a prelude to the annual visit to the pantomime. Amusements were easy to come by both within the confines of *Melrose* and out in the wider arena of Dalkey. In summer the tennis court at *Melrose* took a pounding and the lawn doubled for croquet and as a cricket pitch. On one occasion Willie was at the crease and hit a terrific ball through the thick plate glass of the drawing room window. Luckily the Little Mother was understanding and so managed the affair that there were no recriminations from Papa.

As well as the seaside pursuits, there was plenty of adventure to be found out and about in the local area. One favourite past-time for the two brothers was to engage with peers to battles on stilts, a first pair being a Christmas present one year:

> *They soon became very expert in their use and learnt to walk, run and jump on them with ease, or hop on either stilt while brandishing the other, or using it as a lance to charge an adversary. For many and fierce were the battles waged with other happy possessors of stilts in the neighbourhood.*[7]

Christmas gifts to Charlie and Willie a subsequent year were the much coveted giant stilts with foot-rests some ten feet from the ground.

There were hours of amusement to be found at the local disused quarry and up on the wilds of Dalkey Hill, locations where Willie became an excellent shot. The two boys and their friends shared a rifle and instituted a shooting competition amongst themselves, preceded by hours of target practice. Willie always represented Ireland. Occasionally Papa would come along and watch the shooting and have a go himself:

> *Being somewhat short-sighted, he was not an expert with the gun, and would at times miss the target altogether. But the brothers always acclaimed his shot a bulls-eye or an inner circle, to his great delight!*[8]

The highlight of the year for the young people of *Melrose* was Christmas. Weeks in advance Willie and Charlie would help their sisters make a number of plum puddings and a dozen or so large cakes, not only to be eaten by the household but also to be given as gifts for relatives and friends. As the boys weighed, stoned and stirred the various ingredients they recited verses of scripture, which didn't prevent them from dipping into the fruity raw mass as it was being prepared for the cake tins and pudding basins. The purchasing of Christmas presents was subject to much scheming and planning, as everyone at *Melrose,* including the servants, exchanged gifts. The family budget was stretched to provide extra money at this time so that small presents could be bought. Sil assiduously gathered holly and ivy to decorate the house and the Christmas tree was lovingly dressed a few days beforehand.

Willie and Charlie took an active part in assembling packages for the local poor and polished up six-penny bits to make them look like new. People would arrive at an appointed time on Christmas Eve at *Melrose* to receive their gifts presented by the two boys and checked off a list by Grandmamma. They would be greeted beforehand by a large candle which was blessed and lit, then placed in the drawing-room window, intended to welcome the Christ Child later.

On Christmas Day it was early to Mass in the bright, festive, flower-filled Roman

Catholic Church of the Assumption. On their return home the family exchanged gifts before gathering round a large dining table and a welcome breakfast. The postman would arrive with cards and more presents, to be met at the door by Willie and Charlie who presented him with his Christmas-box. After a day of examining newly acquired treasures, the family went to Mass again, followed by Christmas dinner and then music, songs and games in the drawing-room. Finally, the Christmas tree yielded its trinkets before the children were packed off to bed:

> *Truly Christmas Day was a blessed and happy day, which should appear more often in the Church's calendar! So, at least, thought Charlie and Willie.*[9]

Life either side of Christmas was simple with few luxuries. Food was plentiful, but mainly plain and wholesome. The morning porridge was to be endured rather than enjoyed, to such an extent that their dear old aunt offered the boys a penny for every portion of porridge consumed. She had great faith in the efficacy of this dish to restore some bloom to Willie's pale cheeks. Alas, not many pennies were earned! On Sundays Willie and Charlie were allowed to breakfast with the older members of the household, but only after porridge in the nursery! As the clock was about to strike, Willie would slide down the banisters shouting: *'There's ten! Ghost ... Amen!'*[10] (This was a short formula for the Sign of the Cross favoured by the family as the clock struck the hour.) The two boys then tumbled into the parlour for the much coveted treat of the second breakfast.

If there was any serious rivalry between Willie and Charlie it was to be first in the affections of their adored Grandmamma Byrne. It was her custom to sit beside the fire after dinner with one stool available to sit beside her. This was in much demand, partly because a piece of cake or candy would often appear from one of her pockets. As well as treating her young grandsons, Grandmamma encouraged them to save by buying them a money box, kept under lock and key in her possession, to be brought forth when the boys had a copper or two to deposit. She gave them a head start by inserting a new sixpenny bit and whenever the box came out it was given a good shake to remind the boys of the growing riches inside. Occasionally they would ask to inspect the bank even if they had nothing to put in, as they quickly learnt that on such occasions Grandmamma would drop a coin in!

The substantial sum of seven and sixpence had been saved when the time came for Grandmamma to unlock the contents of the bank to reveal the pennies, halfpennies and farthings. After much discussion on how to spend the money, Willie proposed a treat for Grandmamma from which he and Charlie would also greatly benefit. This was an outing for all three of them in a hired horse-drawn cab, in which Charlie sat next to the old driver and was allowed to take over the reins part of the way:

> *Once on a quiet level stretch of road the reins were handed to him, and with proud delight he drove the cab straight and true for half a mile, while Willie from the window of the chariot shouted encouragement and approval, and urged to greater speed. But he did not ask a seat on the box or the reins himself; these were for Charlie!* [11]

The boys took Grandmamma in that ancient chariot, painted in red and yellow, to see friends and visit convents nearby. Everywhere they went that pleasant day they were given refreshments; the boys anticipated each new destination with glee at the thought of the possible delicacies which might be on offer.

The Melrose flock received pocket money, but Charlie says it was not over plentiful and as they grew older Willie was always thinking up schemes to supplement their income. 'The Penny Torture' was one such example. A group of friends were challenged to pay a penny each to undertake an endurance test, the winner to pocket the purse. This involved walking barefoot in a field of nettles, the victor being the person who could hold out the longest without groaning. Being gluttons for punishment this torture test was endured twice one afternoon with Willie taking both prizes:

> *The gruesome game had a speedy and ignominious end, for that very night watchful and irate mothers discovered the blotches and sores on the feet of their progeny, so 'The Penny Torture' was added to the very long list of forbidden fruit.* [12]

A more conventional penny scheme was the guessing game 'A Penny On', an after dinner game at *Melrose*. The boys were quick to detect that their mother always looked at the object of her clue. Their father's ingenuity, though, came unstuck one evening when:

> *... with great confidence and unwonted liberality he announced 'A shilling*

> *on the I.R.' Without a moment's hesitation Willie seized a whiskey decanter that was on the table and holding it up, exclaimed, 'Ireland's Ruin.' A cleverly earned shilling was at once handed to him.*[13]

Willie in particular was always in need of extra pocket money because he gave so much of it away. His community of friends on Dalkey Hill could rely on him to share his time, money and aid parcels when needed. The games and amusements that occupied his free time were often interrupted when he would leave the cricket crease or tennis court to pay them a visit or:

> *... on his way over the Hill to Vico bathing-place he would dive into a cabin with a joke, or with a word of enquiry for the sick, or a parcel for the needy, and emerge with a shower of blessings accompanying him.*[14]

When his pocket money didn't stretch far enough Willie would beg on behalf of his poor friends; he'd wheedle items such as soup or jelly from the cook, with his mother's permission:

> *Once he ordered several large bottles of cod-liver oil from the family apothecary for a consumptive girl, then presented the bill to his father!*[15]

Willie's selflessness was fostered by the example of his mother who often instructed her children in such terms as: *'Put that chair back in its place, dear. Pick up that piece of paper, and save the maids trouble.'*[16] One of the long-serving maids, Anne, remembers first arriving at Dalkey and as she was finding her way from the station to *Melrose* she encountered Willie and Charlie on their stilts walking along Dalkey Avenue. Willie immediately realised this was the new maid and asked how she was, addressing her by name. He jumped down from his stilts, took her bag, conducted her to the house and made her a cup of tea while she settled in. She wrote:

> *I know I was really awkward after leaving the rough country. I had got orders to have the boots clean that evening. But the good saint took them out to the coach-house and brought them in shining. No one knew, only Kate (the parlour-maid), he did it so quietly. To put it off he said, 'I dare say you have no such thing in the country as blacking.' Not understanding the*

coal fire, and while I was learning, he would run downstairs and have the fire lighting and the kettle on by the time I arrived. Then the breakfast was ready, he would come into the kitchen and ask how I got on with the fire that morning.[17]

(Anne would no doubt be familiar with a turf fire. She probably would not have understood the coal fire because she came from an area where coal was not available, or was a luxury not enjoyed by her family. The working day of a Turf Man south of Dublin involved cutting clumps of turf from the bog land of County Kildare to sell as fuel, a practice repeated in other areas of Ireland.)

These anecdotes were recounted by Charlie and perhaps it is safe to assume that Willie was not unique amongst the Doyle children for kind deeds and sacrifices. They certainly seem to have been surrounded by adult role models in the family. On one occasion Willie was on his way to see an uncle who had recently returned to Dalkey after a period spent travelling. Willie had a whole shilling burning a hole in his pocket, waiting to be spent in the pastry shop *en-route*. However, he encountered a beggar half-way down Dalkey Avenue and stopped to talk to him. After listening to a tale of woe Willie decided the beggar's needs were greater than his. Despite being in sight of the pastry shop, he handed the shilling over to the beggar and cried hot tears all the way to his uncle's. When he left that evening his uncle slipped a new half-sovereign into Willie's pocket. Charlie concludes that: '

Doubtless most of this money went to his many friends on Dalkey Hill.[18]

CHAPTER 3
SCHOOLDAYS:
GENERAL BLUE

'No one can look back on his schooldays and say with truth that they were altogether unhappy'
George Orwell 1903–1950

Willie aged 15 in 1889

Willie's schooldays were largely happy affairs, even though the carefree childhood days spent by the brothers in Dalkey came to an end. In 1883 when Willie was ten, Charlie left home for a substantial part of the year to go to boarding school in England. The following year Willie joined Charlie at Ratcliffe College in Leicestershire, an event they both eagerly anticipated. At the end of the long summer holiday of 1884, the boys' school trunks were packed by their father who prided himself at being an expert at the job. However, the Little Mother had already contributed to the process because when Papa came to start work, he found the trunks contained cakes, pots of jam and other delights such as pork pies. Papa's view was that this was: *'ridiculous nonsense'*[1] but, as always, mother got her own way. At last the day came when the boxes and the boys departed for the railway station, after brave goodbyes holding back the tears. In front of them lay a long, but exciting journey, by train, sea and train again. This was followed by a night in a hotel in Leicester, before arriving at the impressive Victorian Gothic building that was to be Willie's main home for the next six years.

Ratcliffe College is on the long, straight road called Fosse Way, originally built by the Romans as a main thoroughfare stretching from Exeter to Lincoln. The college is about six miles north of Leicester high above the valley of the River Wreake, occupying 100 acres of parkland. It was established in 1841 as a seminary by the Antonio Rosmini-Serbati, founder of the Fathers of the Institute of Charity. Six years later the college became a boarding school.

Willie and Charlie Doyle boarded along with all the other pupils, about eighty in total. The teaching staff was clerical, except the lay music master. The Father President, Father Joseph Hirst IC, had been in his post since 1880 and would continue for a further five years after Willie's departure. Charlie picks out three members of staff whom he particularly associates with Willie. The two Irish brothers Doyle could not fail to empathise with an Irish Lay Brother by the name of Doyle, known affectionately as 'Daddy':

'Daddy' was Irish to the core and a rabid Home Ruler. Willie and he were very good friends. Often would they stop to talk, and discuss the state of their distressful country, and to devise plans for the freedom and glory of Ireland! [2]

Then there was 'Hairy' Tompson, a master with a prodigious amount of hair, who stored his pen and pencil wrapped in his bushy eyebrows! He was another of Willie's friends and his bass voice matched the immensity of his hair:

> *When dissatisfied with lessons or conduct in class, he would open his mouth and emit bellowings that made the windows rattle, the rafters ring, and culprits tremble.*[3]

However, his bark was nearly always bigger than his bite. His pupils loved to try and out-sing him as a group at Sunday evening Vespers, when his great voice filled the church.

As for the French Professor, this unnamed gentleman was a source of much fun. Charlie observes that:

> *He was an excellent teacher, and a simple, kindly man, and the boys liked him. But being a foreigner they doubtless thought they might take liberties with him. They certainly did!*[4]

These liberties mostly involved engaging the willing professor in conversation about a pet project of his on French regular and irregular verbs, in order to divert time away from doing exercises on the same!

Willie was not a brilliant scholar, but what he lacked in academic ability was more than made up for in diligence, organisation and initiative which made him a consistent performer. He was a good 'all-rounder' passing his examinations and often returning home for summer holidays with school prizes. Willie threw himself into the whole spectrum of school life with determined enthusiasm. He brought from home his theatrical and musical interests. Charlie says that although Willie:

> *... never distinguished himself much as an actor, he acquired a knowledge of acting and stage management that was to prove invaluable later on.*[5]

He was also always ready with the banjo and the other area he excelled at was writing and speaking. In his last year he was a prominent member of the Debating Society and writing came as naturally as talking. The Doyle brothers were under orders from home to write once a fortnight, in return for frequent letters from their parents, plus an occasional one from a sibling. Charlie hated the task, but generally managed to pass the chore on to Willie, who only occasionally needed coaxing or bribing to do so.

Where Willie really shone was at sport and outdoor pursuits of all sorts, another extension of his life from back home in Dalkey. He became a member of the senior cricket eleven and also the football team. Charlie is fulsome in his description of Willie's sporting prowess and his leadership skills in general. He describes how the Battle of the Fosse was suggested and organised by Willie, a mock battle staged on a fine summer day about a mile from the college, where Fosse Way goes through a deep cutting. With the agreement of the Prefect, who acted as umpire, Willie organised a red army and a blue army to engage with one another at this spot. The red army was to hold the cutting whilst the blue army, with Willie as its leader, was to try and take it. The red army took to the high ground with improvised shot and shell consisting of mud balls and sods of clay. Knotted towels were dipped in the river to provide heavy cudgel-like weapons for fighting at close quarters. When General Doyle and the blue army advanced waving their towel cudgels they were initially easily driven back by the reds. General Doyle then remembered passing a pile of old tin sheeting en route to the cutting and ordered a party of soldiers to retreat and commandeer those articles. A dozen or so of his soldiers advanced again, shoulder to shoulder, each holding a tin sheet as a shield, with the remainder of the blue troops crouched behind, all protected from enemy fire. In this way the blues were able to deflect red fire and flung themselves over the top of the red trenches, to win the day by 'killing' or taking prisoners. The use of the tin sheets was consistent with Roman or Medieval shields but, reporting years later, Charlie preferred to refer to them anachronistically as:

> *The precursor of the modern tank made its way slowly but surely up to the enemy's trenches, shaking off disdainfully the 'shells' and 'bullets' that fell so plentifully on its stout casing, while the soldiers it covered crept safely along. When they were within a few yards of the foe, tanks and troops dashed forward with blood-curdling yells, flung themselves over the top of the trenches and upon the enemy, whom they buried beneath a shower of tin sheeting, and quickly 'killed' or made prisoners.*[6]

According to Charlie, Willie was a general favourite at Ratcliffe, not only with staff and pupils, but a regular visitor to the college also took a great liking to him. A lady called Miss Rokeby travelled from Leicester to visit friends amongst the priests at Ratcliffe and stroll in the grounds, often stopping to talk to the boys. One day she met Willie and was so impressed by his sunny personality that she issued an invitation for him to visit her, which was also extended to Charlie on request. It was the policy of the college to allow a complete day of leisure activities to those who passed monthly examinations – otherwise this monthly day became one of extra studies for those who had failed. This day of freedom for Willie and Charlie was often spent with Miss Rokeby who greeted them after their early train journey with a: *'sumptuous spread.'*[7] Miss Rokeby's residence, *The Rosary*, provided a base for outings to the city which they explored with enthusiasm. They were lucky enough to attend cricket and football matches: *'when they sometimes saw the best teams in England play'*[8] before returning to *The Rosary* for another good meal, parlour games, music and songs. They could have been home at *Melrose*!

Charlie reports that on one occasion they missed their usual train and were late back from their outing to Leicester. No one appeared to have missed them, however, as the college was locked at nearly midnight and all apparently asleep. Luckily their tactic of throwing gravel up at the window of a friendly master worked, who admitted them back into the building without censure.

On another occasion Willie had to think even more quickly on his feet, when he and three chums were discovered in the furnace-house by Jaspar the furnace man, at a time when he would normally be on a long break from his duties. The furnace-house door was locked, but the boys had gained entrance down the coal chute and were preparing a mid-afternoon feast, for which the furnace would provide the means for cooking the main ingredient – a duck. One of the boys had procured the bird after it strayed from the college farmyard. Its unfortunate early demise to satisfy the appetites of ever-hungry boys was to be accompanied by tuck-box ginger beer, with chocolate and tarts to follow. All was going to plan when Jaspar interrupted proceedings at the point the cooked duck was being divided:

Roasted to a beautiful brown and giving forth a delicious odour, the duck was lifted from the spit and divided into four equal parts, and set before four equal shares of chocolate, tart, and ginger beer. Then squatting on the ground, the boys were about to fall to, when to their horror they heard a key being inserted in the lock; the bolt was shot back, the door opened, and Jaspar walked in![9]

Jaspar declined a share of the duck in return for ignoring the episode, but decided discretion was the better part of valour when Willie suggested a whip-round for him to buy some 'baccy.'

Another feathered casualty was the college farm's best hen, which was taken by a fox when one of the farm-hands had allowed the fox to, initially, collapse in an exhausted sleep in the corner of the barn, after escaping the attentions of the hunt. Leicestershire was one of the renowned hunting shires of England, being home to the Quorn Hunt Kennels, at that time not far from Ratcliffe. The sight of the hunt in full cry was a regular occurrence for the college boys on cold winter days, a close up view being guaranteed when the hunt passed over their playing fields. Willie and Charlie, being keen horsemen, both enjoyed the pageantry of the hunt. Indeed, they enjoyed any enterprise to do with horses.

During a school holiday back in Dalkey the boys once attended a charity bazaar where Willie won a prize in a shooting gallery, a miniature race-course with clockwork horses topped by jockeys, which was soon put to good use. 'Doyle Brothers, Bookies' offered to their friends: *'long odds and prompt payment on horses that would run in a corner of the bazaar grounds.'*[10] This proved to be a popular side-show and a nice little earner until their indignant sister Elizabeth passed by and put a stop to proceedings:

> *'What are you doing, boys?' she exclaimed 'don't you know it is wicked to gamble? Charlie and Willie, I am ashamed of you! Come away at once,' and the 'Bookies' and their race-course were dragged ignominiously away. 'But Lil,' protested Willie, 'the roulette table here isn't wicked, is it? Yet it, too, is a game of chance.' 'The roulette table is making money for the bazaar,' was the crushing reply.*[11]

So the boys had to spend their winnings on raffle tickets, but even when they won a prize, a delicious Jumbo Bun, Lil made them give it back to be drawn again!

Lil (Elizabeth) married a man called Frank Whelan, who was from an Irish family and who lived in Sheffield. She moved to live with him at Shearway House, Endcliffe, a pretty residential district of the city. It became the custom for Willie and Charlie to spend the Christmas holidays with Lil and Frank. Charlie remembers idyllic Dickensian scenes:

> *... with snow deep on the ground and lakes and ponds resounding with the ring of skates. The boys took full measure of the sport King Frost provided, and the holidays slipped by merrily in skating, snow-balling, and tobogganing down the steep and quiet avenues of Endcliffe ...*[12]

On one occasion they were taken coursing by their brother-in-law on a Yorkshire moor when a thick mist descended without warning. They got lost. Luckily, after stumbling around for what seemed like hours to Charlie, Willie spotted a road as the fog lifted for an instant. The direction they opted to take led to an inn:

> *No modern hotel could have been more welcome, and a blazing fire, and cold beef and pickles, washed down with steaming coffee, dried clothes and brought strength and comfort to worn out limbs. By the time they were dry and warm and refreshed, the mist had melted away, and a spirited horse in a hired trap bowled them along home at a spanking pace.*[13]

In March 1887 Willie and Charlie received the sad news that their eldest sibling, Fred, had died seven days after Willie's 14th birthday. Fred was 28 and had been serving as a deacon at the College of Propaganda in Rome when he caught the fever that killed him. Willie himself was to suffer two years of health issues that culminated, in the spring of 1889, in a severe attack of influenza. He went to stay with Lil and Frank in Sheffield to recuperate and relieved any boredom he may have felt by writing long letters to Charlie every week. As his brother had a passion for cricket, Willie would also enclose newspaper cuttings of important cricket matches. During the next academic year at Ratcliffe College Willie continued to suffer from bouts of ill-health, but no longer had the support and friendship of his brother. Charlie had left the college and returned to Ireland, to attend St Stanislaus' College, the Novitiate of the Irish Province of the Society of Jesus. Charlie had decided on a religious life, with a view to becoming a Jesuit, and was now serving as a novice.

As for Willie, when he finally left Ratcliffe College in the summer of 1890 aged 17, he remained so delicate that his family decided he should stay quietly at home for a while in order to build up his strength and think about his future career. This period of reflection lasted four months and a final decision was taken on Christmas Day 1890.

CHAPTER 4
NOVICE:
MAN PROPOSES AND GOD DISPOSES

*'What we want is to see the child in pursuit of knowledge,
not knowledge in pursuit of the child'*
George Bernard Shaw, 1856–1950

Willie Doyle's thirst for knowledge increased when he joined his brother Charlie at St Stanislaus' College, Tullabeg on 31 March 1891, shortly after his eighteenth birthday. The boarding school there had been established in 1818 and was situated in a remote area of King's County (now County Meath). The school authorities later regrouped and switched to become a Jesuit Novitiate in 1896, after the school was amalgamated with Clongowes Wood College in County Kildare, the most popular Catholic residential school in Ireland.

When Willie arrived he was: *'immediately seized upon by Charlie and initiated into the mysteries and black magic of Jesuit life!'*[1] Some months later he wrote to one of his sisters:

The strange part of the whole business is that just before I left Ratcliffe, I told Father Davies, our Spiritual Director, that I would as soon shoot myself as enter a religious Order! But man proposes and God disposes; so it was in my case.[2]

Three of the four 'Brothers Doyle' chose religion for their profession as well as their way of life. Willie's devout faith shone through from an early age, both in his words and acts of worship, and his charitable zeal towards the destitute or needy. Charlie says that in Willie's dealings with the poor cabin residents of Dalkey Hill:

He would skilfully contrive to bring the talk round to religion, remind them of their prayers and the sacraments, lend them good books and papers.[3]

At *Melrose*, Mrs Doyle had a large statue of Our Lady, a cherished possession from her childhood. Often as a boy Willie knelt and prayed before it and continued to do so throughout his teenage years and into adulthood, whenever he paid a visit home. At Ratcliffe College he was a member of the Sodality of Our Lady and went straight to Her altar when visiting any church. Also at Ratcliffe, Willie had become Master of Ceremonies and the leader of one of the three teams of Altar Servers. The solemn and spiritual role was one in which the devout Willie revelled, but it also appealed to the spirited, competitive side of his character. At High Mass and Solemn Vespers one team of Altar Servers would officiate while the other two sat in the stalls in the sanctuary, taking notes of the mistakes of those in charge of proceedings. These defects were reported to the Sacristan and the officiating team marked accordingly in the competition for champion Altar Servers.

Willie's background, character and understated piety predisposed him towards the priesthood. It was just a question of which of his brothers he would follow. Would he be a secular priest like Fred, or would he become a religious novice alongside Charlie? Although Fred had attended a Jesuit boarding school, he went on to study at the Holy Cross College in Clonliffe, the seminary for secular priests of the Diocese of Dublin. Secular priests are subject to the authority of the Diocesan Bishop, and are bound by promises of chastity and obedience. Religious priests, such as Jesuits, are members of a congregation bound by the rule of their particular Order, and profess three vows, of chastity, obedience and of poverty.

Fred's secular career had been progressing at the College of Propaganda in Rome, when he died ten days before he was to be ordained into the priesthood, in March 1887 while Willie and Charlie were at Ratcliffe College. Willie later declared to Charlie: *'I have always wanted to fill the gap left by Fred's death, and to become a secular priest.'*[4] But he didn't. The change of heart appears to have been set in motion when Willie accompanied Charlie to his interview at St Stanislaus' College, where Charlie was to become a Novice of the Society of Jesus. The Provincial (the Head of the Order), Fr Timothy Kenny, obviously saw the opportunity to capture two birds with one stone, because he chatted with Willie and questioned him, in addition to Charlie, who observed: *'Doubtless he judged that Willie had the makings of an excellent Jesuit in him!'*[5]

When Fr Kenny later paid a visit to St Stanislaus' he asked after Willie and suggested to Charlie that his brother should be invited for a short stay at the Novitiate. Willie gladly accepted the invitation and:

*...arrived at the Novitiate looking very manly and handsome in his grey suit and dark soft hat, and carrying his banjo, which had been brought by special request.*⁶

Musical evenings were preceded by days of walking, sight-seeing and sun-bathing. Whilst sitting viewing the surrounding countryside from an elevated position in the college grounds Charlie tackled Willie about his future. Willie's reply was that he wished to follow Fred to Clonliffe and: *'in any case I would never come to this hole of a place!'* ⁷ This led to an animated conversation about religious Orders in general and the Society of Jesus in particular. Willie left Tullabeg unimpressed:

*I uttered a fervent Deo Gratias when I found myself on my way home thanking my stars that I had not the honour of putting N.S.J. after my name.*⁸

He carried back with him a copy of St Alphonsus Liguori's work on the religious state, diplomatically accepted from Charlie with the promise that he would read and reflect on its message.

Four months later, a period in which Charlie was praying for his brother's vocation and which Willie spent in pondering and contemplation, a conclusion was reached. It was Christmas Day 1890:

*I was in the drawing-room at the piano when father came in and asked me if I had yet made up my mind as to my future career. I answered, 'Yes' – that I intended to become a Jesuit. I remember how I played my joy and happiness into the piano, after thus giving myself openly to Jesus.*⁹

The word 'Jesuit' was originally a pejorative term, of mainly 15th Century origin, used by way of reproach to individuals who were seen to make too frequent use of the name of Jesus, or to appropriate His name to their ends. In fact, the name 'Jesuit' was never used by the original founder of the Company of Jesus, Ignatius of Loyola. [FN1] This Society of Jesus was viewed with some suspicion at its inception (from which may be derived the reproving epithet 'Jesuits'), but the term later came to be accepted in a positive sense, celebrating the Society's commitment to the life and example of Christ. The Society's priests, relying on alms for support, are organised for apostolic work, following a defined set of rules, and the Order was the first to prescribe in its constitution the cause of teaching and education, starting with the interior self-reform of the person before preaching the self-reform of others.

And so, the last day of March 1891 saw a whirlwind arrive at St Stanislaus' College – in the form of Willie Doyle!

> *I remember well my arrival at Tullabeg and the way I astonished the Father Socius (as he told me afterwards) by running up to the hall door three steps at a time. He was not accustomed, he said, to see novices coming in such a merry mood, evidently enjoying the whole thing; and though I did not know it then, it was the best signs of a real vocation.*[10]

This real vocation, however, was to be tested by a somewhat mundane way of life. Willie shared chores such as washing up, sweeping, dusting and weeding, which he thought he performed to perfection, only for his work to be found fault with on many occasions. Charlie comments that:

> *…it took more real grit and courage to tackle the little things day after day than it had taken to walk bare-footed through the stinging nettles.'*[11]

Preaching, teaching, converting sinners and pagans would come all in good time. In the meantime Willie:

> *…swept the floor for the love of God … suffered greasy plates glady … tried to smile when ill or depressed, to check the unkind word and utter the kindly, to study when he felt like swinging a cricket bat or turning a cartwheel.*[12]

Willie himself said:

> *Nothing is too small to offer to God. The cross is really light when you take it bit by bit. Big sacrifices do not come often, and when they do, we are generally too cowardly to make them. But little ones are as plentiful as blackberries in September, and stiffen moral courage to do in the end even heroic things.*[13]

Willie had arrived at Tullabeg in a whirlwind and his time there also passed in a whirlwind. On Christmas Eve 1891 he wrote to his mother:

> *The time down here is most extraordinary. They have only twenty minutes to the hour and about six or seven of these are called a day – at least that is the conclusion I have come to.*[14]

Also written the same day, evidently enjoying being swept off his feet:

> *Well, I am happy as the day is long, though at times, I confess I find it hard to keep from turning somersaults, jumping out the window, coming downstairs head first, or from some other mad freak of that kind. I sometimes think that if there was any madness running in the family, it found a resting-place in me! I suppose you heard I have been through the Long Retreat, as it is called; the retreat of thirty days which every Jesuit has to make. It was a wonderful time. I do not think that I ever spent such a happy time in all my life.*[15]

Fitting everything into the swift passage of hours was not helped by the return of a period of ill-health for Willie. He suffered a nervous breakdown halfway through 1892, following a fire at the College and was sent home to Dalkey for some months. There was even the possibility of him not returning at all, according to medical opinion and the views of his Superiors. Luckily he had an influential ally: *'The lad is as good as gold'* said Fr Kenny, *'He has a Jesuit vocation, and God will give him sufficient health.'*[16] Eventually, Willie returned to complete his Novitiate, but this event was delayed for nearly six months because of the break in his studies.

The Novitiate was a probationary period at the end of which Willie took the three vows of Religion. He completed his novitiate and took those vows on 15 August 1893, aged 20. His complete progression to the Religious priesthood was to be a long path, involving teaching practice, undertaking prefect duties and studying at various colleges. His Ordination ceremony eventually took place at Milltown Park Theology College, Dublin on 28 July 1907, after which he still had to spend a further year undertaking a Tertianship. This was effectively another period of probation, making a total of 17 years before Willie was a fully qualified priest of the Society of Jesus.

During Willie's first period of probation as a raw recruit at Tullabeg, a long-held desire intensified and consumed his mind, to the point of recording this burning longing in his own blood in his spiritual notebook. This was towards the end of his time as a novice, when he pledges to Mother Mary on 1 May 1893:

With my blood I promise thee to keep this resolution. Do thou, sweet Mother, assist me and obtain for me the one favour I wish and long for; to die a Jesuit Martyr.[17]

Despite the solemnity of this aspiration Willie's sense of humour, adventure and mischief remained in tact. In April 1892 he had written to his own mother:

I must thank everybody through you for the dear letters and good wishes for my birthday. More especially am I grateful for the big box of sweets from your own loved self. That same box of sweets, I am sorry to say, has met with an untimely end. It is a sad tale, the telling of which makes one's mouth, I mean eyes, water. The box was left in the recreation room for inspection, but when I returned it was gone. The only answer to my anxious inquiries came from a solemn voice in the corner of the room: 'It has been carried off by the influenza!'[18]

Prior to this, on St Patrick's Day, the novices gave the Community a concert to be attended by a favourite retired old Father. Somehow Willie induced Fr Young to exchange his gown for one Willie considered more appropriate for the occasion; one covered in shamrocks. Willie conducted the delighted centurion to a raised throne in the centre of the room to loud applause and introduced him as: *St. Patrick come back to Erin!*[19] On another occasion Willie dressed a bolster in his own hat and gown and threw it out of an upstairs window as a friend, a secular priest, was passing by. The friend rushed to the aid of the 'body' preparing to give conditional absolution when Willie appeared chuckling at the window and the truth of the matter dawned on those below.

Shortly before leaving Tullabeg Willie's notebook is filled with earnestness and devotion. Typically he prays:

O loving Saviour, forgive me the past, accept me repentant, help me, for I am going to become with thy assistance – A thorough Jesuit and a Great Saint.[20]

Footnote 1: Iñigo Lopez de Loyola was born around the year 1491.
He died in July 1556, and is buried in the mother church of the Society of Jesus, the Chiesa del Gesù, in Rome. Beatified by Pope Paul V in 1609, he was canonised as Saint Ignatius of Loyola by Pope Gregory XV in 1622. For further information consult www.ewtn.com or similar.

CHAPTER 5
COLLEGES:
MR DOYLE BECOMES FR DOYLE

'I am afraid that the schools will prove the very gates of hell,
unless they diligently labour in explaining the Holy Scriptures
and engraving them in the heart of the youth'
Martin Luther (1483–1546)

The previous chapter closed in 1893 with a fragile twenty year old Willie Doyle leaving Tullabeg. Whilst his health remained delicate all his adult life, his condition was never life-threatening; he suffered from a chronic, debilitating digestive complaint and was often unwell or run down. Mr Doyle, as he was now called after taking his vows at Tullabeg, was unable to transfer to the next stage of philosophical and theological studies at university because of his health issues. Following a period of rest, Willie was, instead, sent by The Society of Jesus to work at Clongowes Wood College, a large boarding-school for boys in County Kildare. Many of the school pupils became the lucky beneficiaries of Willie's adversity, as he put aside his deep disappointment at this turn of events and threw himself, with all the energy he could muster, into minding unruly youngsters. Willie was employed at Clongowes from 1894 to1898 and again from 1901 to1903. The boys interests were his, he settled their squabbles, played or refereed their games, mended their sports gear and rehearsed theatricals and musicals with them. One former pupil commented:

In the playing fields he was a tower of strength. I can still recall the admiration with which I watched him play full-back, or stump a batsman who had his toe barely off the ground.[1]

Another who lived and worked with him at Clongowes said:

Thinking of Fr Willie Doyle I recall especially his gay, light-hearted ways, that cheery laugh and snatch of song with which he enlivened recreation hours or holiday excursions. Into the latter he threw himself with zest, and was an excellent companion.[2]

Clongowes Wood College has been constructed around a medieval castle and ramparts. These old, extant, fortifications are a link in a long chain of ditched and walled strongholds, known as The Pale, stretching from southern County Dublin, through the present day Counties of Kildare, Meath and Louth. The Pale was directly under the control of the English in the Middle Ages and a fortified border was established to deter the native Irish from ambushing the property of English settlers. The land named Clongowes Wood was first mentioned in a legal document dated 24 February 1417 and a castle was built there in 1450.

The original castle building was, from time to time, re-named as the property changed hands from the original owners of the land to subsequent landowners. Therefore 'Eustace' Castle was first mentioned in State papers of 1583; in 1641 the castle was blown up by the Cromwellian General Monck to make it uninhabitable for rebels and the Eustace's lands were confiscated. Then in 1812 General Michael Wogan Browne inherited Castle 'Browne' from his bachelor brother Thomas. He sold it, to pay off the estate debts, to Father Peter Kenney, S.J. Fr Kenney purchased the castle and 219 acres for £16,000, together with an adjoining farm for £2,753, plus an annual rent of £61. This transaction caused great consternation amongst the establishment both in Ireland and London due to the deep suspicion which The Society of Jesus still aroused. John Gillard wrote in the *Hibernian Magazine* dated 18 November 1813:

The magnificent edifice of Castle Browne in the County of Kildare, which cost over £26,000 in building, has been purchased by a party of Jesuits for £16,000. Ireland now stands in imminent danger. If Popery succeeds, our fairest plains will once more witness days worthy to rank with those of bloody Mary, and the walls of Dublin shall again become the lamentable bulwarks against popish treachery and massacre.[3]

Hansard recorded in full a debate in the House of Commons on 17 May 1814 about the purchase; nevertheless, the following day Clongowes Wood College received its first pupil, James McLorinan, a draper's son from Dublin. In addition to the religious issue which raised such alarm, it also puzzled the great and the good of the ruling classes where the money had come from to fund the purchase, the implication being that it had originated in Rome. Father Kenney was quizzed on the matter by the Chief Secretary for Ireland, Robert Peel, M.P. He was even threatened with confiscation of his property, but would only say that they were private funds. Fr Kenney patiently persevered with promoting his school, giving Robert Peel a prospectus, which unusually did not exclude those of the Protestant religion.

The British establishment needn't have worried. Central to the creed of the Jesuits was the importance of education and moulding their charges for their conventional role in society; the pupils being mainly from fee-paying prosperous business or professional families. Writing about a student who had left the 'Anglophile atmosphere'[3] of Clongowes Wood College seventy years after it opened, and just before Willie Doyle arrived, Irish historian and author Marcus Bourke concludes:

For the Jesuits, religion has been at the very raison d'etre of education; as far as those in charge of Michael Rahilly and his contemporaries were concerned, one of the principal means towards this end was the preparation of the boys for that place in contemporary society to which their family circumstances entitled them ... places in civil or military society for which their education in Clongowes fitted them.[4]

When Willie Doyle commenced duties at Clongowes he would not have found too many differences to the regime he had experienced in England at Ratcliffe College. The curriculum lent heavily towards the classics and had no place for Irish literature or history; the two hundred and fifty or so pupils learned little about their native country. The first secretary of the Clongowes Historical Debating Society, Thomas Francis Meagher, wrote fondly about the College in later life, but even so he complained:

They talked to us about Mount Olympus and the Vales of Thessaly ... They never spoke of Ireland. Never gave us, even what is left of it, her history to read ...[5]

The growth of the Irish Party at Westminster, and rising aspirations for some form of self-government, had no great impact at Clongowes. Even the playing fields of the college resounded to the sounds of rugby, athletics and cricket; Gaelic games did not feature in the timetable. Indeed, Clongowes took pride in being in the vanguard of Irish cricket and was known to entertain Her Majesty's army officers from the nearby Curragh Camp to matches. Marcus Bourke describes the Clongowes Wood College of 1890:

> *...as near to the ideal residential school for boys as one could expect to find in late Victorian Ireland. Then the most fashionable institution of its kind in the country, it was directed in a humane manner and had recently added a high standard of scholarship to the pre-existing qualities of polish and social attainment for which the Jesuits had long been noted.*[6]

Willie Doyle's first year at Clongowes Wood College was spent teaching, thereafter he became a prefect. Charlie says his brother was a gifted and natural teacher, who commanded attention and conveyed information in a clear and interesting way. These gifts notwithstanding, Willie's superiors decided after the first year that he would be more effectively deployed in the demanding field of prefecting. The College operated a three band system which it referred to as 'lines.' Boys under 13 were members of the Lower Line, ages 13 to 15 the Middle Line and 15 to 18 the Higher Line. Each Line had its own prefect to supervise the boys and their territory, in the form of playroom, library and dormitory. Three years after Willie started at Clongowes, new buildings and facilities were added, including a swimming pool and then a gymnasium was constructed in 1902 during Willie's second spell there.

Willie never showed any resentment about the change of role. He went about his prefecting duties in the same whole-hearted manner as when he was teaching:

> *I first met Fr Doyle when I was a small boy at Clongowes. He was then Third Line Prefect, and had under his care some seventy or eighty boys ranging from ten to fifteen years of age. This particular set were rowdy and quarrelsome, and during my first year in the Line, there were two periods, at least, of acute disturbance. Not that the trouble circled round Fr Doyle, or was directed against him, nor was it caused by any act on his part, but arose out of feuds among the boys themselves. The manner in which Fr Doyle dealt with this difficult situation impressed me even at the time, and I have been more deeply impressed again and again in retrospection. Hot tempered by*

nature, I believe, he never allowed himself to be carried into arbitrary action by the intemperate or unreasonable conduct of those in his charge. He was firm but never unjust; indeed if he erred at all, it was on the side of leniency.[7]

On one occasion at Clongowes, Willie had to arbitrate in a dispute between two of the college's cricket teams. Mr Doyle found for the winning eleven, the junior of the two sides. The consequence for the senior eleven was that they were to forfeit their good bats, pads and other gear in exchange for the battered items belonging to the victors. One of the losers was so exasperated that he called the prefect a cheat. Despite clearly hearing the accusation Willie turned the other cheek and ignored the outburst, which made the culprit even more miserable than if he had been flogged in punishment. Several days later the boy apologised to his prefect, but Willie merely laughed and gave him biscuits, lemonade and some sound advice:

Fr Doyle's example worked good. His cheerfulness, his energy, his enthusiasm were infectious and inspiring. His whole conduct was marked by a gentleness and a kindly thoughtfulness that gained him loyalty and affection.[8]

Such testimonies of Willie Doyle's character do not fit into the profile of the staff at Clongowes Wood College as depicted by James Joyce. His novel:

'A Portrait of the Artist as a Young Man' and its numerous interpretations have built up a frightening impression of a strictly-run boarding-school, staffed by callous Jesuits who delighted in the physical and mental punishment of their charges, and patronised largely by self-centred bullies.[9]

However, Joyce's book, although semi-autobiographical, was fiction and took licence with its characters and settings. An example was Father Jimmy Daly (Fr Dolan in the novel) the prefect of studies. Fr Daly's regime was harsh; discipline was frequently enforced by the pandybat. But it was Fr Daly who drove forward reforms starting in 1887, resulting in Clongowes successful participation for the first time in public examinations. This was just one factor for the:

lifelong affection and admiration which hundreds of Clongownians retained for this small, bustling, irascible, efficient teacher…[10]

The Rector of Clongowes Wood College also relied heavily on this older, long serving member of staff. The Rector was Father Matthew Devitt, who transferred in June 1891 from Belvedere College in Dublin. Aged 37 he was reported to be stern, but he was always fair and he had a sense of humour, which compensated for his somewhat aloof and reserved manner.

Willie Doyle may have felt a special connection with Fr Devitt, although it can only be a matter of speculation. Willie never appeared to get involved in any political or overtly nationalist activities, other than proclaiming himself to be a proud Irishman, and it is unlikely he spoke the Irish language. But the fact that Fr Devitt was openly interested in the Irish language revival movement, Irish archaeology and local history would have appealed to Willie's sense of patriotism. Indeed, Fr Devitt was to go on to employ the first teacher of Irish at Clongowes.

During Willie's second period at Clongowes he wrote to his mother in May 1903 apologising for not having been in touch recently:

Indeed I have few spare moments in the day; my hundred odd little ruffians see to that! There is a constant chorus of 'Oh, Sir, you promised to mend my bat.' 'Did you write for my running pumps, Sir?' 'Please, Sir, will you do this or that for me?' And so on all day long till I ask myself, Do these little villains think I have nothing else to do but dance attendance on them. They are, however, really good little chaps that I cannot refuse.[11]

Previously, on Christmas Eve he had written to his father detailing some of the tasks that kept him so busy:

You would throw your hands up in horror were you to see my room at the moment. It is a scene of chaos and disorder that would discourage and frighten even that patient and persevering arranger of confusion and disorder, the Little Mother. For the past week examinations have been in full swing. Now it is a comparatively easy task to sit down and set an examination paper that will keep a couple of hundred boys hard at work for three hours; but it is quite a different proposition to wade through and correct the output of the said boys during these hours. Can you wonder, then, that my pale and emaciated countenance grew still paler and more emaciated, and that my hair, usually so well-behaved, stood on end, as day by day I watched the pile of examination papers rise higher on my table? [12]

Despite coping with such a heavy schedule Willie was always keen to push boundaries and squeeze an extra bit of fun out of academic life. Unfortunately, Charlie does not name the contemporary of Willie's that he quotes as recalling:

After the novitiate and juniorate Fr Doyle and I were together for some years at Clongowes Wood College. In the life there, with its larger liberty of action, new phases in his character showed themselves. He began to display a more common spirit of initiative and enterprise, an energy and resourcefulness in carrying out what he had undertaken and a marked tenacity of purpose. His production of 'The Mikado' may be instanced. For some considerable time elaborate plays had not been attempted at Clongowes, owing to the heavy demands on time and attention made by the Intermediate examinations.

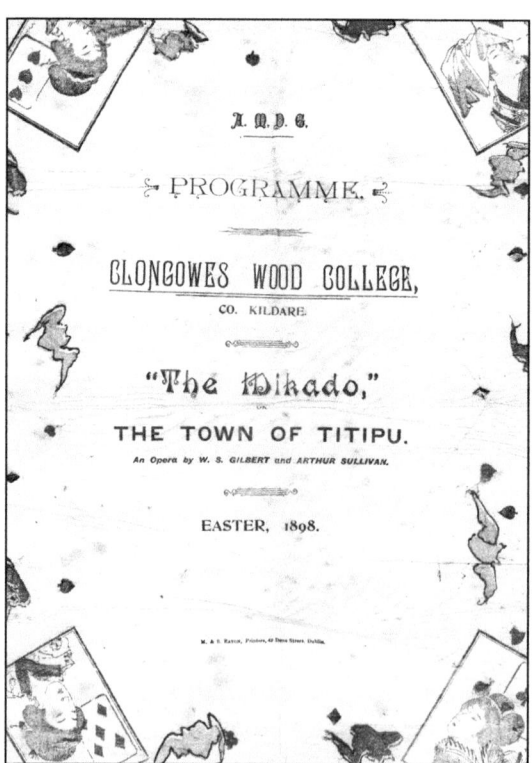

The Mikado *programme, Easter 1898*

When Mr Doyle obtained permission to try his hand at producing this opera, he seemed to be attempting the impossible. Few good singers and actors were known to be among the boys. Everything was wanting, scenery, costumes, and the money to buy them; and above all time to practise, for the studies in no way could be allowed to suffer. There appeared to be a sufficiency of one thing only – cold water; and that was freely poured on the scheme. Mr Doyle kept his own counsel, and set to work quietly and determinedly. He unearthed talent, trained his actors and singers assiduously, enlisted help, and by his tact, energy and perseverance, he overcame every obstacle, and in the end 'The Mikado' was a triumphant success and proved to be one of the most brilliant performances ever witnessed on the stage at Clongowes.[13]

The first edition of the college magazine, *The Clongownian*, appeared during the Christmas period of 1895. Willie Doyle was the founder. He also had great involvement with the foundation of the Clongowes Union, using the vehicle of the magazine to promote the idea, despite not being a Clongownian himself and therefore not entitled to membership.

Life at Clongowes kept Willie very busy, but far from leading a cloistered life, Willie was very well aware of world events. One example was the conflict between Japan and China at this time for control of Korea (for its natural resources of coal and iron):

> *I could stand a siege behind the piles of papers which litter the floor, the table, almost every inch of my room, while the reference books, reports, lists of prize-winners, and lists of those who did not get prizes would supply ammunition enough to drive off even the victorious Japs.*[14]

After Willie had worked at Clongowes for four years his position was reviewed at the end of the academic year in 1898. It was decided that he was sufficiently strong to begin his course in philosophy and so he was sent to a Jesuit House of Studies in Belgium (both Fr Devitt and Fr Daly had experience of studying in Belgium.) Willie's new companions were exiled French Jesuits of the Champagne Province and he soon settled into his new way of life. Indeed, it is somewhat ironic that he was originally sent to Clongowes because he was considered too delicate to continue studying, yet at Enghien the regime was much less demanding. In October 1898 he writes home:

> *Here I am just a month in Enghien and six weeks since I left Ireland. Time works wonders, they say, and certainly a few weeks have altered this place considerably in my eyes. I feel quite at home; strange manners and customs have lost much of their strangeness; I am beginning to realise that life abroad is not half bad, in fact rather jolly – granted, of course that life without tea is worth living! Certainly, compared with the strenuous days in Clongowes, existence here is very quiet and peaceful. Take one item. We are all between the sheets by nine o'clock each night; while in Clongowes at that hour I used to settle down to a solid two hours' work, which as often as not ran on to three or four hours. Then there are opportunities here of quiet reading or of quiet prayer that would not be possible in a big boarding-college, so that I am very much a gainer by becoming a philosopher.*[15]

Where Willie went, opportunities for fun and humour were not far behind. His

French class-mates were not so much willing co-conspirators as innovators. The birthday of their Professor of Philosophy was celebrated by decorating the classroom and:

> *When he was seated, verses and addresses in a dozen languages were read to him and all his qualities, good, bad and indifferent were duly honoured. I took charge of the English verses, copies of which may be had cheap – reduction for large quantities.*

> *Our celebrations paled before the splendour of what the solemn theologians prepared for the feast of one of their Professors. He had been lecturing on the Sacraments, and when he entered the lecture-hall on his feast-day, amid the discordant uproar of musical instruments of all descriptions, he was followed by a comical procession. First came a most substantial baby borne by a strapping nurse to receive the waters of Baptism. Then followed the French equivalent of 'Tommy Atkins' to be made a still more perfect soldier by Confirmation. Next arrived a buxom couple (all theologians mind you) for Matrimony, while the procession was bought up by a corpse, or very nearly a corpse, for Extreme Unction. For this part there had been keen competition, I believe. Assuredly the French are a clever and merry race, and knock all the fun possible out of life.*[16]

The Rector of the College couldn't quite stretch annual celebrations to declare a holiday for St Patrick's Day. However, Willie wasn't forgotten on the patron's day and received a fresh, sweet shamrock from home. He:

> *Had quite an invasion of my room by patriotic Frenchmen seeking a sprig from the old sod. You may be sure the Irishmen decorated themselves lavishly and conspicuously. We made an effort to get the day kept, as far as we were concerned, as a holiday free of class and full of good things, but unfortunately le bon Recteur could not be brought round to our way of looking at things.*[17]

Fate was to deal Willie another ironic hand. Despite the less time consuming schedule at Enghien, Willie's health began to deteriorate. He tried to make light of the situation, writing to his mother in June 1899:

> *You may set your mind perfectly at rest I have still some little sense left, and if I thought there was any danger of getting seriously knocked up here, I should be on my way to Ireland before this. Philosophy may be important, but my health more so. True, I have not been very well lately; the 'malady' to give it a grand name, is nothing new. On and off it has been my companion for the last six years; the only new thing is that it has come at me rather oftener here, as I quite expected. I suffer a great deal from biliousness, and from time to time, whatever goes wrong with the works inside, even a little food gives me cramps. I have seen the doctor both here and in Dublin, but have little faith in their healing arts. Apart from this, my health is excellent; so you see there is no cause for uneasiness, since six years' experience has proved that these attacks are only one of the many ills poor flesh is heir to.*[18]

His Superiors, however, took a different view. Whatever it was about continental life that particularly disagreed with Willie's constitution, his stay in Belgium lasted just a year. In September 1899 he transferred to Saint Mary's Hall, Stonyhurst located at Blackburn in the north of England to continue his studies in philosophy. Unfortunately, Willie's digestive troubles continued but he battled his way through his studies. Maybe he struggled at times to retain his usual infectious bright and cheerful spirit. One such occasion would have been in August 1900 when he had a particular sad cause to write to his sister from Stonyhurst on the twenty-seventh. Addressed to 'My dearest Lena' the letter starts as follows:

> *I have only just heard from the Father the sad news about your little baby. I cannot tell you how much I feel for you in this heavy affliction, for only a mother knows the love she has for her child and what its loss means to her.*[19]

Willie goes on to offer words of solace through expressions of their faith, the wording of which may seem incongruous to the 21st Century reader. Nevertheless, his belief in the sinless little saint's departure to be with the Divine Lord was a devout belief. Willie's letter must have been some consolation to Lena and her husband, as it was retained and remains in the possession of the family.

Whatever his mood, Willie certainly made an impression on the community at Stonyhurst in one way or another. Charlie quotes Fr J. Jagger, S.J. speaking in 1928:

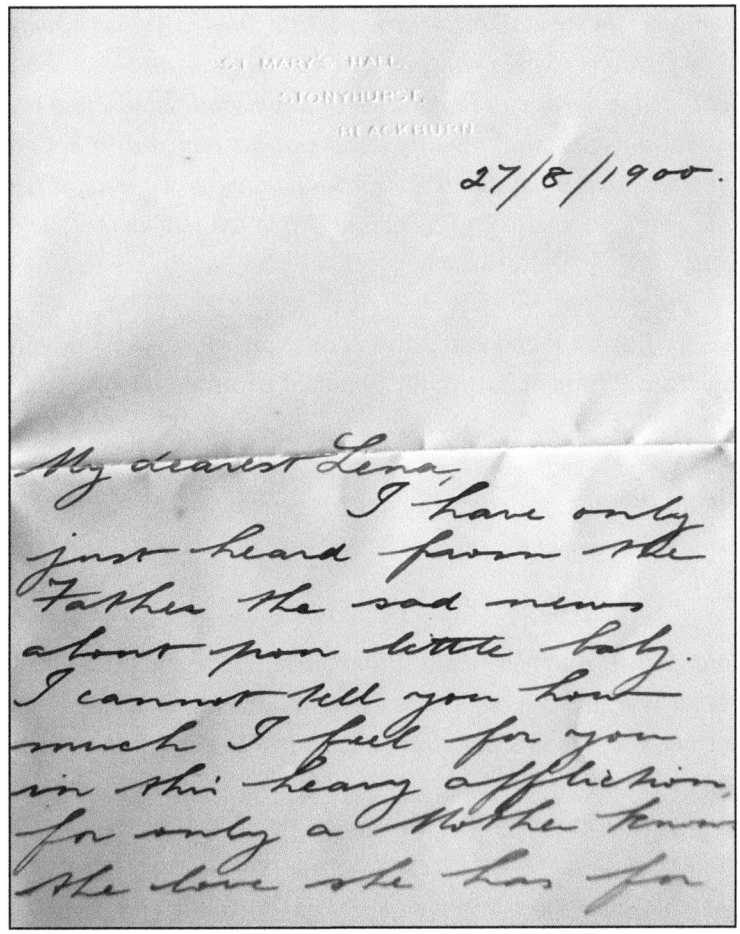

The first page of sympathy letter to Lena, 27 August

Fr Willie Doyle and I were together at St. Mary's Hall during philosophy. I don't remember that his personality impressed me. I don't remember his appearance even. But I do remember this, that when an act of kindness was to be done, Willie Doyle was there to do it. I do remember the words of grateful fellow-philosophers: 'It is easy to see Willie Doyle is in the house.'

It is a pretty good test of true charity if after thirty years one remembers such things.[20]

On the other hand Fr Charles Plater remembered:

I lived for some years with big-hearted Willie Doyle. We were seminarians together at St. Mary's, and I saw much of him. He was always bubbling over with mirth, and generally at the bottom of any harmless mischief that might be afoot, but only the shallow-minded could have mistaken his gaiety for thoughtlessness. Underneath his mercurial behaviour were steadily glowing ideals and enthusiasm. He had a deep and simple piety, and a burning love for Ireland.[21]

Willie's love for Ireland found many forms of expression. A severe winter led to a tobogganing craze at Stonyhurst. Willie obtained permission to ask the carpenter to finish a toboggan for him:

It turned out that the 'finishing' meant the making of it, Willie's part being to furnish the wood and the idea. When "finished" the "Irish Mail" was the envy of all.[22]

Another time, Willie enthusiastically broadcast his pleasure at a British set-back during the Boer War; there was significant Irish opposition, certainly in the Dublin area, to the Boer War. On this particular occasion a Dutch Jesuit remembered:

I knew Fr Willie from 1890-1901 at Stonyhurst. What I best remember about him is that he was very kind, very cheerful, that he was a keen footballer, and that after Sir Redvers Buller's Tugela adventure he came shouting down our corridor, 'Hurrah! The British have lost six guns!' Yet such was his popularity, and he had such a way with him, that the most patriotic Englishmen took no offence.[23]

Equally, Willie took no offence to being referred to as a 'Fenian' by one of the lay brothers at Stonyhurst. A Fenian was a member of an Irish American revolutionary nationalist movement. The old man had spent many years as a missionary in India and had retired to Stonyhurst. 'The Prophet', as he was called, had developed a fondness for the Irish and made a point of making friends with the Irish at Stonyhurst. Inevitably, Charlie reports that Willie was a great favourite:

> *The old man had returned from his labours in India broken in body and mind. From time to time fits of deep depression would seize him, when he would shut himself up in his room and refuse to see anybody. As soon as he felt these fits coming on, he would hang out on his door a large notice: "None but Fenians admitted." This meant that only Irish philosophers might visit him. When his malady grew worse, another notice would appear – "Not even Fenians admitted." One Fenian was excepted. The Prophet had privately informed Willie that no matter what notices were hung out, he had always the right of entry, and would be welcome.[24]*

When Willie finished his studies in philosophy in 1901 he returned to Clongowes Wood College for a second spell of prefecting. Obviously life there agreed with him. He wrote to his sister Mai on 8 April 1902:

> *I really intended to send you my Easter greetings in good time, but with one thing or another I found myself in Holy Week almost before I well realised that Lent had begun. And with Holy Week came a multiplicity of duties which left little spare time; and then the Easter vacation, vacation at least for the boys, but not vacation for us poor prefects, for we had to be on duty all day. Now, however, that I am a bit free, I wish you every happiness and blessing, with abundance of grace to make you all that our dear Lord wishes you to be. May you always be faithful to His call. I was ever so glad to learn that you are keeping well and strong. I have seldom felt better, thank God; and the best proof of this is that I am able to get through my day's work – and it is not always a light one – as well as any man. I cannot tell you how grateful I am to you for your prayers for myself and my boys, and also for your promise to continue the same.[25]*

The start of a new academic year in September 1903 found Willie on the teaching staff at Belvedere College in Dublin City. Belvedere House had been built in 1774 by George Augustus Rochfort, the 2nd Earl of Belvedere, in Great Denmark Street on the then fashionable north side of the city. Its external appearance conformed to the Georgian style favoured by the Protestant ruling class. Its interior decoration was carried out by Michael Stapleton, a leading craftsman of his time. Stapleton was a Catholic and so was not allowed to become a member of his craft guild, yet his name became synonymous with the elaborate ornamental plasterwork of stylish 18th Century townhouses. It would be another twenty years after this house was built before any Roman Catholics, despite being the overwhelming majority in Ireland, were allowed to vote in Parliamentary elections, let alone owning their own property or having other rights. It would take until 1829 for a Catholic Emancipation Act to be passed.

The 19th century brought profound changes in the fortunes of Dublin and its people. For the Protestant ruling class the south of the city had become the new place to take up residence, before Dublin's chic status plummeted completely. The Act of Union in 1801, which had united the Parliaments of the Kingdom of Ireland and the Kingdom of Great Britain, saw Dublin change from being the active first city of Ireland and home to its Parliament, to one whose raison d'etre for its ruling class was purely social. The northside Georgian streets and squares were already in decline, but within a few years even some leading citizens on the southside started to relocate to London or elsewhere. Trades in Dublin lost revenue and many servants lost their jobs. In the north of the city new owners of buildings turned them into tenements to maximise rents. As many poor families were crammed in as possible, whilst the buildings decayed around them. Belvedere House escaped such ignominy. When the Earl of Belvedere died his wife remarried and had a son. George Augustus Rochfort Boyd sold the house and it then came into the possession of The Society of Jesus. The Jesuits opened a school in the building in 1832 and it remains both a school and one of the best surviving examples of Georgian architecture in Ireland.

Fr Charles Doyle said that his brother Willie was even more popular with the Belvedere boys than with those at Clongowes. By this time Willie was 30 years old, and with the benefit of his experiences as a prefect and philosophy student behind him, his teaching gifts came to the fore. Many boys confided in him seeking his help, counsel and prayers. Also, by now Willie was even more mindful of preparing for the priesthood and did much good work for the Apostleship of Prayer.

Willie Doyle was a strong advocate of temperance and his time spent in Dublin gave him an opportunity to do good works in the abstinence movement. When Fr James Cullen, S.J. founded the Pioneer Total Abstinence Association of the Sacred

Heart in 1898, Willie is reported to have been one of its first members. Willie, apparently, served on the Council of the Association whilst in Dublin and Father Cullen had wanted him to be his successor as Central Director.

Hugh Doyle kept a decanter of whiskey at Melrose, but Charles was of the opinion that Willie never tasted alcohol. However, there are references from Willie in years to come, hinting that he was not a total stranger to alcohol, so perhaps he was afterwards persuaded of the virtues of temperance rather than total abstinence. Certainly Willie's charitable visits to the poor on Dalkey Hill, when he lived at home and on return visits, was warning enough of the perils of alcohol, both physically and financially. Indeed, there was one old man that Willie had repeatedly tried to reform and who would promise to give up the drink for Master Willie's sake, only to fall off the wagon shortly after taking the pledge. There was also an occasion whilst at Ratcliffe College, when Willie encountered two pupils who had sneaked off to a local inn during a college excursion. By the time Willie chanced upon them one of the boys could hardly walk. Willie and the other, more sober, boy, linked arms either side of the drunkard to help him along. They politely declined an offer of help from the occupants of a passing carriage, who then realised the problem and their disgust: *brought home to Willie forcibly the object of degradation and aversion drunkenness is in the eyes of many.*[26]

In September 1904 Willie transferred across Dublin from north of the River Liffey to the southern suburb of Ranelagh. Here, a ten minute walk from the centre of the village he took up residence in Milltown Park, a Jesuit house set in landscaped gardens - from northern bustling townhouse to southern leafy country house! The Jesuits had opened a school at Ranelagh in the 1880's and had been teaching theology there since 1889. Willie was to begin, at the age of 31, the study of theology necessary to be ordained a priest - another three years of hard slog!

Willie did not find theological studies at Milltown Park easy. The piecemeal nature of his previous philosophical study schedule, interrupted by periods of ill health, put him at a disadvantage. Once again he relied on diligence and organisation, along with prioritising, to get him through. He concentrated especially on what was likely to be useful in a priestly ministry and gave much time to moral theology. He passed first time, with distinction, his *ad. aud,* the examination in *ad audiendas confessiones*, which entitled him to act as a confessor. Charlie says:

This was rather a feat at the time, since this examination had recently been made very stiff, with the result that failures were many, even among the best.[27]

In addition to his studies Willie found time to read and make notes for future missions and retreats. He filled two bulky manuscript books with extracts from his reading, together with an index of the references. Notes such as those entitled *What is it to be a saint?* On *Heroism* he observes:

How many look upon holiness as something beyond their reach or capability, and think that it is to be found only in the performance of extraordinary actions…With their eyes fixed on the heroic deeds of the few, they miss the daily little sacrifices God asks them to make…[28]

Willie's ultimate aim was to work for the Congo Mission, about which he had heard from a Belgian scholastic whilst at Stonyhurst. Before he left Stonyhurst he had decided he would one day volunteer for the Congo Mission, to work with the poor pagans and share their privations, as soon as he was ordained a priest.

According to Charlie, Willie lost none of his high spirits in spite of the drudgery and monotony of a theologian's life:

He was always 'merry in God', the sunny, happy soul of old, with a bright word instead of a grumble, a smile instead of a sneer, with some innocent bit of fun to relieve the strain of hard work among those around.[29]

Nevertheless, there were some dark demons at work underneath this sunny exterior. A note from Willie's private spiritual diary dated 25 November 1906 agonises over 'The Practice of Humility.'

I will strive to get a great contempt for myself, to think little of and despise myself, and to pray and desire that others may do the same. I have nothing which God has not given me; I can do nothing without God's grace and help. In a few, very few years, my name will be forgotten. What will people think of me if they knew me as I know myself? My pride and desire for praise; my mean uncharitable thoughts about others; my fear of humiliation; the imperfect way I have lived in the Society; the sins I have committed, the scandal given, the terrible harm done to others by making them tepid, breaking rules etc., my resolutions broken in an hour; the many faults not corrected after sixteen years of religious life. In spite of all this I deceive myself that I am pleasing God ...[30]

One suspects this stretches the concept of humility too far, and can only wonder on what grounds he bases such deeply depressive thoughts, and why he was so lacking in self-confidence. There follows one of his many 'to do' lists he constantly wrote to himself:

'What must I do to become a saint?'

1. Excite in myself an ardent desire and determination to become one, cost what it may.

2. Beg and pray without ceasing for this grace and desire of holiness.

3. Take each action and duty as if were the last and the only one of my life, and perform it with extraordinary fervour.

4. Have a fixed duty for each moment and not depart from it; never waste a moment.

5. The spirit of constant prayer.

6. Relentless war against my will and inclination; agere contra at every moment in all things.

7. The faithful practice of little mortifications.[31]

Perhaps this reflection followed one of the scrapes in which he still managed to embroil himself due to his impetuous character, often leading to a rebuke or even punishment for lack of respect. Several times at Milltown Park Willie got into trouble when he was unable to resist poking fun at those in authority. One such occasion was when one of the older Fathers had been particularly vexatious and it was Willie's turn to read the daily menology at supper (a menology is a listing of saints, often with brief biographies, arranged in calendar order.)

Instead of reading the entry for a deceased member of the Society, Willie's obituary was a humorous caricature of the offending Father who was actually present in the refectory.

On another occasion he was ordered to his room by his Superior, a school boy's punishment for a man just into his third decade! Willie obeyed:

but instead of shutting his door, he piled up chair, table, priedieu, etc., at the entrance and during the evening interviewed and entertained friends and sympathisers from behind the barrier.[32]

Perhaps this resulted from an occasion when Willie had challenged his superiors, which he was prone to do when he and his peers believed there had been an injustice or an unfair new regulation. For instance, he reacted angrily when a somewhat officious Lay Brother had locked a gate leading into a field which the theology students routinely had access to. Willie smashed the lock to restore the right of way and incurred the wrath of his superiors. Charlie comments:

For this he justly got a reprimand and a penance, because a religious subject may not take the law into his own hands even to right a wrong.[33]

A rare criticism from Charlie! The two brothers remained close friends and Willie attended Charlie's first Mass following his ordination, which took place at the Carmelite Convent, Drumcondra, Dublin. Willie describes to their sister, in a letter dated 14 August 1905:

I take it for granted that Charlie – I beg his pardon – 'Fr Charles', has given you a full account of his Ordination and First Mass. It has been a wonderful time for us all, for me, perhaps, more than most, since I love my Jesuit brother so dearly; also because the scenes and experiences of those days will soon be my own. As you know, Fr Charlie said his First Mass at the chapel of Hampton Convent that is so familiar to us from childhood. Fr Tom was Assistant Priest, but had nothing to do, as the Celebrant was quite self-possessed, and knew his rubrics perfectly. He gave Holy Communion to dear old Mother Elias, that bit of heaven on earth, who has prayed for us and prayed over us since we were toddlers. I served the Mass of my dear brother, and thought of the long years we had spent together, and of his great happiness that is so soon to be mine. After the Mass we were entertained to breakfast with true Carmelite hospitality, and did full justice to the good things provided. Our party, twelve in number, must have eaten more chops at that one meal than these holy mortified nuns eat in a whole year![34]

The sister receiving this was 'Sister Mary' who was a nun in the order of the Sisters of Mercy. The two other people mentioned in the letter were relatives; Tom was their cousin and Elias their aunt. Willie often asked the family nun for her prayers and they were regular correspondents. A month before his own ordination in 1907 he writes:

I can scarcely believe I have all the long years of study, which I used to dread so much, really over. You know I was never intended by Almighty God to keep my nose buried in books all days. Climbing up chimneys, or walking on my head across the roof of a house, is more in my line! When I came here three years ago, my health was anything but good, and kind friends said I would not spend six weeks at theology. But after the first Christmas things began to improve and, thank God, have gone on improving steadily ever since, so that now, in spite of the hard work – and it has been hard and trying – I am in far better health and able to do more than when I came here. I look upon this as a great grace from God, and I only hope I shall not prove ungrateful to Him for all He has done…. As you may imagine, all my thoughts at present are centred on the Great Day, July 28th. The various events of the year have helped to keep it before my mind, learning to say Mass, the Divine Office etc.; but now that such a short time remains, I find it hard to realise that I shall be a priest so very soon. Were it not for all the good prayers, sister mine, which are being offered up daily for me, I should almost feel in despair, because these long years of waiting (nearly seventeen now) have only brought home to me how unworthy I am of such an honour and dignity.[35]

Just before the ceremony for his ordination, Willie wrote a prayer:

My loving Jesus, on this the morning of my Ordination to the Priesthood, I wish to place in Your Sacred Heart, in gratitude for all You have done for me, the resolution from this day forward to go straight for Holiness. My earnest wish and firm resolve is to strive with might and main to become a Saint.[36]

Willie Doyle was duly ordained into the priesthood, along with a dozen or so others, on 28 July 1907, in the church at Milltown Park. He was aged 34 and lost no time after the ceremony writing to Mai again. Whilst his delight is quite evident, a persistent nagging doubt reared its ugly head.

> *I know that you will be glad to receive a few lines from the hands which a few hours ago have been consecrated with the holy oil. Thank God a thousand, thousand times, I can say at long last, 'I am a priest', even though I be so unworthy of all that holy name implies. How can I tell you all that my heart feels at this moment? It is full to overflowing with joy and peace and gratitude to the good God for all that he has done for me, and with heartfelt thankfulness to the dear old Missionary for all her prayers … I say my first Mass tomorrow at nine at Hampton for the dear Parents, the second (also at noon) at Terenure will be for you … Thank you for all you have done for me; but above all thank the dear Sacred Heart for this crowning grace imparted to your little brother who loves you dearly.*[37]

Doubts notwithstanding, Mr Doyle had become Fr Doyle.

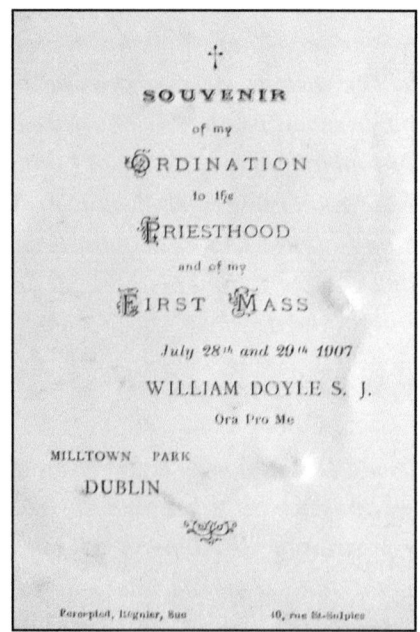 

First Mass Card, 1907, front and reverse

CHAPTER 6
APPRENTICE AGAIN:
MARCHES AND RETREATS

'Domine, quid me vis facere?'
(Lord, what wilt Thou have me to do?) *Acts 9,6.*

'Ego dixi: nunc coepi.'
(I said: Now I have begun.) *Psalm 76,11.*

The year 1907 marked another important milestone for the Doyle family. The month following Willie's ordination his parents celebrated their 50th Wedding Anniversary. A photographer was engaged to record the occasion in August and Christina was presented with a bouquet of flowers. Many of the family assembled and gathered round Hugh and Christina at the front of *Melrose* for the photographs. Mai appears to be the only one of their surviving children who was not present. Once again she was absent from a family celebration, having missed the ordinations of both Charlie and Willie; she obviously could not be spared from her devotions at the Convent of the Sacred Heart. [FN1]

Two months later Fr Doyle was on the move again. In October 1907 he returned to Belgium, to a Jesuit establishment at Tronchiennes near Ghent. He was to stay for a year in order to complete his tertianship which, in essence, was an advanced form of the novitiate. As at Tullabeg, the days were mapped out with menial tasks to perform, each of which brought forth admonitions and corrections, along with spiritual exercises. The tertianship was designed for reflection and to reinvigorate minds and bodies wearying from long years of training and study, before the Last Vows to the Society were made. After assigning fifteen years or more to acquiring so much knowledge, the year of tertianship was to be devoted, as St Ignatius intended, to striving for spiritual perfection. A crucial component of this process was the Long Retreat which occurred right at the beginning of the tertianship. Indeed, altogether, Fr Doyle spent 52 days on retreat; periods of seclusion for prayer and meditation from October 1907 to July 1908.

Doyle family group, 1907

The next couple of years for Willie was also characterised by journeys. Three months into the tertianship the apprentice priest was required to undertake missionary work, by giving missions and retreats, within and outside of Belgium. In addition to which, Willie made a detour via Paris and Lyon during his first journey to Tronchiennes in 1907, which lasted nearly three weeks. Then in July 1908 he embarked on a pilgrimage from Tronchiennes to Liege, about a hundred miles away.

Willie needed to be at Tronchiennes for the start of the Long Retreat on Wednesday 9 October 1907. He set out from Dublin on Monday morning 23 September and wrote an account of his adventures en-route to his father. His journey started by boat from Dublin to Holyhead and he comments:

Glorious morning leaving Ireland. Full boat. Saloon passengers packed like sardines; we steerage ones more so if possible. Longed for a storm to clear the deck, but Neptune only smiled and rippled. Lunch in great demand. A gentleman, a perfect stranger, insisted on standing me lunch. Sorry I could not find him on board the train when dinner hour came! [1]

Willie's next comment illustrates how social mobility had been facilitated by the railway:

Noticed two young girls standing in the corridor of the train. They told me they had left a village near Limerick at twelve the night before, and were going to London, never having been from home before. Got them seats and tea and, with great difficulty, the friend at Euston who had come to meet them. [2]

After disembarking, Willie entrained to Euston, where he arrived late in the afternoon and continued his journey:

Only incident of note in London was the successful endeavour of the driver of the bus I boarded to ram everything in front of him, with no small damage to the paint of the bus or motor ahead, and the creation of an atmosphere decidedly warm. It was interesting calculating the amount of damage he would do to the next vehicle he would ram, and the number of new curse words I should learn! [3]

On Wednesday morning he was on another train en-route to catch the Folkestone to Dieppe ferry. He reached his destination in Paris after a pleasant run through Normandy, although he doesn't specify the means of transport. A late arrival at a religious establishment meant a welcome dinner and straight to bed. Mass was said the next day and:

… in signing my name etc., in the sacristy register, by mistake I wrote Archbishop Walsh's name in the place where mine should have been. The good Curés must have thought me a very youthful Archbishop! [4]

It was a Friday morning, 27 September, when Willie left Paris, early at 7.30 a.m., for Paray-le-Monial, the home of Blessed Margaret Mary, the anniversary of whose death,

17 October, was approaching. He had originally intended to travel by train, Second Class, but decided that, as Third Class looked comfortable enough, he would buy the cheaper ticket, which enabled him to extend his journey to Lyons. He arrived at Paray-le-Monial about 6 p.m. and was directed to the house where two Jesuit Fathers were living. He records that it was a humble abode and an almost blind French Jesuit welcomed him. Willie was invited to take supper, which proved to be a rather frugal helping of soup. He was up early the next morning to undertake his assignment.

Willie's pilgrimage to Paray may have been inspired by the fact that he had a special devotion to Blessed Margaret Mary. Marguerite Marie Alacoque was born in 1647 at L'Hautecour in the province of Burgundy and grew to be a sickly but a very religiously devoted child. She joined the Order of Our Lady of the Visitation at Paray-le-Monial in 1671, where she herself had divine visions. It is recorded that in his revelation to her, God asked Margaret Mary to spread devotion to His Most Sacred Heart. She obtained permission from her superiors to do so and consequently, in 1688, a chapel dedicated to the Sacred Heart was constructed at Paray-le-Monial. Two years later Margaret died at the age of 43; her body rests under the altar in the chapel at Paray.[FN2] Willie says of his visit:

> *Up at cockcrow in order to secure an altar at the convent. Even so, I had to wait nearly three hours before I could get a vacant one. In the end I had the privilege and happiness of saying Mass at the very altar where our Lord appeared to the Blessed Margaret Mary, and revealed to her the devotion to His Sacred Heart with the command to spread it. I paid a long visit to her shrine, and did not forget to pray for you all.*[5]

Later on that Saturday, 28 September, Willie set off for Lyon, via Ars-sur-Formans, for which he had to purchase an extra return ticket as it was off the main Lyon line. The reason for the diversion was, again, to make a devotion, this time to the shrine of the Blessed Curé Jean Baptiste Vianney, who had been beatified in January 1905, and to whom Willie was especially dedicated. Unfortunately, Willie's journey was far from straight-forward. Despite asking advice, he ended up on the wrong train and had to stay overnight in Villefranche. Setting off again on Sunday morning:

> *Next morning I took the steam train to Ars. What a journey it was! The rails were laid anywhere, and anyhow, with no attempt at ballast. You stood on a kind of platform and hung on for dear life to a post, or to your neighbour,*

while the engine jumped up and down from sleeper to sleeper, grunted up the hills, and flung itself recklessly down the other side. Once we stuck in the middle of a steep incline, the train being too heavy for the engine. Nothing daunted the driver backed the machine down and up a hill behind. Then, while all rammed their hats tightly on, and took a long breath, he loosed his brakes, and with full steam on, rushed his engine down the hill, and up the steep incline. I thought we were gone that time, that no respectable engine would stand an insult of that kind. All went well, however, and we reached Ars in safety, though not a little sore after all the bumping. [6]

Again it's a matter for speculation as to why Willie Doyle was drawn to this man. Maybe it was because Fr Vianney was famed for his devotion to hearing confessions, spending long hours in the confessional, in both freezing winter conditions and the sweltering heat of the summer. Or perhaps for the more mundane reason that he struggled with his studies, lacked confidence and doubted his worthiness for office in the same way that Willie did. On the other hand, to put a modern perspective on it, Fr Vianney was a legend in his lifetime and had the fame of sanctity; his story had an element of romance, plus his life had ended a mere fourteen years before the birth of Willie Doyle. [FN3]

Willie discovered that the village of Ars-sur-Formans lies in an undulating plain, its western boundary overlooked by the hills of Beaujolais. A stream meanders through the valley and the village, bypassing the mound at its centre. Fr Vianney, before him, found the church standing on this small hillock, with the presbytery in the shallow. Willie was thrilled to have been able to visit Ars, writing:

In this little country village I saw everything connected with the saintly Curé of Ars. I visited the room in which he died, examined the half-burnt curtains said to have been set on fire by the devil, the little pan in which he cooked the flour-lumps he called his cakes, etc., for everything has been left, just as in his time. The little church is standing, too, unchanged. As a special privilege, one of the priests unlocked the confessional the holy man used so long for eighteen hours a day, and let me sit in it. On Monday morning I said Mass at his shrine, using the very chalice used by the saint. In a gold and glass shrine over the altar reposes his body still quite incorrupt. It gave one a strange feeling to see the holy old man lying before one, calm and peaceful, with a heavenly smile on his face, just as

> *he died fifty years ago. I shall never forget my visit to Ars. I knew all about the Blessed Curé's life, so that each spot had charm and interest for me.* [7]

On Monday evening, 30 September 1907, Willie arrived in Lyon and he spent Tuesday being a tourist. He reported that the weather was beautiful, but very hot, and he went from one end of the city to the other on a river steamer for the sum of one half-penny. He said Mass twice at the shrine of Our Lady of Fourviere and prayed in the church, reputed to be the most beautiful in all of France. Whilst praying he:

> *noticed a priest in front of me, the back of whose head seemed familiar. Went up to him and found a French Jesuit who had been with me in philosophy at Stonyhurst. He was a native of Lyons (sic), had just returned from Egypt, and was delighted to meet me again.* [8]

Willie returned to Paris on Wednesday to undertake a business errand. The train journey went smoothly and he enjoyed the captivating scenery. In Paris he was able to see a lot of the city during the course of the next few days, when intervals of business allowed. Evidently he rued the absence of a contemporary equivalent, in Paris, of the Curé of Ars, who had expended so much energy in attracting parishioners back to the church and away from the taverns and frivolous amusements. Willie says:

> *Visit to what was once our house in the Rue de Sèvres was a painful one. All the Fathers are gone, and now in each room of the huge house a family is living, for it has been let by the Government as a tenement house, whilst the beautiful church has been turned into a cinema hall. In another street where we had a large college, a stage has been erected on the very altar; where people once heard Mass, they now listen to music-hall songs.* [9]

However, he was somewhat cheered by:

> *A stirring contrast to this is the perpetual adoration at Montmartre – bands of women pray all day, and men watch at night.* [10]

By the evening of Sunday 6 October, Willie was in Brussels and slept that night at the Jesuit College which had seven hundred boys on the roll. Willie's life was never a dull moment! He reports:

> *On the way back from a visit outside the city next day I missed my train by a minute. Providentially, for I reached the station just as a poor fellow was run over by the train, and I was able to give him absolution.*[11]

On Monday evening he met the other Irish Fathers undertaking their tertianship, and en-route to the abbey at Tronchiennes they joined up with five Dutch and ten English colleagues. Willie's first impressions of his new home were very good, confirmed when he was given a room facing south and in the sun all day, although he did lament that his carpet must have gone off for spring cleaning! He enjoyed walking along the pathways shaded by huge lime trees in the Abbey gardens and wrote home enthusiastically:

> *My window looks down on the river Lys, which flows past the house; and I am able to study Belgian country life, and inhale Belgian country smells from a couple of farms opposite. The grounds around are very large, with pretty walks; one especially along the bank of the river is a great favourite of mine.*[12]

Consistent with the extensive grounds was the huge size of the house, or rather several houses, which Willie compares to the pontifical university at Maynooth in Ireland. He wryly comments that life is not very exciting at Tronchiennes and his chief amusement is listening to the bells, of which there were eight within the houses used for different people and purposes, including:

> *…a brazen-tongued beast of a bell at the hall door, and to crown it all, the church nearby … has a chime all of its own. May the Lord be good, and send a thunder storm somewhere near that chime that we may have a little peace!'*[13]

Contrary to his previous experience in Belgium, Willie adapted very well to life there a second time.

The truth is, Tronchiennes agrees with me and the food is excellent. I was a bit afraid of this, as one fortnight in Enghien long ago knocked me out of tune completely. It is rather hard work getting accustomed to a second dinner at seven, having dined at twelve; but 'I does my endeavours,' and I think I succeed. I now weigh – no, I won't put it on paper it looks too terrible when worked out in kilos. It is nice to say 'I am nine stone' but if you say two or three hundred kilos, people get a bit alarmed.[14]

Willie's family had to wait for these observations until after the Long Retreat, which began on Thursday 10 October and lasted until Wednesday 13 November 1907. Willie's diary recording the retreat begins on 10 October 1907 with the words:

I begin the Long Retreat this evening with very varied feelings. I feel a great desire and determination to make this retreat as I have never made one before, for I know this is a turning point in my life – I can never be the same again.[15]

His next entry covers the foundation on which the retreat is set. Willie's thoughts on this open with his belief: *God has some special end in creating me, some particular part in His great plan.*[16] However, he goes on to criticise himself for becoming dissipated and careless, then ends with this entry: *I close the Fundamentum with feelings of humility and sorrow at the thought of my past service of God. How little reverence! Thank God, I have still time to make up for it.*[17]

Here is recorded a brief outline of the Long Retreat, as Willie makes his way through the four weeks of the process. (For those readers interested in reading the detailed diary entries, these appear in Professor Alfred O'Rahilly's biography). The first week of the retreat covers the issues of: sin, hell, death, judgement and The Prodigal Son, followed by Willie's summary, 'Fruit of the First Week', which ends: *I am ready to do Your will, no matter how hard it may seem to me.*[18]

The second week examined the subjects: On the Kingdom of Christ, The Nativity, The Flight into Egypt, The Hidden Life, The Two Standards, The Three Classes of Men, The Three Degrees of Humility, Practice of the Third Degree. Then followed the issue of Willie's future (questioning his destiny for the Congo Mission), and his second summary, 'Fruit of the Second Week', which ends: *I see nothing will be dearer to Him than my sanctification, chiefly attained by the perfection with which I perform even the smallest action. 'All for the love of Jesus'.* [19]

The third week pondered the topics of: The Passion, The Scourging, Calvary, A Compact with Christ and Willie's 'Fruit of the Third Week', which ended: *I feel my past sinful life will be a spur for me to aim at great holiness.*[20]

The entries of the fourth week were: Emmaus, Apparition by the Lakeside, Reflections on the Retreat and Resolutions of the Long Retreat, 1907. Willie writes: *At the close of the retreat my soul is full of many emotions,*[21] which is the same sentiment but different words as the opening sentence of his retreat diary. However, the summary which follows indicates that his plethora of emotions was now positive rather than the negative tone of his opening statement. He ends his reflections:

> *Thank You O my God, for all the graces of this retreat, above all for bringing me at last to Your sacred feet. Grant me grace to keep these resolutions and never to forget my determination to strive might and main to become a saint.*[22]

Willie made twelve resolutions as a result of the retreat, the last of which was to read the previous eleven once a week, and the motto *'Agere contra' – all for the love of Jesus and to win His love.*[23]

When Willie finally had the time to write to his family he records that the Long Retreat was a trying time, but easier than he had expected and that he felt a good deal better in the spiritual life. As usual, his letters are full of humour:

> *Lazarus is risen! But by mistake they left him in the tomb thirty-three instead of the scriptural three days; and poor Lazarus is jolly glad to get out and breathe again! We came out of retreat yesterday, having commenced on the afternoon of October 9th. After each eighth day we were given a walk in the afternoon for some hours ... I have nearly forgotten how to talk or write to you, so you must excuse all mistakes. As I wrote to Fr Charles, I have been simply amazed at the good form I have been in all during this trying time, and now at the end I am wonderfully fresh and fit. Many of the fathers were not able to go through all the exercises; but I missed nothing, not even the hour's meditation at midnight. That is perhaps the worst thing in the whole retreat. You go to bed as usual at nine, and then just as you are in the middle of your best dream, a wretch, a perfect villain you think him, puts his head into your room just as all*

the clocks of Ghent are booming twelve and says: Benedicamus Domino (Let us bless the Lord.) By all means, you say, but would it not do to bless Him between the blankets?[24]

Fr Willie in 1908

The year Willie Doyle spent as a tertian was a landmark in his inner life. In addition to his amusing correspondence he recorded at length, in his private journal, intimate thoughts, feelings and spiritual notes. One such instance was his list of pros and cons for proceeding with his wish to volunteer for the Congo Mission. There were thirteen reasons for the project and four against, none of which was actually the most compelling statement he makes elsewhere in his diary, on 13 November 1907, that: *If I go to the Congo, I shall certainly not live long.*[25] (The founder of the Congo Mission of the Belgian Province of the Society of Jesus, Pere Emile Van Hencxthoven, S.J. had died in Africa the year before, aged 54, and had been a novice at the Abbey at Tronchiennes some 34 years earlier).

The Congo Mission was for the future. In the meantime there were other bridges to cross and within a few months of the end of the Long Retreat Fr Doyle, together with the other young priests, were assigned routine retreats of their own, which gave them their first taste of missionary work. In January 1908 Willie gave his first retreat to some fifty girls at a convent near Hamont. Then, during Lent 1908 he travelled to Britain, to give missions in Aberdeen, first, followed by Yarmouth.

During a retreat, the participants are able to withdraw from the usual occupations of their daily lives to a place of shared privacy. Silence and prayer are the order of the day, giving them ample opportunity to meditate on Christ's message and commune with their faith. A mission, on the other hand, is a public event, usually conducted in a church or cathedral, which people fit into their ordinary lives and it is timetabled to facilitate this. Sermons feature prominently during missions as well private prayer and reflection.

Willie spent three weeks helping with missions in Aberdeen under the wing of Fr Matthew Power, S.J., on whom he made a deep impression. Fr Power wrote after Willie's death:

Young and inexperienced at the start of our great mission some years ago, he proved conclusively to me, and to all the local clergy and people, that he was a Jesuit missioner 'to the manner born', and this from the very first sermon he preached. Every day he grew in the affection of the Aberdonians until we parted, to his great grief and mine.[26]

The admiration was mutual as Willie expresses in a letter home to his father:

I was rather uneasy on my way to Scotland as it was the first mission ever given by Jesuits in the 'granite city,' and naturally we hoped it would be successful. Then, though I was very glad to work under such a great man as Fr Matthew Power, who is nearly as famous in Scotland as Fr Tom

Burke was in Ireland, I could not help feeling that I should play only a very humble second fiddle beside him.[27]

This did not prove to be the case. For instance, on the last Sunday Willie started work at 8am with Mass, and didn't finish working until late into the evening, having given four talks in addition to undertaking the rites of his worship duties:

As you may imagine, the work has been hard. We found it necessary to change the original programme, and add to the services. This meant I had to speak on a large number of subjects for which I was quite unprepared, and often had to preach after a few moments' hasty thought, but certainly the grace of God was in abundance. I was not the least bit nervous, and never at a loss for plenty to say. Though the church is very large and lofty, I was easily able to make myself heard in every part of it.[28]

As usual Willie's powers of humorous description didn't let him down:

Fr Power is a tiny creature of only 6ft 6ins and 18 stone weight, but his heart is as big as himself, and from the start he gave me every encouragement, and we soon became great friends.[29]

He explains that the mission had been an unqualified success; they managed to get over a hundred people to go to daily morning Communion, whereas there had been practically none prior to the coming of the mission. He acknowledges that:

I have been most fortunate to begin my missionary career under such a master; for Fr Power has had a vast and varied experience, and I learnt much from him, and I hope to profit by his advice and hints.[30]

Such was their success that they were invited by the Bishop to return the following year to give a renewal of the mission. In addition, Fr Doyle and Fr Power were photographed at various times and the photos were sold for the benefit of the church.

On 20 April 1908 Willie was writing home again, this time describing his experiences at St Mary's Church, Yarmouth. The mission there lasted a week, which he undertook somewhat reluctantly on his own:

> *The mission closed last night with a grand flourish of trumpets, renewal of vows, and general scorching of the Old Boy's tail, not to speak of one lady's hat, who, when I told all to raise their lighted candles, calmly thrust hers into the middle of the flower garden which she carried on her head. She was gallantly rescued from destruction by a young officer behind her; perhaps that encounter may have a happy ending.*[31]

Against all the odds the mission was a great success. It was only announced the week before it started and no posters had been put up to advertise the event, nor handbills sent out. The local clergy had not deemed it necessary to make their presence felt by visiting people and inviting them to attend the mission. Undaunted, Willie took the initiative and asked people to go round to their friends and bring them to the church. However, even at the end of the week Fr Doyle came across families who were not aware of the event but, nevertheless, the church was well filled:

> *Though I cannot say I am quite satisfied – perhaps I expected too much – the Fathers here are more than pleased, thank God, and the people tell me the Yarmouth Catholics surpassed themselves.*[32]

Fr Doyle had found the physical effort of speaking every night for over an hour, together with sole responsibility of this mission, a strain but well worth it in the end:

> *When I was offered this work … I was very much inclined to refuse it. I was rather afraid of facing the music alone, and besides tired after three weeks' work. I cannot say how glad I feel now that I came; it has been a splendid experience for me, and simply invaluable. I was certainly much more at home, and preached better than in Scotland.*[33]

Of course there was the normal touch of dry humour:

> *I have got so hardened about blowing my own trumpet that I make no excuse for doing so again. I was greeted on Friday evening by two ladies from London staying here, with 'Father, we have heard Fr Bernard Vaughan preaching twice on the Passion, but we both prefer your sermon tonight.' Do you live near the Blarney Stone? said I to myself.*[34]

Fr Doyle made two unusual conversions whilst at Yarmouth. The first was a woman of over ninety whom he came across whilst wondering through slums. She had not been to church for many years and told him that she had led a wicked life. However, she also informed Willie that she did pray for God to send her a good friend before she died and now her prayer had been answered:

The next day I came back and heard her confession, and brought her to Holy Communion on Easter Sunday. As the tears streamed down her old withered face, she said, 'Oh, Father, this is the first happy day of my life, for I have never known what happiness is since I was a child'.[35]

The second incident merely sowed the seeds for a most unusual conversion to occur after he left Yarmouth. Late one night Fr Doyle was returning to the Presbytery after hearing confessions in the church, when he came across a prostitute. He couldn't pass her by without stopping and asking her why she was out late and to go home, advising her *Don't hurt Jesus. He loves you.*[36] Some years later he was finishing a retreat in a convent at Bray, county Wicklow, when he was handed a telegram from his Provincial. He was to return to Dublin at once and there it was explained to him that his services were required at a prison in England. A telegram had requested *Please send Father William Doyle, S.J. ... Woman to be executed tomorrow and asks to see him.*[37]

This episode was for the future and can be found in Appendix C. In May 1908 Willie returned from Yarmouth to Tronchiennes to continue his tertianship. At the beginning of July he was fortunate to undertake a pilgrimage in the company of an English tertian, Fr Stanislaus Roberts. Their pilgrimage was to the shrine of Our Lady of Chévremont, near Liege, about a hundred miles away. Fr Roberts had not been able to find a volunteer from his own Province, but was happy to be accompanied by Fr Doyle who was keen to go. They had minimal luggage consisting for each of them of a night-shirt, a pair of socks, a razor and an extra trouser button. They also had a letter of credentials and a purse with some money for emergencies or to save face in case they were accused of being beggars. Fr Roberts recorded: *Fr Willie was a most pleasant companion, always ready to fall in with any reasonable scheme, and never at a loss for timely suggestions*[38,] whilst Fr Doyle said:

We got on capitally together, though the Belgians we met seemed much amused at two 'deadly enemies' traipsing along side by side.[39]

No doubt the locals were equally amused by two priests wearing heavy black soutanes buttoned down to the feet in hot summer weather! Willie, as ever, is vivid in his narrative:

> *We had to depend on our sturdy legs to find us a bed for the night and on our eloquent tongues for food and drink. In the French-speaking parts this was not so difficult; but in the Flemish districts our vocabulary was sorely taxed. However, we found this phrase very useful and expressive, 'Waar is het grubben?' – which sounds very much like 'Where is the grub?' That, with a little pantomime saved us at least from starvation.*[40]

Willie and Stan left Tronchiennes at 6.45 a.m. on Tuesday 7 July 1908, passed through Ghent and arrived at the Jesuit College at Alost at 12.45 p.m. Here they took a shower, refreshment and sleep before making an early start again the next day. Their next port of call was on the Sisters of Charity at Assche who, after offering similar warm hospitality, advised them to divert to call at the Convent of the Sacred Heart at Jette. Willie, always one for a detour, willingly fell in with this plan and was rewarded by being granted the favour of seeing the body of the Blessed Sophie Barat. Like Blessed Margaret Mary, she was devoted to the Sacred Heart of Jesus, becoming the founder of the Society of the Sacred Heart in November 1800. The Society went on to become a world-wide institution during the nineteenth century and was based on the constitution and rules of the Jesuits. Although Sophie died in 1865 at the mother-house in Paris, her body had been brought from France a few days previously to repose at Jette.

Later in Brussels the two pilgrims walked from end to end of the city looking for the Jesuit College of Saint Michel on Boulevard Militaire. They arrived at 5.45 p.m. and made haste to the college's open-air swimming bath. They left Brussels on Thursday morning at 8.30 a.m., en-route to Louvain via the Forêt de Soignes, Groenandal and Overyssche. Willie wrote:

> *The Forest of Soignes was the most beautiful scenery I have seen in Belgium. Four hours march brought us to the other side of the forest, very hungry. A convent loomed in the distance. The Black Sisters, the people called them, and black they were in name and heart! 'No pilgrim*

fathers wanted today, thanks' was all the welcome we got; so we retired as gracefully as we could. When we last saw the convent it was still standing; but I am sure by this it is a heap of ruins, covering the remains of the wretched Black Sisters. Our next attempt was amusing. We saw a fine building on a hill, and were told the Brothers lived there. Hunger led wings to the feet and soon the hill was scaled. We rang; a dream of a maid, gorgeous in all the splendour of her noble calling, opened the door: rather a surprise in a religious house. 'Were the brothers at home?' A smile. 'They were never at home – always at Brussels enjoying themselves,' was the answer. Rather mystifying; but everything was explained when we learned later in the day that the occupants of that magnificent pile were three old bachelors, brothers! The poor pilgrim took in several reefs in his belt and plunged down the hill in search of the Curé's house. The good Curé held up his hands in horror when he heard what we proposed to do. 'Ah! Les Anglais!' That explains all: the English are all a bit mad you know.[41]

Having refreshed themselves Willie and Stan set off again, being fortunate to encounter later a friendly convent of Irish nuns who served them coffee. They arrived at Louvain about 8 p.m. Once again, their destination was at the other end of the town, and they had to walk over a long stretch of cobbled pavé to get to the Jesuit College. Twelve hours later they left Louvain, arriving late on Friday evening in Landen, which Willie noted as:

… ever famous for the death of the great Sarsfield. As I walked across the battlefield, his dying words came back to me: 'Would that this were for Ireland.' Sarsfield left his blood to moisten the plain of Landen, while the big drops of perspiration which rolled from our faces will certainly raise a record crop of wheat.[42]

Patrick Sarsfield (1660–1693) first Earl of Lucan, was a maverick soldier (of 'Wild Geese' fame) from an old Anglo-Norman, Catholic family and a secular hero of Willie's childhood.[FN4]

Fr Doyle and Fr Roberts were dismayed, after their visit to the battlefield, to discover the Curé of Landen was not at home. Off they trudged to the Convent, to find it being repainted and no rooms available:

We had a hearty meal, however, of bread and cheese washed down with cooling water. I could have eaten a haystack, for we were both famished. On the road again. Here was a fix. Nearly nine, no bed, and almost all our Office to say. However, the Lord was good, and we found an old priest who gave us two rooms for the night.[43]

The next leg of their journey was the twenty-six miles to Liege and so they were up with the lark the next morning with umbrellas at the ready – ready to guard against the scorching sun:

Old Sol was up before us sharpening his teeth for a blazing day. I shall never forget the heat of that Saturday. Eighty degrees in the shade. You may imagine what we felt walking along the long dusty road with not a tree to shelter us.[44]

They reached Liege worn out and exhausted, although this state of affairs was exacerbated by yet another diversion that lured them off-route:

On the road we passed a sign-post with the inscription 'Hal a mile to Booz'. The temptation was too tempting to resist. We turned down the road, found a jovial priest; and an hour afterwards two dusty pilgrims emerged from his house singing 'Vive Monsieur le-Curé' – only the heat, nothing more![45]

The Englishman and the Irishman also had a lucky escape that broiling Saturday. They came across a pump and while Fr Doyle seized the handle, Fr Roberts put his head underneath the spout ready to receive a welcome shower. Just in time they were diverted from their task by a Flemish man running towards them shouting. The shower from the spout proved to be liquid manure! Luckily, they were able to have more than a shower in the open-air swimming-bath at the College of St Servais at Liege. They rested at the college on Sunday before starting early on Monday up into the hills for Chèvremont, where they said Mass and breakfasted. Onwards via Liege to Tongres and the novitiate and tertianhouse of the French Jesuits expelled from Toulouse. The rector there insisted that they have a day of rest and relaxation. The next stage of their adventure was to go by train to visit Dutch Jesuits at their house in Maastricht, Holland.

Willie and Stan returned to Louvain via Hasselt, Alken and Diest and said

Mass in the former home in the Seventeenth Century of St John Berchmans in Diest. Once again Willie had the opportunity to make a special devotion at the shrine of a holy person with whom he felt a singular connection. When at Tullabeg Willie had written a pledge in his own blood to Mother Mary; he was copying John Berchmans signing in blood his vow to defend the Immaculate Conception. According to the *Catholic Encyclopedia*, John Berchmans was canonised in 1888 for performing ordinary actions with extraordinary perfection during his short life, which ended when he was only 22. He had an intense love for the rules of his order, the Society of Jesus, and observed them to the highest degree of sanctity. Willie Doyle's background, personal characteristics and interaction with his family and peers found resonance in the life of John Berchmans.

Less than ten years after Willie had made his pilgrimage around Belgium and made his devotion to St John Berchmans, he was back in that country tramping many weary miles and being drawn inexorably towards his own death. After Willie died a former college compatriot wrote from America:

I can safely say he was a perfect Jesuit and often reminded me of St. John Berchmans. His was a combination of real solid piety with a truly human character. Bright and joyous himself, he always made others happy and was evidently happy to do so. To those who knew his self-sacrificing devotedness there could be no doubt as to the identity of the heroic Irish Padre the first despatches recording his death spoke of. So certain was I, that I told my friends here that the hero was Fr Willie. Only three weeks later did I receive corroboration from the Irish papers.[46]

So much for the future. Back in 1908, Willie and Stan were well behind schedule by the time they returned to Louvain and so had to finish the final leg of their pilgrimage by train to Ghent. They reached Tronchiennes in time for the annual retreat, which brought to an end Willie's stay there:

I have finished the tertianship. Looking back on the past year, I see now in how many ways I could have spent this time more profitably, been more faithful to the order of time, more exact, etc.. At the same time I thank God from my heart that this year has been faithful in grace, and, I feel, has worked a wonderful change in me. I feel a greater desire to do all I can to please God and to become holy; a greater attraction for prayer, more desire for mortification, and increased facility in performing acts of self-denial. I know the work of my sanctification is only begun, the hard work and the real work remains to be done.[47]

During that year Willie had been fortunate to have an inspirational Spiritual Director, Père Adolphus Petit, whom he describes:

There is a wonderful little old priest here, named Fr Petit, small in name and small in size – he is about three feet high. He is eighty-five, but as active as a man of thirty, being constantly away giving retreats. I have tried several times to get down to the chapel at four o'clock in the morning before him, but he is always there when I come in. He is a dear saintly old man with wonderful faith and simplicity. In the middle of an exhortation in the chapel, he will turn round to the Tabernacle and say: 'Is not that true, my Jesus?' He is giving a retreat here this moment to a hundred and ten gentlemen.[48]

With such a remarkable figurehead for guidance, Father William Doyle duly and dutifully completed his apprenticeship at the age of 37.

Footnote 1: The author believes that the identity of those seen left to right as you view the photo are: – standing: Charlie, Lil, unknown priest, Jennie, Bob, Lena, Willie. Sitting are: Frank, Fr Willie, Christina, Hugh, Tom Murphy (probably). Children in front are (probably): Eileen (Lil and Frank's daughter), Alice Castles (Bob and Jennie's adopted daughter) and one of Lena and Willie's daughters.
Footnote 2: Following the Church's rigorous examination of cures and blessings attributed to Margaret by pilgrims visiting Paray, she was finally canonised as Saint Margaret Mary Alocoque on 13 May 1920, by Pope Benedict XV.
Footnote 3: Jean-Baptiste Marie Vianney was born in Dardilly in1786 and lived into his early seventies. Fifteen years after his death, Fr Jean Vianney was proclaimed Venerable by Pope Pius IX and, in 1905, Pope Pius X declared him Blessed, and proposed him as a 'model' to parochial clergy. Vianney was canonised by Pope Pius XI in 1925 and, in 1929, he was declared Patron Saint of priests. For further information consult www.ewtn.com or similar.
Footnote 4: It was the concept of an Irish Brigade, taking inspiration from the 'Wild Geese' serving in continental armies, that two hundred years later John Redmond wanted to apply to a similar force serving with the British Army.

CHAPTER 7
MISSIONS AND RETREATS:
WEARY WOBBLERS AND WHOLE-HOGGERS

*'You cannot teach a man anything, you can only
help him find it within himself'*
Galileo Galilei (1564–1642)

I like Father Doyle best because he is holy[1] was the considered opinion of a child attending a mission in Drogheda in 1913, three years after Willie Doyle had been assigned to the mission staff of the Irish Province in Dublin.

Willie's offer to work in the Congo as a missionary at the end of his tertianship at Tronchiennes in 1908 had not been accepted. Indeed, his Superiors initially completely ignored Willie's desire to work in this field and sent him back to Belvedere College to teach there for two years. Naturally this was a disappointment to him as he had been so confident that he would be sent to the Congo, let alone not be appointed to the domestic mission. In preparation for the Congo, he had even found a catechism in the native language with English translation and interleaved the two texts together. Nevertheless, in his usual indomitable manner he reconciled himself to the situation and was able to take positives from it. In 1909 he wrote to his sister Mai:

> *You ask me in my letter about the Retreats for the Workmen. I have nothing but good news to give you. The blessing of God is certainly on the work. You remember what led me to write the little book, my bargain with our Lord that if this project was pleasing to Him (for I had been thinking of it for years) He would station me in Dublin when I returned from the Tertianship, for naturally the start would have to be made there ... what was my amazement to hear that I was to come to Belvedere.*[2]

If Willie Doyle could not be a missionary in the Congo, then he had set his heart on working in domestic missions and, in particular, his ambition was to hold retreats for the working classes of his own country, along the lines of other countries close by, but which was virtually unheard of in Ireland. During the interval he was on the teaching staff at Belvedere College, he wrote the pamphlet entitled *Retreats for Workingmen: Why not in Ireland*, which was published in Dublin by the Irish Messenger Office in July 1909. After two years of teaching and carrying out administrative tasks at Belvedere College, Willie was eventually appointed to the mission staff of the Jesuits. He couldn't wait to write to Charlie:

> *Jesus has chosen me 'to preach the Gospel to every creature,' and to carry the love of His Heart to others. Pray that I may not disappoint him.*[3]

During the next five years Willie gave 140 missions and conventional retreats, and also responded to a large number of requests to give special sermons and talks, almost without break. During missions his confessional was, reputedly, always besieged. Charlie notes that on the Feast of Corpus Christi in 1913 Fr Willie:

> *had been hearing confessions on the day before from half-past five in the morning until eleven at night.*[4]

Obviously, the good Father Doyle had lost no time in aspiring to the work ethic of the Curé d'Ars! On one occasion, the Superior of the mission staff received a request from Monsignor Seagrave, Vicar General at Drogheda, asking that Fr Doyle be one of the missioners sent. The Superior expressed some doubt about the suitability of the appointment because he thought Willie's voice was not commanding enough to fill the large church at Drogheda:

> *'It's not his voice I want, it's himself'*, answered Monsignor *'His presence will sanctify the town!'*[5]

The Superior was also told by the Administrator at Dundalk Cathedral: *There is a charisma of sanctity on Fr Doyle that influences all who come into contact with him.*[6]

It was Charlie's opinion that Willie had few equals as a hunter out and beater up of the most hardened sinners:

His cheery manner, his simple boyish ways, his homely and kindly method of getting to others' troubles, together with his handsome, winning appearance, made an irresistible appeal, and, as among the poor on Dalkey Hill in his childhood days, 'Master Willie' passed from cottage to hovel, from basement kitchen to back-room of tenement, carrying hearts with him, and sinful souls to his confessional.[7]

Fr Willie was always direct in his apostolic approach. When at seaside ports, he would go to the quays at Midnight as ships docked, to try and entice crews to the mission or, at the very least, the confessional. After a few hours sleep, he would be up at six o'clock with shrewd eyes on his next prey; it could be mill hands or factory workers on their way to work. Then he would proceed to the main business of the day.

Missions could be conducted in a variety of situations, from the cathedral at Newry, or the mighty church at Drogheda or in a school or convent. During a mission in a school at Cork, Fr Willie offered prizes to the children who prayed the most and awarded them himself at the close of the mission. He referred to prayers, both his own and others who prayed on his behalf, as: *'ammunition' for the missions, which will mean the capture of many a poor sinner...*[8]

Writing to Mai on Good Friday 1911 after returning from a mission given at Dundalk, he describes two major coups there:

During the course of the mission I heard, by accident, of two men in the town who had been away 40 and 52 years from their duties. One was a hopeless the other a desperate case upon whom missioner after missioner had tried their hand in vain. They were so bad that the Priests of the town did not even mention them among the people to look up – it was a waste of time they said. Clearly no ordinary course of action would do here...[9]

Willie goes on to describe how he tackled these two recalcitrants, starting by going to the chapel to have: *a straight talk with the Sacred Heart.*[10] Fr Doyle was therefore gratified when he arrived at the first house to hear the wayward sinner confide that he had actually already given thought to attending the mission. Unfortunately, words did not translate into action and so Willie returned to see him the following day. Dan explained that he had attended the sermon but when it was time to approach the Confessional, fear had seized his heart and he ran out of the Chapel:

Poor fellow, I felt for him, but he had to face the music. 'Come now,' I said, 'down you go on your marrow bones.' I quickly ran him through his Confession, gave him Absolution and left the old fellow sobbing like a child, with sorrow and joy, beside his bed. Someone else's eyes were not dry either and I asked myself which of the two had received the greater grace.[11]

The next day Dan attended Easter morning service with 1,700 other men filling the church and in the evening when Fr Willie came out to preach:

I found, sitting inside the altar rails which had been reserved for the 'quality', glorious in his Sunday best, with a flaming red tie and a button hole in the most prominent seat of the front bench – my friend Dan.[12]

The other wayward sinner proved more intractable:

I went down one night to his house and was met at the door by a sour, cranky, crabbed old man who made no secret of the fact that I was a most unwelcome visitor – I was not wanted, and the sooner I took my departure the better. In fear and trembling I got in somehow, he leaving the door wide open, that I might lose no time in departing. I sat down uninvited, my friend stood and glared at me snorting. The very helplessness of the case appealed to me for I felt that all human power was out of the question here and that even the Sacred Heart had a hard task to face in tackling this beauty.[13]

Good luck, in addition to Fr Willie's entreaties to the Sacred Heart, came to his rescue. In trying to draw the man out Willie realised that he was well-read and had travelled a good deal as an iron worker and:

…had lived for a long time (of all places in the world) in Sheffield! I was at home at once. We talked Sheffield for an hour and though he did not sit down I saw he was thawing, for 'Sir' was now added to his laconic YES and NO, which eventually reached 'Your Reverence' once. As I left him, for of course there was no word about religion this time - he actually said

> *'God bless you,' his first prayer, I suppose, for years. I went home glad thinking I had done well.*[14]

Bad luck quickly followed this visit. It was several days before Willie could see Mr K again; actually on the Sunday that was the closing day of the mission, and his birthday, as he told Willie afterwards. Willie found him: ... *crouching over the fire looking fifty times as black and fierce as before.*[15] Since Willie's first visit Mr K had been sacked from his job and attributed his misfortune to Willie, who then endured a long tirade against God, the rich and himself for the calamity that had ensued. Nothing Willie said would placate the man:

> *Talk about playing a twenty pound salmon in a river, it was nothing to the tussle with that poor soul!*[16]

Whilst Fr Willie listened to Mr K he repeated a short prayer over and over in his mind: *Lord, You are on Your trial, remember Your promise.*[17] Suddenly, in Willie's words, grace struck the man. He calmed down, turned to Willie and quietly started telling him what had kept him from the Church for over fifty years. Willie does not explain, other than to say it was something trifling that had been magnified out of all proportion, which he was able to provide reassurance about, lifting an enormous weight from the man's mind. Fr Willie offered to hear his confession then and there, but Mr K said he would sooner do it like a man at church. Nine o'clock was the appointed hour, but at half past nine Willie was still waiting, when someone came into the church to tell him that a man had been pacing up and down in the square opposite for the past half hour. With Fr Willie's encouragement Mr K eventually made Holy Communion:

> *Our chat did not take long, the load of fifty years fell from his soul and Holy Communion in the morning sealed his reconciliation with Almighty God. The Sacred Heart <u>had</u> kept His promise.*[18]

Willie reflected:

> *It was only when it was all over that I realised what a strain it was, for I felt perfectly sick.*[19]

Whether it was before or after this event isn't known, but Willie once claimed that:

I have not met a single refusal to come to the mission or to confession so far during my missionary career.[20]

For this he takes no credit:

Why should there be one, because Jesus for some mysterious reason seems to delight in using perhaps the most wretched of all His priests as the channel of His grace? When I go to see a hard, hopeless case, I cannot describe what happens exactly, but I seem to be able to lift up my heart like a cup and pour grace and the love of God upon that poor soul. I can see the result instantly, almost like the melting of the snow.[21]

From the mouth of Willie to that of an army officer a few years later, confirming the Chaplain's gift:

You need not worry any longer about my poor soul, as you call it. I came across a Jesuit, a Fr Willie Doyle, out here, and he settled up my accounts with the Lord. Fr Doyle is a splendid fellow. He is so brave and cheery. He has a wonderful influence over others and can do what he likes with the men. I was out the other evening with a brother officer, and met him. After a few words, I said: 'This is a pal of mine, Padre; he is a Protestant, but I think he would like your blessing.' Fr Doyle looked at my chum for a moment with a smile, and then made the sign of the cross on his forehead. When he had passed on, my pal said: That is a holy man. Did you see the way he looked at me? It went right through me. And when he crossed my forehead I felt such an extraordinary sensation.[22]

Even those secure in their faith were moved by Willie. A fellow religious resident of the mission staff noted:

Though I had seen Fr Doyle several times, it was not until he was starting for the Front that I had my first interview with him. 'For goodness sake, Father,' I said to him laughingly, 'give me a blessing that will drive the spirit of tepidity out of me.' I knelt down, and he gave me a long blessing, and laid his hands on my head. I cannot describe what I felt, but I rose from my knees dazed, and as it were in a dream. I went straight to the chapel, and kneeling before the Tabernacle I realised as never before, that I was far from being a fervent religious, and with this realisation came a great desire to become one. That blessing effected a greater change in my life than all the retreats I had made, or spiritual helps I had received during my twenty years in religion.[23]

Fervent is certainly an adjective that could be applied to Willie Doyle, who once said:

I think there are too many <u>workers</u> in most religious houses, but not half enough <u>toilers on their knees</u>.[24]

Willie often forfeited a good night's sleep in order to put in a long shift of prayer, spending many hours on his knees before the Tabernacle, even after an arduous day in the pulpit and confessional. During a mission in Drogheda the curate was aware that it was Fr Doyle's routine to leave the confessional at 11 p.m. to go straight to the oratory to pray until the early hours, yet he was always up and out of the house before anyone else was astir. At Newry the curate had cause to go into the chapel one night and in the dark stumbled over the prostrate Fr Doyle deep in prayer. Another parish priest, concerned about Fr Doyle's lack of rest, sent the maid to the oratory of the presbytery where Willie was praying to collect his boots for cleaning, in an effort to prompt him to pause and take some rest. Fr Doyle merely left the chapel, removed his boots and his socks and returned inside to continue his prayers. Willie was philosophical about his lack of sleep:

The more I have to do, the greater I feel the need for prayer, so that between the two the poor sleep has a bad time.[25]

On 20 June 1912 he develops this theme:

I learnt a valuable lesson lately, I was thinking what I should do during the Novena of the Sacred Heart when the thought came to me to make

> *the Holy Hour each night. But human prudence pointed to several good reasons why this was foolishness. The mission had begun; I was in bad form, dead tired and badly needing sleep, besides feeling anything but well; then there was an early rise and a long drive before Mass. The Holy Hour each night in such circumstances seemed out of the question. But did not Jesus ask for it? It seemed to me He did, and that He would help me. And I was not mistaken. The result of the first night was that I found myself fresh and vigorous next day, all weariness and pain had vanished; and during those nine days I never felt better.[26]*

Despite such assertions, the lack of sleep must have been detrimental to his general well-being, especially at mission time which he refers to as:

> *... nearly always a time of intense suffering, spiritually and physically. However, I have noticed that with the suffering there usually come special graces for others and myself.[27]*

Readers of Willie's story to date, of whatever religious persuasion – or none - may have little trouble in engaging with his character, with all its frailties and foibles. But there was what many may feel to be a gloomy aspect lingering underneath Fr Doyle's sunny, no nonsense exterior. Willie taxed his already fragile health still further by combining mortification and penance with prayer. His devotion to prayer at the expense of sleep wasn't always self-satisfying enough because, even when he did sensibly retire to his bedroom, he sometimes placed boards in his bed or he slept on the floor. His diary often reveals that he is feeling run-down or unwell, but he rarely relented to give in to, what he considered, self-indulgencies.

There are many diary entries and letters revealing the physical trials Willie subjected his body to in order to aspire to a similar level of suffering as Jesus Christ on the cross. Amongst his papers was one written at Limerick on 22 January 1911, in the form of a spontaneous prayer, in which he refers to crucifying himself several times:

> *... to crucify myself in every way I can think of ... to crucify my body in every way I can think of ... to crucify my appetite ... to crucify my eyes ... to crucify my will ...[28]*

O'Rahilly summarises:

He developed a positive ingenuity in discovering possibilities of denying himself. Thus he was always striving to bear little sufferings and physical discomforts – were it only the irritation of a gnat – without seeking relief; he tried to imagine that his hands were nailed to the cross with Jesus. He gave up having a fire in his room and even avoided warming himself at one. Every day he wore a hair-shirt and one or two chains for some time; and he inflicted severe disciplines on himself. Moreover, between sugarless tea, butterless bread and saltless meat, he converted his meals into a continuous series of mortifications.[29]

Fr Willie Doyle also employed a common technique for living more completely in God's presence; his use of aspirations – short prayers interspersed throughout the day to overcome self-interest and facilitate union with God. For example, in September 1915 he noted in his diary:

This morning I lay awake powerless to overcome myself, and to make my promised visit to the chapel. Then I felt prompted to pray. I said five aspirations and rose without difficulty. How many victories I could win by this easy and powerful weapon![30]

He kept a daily note of the number of aspirations in his notebooks and the figures went into thousands. This subject has caused much debate about the interpretation of aspirations, although suffice to say here that it is an indication of the importance Fr Doyle placed on the use of these short ejaculatory prayers.

Life wasn't all work and self-denial. Willie still found time to visit his family, especially his parents and his sister Mai at her convent. Charlie refers to shared outings and to them both dining at Melrose; whilst O'Rahilly mentions Willie being at Dalkey on Christmas Day 1914. Willie's diary for the previous December reveals that he had been to the cinema to see *Quo Vadis* (albeit a film with a religious sub-plot.) The ending of this Italian silent production with sub-titles prompted a revelation in Willie:

… the words of Our Lord seemed to go through my soul, 'I am going to Rome to be crucified for thee.' Jesus must have given me a big grace, for

I walked home stunned, with these words ringing in my ears 'crucified for thee'.[31]

It is during the years of searching out ammunition for his missions and retreats that Willie Doyle reveals, at length, his belief and practice that every little victory over self helps. On 1 September 1911 Willie writes:

I feel a growing thirst for self-denial; it is a pleasure not to taste the delicacies provided for me. I wish I could give up the use of meat entirely. I long to live on bread and water. My Jesus, what marvellous graces You are giving me, who always have been so fond of eating and used to feel a small act of denial of my appetite a torture.[32]

Despite their best entreaties, and the daintiest dishes to tempt him, by cooks throughout the land, Fr Doyle generally kept to his resolution of sticking to plain food whilst giving missions and retreats. However, on one occasion he appeared to make an exception, much to the delight of the good Sister at the convent who noticed the cakes and fruit left for Willie were disappearing. However, Willie was giving the goodies away! He had discovered that two boarders at the convent were spending their vacation with the nuns, due to difficult family circumstances, and when the nuns were in retreat the girls were left to their own lonely devices. Charlie explains:

When time allowed, Fr Willie used to chat with them and try to cheer them up. He sought to raise their spirits, too, in a way that appeals to most young people. After his dinner he would go round to their recreation room, tap at the window, which would be opened cautiously, and hand in the good things purloined from his dinner-table! It was only years later, when one of the girls entered the convent and became a member of the community, that the true tale was told.[33]

Self-denial of favourite foods was an on-going struggle (but one which actually may have been beneficial in view of his long-standing digestive problems):

One thing I feel Jesus asks, which I have not the courage to give Him –

> the promise to give up butter entirely… For the present I will take butter on two mouthfuls of bread at breakfast, but none at other meals.³⁴

One of the most extreme examples of victory over self was Fr Doyle's regular custom to take discipline with a sheath of thorns (this was not an uncommon phenomenon of the era.) During a mission in Glasgow, when Willie was suffering from a head cold, he decided against tucking himself up warmly in bed and instead explains that:

> *I made the Holy Hour prostrate on the marble flags, and by moving from time to time I continued to get the full benefit of the cold. Then for two hours I made the Stations of the Cross, standing, kneeling, and prostrate, taking fourteen strokes of the discipline at each Station. For the rest of the night I remained kneeling before the Tabernacle, at intervals with arms outstretched, till I could bear the agony no longer.*³⁵

The Stations of the Cross comprises a series of fourteen pictures (or sculptures), possibly in combination with wooden crosses, depicting scenes from the time Jesus is condemned to death, through to being taken down from the cross and laid to rest in the tomb. Appropriate prayers are offered at each of the Stations.

According to Charlie, Willie was planning to endure an even bigger victory over self; one having no implications for his health, but which would have a significant impact on his daily life. Willie knew that his brother was keen to be appointed to the mission staff. For a time they were at Limerick together, and Charlie was teaching at Crescent College whilst Willie was part of the mission staff there: *we would take walks together, when mission work was a favourite topic of conversation.*³⁶ Charlie is a bit vague about the details, but the following St Ignatius Day, which falls on 31 July and is the day when appointments and plans for the coming year are published, he found himself on the Mission Staff - and Willie was to teach at Crescent College! Charlie established that Willie had engineered this situation and, as attractive as the proposition was for him, he was unwilling to accept this sacrifice from his brother, so quickly arranged with the Provincial for the status quo to be restored. Actually, fate had nearly dealt both Doyle brothers a different hand; the Provincial informed Charlie that he had allocated both Charlie and Willie to the mission staff in Australia, but the appointments had subsequently been changed.

MISSIONS AND RETREATS

It was just as well Willie continued on the mission staff; had he not done so he would not have had the opportunity to run retreats, for which he developed a burning passion. His fame as a retreat-giver quickly spread and soon he was in high demand; one particular summer he received forty invitations from religious communities to give them their annual retreat. It wasn't just the fact that Fr Willie seemed to radiate holiness:*The man is a saint! The house was filled with grace after he was in it,*[37] there was his unfailing cheery personality and courteousness: 'Father Doyle', a nun declared with emphasis, *'always treats one as a lady'*.[38] In addition, he applied ingenuity and humour to the retreat sessions:

> *'Don't be a Weary Wobbler,' he would say, 'with a wishing-bone where your backbone should be. Be a Whole-Hogger, and get the best of this world and of heaven; none more wretched than the Half-and-Halfer.'*[39]

Fr Willie would get ready for each day of the retreat by hanging up cards and pictures he had prepared, in which the work to be covered that day was outlined, with illustrations and thoughts for reflection. One or more of these cards would be of a comical nature, experience having proved that humour aids memory:

> *Smile! Keep the corners of your mouth turned up when you feel down in the mouth. 6/8 for this advice please. There are three D's which you ought to avoid – the Doctor, the Devil, and the Dumps. You can cheat the doctor and run from the devil, but the dumps are the divil!*[40]

Sometimes he used lantern-slides, unless the retreat was taking place in a church or chapel. Or he would have his favourite aspirations, for example: *Omnipotent God, make me a saint!*[41] printed on small pink leaflets which parodied a well-known advertisement:

> *Father William's pink pills for pale saints; intended to make pale souls ruddy with the love of God!*

Willie Doyle's sunny exterior not only masked his predisposition to endure, some would even say inflict, unnecessarily hard penances on himself, but it also disguised periods of intense depression to which he was prone:

'Such fear, dread and hatred of the Newry mission came over me,' he writes to a friend, *'that I was on the point of writing to ask not to be sent, and at the last moment I very nearly telegraphed to say I couldn't possibly travel.'*[42]

Travel he did in the end, but his troubles had only just begun:

For three-quarters of an hour I preached in agony, with the perspiration rolling from every pore. I was not afraid of breaking down before the congregation – that would have been a relief – but the physical effort to utter each word was torture, and the longing, time after time more intense, to come down from the pulpit was almost irresistible. They told me I preached well that night, yet I was quite unnerved, and only God knows what I went through.[43]

In a letter of 31 March 1913 he describes the struggle he had with himself and his prayers to overcome his weakness. But his interior battles continued even after finding the strength to fulfil his commitment:

What a battle I went through during these three days! I spoke with ease and confidence during the lectures, but all the rest of the time was simply torture at the thought that I had to speak again – loathing of the work, a resolution made fifty times over that this would be my last retreat or mission, that I could not or would not go on, that I would write to the Provincial, etc., etc.[44]

One person amongst many would have been particularly pleased that Fr Doyle never kept these resolutions. Willie was friendly with a man down on his luck, who had borrowed sums of money he could not repay and become bankrupt, alienating family and friends in the process. Charlie recounts a story of Willie's kindness towards this man:

Mr X retained at least one possession in the days of his misfortune. This was a First Class Pass on any of the routes of the old Dublin and South Eastern Railway. The Company had given him this as compensation for shock received in an accident on their line. Fr Doyle knew of this Pass, and whenever he was giving a retreat in a part of the country served by the Dublin and South Eastern, he would ask the Reverend Mother of the convent where he was giving the retreat if he might have a friend for dinner. When permission was gladly given, Fr Doyle would send an invitation to dinner to Mr X, telling him to come down early. Then having spent a pleasant day in new surroundings, and after a good dinner in the company of one whom he had reason to love, Mr X would return to Dublin happy and refreshed. [45]

Fr Doyle's apostolic work was also carried out by letter and Charlie wonders how Willie managed to fit his enormous correspondence into already well-filled days. He remembers Willie pointing to a bulky package saying: *That is a nice little spiritual letter waiting for an answer, only one hundred and fifty pages!* [46] Certainly, Willie was often tempted to give up at times, writing on one occasion:

When a man takes a pledge for life he generally asks for just one more drink. I have made a resolution this year not to grumble about letters, so I am entitled to have one last growl. The growl is only an apology for not answering your welcome letter sooner. But it reached me with twenty-four others, and ten came by the next post! [47]

Willie's reward, not that he was looking for one personally, were letters of thanks containing statements such as:

It may console you to know that your letter has been the means of saving me from at least one hundred mortal sins since. When these fierce temptations come upon me, I take it out and read it over, and somehow it helps me to fight the devil and say, 'No, I will not offend God again'. That has given me fresh courage. [48]

While giving missions and retreats Fr Doyle was often consulted for advice by those wishing to embark on a religious life in one capacity or another. This prompted him to write two pamphlets, published by the *Irish Messenger Office,* which found a receptive market. *Vocations* was published in August 1913 and as at 1938 had a total print run of 250,000, over 21 issues, and was translated into eight languages. *Shall I be a Priest* was published in March 1915 and by 1938 was in its 14th issue of 140,000 copies, translated into ten languages. The year in-between he published *Synopsis of the Rubrics and Ceremonies of Holy Mass.*

In 1914 Fr Doyle's toils at translation from French of the life of a fellow Jesuit were rewarded when *A Man After God's Own Heart: Life of Father Paul Ginhac, S.J.* (by Arthur Calvet) was published and went on to exceed all sales expectations, after an unpromising start. Indeed, writing on 30 May 1915, before sales had taken off, Fr Doyle wrote:

> *I have the feeling that it will bring much humiliation on me in some way, and I have asked our Lord to make it a source of suffering – I think he will. Not a single Rector except my brother has taken notice of my letter. One criticised the title sharply, but sent no subscription. Yesterday at recreation I gave the book to the Superior; he looked at the cover for a moment but did not even open it, and then passed it on like a sod of turf.*[49]

Paul Ginhac, 1824-1895, was another holy life to whom Fr Doyle felt a special devotion. As well as translating the original book, Willie distributed prayer cards and relics of Fr Ginhac and there are parallels between the two Jesuits. Like Willie, Paul had been persuaded by an older sibling to observe the workings of the Jesuits before deciding on his course in life. Paul originally wanted to become a businessman, but after attending a Jesuit mission he changed course and entered the Jesuit Novitiate in Avignon on 4th January 1843. His subsequent calling included being a college master and giver of retreats, a path Willie later followed.

Another of Willie's side-lines was to help boys and girls obtain places in religious houses once he was satisfied they had a true vocation: *When Ireland failed, he tried England, and even America, Australia and South Africa.*[50] Minor details such as health problems or disabilities did not deter him. He got one girl with a wooden leg, and another with a paralysed left hand, into American convents. On another occasion, having been successful in getting a girl into a convent, without mentioning that she had had spent the previous two years in hospital, he came clean with the Reverend Mother. The good lady was dismayed explaining that the convent could never accept such a delicate girl. Willie's reply being that the girl was not a bit delicate because Hospital in County Limerick where she lives is a very healthy spot! However, he only pushed for such places when he was absolutely sure that the timing was right. Writing from the College of the Sacred Heart at Limerick on 16 February 1912, he sympathised with a young lady who had been offered such a place in America, but was unsure whether to accept:

My dear child, I was about to write to you to suggest that you should wait a little while before going to America when your letter arrived. Some of the girls could not go at Easter, so you can do as you suggest. You are quite right not to make up your mind in a hurry, but for my part I am quite satisfied that God has given you a vocation and so it would not be well to defer entering too long as there is a danger in this. You need not be anxious about the future. God who has called you will give you all the grace you need to persevere.[51]

Willie ends the letter: *Pray for me my dear child*[52] thus leaving the young lady in no doubt that he believes she has a true vocation.

Willie made time to scribble and post a similar note whilst conducting a mission at Dundalk in 1913, offering hope and encouragement to another 'dear child' whose vocation was temporarily on hold due to a health problem:

I can realise what a huge disappointment the present trial must be to you, but as you say so well 'God's will before all things' since He knows best. You will find from this strength and that your happiness will be all the greater for having taken the cross so honestly and lovingly from Our Lord's hands. You must wait patiently till your ear is well and then we shall see what is best to be done. Please excuse this hasty line as I am very busy with mission work.[53]

The Holy Hour was another subject close to Willie's heart. Charlie believed that Willie may have given the first Holy Hour in a public church in Ireland during a mission in the Cathedral at Newry. In response to this unique event the congregation presented the cathedral with a beautiful large Monstrance, a vessel used to display the consecrated Eucharistic Host.

The administrator and Fr Tom Murphy, the Superior of the mission, were discussing what they should call the presentation, when Fr Doyle happened to come into the room. 'Let us ask Fr Doyle,' suggested Fr Murphy. 'Fr Willie, what should the presentation be called?' Without a moment's hesitation came the answer, 'The Mighty Murphy Monster Monstrance Memorial, of course!' [54 FN1]

A subject even dearer to Willie was the issue of retreats for workers. A retreat allowed individuals time to step back, seek personal direction and re-evaluate their relationship with God. In Ireland the opportunities to experience a retreat were confined very much to religious communities and the middle classes; so to establish retreats for workers was a mission for Willie! Charlie says that Willie was a pioneer in this field in Ireland, having seen the good achieved by such retreats on the Continent and England, during his years away when studying and learning his trade. Indeed, one of his friends, Fr Charles Plater, S.J., had recently opened a house of retreats for workers across the Irish Sea. Hence the issue of a pamphlet in 1909, written by Willie whilst still teaching at Belvedere, entitled *Retreats for Workingmen: Why not in Ireland?* While the pamphlet was at the press he wrote to Mai:

> *You know I am very anxious to see these retreats started in Ireland, for I believe they would do a world of good, and be the means of checking the dreadful irreligious spirit which is beginning to creep into even holy Ireland, especially among our uneducated men. I am hoping this little pamphlet may be a means of starting the good work; at least it will help to do so by giving people an idea of what has been done in other countries.* [55]

Willie explains his reasoning with regard to the value of retreats in his pamphlet:

> *There is a vast difference between the methods employed and the fruit resulting from a mission and a retreat. The one makes its influence felt only at certain hours in the evening, the other at every hour; the first uses a few well-known means of moving the heart, the other employs every act of the day, all directed towards one definite end; in the mission it is the preacher who does the work, in a retreat the exercitant himself ...* [56]

When it was published, he sent Mai a copy of the pamphlet, saying:

> *This little book has a history. For some time past I have been studying the question of retreats for workmen. Last year when I saw in Belgium the*

wonderful good brought about by them, and had an opportunity of seeing some of the houses where these retreats are given, I made up my mind to try something here in Ireland. This pamphlet is the result.[57]

Within a few months Willie was writing to Mai again full of enthusiasm because he had secured support from Fr J. McDonnell, the editor of the Jesuits' magazine, the *Messenger,* Moreover:

Best of all, only yesterday a gentleman of this city promised a donation of £2,000 to start the work. He had just read my little book, and was so delighted with the idea that he resolved to make a generous contribution.[58]

Of equal significance was that a deputation from the Guinness Brewery had been to see him to arrange for a retreat for Guinness employees, promising to send an initial 50 to the first retreat, with hundreds to follow. The Guinness Brewery was the largest employer in Dublin with over 2,000 employees and 5,000 at its peak. It covered some 64 acres as the nineteenth century passed into the twentieth, making it the largest brewery in the world. Sales of the famous black stout were in excess of 1.2 million barrels a year across the world. The Guinness family were renowned for charitable works and for the benevolent treatment of their workforce. For instance, restoration work on St Patrick's Cathedral, between 1860-1865, was possible due to a large donation from Guinness. The brewery owned most of the buildings in the surrounding area, allocating many to its employees, and in 1890 the Guinness Trust was established to provide homes for the poor. (Eight hundred of Guinness' employees served with the British Forces in the Great War and, like Willie Doyle, one hundred lost their lives doing so.) Unfortunately, there is no record of what happened with the Guinness retreat project.[FN2]

Willie's only holiday during the five years he was on the mission staff was one vacation of two months spent on the Continent. Although the trip was already approved, his departure was rather sudden following the end of a mission at O'Callaghan's Mills, County Clare:

I have come to the conclusion that I have earned a little holiday; for during the past two years I have given over sixty missions and retreats, almost continuously, and that begins to tell.[59]

During this vacation he was able to visit Lourdres. He writes from there in November 1912:

> *Almost the first thing which caught my eye at the grotto was our Lady's words: 'Pénitence, pénitence, pénitence!' On leaving, I asked Jesus had He any message to give me. The same words flashed suddenly into my mind, and made a deep impression on me.*[60]

Willie had opportunities for similar visits to shrines at Tours, Angers and Lisieux whilst on leave, however, his visit to the Continent was more or less a 'busman's holiday.' The main purpose for the trip was to inspect retreat-houses for workingmen in France, Belgium and Holland. His crusade for workers' retreats had the full support of his Provincial, Fr William Delaney and also that of another colleague Fr J. Walsh. Willie inspected many establishments during the two months he was away.

In spite of giving positive feedback from his expedition to the Continent, the necessary funds for his dream remained insufficient (the promise of the £2,000 had come to nothing, owing to the death of the donor before the donation could be made) and public opinion was largely apathetic. Nevertheless, his hopes were raised on one occasion when his Provincial found a promising residence with grounds and Willie was despatched to ascertain its suitability to adapt for a Retreat House. This proved to be a false dawn when a few days later the house was burnt down by Suffragettes, yet another bitter pill for Willie to swallow. In a letter dated 30 May 1913 to Fr Charles Plater he says:

> *I did not write, because I had nothing but disappointment, opposition, cold shower-baths and crosses to chronicle, the last and biggest cross being the sudden death of my truest supporter, Fr J. Walsh.*[61]

However, he goes on to say, more optimistically:

> *Your news about the success in England is glorious, and yet I am assured that mine will come in Dublin if ever a house is opened. I am confident the real difficulty will be to keep the men out. I never realised till I got on the mission staff the immense amount of faith and love for holy things there is everywhere still in Ireland …*[62]

Nineteen-thirteen passed into 1914 with Fr Doyle diligently going about his duties amid little change to the old routine. He continued to be heavily involved in the spiritual life of those already leading lives guided by the Catholic faith. O'Rahilly records that one of Fr Doyle's flock offered to build a convent if Willie could secure Episcopal permission. Building eventually began on the Colletine Convent in Cork in the Spring of 1914. But still Willie continued to be frustrated by the lack of progress to establish retreats for working men. Perhaps the keen disappointment he felt prompted him to volunteer to be a Military Chaplain in November 1914, a month before the opening of the convent on Christmas Eve. After all, he would find no bigger body of working-class men in need of spiritual direction than in a fighting army. And Ireland had always been a source of willing recruits, for economic reasons as much as any other, to the British Army.

A month after the start of the supposed war to end all wars, the Doyle family suffered a personal tragedy; Willie's sister Elizabeth died in Sheffield aged 40. Two months later Willie had volunteered for the Front and waited for his appointment.

It was a year before Willie received his appointment as Chaplain to the Forces. Before then, Charlie was finally able to record the one instance where his brother did, at long last, get to give a retreat for workmen. Although Willie had been on the mission staff for O'Callaghan's Mills in County Clare, it was at another mill where he was able to put his workers' retreat theory to the test. The Providence Woollen Mills at Foxford, County Mayo, agreed to the arrangement of a three day retreat for its male employees. Sixty of the sixty two men, plus five others from the town, attended the local Convent School of the Sisters of Charity on Holy Saturday, 3 April 1915. Thus the three days were spread over Easter when the school was closed and rooms made available for the retreat. Not only was this a welcome turn of events, but a happy distraction from yet more personal sadness.

The month before, Willie's mother had passed away in Dalkey, a grand old 83, and his niece, Eileen, Elizabeth's daughter, died in Sheffield at the tender age of 17. Willie had just returned from a mission in Glasgow and was with his mother at 7am in the morning of 19 March 1915 when she died. It would have been a huge comfort to him that he was able to say Mass immediately. This sad event, ironically, was followed by such happiness in giving the retreat at Foxford.

Naturally there was some trepidation amongst the Foxford men about the retreat: *We had been accustomed to fiery threatening sermons at missions ...*[63] but they were not coerced and a large number turned up for the first lecture. Indeed, Charlie says they were actually unaware until afterwards that they would be paid for the work time lost, which was Easter Monday and Tuesday morning. The loss of wages for the female staff, who had no choice but to remain idle, was also made up. As the men lived close by and were accustomed to being summoned to work and breaks by the ringing of a bell, it was decided that the nuns need not provide board and lodging. Each day was utilised to the full:

> *Mass was at eight o'clock, there were four instructions, two or three visits to the Blessed Sacrament, the Stations of the Cross, spiritual reading, and the rosary. This was said out of doors, and was very impressive; the men walking in procession followed by Fr Doyle who recited the prayers aloud. The brass instruments of the Mill Band accompanied the Benediction Service and Hymns, in singing which the whole congregation joined.*[64]

As usual Fr Doyle made a deep impression:

> *'His saintly appearance, and attractive manner at once captured our attention,' wrote one of the exercitants, 'and time passed so quickly while he spoke that each lecture, though invariably half an hour, seemed short. His words were simple and clear, and delivered in so kindly and gentle a fashion that they were just what he liked to call them – 'little chats.' ... At the close of the retreat all the men went to Mass and Holy Communion, listened to a farewell talk, assisted at Benediction, and received the Papal Blessing. Then Fr Doyle shook hands with each man as he left the room, and by this simple friendly act captured the last corner of every heart.*[65]

The success of the venture led to a biennial retreat for the mill-workers, although Willie was never to participate again. He had turned his attention to another kind of worker, those who toiled on the battlefields of the near Continent.

Two years prior to the triumph at Foxford, Willie had continued in his letter to Fr Plater:

> *It has been a four years' Calvary, but yesterday the Resurrection, I hope, began, for I heard that Rathfarnham Castle with 53 acres has been purchased at last, and I have the Provincial's promise (when that took*

place) to allow me to make a start in the stables. Ye Gods! Fancy the mighty Doyle preaching in a stable! Very like the Master, is it not? [66]

Rathfarnham had the potential to accommodate some fifty exercitants with communal refectory, library and smoking room, plus a chapel attached. It was situated in picturesque grounds in a south Dublin suburb, well-served by bus and tram. No wonder Fr Doyle found it hard to contain his excitement! And no wonder the Society of Jesus lost no time in moving into the property.

Unfortunately, the premises at Rathfarnham did not ever operate as a retreat house in Willie's lifetime. It was finally ready and opened its doors on 11 March 1921, all set to use a different kind of ammunition on those who walked through its doors, to that which had cut Fr Doyle down in his prime four years previously.

Footnote 1: the term Monstrance is derived from the Latin word 'monstrare', meaning 'to show', and its derivative 'monstrantia', which means 'a showing.' Essentially, a Monstrance is a stand, usually about two feet in height, with a central glass 'window', which is surrounded by a set of 'rays' representing the rays of the sun. A Monstrance is used in a service known as the 'Exposition of the Blessed Sacrament' whereby the Host (consecrated wafers of bread which have undergone transubstantiation, that is, the breads are changed into the Sacred Body of Our Lord) is placed into a crescent-shaped clip known as a lunette, which slots into the window of the Monstrance. The Monstrance is then displayed on the Altar, for the congregation to view, before the Blessed Sacrament is removed from the Monstrance and returned to the Tabernacle. A Monstrance, therefore, is one of the most sacred objects to be found in a church and only Catholic priests would ever joke about it.

Footnote 2: The Archivist at the Guinness Brewery in Dublin could find no record of the project in the files. (Interestingly, the site of the Guinness brewery at St James Gate was traditionally a starting point for Irish pilgrims to begin their journey on the Camino de Santiago. Translated as The Way of St James, this is a large network of ancient pilgrim routes all over the Continent, which fuse at the tomb of St James in Santiago de Compostela, north-west Spain.)

CHAPTER 8
WILLIE VOLUNTEERS:
WAR BREWING, WAR BOILING

> *'It is my Royal and Imperial command that you exterminate the treacherous English and march over General French's contemptible little army.'*
> Remark attributed to Kaiser Wilhelm II, 19 August 1914.[FN1]

By the time Willie Doyle gave his one and only retreat for working men in April 1915, he had spent nearly a quarter of a century under the auspices of the Society of Jesus. The largest conflict the world had ever seen was now in its ninth month of rage and Willie was awaiting his appointment as Chaplain to the Forces. Having had only limited success to date with one ambition, Willie immediately grasped that the war offered the opportunity for the fulfilment of another long held aspiration. When war broke out Willie didn't need to be urged on by recruiting posters and, in November 1914, he volunteered for the front as a Military Chaplain, writing at the time:

> *What I am going to tell you now may pain you. I have volunteered for the Front as a Military Chaplain, though perhaps I may never be sent. Naturally I have little attraction for the hardship and suffering the life would mean; but it is a glorious chance of making the 'ould body' bear something for Christ's dear sake. However, what decided me in the end was the thought that flashed into my mind when in the chapel: the thought that if I get killed I shall die a martyr of charity and so the longing of my heart will be gratified. This much my offering myself as chaplain has done for me: it has made me realise that my life may be very short and that I must do all I can for Jesus now.*[1]

The war which Willie was so eager to join had been brewing for a long time; indeed it followed on from another. *The Irish Times* had reported in Dublin, on Saturday July 16 1870:

> *The die is cast! War was declared against Prussia by France yesterday. Remonstrances are now in vain and arguments useless. The two military giants of the Continent rush to the encounter animated by an ancient rivalry, by ambition for supremacy, by the possession of vast armies fully equipped with the most deadly weapons of destruction, by insults real or supposed on either side, by recent victories or former conquests.*

When the Franco-Prussian war broke out in July 1870, Christina and Hugh Doyle were expecting the arrival of their third son Charles. William would put in an appearance three years later, two years after the end of the conflict between France and Prussia (the latter being in confederation with other German states). The Franco-Prussian war proved to be the supporting act for the main event to follow 44 years later; the words quoted above turned out to be even more apposite in respect of the Great War of 1914–1918. On the domestic front, the same year of Willie's birth, 1873, saw the formation of the Home Rule League in Ireland.

The Treaty of Frankfurt, following the Franco-Prussian war, was signed on 10 May 1871 and led to the creation of a united Germany. The unification of Germany under the first Kaiser altered the balance of power in Europe, tipping it towards the new state with a militaristic Prussian element at its heart. France, on the other hand, was left resentful over loss of territory and precious resources. Germany had taken Strasbourg, Metz, the whole of Alsace and the northern portion of Lorraine. Although Alsace was home to a majority of ethnic Germans, it also contained 80% of French iron ore and machine shops and was rich in coal (the only other significant source of coal readily available to the French was in the area around Lens). Therefore, its loss was a severe blow to the French economy, coinciding as it did with a long period of static population growth in France. The French quickly drafted a plan for military action, should the opportunity arise, to secure the return of Alsace and Lorraine. However, the Germans, ever mindful of French resentments, developed their own plan to strike and, indeed, conquer France should circumstances favour such action.

In July 1888 when Willie Doyle was in his fifteenth year and enjoying life at Ratcliffe College, a third Kaiser succeeded to the throne of Germany. By this time, the hugely populated German state had a vast army, enormous industrial infrastructure and well developed transport and communication systems. This third incumbent to the Imperial throne, Wilhelm II, was aged twenty-nine and a grandson of Queen Victoria. He was born with a withered left arm, which he was very self-conscious about and his was an insecure and unstable character. 'Kaiser Bill's' arrogant behaviour created and exacerbated tensions in Europe; he thought Germany was hard-done-by and encircled by aggressive, less deserving or backward neighbours, some of whom happened to be ruled by his relations.

The family connections in the royal houses of Great Britain and Russia only fuelled the Kaiser's resentments. It seemed to him that the German civilisation was heir to that of Ancient Greece and Rome, but it was not afforded sufficient respect. He made no secret of such feelings. He was openly suspicious of France, contemptuous of feudal Russia and jealous of Britain, particularly her empire and Royal Navy. This third kaiser, having served in the elite Regiment of Guards, and being imbued with the ethos of the Prussian Officer Corps of the Royal Court at Potsdam, was fond of posing in dress uniform, complete with ceremonial sword. He commissioned several paintings of himself as a regal warrior, all of them in profile to disguise his deformed arm. Gustav Steinhauer, the Kaiser's Master Spy, commented:

> *Anybody who knew the Kaiser at all well could hardly help coming to the conclusion that vanity was the predominating note in his character ... the almost unfailing regularity with which he bedecked himself in military garb inevitably prompted the thought that with him uniform was the trump card ... his barber, Erbest Haby ... was the man who invented the Kaiser's famous upturned moustache and, I might add, without him the Kaiser never travelled anywhere ...* [2]

Further insights into the Kaiser's character are worth quoting from Steinhauer, a man who had first-hand dealings with Wilhelm II:

> *I knew the Kaiser as far back as 1889... The Kaiser, in my opinion, was partly the product of his early upbringing and, after he succeeded to the throne, the product of his environment. Like the Prussian princes of days gone by, he was brought up in a strict, narrow-minded military fashion according*

to the ancient traditions of the Hohenzollern dynasty ... There would have been nothing objectionable in this if he had remained heir to the throne until, say, his fortieth year. During that time he might have been enabled, under the care of his parents, to have acquired a sensible knowledge of mankind and a wide outlook on life ... But he came to the throne ... when only twenty-eight years of age, just out of his youth. The people of Germany were not yet mature in the political sense, but were then beginning, under the experienced guidance of Bismarck, to develop their full powers in which the army was the trump card and the military caste had the upper hand ... Even if the young Kaiser had not been extraordinarily headstrong, it would have been strange had he not in some way succumbed to the temptations that surrounded him on all sides. He would need to have been marvellously gifted by God, or to have possessed outstanding mental talents, to keep a cool head when he suddenly found himself German Emperor with an immensely powerful army at his command and a people devotedly attached to the monarchy ... But he would not yield to the advice of his old and sage counsellors; for that, he was too impulsive, much too independent in his own personal character.[3]

True to form, the young kaiser, in 1890, dispensed with the services of the first Chancellor of the German Empire, Otto von Bismarck. The experienced Prussian statesman had worked tirelessly to make Germany a great power and believed that Wilhelm II was inheriting from him a firm basis for German security. Unfortunately for Germany:

The Kaiser was neither especially favoured by God nor did he possess anything but an ordinary intellect ... Fulsome flattery haunted his footsteps day and night ... ridiculously exaggerated flattery (that) was showered upon him right up to the last.[4]

Although the Kaiser inherited the tensions caused by the Alsace-Lorraine situation at the end of the nineteenth century, it wasn't many years into the new century before he added to them, provoking both France and Britain and edging those two former bitter foes into a formal declaration of friendship in 1903. Ten years previously, France and Russia had formed an alliance, which was cemented by a formal pact.

The Franco-Russian pact of 1893 quite openly stated that Kaiser Wilhelm II's Imperial Germany was the potential aggressor. France's motivation for this pact is accounted for partly by her static population growth and need for a bilateral defence treaty. Russia was conscious that her former ally Germany was now allied with Austria-Hungary and Italy. This Germanic Triple Alliance identified Russia as a likely enemy, owing to Russia's paternalistic attitude towards Slavs in the Balkan states, some of whom were part of the Austro-Hungarian Empire.

As one century passed into another, while Willie Doyle was passing between England, the Continent and Ireland, Europe was in the grip of a network of every kind of alliance, pact, treaty, understanding, agreement and guarantee. Simultaneously, political agitation in Ireland increased, although John Redmond, Member of Parliament for Waterford City, temporarily united the Irish Parliamentary Party, both at Westminster and in Ireland.

During the early years of the twentieth century, an escalating arms race took place in Europe, largely in response to the Kaiser's military posturing. For example, in 1900 the Reichstag had passed a second Navy Act that set out to double the size of the Imperial Navy by 1920. Germany antagonised France by interfering in French territory in Morocco, at Tangier in 1905, then again in 1911 when the German gunboat *Panther* was deployed at the port of Agadir. In 1907 Germany refused armament limitations proposed by the Hague Peace Conference and in 1912 Britain's request for a mutual freeze on warship construction was rejected by the kaiser.

As a consequence, Britain began to modernise her fleet and agreed naval defence measures with France. The French were to be responsible for securing the Mediterranean, while the British undertook the security of the French Channel ports and the North Sea. Britain also made no secret of its desire that Belgium should remain neutral, partly driven by the same strategic imperatives; that the Germans must not gain possession of Belgian ports any more than the French ports. The inevitable result was that Wilhelm II interpreted this as a threat to Germany. However, his own behaviour had fostered the continent-wide belief that it was Germany who was actually the aggressor. During a visit to Brussels in 1904 Wilhelm II said to Leopold, King of the Belgians: *I told him I could not be played with. In the case of a European war, whoever was not for me was against me.*[5] Therefore, it was no surprise that from 1910 onwards, under the guidance of the Francophile Major General Sir Henry Wilson, Director of Military Operations, the British army started to make advanced plans in the event of war with Germany.

When the Serbian student Gavrilo Princip took aim and fired at Archduke Franz Ferdinand, heir to the Austro-Hungarian Empire on a fine summer's day in the Bosnian capital of Sarajevo in June 1914, Willie Doyle was busy in Ireland organising missions and retreats. The sense of resentment felt by Bosnian Serbs under Austro-Hungarian rule may have struck a chord with Willie, in view of the Irish situation, but the means of addressing the issue would not. There is no record in the public domain of Willie expressing a view about the assassination. He was probably, like many people that balmy summer, blissfully unaware that a slow burning fuse had been lit. Many, but not all; Gustav Steinhauer later observed:

Sunday afternoon, June 28, 1914. The most fateful day in the history of the world if one had only known it. On the surface, all was calm and peaceful. My Imperial master, Wilhelm II of Germany, stood on the deck of his racing yacht 'Meteor' interestedly watching the brilliant panorama of the Kiel Canal. It was regatta week, with hardly one outward sign to herald the coming of the storm.

Thickly clustered round us were the warships of the Great Powers – British, French, Russian, Japanese, Austrian and German. The strong detachment of the British Fleet, significantly impressive in its overwhelming superiority, lay anchored in the canal, outnumbering the warships of all the other nations as if to demonstrate that Britannia still ruled the waves.

Luxurious private yachts, leviathan passenger liners belonging to the North German Lloyd and Hamburg-America companies, crowded with sight-seers, battleships, cruisers, destroyers and dozens of smaller craft made as gay and brilliant a spectacle as one could wish to see.

Who could have imagined that 'Der Tag' had come at last? The Emperor knew, of course, that the time was drawing nigh. So did I.[6]

Despite Steinhauer's assertion, and the Kaiser's years of military bluster, Wilhelm II initially did not appear to see the need to go to war. He continued his holiday, cruising the Baltic on the imperial yacht *Hohenzollern* whilst Austria-Hungary and Serbia were jockeying following the assassination. He hinted that any cause for war had been dispelled, once Austria-Hungary and Serbia engaged in talks (albeit aggressively by the Austrians). He was quick to assure his cousin Nicky (the Russian Tsar, Nicholas II) that Germany was not anxious to go to war with Russia. Indeed, on his return to

Berlin, there was an exchange of telegrams, in English, between the Kaiser and the Tsar, precipitated by Wilhelm urging Nicholas on 29 July: *to smooth over difficulties that may still arise ... without involving Europe in the most horrible war she has ever witnessed.*[7] Wilhelm represented himself as a mediator, but his main concern was his reluctance to take on the country of his cousin King George V; so the German Ambassador in London was instructed to sound out British intentions.

To begin with, there was a ground-swell of sympathy for Austria-Hungary; had they invaded Serbia immediately perhaps the conflict would have been confined to the Balkans. *The Irish Times* on Monday 29 June 1914 stated:

> *The news may have an effect upon the immediate Parliamentary arrangements..... The Prime Minister will, of course, make sympathetic reference to the blow that has fallen upon the Austro-Hungarian peoples and their Monarch, and after that the House will, perhaps, proceed to other business, or even adjourn as a mark of respect.*

Although ultimatums were issued by Austria-Hungary and rejected by Serbia, weeks passed before any military action was taken. This passage of time increased tensions while each side rallied their allies, despite diplomatic manoeuvres to dampen the powder keg sparked by the assassination. Indeed, there was a general feeling that a brief European war – famously to be 'over by Christmas' – might clear the air, resolve problems and lead to a fresh start. In Berlin, Paris, Moscow, Vienna and London, crowds, some singing patriotic songs, some cheering, and some simply apprehensive and inquisitive, took to the streets. In the East Prussian town of Schneidemühl, a twelve year old girl, Piete Kuhr, writes on 1 August 1914:

> *From today Germany is at war. My mother says I should write a diary about the war ... We have no idea what war will be like. There are flags on all the houses in town, just as if we are having a festival.*[8]

Two days later she writes:

> *At school they talk of nothing but the war now. The girls are pleased that Germany is entering the field against its old enemy, France. We have to learn new songs about the glory of war. The enthusiasm in the town is growing*

by the hour. People wander through the streets in groups, shouting: 'Down with Serbia! Long live Germany!' [9]

At the end of July a party of English holiday makers based in Switzerland, which included the Reverend Charles Doudney from Bath, had debated about continuing their tour:

We crossed the Austrian border at a point just south of the lake near Bregenz, and the hostile attitude of the soldiers ought, perhaps to have made us turn back ... In Austria we found intense excitement... Every market square was filled with a gesticulating crowd ... [10]

The Irish Times reported on Wednesday 5 August 1914:

We believe that the people of these kingdoms are today more cheerful than they have been at any time since the war clouds began to gather over Europe. The period of suspense and uncertainty is ended. In Ireland today the national feeling is not merely one of courage and confidence. Faced with terrible and urgent danger though we be, our hearts find room for thankfulness – even exultation.

Ultimately, diplomatic moves and ultimatums notwithstanding, there was a domino effect, tumbling to war, during the closing days of July into the early days of August. Serbia mobilised, Austria-Hungary declared war and Russia started the laborious process of mobilisation in support of Serbia. Within days, the other major powers entered the conflict, either through choice or by being drawn in because of the actions of others.

Irrespective of the fact that Germany was in alliance with Austria-Hungary anyway, the German Generals were eager to utilise this window of opportunity to put their own, long devised, plan into operation. The Schlieffen Plan had aimed to break Germany's encirclement by France and Russia, thus making Germany the master of Europe on two fronts. France, as Russia's ally, entered the fray and, indeed, was eager to do so, to grasp the opportunity to put into operation her strategy for regaining Alsace-Lorraine (known as Plan XVII). Britain had no obligations other than to Belgium, but when Germany invaded Belgium, Britain, bound by her commitment to guarantee Belgian neutrality enshrined in the 1839 Treaty of London, felt obliged to enter the fray.

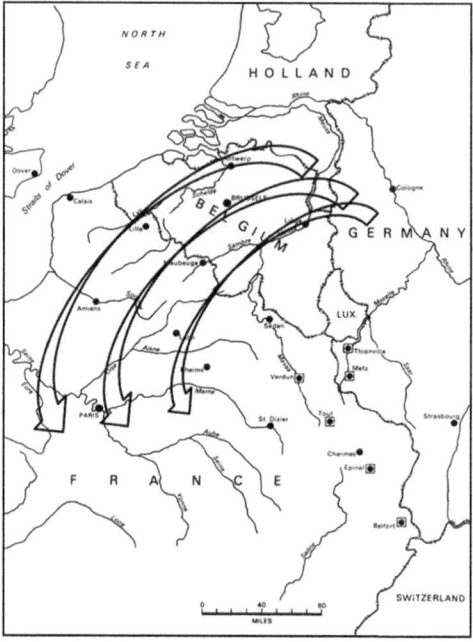

Schlieffen Plan

Count Alfred Von Schlieffen, Chief of the Imperial German Staff from 1891 to 1906, had overseen the development of a war plan to strike firstly against France and then against Russia. Schlieffen's successor as Chief of the General Staff, Helmuth Johann von Moltke (known as 'Moltke the Younger', and a nephew of Helmuth Karl von Moltke, one of the architects of the 1871 victory), had undertaken modifications of the original plan. This revised version came into action on Saturday 1 August 1914. Basically, the plan involved three separate deployments of German troops to engage with the French, firstly, in the Alsace-Lorraine area, to provide the little encouragement the French needed to concentrate her troops there in large numbers in order to regain that territory. More German troops were to be deployed to the right to cross a shortened area of shared border, which the French had strengthened with a chain of fortresses and fortifications. As it was anticipated that it might take weeks, perhaps months to smash through those defences, a third, larger, German force was deployed on the German extreme right wing, to traverse through Luxembourg and Belgium, with the aim of sweeping through Brussels to Paris, securing the French capital and, by isolating and defeating the French army, forcing the French government to capitulate.

Simultaneously, a smaller German force was deployed in the east to prepare for the subsequent assault on Russia. The Schlieffen Plan envisaged a quick, decisive blow at the French, before transporting the mighty German army east by rail, to strike before the unwieldy war machine of the Russian Empire could grind into action. The key to this plan working was speed – and lack of speed. France had to be conquered quickly, hence the need to access Paris via Belgium. (It was widely anticipated that, in a repeat of the Franco-Prussian conflict of 1870/71, France would capitulate once Paris came under threat; the Schlieffen Plan envisaged a total of just four weeks to complete the defeat of the French). On the other hand, it was calculated Russia would take much longer to effectively mobilise, due to the inefficiency of the Russian army, the inadequacies of the Russian railway system and the sheer size of the Russian Empire. This would buy Germany precious time.

Unfortunately for Germany, this plan did not work, although it nearly did because the French were very obliging. They concentrated a large army, as per their 'Plan XVII', in Alsace Lorraine which out-numbered the enemy. But this numerical superiority proved to be of no advantage to the French. The smaller German force easily held them, partly due to French troops being slaughtered en-masse, advancing across open ground in conspicuous uniforms of bright red and blue.

Peter Hart points out:

... it is shocking to record that some 27,000 Frenchmen died on 22 August alone. This was an almost unprecedented slaughter in the long history of warfare.[11]

John Lucy of 2nd Bn Royal Irish Rifles described seeing French troops on his arrival at Le Havre on 14 August 1914:

Strange-looking soldiers like those in the coloured prints of 1870 scampered about on shore, gesticulating wildly at the sight of our ship. They were clad in huge red trousers, dark-blue long-tailed coats, and peaked caps.[12]

Then, in a reversal of the numbers game, the Germans advancing on the right were checked by a significantly smaller British Expeditionary Force at Mons and things just went from bad to worse, both for the Germans and a large part of the continent of Europe.

Following Mons, the Germans made poor tactical decisions, misjudgements and manoeuvres and within months the opening war of sweeping movements became a continuing war of static stalemate. John Lucy's wry observation, early in September, was that: *The Germans appeared to go crazy. They suddenly stopped short of Paris, and no longer pursued us. They went after bigger game, or thought they did.*[13] The reality for Germany was that there was no 'Plan B'; they had no realistic long-term strategy to replace the failed Schlieffen Plan. [FN2]

Under the Quintuple Treaty of London, Britain had long been a guarantor of Belgian neutrality in the event of war. Indeed, all the major European nations, Austria, France, Prussia and Russia, were joint signatories to the guarantee. Therefore, Britain had started mobilising on the day Germany flouted that guarantee, by invading Belgium on Saturday 1 August 1914, and Britain finally declared war on Germany the following Tuesday. The men of the BEF who embarked for France that month were seasoned professional soldiers, and reservists called back to the colours following a period of previous service. It never amounted to more than about 160,000, a large proportion of whom were ready for action and advance parties began crossing to France on Friday 7 August 1914. Crossing the Channel seven days later were the Lucy brothers from Cork and their battalion of Royal Irish Rifles. The elder brother John recorded his pride in the BEF:

> *The British Army in 1914 was more used to battle than that of any other nation. It possessed the highest and bravest traditions that can be engendered in a fighting force, and its experience of wars was such that our own regiment, though a young one in the army, had so many battle honours they were difficult to memorise... Our reservists came streaming in to make up our war strength; cheerful, careless fellows of all types, some in bowler hats and smart suitings, others in descending scale down to the garb of tramps. Soon, like us, they were uniformed and equipped with field kits, and the change was remarkable.*[13a]

In stark contrast, Germany could mobilise in the region of 1,500,000 men and France approximately a million, both countries maintaining much larger armies based on a system of conscription. Nevertheless, the *British Official History* claims that the BEF who went to France in 1914 was:

> ...the best trained, best organised and best equipped British Army that ever went forth to war ... except that in the matter of numbers; so that though not 'contemptible' it was almost negligible in comparison with continental armies, even of smaller states.[14]

The BEF's role in its opening skirmishes of the war was to support the left wing of the French Army. This was done with distinction and valour in the vicinity of the small Belgian town of Mons, towards the end of what had begun as an ordinary, peaceful late summer month. They checked the advance of a mighty German force of arms, despite being heavily out-numbered. Indeed, the role of the 1st Battalion Royal West Kent Regiment, deployed either side of a stretch of the Mons-Condé canal, led its historian, Major C.V. Molony, to claim: *The odds of Agincourt once more, ten to one – truly the men of Kent have not degenerated in 500 years!*[15]

During the afternoon of 23 August 1914 John and Denis Lucy, together with their colleagues of the Royal Irish Rifles, experienced their first actions of the war. They were waiting in a temporary kneeling trench (about three feet deep) outside Mons when:

> ...the Germans discovered us before we saw them, and three or four dull thuds to our distant front followed by a whirring noise rapidly approaching us marked the discharge of enemy guns, and our first moment under shell-fire. The salvo of shells passed over our heads, and burst about eighty yards in rear with a terrific clattering clash ... Then the enemy gunners shortened, and the shells exploded above our trenches, and the men, already taken in hand for exposing themselves, crouched low ... The Germans now ranged well, and their shell-fire seemed to concentrate heavily on the trenches ... One shrapnel bullet hit my pack ... A dispatch rider coming towards us on the road from the west fell off his motor bicycle when a shell burst over him ... Finally the shelling ceased, and we put up our heads to breathe more freely. Then we heard conch-like sounds – strange bugle calls. The German infantry, which had approached during the shelling, was in sight, and about to attack us.[16]

John Lucy started to write his memoirs in 1936 (first published 1938) aided, perhaps, by a hint of rose-tinted spectacles. Nevertheless, his account lends support to the oft cited claim that the commander of the German First Army, General Alexander von Kluck, initially had no idea British troops were in the line, until the start of sustained heavy and accurate rifle fire from positions around Mons. Some German accounts commend the skill of the British musketry. John Lucy continues his narrative:

> *Not a shot had been fired from our trenches up to now, and the only opposition to the Germans had been made by our field-gun battery, which was heavily engaged behind us, and making almost as much clamour as the enemy shelling ...In answer to the German bugles or trumpets came the cheerful sounds of our officers' whistles, and the riflemen, casting aside the amazement of their strange trial, sprang into action. A great roar of musketry rent the air, varying slightly in intensity from minute to minute, as whole companies ceased fire and opened again ... The clatter of our machine guns added to the din.*
>
> *For us the battle took the form of well-ordered, rapid rifle-fire at close range, as the field-grey human targets appeared, or were struck down ... The leading Germans fired standing, 'from the hip', as they came on, but their scattered fire was ineffective, and ignored. They crumpled up – mown down as quickly as I tell it ...*
>
> *Our rapid fire was appalling even to us, and the worst marksman could not miss ... Such tactics amazed us, and after the shock of seeing men slowly and helplessly falling down as they were hit, gave us a great sense of power and pleasure. It was all so easy.*[17]

A few weeks earlier, on Thursday 6 August 1914, Horatio Herbert Lord Kitchener, Baron Kitchener of Khartoum, had been appointed to the post of British Secretary of State for War. He quickly concluded that Britain was on the brink of a world war, which would last at least three years, and that she would need one million men to fight it. He realised that a vast new army of volunteers would be required to match the might of the German armies and to provide an effective fighting partnership alongside the equally huge French armies. He preferred to create a new structure to augment the Regular Army under the direction of the War Office, rather than expand and change the role of the Territorial Force, which was operated by the County Territorial Associations for home defence. He proceeded to put a framework into place to deal with the logistics of recruitment, training and deployment of his New Army divisions, which were raised on a regional basis throughout the British Isles. Hundreds of thousands immediately responded to the 'Kitchener Needs You' appeal and new armies were created in groups of 100,000 men each. The 10th (Irish) Division started recruiting in August, part of the First Hundred Thousand known as K1. Recruitment for K2 and Willie Doyle's 16th (Irish) Division commenced in September and to complete representation from Ireland the 36th (Ulster) Division was authorised on 28 October 1914.

By the time Willie Doyle's family had been informed of his intention to go to the front as a temporary army chaplain, the original BEF had been involved in several further major engagements; at Le Cateau, the retreat to the Marne quickly followed by the advance to the Aisne, and the first battle of Ypres.[FN3] By the end of the First Battle of Ypres in November 1914, the BEF had been almost totally destroyed; one of the casualties was Denis Lucy who had been killed on the Aisne on 15 September. But eager recruits to Lord Kitchener's New Armies, together with volunteers for service overseas from the Territorial Army, were swelling the ranks of the British army in Flanders' fields. The war was no longer a war of movement; the degeneration to digging in for a war of attrition had begun; digging into the ruins of communities and into trenches separated by open spaces of 'no man's land.'

Arriving in Ypres on 1 November 1914 John Lucy observed:

Ypres was a pleasant town, busy, with lighted shops, the names over which reminded us that we were again in Flanders. The streets were full of motor cars and other civilian traffic. A prosperous place. The inhabitants, including some nuns, greeted us cheerfully, and did not pay very much attention to a couple of shells which swished overhead, and landed somewhere in the outskirts at the back of the town. At Hooge the people also flocked to their doors, and waved us on.[18]

A little over six months later, Captain F.C. Hitchcock, an Irishman serving with the 2nd Battalion of a famous Irish Regiment, the Leinsters, gave a description of the devastation now wreaked by the war:

Macartney, the Padre, and I went down in the evening to see Ypres. The city was deserted and desolate. The atmosphere was heavy with the smell of decaying bodies, for the first shells had surprised the inhabitants, and caught many in their beds. A number of the houses had been knocked down by direct hits, and others had one of the walls blown down, showing the furniture of the stories above, like scenery in a theatre.

Few houses had been left unscathed. The square in front of the Cloth Hall was in a dreadful state, strewn all over with parts of British G.S. wagons, bones of dead horses, broken rifles, and web equipment. The streets throughout Ypres were pitted with shell craters, beside the Cloth Hall there was a crater of a 16-inch shell. I measured it, and found it was fifty-two paces round, 30 feet deep and 48 feet across from lip to lip.[19]

Willie Doyle would have appreciated the humour and enduring optimism in the face of such bleakness mirrored in Hitchcock's diary entry a day later, 18 June 1915:

Marsland and I took up our platoons to Ypres, and took down a number of the hall doors off the houses for dug-out roofs, and brought them back to La Brique in hand-carts. I got some dozen bottles of wine which I looted from a cellar. At dark, I brought the 'hall doors' up to the line, and as the knockers had been left on most of them, at every halt the men amused themselves by knocking a tattoo! We dumped our loads in the support trenches, and returned early to our dug-out line.'[20]

Fr Doyle was waiting for his appointment whilst such events were going on. He eventually received his appointment as a Chaplain with the 16th (Irish) Division on 15 November 1915.

Footnote 1: The original German text contains a word which means 'insignificant', but may be translated into English as 'contemptible' or 'contemptibly'. Therefore, Wilhelm II may have meant 1) a little army that is contemptible; or 2) an army that is contemptibly little.

Footnote 2: The original Schlieffen Plan had been seriously compromised (arguably, fatally so) by the modifications made by the younger von Moltke, and in particular, by his decision to switch substantial numbers of troops from the right wing attack, to bolster the forces in the German centre against the anticipated French assault. As a result, the planned sweep by German right-wing forces down the North Sea coast of Belgium and into France, capturing the Channel ports, had to be abandoned. This plan had been an integral and key element of von Schlieffen's original proposal and, if successful, could have seriously compromised Britain's ability to mobilise, and then to re-supply, an expeditionary force in France.

Moreover, the British failed to co-operate in the unfolding of the Schlieffen Plan. The Plan had envisaged that Britain would need at least four weeks to bring its army to France, by which time it was anticipated that France would have been defeated. In the event, the British army put in train an extremely well-written, carefully thought-out, and meticulously rehearsed, War Plan, which was assisted by the fact that the Territorial Force battalions had undertaken their annual training camps in the last two weeks of July 1914. When, over the weekend of 1st and 2nd August, it became self-evident that war was unavoidable, the Territorial troops, already embodied in their respective units, and fresh from a fortnight's military training, were sent directly to their Regimental home Headquarters, to take over the running of the depots, and to take in hand the myriad administrative and logistical tasks involved in mobilisation. The Regular battalions on home stations were left to concentrate on their transport arrangements and on moving quickly to their points of embarkation, with the result that the entire British Expeditionary Force had crossed over to France, and had reached its pre-planned forward concentration areas, within just twelve days of the British Declaration of War.

Footnote 3: Following the action at Mons, and the collapse of the French left wing, the BEF.had been forced to withdraw to the south. At the village of Le Cateau, the British II Corps, under the command of Lieutenant General Horace Smith-Dorrien, held up the advance of von Kluck's First Army by a day and a half, and further small 'stopping' actions followed. In the face of these checks, the German advance became slow and increasingly more cautious, throwing the Schlieffen timetable into disarray and, by 1st September, by which time the German armies should have been celebrating the fall of France, they were still being pressed by the British, in an action in the village of Néry, a small and relatively insignificant action, but one which nevertheless held up the German advance some 60 miles short of their target. The British and French forces consolidated along the line of the River Marne, forcing the German armies to withdraw to the Aisne, and the first Battle of Ypres quickly followed.

CHAPTER 9
ON THE CUSP:
LORD KITCHENER POINTS HIS FINGER

'Padre is a term of endearment for a military chaplain'
from Latin – *pater patri father*

On 15 November 1915 Willie Doyle signed his appointment letter as *Acting Chaplain engaged for duty with Expeditionary Force.* The Rev William Joseph Doyle, S.J. of Rathfarnham Castle, Dublin confirmed to His Majesty's Principal Secretary of State of the War Department that he was a duly ordained priest of the Roman Catholic Church. His signature was witnessed at Rathfarnham by Fr Patrick O'Mara, S.J. Willie was to be Chaplain to His Majesty's Forces, 4th Class, with the relative rank of Captain in the army whilst so employed. He agreed to abide by six conditions of service. Broadly these were: his service was to be for 12 months; his pay was to be 10/- (shillings) a day with other allowances as appropriate; he would receive free passage to and from his place of service; while in the field he would receive free rations for himself and forage for any government horse put at his disposal; he would obey all orders given to him by his superior officers; and an annuity of 60 days pay would be paid on completion of service according to certain terms and conditions.

Willie was directed to obtain a medical certificate from an Officer of the Royal Army Medical Corps, confirming his fitness for general service and have an anti-typhoid inoculation; then he was to report to the General Officer Commanding 16th (Irish) Division at Aldershot as early as possible. He had to provide himself with uniform, field and camp kits.[1] His appointment was effective from 30 November 1915 and appeared in *The London Gazette*, entry number 29404, on 14 December 1915.

It must have been a daunting thought for Willie to even contemplate leaving the protection of the Society of Jesus, let alone expose himself to the dangers of warfare. From the close of the 19th century until he volunteered to be a Military

Chaplain, Willie Doyle's life had been totally tied up in Jesuit establishments - studying, teaching, writing religious pamphlets and leading Catholic spiritual exercises. By the outbreak of war he had established himself in a vocation that, in addition to fulfilling him spiritually, was his way of life, the means of his support and had given him the chance to widen his horizons and travel. His life was secure and comfortable, if somewhat spartan at times. However, any privations he suffered were entirely self-inflicted in the cause of testing his faith, or helping people less fortunate than himself. Willie made his intentions known to the Provincial at Rathfarnham, who put the 42-year-old priest's name forward for consideration by The Rt Rev Mgr M.J. Bidwell, D.D., at the Roman Catholic Archbishop's House, Westminster.

It is interesting to speculate about Willie's motive for volunteering. It may have been because he had spent a number of happy years in Belgium; or that, like some others of his compatriots, he drew a parallel between Belgium as an invaded country and the political situation in Ireland; and because he had always championed the cause and spiritual well-being of ordinary working men, tens of thousands of whom were now caught up in the war. What is certain is that a burning desire for the 'grace of martyrdom' seems to have made a possibly difficult decision easy. Despite being an exuberant, engaging, larger-than-life personality Willie's ambition was to be a martyr, to lay down his life for Christ. During the year between volunteering and receiving his appointment, Willie wrote several letters repeating the same desire. A brief entry in his diary, on the day he signed and returned his appointment paper, states:

> *Received my appointment from the War Office as chaplain to the 16th Division. Fiat voluntas Tua. What the future has in store I know not but I have given Jesus all to dispose of as He sees best. My heart is full of gratitude to Him for giving me this chance of being really generous and of leading a life that will be truly crucified.*[2]

Frederic C. Spurr in his book *Some Chaplains in Khaki* sentimentally describes the upheaval and change of culture Willie was soon to experience:

> *From peaceful village, sleepy country town, quiet suburb, and crowded city, men who spent their Sundays at church and school; in a religious*

atmosphere and in the service of God and man, found themselves suddenly cut off from this their familiar environment, and plunged into an atmosphere wholly foreign to them ...³

Spurr records many temptations of camp life, including alcohol, prize-fighting and gambling, which the chaplains had to contend against. He quotes anonymously the feelings of one new, devout and disorientated recruit:

The life is very hard, but none of us mind that ... The thing that hurts is the conversation of the men around me. It is an awfully difficult thing to sit day by day and listen to a flood of blasphemy and obscenity, and to get scarcely a quiet moment for thought or prayer. To rebuke these men openly exposes oneself to the charge of Pharisaism; to remain silent exposes one's own conscience to the charge of cowardice. I have tried, however, privately to speak to some of the men and to put a better view of life before them, and I hope in some measure I have succeeded.⁴

There are more upbeat views of life in an army training camp. One example is from the letters of Frederic (known as Ben) Keeling. He was a man in his late twenties, of independent means at the outbreak of war, who lost no time in volunteering. A university friend of Rupert Brooke and other Cambridge alumni, he actually stuck to their pact of not accepting a commission.[FN1] By the end of August 1914 Ben Keeling had transferred from drilling with the Artists' Rifles to duties as a private with the 6th Battalion Duke of Cornwall's Light Infantry. Many of Keeling's observations were written from Watts Common, Aldershot, and he evidently shared the same kind of empathy for the ordinary working man as Willie Doyle. Writing on 27 September 1914:

I was canteen corporal yesterday, which means a sort of official pub chucker-out. ... That job bought me up against a rougher type of man in the battalion than I had got to know before. They're all right if you remember they are just overgrown children ... Take it all in all this is a fine life. I feel more and more that all these young fellows will be far finer fellows for the experience, whether we get fighting or not. ... The camp was a fine sight this afternoon, a series of football matches between the companies, impromptu miniature range firing, bayonet fighting, and tent-pitching and rapid-firing competitions and a few of us having cold baths in the sun ...[5]

Later in his training he concludes: *I have very definitely formed the impression that drunkenness, or even excessive drinking in any sense, in the New Army is confined to a relatively small minority of men in most battalions. ...*[6]

Thus, there were many challenges in store for Willie Doyle and to begin with some of them were safely routine; the exact kind the focused and highly motivated hunter-out of souls relished!

Rewinding to just over a year before Willie Doyle's appointment, there were 117 commissioned Chaplains and 37 Acting Chaplains in the Army Chaplains' Department under the Chaplain General in August 1914. Only seventeen of these were Roman Catholic, six of whom were stationed overseas in Cairo, Gibraltar, Malta, South Africa and attached to the Royal Navy. Britain's small regular army comprised approximately 247,000 soldiers, a third of whom were stationed in India, where a separate ecclesiastical establishment took care of the soldiers and their dependents. Once war broke out it quickly became evident that the number of chaplains was insufficient to meet the needs of a rapidly expanding army, both at training camps and overseas. More than 200,000 reservists had been recalled to the colours, volunteers from the home defence Territorial Force were mobilised and, once Lord Kitchener started pointing his finger, a vast 'New Army' of civilian volunteers was raised.

In August 1914 only eleven of the seventeen Catholic chaplains were available for immediate service. In War Office planning terms this was enough, as one Catholic chaplain was allocated to each division of the BEF. Consequently, seven travelled, leaving four available for immediate service elsewhere, with the remaining six unavailable.

A division was a self-contained entity, consisting of the fighting men in units of the infantry, cavalry and artillery, along with support services; in round figures about 18,000 men when at full strength. A division could be spread over a wide area, especially in the early months of the war when it was one of fight and movement and non-combatants had to be kept to a minimum. Nevertheless, the paucity of Catholic chaplains speaks for itself and provoked floods of letters from Catholic priests throughout Great Britain and Ireland offering their services.

Despite the obvious urgent need for extra chaplains of all denominations, even before the huge deployment of newly enlisted soldiers, Fr William Doyle's services were not required by the British Army for twelve months after he volunteered. The Chaplain General had been inundated with applications, over twelve hundred across all denominations by October 1914, and his department was woefully unprepared to meet the demands of processing the human resources at its disposal, both in recruitment and to their appointed posts. By the end of the war, four years later, there were nearly 3,500 chaplains representing eleven denominations.

The despatch of existing regular chaplains to the Front in the early stages of the war was disorganised, resulting in too few chaplains in the field and in reserve. Wheels ground so slowly some candidates for new posts were frustrated and turned to other types of military service. Willie Doyle was eventually assigned to a new division mainly of Irishmen. The logistics of large-scale army recruitment in Ireland were, largely speaking, more time-consuming than in the rest of the United Kingdom, which was another factor that delayed his appointment.

Fr Doyle was to serve in the 16th (Irish) Division. A division was managed like any large organisation, by allocating the workforce to smaller units that fitted together like building blocks to form the whole. The world of the average 'Tommy' centred on his battalion (approximately 1,000 men at full strength), but more especially on the smaller components within that framework: platoons and sections. Battalions derived their identity from the regimental system, which was the cement which held together the whole of the British army during the Great War. An individual battalion of a regiment could serve in one division, whilst another battalion of the same regiment could serve in another division. Battalions (from several regiments) were at first grouped into fours (although later in the war into threes) to form an Infantry Brigade. The 16th (Irish) Division had three brigades – the 47th, 48th and 49th Infantry Brigades.

In 1914 there were already some 30,000 Irishmen serving in the British regular army and thousands more were in reserve, to be called upon for active service should the occasion arise. In spite of the vicissitudes of the political situation in Ireland, there had been an Irish presence in the British army from the late 1600's. Britain had long achieved dominance over Ireland by military conquest and in 1914 Ireland had numerous army barracks across its width and breadth. Ireland was one of seven separate commands for the whole of the British Isles, administered under the direct control of the War Office in London. Troops garrisoned on the island hailed from all parts of the British Isles, not just from Ireland. Individual Irishmen had joined the army through a variety of motives, not the least of them being economic; many families had a tradition of service going back generations.

Irish regiments had been formed with their own recruitment areas. Looking, for example at the two regiments with which Willie Doyle served, the Royal Dublin Fusiliers recruited from the area of County Dublin and three adjoining counties in the province of Leinster, whilst the Royal Irish Fusiliers recruited from three counties further north in Leinster and one county in the province of Ulster.

Royal Irish Fusiliers Cap Badge   Royal Dublin Fusiliers Cap Badge

Battalions of both these regiments served with the BEF in the opening months of the Great War as part of 4th Division. Whilst these regular army soldiers were in the thick of it, new battalions of their two regiments, together with five other Irish regiments, were formed into the three brigades of the new 16th (Irish) Division, in which all four provinces of Ireland were represented.

John Lucy lost his brother and many close comrades of his regular battalion of Royal Irish Rifles during these early months of fighting. His poignant diary entry for 19 November 1914, on being relieved in the Ypres Salient, was:

My eyes weakened, wandered and rested on the half-hidden corpses of men and youths. Near and far they looked calm, and even handsome, in death.

Their strong young bodies thickly garlanded the edge of a wood in rear, a wood called Sanctuary. A dead sentry, at his post, leaned back in a standing position, against a blasted tree, keeping watch over them.

Proudly and sorrowfully I looked at them, the Macs and the O's, and the hardy Ulster boys joined together in death on a foreign field. My dead chums.[7]

John Lucy's opinion of the New Army recruits was grudgingly complimentary. The man from Cork said:

Towards the end of 1915 there was no professional army in France. The British civilian had taken over the war. Many of the straight-spined old soldiers looked askance at the civilian warrior, and, indeed the civilian under arms presented many a strange sight to our conservative eyes.

He was undersized. He slouched. He was bespectacled. He wore uniform in a careless way, and he had a deadly earnestness, which effectively took the place of our cold-willed esprit de corps. He saluted awkwardly, and was very clumsy with his weapons. His marching was a pain to look at, and the talkative methods of his officers and NCOs made us blush. His childish admiration for what was left of the old army was very disarming.

The old army was distinctly queasy about the future. One consolation was the sight of recently captured German prisoners, whose poor physique filled us with satisfaction and the hope that the New Army might be able to cope with them somehow.

The New Army did, and when we learned that they could fight we forgave them everything and allowed our prejudices to slide away.[8]

It was to a new service battalion, 8th Royal Irish Fusiliers, in 49th Infantry Brigade, that Father Doyle was eventually sent. Princess Victoria's (Royal Irish Fusiliers), to give the regiment its full title, had been formed in 1881 from an amalgamation of two Regiments of Foot, identified under the then system of naming/numbering as the 87th and 89th of Foot, which had been raised in response to the Napoleonic crisis. The regiment was nick-named the Faughs, after their battle cry *Faugh a Ballagh!* (Clear the Way.)

The other battalions of the 49th Brigade were the 7th Battalion Royal Irish

Fusiliers, together with the 7th and 8th Battalions Royal Inniskilling Fusiliers. There is no battalion history for Willie Doyle's 8th Royal Irish Fusiliers, but there is a battalion history for the 7th Royal Inniskilling Fusiliers, which opens with the following statement:

> *In accordance with Army Council instructions, and the approval of His Majesty King George V., the 16th (Irish) Division was formed on, or about, the 14 September, 1914.*[9]

The nucleus of all four battalions of that division's 49th Infantry Brigade was created on 1 October 1914. However, the history of the 7th Battalion Royal Inniskilling Fusiliers, tells us it was not until mid-February 1916 that they arrived in France (Willie Doyle's 8th Royal Irish Fusiliers followed three days later.) During the interim period the raw recruits had to be knocked into fighting shape and the time needed for this was a source of frustration for those raring to get to the sharp end.

David Starret was one such impatient Irishman serving in another Irish division. He became a senior officer's batman shortly after enlisting in September 1914. He went straight to training camp in the north of Ireland and into an Ulster regiment, the 9th Battalion Royal Irish Rifles, in 36th (Ulster) Division. He wryly commented nearly a year later:

> *The war had been going on now for ten months and 1915 was well on its way when we got marching orders for England. 'Bit nearer France,' we said cheerfully ... By the end of that September (1915) we were all ready, packed and waiting so to speak, but it was October before we marched through a darkened Folkestone and boarded the transport. With mixed feelings, to speak for myself, remembering the good friendships left behind and wondering what the future had in store.*[10]

The logistics of assembling the new divisions varied from place to place. The situation with regard to the three Irish Divisions, 10th (Irish), 16th (Irish) and 36th (Ulster), was unique in that it was heavily influenced by the political situation in Ireland. Even though the 'Irish Question' and the issue of Home Rule was immediately eclipsed upon the Declaration of War, when, for varying reasons, the main political agitators in Ireland offered support to the British government, the mechanics of recruitment were not as easy as on the British mainland. Although some of the Irish populace could be swayed by oratory, and others enlisted for their own personal reasons, many potential recruits in Ireland viewed the British with suspicion. The 7th Battalion Royal Inniskilling Fusiliers' history notes that after a rush of recruits in late Autumn 1914, there was a need for a recruiting tour in March 1915. The Inniskilling recruiting area was the four north-western counties in the province of Ulster. Despite the best endeavours of the recruiters, complete with fife and drum band, there was a poor response, leaving the battalion still far short of its complete establishment. Indeed, when a new Commanding Officer, Lieutenant Colonel Michael Hughes, took over in April 1915 the battalion remained substantially under-strength, with approximately 32 officers and 550 other ranks.

In addition to the problem of recruitment, the period between approving the 16th (Irish) Division and its departure for the Front had to be spent in setting up a command and training structure, equipping the men, and basic training in Ireland, followed by advanced training in England. Much of the training was piecemeal, as revealed by the history of the 7th Royal Inniskilling Fusiliers. Whilst they were still in Ireland:

> *Preliminary instruction in trench digging began early in 1915, but it was not for many months to come that this form of training got anything like the amount of time devoted to it that was necessary for proficiency.*[11]

By the end of the year they were across the water in England:

> *All our efforts were directed on the field training and trench duties. Peculiar as it may seem, we had up to this had very little instruction in trench life, and the established routine of 'manning and relieving'. True, we had many lectures about the life and routine of stationary warfare in France, but we needed some practical work in this branch to appreciate it fully.*[12]

The process was not helped when battalions were required to supply drafts of trained men elsewhere, coupled with the fact that there was always a percentage of men that had to be released subsequent to recruitment owing, for example, to previously undiscovered health issues. Consequently, it was a constant battle to get the battalions up to full strength, or as near as possible. That this continuing need for piecemeal recruiting disrupted the training process, is revealed by the historian of the 7th Inniskillings, G.A. Cooper Walker:

Almost coincident with the latter stages of the musketry course, the C.O. received orders to detail 300 other ranks as a draft to reinforce the 10th Division, prior to their departure overseas. Needless to say, at our present strength this would leave us a mere skeleton unit once more. The other battalions in the Brigade received similar instructions ...[13]

As a consequence of this draft, during the month of June 1915 the 7th Inniskilling's Commanding Officer, together with Lieutenant E. Gallagher, personally supervised another recruiting drive, both in Northern Ireland and throughout the estates of Lieutenant Colonel Hughes in England, raising 670 more men.

Other personal recollections confirm that issues of recruitment, and the posting of troops to other units, were constant problems throughout the war. For example, Captain F.C. Hitchcock of the 2nd Leinsters recalls in July 1916:

On account of the large casualties, drafts were being sent up the line to feed fighting battalions daily. Owing to the heavy demands for reinforcements from the Somme area, there seemed to be no discrimination with regard to men being sent to their own units. Two hundred men of the Connaught Rangers were sent up the line to join the Munsters, who had suffered severely in the attack on Mametz Wood. A Leinster draft of over fifty was sent to the Black Watch! Posting men of one Irish regiment to another was reasonable, but sending Leinsters to join any regiment but an Irish one gave cause for much legitimate grousing.[14]

Willie Doyle finally joined the battalion to which he was to attached, 8th Battalion Royal Irish Fusiliers, at the end of November 1915 when they were ensconced at Witley Camp in Surrey. Willie's resolve had not weakened during the intervening year, although his one regret, revealed in a letter, was leaving his recently widowed father. On the eve of starting out for England he wrote:

A last farewell for I shall be far away when you receive this. My via crucis is nearly over; but only in heaven will you know how I have suffered all this week. It is all for Him and I do not regret it; but He filled my cup of bitterness this evening when I left my darling old Father. Thank God, at last I can say, I have given Him all; or rather He has taken all from me. May His sweet will be done.[15]

Willie would have crossed the Irish Sea to Holyhead and continued his journey to training camp by train. Perhaps his experience was similar to that of Fr Charteris, a Chaplain of one of the non-conformist denominations, who found himself at Wareham in Dorset.

When I arrived on the scene, everything (town, camp and men) was in a state of transition. The town was changing from a little town of 2,000 into a garrison town of 10,000. The camp from a turnip field, (a foot deep in mud) into a well-planned town of wooden huts, with macadamised roads. The men from a mob of raw recruits, into an army of khaki clad, disciplined soldiers.[16]

Maybe Willie arrived in time to take part in the inspection of the 16th (Irish) Division by Her Majesty Queen Mary on 2 December 1915 at the Queen's Parade, Aldershot. For two weeks prior to the inspection the men of the division:

… were given a thorough exercise in 'ceremonial'. Numerous practices were held in the drill field adjoining the barracks in marching past and forming up in review order. Up to this we had done very little ceremonial drill, and the consequence was that the parades were not altogether perfect.[17]

All went well however:

Unlike the rehearsal a few weeks before, the weather was fine, which made the drill and movement much easier than on the previous occasion. The 49th Infantry Brigade, with ourselves as leading battalion, presented a smart appearance on parade, and marched past in very good line.[18]

If Willie settled in at Witley with no preconceived notions other than to save souls then he was not disappointed. Whilst army histories and war diaries reveal intensive training procedures for the officers and men, there was no such preparation for the padre. The men had a rigid daily routine: the padre sorted himself out. The men received instruction in squad drilling, physical training, route marching, trench digging, rifle practice and anti-gas procedures. They attended lectures and musketry courses. The padre was left to his own devices.

This particular padre was bitterly disappointed with one aspect of training camp life – the empty huts provided for worship. Army Council Instructions dated 29 May 1915 – 266 Huts for Religious Meetings stated:

> *Ref. L.* Gen. No. 9/427 (D.F.W.) of 19 Oct., 1914, it is notified that in addition to the huts for religious purposes thereby authorised, two similar huts may be provided in each divisional hutted camp; one for Roman Catholics, and the other for Nonconformists of various denominations.' (L. Gen. No. 9/427, D.F.W.)*

Fr Doyle had no choice but to use the hut for his flock, but he was determined to seek alternative provision for himself, writing shortly after his arrival:

> ***There is one thing I cannot, (I almost wrote 'will not'), bear, the loss of our dearest Lord ... I have found a tiny chapel some miles from here, but I can seldom get there. The thought of Jesus in that lonely Tabernacle haunts me always, and at night I seem to hear Him calling gently and sadly. Oh! how I wish I could go to him through the mud and rain.*** [19]

It is not that proof of Willie Doyle's faith is needed, but this single quotation, perhaps more so than any other, seems to reveal the true depth of his belief. In the celebration of the Eucharist during Mass, altar breads are offered in sacrifice, in the 'making new' of Christ's sacrifice. Following the Consecration, the breads become changed, through a process known as 'transubstantiation'. In outward form and appearance, they continue to look like bread, but their inner 'substance' is changed, to become for Catholics the 'Host', the Precious and True Body of Jesus Christ. In Catholic churches, one Host, revered as the 'Blessed Sacrament', is always reserved in the Tabernacle, ensuring that Christ is always truly present in the church.

It seems typical of Father Doyle that he could think of his Lord, truly present, but alone, unvisited, and isolated in the Tabernacle of that remote chapel. His worry that, in the midst of all his other concerns, he could not find the time to visit the chapel, attests to a true servant of God.

Unfortunately for Willie, the provision of a suitable building for consecration was low on the list of priorities, when the training camps struggled to meet even basic accommodation needs at times. When the Royal Inniskilling Fusiliers arrived at nearby Woking it was into cramped accommodation, the two battalions sharing billets normally sufficient for just one. When they moved to Bordon it was the same story once final drafts arrived. Nevertheless, the men just got on with it.

Willie also got on with keeping his family in Dublin up to date with his news. His main letters home were to his father, who passed the missives round to the others. However, Willie also found time to scribble post cards to other members of the family. He sent his nieces Mollie and Nora picture post cards of sentimental drawings with humorous captions.

A postcard, dated 27 December 1915, to Mollie thanked her for what was, no doubt, a Christmas gift:

> *Ever so many grateful thanks for the box of leads which are most welcome. We are nearly swamped with fearful rain but otherwise all well and going strong. Sending all news to the Father. Much love Will.*[20]

Earlier in the year, prior to Willie Doyle's arrival, Ben Keeling records the progress of the Duke of Cornwall's Light Infantry recruits at Witley Camp, the kind of routines that the Irishmen would later be locked into:

> *In the course of a fortnight we have certainly made some progress in the way of transformation from a rabble into a military unit. After two or three days the task of serious training began. Reveille is at 6am, parade at 7, breakfast at 8, morning parade from 9 to 1, and afternoon parade from 2 to 5. ... Little time is wasted in ceremonial drill. The number of formal drill rifle exercises to be learned is reduced to an absolute minimum. Extended order drill, taking cover, and skirmishing are practised almost from the first day of training. And we are already become proficient in certain new movements which have been devised in order to meet special features of the tactics adopted by the Germans during the present war, and on which the C.O. gave an excellent lecture to all officers and NCOs.. ... The regimental*

sergeant-major ... instructs a special class of about thirty lance-corporals and possible lance-corporals every afternoon and evening on such subjects as musketry, judging distance, patrols and bivouacking.[21]

Then, as an NCO, three months later Keeling reports:

We have learned to march, to bivouac, to cook our own dinners in mess-tins over a fire of a few sticks, and, last but not least, to wait for hours in every variety of weather by day or night. We have had experience of life under canvas, in huts, and in billets. Our musketry is good, but not on the average as good as that of the old Regular Army, though we have had plenty of crack shots. Our specialists, such as signallers and machine-gunners, are thoroughly trained and keen. Our drill on the barrack square is not generally up to the standard of the Old Army, but when we turn out for an inspection and really put our minds to the job, I think we can do a march-past or a rifle movement as well as a line battalion. ... Incidentally, the important part which athletes have played in the training of the New Army is worth noting. Cross-country running, football, and boxing have encouraged physical development, bred esprit de corps, and relieved the monotony of life.[22]

In contrast, Chaplain A.E. Crosse's memories of his early experiences of military service are somewhat different:

(The chaplain) received no sort of preliminary training to equip him for his new life. He went straight from his parish to his unit, and was left almost entirely to gain his experience for himself. Even one month spent at some preliminary school of army training would have paid a handsome dividend, and saved him from many needless efforts.[23]

Padre, R. Bulstrode, commented on his ad-hoc role in September 1914:

Route marching, Hospital visiting, concerts, boxing, meetings and classes – each and all of these (even boxing) gave scope for what, I can only repeat, is the essence of a chaplain's work under such conditions – personal touch with officers and men, and the endeavour to use each 'contact' as a spiritual opportunity ... On Salisbury Plain we had the great advantage of large and well equipped YMCA Huts with good canteens. This made social and religious activities possible on a larger scale. I made it an invariable practice to close Concerts and Meetings of any kind with very short 'family prayers'... This may have been open to criticism, but I have never found it resented either by the audience or by the artistes .... Occasionally manoeuvres took place, and a chaplain might either take the day off or accompany the men as a free-lance – no duties were assigned to him and he was responsible to no man.[24]

And so it was with Willie Doyle. He quickly discovered for himself how to prepare for the rigours that lay ahead. For instance, an observation in December 1915:

I cannot say I am quite in love with camp life, which in many respects is very repellent .... For example, this morning a regiment marched out of camp at 5am in torrents of rain merely for exercise. When they return tonight, they will dry their wet underclothing by sleeping in them! [25]

But by February 1916 he was joining them on the route march!

... once I did a hard day's work ending up with a fifteen miles' march on a cup of tea.'[26]

In-between times, on New Year's Day 1916, Fr Doyle and his new flock had moved barracks to Bordon in Hampshire. There he made a most welcome discovery:

Before I thank you for your letter which was doubly welcome in my exile, I want to tell you the New Year's gift our Lord gave me. We had an awful time of storm and rain coming over here, but the first thing I saw on reaching the barrack square was a hut marked R.C. Church. I took it for granted that it was just the usual hut set apart for Sunday Mass, but on trying the door you can imagine my delight to find a small but beautifully furnished chapel with lamp burning before the altar, which made my heart leap with joy. I felt as if all the hardships of my life had vanished,

> *for I had found Him again who makes the hard things easy and the bitter things sweet….. But His goodness did not stop here; the other priest who had the key gave it to me without my even suggesting it, so I can go to Him at any hour of the day or night if I want to – do you think I shall?*[27]

Further detail in Willie's letter reveals how vast the army camp was, the spartan living conditions and how the religious mix reflected the recruiting areas of the battalions of the brigade:

> *Is He not good to have put the little chapel where He did, as it might have been in any other part of the camp, miles away? I do not think there is a happier man in England than I today. I am writing this, sitting on a piece of wood – no chairs in our quarters. There are about 1,200 Catholics in our brigade now. I get a few 'big fish' each evening.*[28]

The two regiments which made up the four battalions of Willie Doyle's 49th Infantry Brigade had recruiting areas in all of Ulster. Hence there would be more Protestant recruits than Catholic. In a brigade at full strength, twelve hundred Catholics would represent a little over a quarter of the total.

The process of familiarisation of his new surroundings and way of life did not prevent Willie from continuing a regular correspondence with friends and family, which became a mixture of humour and the reiteration of his mission to save as many souls as he could. He writes:

> *There is nothing like the prospect of a German shell for putting the fear of God into one; and many an old rooster whom no mission ever moved has been blown out of his nest by the news of our departure. I cannot help thinking that when the final day of reckoning comes, in spite of all the misery and suffering caused, this war will turn out to have been the biggest act of God's love, saving the souls of scores of poor fellows, certainly among my men.*[29]

When he wasn't using his pen for keeping in touch at home, or writing on behalf of illiterate men, or writing in the course of his pastoral duties, then Willie continued his old habit of scribbling daily aspirations in his diary, such as on 4 February 1916:

1. I am to kiss the floor every time I enter, leave or pass before the Tabernacle.
2. I am not to ask remedies for small ailments, toothache, etc.
3. Not to shrink from or relieve small pains
4. Absolute abandonment to God's will in all things; to have no will or wish of my own.
5. To ask Fr B to treat me like Luisa Cavajal.
6. Every night to tell my Master how many aspirations I have gathered up.[30]

Such were Fr Doyle's preparations for active service! Ten days later he describes how he has prepared his charges and his intentions to continue a full ministry even in transit:

We are having desperate work these days. The good God is simply pouring out His grace on these poor fellows and reconciling them before they die. It has to be quick work, no time for 'trimmings.' I have positively a pain in my arm giving Absolution and Communions in the morning. I was able to manage Exposition all day last Sunday, which bought in many an erring sheep. I realise that from this on my life will be a martyrdom in a way I never thought of. I have got to love my brave lads almost like my own brothers and sisters. They are so wild and reckless, and at the same time so full of faith and love of God and His Blessed Mother. Yet soon I shall have to see the majority of them blown to bits, torn and mangled out of shape. Our Brigade is leaving tomorrow for France. I am waiting till Friday night, so as to get in all the confessions I can. Do pray I may be able to say daily Mass. I shall carry everything necessary on my back, and so may manage the Holy Sacrifice in the train.[31]

The same letter reveals that Willie had not given up enduring hardships for his faith; he had recently fasted and spent a whole night in prayer.

The day finally came that was to signal the end of camp life; orders were received on Thursday 17 February 1916 to proceed overseas. Prior to and immediately after this, the sequence of proceedings would have involved all, or most, of the following actions:

All necessary kit and documentation, including field dressings and field postcards, would be issued. Soldiers were subject to medical inspections and inoculations.

Weapons, ammunition, transport, tools, catering supplies etc. had to be checked and made up to the scale required for the job in hand, and extra horses requisitioned. Items not required on active service, such as full dress uniform, were to be returned to store; loan books were returned to the garrison library and the mess silver and trophies were put into a bank for safe-keeping; hunting horses and other private property had to be disposed of.

A particular piece of kit was issued solely to the Chaplains – Field Service Communion Sets. It's not clear whether Fr Doyle received one at this stage, or once he was in-situ overseas. He makes reference to carrying everything necessary for daily Mass on his back during the journey, but such an item would have been an awkward burden to transport in such a way. A typical Field Service Communion Set is contained within a wooden box measuring approximately 18 inches wide, 11 inches long and 6 inches deep (455mm × 280mm × 152mm) with a suitcase type handle. Three of the sides opened up to reveal a purple silk-lined interior with all the accoutrements necessary for celebrating Mass: crucifix, breads, glass/tin vessels, cloths, candles and an army prayer book.

Once he was issued with the set Willie would have been left in no doubt as to his responsibility for it. An Army Council Instruction dated 17 May 1915 stated:

164 Field Service Communion Sets. In order to prevent misunderstanding, it is notified to chaplains to whom field service communion sets are being supplied at the public expense, that these articles remain public property and are held on ordnance store charge. Chaplains to whom they are issued are held responsible that due care is taken of them, and that when the necessity for using them ceases they are returned immediately to the nearest ordnance store. When the communion set is handed in, a receipt should be obtained from the ordnance officer and forwarded to the W.O. (Chaplains' Department). Unless this is done the chaplain cannot be relieved of his responsibility for the set. (L 57 Gen. No./4216, Chaplains.)

Willie anticipated the journey overseas with a mixture of excitement and dread, writing to his father with customary humour, naming this letter *On the Road to Mandalay or elsewhere*:

In some respects I am sorry to leave Bordon, I suppose because it was such a paradise after the month's purgatory (without fire) at Whitley (sic), and also because the little chapel, with the Blessed Sacrament, has been such a comfort …I set out to face the future with a certain amount of trepidation: General Roberts admitted that he began every campaign with his heart in his boots so I am in good company, even if my spirits have not gone so far as that.[32]

Turning to practicalities, Willie records:

Our first regiment marched yesterday with most of the artillery, though it is no joke to get over 4,000 horses on the move, with wagons, guns and baggage. Two more are leaving today and the last tomorrow. I had hoped to remain till the end but I received orders unexpectedly yesterday from our general, to proceed overseas with his staff this afternoon.[33]

From Wednesday 16 February to Friday 18 February 1916 the battalions of Willie Doyle's brigade paraded in turn outside the barracks and then marched to Bordon railway station. In military parlance, they entrained to Southampton where they embarked on a ship bound for Le Havre.

Footnote 1: Second Lieutenant Rupert Brooke was to gain posthumous fame as a poet, especially through his immortal lines: *If I should die, think only this of me: That there's some corner of a foreign field that is for ever England.*

PART 2

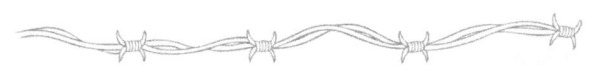

INDUSTRIAL WARFARE

CHAPTER 10
ABOUT CHAPLAINS:
PADRES, NOT OFFICERS

'The present war would be run on much the same lines' (as the Boer War)
'none of us would be allowed within forty miles of the front line.'
Jackson, H.C., *Pastor on the Nile* [1]

The previous war fought by British soldiers was the Boer War, from 1899 to 1902, in South Africa. There, it was War Office policy that chaplains should neither be in the front line, nor anywhere near the front line. This was actually still official policy in 1914, even if the distance of 40 miles, indicated by Pastor Jackson, was much reduced. Chaplains were to remain with their respective field ambulances and these orders were in keeping with the Geneva Convention of 1864. Leading churchmen criticised this stance. For example, four months into the war Archbishop Randall Davidson (Archbishop of Canterbury from 1903 to 1928, later Baron Davidson of Lambeth) derided as short-sighted: *the unwillingness of the War Office authorities to send non-combatants to the fighting line with all the addition to the cost and trouble of transport and supply.*[2]

Even more scornful of this diktat was the Irish Roman Catholic Church hierarchy, in view of the Sacramental needs of Roman Catholic soldiers. The *Catholic Herald*, in its edition of 21 October 1914, reported a speech given at Maynooth by Cardinal Michael Logue, (Archbishop of Armagh, and Primate of All Ireland):

> *What we want is that chaplains will be permitted to go to the Front – not merely to go to the French hospitals, but to go to the firing line, so that when the poor fellow drops he may have a priest beside him to give him the last consolations of religion.*[3]

An alternative viewpoint was mooted within the Catholic Church, *The Tablet* commented a month later, on 7 November 1914:

> *Some disappointment is expressed in some quarters that the Catholic Chaplains cannot be in the Firing Line, instead of being kept with the ambulances, but is complaint reasonable?* [4]

The frustrations of the clergy resulting from this policy are illustrated by an incident within the first week of the war. On Thursday 27 August 1914, the 2nd Battalion, Royal Munster Fusiliers, commanded by Major Paul Charrier, had taken up positions astride the Landrecies to Guise road, to the south of the Forêt de Mormal. The Battalion had been detailed to form the rearguard to 1st Infantry Brigade, covering the withdrawal southwards of the British I Corps after its disengagement from Mons. Unfortunately, the Munsters lost touch with the other units of the brigade before encountering the enemy about mid-morning. There followed a fierce action, in which this single Battalion faced attacks from five, and later six, German regiments.

Under heavy fire, the Munsters slowly withdrew down the main road towards Étreux. They fought on until, around 9.30 p.m. that evening, with Major Charrier and most of the officers killed, the remnants of the Battalion found themselves trapped in an orchard on the northern edge of the village, surrounded on all sides by German troops. Fighting until the last of their ammunition had been expended, the surviving Irishmen finally surrendered.[FN1]

The Regiment's first chronicler, Mrs Victor Rickard, records from personal testimony:

> *It is told that the German officers said that men had never fought more bravely; it is also said that they sent back to their headquarters for a chaplain to bury the Irish dead.*[5]

Hence, in the absence of any BEF Chaplain close enough to undertake the duty, the needs of the Munsters were ministered by an enemy padre. The man's nationality was almost certainly of no concern to the Irishmen; it was spiritual solace they needed – and received. But the incident must surely have been foremost in the mind of Fr Francis Gleeson, the Munsters' Chaplain when, on 21 December 1914, ignoring official War Office policy and the few doubters within his church's hierarchy, he accompanied his Royal Munster Fusiliers into battle at Givenchy. After the attack:

> *Stretcher parties, helped by the chaplain, Fr Gleeson, heroically scoured the fire-swept battlefield searching for the wounded.*[6]

Again at Aubers Ridge in May 1915 Fr Gleeson was at the side of his flock in the front line and recorded in his diary:

> *I gazed out over the scene, there were hundreds of giant men sitting in the fresh grass under the shade of the thickly-blossomed fruit trees, praying, meditating, reading their prayer-books, saying their rosaries – silent, absorbed, reverential to a degree.*[7]

A few hours later, on 8 May, Fr Gleeson was at the front line at the village of Rue du Bois, giving Absolution prior to the attack in which the Munsters were annihilated. An extract from a letter written 9 May 1915 by Sergeant Louis Moore, 2nd Royal Munster Fusiliers, to Mrs Victor Rickard, the widow of the Battalion's Commanding Officer, describes the scene:

> *On his way up to our position on that Saturday evening, and just before reaching our trenches, we passed one of those little shrines. The Major halted his Regiment, and the Father, still mounted, gave the Regiment a general absolution. After that they sang the 'Te Deum'. I know you can see the whole picture. The semi-light, the Major on his horse in front, and then the whole Regiment uncovered. It was a sight never to be forgotten.*[8]

The Major was, in fact, Lieutenant Colonel V.G.H. Rickard who died in the battle. Afterwards, the padre, steadfast to the end, conducted a memorial service in an improvised chapel erected in a field tent.

An apposite comment from an Anglican commentator illuminates the front line debate further:

> *The Church of Rome sent a man into action mentally and spiritually cleaned. The Church of England could only offer you a cigarette. The Church of Rome, experienced in propaganda, sent its priests into the line. The Church of England forbade theirs forward of Brigade Headquarters, and though many, realising the fatal blunder of such an order, came just the same, the publication had its effect.*[9]

However, as the war progressed it became increasingly accepted that those padres who wished to do so worked in the front line. Whereas the Anglican Rev E. C. Crosse remembers joining his division in France in September 1915 and was: *absolutely forbidden* [10] to venture into the front line, by 1916: *no sort of general restrictions prevailed ... and most chaplains came to regard visits to the trenches as the best part of their work.* [11]

On the other hand, there was a role for chaplains further back, even if their thoughts did turn to the front lines. Father Henry Gill, S.J. wrote to his Father Provincial from the base hospital where he had been sent:

Medical department wonderfully well organised. It is certainly not the kind of life to select as an amusement. I hope however that one may go nearer the firing line. [12]

Father Gill eventually got his way, serving with the 2nd Royal Irish Rifles, he writes:

The Commanding Officer gives every encouragement, but between being in the trenches and sudden moves it is not always possible to hold Mass. Confessions in fields, roadside, generally in several inches of mud ... Whole battalion have been to confession and Holy Communion in the last week to ten days ... [13]

Tom Johnstone and James Hegerty note:

The encouragement of the CO was probably because of the effect Fr Gill was having on his battalion, where military 'crime' had been greatly reduced due to the chaplain 'who moved about constantly among men'. [14]

Debate continued about the role of chaplains, and the numbers required throughout the war. Willie Doyle evidently thought that his ministry would take him to the front line, writing to his father before departing for France in February 1916:

Strange to say, I have not the smallest anxiety about the possible dangers of warfare, not so great for me, as for others, but I do dread the horrors of the battlefield which all say no words can picture. Still it is a consolation to know what a comfort the mere presence of a priest is to both officers and men alike. They are one and all going to face their duty with the joy of heart which comes with a clear conscience; many of them had not been to confession for over twenty years.[15]

Willie Doyle was to strike up a fond working relationship with another Jesuit priest, Fr Francis Browne, S.J. Indeed, chaplains as a breed often tended to co-operate and work in harmony whatever the denomination, as noted by Frederic Spurr:

Those six men represented several denominations, yet no stranger suddenly appearing in their midst could have determined, by any outward or visible sign, the denomination to which each belonged. Anglican, Presbyterian, United Board, Wesleyan and Catholic – they are dressed alike; for the most part they hold common rank; they confer together, they pray together, they work together. They respect each other, although some of them profoundly differ from each other ...[16] *One of the Free Church Chaplains ... was enquiring about some of his boys when a Roman Catholic priest, fresh complexioned, and hearty, came forward and in 'lovely' Irish brogue he said: 'Can I be of service to ye to show ye where your boys are? I know lots of Baptists and Congregationalists and others.' Away we went, and from that day I have not wanted a friend.*[17]

Throughout the course of the Great War the Chaplains' Department shared a common experience with the armed forces and sections of society as a whole; its role evolved and adapted as the impact of the huge conflict started to bite and gnaw away at its core being. That is not to say that it evolved as one cohesive force and certainly those of the Roman Catholic faith had one advantage over other faiths. Robert Rider, a Wesleyan chaplain reflected that:

The war had been fought in countries where 'Roman Catholic' was the state religion (sic). The general populace was of that faith; most villages had, at both entries, the sacred figure of the Crucifix, as well as a common public shrine inviting mens' religious courtesies; and the village church with its resident priest and in many cases its general ecclesiastical equipment was at the service of Roman Catholic troops.[18]

Thus, it was natural that when Father Doyle first arrived in France he stepped into the vacant shoes of the parish priest of Mazingarbe, the ruined village where, on several occasions, one of his Irish battalions was stationed.

The logistics of coping with the huge expansion in the chaplaincy service from 1914 onwards was exacerbated by a general lack of instruction for the chaplains. All that was certain was that the King's Regulations required all soldiers to attend a parade service, conducted by a chaplain, once a week whenever practicable; troops also had the option to attend any voluntary services conducted by the chaplain. Other than such services, it was generally accepted that the padre presided at burials and he might also write to the next of kin of the dead. He could assist other officers with censoring duties and he might be disposed towards helping illiterate troops with letters. In due course, chaplains were to play a pioneering role in the establishment of clubs, canteens and other recreational amenities for the troops, although Edward Madigan points to the perception that Catholic padres focused more on the spiritual than the recreational needs of their charges.[19]

The range of the padres' activities is illustrated by Rev Pat Leonard, writing on 17 December 1915, two months after his arrival in Belgium:

Today (Friday) has been filled with small fry of various sorts. Celebration in the YMCA at 7.15am. [at Reninghelst], breakfast at 8.15am, writing and sending in Returns and various official work until 11 am. Then walked up to Headquarters and saw the Adjutant about various things and arranged a gramophone concert for this evening. Back to lunch at one o'clock. Then down to the cemetery with the Pioneers to put up a cross over Major Williams' grave, then in to see the Senior Chaplain and help him with the censoring of the day's mailbag. Then after ten (sic), once more up to the King's Own camp to arrange for the concert, then the concert itself, which by the way was very cheery. Then a little sick visiting until dinner time, and now I'm back once more in my hut thinking it is nearly time for bed as my candle is flickering out and Mr Dream Man is throwing dust into my eyes.[20]

It is evident that many chaplains aspired to expand their pastoral role by improving the morale, comfort and education of the men wherever they could. When the Reverend John Sellors arrived in France in 1917, he was advised by a helpful sergeant to: *mix with the boys, join in their lives and interests and see the boys made more contented and happy.*[21]

The padre was, to a large extent, left to determine his own role and workload. In addition to this somewhat challenging open brief, the new chaplain at the beginning of the war had practical problems to contend with. The question of transport was one, which proved an intractable problem throughout the war. Incredibly, no thought had even been given to the process of mobilising the chaplains. The Reverend Harry Blackburne, a pre-war regular chaplain, remembered:

> *The Medical authorities, into whose arms we were thrown, did what they could for us, and provided us with homes in the Field Ambulances and Hospitals; but for the first few weeks of the war it was always a matter of some difficulty to get one's modest kit carried on wagons which were already fully loaded with authorised equipment, as laid down in those carefully constructed mobilisation regulations; and in which, except for the Principal Chaplain, the Chaplains did not appear.*[22]

The Reverend E.C. Crosse pointed out that the terms of the annual contract signed by temporary Chaplains entitled each to his own horse. However, only a few could ride when they joined the army and: *by no means all*[23] bothered to learn. When the Reverend Geoffrey Studdert Kennedy was given a horse in 1916 to help him get around in order to perform his duties, the horse threw him the second he got in the saddle.

The Reverend Pat Leonard wrote home on 12 October 1915, shortly after arriving in France:

> *I am becoming quite an expert horseman. On Sunday I borrowed a blood mare from one of the officers here, and went for a long tour of inspection, and incidentally tried my luck over a few jumps, luckily without disaster but with a marked absence of finesse or elegance. However, I am becoming quite good by degrees.*[24]

Willie Doyle, in keeping with his semi-rural, middle-class upbringing and athleticism during his youth, was a horseman. He had access at different times during his army service to horses and bicycles, although these modes of transport were not always readily available or practical, so Willie often found himself walking long distances in order to carry out his duties. On occasions when his flock were en-route between destinations he would walk with the 'other ranks'. In a letter home, he writes in August 1916:

> *The Officers, from the Captain up have horses; but I prefer to shoulder my pack and foot it with my boys, for I know they like it, and besides I don't see why I should not have a share of their hardship.*[25]

On Sunday 19 June 1915, the Reverend Charles Doudney writes from the Ypres Salient about the difficulties of getting around in order to carry out his duties:

> *Spent the rest of the day in arranging services for tomorrow ... I have borrowed a horse from a friendly gunner for the day. I have indented for a horse for myself, but expect it will be a week before it arrives.*[26]

Then he struck lucky a month later when:

> *He was presented with a brand new Triumph motor bicycle with all the extra equipment: leggings, luggage case, plugs, etc. (all bought at the cost of £50 18s 9d.).*[27]

This generous gift was from his former parishioners in Bath whilst he was home on sick leave for the treatment of eczema in the summer of 1915. Charlie was delighted and lost no time in reporting this improvement in his transport problems in August 1915:

> *This morning I had occasion to test my new method of travel as services had been fixed in to places beyond (Ypres.) Instead of relying on passing vehicles or slowly working in on a horse, I swung down the road at about 15 miles an hour, and was in the city in about 20 minutes. At that pace one is not bumped too much, appalling as the road is. Then came the advantage. Instead of the slow weary tramp, I went right up to Z-, round Suicide Corner like a streak and was at the dug-out in no time.*[28]

The second most common problem faced by Chaplains was the logistics of organising church parades and other services, an issue complicated by periodic and regular movement of troops. In addition, gathering together large numbers of men in, or even near, the front line for non-combat reasons was frowned upon. Behind the lines, scattered support services at supply depots and workshops also provided a challenge for the padre to co-ordinate his ministry.

The Reverend Pat Leonard writes home ruefully on 6 November 1915:

Today has been proclaimed a general whole holiday and the sun is shining brilliantly. Nearly everybody has gone off to see the final of the GOC's cup. I, poor wretch, am the only one who can't make holiday for it is the day of preparation, and when I have finished all this I will have to visit innumerable Orderly Rooms and make arrangements for tomorrow. I have a Celebration and four Church Parades tomorrow, each one separated from the other by distances varying between one and three miles. It is like fitting in a Chinese puzzle, and I anticipate dashing madly à la John Gilpin on a foam-flecked steed from Service to Service, stung to a frenzy by the fear of being late.[29]

Church services in front-line trenches were virtually forbidden and Willie Doyle sometimes found himself pushing back boundaries in order to celebrate Mass. Fr Doyle invariably always accompanied his flock to front-line trenches even though he was not allowed to have Mass there. He tried to return to the reserve area every morning, in order to give Holy Communion to those who were free to attend. Early in February 1917, however, he felt confident enough to improvise a chapel in a dug-out of a front-line trench, which held about ten to twelve men:

But as my congregation numbered forty-six,' he says *'the vacant space was small. How they all managed to squeeze in I cannot say.*[30]

Chaplains wore badges of rank, together with a Maltese cross on their lapels and cap badges. Most, like Willie Doyle, were Chaplain IV class, which was afforded the equivalent rank of Captain, but not the same salary or the right to be addressed by the title of their military rank. Harry Blackburne observed in a letter to his wife that the Canadian Chaplains used military titles and:

It is all right for the Canadians, for they have always done this; but we do want it to be clear that padres are padres and not officers. [31]

However, chaplains were permitted the same courtesies and privileges as officers, including the services of a servant. Willie Doyle had grown up in a household which employed several servants, but he was known to have frequently eased their workload by performing some tasks himself. Even as a child he would often volunteer to do work for the parlour-maid if he thought she looked tired. Some thirty years later, hours before the Battle of Messines, and fatigued following a rest of just one hour on 6 June 1917, Fr Doyle left his exhausted servant to sleep an extra hour, whilst he and Fr Browne prepared the makeshift altar at 1a.m. in their improvised chapel of sandbags.

Chaplains who were religious priests i.e. members of religious orders, such as Willie Doyle (Society of Jesus), were not allowed personal spending money. After expenses had been met, they were expected to send surplus funds to their religious house or Diocese.

Unlike other officers who were tied to the army for the duration, chaplains were on annually renewable contracts and could walk away on the expiry of the contract. Even if they signed up again, chaplains could still get some breathing space from the Front and return home for a period of leave. Interestingly, Bishop Francis Bourne, the Senior Roman Catholic Chaplain, expected his priests to serve for the duration, but that didn't always prove to be the case. Father Francis Gleeson served with the 2nd Royal Munster Fusiliers for the year between November 1914 and November 1915; one month later he was working as a curate in the Church of Our Lady of Lourdes, Gloucester Street, Dublin. However, he subsequently returned to France for a second stint as Military chaplain for two years from May 1917.

The biggest difference between chaplains and other officers, of course, was that the padres had no military authority, so could not give orders which might endanger the soldiers. Consequently, they tended to be more popular with the Other Ranks than other officers. A famous padre of the Great War was the Reverend Geoffrey Studdert Kennedy, who became known as 'Woodbine Willy' because of his predilection for giving out cigarettes to the troops. When a new Anglican chaplain asked for guidance in 1916, Studdert Kennedy recalls telling him:

I remember the conversation very well, and the memory has never left me ... He asked me to tell him what the best way of working up there was. I said

Live with the men. Go everywhere they go. Make up your mind that you will share all their risks, and more if you can do any good. You can take it that the best place for a Padre (provided he does not interfere with military operations) is where there is most danger of death. Our first job is to go beyond the men in self-sacrifice and reckless devotion. Don't be bamboozled into believing that your proper place is beyond the line; it isn't. If you stay behind you might as well come down, you won't do a ha'porth of good. Your place is in the front. The line is the key to the whole business. Work in the front, and they will listen to you when they come out to rest, but if you only preach and teach behind, you are wasting your time, the men won't pay the slightest attention to you. The men will forgive anything but lack of courage and devotion; without that you are useless.[32]

The rookie listening to this advice was the Reverend Theodore Bayley Hardy who went on to become the most decorated chaplain of the Great War (VC, DSO and MC).

Father Doyle did not need any such advice, he felt it instinctively. Like Woodbine Willy, Willie Doyle often appeared with pockets full of treats for the men, mystifying one of his battalion officers, Captain Healey:

Whenever he came up to the men he always had his pockets stuffed with sweets and cigarettes, where he got them we could never make out, he had them when we officers had not.[33]

And from the moment Willie Doyle arrived in France, he inadvertently courted danger by sauntering in danger zones. This unintended casualness proved to be an unwitting morale booster for his charges, for which he became infamous, and he was often scolded by Captain Healey and other officers. Another battalion officer, Frank Laird, recalled:

When shells dropped round ordinary mortals took cover or an opposite direction. Father Doyle made for them to see was he wanted. One morning in the line I was standing watching the communication trench a short way down getting a very nasty shelling. In a few minutes Father Doyle arrived smiling, having just come through it on his usual visit to the front line, without his tin hat, which he could not be induced to wear. In fact it was with great difficulty that he was got even to carry a gas helmet. His gentlemanly, reserved manner with his quiet humour and pleasant conversation, which often contained some canard such as that the French were going to give in next month, all made him a very pleasant man to meet at any time, and most of all in a bad time. Is it any wonder that he was welcome in every mess, that the men worshipped the ground he trod on, and that he was worth several officers in any hot spot when endurance was tested to its height?[34]

Fr William Doyle, SJ, CF

Footnote 1: As a result of the rearguard action by the 2nd Munsters, the southward advance of General von Bülow's Second Army had been seriously delayed, and precious time had been bought, allowing British I Corps to reach and to consolidate positions around Guise.

CHAPTER 11
THE NOVICE CHAPLAIN ARRIVES:
WITH FAUGHS AND SKINS

Royal Irish Fusiliers – RIF – Irish Fusiliers - the 'Faughs'
Royal Inniskilling Fusiliers – RInnF – Inniskillings - the 'Skins'

Willie Doyle was a seasoned sailor. He had crossed the Irish Sea many times to England and, on at least half a dozen of those occasions, made the onward journey across the Channel to the Continent. However, the voyage from Southampton to Le Havre would be something of a novelty for the novice Military Chaplain. Whether the voyage was quite as original as that experienced by the 7th Battalion Royal Inniskilling Fusiliers, a few days beforehand, is unknown. The 'Skins' travelled to Le Havre on the *SS Mona Queen*, a paddle-steamer with very limited accommodation. Their baggage, transport and quartermaster's staff went on a separate steamer. Willie does comment, however, on the dearth of bunks on the vessel in which he sailed:

> *The moon was surrounded by a magnificent halo or crown, which I promptly bagged for myself. I was fortunately able to get some tea on shore, for though they served us out with lifebelts, nothing in the shape of a dinner or rations came along. There were only a few bunks which I left to the other officers, and as there was no place to sleep, except the stoke hole, which I was not having this journey, I picked a comfortable (?) corner on deck and prepared for a snooze, when alas! down came the rain. Providence however came to my rescue: the second engineer passing by very kindly offered me a share of his cabin, and I slept like a top on the settee.[1]*

The ship arrived off-shore at 4a.m. and when Willie awoke a few hours later the

Second Engineer offered him breakfast of hot coffee and buns. However, Willie was too busy making his preparations to celebrate Mass on shore to accept the kindness. By 9a.m. he had regretted that decision because he was still waiting to disembark. Finally, he stepped ashore at Le Havre at 11.30a.m. on Sunday 20 February 1916:

> *Just landed. Seeing there was no chance for Mass I rooted up a Chinaman and secured a welcome cup of tea; he brought me also a plate of cold liver and potatoes likewise cold – a dish to tempt one's appetite after a channel crossing!*[2]

The troops of the 8th Battalion Royal Irish Fusiliers had started disembarking at 7a.m. and marched to Rest Camp Number One. It was the lot of the British Tommy to spend many a tiresome time at Channel ports, hanging around waiting to be directed on to the next stage of their journey. If the boredom didn't put a damper on any sense of excitement and expectation the Faughs felt initially at Le Havre, the unceasing rain certainly must have. Finally, they began to entrain at 6p.m. on Monday, which proved to be just another tedious leg of a long, long journey. Willie wrote to his father on 21 February 1916:

> *After a long tiresome day at H____, the rain never ceasing for a minute, we reached the station at nine o'clock to begin our journey to the front, only to be told the train would not start until Midnight. We also learned that we should stop at 6am for breakfast; and again at one o'clock for dinner, reaching our destination about six, which turned out to be 9.30 as a matter of fact. We three Chaplains, a Reverend Mr. Moore, Father Kelly and myself, had a carriage to ourselves, and though the night was fairly cold, and we had no rugs or blankets we made ourselves comfortable and slept some hours at least.*[3]

Three days previously, during the evening of Friday 18 February, the Fusiliers of the 7th Battalion Royal Inniskillings had preceded their brigade colleagues on the train out of Le Havre:

> *That evening we were initiated into that mysterious and depressing mode of travelling known as the 'French troop train'. By 9 o'clock the battalion*

arrived at the station, and entrained for an unknown destination. With the exception of one very dilapidated first-class carriage labelled 'officers', a few open trucks for the limbered wagons and miscellaneous vehicles, the train was composed of covered-in cattle trucks – 40 Hommes, 10 Chevaux – nobody seemed to object if you cared to mix them. At 10.30 o'clock the train pulled out of Havre, and judging by our ultimate time record it must have toured most of France during the night. Sometimes we would jog along at 20 m.p.h. for several hours, then for the next hour the train seemed to crawl, shunt, stop and start alternately. During a rather longer halt than usual outside Calais (Les Fontinettes), our mascot 'Tip' jumped off the train and was never seen again. A stop at St. Omer gave us an opportunity for a wash, of which we felt badly in need. By 7pm we arrived at Berguette Station (about five miles north of Lillers), and here we detrained and made tea before starting out for billets.[4]

The trains ambled through gently rolling countryside not dissimilar to that of the English South Downs from whence Willie had started his journey. The views were to prove the only source of comfort to the three Chaplains. Willie continues his letter:

Morning broke at last, bringing with it the first of our adventures and disappointments. We had reached the breakfast station, spirits and hopes rising accordingly, but to our dismay breakfast turned out to be a mug of black coffee only, which we had barely time to swallow before the train moved off. It was my first experience of warfare, but not the last – and then seven hours more would bring dinner and comfort for the inner man. It was only when one o'clock arrived that we discovered the mistake we had made – the men had their field kitchens, but we officers were supposed to provide for ourselves. No one had told us this, and only an officer came to our rescue we should have starved. [sic] We managed to get some coffee at the station, and that with a couple of sandwiches made a capital meal.[5]

The journey took twenty-one and a half hours, but:

Nothing however seemed to damp the spirit of the Tommies. They had only horse boxes to travel in, but very soon the foot-boards on both sides of the

> *train were lined with men, who sat and smoked and sang to their heart's content. How they did not fall off, will ever be a mystery to me. There was never any question where our regiment hailed from, they seemed only too anxious to let everyone know they were Catholics. One little man at a station was the recipient of a volley of cheers, which must have made some of the Frenchmen think!!* [6]

When they finally arrived in Berguette, there was still the job of detraining horses, wagons etc. but journey's end meant a good night of rest. Then came the unwelcome news that there was still a march of twelve miles to be endured, largely over roads made of worn cobble stones, in the grimy mining district of north-west France. Willie observed:

> *Eleven was just striking as the column, led by a guide set out. Fortunately it was a lovely moonlight night. As we emerged round the corner of the little town, into the country, I heard for the first time, the deep, dull, boom of the guns, real war at last. I quite expected I should have had the 'creeps' but to my surprise it seemed the most natural thing in the world to listen to the angry growl which meant death perhaps to some poor fellows.* [7]

Whereas the men would have been used to marches of twenty or thirty miles on metalled roads the other side of the Channel, the French *pavé* roads played havoc with their feet; their heavy, hob-nailed boots had trouble gripping the stones. Willie wrote:

> *I shall not try to describe that march, but you can gather what it was, with strong, big men falling down now and then from sheer exhaustion. Under other circumstances I would not have minded the tramp, but I was near the end of my tether and was carrying a great coat, pack and water-bottle.* [8]

The minimum load the Tommies carried weighed about sixty pounds, but extras could be put on top of this, such as rations, pick or shovel, periscope and souvenirs. The standard load included clothing, toiletry items, First Aid, rifle, ammunition and other equipment. If anyone had bothered to tell the men, the destination for the Faughs was Bellery and Father Doyle was to be billeted in the convent at nearby

Amettes. The path of Willie's journey proved not to be smooth in more ways than one. The forty-two year old priest marched with fortitude over the endless cobblestones, alongside much younger men, some of whom were less than half his age. All were burdened with heavy kit. They were escorted by officers, some of whom had the good fortune of being on horseback. After about two hours an officer noticed Fr Doyle was exhausted and persuaded him to take a ride on an artillery wagon:

> *At the first turning the infantry left us. I was too tired and worn out to wonder at or take much notice of this, and besides it was as much as I could do to keep my seat on the limber. I would suggest to anyone thinking of taking a 'joy-ride' on an artillery limber to make quite sure that his ribs were securely fastened to his spinal cord, and his head well settled on, otherwise he might have difficulty keeping them in their proper position.*[9]

When the wagons stopped after some hours Willie discovered he was separated from his regiment which had proceeded to its destination without him. He was stranded! Willie did not let this minor inconvenience trouble him:

> *We had travelled a long way when orders came to stop, and rest the horses. It was only then I discovered that the officer had put me on the wrong wagon, and that I was with a column of reinforcements, on its way to the trenches, and separated from my own regiment. There I was, at 2am 'somewhere in France' certainly, but where, the Lord only knew – I was lost!! To make matters worse, I did not know the name of the town or village that my regiment was bound for, and no one could tell me either. This did not trouble me very much however. I was much more troubled to find some place to sleep. There was no lodging to be had – all the houses and barns were packed with soldiers, there was not even a welcome haystack to furnish a bed. At last I saw a cart under a sort of shed or roof, supported on four poles – it was very inviting, even now I cannot tell if the boards were soft or hard, for almost before I had laid my head on my pack, and stretched my legs, I fell asleep.*[10]

Willie slept for three hours; when refreshed he walked on for a couple of miles and found himself in, what he described as a good size town, during early morning of Thursday 24 February 1916. Although he had eaten very little since detraining at Berguette the previous Tuesday evening, his first thoughts were to celebrate Mass before finding breakfast. The active military life had certainly focused Willie on his appetite; he was in no mood for fasting!

> *The Curé of the place was very much amused at my adventures; and hoped I would soon pick up my regiment again, but never asked if 'I had a mouth on me.' However after washing off the dirt of two days and getting a good breakfast in town, I proceeded to find the station.[11]*

His next dilemma was discovering there were no passenger services, but he was resourceful as ever and his boyish enthusiasm for adventure undiminished:

> *There was no passenger train to be had, but I noticed that the goods trains when passing the station slowed down greatly, and as they were going where I was wanting to get to, I seized my opportunity and boarded one. But where had I landed? If one of the shells I was sitting on went off, I think Captain W. Doyle, C.F. would be on the missing list for many a long day; and even at the day of judgement, I think the Lord's angels would have difficulty gathering up the bits. In this way I got a good bit on my journey, and eventually was lucky enough to come across a Major of our Division – an excellent Catholic, who took me in his private motor car to my journey's end, and put me in a nice little convent, which is a kind of hospice, where I have a room to myself, and a most comfortable bed. The good Sisters are kindness itself to me, and I believe I am to remain here for the present as we are not to go to the firing line just yet.[12]*

Once again Willie was able to rise above adversity and take the positives from what fate threw at him, ending his letter thus:

> *You see God has made up to me for all I had suffered ... A strange coincidence has happened. Since reading the life of Saint J. Benedict Labré, when at College I have always had a great devotion to him, and now I find I am billeted in the town in which he was born, and I celebrate*

the Holy Sacrifice in the very chapel in which the Saint prayed so often. Strange certainly.[13]

Just before ending the letter advising this lucky coincidence, which he had started composing on 21 February 1916 but added to over the following days, Willie had informed his father that the weather was very cold with snow and frost. There is no detailed record of the fate of the men of the 'Faughs' shivering in their billets whilst Willie was spoilt by the nuns, so we turn once more to the history of 7th 'Skins' for a flavour of life on the road. They were billeted at nearby Nédonchelle; officers responsible for billeting preceded the men by car to the village and their efforts were duly rewarded:

The inhabitants of this pleasant village received us in a most friendly and benevolent manner, which greatly added to our comfort.[14]

The men who found themselves in this bleak area far from home appreciated every comfort they could get:

Life in billets might have been very pleasant had it not been for the extreme bitterness of the cold and wintry weather. Snow lay half a foot deep over the country the following morning, and during the night the thermometer registered 25 degrees. The state of the roads made training almost out of the question, and most of the time was spent in giving the men lectures and reading the 'standing orders' regarding the duties and restrictions of a soldier's life on active service. The C.O. gave special instructions and was most particular about the mounting of guards, the general smartness of the men in billets, the correct method of saluting, and the exchange of compliments.[15]

Perhaps the warmth of their reception was aided by some French speakers amongst their ranks. For example, in March 1916 another Irish regiment, 8th Royal Munster Fusiliers, deployed French-speaking Second Lieutenant J.H. Hall as billeting officer, to persuade farmers' wives in the same area to provide billets. He explained:

My procedure is always the same. I first compliment them on the beauty of their children, the gallantry of their soldiers and the cleanliness of their stores (they are always grumpy and disobliging and singularly unembarrassed by the ordinary conventional decencies of life.) Then after a few more sugary compliments and patting all the children on the head, I suggest ... They grumble but I always prevail'[16]

Willie Doyle had caught a bad chill after three nights exposure *en-route* to Amettes, where he spent several days being spoilt by the nuns. Willie's battalion received orders to march again, leaving Bellery on Saturday 26 February 1916. Willie ruefully remarked:

To leave such comfortable quarters was not pleasant, especially as it had been freezing hard, and the ground inches deep in snow. Fortunately we had only fourteen miles to go, and the morning was fine and bright, a pleasing contrast to the blizzards of the previous evening. We officers marched with the men to encourage them, for marching in full kit with haversack, water-bottle, entrenching tools, a rifle, and 120 rounds of ammunition is no joke.[17]

A typical list of full kit would be: Greatcoat 1, Tin (mess) 1, Tin (mess) cover 1, Shirt 1, Socks - pair 1, Soap 1, Towel 1, Housewife 1, Holdall 1, Razor 1, Razor case 1, Lather brush 1, Comb 1, Fork 1, Knife 1, Spoon 1, Toothbrush 1, Cardigan 1, Cap (fatigue comforter) 1, Pay-book 1, Disc (identity) 1, Sheet (waterproof) 1, Grease (tin of) 1, Field-service dressing 1, Respirator 1, Spine protector 1, Set of equipment 1, Laces (pair) 1, Rounds of ammunition 150, Rifle and bayonet 1, Rifle cover 1, oil-bottle and pull-through 1, Entrenching tool 1.[18]

A few days later Willie scribbled a postcard to his sister Lena, on 2 March 1916, in which we learn of his intended routine of sending detailed news to his father, whilst keeping briefly in touch with other members of the family via post-cards.

Many thanks for your welcome letter. You will have seen mine to the father by this. So far we are well behind the firing line near the town where I said we were likely to go, but on Saturday we got a move on. I am ever so well thank God.[19]

The 'Faughs' marched from Bellery to Gonnehem where, luckily, the weather turned milder, fine and dry, a few days later. On arrival Willie made the Curé's house his first port of call, describing the welcome:

> *When he heard I was an Irish priest, he welcomed me with open arms: but when I told him I had brought close on 2,000 Catholic soldiers, the good man fairly wept on my neck, and insisted on my occupying his best room. I did not quite tumble to the meaning of this warm welcome, until his Reverence dropt a discreet hint about the Sunday collection, which, poor man, meant a great deal to him. His face fell when I told him that the men had not been paid for a fortnight, and did not possess a red cent between them.*[20]

As ever Willie made no secret of his pride in his Irish boys:

> *I was hoping to make it up to him next Sunday, but alas we move on again tomorrow. However the men have made an extraordinarily good impression on the people, by their attendance at Mass and the Sacraments, and the good old Curé is grateful for their visit. I expect we shall be back here later, when please God, we shall fill his bounty more for a while.*[21]

Fr Doyle and his men were edging closer and closer to their ultimate destination and the character of the environment started to change:

> *So far we have been behind the firing line: no doubt the Germans could reach us with their big guns, but have never tried to do so. Tomorrow the men move on nearer the trenches, to break them in by degrees. The enemy aeroplanes constantly fly over us. Yesterday I watched several being shelled by our guns, and later on I saw an air fight for the first time. The unfortunate German had no chance as he came right over our aerodrome, with the result that six of our 'flyers' were after him in a moment. The sky was quite clear, and one could hear distinctly the rat-tat of the machine guns overhead. The fight took place directly over the spot I was standing, so I had a magnificent view. A bullet must have hit the German engine, for I saw a jet of black smoke behind, and the machine at once dived for the ground. He came down and was captured half a mile away: one of the two officers was wounded, but neither was killed.*[22]

Not only was there a change of environment but also one of administration. The change to the continental system of timing was recorded in the history of the 15th Scottish Division, from whom the 16th Division had taken instruction on arrival in France. It said:

It certainly tended to lessen confusion as regards orders etc., but the Scotsmen found it rather difficult at first to grasp the fact that 23.59 hours meant one minute to Midnight.[23]

The war diaries for the 16th (Irish) Division continued with a.m. and p.m. and Willie doesn't mention this change, or whether he adjusted easily to it, but he did become a fast learner in the mechanics of warfare:

Just now I got a bit of a start. As I was sitting writing, three bombs exploded in rapid succession in a field right opposite my window, with such a crash that I thought every pane of glass was gone. I could see the flashes quite distinctly, as they were in a direct line from where I sat. It was a wee bit 'creepy' wondering would the next one come through the roof, or just miss the house. Then I noticed there was no whine of the aeroplane engine, so I knew at once it was only our bombers keeping their eye in.[24]

Shortly the 'Faughs' would arrive for service in the Loos sector, some 150 miles as the crow flies from Le Havre. They were en-route to a landscape portrayed by Rudyard Kipling thus:

It was a jagged, scarred and mutilated sweep of mining-villages, factories, quarries, slag-dumps, pitheads, chalk-pits and railway embankments – all the plant of an elaborate mechanical civilisation connected above ground and below by every means that ingenuity and labour could devise to the uses of war.[25]

CHAPTER 12
FINDING HIS FEET:
AMONGST FOSSES AND CRASSIERS

Fosse = pithead/mine workings
Puits = pithead/mine workings
Crassier = slag-heap

Loos Double Crassier, 1916

Even before the Great War, the landscape between the La Bassée Canal and the mining town of Lens was dirty, dusty and dreary. It was dotted with mining communities, with their pitheads, winding-gear, uniform rows of red-brick houses and black slag-heaps. The flat ground between the villages was criss-crossed by ditches, hedges and fences around fields devoted to arable farming. The only rising ground was east of Loos-en-Gohelle[FN1] which, together with a towering double crassier, provided perfect observation points for the occupying troops. Despite this, wherever possible, the local people carried on as normal. A chaplain to the 3rd Brigade, Harry Blackburne, commented in 1915: *What wonderful people the French miners are: they go on working the mines quite close to the line.*[1]

Chaplain Blackburne also noted, the year before Chaplain Doyle's arrival:

We are now billeted in a wonderful chateau at Mazingarbe, quite near the trenches. The owner, who is a mine magnate, keeps up his garden as if there were no war! There are eight old French gardeners, and if a shell comes, they at once fill up the hole and put turf on it, and then go on in the garden as if nothing had happened.[2]

There was, at least, one distinct advantage for a soldier serving in this area; it had the best bath houses on the Western Front for men being relieved and coming away from front line duty:

The colliery baths of the Loos area were put to good use and each man was provided with a clean set of underwear in exchange for his own. These were then washed and passed on to another unit in their turn at the bath. While the men were bathing, their uniforms were cleaned pressed and had insect life removed by locally employed women.[3]

When the soldiers of the 16th (Irish) Division arrived in the Loos sector in stages, between the end of 1915 and beginning of 1916, it was to a static situation of stalemate. The Battle of Loos had been fought a few months previously, from 25 September 1915 to 14 October 1915, for control of the French coalfields, which, following the German annexation of Alsace and Lorraine, provided France's only remaining substantial source of coal. The British mounted an attack in this sector, as part of a larger offensive with the French in the region of Artois, to drive the Germans back and to gain full control of Lens and all the coalfields. This battle marked the first use of New Army units raised by Lord Kitchener's recruitment drive; it also had the dubious distinction of being the first time the British had used poison gas in the war.

Whilst the British did make gains on this front, capturing the mining village of Loos for example, nothing of significance was achieved by this battle, or indeed by the wider Anglo-French offensive. Unfortunately, the novice British troops were hampered by inexperience, both practically and in terms of lack of fully-trained officers and experienced staff officers. They also had to contend with a shortage of artillery shells and ineffective gas masks, with some British soldiers being gassed by their own chlorine gas blowing back across their lines. In addition, the British High Command seemed to miss a trick, which was to overlook the possibilities of the valuable role underground warfare could play at Loos. The Tunnellers history comments:

> *As news of the impending offensive percolated along the front – for secrecy was not the Allied strong point in 1915 – Tunnellers naturally began to visualise their share of the battle. Lens was a mining area: the possibilities were obvious. Keen company commanders studied maps and made provisional plans. Some bold spirits went so far as to throw out hints to the powers above. They discovered to their dismay, however, that mining was to form no part of the preparations for battle. The newly formed 180th Tunnelling Company was indeed ordered to the Loos sector, but there it found itself engaged in the construction of saps and communication trenches; nothing more.[4]*

At the end of the battle, the advances made by the British had been at a heavy cost of over 50,000 casualties, fifteen thousand of whom were killed or reported missing during the first two days. The Germans had sustained half that number in losses of killed, wounded or missing. In addition, six of the most senior British Army officers were killed: Brigadier Generals Wormald, Pollard and Nickells; Major Generals Capper, Wing and Thesiger; whilst Brigadier General Pereira was wounded and Brigadier General Bruce was captured by the enemy. Ironically:

> *Immediately after the battle tunnellers were given free rein, and for two years this sector was a hive of mining activity: Hohenzollern Redoubt, the Quarries, Hulluch, and the Chalk pits are names that will conjure up memories to thousands of miners.[5]*

Lessons had been learned and the Germans now also realised the value of mine warfare; they had started to dig their own tunnels, getting underneath sections of British trenches. There was daily fighting for possession of mine craters, with listening posts established on the near lips of craters. As 1915 drifted into 1916 at an impasse, life in the Loos sector once more settled down to a rhythm; the British watching the Germans watching the British, from slightly altered trench lines, separated by the land of 'No Man.' Rudyard Kipling described the area thus:

> *The ground was trenched and tunnelled with cemented and floored works of terrifying permanency that linked together fortified redoubts, observation posts, concealed batteries, rallying points and impregnable shelters for waiting reserves. So it ran along our front from Grenay north of the plateau of Notre Dame de Lorette, where two huge slag-heaps known as the Double Crassier bristled with machine guns, across the bare interlude of crop land between Loos and Hulluch, where a high German redoubt crowned the slopes, to the village of Haisnes with the low and dangerous Hohenzolern Redoubt south of it. Triple lines of barbed wire protected a system of triple trenches, concrete faced, holding dug-outs twenty feet deep, with lifts for machine guns which could appear and disappear in emplacements of concrete over iron rails; and the observation-posts were capped with steel cupolas. In the background ample railways and a multitude of roads lay ready to launch fresh troops to any point that might by any chance be forced in the face of these obstacles.[6]*

Into this stalemate Fr Doyle's 8th Royal Irish Fusiliers arrived at Gonnehem, well behind the front line, during the late afternoon of Wednesday 26 February 1916. They remained in billets throughout the following day and the next day started practising drill and field operations. Willie Doyle ended his letter dated 3 March 1916 commenting on the fact that the snow had gone and, despite some rain, Spring was on its way. His next letter dated 10 March starts:

> *Before I begin my budget, I want to take back all the nice things I said about the weather, which has been simply on its worst behaviour. The day after I wrote to you, we left our last billet to come here, in a blinding snowstorm, and almost every day since snow has fallen. It melts during the day with the result that we are living in slush, not too pleasant for those who have not provided themselves with a pair of 'gum' boots, which*

makes trudging through the mud and water quite a pleasure. I marched with the 8th Fusiliers, but as I also have charge of the 8th Inniskillings, my first step was to find out where they were quartered, so as to arrange for Mass the next day (Sunday). I found them 4 miles away, in what was once a flourishing town, but now a mass of ruins.[7]

Both of Willie Doyle's battalions were creeping closer to the front line. To get a flavour of the area, the 7th Royal Inniskilling's history describes nearby Philosophe West:

Philosophe 1916

It was getting late as we marched in, and all that one could see of the village was the two long straight rows of deserted houses on either side of the main road; at the top of a hill, about 600 yards further on, loomed up Fosse 3, and the slag heaps above the mine shaft. The houses, needless to say, were uninhabited, except by soldiers – this, we were informed, was the reserve position of the brigade holding the front line. The houses at first sight looked in good repair and to be unaffected by the hostile shelling, but closer examination showed they had received some attention from the Hun. Perhaps the worst fault to be found with them was the dirt and the lack of windows, which made them so uncomfortable in this wintry weather ... The following morning was spent in inspecting the men before proceeding to the line in the evening – gas helmets, field dressings, rifles, ammunition and other numerous details ... The hardships and privations suffered by our men during their initiation to trench warfare were most severe – snow and frost reigned alternately, and the unaccustomed exposure brought its toll of sickness and trench feet.[8]

Philosophe East on the other hand, although nearer the front line, was described as much preferable both for accommodation and cleanliness, with an elderly Frenchman still living in and operating the bakery. Unsurprisingly, the battalion's headquarters were established there!

Returning to Willie Doyle's letter, he describes what he found where he was billeted:

In the midst of the desolation stands a little convent of the Sisters of Charity, absolutely untouched with the exception of some broken panes of glass. The Superioress said they had had a charmed existence, shells flying in all directions, one having actually burst in the garden, but no one received a scratch. She then brought me to the Parish Church next door, its roof and walls pierced with shell holes, with bullet marks on every side, and pointed out the altar, where I was to celebrate the following morning. On the principle I suppose of 'making my flesh creep' she pointed out the spot behind the altar, where a shell had burst making a big hole in the wall, and blowing the priest into the middle of the congregation without hurting him or them. However she told me, the Germans had not bombarded the town for the past 12 months, and so I began to breathe freely again, and went back to my own quarters with a light heart, little thinking what was in store for me the following morning.[9]

Just as there had been no formal training for temporary chaplains in the training camps, Fr Doyle could expect none whilst on active service, if the experience of those whom went before him was anything to go by. One Catholic chaplain with the original BEF of 1914 remembered that:

> *We were a disorganised body, each playing his own lone hand. There was no definite public policy, no one to train us, no one to lead. Each had to learn his work by experience of his failures.*[10]

Colonel H.A.R. May of the Artists Rifles, who saw active service in France during 1914 and 1915, reinforces this state of affairs:

> *Most of the Chaplains (so it seemed to me) had come straight from their parishes at home, and had had but little military preparation, and though most of them were keenly anxious to help in any way in their power, they were sometimes severely hampered in their work by their want of knowledge of military affairs.*[11]

Colonel May goes on to tell an amusing anecdote illustrating this point, albeit in a minor way:

> *On one occasion when walking with a 'General' at St. Omer, we passed a Chaplain newly arrived (apparently) from England (he was wearing a very new khaki kit!) and (apparently) inexperienced in military matters. He gave a most original flourish of his arm as he passed. 'Who the deuce is that?' asked the General, wrathfully, 'And what is he doing? – blowing me a kiss or what?' 'He's a Chaplain, sir, and he's saluting you,' I replied. 'Well, why the devil doesn't someone show him how to do it?' responded the General.*[12]

More pressing issues, rather than how to salute, needed addressing by the new padres in the Loos sector. In the summer of 1915 Rev Harry Blackburne recorded:

> *My job is to do all I can for the troops out of the line ... I have found up at Vermelles a glorious place for a Divisional Club, where we can have tea and buns for the men going in and out of the trenches. It is a huge cellar under a brewery which has been knocked to bits; but the cellar is all right ... We have arranged for a Cemetery and are trying to prevent indiscriminate burying all over the place ... We spent a long day clearing out the bricks and rubbish from the brewery cellar; and my arms ache ... The cellar club is now in full swing. At one end is the bar for buns, tea and cigarettes. I have*

found a baker in Bethune and have taught him to make English penny buns ... On Sundays we turn the club into a church and have relays of services there all day long.[13]

As for Willie Doyle's lack of practical preparation for active service, no amount of training would have readied him for his first experience of what should have been routine, the celebration of Mass on Sunday 5 March 1916. He tells his father:

Having finished my first Mass at 9 o'c, I mounted my bicycle, which I sometimes find more convenient than a horse, and set out so as to be with the Inniskillings at 11 o'clock.

On my way I noticed that heavy firing was going on ahead, but it was only when I reached a bend in the road that I realised the enemy were actually shelling the very spot I had to pass. Some soldiers stopped me, saying it was dangerous to go on; at the moment I was wondering what had become of the side of a vacant house, which had suddenly vanished in a cloud of smoke, and was painfully aware of the proximity of high explosive shells.

Here was a fix. I knew my regiment was waiting in the village for Mass, and also that half of them were going to the trenches that afternoon for the first time: if I did not turn up they would lose Confession and Holy Communion, but the only way to reach them was by the shell-swept road. What really decided me was the thought that I was carrying the Blessed Sacrament, and I felt that having our Blessed Lord Himself with me, no harm could possibly come to me. I mounted the bicycle and faced the music.

I don't want you to think me very brave and courageous, for I confess I felt horribly afraid, but it was my baptism of fire, and one needs to grow accustomed to the sound of bursting shells.

Just then I was wishing my regiment in Jericho and every German gun at the bottom of the Red Sea, or any other hot place. Call it a miracle if you like, but, the moment I turned the corner the guns ceased firing, and not a shell fell, till I was safely in the village Church. My confidence in God's protection was not misplaced.

Naturally I did not know this was going to happen, and it was anything but pleasant riding down the last stretch of road, listening for the scream of the coming shell. Have you ever had a nightmare in which you were pursued by ten mad bulls, while the faster you tried to run, the more your feet stick in the mud? These were just my feelings as I pedalled down that road, which seemed to grow longer and longer the further I went.

At last I turned the corner, reached the Church, and had just begun Mass, when down came the hail of shells once more. One or two must have burst very close, judging by the way the walls shook, but I felt quite happy and quite ready to be blown from the altar, for I saw a fine, plump Frenchwoman just behind me. She might have been killed, but I was quite safe.

I mention this little adventure, as I think it will console you, as it has consoled me, showing that all the good prayers are not in vain, and that this is a happy omen of God's loving protection from all dangers. I have just heard that one at least of the men, to whom I gave Holy Communion this morning, was killed the same night in the trenches.[14]

Fr Doyle quickly settled down to work, both ministering to his military flock and taking the native population under his wings. The 8th Faughs were stationed in Noeux-les-Mines, while the 8th Skins were in the ruined village of Mazingarbe. The villages may have been in a derelict condition but residents still clung to their lives there and Willie became the unofficial Curé of Mazingarbe. Writing early in March to his father:

You may be pleased to learn, that without ever having been a C.C. I am now a full P.P. of this parish, the Curé being away at the war, and no one to take his place. (If Father Tom wants a good thing in parishes send him on at once.)

Last evening I heard quite by chance that an old woman was very ill, her family evidently not thinking it worth the trouble of sending for the priest. Almighty God seemed to have kept the poor old creature alive till I reached her and gave her the Last Sacraments, for she died almost before I got home. You see my life has many consolations, and it is just as well, for this is a sad, sad war, of which you at home have but the faintest idea. May the good God end it soon.[15]

The tone of Willie's letters to his father was generally more light-hearted than to others of his correspondents. At the beginning of March 1916 he tells his father:

> *You need not be uneasy about me starving in any case ... Things are naturally a bit rough, but the food is abundant and excellent – officers and men getting exactly alike, though we generally supplement our rations.*[16]

However, writing to an acquaintance a few days later he advises:

> *I am suffering in every way, most of all, perhaps, from sheer fatigue. As regards food and lodging I am not badly off, but the discomforts of the life would be long to tell.*[17]

He modifies his tone again to his father on 10 March, but at the same time tries to address the problem so many soldiers came across throughout the war; that of people at home romanticising events.

> *Thank you very much for the interesting number of the 'Irish Catholic News'. I quite agree with all Father O'Connor says about the universal kindness shown us by all the officers, and even great respect, but he wrote the rest of his letter with pen well dipped in 'couleur de rose', (or was it a bottle of red wine?), for I have not yet met a Chaplain who looks on the life as a picnic.*[18]

As well as the hardships, military life was subject to minor irritations such as mail going astray, which was very trying for men whose burdens were lifted with news from home. Willie was not immune from such disappointment, especially when he had a hand in the chain of misfortune:

> *As an old friend of mine, who had a wonderful way of mixing things up, used to say; 'it is an ill wind that blows nowhere.' The returning your envelope for the full address gave me the advantage of getting two letters from you instead of one. Nearly all my letters have gone astray for a time or have been delayed, because '8th R.I. Fusiliers may mean 'Royal Inniskillings' as well as 'Royal Irish', it was my mistake originally.*[19]

Meanwhile, whilst Fr Doyle busied himself with his duties and corresponding with home, orders had been received from 49th Infantry Brigade Headquarters that 8th Battalion Royal Irish Fusiliers were to be attached to 3rd Infantry Brigade for instruction in trench warfare. Therefore, on Monday 6 March 'A' Company was attached to 1st Battalion South Wales Borderers and 'B' Company was attached to 1/6th Bn Welch Regiment; they moved up to the front trenches. 'C' Company was attached to 1st Bn Gloucester Regiment and 'D' Company to 2nd Bn Royal Munster Fusiliers; they remained at rest but provided working parties for maintenance of communication trenches. At full strength a company comprised approximately 200 men and life for those men now settled into a pattern of triple rotation between being in the front-line, behind the front in support and further back still in the relative safety of the reserve positions. This made Willie's life complicated:

> *As things are at present, I find it quite impossible to do my work as I should wish, simply because I cannot be in four places at the same time.*
>
> *I have charge of a half Brigade (two regiments) which are billeted about five miles apart; that would not matter so much, but one half of each regiment remains in the village while the other is up at the firing line. If I go up to the 'dressing station' to look after the wounded, the men at the base cannot get to Confession and vice versa. I can only do what I can; later on things will be better when the whole brigade comes together, for at present they are holding the trenches with other troops, to train them to their work.[20]*

This letter was written on St Patrick's Day and the 8th Royal Irish Fusiliers' War Diary for 17 March records receipt of a telegram from General Sir Charles Munroe, commanding First Army. He says:

> *Please convey my thanks to all ranks my best wishes on St. Patrick's Day and my feeling of confidence that they will prove themselves to be the stern, hard fighters that Irishmen have always shown themselves to be.*

The diary also records that a:

> *Shamrock was received from Mr John Redmond M.P. and distributed to A&B Companies on parade. Shamrock was sent up to the trenches to be*

distributed to the companies in the trenches.[21]

St Patrick's Day was a holiday for as many of the men as possible. Mass was the first priority, followed by brigade sports competitions, football matches and evening concerts. For the Irishmen who found themselves in the trenches instead, they had to endure very poor conditions. Foul air, stagnant water and mud, swarms of rats, enemy bombardments and constant fatigues to repair everlasting lines of chalk trenches. The main support line in 49th Brigade's sector was Tenth Avenue, which had been the chief communication trench to the Germans' own front lines prior to the outbreak of the battle of Loos on 25 September 1915. It had been converted by the British as a support position and:

Fire-steps had been dug on the reverse side, traverses put in order, and a formidable belt of wire erected in front of it.[22]

There were casualties even during quiet periods, some of which were self-inflicted. The War Diary for the 49th Infantry Brigade records on 18 March, the day after St Patrick's Day, that there was an accidental explosion of a Mills grenade in the 7th Royal Irish Fusiliers' sector, killing four rank and file, wounding three officers and ten other ranks.

Once trained all the battalions of the 49th Infantry Brigade would be a cohesive unit implementing their own triple shift patterns, working within the triple shift patterns operated by the three brigades of 16th (Irish) Division. The pattern of rotation saw two of the brigades manning the front lines and the third in reserve. Each of the two front-line brigades deployed two of its four battalions forward, one behind in support and the other further back still, attached to the brigade in reserve. The smaller units within the front-line battalions were also deployed in stages as described by Tom Johnstone:

... with two companies actually in the line, with a company in support trenches 100-200 yards behind and another in reserve 400-500 yards further back. Each battalion manned the Front for equal specific periods during the brigade's front-line tour of duty of eight days. This was followed by four days in reserve behind the lines. Such was the distance between the Front and rear areas that the journey between front and billeting areas might take

up to twelve hours. During the period of 'reserve' duty, battalions provided work parties for division and brigade, on the constant fatigue of maintaining and repair of roads, trenches and communication lines. Those not on fatigue duty continued training.[23]

This theme is expanded in a memoir of the Loos sector, albeit from a few months further on from Willie Doyle's arrival there. An Irish officer, 2nd Lieutenant J.F.B. O'Sullivan, 6th Connaught Rangers, writes in *At Rest in Philosophe, June 1916*:

This term 'rest' became a standard joke. Everyone made it, each with an air of great originality – and always got a laugh – or at least a sympathetic snigger… The period when a battalion was not holding the front trenches were so filled with fatigues, raids, and back-breaking work parties that many a tired man welcomed the return to the death-dealing 'line.[24]

There were periods when Willie Doyle had a little more spare time than the men and also had the luxury of being able to indulge his curiosity:

One day is very much like another, and yet each one is full of interesting and stirring events; it is quite delightful never to know what may happen yet. Aeroplane flights are a daily occurrence. I believe we have got new fast machines, but the German 'Fokkers' that I have seen simply walk away from our men, and seem to be able to do what they please.

Yesterday I was watching the bombardment of an old mill, and some houses about half a mile away, by the Germans. Their guns were so far away I could not even hear the report, but they kept dropping shell after shell with marvellous precision, on the little mound, believing, I understand, that we had some heavy guns there, which was quite true, but they had been removed.[25]

The next part of the letter reveals evidence of Willie's prosperous background, when he refers to a gift of a periscope (or binoculars) from his sister Lena:

With Lena's glass I could follow the whole thing as distinctly as if I had been standing near. I can say with truth I was jolly glad I was not. But now comes my part of the story. This morning I thought I would stroll over to the mill and take a look at the damage done. Not much was left, as you may imagine, while the ground all around me was ploughed up by huge shell-holes, though within a narrow radius, showing the accuracy of the enemy's fire. I wandered round for some time, when it flashed across my mind that if the Germans thought it worth their while to bombard that spot yesterday, they might think the same today. I thought also of several useful maxims: 'A living ass is better than something else' and 'He who runs away will have a chance of a second innings.' I turned round and started down the hill. Just as I did so I heard a scream – the diabolical scream – of a shell coming straight for where I was. This time it seemed like 'Abraham's Bosom', but to my relief the beastly thing went on and burst close to the road a couple of hundred yards away. Fortunately for me the Germans had changed their target for the moment, as an hour later they started shelling the mill again.

Moral: 'Leave mills alone unless they have a good, deep well, which you can drop into in case of necessity.' [26]

Did Willie 'over egg the pudding' in his descriptions to make a more interesting read for his father? Maybe, but conversely, he was certainly a master of understatement when he continues:

These little things give a zest to life, and prevent things becoming too monotonous, but they also turn one's thoughts with gratitude to the good God, and make one trust more in His loving protection.[27]

For those actually in the trenches, trench routine was exactly that – routine, regular, repetitive. Each day began with 'stand to' an hour before daybreak. Every available man would be in the line prepared for an enemy attack, which, if there was one, invariably took place as the sun dawned, although not always. Once the sun was up, sentries were posted and the remainder of the men spent the day cleaning equipment, some trench maintenance, cooking rations, brewing tea, or resting as best they could. Turning once again to 2nd Lieutenant O'Sullivan, he describes:

> *On 24 June the 6th Battalion in the front trenches had had a quiet morning of digging and trench repairing till noon. Then shelling and mortaring started pouring havoc all along the sector till finally, at 6:40 p.m. an hour's concentrated 240-pounder 'minnie' barrage completed the devastation of our carefully built up parapets. In the midst of this hullabaloo unexpected word from Brigade warned us to prepare for immediate relief; and at midnight the 6th Royal Irish took over. So we crawled back to rest, reaching Philosophe at 1.30 a.m. of Sunday 25th.*[28]

Night time was a hive of activity, both behind and in the front line, as explained by J.H.M. Staniforth, who served briefly with the 6th Connaught Rangers and then with the 7th Leinsters:

> *At night the whole population rises silently and hosts of dim ghostly figures appear above ground like stokers coming up to breathe on deck. It's then that all our working parties do their jobs: mending shell-torn trenches, bringing up rations, water, ammunition, and other stuff, relieving the trench garrison, sandbagging more cellars, and all that kind of thing.*[29]

Amongst all this bustle officers had the dubious compensation of slightly better living and sleeping conditions. Captain Staniforth describes his introduction to an officer's dug-out in the Loos sector at the end of 1915:

> *I was told off to the headquarters dug-out, which of course was in the third or rearmost line about 500 yards behind the fire-trench. You bent your back and scrambled down a flight of wooden steps. The dug-out itself, which was twenty feet below the surface, gave one the impression of being in a coal mine. There were the same enormous pit-props shoring up the roof, the same eternal drip, drip from the ceiling, the same heavy atmosphere and absolute silence. It was about as big as your bathroom, and six of us slept there: one on the table, one under it, the colonel on his bed (a hospital stretcher raised on two trestles), and another under that, and two of us side by side on the floor.*[30]

But he still had to work and move around in the same conditions as the men:

After I had dumped my things down; I went out to explore the front line. The water in some places was up to the thighs, and nowhere under the ankles; the wet walls of the trench smeared one all over as you pushed along between them; so you can believe that when men come out after four days on duty there is absolutely nothing to be seen of man, uniform, cap, equipment, face, or rifle. And the mud is of every consistency, from thin gravel that is half water to the stiff gluey clay that pulls the boots off your legs.[31]

Despite the hardships of warfare, the men tried to carry on life as normally as possible, whenever the opportunity arose, even when handicapped by foreign language. Willie Doyle gives such an insight:

I thought my days of French speaking were a thing of the past, but the little knowledge I have has proved of immense service to me. Very few of the officers can make any hand at all, except by gestures, so I have to act as interpreter, and get them out of difficulties. The foreign tongue does not bother the Tommies a bit, for they talk away and make love to the girls, as if they had been born in France, but what they say Heaven only knows.[32]

Willie at this time was also still firmly grounded in the normality of civilian life, remembering the first anniversary of the death of his mother:

I have had to write this in bits and scraps as best I could. If I do not post it now you may not get it in time. Au revoir, much love to everyone, ever your loving son Willie. I shall not forget the dear anniversary on Sunday, though I doubt if she needs our prayers.[33]

Not forgetting either the usual observations about the weather!

The weather has taken a turn for the better, and is now fine and warm, in fact almost too hot for Winter clothes.[34]

Willie's next letter to his father, dated 24 March 1916, just before the 8th Royal Irish Fusiliers finished its apprenticeship attached to 3rd Infantry Brigade, starts with a protest that he has no news; nevertheless he manages to fill quite a few pages:

> *Unless I draw upon my imagination I am afraid this letter will prove rather uninteresting, as I have little news to give you, no thrilling hair-breadth escapes to recount (possibly because I have had my few remaining locks cut recently) nor can I even say that thanks to a magnificent piece of horsemanship I escaped happy despatch to a better world by jumping over a passing shell. I must only fall back upon a description of my day's work last Sunday, which will show you that at times at least, I am kept pretty well on the go.*
>
> *I started at seven in the morning by giving Holy Communion to the men whose Confessions I had heard the previous evening, a goodly number I am glad to say. This was followed by a number of Confessions in French for the townspeople and some French soldiers. I am quite ready to face any language at the moment. This brought me up to nine when my men had Mass Parade.*
>
> *By chance the whole Regiment were in the village which meant of course that the Church would not hold them, so I had arranged for Mass in the open. The spot I selected was a large courtyard in front of the school (whereby hangs a tale.) Armed with the Mayor's permission I approached the schoolmaster for his sanction, and I must say I found him most obliging and very gracious, even helping to get things ready. It was only afterwards that I discovered that this man was a red-hot anti-clerical, anti-everything that was good in fact, quite a bad lot, so that my request was about the same as asking the Grand Master of the Orange Lodge in Belfast for permission to have Mass in his hall. He was so staggered I suppose, by my innocent request he could not find words to refuse, but the good folk of the town are wild with delight and immensely tickled by the idea of Mass in the Porch of his school above all people, needless to say they have rubbed it into him well.*[35]

Willie Doyle's reference to the Grand Master of the Orange Lodge in Belfast, shows that he had not lived his privileged life cocooned from the problems and issues which affected his native country. He continues:

I had never celebrated Mass in the open air before and I think the men were as much impressed as I was. It was a glorious morning, with just a sufficient spice of danger to give the process a warlike touch to the picture by the presence of a German aeroplane scouting near at hand. I was a wee bit anxious lest a bomb might come down in the middle of the men, but I fancy our unwelcome visitor had quite enough to do dodging the shells from our guns which kept booming all during Mass, besides I felt confident that for once our Guardian Angel would do their duty and protect us all till Mass was over. (This Sunday I had only one Mass as a rule I have two.)

When I finished breakfast I found a big number of men visiting for Confession. I gave them Communion as well, though they were not fasting, as they were going to the trenches that evening and being in danger of death could receive the Blessed Sacrament as Viaticum. It was the last Communion for many poor fellows who I trust are praying for us in Heaven now.[36]

A less conscientious chaplain may have retired to rest for the remainder of the day, but not Willie:

Having polished off all who came to the Church I made a raid on the men's billets, and spent a few hours in stables, barns, in fact anywhere, shriving the remainder who gladly availed themselves of the chance of settling up accounts before they started for the front. The harvest, thank God, was good and consoling. Just before they marched at six in the evening I gave the whole regiment (the RCs at least) a General Absolution, so the men went off in the best of spirits, light of heart with the joy of a good conscience. 'Good Bye, Father,' one shouted 'we are ready to meet the divil himself now'; which I trust he did.[37]

Fr Doyle does seem to have had an almost casual attitude to the likelihood of casualties, particularly fatal ones, amongst his flock. But, of course, in his mind those that might perish would be going to a better place. The actual casualties for the 16th (Irish) Division for January to March 1916 were 89 killed, 470 wounded and 20 missing.[38]

Willie's letter of 24 March 1916 recounts one further incident of note. Luckily for him, not only did he have a horse at his disposal at this time, but one with a calm temperament:

I dined with the two transport officers who bring up the rations and ammunition to the soldiers and then mounted my horse and rode up to Headquarters at the communication trenches. I have a good old beast of a horse, quiet but with plenty of pace, who simply turns up her nose at a bursting shell with supreme contempt. All went well till suddenly six of our guns, hidden by the roadside (they seemed to me to be in the middle of the road judging by the noise) went off with a bang. This was not playing the game, and 'Flunkibrandos' (the 'oss's name) stopped dead, or rather reversed engines and began to go astern. I tried to think of all the manoeuvre, and was devoutly wishing I had a bridle tied to her tail, for 'Flunki' backed and backed until she pulled up with a bump against a brick wall which the Germans had kindly spared – one of the few, it must be confessed, left in that town, when she sailed ahead again as if nothing had happened. I am bringing home a brick of that wall, for if it had not been there I certainly should be half way across Germany now.

My work done I mounted again and made for home. It was rather weird riding past the shattered houses in the dark, with the ping of a stray bullet to make you uncomfortable, while every few minutes a brilliant star-shell would burst overhead and the guns spat viciously at each other. An officer told me in the early days of the war our star-shells were a miserable failure, and when at last we got the right thing, the Germans greeted their first appearance with a great cheer; the war has its humorous as well as its tragic side. I reached my billet and tumbled in just as the clock struck midnight.[39]

Three days after this letter was written, the 16th (Irish) Division's front-line training ended and it joined I Corps, part of First Army, to hold the line opposite Hulluch, north-east of Loos, where life settled into a mundane rhythm. Willie's next letter to his father, dated 31 March 1916, began:

The task set the Israelites of making bricks without straw, was a light one compared to mine, viz – writing a letter without news to give. We have had a quiet uneventful week here in 'rest billets', to which the men return after a spell in the trenches and hence there is little to record. The days pass very quietly, one very much like another, except that this week I have both my regiments together and have not to go hunting for them in the desert. They are really a fine lot of fellows, and make a good impression on the people wherever they go, more especially here in the north of France, the mining district, where most of the men are too busy washing the dirt out of themselves on a Sunday to bother about much else. Hence it is an object lesson to the 'Parley-vous' to see the crowds who come to Mass and Communion daily, and Benediction in the evening; poor old Ireland is doing more than teaching the Germans how to behave themselves in the future.[40]

At long last there was to be a long time frame in one location, during which Willie could establish a settled ministry, living and working with his flock of Fusiliers and other 'parishioners.'

Footnote 1: Loos-en-Gohelle is the full name, but usually the place is referred to as Loos. Although the name of Loos was pronounced by the troops as if it rhymes with 'goose', in fact it is pronounced locally as 'Loss' to rhyme with 'moss'.

CHAPTER 13
DIFFICULTIES AND OPPORTUNITIES:
LOOSE ENDS

'England's difficulty is Ireland's opportunity'

Willie Doyle, in his letter of 31 March 1916, and ingenious as always, hedged around the rules by conveying his whereabouts to his father thus:

> *The name of the place I move to next, all the King's horses could not drag from me, for it is possible the Germans might get wind of it, and spoil all the fun by flying away. However when I do get there I sincerely hope I may not go on the <u>loose</u> altogether: A little joke, which you will probably understand.¹*

A little joke played by Irishmen at Loos earlier in the month may not have been quite so appreciated by the Germans, as explained by Captain Stephen Gwynn of 6th Connaught Rangers:

> *On Saint Patrick's day of 1916 the 16th Division lay opposite the most conspicuous feature of all the British line: the one survivor of what had been twin pylons, the 'Tower Bridge' erection at Loos. Day and night that was a ranging mark for German shell; shrapnel and high explosive screamed and burst about it, machine-gun fire swept it in search for some sniper's post. But on Saint Patrick's day morning the German gunners had something new to shoot at – a square of green flag run up there in the moonlight by some bold climber from the Munsters. That flag certainly spoke for Ireland; its challenge would have been cheered from Cork to Donegal.²*

DIFFICULTIES AND OPPORTUNITIES

Tower Bridge, Loos, 1916

There again, maybe 'Fritz' did appreciate 'Paddy's' mentality because, in another part of the Loos sector, the Germans had a trick or two of their own up their sleeves that same day. Willie Doyle recounts:

By the way, it is simply marvellous how the enemy get all their information. They knew when my men were going to hold the front trenches, the name of the regiment, and sending it all over the night before, to our lines, and shouting scores the next day, to welcome the 'Paddies,' they even went as far as to cease firing on St. Patrick's Day, and invited the RIFs to come over and have a drink.[3]

Of course, none of the Fusiliers could be tempted by this offer and, in particular:

One poor fellow at the moment did not want any drink: he had found a jar of rum in a quiet corner of the trench and had taken a long deep pull, before he discovered that it was diluted Candy's fluid. He has taken the pledge for the rest of his mortal life.[4]

Presumably this unlucky man was not the same miscreant who appeared in another of Willie's anecdotes:

Some of them have proved themselves to be Trojans in more things than prayer. For example, the other day one of the fusiliers finding himself alone in company with a box containing twelve tins of jam, (about the size of a condensed milk tin) promptly ate the lot, minus the tins fortunately, since when he has been feeling and looking very much like a jam dumpling.[5]

These incidents lend support to other accounts of the high morale, unfailing good humour and propensity for mischief of the Irishmen in the Loos sector. Mischievous or serious, Irishmen had enlisted for the same range of reasons as their British Empire counterparts: for some it was out of patriotism, loyalty or sympathy; for others it was economic and for yet more others it was for adventure.

John Lucy and his younger brother were pre-war regular army men who had enlisted as raw teenagers in January 1912. John describes being tired of their dull southern Irish lives, their father and advice from relations, and about wanting to spread their wings:

> *My brother persuaded me to join the army. We had hardly left school. Our mother had just died, and we had gone a bit wild ...*[6]

They chose to serve with an Ulster Regiment, the Royal Irish Rifles, putting plenty of distance between themselves and their home in Cork.

Two years later, thirty-five year old Frank Laird, from County Dublin, witnessed great fleets of steamers arriving in Dublin Bay to transport troops from Ireland in August 1914. He then spent several months reflecting on his own situation:

> *By now I had begun to experience searchings of heart.... Every day word came that someone had joined up.... I had never considered soldiering as at all in my line.... On the one hand were all the prepossessions of my life, for I was naturally a man of peace. On the other was the awkward question of how my friends would regard me afterwards if they found me still at home when the war was over. It seemed a poor affair to be peaceably pen-pushing while men were fighting and dying out yonder. There was the reflection too, that a Civil Servant's life, though agreeable, did not offer great variety. Here was a chance to get out of the groove with a vengeance.*[7]

Frank Laird went into hospital in November 1914 to have his varicose veins removed prior to enlisting with the Royal Dublin Fusiliers.

A much younger Tom Barry, who served with the Royal Field Artillery and was to subsequently become a prominent member of the IRA in Cork during Ireland's War of Independence, recalled his situation:

In June 1915, in my seventeenth year I had decided to see what the Great War was like. I cannot plead I went on the advice of John Redmond or any other politician, that if we fought for the British we would secure Home Rule for Ireland, nor can I say I understood what Home Rule meant. I was not influenced by the lurid appeal to fight to save Belgium or small nations. I knew nothing about nations large or small. I went to the war for no other reason than that I wanted to see what war was like, to get a gun, to see new countries and to feel a grown man. Above all I went because I knew no Irish history and had no national consciousness.[8]

Immediately prior to the outbreak of war there had been much political turbulence in Ireland and animosity towards Britain, for different reasons, both in the south and the north. Indeed, in some parts of Ireland, unrest had been a fact of life for centuries. During the early months of the war the complex relationships between the leading personalities and parties, both in Ireland and on the mainland, were so fraught that it is surprising so many Irishmen ended up marching in harmony with the British army, both on the Western Front and elsewhere. Major Bryan Cooper of the 10th (Irish) Division, which fought in Gallipoli in 1915, recalls:

... many of the officers and men had played, or, at least, had relatives who had played, an active part in the agrarian and political struggles that have raged in Ireland for the last forty years. Yet all this went for nothing; the bond of common service and common sacrifice proved so strong and enduring that Catholic and Protestant, Unionist and Nationalist, lived and fought and died side by side like brothers. Little was spoken concerning the points on which we differed, and once we had tacitly agreed to let the past be buried we found thousands of points on which we agreed...[9]

Despite the long history of Ireland's role in the British Army, the omens prior to the outbreak of war would not have suggested an enthusiastic response by Irish volunteers for a call to arms. According to the Protestant Dr. Charles Dowse, the Church of Ireland Bishop of Cork, the war *was not of our asking. It was thrust upon us.*[10] Nevertheless, there are many accounts of soldiers, and reservists, based in Ireland getting rousing send-offs at the railway stations and ports from local populations. Dundalk man Thomas McCrave recalls watching the British military garrison as: *They were conducted to the railway station by the Dundalk Emmet Band, and they got an enthusiastic send-off from the townspeople.*[11]

As recently as March 1914 the nagging question in the minds of the British political classes had been that of Ireland; how to keep the lid on a boiling situation which threatened civil war. A crisis point had been building up since the introduction by the Liberal government of the *Third Home Rule Bill* (the previous two having been rejected) on 11 April 1912. Although passed by the House of Commons on 16 January 1913, it was thrown out by the largely Conservative House of Lords and the same process was repeated in July. By the terms of the 1911 Parliament Act the Lords could now only delay the Bill and its successful passage would become inevitable.

Southern Irishman John Lucy remembered the commercial northern garrison town he and his brother Denis were sent to on enlisting in the army in 1912, which was:

...a strange place to us. Slogans: 'To hell with the Pope', and 'No Rome rule', were white-washed on the gable ends of the houses in the poorer districts.[12]

However, by December 1914 John was happy to report that:

Two of my best chums were Belfast Orangemen, and we all shared and suffered together, and made merry too.[13]

In March 1914, fifty-seven out of seventy British Army cavalry officers, led by Brigadier Hubert Gough and stationed at the Curragh Camp in County Kildare, the main British Army base in Ireland, had threatened to resign if they were ordered north to take action against anti-Home Rule agitators in Ulster. This amounted to a threat of mutiny, which did not in the event take place, but this notorious *'Curragh Incident'* caused great consternation within the Establishment. The *Home Rule Bill* was finally carried on 25 May 1914 and *The Irish Times* reported on 29 June 1914:

Speaking at a temperance demonstration in Dublin yesterday, Mr. T.W. Russell said that within twelve months – it would certainly not be later – they would see the largest crowd of Irishmen – from the four corners of the world – assembled in Dublin to witness the inauguration of the Irish Parliament, which had been closed so cruelly but which would be opened so gloriously.'

By the time of this optimistic statement, two opposing, voluntary, para-military organisations had been formed. Approaching the issue from differing standpoints, both the Unionist Ulster Volunteer Force and the Nationalist Irish Volunteers were ready to take advantage of the popular maxim *England's difficulty is Ireland's opportunity.*[FN1]

The Ulster Volunteer Force, under the former Conservative, but now Ulster Unionist, Member of Parliament, Sir Edward Carson, was about 85,000 strong. They opposed the re-introduction of a Parliament for the whole of Ireland in Dublin. The U.V.F. openly trained, paraded and drilled, ready to resist the *Home Rule Bill* when it became law. The same edition of *The Irish Times* reported:

> *The First Battalion South Antrim Regiment of the Ulster Volunteers were engaged in field operations near Lisburn on Saturday. On Friday night the Clogher, Fardross, and Killyfoddy companies of the Ulster Volunteers engaged in mimic battle at Killfoddy Hill.*

Already by April 1914 the Ulster Volunteers had obtained a consignment of guns from Germany. When war broke out in August, the implementation of the *Home Rule Act* was suspended. Sir Edward Carson was eager to show his patriotism by supporting the war, but was wary of the *Home Rule Act* unexpectedly coming into play, whilst his Volunteers might be away fighting on the Continent. Nevertheless, after some prevarication (during which time many impatient Ulstermen joined the 10th (Irish) Division) the 36th (Ulster) Division was raised, largely from the ranks of the Ulster Volunteers. Other Protestant Ulstermen also found themselves alongside Catholic comrades in the 16th (Irish) Division and Willie Doyle's 49th Brigade in particular.

In the south of Ireland the Irish National Volunteers were stronger, about 180,000, but opinion was divided between those who accepted the British Crown's constitutional solution of Home Rule now, and those who wanted to hold out for a fully independent Irish Republic. The Irish Volunteers had also negotiated a supply of arms from Germany, but the attempt to land them in late July 1914 went disastrously wrong and resulted in a small number of undisciplined British troops killing four unarmed civilians in Bachelor's Walk, Dublin and wounding fifty. The killings profoundly shocked people in both the Irish and British isles. Normal business came to a halt in Dublin on the day when three of the victims were buried.

The funeral procession was over a mile long, with 200,000 people lining the streets, and ended with Volunteers firing a volley over the graves. The funeral was filmed and the newsreel screened at cinemas throughout the country, which boosted recruitment to the Irish National Volunteers. The following month Frank Laird observed:

> *The East Surreys passed jovially by me one day ... To my surprise the common folk who had regarded the English soldiers with scant affection of late gave them a hearty cheer as they went by. The only British regiment which got a bad send-off was the King's Own Scottish Borderers. Their action some weeks before in firing on the Dublin mob was deeply resented.*[14]

The leader of the Irish Volunteers, John Redmond, was also leader of the Irish Parliamentary Party, having been a Member of Parliament almost continuously since 1881. He told the House of Commons:

> *Let the House clearly understand that four-fifths of the Irish people will not submit any longer to be(ing) bullied, or punished, or shot, for conduct which is permitted to go scot-free in the open light of day in every county in Ulster by other sections of their fellow countrymen.*[15]

John Redmond was an Irish Nationalist but reluctantly accepted that a compromise was inevitable; that Home Rule was needed as a stepping-stone towards full independence. Redmond was pragmatic, believing that Ireland should support England and that such support would ultimately be rewarded. He and many others of his ilk also believed that the cause of supporting 'little Belgium' was akin to the Irish quest for freedom from foreign interference; that the war was an opportunity to weld the Irish people, north and south, together. By encouraging his Irish Volunteers to join the British army he split the organisation. His short-term goal was to raise an all-Irish force with its own officers and colours, to be used both in defence of the state on Irish soil as well as fighting on the Continent. Unfortunately, these plans were frustrated by Lord Kitchener and the War Office, even though a concession was made that the 16th Division, to which Redmond's supporters flocked, was styled specifically as 'Irish', in the same way that the 36th Division was specifically named 'Ulster'.

The Dublin based newspaper, *The Irish Times*, was not likely to be representative of the views of the whole of Ireland, but in all probability was close to those of the region and class of people from which Willie Doyle came. The editorial on Wednesday, 5 August 1914 claimed:

In this hour of trial the Irish nation has 'found itself' at last. Unionist and Nationalist have ranged themselves together against the invader of their common liberties. A few weeks ago it was said by despairing English politicians that Ireland was two armed camps. Today she is one armed camp, and the menace is directed against a foreign foe.

The day before, Captain George Berkeley, an Irish National Volunteer Commander in Belfast, recorded in his diary that the outbreak of war *meant peace*.[16]

There was optimistic cause for such proclamations when, in November 1915, John Redmond made a tour of the Western Front visiting the Irish battalions, accompanied by Divisional and Corps Commanders. John Lucy remembered:

John Redmond inspected our battalion late in the year, and everyone – Orangemen as well Nationalists – gave him a cheer. We buried the hatchet of bigotry during the war.[17]

Although it was to be over a year before the Irish and Ulster Divisions were to fight side-by-side, the war did seem to unite all serving Irishmen at that particular space and time. In 1917, despite their polarised views, Edward Carson and John Redmond both contributed an appreciative review of Bryan Cooper's history *The Tenth (Irish) Division in Gallipoli*. Carson commented:

Their magnificent bravery in the face of almost insurmountable difficulties and discomforts stands out amongst the countless acts of heroism in this war ...[18]

John Redmond's review was much longer, but makes the equally pertinent point that:

Irishmen of all political opinions were united in the Division. Its spirit was intensely Irish ... For my part, I am convinced that nothing that can happen can deprive Ireland of the benefit of the united sacrifices of these men.[19]

Had the powers-that-be bought into the vision of John Redmond and General Sir Alex Godley, maybe the united camaraderie would have extended beyond the end of the war. Godley stated:

> *I have always thought that if those in authority had had the vision and foresight in the early stages of the War, to raise three divisions in Ireland – one in Belfast, one in Dublin and one in Cork – and to turn them into an Irish Army Corps under command of John Redmond, the history of my distressful country might have been very different ... And what a nucleus for that corps would have been all the splendid Irish regular regiments with their glorious records and traditions. But the English politicians, and I am afraid many English soldiers, were totally unable to understand Irishmen. They would not trust them ...*[20]

General Godley's brother John was Under-Secretary of State for War and it is an easy assumption that the General's barbed comment was directed at his brother's superior, the Secretary of State for War, Lord Kitchener. Kitchener had been born into an English family in Ireland in 1850 and was brought up in County Kerry. He was opposed to any manifestation of Irish agitation and nationalism and considered himself to be an expert on all things Irish. He once told John Dillon, an associate of John Redmond, who accused him of having no understanding of the country or the people: *'Mr Dillon, I understand everything about Ireland.'*[21] However, Augustine Birrell, the government's Chief Secretary for Irish affairs was in agreement with Dillon, describing Kitchener as an *accidental Irishman,* and that he had once had: *the pleasure of telling him he might as easily have been born on the London and North West Railway on the way to Holyhead as in Ireland.*[22]

Unfortunately, Kitchener had little respect for politicians in general, and regarded the Irish Unionist and Nationalist leaders in particular as an awkward, irritating sideshow which distracted from the main event. Whilst he held existing Irish soldiers and the fighting potential of new recruits in high regard, he thought it dangerous to give any consideration to an Irish Army Corps. Eventually he had to compromise and sanctioned the raising of separate Irish divisions to serve with different army Corps.

It is somewhat ironic that Kitchener was to perish at sea, during a Force 9 gale west of the Orkneys, on 5 June 1916, when a year previously men of the 10th (Irish) Division had sailed, in the summer heat of the Mediterranean, bound for Turkey and the ill-fated Gallipoli campaign, which Kitchener had agreed to support. On board those vessels was a force:

> ... *17,000 strong and thus one of the biggest bodies of soldiers to leave Irish shores, with men from every county in Ireland as well as every kind of political allegiance ... It would be the first time that so substantial and well equipped a body of men had entered a war bearing the title 'Irish'.*[23]

Kitchener was en-route to Russia on a diplomatic mission, aboard the armoured cruiser *HMS Hampshire,* which struck a mine laid by a German U-boat. He would have been aware of the risks associated with such travel, as in May 1915 the enormous Cunard passenger liner, *Lusitania,* had been torpedoed by a German submarine, killing most of the passengers on board. The *Lusitania's* sister ship, the *Mauretania,* had been converted for use as a troop carrier and survived its mission as one of several vessels that conveyed the Irish troops to Gallipoli.

As for John Redmond and Sir Edward Carson, they chose different paths. The so-called 'shell scandal' of 1915 (simplistically, this was a lack of sufficient shells to do the job in the front line on the Western Front) brought down the Liberal government and a coalition administration was formed. Both Irishmen were offered ministerial positions in January 1916. Redmond declined; Carson accepted. Two months later, at the 'sharp end', Willie Doyle continues his correspondence with his father thus:

> *When I posted my letter to you this morning it occurred to me that perhaps if I kept a diary for the next couple of weeks, it might interest you, and others, even if I had nothing of very great interest to relate. I know however, that what seems common-place to us out here may appear in quite a different light, when read at home, so I shall begin and jot down day by day when I get a few spare moments, the various episodes of my life during the coming week, which by all accounts promises to be lively.*[24]

Footnote 1: *England's difficulty is Ireland's opportunity.* Remark attributed to Daniel O'Connell, 6 August 1775 – 15 May 1847, Irish political leader who campaigned for the repeal of the Act of Union and for both Catholic and Jewish emancipation. Known as the 'Liberator' or the 'Emancipator'.

CHAPTER 14
SCRIBBLINGS FROM THE FRONT:
LOOSE INFORMATION

'Another lesson I have learnt is the powerful weapon we have in prayer. How much His interests may be helped at any moment of the day, easily and surely! Oh, how much we could all do for Him and His interests, how many poor souls would be saved daily, if only we filled in the chinks of our full lives with aspirations.'
Willie Doyle, April 1916 [1]

By the end of April 1916 Willie's life had begun to settle into the tempo of trench timetables. He wrote as often as possible, a diary type account that he referred to as a 'budget', sent to his father – always his 'Dearest Father' and signed off with much love from 'Ever your loving Son.' The next dispatch Hugh Doyle received from Willie, commenced on 31 March 1916, openly confirmed his location and went on to cover the next twelve days activities:

You will forgive, I trust, bad hasty writing, pencil at times, and frequent 'swear words' when a shell bursts uncomfortably near. I understand that when the regiment has left any place, one may speak more freely about it. You will not receive this till we are miles away from the hot spot we go to tonight, so I can say it is 'Loos', the scene of the desperate fighting last September, when our casualties alone were close on 80,000. I am writing from a town called Noeux-les-Mines, not far from Bethune, which we leave this evening at 6 for the firing line. [2]

Willie notes a change to his usual routine thus far:

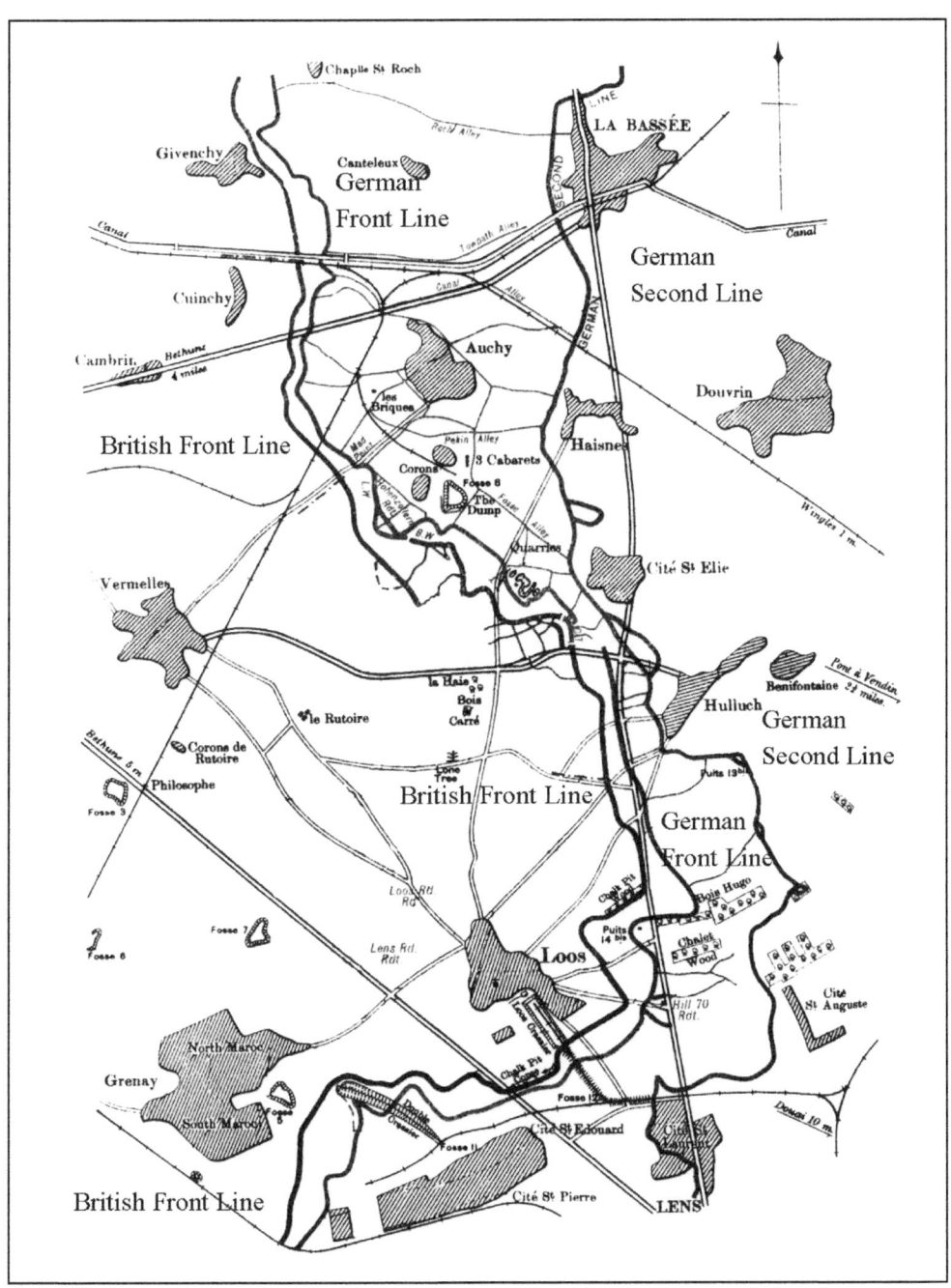

16th (Irish) Division sector, Hulluch, 1916

*The whole regiment, or should I say, the whole 49th Brigade (four regiments) is going up this time, so I shall go with them. Up to this, half remained behind and I stayed with them, as practically nothing can be done in the trenches themselves, while at the rear I had my hands full, with just an odd visit to my absent men, to cheer them up in their mud and slush.*³

The chaplain's position had been somewhat difficult up to this point, for he could neither be in two places at once, nor could he travel conveniently between the two. But on 31 March the whole of 16th Division's 49th Infantry Brigade had relieved the 47th Infantry Brigade in the Puits 14 Bis Section of the Loos sector.

Facing them across No-Man's-Land were Germans of the Bavarian 4th Infantry Division (Bavaria, coincidentally, was a predominately Catholic state.) Puits 14 had been a sugar refinery located on the La Bassée-Lens Road, east of Loos town, south of a copse renamed Chalk Pit Wood. Fr Doyle quickly became familiar with the trench system; the support trench Tenth Avenue (the old German front-line) would provide one of his dug-outs (depending on dispositions of battalions). This dug-out also doubled as his 'church' and was near the doctor's dressing station; Willie was therefore on hand to help out looking after the sick and wounded.

Willie Doyle's battalion of 8th Royal Irish Fusiliers relieved the 6th Connaught Rangers in the right sub-sector: Gordon Alley (inclusive) to 1st. Boyau, south of Railway Alley on the left. The 7th Royal Inniskilling Fusiliers relieved the 7th Leinster Regiment on the left sub-section: Posen Alley inclusive. The 7th Royal Irish Fusiliers relieved the 8th Royal Munster Fusiliers in the support position: Tenth Avenue and Gun Trench, with one company at Philosophe. And at Philosophe, the reserve position found the 8th Royal Inniskilling Fusiliers relieving the 6th Royal Irish Regiment.

Over the next twelve days the four battalions would rotate until they themselves were relieved on 13 April. In addition to the positioning of the four infantry battalions, other units and personnel also received their orders: Machine Gun Company, Lewis Guns, Trench Mortar Batteries, Grenadiers (bombers), Snipers, Signallers, Trench Stores and Traffic Control and Communications. The historian of the 7th Royal Inniskilling Fusiliers, who were located in the left sub-sector, notes:

The enemy had superiority of visibility in this sector, due to the natural advantage of having the higher ground in his possession, not only from Bois Hugo, but more effectively from Hill 63 to a flank.[4]

Before Fr Doyle departed to the right sub-sector he received plenty of advice:

The usual 'Job's Comforters' have been about in plenty today, telling us of the sweet time we shall have in Loos, perhaps the worst spot in the whole line; for this reason, elsewhere the trenches run in parallel lines facing the Germans, but Loos stands in a salient or horse shoe and so the enemy can fire on us from three sides.[5]

At this point in his document he has drawn a horse shoe to represent the salient at Loos, marking *us poor chaplains* in the drawn curve of the trench system. The Irish battalions soon made their mark in the sector. Just as the Scottish regiments had adopted familiar names for trenches in 1915 – Cameron, Gordon, Black Watch, Scots, Seaforth, so the Irish had their Meath, Bray, Connaught, Leinster and, indeed, Dalkey!

As always, Willie's missive is very informative, entertaining, but also speculative in places. However, he could afford to write, to a degree, in a fairly flippant fashion, knowing that the letter would not be sent until he was back, intact, behind the hot-spot of Loos. His budget is worth recording fully:

Advice came in to us: 'Mind the pump in the square,' said one thoughtful officer, 'the Huns have a machine gun trained on it and they do a little pumping too: I should think the well must be half full of dead bodies by this time.' 'Mind the door of your Mess dug-out' was the parting shot of another cheerful individual, 'a bullet comes through the broken window every few minutes, you are never safe there.' Cheerful prospect!

In fact I got so many spots to mind, that I made up my mind, not to mind any of them. N.B. This bit of information was true, I have a bullet in my pocket, which came through the door just before I did, and obligingly went into a sand-bag instead of my poor carcass!

We shall be off in a few moments, with a twelve hard days before us, twelve days sleeping and eating in a dark damp cellar to the music of bursting shells overhead, with no chance of course of taking off one's clothes at night. We are waiting for dark, as the road to Loos is commanded by German guns, and our only chance is to slip through in the dark.

We shall be shelled, they tell us, and sniped and potted and machine-gunned. 'Are we downhearted?' – personally I am looking forward to this adventure, with keen interest; the company of others takes away the natural fear, which one always feels alone.[6]

The budget continues after Willie reaches Loos, which he indicates preceded by a line of dashes, written as if he was writing en-route and describing events in real time:

------------(Safe in Loos.) We have moved off, the men in great spirits: I had given them a General Absolution and nearly all had been to Holy Communion that morning or the morning before. The night fortunately is very dark, with no moon, in fact we might go anywhere were it not for those blessed star-shells, which light up the country for miles around.

'Single file, no smoking,' comes the order. We are in the danger zone. Another mile and a halt is called. 'Men will advance by twos, twenty paces apart,' is the second order. I stick close to the Doctor: he might be useful if a leg comes off, as evidently shells are expected. So far none have come, though stray bullets are buzzing about like so many angry wasps. Another half a mile will bring us to our destination when down the line comes the command: 'No noise of any kind – walk as quietly as possible,' and then suddenly: 'Every man lie flat.' Some villainous German machine gunner has seen or heard us and is sweeping the road with bullets. 'Too high old chap, try lower next time.' The leaden hail has stopped and we move on again: most hearts beating faster if I mistake not.

The Headquarters, Colonel, etc. remain in the town, while the men go on to man the trenches. It is just 11.30pm when we sit down in our cellar, deep underground, to dinner: not a luxurious meal certainly, some cold meat and bread, but most welcome to hungry men. Our only visit tonight are the rats, who treat us with absolute contempt, running round and chasing one another like so many kittens. The meal over I make my way through the deserted street to my dug-out, five minutes away, which I have to share with four other officers, part of the staff. An uncanny creepy walk, surely. The road, in parts, is in full view of the German trenches, the crack and whiz of bullets is unceasing – very few probably are crossing the road, but one feels as if every bullet were aimed at him and all the Kaiser's men doing their best to make him like a kitchen sieve. Why did the Lord make us so big? I am certain I must be 20 ft high and 10 broad in spite of my efforts to present as small a target as possible.

A good night's sleep in spite of the rats, who had the time of their lives running over me, as I slept on the floor. They had plenty to eat outside so I was not afraid, and to tell the truth, too tired to care.[7]

The narrative continues covering the next day's events, starting casually in what was to prove pronounced understatement, befitting April Fool's Day, in view of what was to come:

The only item of interest during these days occurred on Friday 1st.[7a]

Willie continues this budget on 1 April by noting the personal significance of the date:

Anniversary of my entrance into the Society 26 years ago. At a reasonably respectable hour, yours truly might have been observed emerging from his 'cellar deep' bucket in hand for, even at the front, we wash sometimes. It was a glorious morning, brilliant sunshine and warm, while the sparrows chirped to one another as if war was a thing unheard of. Peace reigned in the Heavens, but on earth what a sight! No words could ever describe, nor photograph give even a faint idea of the havoc and ruin on all sides. One must see it with one's own eyes. I do not know what the 'abomination of desolation' mentioned by our Lord is like, but Loos at this moment must be something near it. Our guns raked it for days from end to end, and the Germans must have been shelling it ever since while every inch of ground was fought for fiercely as one can see, by the bullet-splashed walls.

My chief thought, as I washed in a narrow bucket (not an easy feat by any means) was, where could I celebrate Mass. The church was a mere pile of stones, for the Germans filled it, I believe purposely, with tons of dynamite and when driven out of the town, at once turned their guns on the church, so as to explode it, and blow Loos and our army to bits: thank God they failed. As I was dressing I saw at the corner of the road, a tiny wayside chapel of 'Our Lady of Consolation', with the altar still standing. It cheered me up more than I can say, for I felt that Mary would be my 'Life, my Sweetness and my Hope' in this inferno of shot and shell, which never seems to cease for a moment and under her mantle I would be safe from all danger. It was a memorable Mass. Every now and then a big shell would burst with a crash, some far off, others quite near, while our guns behind roared back their defiance, and the wasps hummed by.

Out in the middle of the road a little group of Tommies had gathered to kneel and pray as they had done many a time in the peaceful chapels of holy Ireland. Poor lads, they needed the help of Notre Dame de Consolation more than I did, and Mary I am sure did not fail them, then nor since.[8]

A bit later that day when Willie (continuing his graphic and colourful account) was:

Taking a short-cut across to our lines I found myself in the first battlefield of Loos, the place where the French had made their attack. For some reason or other this part of the ground had not been cleared, and it remains more or less as it was on the morning of the fight. I had to pick my steps for numbers of unexploded shells, bombs and grenades lay all around. The ground was littered with broken rifles, torn uniform, packs, etc., just as the men had flung them aside, charging the German trenches. Almost the first thing I saw was a human head torn from the trunk, though there was no sign of the body. The soldiers had been buried on the spot as they fell; that is, if you can call burial, hastily throwing a few shovelfuls of clay on the corpses: there was little time, I fancy, for digging graves, and in war time there is not much thought or sentiment for the slain. As I walked along I wondered had they made certain each man was really dead. One poor fellow had been buried, surely, before breath had left his body, for there was every sign of a last struggle and one arm was thrust out from its shroud of clay. A large mound caught my eye. Four pairs of feet were sticking out, one a German, judging by his boots, and three Frenchmen – friend and foe are sleeping their long last sleep in peace together. They were decently covered compared with the next I saw; a handful of earth covered the wasted body, but the legs and arms and head were exposed to view. He seemed quite a young lad with fair, almost golden, hair. 'An unknown soldier' was all the rough wooden cross over him told me about him; but I thought of the sorrowing mother, far away, thinking of her boy who was 'missing', and hoping against hope that he might one day come back. Thank God, Heaven one day will reunite them both. I found a shovel near at hand and after a couple of hours' stiff work was able to cover the bodies decently, so that on earth at least they may rest in peace.[9]

In the next section of his sketch from the front Willie refers to the Field Ambulance Station and to the Regimental Aid Post. Field Ambulance was a generic term covering a whole gamut of medical services, whilst the Regimental Aid Post (RAP) was the place where such services were provided. The Regimental Aid Posts were the first port of call for the injured and they were set up as close to the front Line as practical, but in as safe a location as possible in the circumstances. R.A.P.'s could be established in the remains of any suitable building if applicable or, more likely by 1916, in a dug-out towards the back end of the trench system. Here, a few personnel with basic facilities allowed the wounded to be patched up before being transferred to the next stage of their treatment. In many cases this would be to an Advanced Dressing Station, located in a much safer place back behind the lines and staffed by larger numbers of Royal Army Medical Corps personnel, working with more advanced facilities. (Further back still would be the Base Hospital.)

When Willie refers to the Field Ambulance Station, he more than likely means the Advanced Dressing Station, because, technically, the term 'Field Ambulance' is normally used to refer to the service structure under which the various echelons of First Aid and medical facilities operated. Each Division had its own Field Ambulance, which was sub-divided into three operations: stretcher-bearers with access to horse-drawn or motorised ambulance wagons; tented accommodation; and staff to provide medical treatment. Whilst the Field Ambulance service would move from area to area along with the rest of its Division, the locations of the various R.A.P.'s and Dressing Stations (if the area remained active) would stay in-situ, ready to receive a new Division with its Field Ambulance. And so Willie continues his description of his day thus:

This afternoon I had the most exciting experience of my whole life. Looking back on it now, when all is safely over, one can afford to be amused, but I can assure you that half hour was far from being amusing at the time. The Doctor and myself set out to visit the Field Ambulance Station [Advanced Dressing Station] at the other end of the town, where the wounded are sent at night from the Regimental Aid Post to be forwarded to the Base Hospital. The wounded men from the trenches are brought to the Aid Post first, where I am able to see them and do all I can for the brave fellows. We walked up the trench, as the road is not safe in the day time, nor much better at night indeed, but found it only went a certain distance.

The sentry pointed out the Ambulance Station [Advanced Dressing Station] in the distance and told us we might walk along a certain road, which we did without mishap. In the cellar of the house, where the Ambulance is located, we found some officers, who opened their eyes when we strolled in. 'How did you get here' they asked 'no one can ever come except under cover of darkness. Did no one tell you that the road to this from the trench you left is in full view of the Germans? They watch it like cats, and the wonder is no one tried to 'plug' you. However they have certainly seen you enter this house so go and get ready for what is coming.[10]

What 'came' was a pleasant diversion for a time until the prediction was fulfilled.

The singer Willie next refers to, John Francis McCormack (1884–1945), was a world-famous Irish tenor and the first artist to record, in 1914, one of the most popular and famous songs favoured by the troops: *It's a Long Way to Tipperary*. He also sang songs of Irish nationalism and his recording of: *The Wearing of the Green*, a song about the Irish rebellion of 1798, was adopted by those pushing for Home Rule. Willie continues:

They all seemed to enjoy the whole thing hugely, invited us to join them in a cup of tea and 'shell' (without fish.) They had an excellent gramophone with some fine records, so our tea party was quite a jolly one. John McCormack had just finished the last bars of 'She is far from the land' which brought back old memories, when suddenly Bertha Krupp opened her mouth in a most unlady-like way, even for a German, let a screech which you could hear in Dublin, and spat a huge shell right into our courtyard. It was a 6 inch gun, so the artillery officer who was present said, but I am certain that 60 inches would be nearer the mark. I shall not easily forget the roar as the shell burst only a few feet from where we sat: had we not been safe under cover, there would have been few 'Fragments from France' to send across the water. A moment later there was a deafening crash: a second shell had hit what was left of the upper wall, and brought it tumbling down half smothering us with the dust that came through the open slit which served as a window and chimney combined. Not bad shooting so far.

The next shot went wide, but did useful work among the stables and out houses, and then came a fearful dull thud, the walls quivered, I was nearly knocked off my chair by the concussion, while the cup in the officer's hand sitting next me was sent flying – a shell had landed clean on top of our cellar. That was too much for Messieurs les Rats: out they came from hole in the corner, scores of them, and scuttled for the open, evidently they thought the poor ship was in a poor way. For once I said a fervent prayer for the Germans who had formerly occupied the house. They had done their work well, propping up the cellar roof with huge beams, otherwise we must have all been buried in the ruins. Shell after shell kept raining down, six at least falling on our heads. We were perfectly safe as the battered in roof and walls on top of our cellar made a natural dug-out, but we all knew that there was just the chance of a shell coming through and possibly smashing the cup and gramophone. It was an exciting half hour, and as I said one also that none of our party have any great anxiety to repeat for some time at least.

As we went home in the dusk of the evening I came to the conclusion that there are worse places to live than in than poor old Ireland, and also that I had had quite enough thrills for one day. It was not to be for another experience awaited me. I found that a dead man had been brought in for burial, a by no means pleasant part of my life. The cemetery, part of a field, was outside the town, in the open country, so exposed to shell and rifle fire that it could not be approached by day.[11]

This was to be Fr Doyle's first war burial and it appears he lent a hand digging the grave as well as performing the funeral service. He continues:

As soon as it was dark we carried the poor fellow out on a stretcher, just as he had fallen, and as quietly as we could, began to dig the grave. It was weird. We were standing in front of the German trenches on two sides, though a fair distance away, and every now and then a star-shell went up, which we felt certain would reveal our presence to the enemy. I put my ritual in the bottom of my hat, and with the aid of an electric torch read the burial service, while the men screened the light with their caps, for a single flash would have turned the machine guns on us. I cannot say if we were seen or not, but all the time bullets came whizzing by, though more than likely stray ones and not aimed at us. Once I had to get the men to lay down, as things were rather warm, but somehow I felt quite safe, as if the dead soldier's Guardian Angel was sheltering us from all danger, till the poor dust was laid to rest. It was my first war burial, though assuredly not my last – may God rest his soul and comfort those left to mourn him.[12]

It wasn't long before Fr Doyle knew the burial ritual off by heart. He doesn't record any burials for the next day, but he was busy helping tend the wounded at the Regimental Aid Post as a result of heavy shelling from across the way. He continues his budget on Sunday 2 April:

Quite a good night's rest in spite of the hard floor (I shall probably not be able to sleep in a soft bed when I get home) and the friendly attention of one sweet little rat, a darling, with a long tail, who would persist in burrowing his way under my makeshift of a pillow. I am not exaggerating when I say the rats share our beds, why should they not? They were in the field before we were and have been feeding ever since on luscious German, French and English corpses. I have serious fear for the end of my nose.

The only thing to record today was heavy shelling by the Germans from seven in the morning till three in the afternoon. Only one came really near me. I was sitting close to the door of my dug-out when I heard the beastly thing coming very close. The Abbot, unmindful of his dignity, took one dive down the steps like Brere Rabbit, and chuckled in safety as he heard the crash overhead.

Busy all day as there were many wounded, mostly through their own

> *fault in not taking cover. One poor sapper just carried in with face burnt black by exploding shell, which buried a dozen of his comrades, he alone escaped by a miracle.'*[13]

Willie doesn't mention the visit of Major General Hickie, Officer Commanding 16th (Irish) Division to 49th Infantry Brigade Headquarters, which is recorded in the Brigade War Diary, presumably because he was too busy helping with the wounded to make it back to HQ.

In his report for the next day Willie refers to one of the wonders of the war, a landmark at Loos. Whilst mention of a Loos landmark would trigger, in the minds of most British troops, the thoughts of either the huge double crassier slag heap, or the pit-head popularised as Tower Bridge, for Fr Doyle it was something else. His budget continues on 3 April:

> *Up at cock crow, in fact before it, through the zeal of my orderly who pulled me out of bed at 3.30am. I had to get to a certain place before eight, to bury some men, which meant three hours' walk through the trenches, as the roads cannot be used in daylight. Fortunately it was a foggy morning, so I was able to use the road, and shorten my tramp by two hours, get Mass over, and a bowl of coffee stowed away before the appointed time. I had an opportunity, a rare one, thanks to the fog, of examining closely in daylight one of the wonders of the war – the famous crucifix or Calvary of Loos. This is a very large cross standing on a mound, a most exposed position, the centre of fierce fighting. One of the four trees standing by it has been torn up by a shell: the branches of the others smashed to bits: a tombstone at its foot lies broken in half, and the houses on either side are a heap of ruins, but neither cross nor figure has been touched. I looked closely and could not see even one bullet hole. Surely if the Almighty can protect the image of His Son, it will be no great difficulty to guard His priest also, as indeed He has done in a wonderful way.*[14]

The crucifix Fr Doyle referred to was located to the north of Loos on the Grenay to Benifontaine Road, but ultimately it did not survive. Willie continues his account:

> *This afternoon I saw my first live German, and a very much alive German*

saw me, which was quite a different story. I was passing down through the front line trench, which in parts is only 30 yards from the enemy, when one of our men called me to look through a spy-hole. Just opposite was a German standing with head and shoulders over the parapet, looking about him quite calmly, in full view of where I was. I happened to mention this to my new Colonel, who told me that though he had been out for more than a year he had not once seen a living man of the enemy. It is a funny war.

On my way back a sniper, hidden Goodness knows where, caught sight of the officer who was with me, and myself. At each bend of the trench he had a shot at us, crack, crack, crack all the way down most uncomfortably near for my taste, especially as I was the last, and our German friend was firing from behind. Strange to say I did not feel afraid, but very angry, there was something so annoying in being potted at, by a man under cover who you could not see, and I found myself humming that beautiful song:

'When I get hold of Hun Hooligan his mother will lose a son.'[15]

There follows one of the many amusing anecdotes Willie was so fond of recounting to his father:

There are many sad scenes out here as you may imagine, but the war furnishes many an amusing episode also. For example, the other night a shell burst close to some men. It is well known that a man may receive a bad wound without feeling pain, and as one of the Tommies concluded he must be seriously hurt, as he heard the blood gurgling from his side, and streaming down his leg, he felt no pain whatever, but the blood was pouring fast, his boot was full of it, his uniform soaked through – his head began to reel, would he live till they carried him to the Doctor? Just then someone brought a light, which revealed a large, gaping wound in the poor fellow's water-bottle: while he had not received a scratch.[16]

This episode may have taken place during the period, recorded in the 49th Infantry Brigade's War Diary, of enemy shelling on Gordon Alley and English Alley between 3 p.m. and midnight on 3 April 1916. The 8th Royal Irish Fusiliers were spared further shelling when they were relieved by their 7th Battalion comrades;

the relief started at 7.30 p.m. and was completed by 4am on the morning of Tuesday 4 April. As companies were relieved they marched back to Philosophe into billets to form the brigade reserve, taking over from the 8th Royal Inniskilling Fusiliers. Their three days duty in the front line was now at an end and Fr Doyle decides to discontinue his budget for the time being, informing his father that day:

> *The men having spent their three days and nights in the front trench, we have moved back again for three days to a village, in comparative safety, out of range of rifle fire, though not of shells which come our way from time to time. After three days here we move up to the 'Support Trench' and three days later return once more to the joys of Loos, our cellars, shells and rats. My life will be more or less routine during these days, so I shall discontinue the diary. Burials in the morning, followed probably by a visit to some trench, confessions for the men in the afternoon, winding up the day most likely by more burials at night. I had six at 11.48 last night – a gruesome sight, as two bodies fell to pieces when we lifted them off the stretchers. I had to shovel the remains of one poor fellow into his grave, not a very pleasant task I can assure you.*[17]

The 49th Infantry Brigade War Diary for this period gives a snap-shot of the routine work done at the front by all those involved. For the Officer Commanding there would be daily visits and inspections to various sectors of the line; every three days there would be battalion reliefs and changeovers; the Pioneers (11th Hampshires) attached to the 16th (Irish) Division constructed new trenches, whilst men of the Irish battalions would carry out trench maintenance; the men considered unfit for service were inspected by the General Officer Commanding First Army and all 74 were sent to the 16th Infantry Base Depot. Meanwhile, mining experts had been summoned to investigate the neighbourhood of Scots Alley and Chalk Pit Quarry, in which mining operations by the enemy had been heard. And, of course, an unvarying 'routine' for all was the enemy shelling. On several occasions the War Diary records that: *our heavy artillery retaliated but the greater number of their shells failed to explode* [18] (indicating that the major problem during the battle of Loos the previous year had not been entirely resolved!)

When the 8th Royal Irish Fusiliers went back in reserve, they formed working parties for maintenance work on a communication trench, Railway Alley, which ran west from the crucifix Fr Doyle referred to. Two days later, on Thursday 6 April, the reserve battalion at Philosophe was ordered to Stand-To about 6.30 p.m. and companies were moved forward to the positions of the support battalion, in the neighbourhood of Tenth Avenue. This was due to an intense bombardment of the left sub-sector of Puits 14 Bis which damaged the trenches. The 7th Royal Inniskilling Fusiliers had borne the brunt of the heavy shelling, between Chalk Pit Quarry and Posen Alley, resulting in support and fire trenches being destroyed, eighteen men were killed and eight wounded. Again it was noted that: *Our artillery retaliated but only partially successful.*[19] At 6 p.m. one company of 8th Inniskillings were sent to assist the 7th Inniskillings in digging out men and repairing trenches. The history of the 7th Battalion Royal Inniskilling Fusiliers puts more flesh on the bare bone of the brigade War Diary, confirming the flesh and bone number of casualties:

> *Undisturbed as were the first few days of April, comparatively speaking, the 6th of the month brought with it a most unprecedented bombardment on our trenches. 'B' Company (Captain R.G. Kerr) was the objective of the severest gun fire. Shortly after 1.30 p.m. – in fact just as the men were eating their dinners – the bombardment opened. Captain R.G. Kerr and the officers were having lunch in their company headquarters when the first shell burst within a few yards of the door, followed in quick succession by several more. The officers quickly got up, followed by the mess servants and batmen, and tried to get out to the trench. Before the officers got to the trench a 5.9 registered a direct hit on the dug-out, and it collapsed. The officers were fortunate to escape unhurt, but two batmen were severely wounded, and four signallers were buried in the debris, and, despite the efforts of a continuous working party for the next twenty-four hours, their bodies were never recovered. Within ten minutes of the opening of this artillery onslaught, the enemy concentrated all his fire on 'B' Company's support line. Salvo after salvo burst on, or near the trench, with most terrifying rapidity. For two hours the enemy kept up the demolition of our defences and then ceased, but not before he had suffered heavily from our artillery. This was the first occasion we had observed in which our guns were not stinted with ammunition. The courage and devotion to duty shown by the men during this terrible ordeal was beyond praise, and was*

recognised, as we shall see later by the Army Commander. About twenty casualties was the result of the shoot, the object of which was never quite understood, as no infantry action followed, unless it was in retaliation for our trench mortar activity.[20]

As recognition for especially good work during the enemy bombardment of 6 April 1916, 'B' Company of the 7th Battalion Royal Inniskilling Fusiliers were awarded the Parchment of Merit of the 16th (Irish) Division:

The inspection took place on the Market Square at Noeux-les-Mines, and was attended by the Battalion, Brigade, Division and Corps Commanders. The G.O.C. First Army shook hands with the officers and N.C.O.'s ... and expressed great satisfaction with the appearance and smartness of the company on parade. He expressed a hope that the company would live up to the reputation they had earned and would get their own back on the enemy with interest at no distant date.[21]

Although lacking the same flair for anecdotal description, the history of the 7th Inniskillings also contains incidents similar to those recorded by Willie Doyle:

Another unpleasant incident, but happily not attended with any serious consequences, was the organised shoot by the enemy on our Battalion Headquarters. It was the custom to have sent up a daily basket containing two pigeons, as an alternate means of communication to the rear, should all other means fail. These birds were kept in the battalion signal office for twenty-four hours and then released with a practice message if not required tactically. During one afternoon they were released, in clear visibility, within a few yards of the headquarters, and evidently within observation of the Boche. Next morning he 'strafed' the neighbourhood for half-an-hour with 'heavy stuff,' but his range, though at times uncomfortably accurate, was not correct, and, save for some damage to the trenches, he caused no casualties. The incident was one which is worth recording, as it was through all these and countless other details we gained that great essential 'experience,' which nothing can supplant, and which can only be gained by the analysis of the thousand-and-one things which happen, or don't happen, daily.[22]

The history confirms some of the observations made by Fr Doyle about his abode in Tenth Avenue:

> *The battalion in Brigade support was generally looked on as having a 'cushy' job compared with those in the front system. The fatigues were wearisome and continuous, but they were chiefly done under cover of darkness. Hostile activity was very seldom directed on 10th Avenue, excepting, of course when the enemy contemplated a raid or a local attack; on such occasions he would shell the trench, but never with any degree of accuracy, chiefly due to the fact that direct observation from the ground was not easy, as the trench was, for the most part, on the reverse slope ... The greatest drawback to Tenth Avenue was the abundance of rats that it harboured. After dusk the trench was alive with these vermin in all shapes, sizes and colours. Dug-outs swarmed with the pestilence, and great supervision had to be preserved over the rations, or they would often disappear with alarming regularity.*[23]

Returning to Willie Doyle, who reflects, in his next instalment, on the new experiences which the early days of April have brought him, and his trust in God that he would remain safe and well. His budget continues:

> **9 April:** *I am glad I have been able to bring this letter up to date, as we are going back in an hour's time to charming Loos – to 'St. Patrick's, or if you like St. William's, Purgatory,' to the cellars, the smells and the rats.*
>
> **12 April:** *We have just got back safe and sound from Loos, having finished our three days' scourging, deeply grateful to have come away with whole skins, all save the brave lads we have left behind to wait there the Last Roll Call.*
>
> *Perhaps it will be just as well to send you on what I have written, as ink and paper are running out, and I can reserve further scraps of news for a later date. Besides these three days have been almost as uneventful as the first three were exciting. Possibly I have become more hardened to sad sights, and more accustomed to the ceaseless bombardment, and so things have not struck me so much as they did in the beginning.*[24]

Willie's next comment is strange, as it implies that his time at Loos is at a permanent end, whereas, in fact, the respite is only temporary:

> *You must not let this letter make you uneasy about me, or my safety. First of all I can never again be in so much danger, for we do not return to Loos, and there is no other place on the line like it, and secondly I have, through God's help, come through the ordeal untouched, and am now miles away from danger.*
>
> *It was a memorable six days for us all, living day and night literally face to face with death at any moment. When I left my dug-out to go up or down the street, which I had to do scores of times daily, I never knew if I should reach the end of it without being hit by a bullet or piece of shell, and in the comparative safety of the cellar at meals, or in bed, there was always the pleasant prospect of being blown to bits, or buried alive, if a large shell came in a certain direction. The life was a big strain on the nerves, for it does make one 'creepy' to hear (as happened to myself yesterday) the rattle of shell splinters on the walls, on either side of the road: almost to feel the thud of a nice jagged lump right behind, and see another fragment go hopping off the road a few yards in front. Why, Daniel in the Lion's Den had a gay and festive time compared to a walk through the main street of Loos. Yet through it all, I was filled with a strange feeling of confidence that no harm would befall me, that our Blessed Lord just wanted me to trust Him. I tried to do so all along, and so I have come safe out of the furnace, a mighty hot one at times!!!*[25]

Willie updates his budget with a mysterious comment, as we only have one side of the correspondence, about unexplained news of someone called Lizzie:

> *Your ever welcome letter has reached me. I cannot tell you what a treat it was to read it and it made me forget there was ever such a thing as a bursting shell. However, please don't try and write too often, for I know how busy you are with the 'Penny Bank' accounts. The good news you gave me about Lizzie was a most agreeable surprise. God has rewarded her for the sacrifice she made years ago, but only for your goodness to her, her desire would never have been realised.*[26]

Loos in ruins, 1916

Hugh Doyle had evidently taken over from Willie's aged aunt as custodian of the 'Penny Banks' for the next generation of Doyles, his daughter Lena's children!

The day before this was written, on Tuesday 11 April, before reliefs had taken place, a raid had been ordered by Captain Watson of the Divisional Staff, the objective being to take a German soldier. Two patrols of 8th Royal Irish Fusiliers in the right sub-sector and two patrols of 8th Royal Inniskilling Fusiliers in the left sub-sector had been sent out in the attempt to secure a German prisoner for intelligence purposes. The attempt proved unsuccessful, after the patrols on the right were fired on from enemy sap heads and they had to retire, and those on the left found the enemy saps unoccupied. Following this, reliefs commenced later that evening at 7.30pm and were completed by 12.30 a.m. on the 12 April, at which time 8th RIF found themselves at Mazingarbe. Here they were billeted and kept busy on drill parades, rifle and physical exercises, with extra training for bombers. 'D' Company were unlucky to suffer shelling of their billets, sustaining four slight casualties.

Willie's next letter to Hugh was dated 22 April, Holy Saturday 1916. He seems to contradict previous comments made to his father about safe areas, but such reassurance is in keeping with the philosophy he has practised thus far, to advise his family of the dangers, whilst making light of it and adapting what he says to suit his every circumstance:

> *I certainly did not think six months ago that I should find myself sitting down in an old German dug-out of the former German Front line, to send you my best Easter wishes. Good fortune has even given me the 'lend of a loan' of a typewriter for an hour (please excuse the beast when it starts writing red, or doing other queer things – I am sure it was made in Germany.) So I hope to send you a good Easter egg, in the shape of a decent letter, since you tell me you have found what I have written so far interesting.*
>
> *Well, here I am settled down in the trenches for the next 8 days, having got here on Holy Thursday evening. I have a very comfortable dug-out, no great luxury, as you may imagine, and its dimensions are better given in feet than yards, but I have a dry floor under me, a rain proof, if not shell proof roof on top, a plank bed, which I fear I must count as a 'luxury,' and a small stove which smokes like 'Billy-O' whoever he is.*
>
> *I hope you will not picture to yourself all kinds of possible dangers when I say I am living in the trenches. As a matter of fact one is far safer where I am than in the village billets, as the Bosches shell these constantly, knowing they will hit something, whereas the back trenches offer a very poor mark, not worth the waste of powder and shot.*
>
> *You will understand this better if you remember that the Front line consists of 8 lines – the Firing line or Front trench: the Reserve: and the Support lines, one behind the other, and all connected by Communication trenches. The Doctor's Dressing Station and my dug-out are in the Support trench, hence quite a long way from the danger point. Again even this viz: the Front line is not really dangerous except at night when most of the fighting takes place (and I am in bed.)*
>
> *So much for my present position, so I shall give you news of the past week. As I said in my last letter, nothing of very special interest happened during our second three days at Loos, though every moment was of interest in one sense, as the Germans kept peppering us from morning to night. In fact I used to go up to the Front line trench for safety.*[27]

Wherever Willie was – he was safe! His narrative continues:

> *When introducing you to my friends the rats, I made a serious omission in forgetting another class of most attentive friends, smaller in size but more active, in a personal way: they are not called 'Teas' but something very like that. You must remember that the unwashable Hun lived in our cellar for months, and 'departing left behind him' a large number of small fierce warriors from across the Rhine. Next came the French. There is not much picking on a Frenchman, so it is small wonder that when they in turn departed their small companions remained in hope of better things to come. Tommy Atkins then appeared, and not to be outdone left a legacy also. Fortunately, these visitors were natives of different countries, speaking different tongues, otherwise, had they been friends and united in policy, we should have been literally pulled out of bed. These are some of the pleasures of a military campaign and prevent one from ever feeling lonely.*
>
> *I am glad to say that the casualties among my men were light. The Inniskillings during their three days had nearly 20 men killed, whereas we during the same time, had only one man fatally hit and two others who died from wounds, both of whom I was able to anoint. I had tried to drive home to them that their safety lay in prayer, and I really believe God watched over them on that account. For example: a group of men were standing together when a big shell dropped in the midst of them but did not burst. Another man told me that before he went past a dangerous corner he stopped to say a Hail Mary. The next moment a bullet struck his helmet, but glanced off, and did him no harm.*[28]

As with many previous letters, Willie has included an episode a little out of the ordinary for his father's entertainment:

> *I was anxious to get some little souvenir of Loos before I came away, so the last evening when it got dusk, I set out for a hunt among the ruins and had the good luck to pick up a fine solid brass crucifix about 6 inches long, which I can get mounted again on a wooden cross. It was a very wet evening and I wore my big waterproof and was well muffled up: my dress and suspicious movements evidently attracted the attention of the military*

police, for passing a corner one of them sprang out on me, quite suddenly and demanded who I was. A German spy had been round the previous day, which made us on the qui vive. A little further down the road I was again challenged 'Halt. What sort are you?' There was no mistaking the country that sentry hailed from, even if he had not added: 'God forgive me, your Reverence, for taking you for a b----y Jarman'.[29]

Willie follows this with an appreciative insight into the lot of the ordinary Irish Tommy in his brigade:

Our poor lads are just grand. They curse like troopers all the day, they give the Bosches Hell, Purgatory and Heaven all combined at night and next morning come kneeling in the mud for Mass and Holy Communion when they get the chance, and beam all over with genuine pleasure when their padre comes past their dug-out, or meets them in the trench. They are going through their own Purgatory, a damp one, just at present, for it has been raining steadily the past two days, and the trenches are a sight to see, just a big ditch full of slush and water. I have a fine waterproof and big gum boots and so keep dry as a bone, but the Tommies are not so well off, more especially as many of their dug-outs are flooded. Yet in spite of it all they keep in the best of spirits, though there are not many of us, on either side, who are not wishing in their hearts it were all over.[30]

Next, Willie responds to Hugh Doyle, who had evidently written with news of a fellow priest they both knew:

It may be news to you that the venerable Rector of Limerick volunteered as chaplain before I did, but being a useful man would not be let go. He would be welcome all the same, for I recently discovered that the other two Brigades of the 16th Division have 4 and 8 chaplains respectively, whereas we are only 2 in the 49th though most of the men are Catholics.[31]

The last comment is surprising and perhaps it was just wishful thinking on Fr Doyle's part, as he refers several times during his military career to attracting converts. The battalions of 49th Infantry Brigade were Royal Inniskilling and

Royal Irish Fusiliers. Both these regiments had their recruiting areas in Ulster, so it would be expected that there would be more Protestant than Catholic personnel. Willie continues and yet another tale of a 'rat' sporting a different tail is related:

> *I had rather an amusing experience the first night I spent in the trenches. On arriving here I found two officers in the dug-out, which was intended for me, but as they were leaving the next day, I did not care to evict them. After some search I came across an unoccupied, glorified rabbit hole (any port in a storm.) It was not too inviting looking, and rather damp, but I got a trench-board which made a capital foundation for a bed and spread my sleeping bag over it. Let me say here that I do not recommend 'trench-boards' for beds. It is simply a kind of ladder with flat steps, which is laid at the bottom of the trench, but being rather narrow requires great skill to prevent yourself from rolling off during the night. In addition, the sharp edges of the steps have a trick of cutting into your back and ribs making you feel in the morning as if you had been at Donnybrook Fair the night before.*
>
> *In spite of it all I slept soundly till I was awakened by feeling a huge rat sitting on my sheet. The rats round here beat anything I have ever seen. If I told you they were as big as sheep you would scarcely believe me, so let me say a lamb: in any case this fellow was a whopper, weighing fully 7 pounds as I proved afterwards. I thought first of all that 'I had them again', but as I was gradually awoke more fully I felt his weight and could dimly see the black outline. Before I quite realised what was happening, a warm soft tongue began to lick my face, and I recognised my old friend – the dog.*
>
> *I have kept my Easter wishes for the end, they are none the less hearty for that. Please God we shall spend the next one together in the dear old home. Au revoir. God bless you all.*[32]

Willie had commenced this letter whilst the 8th RIF were in brigade support in the Hulluch Sector; the day after he wrote the battalion moved to front-line duty in the left sub-sector. The right flank of the battalion resting on Holly Lane and the left on Stone Street. Battalion Headquarters was in Ninth Avenue near Hay Alley.

In front of all the Irish positions, along almost the entire length of No Man's Land, was a mass of mine craters. Special arrangements were made for the defence of the strategically important mine craters by company bombers. During this spell of duty, the bombers of 'C' and 'D' Companies, 8th RIF, assisted by one officer and twenty-four bombers from 'A' and 'B' Companies, were under the command of Major E.W.P. Uniacke. The bombers manned the near lips and flanks of the craters, as well as occupying where communication trenches ran from the support trench to the fire trench. The latter, immediately to the rear of the craters, was in a bad condition owing to mining operations and, to make matters worse, sandbags taken from the mines blocked the firing trench to a considerable degree.

The War Diary for the 8th Royal Irish Fusiliers[33] notes that at 3.40am on Wednesday 26 April the Royal Engineers fired two small mines south of Munster and Tralee craters, following reports of a suspected hostile mine just north of the two craters. Acting on the advice of the Tunnelling Officer the front line between Sixth Avenue and Connaught Lane was evacuated in order to minimise the casualties. Subsequently, Captain E.R. Cooke was killed in action while visiting the bombers in Munster Crater. The Germans were luckier. The regimental history of the Bavarian Infantry Regiment 9 (their times being an hour ahead of the British who conformed to Greenwich Mean Time) records: *At 4.34 a.m. on 26 April the enemy blew two mines opposite Offensive Mine 6, without causing any damage or casualties.*[34] This activity was the prelude to gas attacks launched by the Germans which Fr Doyle briefly alludes to in a note written on Saturday 29 April 1916:

> *One line to let you know all is well.*
>
> *I am back safe in billets, but just dog-tired, as we had a fierce German attack, which our boys stood well, and gave the Bosches beans.*
>
> *When I have had a good soak I shall send you my budget. The 'soak' will be a double one, in a tub (to get the mud out) and in bed to rest my old bones, otherwise I am ever so fit and well.*[35]

He mentions the fierce German attack almost as if in passing. However, the details of this engagement were to follow in his next correspondence and took up many pages of paper in the telling.

CHAPTER 15
GAS ATTACK:
GALLANTRY AND DEVOTION

GAS! GAS! Quick, boys! – An ecstasy of fumbling,
Fitting the clumsy helmets just in time;
But someone still was yelling out and stumbling,
And flound'ring like a man in fire or lime …[1]

Willie Doyle's next letter to his father, Hugh, dated Wednesday 3 May 1916, begins as so often with an apology and hints at what is to come, whilst providing reassurance about his safety and well-being:

You would have had my promised letter before this if I had had a chance of writing to you, but our time of 'rest' turned out to be days of very strenuous work indeed, and it is only now I have got away to the rear for a while. I began well last night by sleeping 18 hours without waking and am feeling all the better for it this morning. I suppose it was the luxury of a real bed, and the additional comfort of getting off one's clothes (the first time in the past fortnight) which is responsible for such laziness.

To tell the truth I had nearly reached the end of my tether, from exhaustion, want of sleep, and the strain of the terrible time we have gone through, not to speak of the heart-breaking scenes I have been witnessing, which you will realise better when I tell you that the casualties in our Brigade alone came to 800 men, though we were not in the hottest part of the fight.

Now however I have absolutely nothing to do except rest, for some days at least, which may be extended at the end of the week. I am really only tired and quite well otherwise, so you need not be uneasy.[2]

Whether Willie actually wrote 800 men, or whether it was an error of transcription is hard to say, but the casualties he refers to, whilst high in number, were not as severe as stated. A few days prior to the events which had exhausted him, it had been the Easter weekend and Fr Doyle did his utmost to observe the festival with the limited means at his disposal:

You will have received my typed letter from the trenches, posted on Easter Sunday, which turned out a glorious day, warm with brilliant sunshine, in fact we have had nothing else since.

I had quite a little congregation, of officers chiefly, the men not being able to leave their posts, for my first Mass in the trench. My church was a bit of a trench, the altar a pile of sand bags, and though we had to stand awhile deep in mud, not knowing the moment a sudden call to arms would come, many a fervent prayer went up to Heaven that morning and surely the Almighty looked down in pleasure on those who had not forgotten His glorious Resurrection.

The next few days were rather quiet and uneventful.[3]

The situation rapidly changed. During the afternoon of Wednesday 26 April 1916, British front line trenches in the Hulluch area (north-east from Loos), between Fly Lane and Leinster Lane, in front of 6th Avenue, were evacuated in order to allow 8-inch guns to fire on the German front line trenches.

Intelligence had been gathered of the existence of gas cylinders in position and the likelihood of an enemy attack using gas. Aerial reconnaissance had also observed swarms of rats running from the German trenches into No Man's Land, escaping from leaking gas cylinders. The history of the Seventh Royal Inniskilling Fusiliers records a report from the General Staff, I Corps, which stated: *... there are gas cylinders on the front occupied by the 4th Bavarian Division, that is to say, approximately between Puits 14 bis and Hulluch.*[4]

Information from a German deserter, captured on the night of 23 April, had prompted the bombardment. The deserter, apparently, reported overhearing officers' conversations which, whilst only hearsay, gave the British cause for concern. A proposed raid was to be made with the assistance of gas when the wind conditions were favourable, with the objective of destroying the British mining system. The British objective, therefore, was to destroy the gas cylinders before they were used. The 8th Royal Irish Fusiliers' War Diary entry for that day concluded, however, that: *'Although the shooting was good, no gas was discovered.'*[5] Nevertheless, General

Hickie had ordered all wire defences to be strengthened and blankets, soaked in the anti-gas agent Vermorel, to cover the entrances of all dug-outs. Vermorel sprayers and personal respirators were also to be checked. Little more than twelve hours later the enemy did, indeed, launch a poison gas attack, during which our intrepid chaplain found himself in the thick of the action. This was followed by a second gas attack on Saturday 29 April. Whilst he was recovering from his exertions during the gas attack, Willie Doyle continued his letter to his father describing his traumatic experience:

On Wednesday morning the enemy began a slight bombardment, which gave me a chance of anointing some of my men, who were rather badly hit.

I little thought that an insignificant act of charity on my part would have led to such big results, but events proved that our Lord does not forget even 'the cup of cold water' given in His Name. The incident was this: I came across an officer who had been badly shaken by an exploding shell, though he had escaped with a slight scratch. I brought him to my dug-out and made him sleep in my bunk, for I knew in any case I could not turn in before 1.30 that night. However, when I did lie down, I found I could not sleep without a blanket, on account of the cold, the night air being still very chilly. About 4 o'clock the thought struck me that it would be a good thing to walk back to the village to warm myself, and say an early Mass for the nuns, who usually have to wait hours for some chaplain to turn up. They have been very kind to me and I was glad of this chance of doing this little service for them. The village is about two miles behind our trench, in such a position that one can leave cover with perfect safety and walk there across the fields. As I left the trench about 4.45 the sun was just rising. It was a perfect morning, with a gentle breeze blowing. Now and then came the crack of a rifle, but all was unusually calm and still: little did I think of the deadly storm about to burst, and hurry so many brave men into Eternity. I had just reached the point marked X halfway between our trenches and the village, when I heard behind me the deep boom of a German gun, quickly followed by a dozen others.[6]

Willie had drawn a very rough sketch showing the location of the trenches, the village he was headed towards, woods to his right, 'X' marking the spot that he had reached and an arrow pointing to the direction of the attack:

GAS ATTACK

In a moment our gunners replied, and before I could well realise what was taking place, the air was alive with shells. At first I thought it was just a bit of the usual 'Good morning greeting' and that after ten minutes artillery 'strafe' all would be quiet once more, but I soon saw this was a serious business, for gun after gun, and battery after battery was rapidly coming late into action, while at the lowest number 500 guns were roaring all round me. It was a magnificent if terrifying sight. The ground fairly shook with the roar of the guns, for the 'heavies' now had taken up the challenge, and all round the horizon I could see clouds of smoke, and dust from the busting shells, as both sides kept searching for their opponent's hidden cannon.

There I stood in the very centre of the battle, the one man of all the thousands engaged, who was absolutely safe, for I was away from the trenches, there were no guns or troops near me to draw fire and though tens of thousands of shells went over my head, not even a splinter fell near me. I felt that the good God had quietly 'dumped' me there till all danger had passed.

After a while, seeing that this heavy shelling meant an attack of some kind, and that soon many a dying man would need my help, I turned and made my way towards the ambulance station.

As I approached the trenches I noticed the smoke from the bursting shells, which was hanging thickly over them, and was being driven towards me across the fields. For once, I said to myself, I am going to smell the smoke of a real battle and I stepped out quite gaily – the next moment I had turned and was running back for my life. The Germans had started a poison gas attack, which I had mistaken for shell smoke, and I had walked straight into it![7]

Willie hadn't actually made a mistake. Two gas clouds were dispensed; the first one, designed to deceive, was principally of thick black smoke and largely innocuous, but this was followed by a very strong gas cloud, which caused the most harm. Willie's tale continues:

After about 20 yards I stopped to see what was to be done, for I knew it was useless to try and escape by running. I saw (assuredly again Providentially) that I had struck the extreme edge of the gas (at the point marked by the arrow on sheet 3) and also that the wind was blowing it away to my left, a hundred yards in the opposite direction, and I was safe.[8]

Willie's next comment is interesting in view of the intelligence that had been gathered and the precautions that had been ordered by General Hickie; but then Willie's version makes for a better story!

I must confess, for a moment I got a shock, as a gas attack was the very last thing I was thinking about, in fact we thought the Bosche had given it up. Fortunately too, I had not forgotten the old days of the chemistry room at Ratcliffe nor Brother Thompson and his 'stink bottles,' so I knew at the first whiff it was chlorine gas, and time for this child to make tracks.

But I was not yet out of the wood. Even as I was congratulating myself on my good fortune, I saw both right and left of where I stood the green wave of a second gas attack rolling towards me, like some huge spectre stretching out its ghastly arms. As I saw it coming, my heart went out to God in one fervent act of gratitude for His Goodness to me.

As probably you know, we all carry 'smoke helmets' slung over our shoulders in a case, to be used against a gas attack. That morning as I was leaving my dug-out I threw my helmet aside: I had a fairly long walk before me, the helmet is a bit heavy on a hot day, and as I said, German gas was as likely as the burning of Sackville St so I made up my mind to leave it behind. In view of what happened, it may appear imagination now, but a voice seemed to whisper loudly in my ear: 'Take your helmet with you, don't leave without it.' I turned back and slung it over my shoulder.[9]

The reference to Sackville Street in Dublin is intriguing. It was either a huge coincidence, or included deliberately for dramatic effect. On Easter Monday, 24 April 1916, a rising against British rule had started in Dublin. Ultimately, it failed and on the following Saturday when Willie started writing this letter, the ring-leaders had surrendered. It is inconceivable that news of the insurgency had not already filtered through to the forces in France; indeed the Germans opposite were always quick to try and play on Irish sensitivities. A placard had been erected announcing: *'Irishmen, heavy uproar in Ireland. English guns are firing on your wives and children'.*[10]

Willie doesn't make a direct reference to the Easter Rising until his next letter written on 13 May, yet here he is talking about the burning of Sackville Street, the main boulevard in Dublin city centre, where the freedom fighters had established their headquarters in the General Post Office. The GPO and several prominent premises on Sackville Street (now renamed O'Connell Street) were badly damaged or destroyed by shelling and fire. Having made his probably staged comment, Willie continues his narrative:

> *Surely it was the warning voice of my Guardian Angel, for if I had not done so you would never have had this letter, and the poor Abbot would have at last turned into a real gas bag.*
>
> *I wonder can you picture my feelings at that moment? Here was death in its most awful form sweeping down towards me: thank God I had the one thing which could save me but with a carelessness, for which I ought to be scourged, I had never tried the helmet on, and did not know if it were in working order. In theory, with the helmet on I was absolutely safe, but it was an anxious moment waiting for the scorching test, and to make things more horrible I was absolutely alone.*
>
> *But I had the companionship of One who sustained me in the hour of trial, and kneeling down I took the Pyx from my pocket, and received the Blessed Eucharist as Viaticum. I had not a moment to spare, and had just my helmet fixed, when I was buried in a thick green fog of poison gas.*[11]

Fr Doyle carried a small red leather pouch round his neck at all times, specially designed to hold his Pyx, a metal container which houses the Sacred Host.

On this occasion, he took the Blessed Eucharist as Viaticum, meaning that he performed the Holy Sacrament because he and those around him were in danger of death. In an earlier letter to a friend Willie had revealed what a comfort the Pyx was to him:

> *I have been living in the front trenches for the last week, in a sea of mud, drenched to the skin with rain and mercilessly peppered with all sorts and conditions of shells. Yet I realise that some strange purifying process is going on in my soul, and that this life is doing much for my sanctification.... Then in addition there is the great privilege and joy of carrying our dear*

Lord next my heart day and night. Long ago when reading that Pius IX carried the Pyx around his neck, I felt a foolish desire, as it seemed to me, for the same privilege. Little did I think then that the God of holiness would stoop so low as to make me His resting-place.[12]

Returning to Willie's narrative to his father of the gas attack, he continues:

In a few moments my confidence returned, for the helmet worked perfectly, and I found I was able to breathe without any ill effects from the gas. By the time I got down to the dressing station the guns had ceased fire, the gas blown away, and the sun was shining in a cloudless sky.

Many a stream of wounded was coming in and I soon had my hands full when an urgent message reached me from the front trench. A poor fellow had been desperately wounded, a bullet had cut him like a knife across the stomach, with results you can best imagine. He was told he only had a few minutes to live, and could they do anything for him. 'I have only one wish before I die' he answered, 'could you possibly get me Fr Doyle? I'll go happy then.'[13]

More injuries were caused by conventional weapons than by the gas, as in the case just described by Fr Doyle. As well as shelling, there had been hand to hand fighting in some places. Willie continues:

It was hard work to reach him, as parts of the communication trench were knee deep in water and thick mud. Then I was misdirected and sent in the wrong direction, but I kept on praying I might be in time and at last found the dying man still breathing and conscious. The look of joy which lit up his face when I knelt beside him was reward enough for the effort I had made. I gave him absolution and anointed him before he died, but occupied as I was I did not notice that a third gas attack had begun. Before I could get my helmet out and on, I had swallowed a couple of mouthfuls, but which did me no serious harm beyond making me feel rather sick and weak.[14]

The history of the Seventh Royal Inniskilling Fusiliers confirms Fr Doyle's account of the conditions prevailing that morning:

On the morning of the 27 April, shortly after 4.30 o'clock, the enemy opened up intense rifle and machine-gun fire opposite the centre of the divisional front, viz. – the 8th Royal Irish Fusiliers, the 8th Royal Dublin Fusiliers and ourselves.

A slight easterly breeze was blowing from the direction of the enemy, visibility was good, and altogether it was an excellent opportunity for the enemy to release gas and carry out a raid under cover of it.

About 4.45 a.m. our front, support and reserve lines were subjected to an intense hostile bombardment, and almost simultaneously the enemy released dense volumes of smoke and gas over the whole divisional front. With a favouring wind the gas cloud drifted across 'No Man's Land' and over our trenches, and so exceedingly concentrated was it, that objects two or three yards away were rendered quite invisible.

For a time the cloud seemed to hang between the front and support lines, then gradually drifted in a south-westerly direction towards Loos, finally moving west over Mazingarbe towards Noeux-les-Mines.[15]

The 7th Inniskillings were situated to the right of the 8th Royal Irish Fusiliers, who themselves were at the extreme left edge of the 16th (Irish) Division's Front, facing Hulluch. On the extreme right edge of the divisional frontage in front of Loos were the 9th Royal Munster Fusiliers. The 8th Royal Dublin Fusiliers were the other centre battalion between the Inniskillings and the Munsters. The two centre battalions sustained the most casualties during this gas attack.

The gas was emitted from 3,800 cylinders from the trenches of the 5th Bavarian and 5th Bavarian Reserve Regiments of the German 4th Infantry Division and the smell of gas was noticed as far as fifteen miles away. The British 47th Brigade were in reserve a mile behind the front line and Captain Staniforth of 7th Leinsters reported:

There was a blizzard of shells in the street, all smashing on a cross-roads at the end. When we got to HQ there was a telegram from Division ordering all ranks to stand-to, and a warning of a possible attack.... Then it came. First thin broken wisps of greenish film in the sunlight, and then stronger whiffs, until our eyes were all bloodshot and dripping.[16]

Captain J.C. Dunn, a Medical Officer, Royal Army Medical Corps, attached to 2nd

Battalion Royal Welch Fusiliers, records gas drifting to their location well behind the front lines at Annequin North on 27 April:

> *... gas drifted through the village at 5 and again at 7.30 this morning. The Germans put it over at Hulluch, a couple of miles to our right, and entered 300 yards of front and support trenches ... Here the gas crept along the ground in thin dilution, at a fair pace, well below the height of a man standing. It didn't inconvenience any of us ...*[17]

Back at Hulluch, cylinders were also in position in the trenches of the 9th Bavarian Regiment, but these were not used because the direction of the wind was not favourable. However, their troops did participate in the raid. The 9th's regimental history notes:

> *On 27 April the three regiments of 4th Infantry Division (Infantry Regiments 5 and 9 and Reserve Infantry Regiment 5) were to have been involved in a gas attack, followed by raids. The gas cylinders had been in position for some considerable time. Because on the frontage of Infantry Regiment 9 the direction of the wind meant that the use of gas would have endangered 3rd Division, no gas was released. Proof of the offensive spirit and willingness to raid within the regiment is provided by the fact that, in broad daylight, at 7.45 and 9.00 a.m. patrols commanded by Res. Leutnant Cremer and Unteroffizier Eichenmüller of 11th Company and Unteroffizier Philipp of the Machine Gun Company, forced their way into the British positions, caused casualties amongst the fleeing British and returned with a machine gun and other captured materiel.*[18]

When the gas attack commenced, Fr Doyle's 8th Royal Irish Fusiliers held a 1,000 metre front line between the Hulluch Road (which crossed the battlefield west to east) down south to Holly Lane. On the left at the Hulluch Road end was 'B' Company under the command of Captain Barry St John Galvin. On the right at Holly Lane were Captain N.G. Alexander and 'A' Company. In the middle were the men of 'D' Company commanded by Major T.H. Boardman. In front of 'D' Company were mine craters, the lips of which were occupied by special bombing parties commanded by Major E.W.P. Uniacke. Between centre 'D' Company and the line of craters, there was an area linking 6th Avenue, Connaught Lane and

Tralee Crater which was not held, as advised by the Tunnelling Officer from the Royal Engineers, owing to a hostile mine having been detected immediately north of Tralee Crater. This portion of the front line was monitored by patrols instead.

In reserve some 500 metres back were 'C' company commanded by Captain E.M.H. Greville in the appropriately named Reserve Trench. Battalion Headquarters was another five hundred metres west in Ninth Avenue near the junction with Hay Alley. Another 100 yards beyond was Tenth Avenue, where Fr Doyle had his dug out, running parallel with Ninth Avenue.

'B' company, on the left, was the first to send back word that the enemy was using gas. As telephone communication was broken very soon after the commencement of the bombardment, Captain Galvin asked for a volunteer to go to Battalion Headquarters with the message. Private J. Costigan volunteered and arrived with the dispatch despite being gassed. At 7.35am, an hour after the second gas cloud had been released by the Bavarians, a message was received at HQ from Major Boardman of 'D' company, at centre position, that the enemy had advanced into the craters and penetrated the unoccupied section of the front line near 6th Avenue. Six of Major Uniacke's bombing party were posted at the junction of 6th Avenue and the fire trench. They managed to hold the Bavarians off and slowly drove them back, at a cost of two Irishmen killed, Privates Carey and O'Neill,[FN1] and the remaining four sustaining injuries. Second Lieutenant J.A. Culliemore showed good initiative by organising the bombers to hold on to Munster Crater, even though he was not a trained bomber. Major Uniacke traversed the fire trench from Smiths Crater and requisitioned three bombers, returning to Tralee Crater to bomb the enemy out. However, fourteen fusiliers had already paid the price of keeping Tralee Crater and the surrounding area clear, as a precaution against the suspected German mine. Other small parties of Bavarians elsewhere on the 8th Royal Irish Fusiliers' frontage were driven off by machine gun fire, but not before they had forced their way into British positions causing casualties and returning with captured materiel including a British machine gun.

Elsewhere along the line, under cover of gas and smoke, Bavarian units also advanced close up to, and gained entry to, other trenches. Bloody hand-to-hand fighting ensued. Some prisoners were taken, nearly all of whom lost their lives either attempting to escape or were killed alongside their German captors by the British counter-barrage. When a second gas attack was launched a few hours later, the direction of the wind suddenly changed and blew the gas back into the Bavarian lines. They tried to escape from their own trenches and were caught by machine-gun fire from the Irish battalions. However, by this time, as recorded by Tom Johnstone:

The front-line trenches of 16th Division were smashed. Parapets were blown down, trenches filled in, material and equipment lay scattered all over the battlefield. Prevailing all else was the stench of chlorine. Fire-bays and dug-outs were filled with dead and badly wounded and gas cases, blinded, choking and retching green bile, supported each other or, leaning on fit friends, formed long lines down the choked and chaotic communication trenches, making their painful way back to the Regimental Aid Post before being evacuated to the Casualty Clearing Stations.[19]

The Officer Commanding 8th Royal Irish Fusiliers, Lieutenant Colonel S.T. Watson, in his report dated 30 April 1916, picks out and names 20 men who performed acts of initiative as well as bravery, representatives of every rank from Private to Major. For example:

Captain Alexander obtained a machine gun whose team had become casualties and in spite of not knowing how to handle the guns took it to Southern Sap and found a man who said he could work it and opened fire. One of the enemy was killed by the gun and another shot by revolver fire. The remainder withdrew. Captain N.G. Alexander remained with his company until the battalion was relieved in spite of his previously having his finger shattered and receiving another shrapnel wound in his neck.

Private S. Connor showed great resource in digging out men who had been buried in the support line and dressing wounded. He rescued two comrades who were in a dugout which had been blown in on them, thus saving their lives.

I should also like to bring to notice the good work done by Lieutenant G. Buchanan, R.A.M.C. medical officer in charge of the battalion. About seventy casualties passed through the aid post in one day all of which he attended to and all were evacuated by 3.30 a.m. the following morning.[20]

This is the context in which Fr Doyle found himself that day and his chronicle continues:

GAS ATTACK

As I made my way slowly up the trench, feeling altogether 'a poor thing,' I stumbled across a young officer who had been badly gassed. He had got his helmet on but was coughing and choking in a terrible way. 'For God's sake' he cried 'help me to tear off this helmet – I can't breathe, I'm dying.' I saw if I left him the end would not be far, so catching hold of him I half carried, half dragged him up the trench to the medical aid post.

I shall never forget that 10 minutes, it seemed hours. I seemed to have lost all my strength: struggling with him to prevent him killing himself by tearing off his helmet made me forget almost how to breathe through mine. I was almost stifled though safe from gas, while the perspiration simply poured from my forehead.

I could do nothing but pray for help, and set my teeth, for if I once let go he was a dead man. Thank God we both at last got to the aid post and I had the happiness of seeing him in the evening out of danger, though naturally still weak.

Fortunately this last attack was short and light so that I was able to take off my helmet and after a cup of tea was all right. The best proof I can give you of this lies in the fact that since then I have put in three of the hardest days' work in my life, which I could not possibly have done had I been really gassed, as its first effect is to leave one as helpless as a child.

I shall not attempt to describe my work for the next two days, nor the harrowing sights I saw. On paper every man with a helmet was as safe as I was from gas poisoning, but now it is evident many of the men despised the 'old German gas', some did not bother putting on their helmets: others had torn theirs: and others like myself had thrown them aside or lost them.

From early morning till late at night I worked my way from trench to trench, single handed the first day, with 3 Regiments to look after, and could get no help.

Many men died before I could reach them: others seemed just to live till I anointed them and were gone before I passed back. There they lay scores of them (we lost 800 as I said, nearly all from gas, though many will recover) in the bottom of the trench, in every conceivable posture of human agony, the clothes torn off their bodies in a vain effort to breathe, while from end to end of that valley of death came one low unceasing moan from the lips of brave men fighting and struggling for life.

> *I don't think you will blame me when I tell you that, more than once, the words of Absolution stuck in my throat, and the tears splashed down on the patient, suffering faces of my poor boys, as I leant down to anoint them. One young soldier seized my two hands and covered them with kisses, another looked up and said 'Oh Father, I can die happy now: sure I'm not afraid of death or anything else since I've seen you.*[21]

Words of Absolution may well have stuck in Fr Doyle's throat momentarily but his devotion to his ministry was unwavering:

> *Don't you think dear Father that the little sacrifice made in coming out here has already been more than repaid, and if you have suffered a little anxiety on my account, you have at least the consolation of knowing that I have, through God's Goodness, been able to comfort many a poor fellow, and perhaps open the gates of Heaven for them.*[22]

The final part of Willie's letter addresses concerns evidently expressed by his father:

> *You need not be uneasy about the burials, which are part of my duty, as the scene at Loos will not be repeated, and I know the service by heart now.*[23]

Indeed, the 7th Inniskillings history records that two days prior to Willie writing his letter home, he had been very busy at the cemetery behind the lines. The author records sixty-six out-right deaths during the recent gas attacks, and an unspecified number who had died subsequently. He describes:

> *On the afternoon of the 1 May, the officers and other ranks who had been killed in the recent operations, and others who had succumbed to gas poisoning, were laid to rest in the battalion cemetery at Philosophe East. The C.O., adjutant and many of the battalion attended the funeral service, which was conducted by Father Doyle.*[24]

Willie's letter continues with thanks to his brother Bob and sister-in-law Jennie who, conscious of the reams of news written by Willie from the front, had sent him a practical gift:

Ever so many grateful thanks for your dear welcome letter and to 'all the family at large' none forget me. Please thank Bob and Jennie especially for their useful gift of writing material, which was most acceptable.

I am due for my week's leave in a fortnight, but as the other chaplain goes first, I do not expect to get home till early in June. In the meantime 'keep the camp fires burning' under a large pot, as I shall want a liberal supply of hot water to wash away the dirt.[25]

This is a curious comment. Earlier Willie had referred to looking after three regiments during the gas attack (i.e. battalions), presumably the two from 49th Brigade in the front line - his own 8th Royal Irish Fusiliers, plus 7th Royal Inniskilling Fusiliers - and the third was the one in support 7th Royal Irish Fusiliers. This left the fourth battalion of the brigade, Willie's 8th Inniskillings, in reserve behind the lines. This begs the question: where was the other chaplain and why was his leave scheduled first, when he wasn't around for the gas attack and didn't even perform the burials for his own 7th Royal Inniskillings?

Willie's final comment in his letter of 3 May 1916 hints at his knowledge of the Easter Rising again, which he chose not to refer to directly until a letter written 10 days later:

I know you will forgive this letter being so much 'I.I.' but I think you would prefer to hear of the doings of this child to anything else, judging by what I hear real war news is very stale in Dublin just at present. In case of necessity I can offer you a nice dry trench as a place of safety.[26]

An even longer delay in revealing his thoughts occurred in a letter a year later, when Willie returned to the post-Easter Gas Attacks of 1916. The letter is included here to keep to the chronology of the story:

I have never told you the whole story of that memorable April morning or the repetition of it the following day, or how when I was lying on the stretcher going to 'peg out', as the doctor believed, God give me back my strength and energy in a way which was nothing short of a miracle, to help many a poor fellow to die in peace and perhaps to open the gates of heaven to not a few.

> *I had come through the three attacks without ill results, though having been unexpectedly caught in the last one, as I was anointing a dying man and did not see the poisonous fumes coming, I had swallowed some of the gas before I could get my helmet on. It was nothing very serious, but left me rather weak and washy. There was little time to think of that, for wounded and dying were lying all along the trenches. And I was the only priest on that section at that time.*[27]

It is not altogether clear whether Willie was referring to the gas attacks which took place on 27 April or whether he has moved on to that of the 29th. In between these two dates the 8th Royal Irish Fusiliers had been relieved by their regimental counterparts in the 7th Battalion, and went into brigade reserve at Philosophe West. Despite now being in reserve, working parties had been detailed to clear the front line trenches where mining operations were being carried out, and no doubt Fr Doyle also thought it was his duty to carry on working where he was most needed.

At 4 a.m. on the 29 April the Klaxon and Strombos horns blared out again warning of another attack. Philosophe was actually bombarded with 8-inch shells, but these did not do much damage to Fr Doyle's boys as they were directed nearer to Vermelles Railway Station. Once again, gas was let off from over 3,000 cylinders in front of the Hulluch Sector. The chlorine gas hung immobile for some time causing numerous Irish casualties and killing off all vegetation, while the enemy massed ready for an attack behind the craters. Unfortunately for the Bavarians, the wind let them down again and blew the gas back into their trenches; they could not close the cylinders quickly enough before sustaining many casualties, not only from the gas but also from British shrapnel. At 5.40 a.m. the bombardment ceased, but not before the 8th Royal Irish Fusiliers' working party in the trenches were caught by the gas. Of the total of 45 men, only four were not gassed and the Officer Commanding 2/Lt D.J. Henry was amongst those gassed.

There are many accounts of Irish exploits in the front line that day, such as that of Private D. Lynch of 6th Connaught Rangers. He was caught in the gas and witnessed nine of his fellow machine-gunners also struck down by the gas, four of whom died, including the section commander. Nevertheless he continued alone to man his own machine gun for several more hours, attacking the enemy, stopping a new surge by the Bavarians and knocked a gas cylinder back into one of their trenches. Lynch was later awarded the Distinguished Conduct Medal.

Fr Doyle continues to reminisce:

> *The fumes had quite blown away, but a good deal of the gas, being of a heavy nature, had sunk down to the bottom of the trench and gathered under the duck boards or wooden flooring. It was impossible to do one's work with the gas helmet on, and so, as I knelt down to absolve or anoint man after man for the greater part of that day, I had to inhale the chlorine fumes till I had nearly enough gas inside to inflate a German sausage balloon.*
>
> *I did not then know that when a man is gassed his only chance (and a poor one at that) is to lie perfectly still to give the heart a chance of fighting its foe. In happy ignorance of my real state, I covered mile after mile of those trenches until at last in the evening, when the work was done, I was able to rejoin my battalion in a village close to the Line.*
>
> *It was only then I began to realise that I felt 'rotten bad' as schoolboys say. I remember the doctor, who was a great friend of mine, feeling my pulse and shaking his head as he put me lying in a corner of the shattered house, and then he sat beside me for hours with a kindness I can never forget. He told me afterwards he was sure I was a 'gone coon' but at that moment I did not care much. Then I fell asleep only to be rudely awakened at four next morning by the crash of guns and the dreaded bugle call 'gas alarm, gas alarm'. The Germans had launched a second attack, fiercer than the first. It did not take long to make up my mind what to do – who would hesitate at such a moment, when the Reaper Death was busy? – and before I reached the trenches I had anointed a number of poor fellows who had struggled back after being gassed and had fallen dying by the roadside.*[28]

The 7th Leinsters participated in mopping-up operations. Captain J.H.M. Staniforth was horrified at the condition of the trenches and the sights therein:

> *The bombardment of the last three days had flattened them into mere hammocks and morasses, and has prevented the evacuation of casualties. Everywhere we picked our way over dead and dying, all gassed. Up to the present we have evacuated 440 men killed by gas. It's a nightmare of a job;*

*the expressions of men caught suddenly and choked aren't pretty.*²⁹

Lieutenant C. Weld also worked, in what were already extremely unpleasant conditions, on 29 and 30 April, and exacerbated by hot weather:

*It was a ghastly sight. Hundreds of men who were gassed lay three deep in the firing step. They had died in terrible agony with faces all purple from the gas. Many others not yet dead gasping out green foam. This is about the most fearful sight I have yet seen ... I thought I was accustomed to war and all its frightfulness, but this fairly staggers me ... what with the dead lying in the trenches, the dreadful smell, the collection of the wounded and the half-gassed, and the enemy attacks, rest or sleep is out of the question. We are all very weary.*³⁰

Perhaps only a religious man like Fr Doyle could seek and find some comfort from the horrendous sights of the last few days of April 1916:

*The harvest that day was a big one, for there had been bloody fighting all along the Front. Many a man died happy in the thought that the priest's hand had been raised in absolution over his head and the Holy Oils anointing had given pardon to those senses which he had used to offend the Almighty. It was a long, hard day, a day of heart-rending sights, with the consolation of good work done in spite of the deadly fumes, and I reached my billet wet and muddy, pretty nearly worn out, but perfectly well, with not the slightest ill effect from what I had gone through, nor have I felt any since. Surely God had been good to me. That was not the first of His many favours, nor has it been the last.*³¹

Fr Doyle's heroic efforts beyond the call of duty were noted in his battalion commander's report. Lieutenant Colonel S.T. Watson stated in his hand-written report of 30 April 1916:

Splendid work was done by Revd Father W. Doyle, chaplain to the forces. Though gassed in the early part of the day he continued to work amongst the wounded and dead and his energy was unlimited. He paid frequent visits to the front line trenches and refused rest until forced to do so. Since the battalion came out of the trenches he has again visited the front line attending the wounded and burying the dead.[32]

Professor Alfred O'Rahilly asserts in his biography of Fr Doyle that: *His Colonel recommended him for the Military Cross but was told that Fr Doyle had not been long enough at the Front. So he was presented with the Parchment of Merit of the 49th Brigade.*[33] However, although Lt Col Watson had recorded Willie's exceptional conduct in his report, the name of Fr Doyle did not appear in the list noted in the War Diary as having been submitted for gallantry awards. Indeed, the same applies to Major Uniacke who was singled out for particular praise in Lt Col Watson's report but was not recommended for immediate reward. But this is a perplexing issue because Fr Doyle's name was submitted for Mention in Dispatches.

Professor O'Rahilly was correct about the Parchment of Merit in which Major General W.B. Hickie, Commanding 16th (Irish) Division, said of The Rev Father W. Doyle:

I have read with much pleasure the reports of your regimental commander and brigade commander regarding your gallant conduct and devotion to duty in the field on April 27 and 29 and have ordered your name and deed to be entered in the record of the Irish Division.[34]

This certificate is in the possession of Fr Willie's great-nephew (Lena's grandson) living in County Dublin.

Footnote 1: The bodies of Privates Thomas O'Neill and John Carey were not recovered and they are commemorated on the Memorial to the Missing at Loos, Dud Corner, Panel 124

CHAPTER 16
BAD GAS DISCIPLINE?:
MENTION IN DISPATCHES

*The gallantry of the Irish troops is an answer
to the German plots and attempts to
rouse sedition in Ireland* [1]

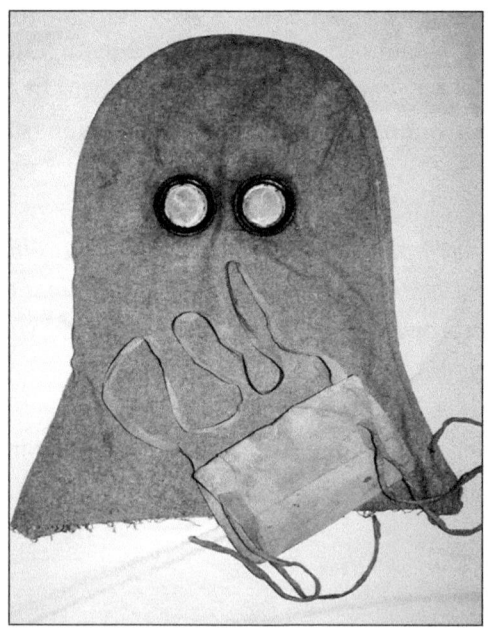

Late type hypo helmet

The chlorine gas attacks launched by the Germans at Loos on Thursday 27 and Saturday 29 April 1916 spawned a plethora of reports; preliminary reports, reports, and recommendations of reports. Reports at battalion level, such as that compiled by Lieutenan Colonel S.T. Watson, Officer Commanding 8th Royal Irish Fusiliers, who commended the work of Fr Doyle during the gas attacks. Yet more reports at

Brigade, Division, Corps and Army levels and from the Field Ambulance Service. Reports which were included in personal diaries and, later on, in memoirs. The composition of the reports started immediately after the first attack on the 27 April and continued on through into early May.

All reports had one or more of the following elements: a narrative of events; how the British responded to the German attack; how the whole gamut of equipment used (ordnance, protective and preventative gear, communications) responded to the proximity of gas; what intelligence was gained from German prisoners; what lessons could be learned; recommendations and, most crucially, the casualties. Willie Doyle's next letter to his father, dated 13 May 1916, touches on the issue of casualties, albeit only within his own parochial field of operations:

> *Since I wrote last we have been back here some miles from the firing line, as the poor men always get a rest after a spell in the trenches. This time they wanted it badly, poor chaps, having had a hard time of it, an experience none of us are likely to forget. Once again we have had all the luck, even with our share of fighting, for though one regiment of the brigade is reduced to 200 men, the casualties of the 8th Fusiliers only came to a little over 100.*[2] [25 were deaths.]

The report of 49th Infantry Brigade, to whom the 8th Royal Irish Fusiliers was attached, gives a picture of German losses after the first attack. Two wounded prisoners were taken alive; equipment secured; and correspondence etc. belonging to a dead German officer was found lying outside the parapet. Over one hundred fresh German bodies were counted in No-Man's-Land between the Kink and Smith's Crater, some of which were lying in or near British barbed wire, but the majority were lying about mid-way between the opposing lines. It was asserted that the enemy must have suffered severely from artillery fire aimed into their trenches and from gas blowing back. About forty or fifty large motor ambulances were seen to come up rapidly to Bois Benifontaine in the afternoon and, after a short time, go slowly away. An interesting cameo emerged from one of the prisoners.

Private Frederick Habenstein, 5th Company of 5th Bavarian Regiment, Second Army Corps, was 21 years old and had joined the army as 'Uberschreibon' in September 1914, having been a Blacksmith by trade. For his latest spell of duty he had been three days in the trenches, his battalion having relieved a Prussian

Regiment; his 5th Bavarian Regiment were to the right of the 9th Bavarians. His unit had one Company in the Firing Line, one Company in Support and one Company in Reserve; each was about 250 men strong with three or four machine guns. He reported that German rations were satisfactory, but their trenches were in a worse condition than the British, being a lot wetter. They must have been extremely miserable places, because the 16th (Irish) Division's trenches were infamous for their poor conditions, dug in the flat, low-lying water-logged landscape. Indeed, Major General William Hickie, Officer Commanding 16th (Irish) Division, later wrote: *It is suggested that the Germans, knowing they were attacking an untried Division in not very good trenches, hoped to clear those trenches with gas and by the bombardment.*[3]

Habenstein had known nothing about plans for the attack, nor did he know what the objective was. However, he expected the war to be over soon, as the English were bound to give in, and because there were many reserves in Germany. Private Habenstein's war proved to be soon over; he and the other prisoner died during the night.[4] Whether Frederick Habenstein received absolution and was anointed or not is not stated, but he certainly achieved release and peace from the horrors of war. Willie Doyle also escaped eventually to a temporal, albeit temporary, peaceful idyll away from the Front Line, continuing in his letter:

> *As a result of our stay here things have been singularly uneventful and quiet. They say a war is going on somewhere, but it is not easy to realise that at present. I was not sorry to get a little rest, for the beastly gas took more out of me than I thought, but I am feeling fit and well again now, thank God, ready for another spell before my trip to 'Blighty'.*[5]

The gas affected Fr Doyle because he removed his helmet in order to properly carry out his duty to his own satisfaction, which was hindered by the helmet. Several reports conceded that there were issues with gas helmets such as: *a prickling irritating sensation is to be expected in the eyes, nose and throat*[6] thus: *causing a man's field of vision to be very limited and his hearing to be dulled*[7] and: *the difficulty of seeing owing to gas helmets and goggles becoming blurred with moisture.*[8] Therefore, some men, like Fr Doyle, had no choice when it came to properly executing their duties; for example the men of Machine Gun 9 were slightly gassed owing to removing their goggles in order to remedy stoppages when the gun over-heated. They had no other option in view of the fact that three of their fellow Machine Gun teams had been killed, and their guns knocked out.[9]

There were also numerous other incidents of men who, for one reason or another, either didn't get their helmets on in time or took them off too early. Fr Doyle had struggled with an injured, gassed officer he was trying to assist, who had his helmet on and was trying to tear it off because he was choking. Perhaps he was one of those officers who had tried to assist his men before getting his own helmet on first. This phenomenon was noted in several reports, along with the fact that some officers removed helmets in order to deliver orders to their men. Major Rudkin, 49th Infantry Brigade said:

> *It is feared the lives of Officers and NCOs were lost owing to the fact that they moved along the trenches giving instructions to the men during the gas attack, and in doing so removed the tube from the mouth. The necessity for not talking during a gas attack should be impressed on all ranks and also for as little movement as possible.*[9a]

There was also the issue of men emerging from mines, to find a gas attack in progress, and not being able to get their helmets on in time. Or men in forward saps and listening posts who did not have sufficient time to put their helmets on. Men were caught in latrines and, further behind the front line, at other ablutions. The 2nd Bn Royal Welch Fusiliers were well behind the line at Annequin North, where wispy gas penetrated; they responded appropriately to the gas alarm, which was no great inconvenience to anyone:

> *...except Moody, who was having a bath when the alarm sounded. He pulled on his gas helmet and stood waiting for the 'all-clear,' forgetting that he was defenceless because he had not a garment on into which to tuck the free end of the helmet. From that ridiculous attitude he was released by the entry of his servant.*[10]

The history of the 7th Inniskillings, who took a severe battering in the front lines, records a similar incident. 'A' Company were holding the reserve line and had only a few minutes notice of the approach of the gas cloud. Unfortunately: '*Private Cassidy, who was changing his socks and was in his bare feet at the time, was ordered to put on his gas helmet. He did so, but put it on back to front.*[11] Despite their subsequent heavy losses, the history of the Inniskillings, with typical Tommy humour, continues on an amusing note: *'Rushing madly round the trench he kept clutching blindly at his helmet and was heard to remark: 'I wish I could find the b----- windows.*[12]

An unforeseen cause of poisoning was recorded in Lieutenant Colonel S.T. Watson's report:

> *When gas was detected helmets were adjusted with promptitude and all men rearmed. This action prevented any casualties occurring from gas with the exception of a few men who, subsequent to the attack, drank tainted water.*[13]

There is no definitive answer to the question of how many casualties were sustained from the gas attacks, each source consulted varies from the one before, but the margins are relatively small. A man on the ground, just behind the Front Line, Captain J.H.M. Staniforth of 7th Leinsters, refers in his diary to evacuating 440 men killed by gas.[14]

Research undertaken by Terence Denman provides an interesting set of figures for the 16th (Irish) Division, who suffered casualties far in excess of flanking divisions. He compiled casualty figures on a monthly basis from January 1916, when the first units arrived in France, until 31 March 1918 when the division was no longer a viable unit. The number killed for April 1916 shows 538, compared to 643 deaths sustained in September 1916 during the battles of the Somme and 563 for August 1917 during the battles of Third Ypres; every other month ranging from 7 to 156.[15] So the deaths largely attributable to the gas attack, were comparable to the two major battles of the war the Division was involved in. Denman's complete figures for the whole of April 1916 are 538 killed, 1,526 wounded and 64 missing.[16] The 7th Bn Royal Inniskilling Fusiliers and 8th Bn Royal Dublin Fusiliers bore the brunt of the casualties. One company of the former ('B') lost 90 men alone, whilst 60 men of the latter were buried together in one shell hole.[17]

The *Official History of the War* quotes casualties, for 27 and 29 April only, as 570 killed (232 from shelling, 338 from gas) and 1,410 wounded (488 from shelling, 922 from gas).[18]

There is no single consolidated figure for the German's losses. However, the 15th Division's history notes:

> *In connection with this attack on the part of the enemy, it is interesting to note that in October 1918, at the commencement of the 'Advance to Victory' an officer of the 15th Division saw, in the German cemetery at Pont-a-Vendin, the graves of 400 Germans killed on April 27 and 29, 1916, 'gassed with their own gas'.*[19]

Pont-a-Vendin is approximately three miles diagonally opposite Hulluch. Bavarian deaths appear to be similar to Irish deaths despite the Germans having a superior gas mask.

Amongst the plethora of reports that mushroomed like the gas clouds, there was some suggestion that, whilst the Irishmen had undoubtedly conducted themselves in a courageous manner, it was their lack of discipline which led to such horrendous casualties. After the war this viewpoint may have been driven by other political factors, but at the time it provided a convenient cover-up to focus attention away from any possible defects in the equipment, particularly the gas helmets.

Lieutenant A. Bowen of the Royal Army Medical Corps attached to 16th (Irish) Division concluded on 1 May 1916 that there was a: *want of drill in the use of the gas helmet and not to any defect in the helmet.*[20] His reasoning can be followed when he asserts that: *Some men stated they never had a gas helmet on before.*[21] However, Lieutenant Bowen does not state whether those men who had never practiced with a gas helmet were experienced in the front line, or members of a new draft of the 7th Royal Irish Rifles, who had literally only arrived in France days before-hand.[22] He continues: *One officer was reported to have been seen walking about with his helmet pulled on and no attempt made at tucking it in.*[23] Conversely, Bowen's argument is less clear when he asserts:

> *Another officer reported that he put on the 'P.H.' helmet and being alarmed at the choking sensation changed it for his old helmet, which he stated was perfectly efficient. Several men stated on pulling on their helmets, they were alarmed by the sensation of choking and pulled them off again.*[24]

On the other hand:

> *One man admitted to No.112 Field Ambulance, suffering from Grenade Wounds, received subsequent to the gas attacks, was (sic) through both gas*

attacks and was in no way affected, only one helmet being used by him, which is apparently still quite effective.[25]

Quite evidently there were inconsistencies in the performance of helmets and there is a telling, final, observation from Lieutenant Bowen, which may have affected a man's ability to cope under exposure to gas: *There is also considerable evidence pointing to the men in several cases being exhausted from want of food.*[26]

The P.H. helmets then in use were rudimentary (and in time replaced by the box respirator already used by some Machine Gun crews).

Known as a smoke helmet, it was a flannel hood, with two round glass eye pieces; inside was a flat breathing tube to go in the mouth, connected to a rubber valve on the outside of the helmet. The flannel material was impregnated with anti-gas chemicals Sodium-Phenate and Hexamethalyne-Tetramine. The bottom of the helmet had to be tucked in the top of the tunic for the helmet to be effective. It worked by the wearer breathing in through the nose, through the fabric, and out through the mouth via the tube. It was a crude, clumsy arrangement that demanded practice; unfortunately, use of the helmet, during practice as well as in a gas attack, diminished the level of protective chemical. The intricacies involved of using these helmets is described by an American serving with the 56th (London) Division, Arthur Guy Empey:

Gas travels quietly, so you must not lose any time; you generally have about eighteen or twenty seconds in which to adjust your gas helmet. A gas helmet is made of cloth, treated with chemicals. There are two windows, or glass eyes, in it, through which you can see. Inside there is a rubber-covered tube, which goes in the mouth. You breathe through your nose; the gas, passing through the cloth helmet, is neutralized by the action of the chemicals. The foul air is exhaled through the tube in the mouth, this tube being so constructed that it prevents the inhaling of the outside air or gas. One helmet is good for five hours of the strongest gas. Each Tommy carries two of them slung around his shoulder in a waterproof canvas bag. He must wear this bag at all times, even while sleeping. To change a defective helmet, you take out the new one, hold your breath, pull the old one off, placing the new one over your head, tucking in the loose ends under the collar of your tunic.[27]

The previous year John Lucy had received:

Instruction in protection against poison gas was given to us ... I imagine that none of these P.H. helmets as they were called, would have been of any earthly use except against tear gas, but the fact of having some gadget gave us spurious confidence, which was maintained by the repeated publication of Army Orders extolling the efficacy of the masks.
   I am grateful that we never had to test the masks in battle.[28]

Major General O.H.D. Nicholson's report (General Staff, First Army) dated 5 May 1916 set out six reasons why men were gassed the week before, the first of which commenced:

The helmet was not put on quickly enough. This was probably the result of the helmets being carried in the satchels, instead of being rolled up on the head.[29]

The satchels in which the helmets were carried had an inner as well as an outer cover. The inner cover was designed to keep the helmet lubricated by the protective chemicals; wearing the helmets for long enough rolled up on the head would counteract the integrity of the performance. Obviously there was a fine balancing act to be achieved between being prepared quickly enough for an attack and being prepared for an attack with uncompromised equipment; 48th Infantry Brigade reported gas helmets being too dry and four authentic cases of men gassed dead with their helmets on after the attack of the 29 April.[30]
   Many of the reports issued in the days following both gas attacks arrived at a similar conclusion with regard to gas helmets. Major General Nicholson stated:

Where helmets and box respirators were inspected adequately, adjusted properly, put on in time and not taken off too soon, they were found to give sufficient protection.[31]

In fact, there were variations in the performance of the gas helmets; the one simplistic reason for the high number of casualties for the 16th (Irish) Division is where troops were located in relation to the release of a high concentration of gas from cylinders. The obvious conclusion drawn by Staff Officers located behind the front line, that helmets should be put on promptly and remain on, is valid in a situation where gas is released with plenty of warning, with no prior artillery bombardment, and all the men had to do was sit calmly and wait for it to clear, while the enemy also sat equally quietly opposite. Quite evidently this wasn't so. Moreover, fully functioning gas helmets were crucial and, tellingly, 16,000 new helmets were issued in the Loos sector after 27 April 1916.[32]

Whilst reports criticise men for taking their helmets off too early, Lieutenant General L.E. Kiggell, Chief of the General Staff, First Army, in his report on the first gas attack on 27 April, notes mitigating circumstances. He refers to a ruse played by the Germans in delivering an innocuous, mostly smoke cloud, first, before a very strong gas cloud, by which time a few men had been fooled into taking their helmets off.[33]

Irrespective of the cause, the 16th (Irish) Division was not the only Division to suffer. The historian of the 15th (Scottish) Division records:

On the 29th another, and very different, gas attack took place. This time it was directed mainly against the line held by the 16th (Irish) Division on the south, the northern edge of the cloud only passing over the right battalion of the 44th Brigade (9th Black Watch.) This time the gas was much stronger, and not mixed with smoke as it had been before. It was very difficult to see, and the Black Watch suffered a good many casualties from a change of wind which blew the gas back over their area after the men had removed their masks.[34]

The casualties were 107 men killed and wounded, mostly in the Black Watch, of whom two officers and sixteen Other Ranks were killed.[35]

Willie Doyle passed a few remarks to his father in letters home that are odd – and not just for the reason that his letters appear to be uncensored. He said in his letter of 3 May 1916 that he thought the Bosche had given up the deployment of gas, and that as the helmet is a bit heavy he nearly didn't take it with him when he set out to walk to the village early that morning of the 27 April. In fact, he says he had never even had the helmet on before. Fr Doyle, it must be remembered, was a bit of a maverick who was often reprimanded for his careless attitude to his own safety. In addition, Willie could have been embellishing his story to add melodramatic value, as he surely must have been aware of the gas alerts and precautions that had been put into place. Nevertheless, he also goes on to say that some men did not bother putting on their helmets, or had torn them, or cast them aside or lost them. These are disturbing comments indeed, but which could indicate, rather than a lack of discipline, the confusion and chaos caused by the smoke cloud, followed by a high concentration gas cloud, and the fact that some equipment just was not fit for purpose, and the wearers knew it.

The two issues – of timing being crucial, and that of defective equipment, was not confined to the Irish casualties in April. Arthur Guy Empey was wearing his helmet during a gas attack at Ypres a few days later when it started to leak and he had to change it:

*Suddenly, my head seemed to burst from a loud 'crack' in my ear. Then my head began to swim, throat got dry, and a heavy pressure on the lungs warned me that my helmet **was leaking**. Turning my gun over to No. 2, I changed helmets. The trench started to wind like a snake, and sandbags appeared to be floating in the air. The noise was horrible; I sank onto the fire step, needles seemed to be pricking my flesh, then blackness. I was awakened by one of my mates removing my smoke helmet. How delicious that cool, fresh air felt in my lungs. A strong wind had arisen and dispersed the gas. They told me that I had been 'out' for three hours; they thought I was dead.*[36]

The Reverend Pat Leonard, working in the same sector as Empey, noted in his diary on 1 May 1916:

At 1am all the guns in the neighbourhood gunned with colossal speed & noise, and hard on the heels of the first salvo began a great clanging of gongs – the dread signal that the Germans were making a gas attack.... After breakfast I got word that some cases were coming down to the Field Ambulance from the trenches where the attack had been made, so I hurried down to see if I could do anything. Nothing that I have ever read prepared me for the agonising sight that I saw. There were some twelve or thirteen men lying on their stretchers in tents, writhing in their gasping efforts to get their breath and tearing at their throats, coughing and moaning and wrestling with the poison. I never shall forget their damp greenish faces, *contorted with pain and flecked with froth which continually forms at their mouths.*³⁷

On Friday 5 May 1916, after most reports had been compiled in the 16th (Irish) Division sector, the Commander-in-Chief of British forces, General Sir Douglas Haig, visited the Division. He observed that the gas attacks: *seem to have been the most severe which we have yet encountered. The Irishmen did very well.*³⁸

One incident, though, leaves no doubt of indiscipline, but relates to a report about a Scottish battalion of Cameronians:

> *On the morning of the 27th, just at dawn, we experienced our first gas attack, but the release of the gas developed mainly upon the Irish Division which was holding the trenches on the right of the Hulluch Road. The story is told of how two of our men, in one of the front lines both claimed the same gas-mask, and solemnly fought it out with their fists while the gas steamed overhead. Of course the gas mask was torn to bits, but those two warriors, who, by all the theories of science, should have been as dead as roast pork, emerged unscathed from the fray.*³⁹

First Army reports, in particular, and other reports at the time, were adamant that the P.H. helmets functioned properly when used correctly. This initially seems to be borne out years later in the history of The Special Gas Brigade, which states that the helmets: *gave absolute protection against much higher concentrations of gas than could be experienced from a gas cloud, provided that they were in good condition and properly adjusted in time.*⁴⁰ Curiously, however, the words 'absolute protection' later gave way to noting that none of the P, P.H. or P.H.G. helmets were: *as efficient as the box respirator which was introduced later.*⁴¹ ᶠᴺ¹

One of the official Historian of the Great War, Brigadier General Sir James E. Edmonds, reviewed the gas attacks, and also the one (noted by the Rev Leonard) that took place at Wulverghem near Ypres on 30 April 1916. He notes in the latter instance that:

> *The prospect of a gas attack in daylight, with **no more protection than the P.H. helmet** and the enemy little more than a stone's throw away, was bad enough ...*⁴²

These contradictory reflections after the war give pause for thought, without even knowing the conclusions drawn by Edmonds about the issue of alleged bad gas discipline at Loos:

> *All units practised gas alerts daily... The gas alert, for which everyone was ready, was given ... It was light when the gas clouds were released, and the men of the 16th Division had full warning and were ready – not a dead man was found without his helmet properly on – yet the gas casualties were somewhat heavy. Although it was not admitted at the time, and the casualties were unjustly attributed to the bad gas discipline of the 16th Division,* **the helmet was obviously insufficient protection** *against the strong concentration of gas which the enemy was able to produce, the heaviest incidence of casualties and the highest mortality occurring at those parts of the front line nearest to the enemy's trenches. The manufacture of the gas respirators, therefore, was pushed on with all speed.*[43]

Unfortunately, despite these findings, inflammatory statements post-war, alleging non-existent gas discipline, along the lines of 'wild Irishmen' completely losing their heads and severe casualties due to the 'Irish temperament', had already been made by former personnel of 12th and 15th Divisions and I Corps.[44]

Returning to 1916, normal routines were re-established after the gas attacks and the resultant mess cleared up. Lieutenant Lyon of 7th Leinsters was one of the officers responsible for burial parties on the 27 April, a most gruesome task collecting dead comrades: ... *in all sorts of tragic attitudes, some of them holding hands like children in the dark,*[45] whilst at the same time being pestered by: *half-poisoned rats by the hundred.*[46] His colleague, Captain Staniforth, noted the effect of gas on equipment, which then had to be promptly cleaned: *every rifle, machine gun, cartridge, bandolier, telephone wire, and metal of any sort turns a dull arsenic green, with a corroding film.*[47]

The evening of the second gas attack on 29 April bought relief for the 7th Royal Inniskilling Fusiliers:

> *The battalion was relieved on the same night by the 7th Camerons and moved into Philosophe West. The 8th R.I.F., who had come out of the line*

the night before, provided us with a hot meal and, thanks to their hospitality, billets also, and sleep was appreciated by us all.

The following day was spent by the orderly room in estimating and checking casualty returns, collecting and collating reports from the companies, and consolidating various returns and indents for lost and damaged material. The men spent their day washing and shaving, and generally cleaning up arms and equipment. Buttons had been rendered black by the action of the gas, and rifles were to a large extent polluted by it.[48]

Way back beyond the line Captain J.C. Dunn, 2nd Bn Royal Welch Fusiliers had previously noted diluted gas creeping along the ground below standing height and described its effect on the surroundings:

Horses and tethered cattle were startled, and tugged at their head-ropes. A little dog on a heavy chain, unable to scramble on to his kennel, ran about frantically; hens flew on to walls and outhouses, clucking loudly; little chickens stood on tiptoe, craning to raise their gaping beaks above the vapour; mice came out of their holes, one climbed the gable of a barn only to fall back when near the top. Seedling peas and other vegetables were bleached, and wilted. Bethune buzzed with excitement, we were told, and pealed every bell.[49]

In the ensuing days of May 1916 Willie Doyle and his flock were moved even further back. His letter, started on Saturday 13 May, after referring to recovering from the gas, continues:

I paid a visit recently to another wonder of the war, the church of Vermelles. Little remains of it now, for the town has been held in succession by the Germans, French and ourselves, and every yard of ground was lost and won a dozen times. The church is just a heap of ruins: the roof has been burnt, the tower shot away, while the statues, Stations etc. are smashed to dust, but hanging still on one of the broken walls is a large crucifix absolutely untouched. The figure is a beautiful one, a work of art, and the face of Our Lord has an expression of sadness such as I have never seen before. The eyes are open, gazing as it were upon the scene of desolation, and though the wall upon which the crucifix hangs is riddled with bullet holes and shell splinters, the image is untouched save for one round bullet hole just through the heart. The whole thing may be only chance, but it is a striking sight and cannot fail to impress one, and brings home the fact that if God is scourging the world, as it well deserves, He is not indifferent to the sorrows and sufferings of His children.[50]

Willie breaks off this letter to hear confessions and next day, following church service. He resumes:

Sunday 14th: *I was not able to finish this yesterday as the men kept me going 'scraping their kettles.' (I wish mine was half as clean as some of theirs.) Between 600 and 700 men were at Holy Communion this morning, the last probably for many of them, for we are due back in the trenches tomorrow, though the part we are going to is quiet compared with the last position we held.*

One cannot help feeling proud of our Irish lads, everyone loves them – the French girls, naturally, that goes without saying, as poor Aunt Polly would have written; the shopkeepers love them for their simplicity in paying about five times the real value of the goods; Monsieur le Curé would hug them each and everyone if he could, for he has been simply raking in the coin these days, many a one putting three and five franc notes in the plate, to make up, I suppose, for the trouser buttons of the knowing ones; and surely our Blessed Lord loves them best of all for their simple, unaffected piety which brings crowds of them at all hours of the day to visit Him in the Tabernacle. Need I add that the Padre himself has a warm corner in his heart for his boys, as I think they have for him, judging by their anxiety when the report spread that I had got knocked out in the gas attack. They are as proud as punch to have the chaplain with them in the trenches: it is quite amusing to hear them point out my dug-out to strangers as they go by: 'That's <u>our</u> priest,' with special emphasis on the our.[51]

He ends his letter with a bit of news:

> *My Dear Father Let me end up this note with a little bit of news, which I mention because I think it will please and gratify you: I have just been told (unofficially) that my name has been sent on to the Commander-in-Chief for 'Mention in Dispatches'. I hope the Angels have done their work as well and that I shall get a little corner in their report to Head Quarters. This is only for yourself.*[52]

The 'M.I.D.' was not gazetted until 4 January 1917, being one of many that were grouped together in one special edition of the *London Gazette*.[53]

Footnote 1: The letters assigned to the three sack type gas helmets refer to the type of chemical in which the cloth had been impregnated. The small box respirator was a self-contained unit, which had a close-fitting rubberised mask with eyepieces and a mouthpiece connected via a hose to a box filter, which contained granules of chemicals that neutralised the gas.

CHAPTER 17
EASTER RISING:
'WAS IT NEEDLESS DEATH AFTER ALL?'[1]

Now and in time to be,
Wherever green is worn,
... changed, changed utterly:
A terrible beauty is born[2]

The budget Willie Doyle commenced writing to his father on Saturday 13 May 1916 ended with the news he was to be 'Mentioned in Dispatches.' It had begun, however, by referring to the Easter Rising, before going into further details about the gas attack. On the Easter Rising in Dublin he comments:

> *I was on the point of writing to you when your ever welcome letter reached me – a thousand thanks for it (you cannot imagine how welcome your letters are) and also for the paper giving an account of the dreadful riots in Dublin. I am glad I was safe in the trenches during that time, for apparently the Bosches cannot hold a candle to the Sinn Feiners.*[3]

Willie Doyle may have been serving in the British Army but there had been previous testimony of his burning love for Ireland and opposition to British policies. Just before his twenty-seventh birthday, whilst at Stonyhurst College in Lancashire, he gleefully celebrated a British set-back in the Boer War in February 1900. There had been substantial Irish opposition to the Boer War, especially in the Dublin area, the same area which saw the gestation of the Easter Rising. Historically, the Catholic Church had always been opposed to Republicanism, which may not necessarily have influenced Willie, who did not object to being labelled a Fenian (a member of an Irish Republican group founded in America in 1858) by one of the Lay Brothers of the college.

This patriotism notwithstanding, from all that we know of his character, Fr Doyle instinctively opted for the rule of law over that of a mob, no matter how just the cause. And 'mob rule' is how the instigators' of the 'rebellion' were portrayed by the middle-class press, such as the *Irish Independent,* who represented Catholic business interests (businesses were badly disrupted for days) and the pro-Union *The Irish Times.* In County Louth, *The Drogheda Independent's* editorial on 2 May 1916 ran thus:

> *It would appear that an armed conjunction of the Liberty Hall heroes, with some of the Sinn Fein Volunteers, has made an attempt at some kind of miserable rising. The King's troops and the police force have now got the Larkinites and the Sinn Feiners well in hand, and the ridiculous 'rising' has been crushed and broken.*[4]

A small military council of the leaders of the Irish Republican Brotherhood formed an alliance with the socialist Irish Citizen Army, aiming to overthrow British rule in Ireland. The rank and file of the rebels were drawn largely from the Irish Volunteers, the rump of the Irish National Volunteers, which broke away when John Redmond declared he was paving the way for the I.N.V. to go to war, serving with the British Army. Other organisations were also involved in the Rising, but the rebels tended to be labelled with one universal name, Sinn Fein, although this was a misleading term. The fact that there was a range of groups and competing personalities lead to disorganisation, confusion and a split in the leadership, which was compounded by sheer bad luck, and ultimately the collapse of the rising.

Yet it all started well, catching much of the British garrison unawares. Frank Laird, who had served and was wounded in Gallipoli, had been assigned to the 10th Royal Dublin Fusiliers in the Royal Barracks Dublin. He remembered that:

> *Just before Easter 1916, a special emergency body was formed of those who had seen service. We were instructed to fall in at a moment's notice when the alarm was sounded, and to this end we had alarms sounded at odd times, when we had to rush on the parade ground at our best speed, induing our accoutrements and arms as we went.*
>
> *In spite of these warnings of the coming storm, Easter Monday found us unsuspicious. I had managed to leave barracks early in the day and gone to my wife's home to go for a walk up the Dublin mountains with some friends. Just before we started my mother-in-law came in and said a tram conductor*

had told her the rebels had taken the G.P.O. We thought nothing of it and set out for Milltown station. After waiting some time vainly for a train we were informed by a man who walked up the line that the rebels had taken Harcourt Street station.[5]

Viewed from his position over in war-torn France, as far as Willie Doyle was concerned, there was no excuse for the mayhem caused by the rebels:

One good result will follow from what has happened: the ridding of Dublin of a most undesirable element which was doing much harm among our ignorant people. Incidentally, I am chuckling to myself over those that said that 'Retreats for working men' were not needed in Ireland, and I hope the project will be helped by these sad scenes.[6]

Sad scenes they were indeed for the ordinary peaceable population of Dublin. Although, initially, when the fighting first broke out, curious crowds of citizens gathered to watch the events unfolding, as if they were spectators at a sporting event. At the turn of the 21st Century, Irish Historian Tim Pat Coogan interviewed:

Mabel Fox, who lived in Rialto near the South Dublin Union (now St James's Hospital), told me her memory of being taken as a six-year-old by her father to see the soldiers firing on rebel-held positions in the Union. 'I remember peeping out from under his coat, holding his hand. The bullets were flying. It was very exciting.'[7]

Another child of a similar age, May Hanaphy, had a different reaction, as told to oral historian Kevin C. Kearns nearly eighty years after the event:

And I remember the rebellion so well because there was a policeman down at the very end of Ship Street we used to call 'Daddy' and he was shot and we were horrified.[8]

Monk Gibbon, serving with the Army Service Corps, was the son of a Church of Ireland rector in the Dundrum area of south Dublin; he joined up at the outbreak of war and was in Dublin when the Rising started. He observed that:

> *For the duration of the rebellion it could be said that the sympathies of all parts of Dublin, including the slums, were on our side. There were far too many Dubliners fighting with Irish regiments, in France and elsewhere, for the population to feel that this was the right moment to embarrass England. The insurrection had little approval.*⁹

Before too long the excitement shared by many citizens gave way to blinding realisation that this was not a game, as stray bullets killed civilians, the centre of Dublin was gutted (61,000 square yards of buildings destroyed) and all normal routines came to a complete halt:

> *Traffic had ceased, shops, cinemas and theatres had closed, the post had stopped, even the 'very clocks on the public buildings had stopped because there was no one to wind them up' The tramways came to a halt on Monday, and even street lighting (already reduced by a cash-strapped Dublin Corporation) was cut off. Works closed down, and wages dried up; banks closed too, but even people with money found it hard to buy food.*¹⁰

The 178th Brigade, 59th North Midland Division, of the British Army helped quash the Rising and it was observed that:

> *By the time the rebellion collapsed there was considerable shortage of food in Dublin, and bread carts were looted in full view of the guards at the Royal Hospital.*¹¹

Some citizens tried to carry on as normal and soldiers of 177th Brigade south of Dublin were distracted from their military duty:

> *Within the cordon formed by our troops a savage war was being waged – incessant rifle firing, bursting of bombs and burning houses – whilst outside an enterprising tradesman was occasionally heard going round with the milk!... At Balls Bridge – where some Battalions were stationed – a cattle show was in progress. With true philosophy the persons responsible for the show, being prevented from moving the various beasts away, were 'carrying on'; the exhibits being frequently, and critically, studied by soldier experts*

from the farms of Lincolnshire and Leicestershire.[12]

Other people, far from even trying to carry on as normal, poured into the mix of chaos, confusion, death and devastation - adding looting, drunkenness and wanton destruction, largely by the poverty-stricken underclass of the Dublin slums.

May Hanaphy remembered:

Then the looting started. Now my Ma wouldn't allow us outside the street when the trouble started. But my brothers were older than us and they went with a crowd of fellas down Grafton Street and it was terrible they told my mother. People were getting trampled on when they were looting, taking things out of the shops. It was shocking. Anyone was doing it. See, we were curtailed for food during the Rebellion and there was nothing coming to anybody. They smashed all the windows in Grafton Street and they had all the best quality of stuff ... they were bringing up pianos on carts ... and chairs ... Beautiful chairs.[13]

Ernie O'Malley remembered:

... shops had been looted. Lawrence's Toy Bazaar and some jewellers... Diamond rings and pocketfuls of gold watches were selling for sixpence and a shilling, and one was cursed if one did not buy ...Women and girls wore rings on every finger ...Ragged boys ... tramped up and down with air rifles on their shoulders or played cowboys and Indians armed with black pistols supplied with long rows of paper caps ... Little girls hugged teddy bears and dolls as if they could hardly believe their good fortune ... Some of the women with wispy, greasy hair and blousy figures, walked around in evening dress. Young girls wore silk dresses ... In the back streets men and women sprawled about, drunk, piles of empty and smashed bottles lying around.[14]

Privation drove these people to join in, amongst whom were some wives of soldiers serving with the British forces, known as 'separation women,' whose only income was the separation allowance. When, eventually, the rebellion was quashed and prisoners transported through the streets of Dublin, cat-calls from separation women followed them:

Bleedin' bastards, my husband's out in the war fightin' for you bow-sies and yiz go and yiz stab them in the back.' 'Yiz are too cowardly to fight, and too lazy to work.[15]

On the other hand, the 178th Brigade reported on the bravery of rebels, following a grim duty that the North Midlanders had to carry out:

At 3 a.m. on the 3 May three of the ringleaders of the rebellion were shot, the execution being carried out by the Brigade. They met their fate bravely.[16]

178th Brigade had previously noted on Wednesday 26 April:

That the general feeling of the people was against the Sinn Feiners was clear from the fact that they streamed out from alleys and courtyards and cheered 'the Ginerel' as the Brigade Commander went up Lower Mount Street, which was brilliantly illuminated by the flames from Clan-William House.[17]

Irish soldiers serving in Irish regiments also took part in quelling the rebellion in Dublin City centre. The 3rd Bn Royal Irish Regiment was garrisoned at Richmond Barracks, 10th Bn Royal Dublin Fusiliers at Royal Barracks and 3rd Bn Royal Irish Rifles at Portobello. The 5th Leinsters were at the Curragh when orders were received on Easter Monday for every available officer and man to proceed to Dublin as part of a mobile column. Elsewhere, Subalterns of 3rd Leinsters were at the Young Officers Corps at Fermoy, and were dispatched to Wexford to guard the munitions factory and other strategic points. Later they were divided into flying columns and were engaged in rounding up suspects. The 4th Leinsters were at Limerick when the Rising broke out:

The news of the seizure by the rebels of the General Post Office in Dublin on Easter Sunday, 23 April, reached Sir A. Weldon at 4.30 p.m. the following afternoon, and within twenty minutes the Battalion – strength 49 officers and 490 other ranks – turned out with 120 rounds per man. All communication with Dublin had now been severed, but the telephone to headquarters, Queenstown, was intact. The Battalion remained under arms all night and as the wildest rumours were afloat the commanding officer visited the police authorities from whom was gathered tidings of the serious state of affairs in County Galway. Picquets were now sent to hold the post office, gaol and the railway bridge across the Shannon.[18]

Two days into the Rising, Major General L.B. Friend (Commanding Troops, Ireland) issued a proclamation of Martial Law, which started with the order that:

All persons in Dublin City and County shall keep within their houses between the hours of 7.30 p.m. in the evening and 5.30 a.m. on the next morning, on all days until further notice ...[19]

Dalkey in south County Dublin was as peaceful as ever, but one surprising person to be significantly affected by the general turmoil (other than the inconvenience of the curfew) was Willie's father. Hugh Doyle may have been in his 84th year, but he was still employed as Chief Clerk in the Bankruptcy Court, Dublin (he actually retired in 1922 aged 90 after 73 years' service.) The Four Courts district of Dublin was a strongpoint for the rebels, being on the Quays and in a position to impede the movement of British troops from the Royal Barracks further along the River Liffey to the west. The 1st Battalion of Volunteer rebels, one of four strategically placed in the city, established a garrison in the Four Courts on Easter Monday 1916, until the breakdown of the Rising and surrender the following Saturday. Hugh must surely have not made any attempt to travel into Dublin, instead staying safely at *Melrose* until after the Rising had collapsed.

For the next ten days the South Staffordshire Regiment combed the Four Courts area looking for general military debris (of which they made significant finds) and rebels who had defied the surrender order (of whom they found none.) Unfortunately, Hugh Doyle's side of the correspondence between him and his son has not been located, so we know nothing of his reaction to the Rising and his enforced absence from the Four Courts. Willie also quickly moved on to other topics in his correspondence; the issue of the gas attacks being more pressing in his world than the Easter Rising.

At the time the Rising took place there was a range of reactions from serving Irishmen at the Front, most, like Willie Doyle, against it or simply bewildered. Eighteen year old Lieutenant Emmet Dalton, 9th Royal Dublin Fusiliers, went on to win the Military Cross for valour at the Somme a few months after the Rising; a few years after the war ended he was a General in the IRA. He said:

> *I thought the insurrection was a mistake, but then I think the rest of the world might have judged it to be a mistake at that time ... I thought that the insurrection as such was a hopeless gamble because it had no earthly hope of success as far as I could see ... I can only speak of the people that I met and associated with at that time, and they were my contemporaries in the war and looked askance at the 1916 Rising ... I think it should never have happened. I think if it had not happened the Home Rule Bill ... could have been achieved ...*[20]

Lieutenant Noel Drury, a southern Protestant committed to the union was, naturally, equally as scathing about the Rising, but also claimed to represent the opinion of his mainly Catholic battalion, 6th Royal Dublin Fusiliers:

> *We got the most astonishing news on the 27th that a rebellion has broken out in Ireland. Isn't it awful? Goodness knows what they think they are going to gain by it. It's a regular stab in the back for our fellows out here, who don't know how their people at home are ... I don't know how we will be able to hold our heads up here as we are sure to be looked upon with suspicion. The men are mad about it all, but don't understand who is mixed up in the affair.*[21]

Mostly the Irishmen had no time or inclination to dwell on the matter. Lieutenant Michael Fitzgerald of the Irish Guards was training in England at the time:

> *Curiously enough, that was not talked about at all. On Easter Monday 1916 I was one of a battalion of Irish Guards marching near Worley in Essex. We passed by the newspaper shops as we marched along and, of course, saw what were the headlines on the billboards, 'Rebellion in Ireland – Heavy Casualties' or something like that. We looked at one another. When we got back to our rooms, of course, we discussed it briefly. We were angry, but we didn't know the whole story, so we got on with our ordinary conversations until we could get the whole story. But I must say we were not impressed*

by the whole thing. We were too preoccupied with what was in front of us and what we had to do, and we were committed to what we had to do, and whatever might happen in Ireland after we'd gone we could do nothing about that. That was our attitude.[22]

An Irish officer with the 1st Bn Irish Guards (the Irish Guards being the senior Irish regiment, recruited from all over Ireland, but strongly rural catholic) remembered:

It must, I suppose, have been in the late spring or early summer in 1916 that news reached us of the Easter Rising in Dublin; I am uncertain for the good reason that it made no impact on the men of the battalion. All company officers got to know their men ... one took part in countless discussions and could not help overhearing the men discussing things amongst themselves, but I can recollect no talk about the Rising or its implications. Perhaps the problems, all day and every day, of staying alive made news from home unreal and irrelevant. If there were differing views among guardsmen on the future of Ireland, they were as unimportant on active service as the fact that the battalion contained protestants amongst its massive majority of catholics.[23]

However, some Irish sympathies were expressed for the Rising. Tom Barry went to war as a young man for adventure, before becoming radicalised and subsequently joining the IRA, after his exploits with the British Army came to an end at the finish of the war. He read the news of the Rising in a bulletin posted in his unit's orderly room, whilst serving with the Royal Artillery in Mesopotamia:

It was a rude awakening, guns being fired at people of my own race by soldiers of the same army with which I was serving.[24]

On the other hand, Private F. Nulty from Drogheda wrote to his local paper, the *Drogheda Independent*:

All the men from the town heartily agree with the measures taken to stop this rebellion said that even if it came to shooting down of our own countrymen it would be carried out to the letter.[25]

John Lucy profoundly disagreed:

> *My fellow soldiers had no great sympathy with the rebels, but they got fed up when they heard of the execution of the leaders. I experienced a cold fury, because I would see the whole British Empire damned sooner than hear of an Irishman being killed in his own country by an intruding stranger.*[26]

Lucy, who was awaiting a commission in June 1916 following a period of sick leave, was introduced to a sergeant of the firing-squad:

> *He was the first of a number of unhappy Englishmen who tried, and tried vainly, to square their acts against Ireland with me ... He described in detail the way the leaders met their death. I cannot remember them all because my blood was racing ... mentally I was wishing him and his like non-existent ... I also refused to drink with him.*[27]

Lieutenant Colonel Edward Bellingham, a Catholic from a land-owning family in County Louth, was the Officer Commanding 8th Royal Dublin Fusiliers in April 1916 and was sad to hear the news of the Easter Rising. Three days after the first shots were fired on Easter Monday in Dublin, his battalion took the brunt of the first German gas attack at Loos. He and his men were commended for their gallant stand by The GOC of 16th (Irish) Division, Major-General William Hickie. Subsequently, Lt Col Bellingham wrote to his father, asking him to express his profound sympathy to the families of five local men from close to the family estate, Castlebellingham, who lost their lives in the gas attack. The letter was published in the *Dundalk Independent* on 20 May 1916. Lt Col Bellingham also said:

> *We had heavy casualties, but 50 per cent will return eventually. Our men were furious with the Sinn Feiners and asked to be allowed to go and finish them up. We were defending the empire, with serious losses, the very day those people were trying to help the Germans that we were fighting. It is all too sad.*[28]

Reaction from British officers wasn't always fierce fury, as remembered by Ernie O'Malley. O'Malley was a republican Irish Volunteer whose brother was serving in the British Army; he also had friends in khaki and was tolerant of their motives for serving in the war, for which he was accused by his republican associates of fraternisation. Ernie recounts encounters with British officers:

> *They were indignant at what they misnamed the Sinn Fein Rebellion; but there was a half understanding; risings and attempted risings were part of the country. I heard an English officer say with dawning surprise: 'Why those people look upon us as the Belgians do the Germans.' He had been used to Ireland as a good hunting country in the same way that he looked upon Northern Scotland as a fine place for grouse, deer, fish, and the wearing of kilts.*[29]

Monk Gibbon, after initially condemning the Rising out of hand, began to have reservations following the execution of the leaders. He had a discussion with a fellow officer:

> *It would have been useless to point out to him that a traitor is someone who, having subscribed to a certain loyalty, subsequently turns his back on it. You cannot betray what you have always opposed. I enraged my companion by pointing this out to him. But his indignation soon passed. He refused to take me too seriously. The Irish were all mad. Supported by this premise, you did not allow yourself to be worried too much by any particular manifestation of their madness.*[30]

Back at Loos, in the Hulluch sector, the Germans in front of the 8th Bn Royal Munster Fusiliers nailed placards in relation to the rebellion to two poles in view of the Irishmen. They were invited to:

> *Throw away your arms; we give you a hearty welcome. We are Saxons. If you don't fire, we won't.*[31]

The invitation was declined:

> *The Munsters, Catholic and Nationalist to a man, reacted with that extraordinary characteristic which bemuses and bewilders Englishmen.*

First the Munsters replied firing shots into the placards. Then they sang God Save The King. A night patrol cut their way through the enemy's wire, strafed the Huns and captured the placards.[32]

Almost concurrent with the Easter Rising, the German gas attacks on two days in the Loos Sector left casualties of 570 killed from shelling and gas poisoning and 1,410 wounded. In comparison with the regular carnage on the Western Front the casualties of the Rising were not high. Tim Pat Coogan refers to some 1,350 people being killed or severely wounded in the Rising, which more or less ties in with the 1,306 stated in the history of the 2/7th Bn Sherwood Foresters, specified for the entire Rising as: 300 killed, 997 wounded and 9 missing. The casualty table shows the casualty rate for natives of Ireland (civilians, insurgents and police personnel) was nearly double that of British Army personnel (197 deaths compared to 103 - 640 wounded compared to 357.)[33] Compared to British Army units as a whole, four battalions of the Sherwood Foresters took the brunt of the casualties.

Between 3 May and 12 May 1916 thirteen men were executed at Kilmainham Jail, Dublin, shot for their part in the Rising. Many more sentences of execution were commuted as a tide of condemnatory opinion slowly swelled, breaking against the British Government and Army's handling of the whole aftermath of the Rising. This included the murder of a well-known, well-connected pacifist on the orders of a demented British army officer; the arbitrary nature of some of the rebel executions; together with the shooting of a badly wounded man, who had to be propped up in a chair, provoked particular revulsion. But that is another story. In the long term, the Easter Rising changed Irish history; in the short term it slowly started to impact on the lives of the Irish soldiers serving with the British Army.

Meantime, Willie Doyle opened up new chapter of adventures when he commenced writing his next budget home to his father on 22 May 1916, in which he makes no further mention of the Easter Rising.

CHAPTER 18
TRIPS AND RAIDS:
MOVING ALONG THE LINE

'War hath no fury like a non-combatant.' [1]

For the troops of the 16th (Irish) Division holding the line around Loos (as for many other British units) a perceptible change came over the Western Front during the weeks following Easter 1916, as the focus of operations began to shift southwards in preparation for the planned summer campaign on the Somme. True enough, the line at Loos had to continue to be manned, and local operations mounted, both to keep the enemy busy and dissuade him from moving troops south to reinforce the Somme garrisons.

As Willie Doyle often says in the next series of letters, life in the Loos sector was relatively uneventful (compared to the horrors of the gas attacks) but as more and more troops were concentrated further south in the Département of the Somme, hopes were raised and dashed several times that the 16th (Irish) Division would get the sustained break it was due and deserved. However, Willie just managed to squeeze in the leave of absence to which he was entitled before all such vacations were temporarily cancelled. Willie's letters during this period dwell on the hot weather, the tiredness of the men, his usual lucky escapes from shelling, and the final destruction of his haven at Mazingarbe, before the division started the trek south to the Somme.

Willie's next two letters home, dated 22 May and 19 June 1916, are positioned either side of his period of leave, during which he visited his father and sister in Ireland. It was during this holiday from the front that one of the last photographs of him was taken in his Military Chaplain's uniform. Standing at the bottom of the steps leading to the front porch of *Melrose*, Willie's benign, enigmatic smile belies his 43 years and the horrors he has witnessed. One assumes the photo was taken either on his arrival home or just before his departure back to France.

In the six months since Willie had taken up his appointment and joined his battalion at Witley Camp in England, his life had been crammed with so many

Fr Doyle on leave outside Melrose, 1916

incidents; but it must have felt like much more. His focus switching to his impending period of leave, Willie's excitement is palpable at the start of the letter advising of his departure from the Front:

> *At this present moment I feel just like a big schoolboy counting up the days till the holidays, for I have applied for leave of absence (10 days including the journey) to which we are entitled after three months service and I hope to get off on 2 June, the day we leave the trenches. My intention is to cross*

*via Rosslare and see Mai, not to mention other friends, before coming to Dublin.*²

Yet another colourful account follows:

Had you seen me last evening you might have thought I was sorry to leave Belle France, for I spent several hours weeping buckets-full, not crocodile tears by any means I can assure you. Our dear friends the Bosches flooded us with 'Weepers' so in gratitude for their generous gift we sat down and wept! It was a most ludicrous sight to see grizzled, old soldiers and dignified majors crying like so many school-girls, for though the lachrymous gas has no injurious affect, it makes one's eyes smart and simply stream with water. We are annoying Mr Hun a bit so he punished us in this way. We are going to be good in future and not give trouble.

I do not think I ever looked forward to a holiday with such keenness in my life before. At the present moment I am just 'fed-up' as we say out here with trench-trotting: the apparently never ending stream of soldiers and ceaseless sound of war-fare, and am longing for a few days calm and peace. Then there is no doubt that the life itself is a constant nerve strain, which tells on everyone, on myself less than others, naturally, as I am not exposed to the same amount of danger, but I am beginning to feel the effects of the past three months. To crown all the weather is intensely hot and sultry, which the glare of the chalk trenches does not tend to lessen, hence the prospect of 'Home sweet Home' very soon is just delightful.

*By the way you can do me a service. At present we are all spy-hunting, the country round is supposed to be full of them and the royal reward for the capture of one is 2,000 francs (£80) in cash, and a whole month's leave of absence. Will you come over here and do a little spying for the Kaiser? I shall arrest you – pocket the cash and spend a glorious month in Ireland. You of course will be shot, but that is only a matter of detail! I am open to unlimited offers!*³

Next follows bad news of the chapel at Mazingarbe that Fr Doyle was so fond of:

You will be sorry to hear that I have lost the good nuns and my little

Chapel. I call it 'mine' as it was associated with so many stirring events in my life at the front. I was on my way there the famous Sunday morning when the shells miraculously stopped falling on the road I had to pass. I was going to the same little chapel when the bombardment and gas attack of 27 April began, and several times I have said Mass at the Altar, which is now in fragments. A few mornings ago a big shell hit the chapel, burst inside, and literally blew it to bits, not a brick being left standing on another. It was the most complete bit of destructive work I have ever seen. I remember the poor nuns telling me that they had become so accustomed to the shelling they did not bother taking shelter in the cellar. For some reason or other (God's providence over them no doubt) they had gone down to the lower regions – Limbo only – this morning and so escaped without a scratch. I am very sorry to leave them, for we had become fast friends and more than once they had bound up my wounds, internal ones be it noted, pouring in rolls and coffee, hot and strong. I think I never met four pluckier women – three times they were sent away by the military authorities and as often came back. I should not be a bit surprised to find them one morning camped once more on the ruins of the convent.

I shall not delay this letter any longer (this is the 26th) but send it to you with my love. Don't forget the 'Camp Fires' under that pot of water which I asked you to get ready. If you like you can put the 'fatted calf' (I don't mean the cook) in it.[4]

Before Willie posted this letter he received one from his father and so a postscript was added to his letter by the good chaplain. (It is such a shame that we only have Willie's side of the correspondence!)

P.S. Your welcome letter of the 20th just arrived as I finished mine. I think I can count on leaving on the 2nd, but in any case it will only be a question of a few days. I shall let you know definitely later. All well. Things very quiet where we are. With all these prayers going on a fellow has no chance of getting hit. It's not fair I think![5]

There is now a longer break than usual between letters as Willie saves any further news until he reaches home. Fr Doyle's leave coincided with one of the battalions he was responsible for, 8th Royal Inniskilling Fusiliers, being away from the front Line, as noted by the historian of the 7th Royal Inniskilling Fusiliers:

> *The battalion was relieved by the 5th Royal Berks Regiment on the night 29–30 May ... To be relieved by a battalion of the 'Berks' was unusual. The reason for this was that the 8th Royal Inniskilling Fusiliers, who were generally our 'opposite number' for relief, had gone away for a fortnight to the seaside to recuperate after the gas attack of the 29 April.*[6]

The War Diary places the 8th Inniskillings firstly at Drouvin, a village in the Pas de Calais, and then 'under canvas' at nearby Condette, which was on the coast. They returned to Philosophe on 14 June 1916.

Unfortunately, there is no record of any adventures that may have befallen Fr Doyle en-route to Ireland, or many details of how his visits went to his family and friends back home. However, Willie's letter of 19 June 1916 does record a somewhat unusual route back to France:

> *My postcard will have told you of my pleasant crossing, both from Ireland and England, and of my safe arrival here on Thursday evening. On my way over I suddenly remembered a promise I had made, to visit the Sisters of St. Joseph at Newport, Mon., if at all possible and as I had a day to spare I thought I should not do better than drop down there. As luck would have it my ticket ran from 'Dublin to France' so I changed at Chester and went down South by the Great Western Railway.*
>
> *Ticket collectors looked rather puzzled to find me so far off the track, but I ended all argument by asking them to deny the fact that I was making my way, surely if slowly, towards France. Had I examined my ticket sooner I might have gone round by the North of Scotland, taken a dive for Cornwall, and so worked on towards the land of frogs and Frenchmen.*
>
> *I had a very warm welcome from the good Sisters, but unfortunately the Mother Provincial, whom I wanted to see, was away on visitation, and the girl whom I had sent to Newport as a novice was in another house some distance away, so I saw neither of them.*
>
> *The following morning I went to London, slept at Farm Street, crossed to Boulogne on Thursday, reaching Bethune about eight the same*

evening. My travelling companion was a corpulent Major who spent most of the journey getting outside a formidable pile of eatables, with which he provided himself, the whole being steadied by two large baskets of strawberries. For a while I feared he would 'burst' as the Yanks say, and then uncharitably I hoped he would, as I had had to run for my train and was starving in consequence, but my friend did not offer me a bite.

I put up in the hotel that night, and the next morning, Friday, made my way up to the trenches where the Brigade had gone.[7]

Just as Fr Doyle caught up with his flock in the Loos sector, another of his fortuitous escapades occurred:

I had barely got there when I met with an adventure, which at first I did not intend to mention, fearing it might make you more uneasy about me, but on reflection it seemed right that I should not keep from you this last mark of the good God's wonderful protection, which has been so manifest during the past four months.

I was standing in a trench, quite a long distance from the firing line, a spot almost as safe as Dalkey itself, talking to some of my men, when we heard in the distance the scream of a shell. It was evidently one of those random shots which Brother Fritz sends along from time to time, as no other came after it. We very soon became painfully aware that our visitor was heading for us and that if he did not explode in front of our trench his career would certainly come to an end close behind us. I did not feel uneasy for I knew we were practically safe from flying fragments which would pass over our head, but none of us had calculated that this gentleman had made up his mind to drop into the trench itself, a couple of paces from where I stood.

What really took place in the next ten seconds I cannot say: I was conscious of a terrible explosion and the thud of falling stones and debris. I thought the drums of my ears were split by the crash and I believe I was knocked down by the concussion, but when I jumped to my feet I found the two men, who were standing at my left hand, the side the shell fell, stretched on the ground dead, though I think I had time to give them absolution and the Last Sacraments. The poor fellow on my right was

> *lying badly wounded in the head, but though a bit stunned and dazed by the suddenness of the whole thing, I was absolutely untouched though covered with dirt and blood.*
>
> *My escape was nothing short of a miracle, for a moment before I was standing on the very spot where the shell fell, and had just moved away a couple of paces. I did not think it was possible for one to be so near a high explosive and not be killed, and even now I cannot account for my marvellous escape. In saying this I am not quite truthful, for I have not a doubt where the saving protection came from. I had made up my mind to consecrate some small hosts at my Mass the following morning, and put them in my pyx as usual, but as I walked through the little village on my way to the trenches the thought came to me that with so much danger about it would be well to have Our Blessed Lord's company and protection. I went into the church, opened the tabernacle, and with the Sacred Host resting on my heart set out confidently to face whatever lay before me: little did I think I was about to be so near death, or how much depended on that simple action.*[8]

Willie's next comment seems somewhat harsh in view of the fact that at least two men died in the incident he was describing. One can only ascribe it to the over-exuberance of his sincere devotion:

> *That is the explanation of the whole thing, I trusted Him, and I believe He just allowed this to happen, on the very first day I got back, to make me trust Him all the more, and have greater confidence in His loving protection.*[9]

Death and injuries remained a stark fact of Loos life, with new men and officers being drafted in to replace those that fell by the wayside. For example, at about this time a new subaltern, 2/ Lt C.L.Porteous, joined the battalion on 11 June, only to be injured by shelling twelve days later on 23 June.

There follows an insight into Willie's trip home. His sister Angelina (Lena) and her husband William had evidently acquired a motor car and Willie was taken for a spin in it. Subsequently he complained of some ailment to the nun of the family, Mary (Mai), who dosed him up with medicinal pills; and he was treated to plenty of good food at every establishment he visited:

> *Whether it is my trip, or Lena's motor, or Mai's vile pills, or the fearful feasting of those memorable days at home, I never felt better or fitter in my life. All the same I am hoping that my next trip will be the last and will see the end of this dreadful war, a thing which is not impossible. Au revoir, my time is up. Love to all.*[10]

Nine days later Willie briefly puts pen to paper again, writing to Hugh on 28ʲᵘⁿᵉ 1916, commenting on a new friend he had told his father about during his trip home, a replacement for the nuns who used to look after him at Mazingarbe:

> *We had a very uneventful time in the trenches, intense heat varied by much rain, which threatened to flood us out, so that I have little news to send you this time. We are back again in billets for a week, a rather busy time for me as the men take advantage of this to get to Confession and Holy Communion. As I told you, I have a great friend in this particular town, the 'Miller's daughter', who has a little room for me whenever I come, and does everything in her power to make me comfortable.*[11]

Fr Doyle had charmed the miller's daughter and was himself a good luck charm; most certainly he must have charmed his father with his pithy turn of phrase! He continues:

> *Though we are well behind the firing line, the Germans some days ago turned their long range guns upon the place and did a good deal of damage: one shell hit this house, came slick through the brick wall into my poor bedroom of all places (very shabby I call it) missed my bed by just an inch, took a dive through the floor of the room below, and having amused itself with the furniture, coolly walked out through the opposite wall without condescending to burst, in indignation I suppose because I was not there. No one was hurt and not much harm done. I have put the head of my bed in the hole in the wall, for it is a point of honour among shells not to come twice through the same spot, and in consequence sleep securely.*[12]

Willie then echoes the humour of Bruce Bairnsfather's *'Old Bill'* post cards, continuing:

I saw an amusing picture yesterday of two Tommies consulting 'Old Moore' to find out how long the war would last. 'I see Bill' says one 'by this 'ere book, that the seventh year of this b--- war is to be the worst, and after that the fourteenth.' I have come to the conclusion that by that time I shall have had enough of soldiering, and intend to resign my Commission in 1928 if not before.[13]

Bruce Bairnsfather cartoon 'Old Moore'

Bruce Bairnsfather was fifteen years younger than Willie Doyle, but they evidently shared the same sense of humour. Bairnsfather's background and education had naturally pushed him towards a military career, but in 1908 he changed direction to study at the John Hassall School of Art. He returned to the army and joined the Royal Warwickshire Regiment in 1914, serving as a machine-gun officer in France, until he was hospitalised in 1915. He was posted to a Staff job with 34th

Division on Salisbury Plain., where he continued submitting humorous cartoons for a weekly magazine, *Bystander*. The cartoons featured Bairnsfather's well-known BEF infantrymen characters 'Old Bill' and the much younger 'Alf'. These are the two Tommies Willie refers to, who were credited, despite official disapproval, with helping to maintain cheery morale amongst the troops.

Willie had recently received some gifts from home that Bill and Alfie might have appreciated – something to read and something to dispose of unwanted visitors, an insecticide called Keating's Powders, thoughtfully supplied by his practical minded sister-in-law:

> *All last week there was fearful slaughter in our trenches, in fact I am quite worn out carrying off the dead and burying them. To save time and trouble I made a big grave behind my dug-out and just pitched in the dead bodies anyhow, one on top of another – one gets very callous I fear during war – as I could feel no pity for the slain: I was helped in this much by a lady you well know, Jennie Doyle, as it was her tins of deadly explosives which laid this enemy low – I have only to say 'Keatings' once to make the foe flee (no joke intended). Au revoir for the present, many thanks for the magazine I asked you to send me.[14]*

Willie's next letter was to his sister, dearest Mai, on 8 July:

> *Ever so many grateful thanks for the grand box of rosaries which has just reached me and also for your more than welcome letter. You are too good to send me such a number of fine 'bades' as the poor fellows call them, and I need not say that if they were made of gold they could not have been more acceptable.[15]*

This was written seven days after the opening of what became, arguably, the defining campaign of the war, the Battles of the Somme. The history of the 7th Royal Inniskilling Fusiliers recorded a hive of activity in the Loos sector during the second half of June 1916, trying to put the enemy off the scent of what was building up further south in the Département of the Somme:

> *To appreciate the reasoning for this strengthening of the garrison, the*

sudden appearance of gas cylinders in the front line, and the recent attempts to raid the enemy for identifications, one must bear in mind that the British were on the eve of their Great Push, which, though more or less common knowledge that it would be launched somewhere south, yet every effort was being made along the whole British front to make the enemy believe that it wasn't where he might imagine it was going to be, and at the same time stop the enemy moving troops by our constant aggressive activity. With these points in view, it did not come as any surprise that we were ordered to dig assembly trenches under cover of darkness on the night of the 21st ... it was meant to make believe that we contemplated an attack on a large scale ... '[16]

One amusing incident was noted:

On the afternoon of our third day in Duke Street, the vigilant Hun observers must have spotted the activities of our shelter construction parties, and just to remind us there was a war on, they subjected us to ... salvoes of 5.9s, fired in quick succession. Luckily we managed to get clear without any casualties ... The staff captain at Brigade Headquarters was tactless enough to ring up the C.O. at this inopportune moment to enquire 'if he considered the present ration of sugar issued to the troops could be replaced by half the quantity of jam and part golden syrup'.[17]

While the British were trying to fool the Germans in the Loos sector, preparations were proceeding apace in the Somme area for the 'Big Push,' including a sustained and heavy seven-day bombardment of the German front line, which preceded the start of the main battle on Saturday 1 July 1916. The 16th (Irish) Division, however, took no part in the opening actions of the battle, as Willie explains to Mai:

I have little news which I can give you as the conditions of letter writing are very stringent. You will have seen by the papers that at last our big 'push', which has been so long and carefully prepared has at length started, and so far all is going well. The line of advance is a good distance from where we are, so that we are not much affected by the present struggle, but no doubt our time will soon come to move on the enemy who will have a hot time when the Irish boys get going.[18]

Willie then expresses sentiments similar to those which prompted Siegfried Sassoon to rail, in his poetry, against complacent men, tucked safely away the other side of the Channel, some of whom glorified the war. He goes on to reassure Mai about both his safety and the consolation to be found in the Catholic Church.

> *Naturally we know nothing of the plans, but it seems clear that this attack is to be pushed home with the determination of ending up this business once and for all: for everyone, except the gentlemen who sit in comfortable arm-chairs in London, is deadly sick of this long, wretched business. I hope you are not uneasy or anxious about my safety; there is little need to be so, for as far as the Blessed Curé d'Ars used to say 'Qui le bon Dieu garde est bien gardé', and certainly so far le bon Dieu has done His work well and will to the end I have not the smallest doubt.*
>
> *Though the life at times is rough and hard enough (at least the floor feels so at night) there are many consolations for a priest, not the least of which is the number of converts, both officers and men, coming into the Church. Many of them have never been in contact with Catholics before, knew nothing about the grandeur and beauty of our religion and, above all, have been immensely impressed by what the Catholic priests, alone of all the Chaplains on the Front, are able to do for their men, both living and dying. It is an admitted fact that the Irish Catholic soldier is the bravest and best man in a fight, but few know that he draws that courage from the strong Faith with which he is filled and the help which comes from the exercise of his religion.*
>
> *Will you please send this hasty line on to the dear Father as I shall not be able to write to him this week, though I owe him a letter also in return for his. If you are only half as well as this enfant, the doctor won't make a fortune out of you and your grave digger will be sodded years ahead. Everything kind to Rev. Mother and all the holy (and unholy) nuns.*[19]

Willie continues to be circumspect in his next letter to Hugh, writing from the brigade support position at Philosophe East on 14 July:

> *This morning I was sleeping the sleep of the tired, if not the just, in my cellar deep, when I was awakened by an unearthly crash. For a moment I*

thought it was the day of General Judgement and then I was certain of it, for I could hear the dead rising from their tombs, sending brick and clay and rubbish tumbling down the steps nearly on top of me.

I waited patiently for a blast or two of the Archangel's trumpet before rising, or at least the vision of a few resurrected Bosches whose uneasy spirits haunt my coal-hole, but as neither one nor the other made their appearance I decided to risk it being Resurrection Day and so turned over and went to sleep. Daylight revealed the fact that the disturbance was only the enemy saying his morning prayers in the shape of half a dozen high explosive shells, but it served to remind me that I owe you a letter even if the time for my budget was not due.

I wish however that friend Fritz had sent over some news with his dose of 'morning hate', for though we have rats and mice by the million, innumerable flies, which eat the jam off your bread before you can get it into your mouth, smells wondrous and varied, not to speak of other unmentionable things, the supply of news has sunk to vanishing point. You must be tired out by this time hearing 'I am well and fit and never felt better in my life' but facts are facts and there is my whole stock in trade of news, seeing that, like Washington, I never tell a lie – unless it turns in handy.

There are of course many little interesting things happening daily, but unfortunately regulations about writing military matters have become exceedingly strict, as much information seems to have leaked out in this way to the enemy. However, this line written on my knee, since I cannot boast the luxury of a table, will show you that in imitation of Johnnie Doolin's cat 'I am still alive and prowling, if not howling.' I hope you enjoyed your trip to dear Mai, but that is a foregone conclusion. Heaps of love dearest Father.[20]

It's not long before Willie gets back into his more detailed stride, writing another long letter to his father from billets in Mazingarbe on 20 July 1916:

If this letter does not reach you for some time, you must not put the blame on my poor head, but pour the vials of your wrath on the real culprits – the commander-in-chief! We have just come out of the trenches after our usual sixteen days 'hard labour' to begin a week of comparative rest, when like a bombshell came the news this morning that we are to return at once for two days, they say, but who knows? I pity the poor men, without sleep practically all that time, worn out, dirty and exhausted, shouldering their packs and facing off again for the same dreary round. They are wonderfully cheery over the whole business, but I fancy the Kaiser is being consigned (mentally at least) to a cosy corner somewhere 'out in France' by more than one weary Tommy.[21]

Willie continues, unsurprisingly, with the observation:

I had a couple of little adventures since last I wrote, coming through all, as usual, without hurt or harm, thank God.

I had occasion a short time ago to go to a certain village which our men were holding. The journey by 'the underground' otherwise 'trench street' would take a good couple of hours, whereas a quarter of an hour on a bicycle would cover the same distance following the high road. There was just one little inconvenience in choosing the latter route, viz the road was in full view of the German trenches, unpleasantly near as well, so that in daylight no one ever ventured that way unless he was anxious for a nice little cross over his head in the peaceful cemetery. Now, just at present, this child has not a burning ambition to fill a hole on French soil, but the case was urgent, speed was everything and there was no room for choice - the road in had to be trusted to Providence and a fast pair of heels, or rather wheels, would look after the German bullets.

The first part of the journey was uneventful: the road was up a slight hill, which hid me from any hostile observer, so I pedalled slowly in preparation for the coming burst down the other side. I had laid my plans carefully: I had calculated, and rightly, that since the road was not used in the daytime for the reason stated, Brother Fritz would not expect a visitor that way, and possibly might not trouble watching it, all the same I meant to keep my ears well cocked and at the first sound of a coming shell the bicycle might go where it liked but my billet was the bottom of the deep ditch where I would be as snug as a bug in a rug. As a matter of fact I had no fear from shells, big or little, as the artillery never fire at a single man, but they might.

Rifles and machine guns were both on the cards: the latter, if you lie flat on the ground, I knew were quite harmless, while as regards the former, I felt safe in betting a franc with my Guardian Angel that it would take a jolly good shot to hit me as I flew along at sixty miles an hour, more or less.

A few moments brought me to the top of the hill, and then right before me on the opposite slope were line after line of German trenches, about half a mile away. As I capped the rise, a thousand pairs of angry eyes, each more ferocious than the other, were fixed upon me: from every observation post and broken window, telescopes and glasses were thrust out, while mingled with the rattle of the rifle bolts and the sharp click of the gun breach, came the deep roll of guttural German curses. At least these were my sensations at the moment. You know the feeling, when having dined unwisely on a surfeit of lobster salad, you fall asleep on your back. For a little distance my road went straight down, every yard nearer and nearer the hidden enemy, and then turned sharply to the left, running parallel with the trenches. I was a little uneasy about this last bit of the trip, for each second increased the chance of being seen, and besides I was close to the Bosches without cover of any kind.

Down the hill I went like a hundred 'John Gilpins' but I had forgotten one thing: the surface of the road was pitted with shell holes which forced me to slacken speed and dodge and twist to get round them. Down I went, past the spot where some weeks before five of my poor boys had been blown to bits, thinking it was dark enough to venture up the road. I had buried their mangled bodies under cover of darkness, so I felt I had their protection now. It seemed very much like running into the Lion's jaws but all the time I had a strange feeling of security and rather enjoyed the adventure. At last the corner was reached: the ground was level and fairly good and you may guess I did not waste too much time getting up speed. So far all had gone well, not a single shot had been fired when suddenly I heard a rattle and a bang ----[22]

Willie then breaks off and Lena has transcribed his next few words of text in bold:

(To be continued in our next!)

Fearing you might not have the patience to wait till next week I resume the thrilling adventure of 'Chaplain Bill and his Bounding Bronco'.

I gave a groan, for I knew what had happened, the pump of my bicycle had jerked off (I had nearly done the same a moment before) and was lying in the middle of the road 20 yards behind. There was nothing for it: I jumped off, ran back, picked it up and mounted once more, deeply thankful that the Huns had missed their best chance of letting daylight through me. I don't know how Daniel in the Lion's den felt but I was mighty uncomfortable.

In a few minutes more I dashed into the village, to cover and safety, having ridden the whole way without one bullet being fired, probably because the Bosche did not think it worth his while wasting ammunition on a wretched chaplain. Judging by some remarks which have reached me since, people cannot make up their minds whether I am a hero or a fool (I vote for the second) but then they cannot understand what the salvation of even one soul means to a priest, so I just laugh and go my way, happy that I was in time.

My second adventure if I may style it was of a different kind: preparations had been made for the blowing up of a gigantic mine going under the German trenches, while at the same time our men were to make a raid, or night attack, on the enemy.[22a]

Raiding was a regular activity and the purpose is succinctly stated in the War Diary for the 8th RIF. Lt Col Watson, O.C., on 2 July set out the scheme for a battalion raid, its object being:

To inflict casualties on the enemy, capture prisoners, obtain identification, damage trench mortars and machine guns.[23]

There follow nine further headings: boundaries of the raid; strength of party; description of area to be raided; preparation; method of attack; timetable; the return signal; countersign; and dress and equipment. The personnel concerned then had nine days to prepare; there were to be two raiding parties, left and right, each consisting of two officers and thirty-three Other Ranks. When the time came, once all personnel had arrived at their appointed places, the timetable of the offensive on the morning of 11 July was recorded in Lt Col Watson's report as follows:-

01.16 bombing started
01.17 our guns opened fire
01.18 red rocket fired by enemy; enemy opened fire with artillery
01.20 green rocket fired by enemy
01.21 hostile machine gun fire opens
01.33 enemy opens artillery fire from a north east direction
01.50 our guns ceased
01.56 hostile artillery ceased

Although some intelligence was gathered about the enemy's trenches and the fact that some Germans were wearing steel helmets, whilst others wore soft round caps, the raid did not produce the desired results:

> *It is regretted that no prisoners or means of identification of the enemy was obtained.*[24]

The cost to the battalion was two men slightly wounded in the right party and heavier casualties in the left party. They had six men wounded, and two missing and both officers, Captain Barry Galvin and Lieutenant Gavin Paterson Bryars, were wounded. The battalion War Diary records:

> *Captain B. St.J. Galvin ... and Lieut G.P.Bryars ... were both wounded within a very short time of leaving the front trenches. This did not prevent these two officers from pushing on and gaining the enemy's trenches. They were both wounded again and Capt. Galvin fell when returning to our trenches and remained out on the Lens Road until his absence was discovered. Lieut A.E. Kinghan, 2nd Lt E.E. Sergint (7th Bn. R. Irish Fusiliers) 2nd Lt J.E. Rea and Capt. G.W. Eaton went out and carried in Capt. Galvin.*[25]

Captain Galvin sustained a perforating gun-shot wound to the right chest, the entrance being three inches from the right nipple and exiting at the posterior lower part of right chest; another entry wound was sustained in the left shoulder leaving numerous pieces of metal in soft tissue. Twenty-one year old Captain Galvin nearly died and was to keep Fr Doyle busy over the course of the next few days. However, Willie makes no mention of this as he continues:

The hour fixed was eleven o'clock, so shortly after ten I made my way up to the firing line where the attacking party were waiting. They were grouped in two bodies, one on either side of the mine, waiting for the explosion to rush over the parapet and seize the newly formed mine crater. As I went along the trench I could hear the men whisper 'Here's the priest' while the faces, which a moment before had been marked with the awful strain of the waiting, lit up with pleasure. As I gave them Absolution and the Blessing of God on their work, I could not help thinking how many a poor fellow would soon be stretched lifeless a few paces from where he stood: and though I ought to be hardened by this time, I found it hard to choke down the sadness which filled my heart. 'God Bless you Father, we're ready now' was enough reward for facing the danger, since every man realised that each moment was full of dreadful possibilities.

It was well known that the Germans were counter-mining and if they got wind would certainly try and explode their mine before ours. It was uncanny walking along knowing that at any moment you might find yourself sailing skywards, wafted by the gentle breath of four or five tons of explosives. Fortunately, nothing happened, but the moments were running out, so I hurried down the communication trench to the dressing station in a dug-out about 100 yards away, where I intended waiting for the wounded to be brought in.

On the stroke of eleven I climbed up the parapet out of the trench, and as I did there was a mighty roar in the bowels of the earth, the ground trembled and rocked and quivered, and then a huge column of clay and stones was shot hundreds of feet in the air. As the earth opened, dense clouds of smoke and flames burst out, an awful and never-to-be-forgotten sight. God help the poor fellows, even though they be our enemies, who were caught in that inferno and buried alive or blown to bits.

For a second there was a lull and then it seemed as if hell were let loose. Our artillery in the rear were standing ready, waiting for the signal: the moment the roar of the explosion was heard, every gun opened fire with a deafening crash. Already our men were over the parapet with a yell, which must have terrified the Bosches, up the side of the crater and were digging themselves in for their lives. Under cover of our guns the raiding party had raced for the enemy's trench, fought their way in and out again, as our object was not to gain ground.

By this time the enemy's guns had got into action and shells were coming over like hailstones, so on the principle that 'discretion is the better part of valour', I retired gracefully down my dug-out, 20 feet or more underground, and was soon busy with the wounded and dying.[26]

Fr Doyle's account and timings conflict with that of his commanding officer, Lt Col. Watson, whose report made it clear that no one from the battalion was killed and no prisoners were taken. However, it may be that other raids were being conducted simultaneously in that part of the Loos sector, leading to losses, or Willie's reference to the dying may just be one of the figures of speech he habitually used. He could have been confused on timings. Alternatively, he may have combined accounts of two different raids he had witnessed for dramatic impact. Although the 8th RIF may not have captured any prisoners, it may be that another unit did, either during this raid or a previous one, and the wounded man came under Fr Doyle's care:

One German prisoner, slightly wounded in a couple of places was carried in. Poor beggar he was certain his last hour had come, for he had been told the English kill all their prisoners. He was only a young lad and his teeth chattered with fear: I tried to get him to take a drink, but he pushed it away, thinking I suppose it was poison. How I wish that our Charles, with his Apostolic gift of tongues, had been near to tell him we mean no ill, for my knowledge of German is limited to 'der Hund', but the repetition of this word only increased his terror and convinced him we had sent for the dogs of war to tear him to pieces. By degrees I calmed him down and, with the help of a few French, Flemish and Latin words, found out that he was a Bavarian and a Catholic. I gave him a rosary, which he devoutly kissed and then hung it round his neck: and then evidently reassured that no harm would come to him with a priest by his side, he fell asleep. Next morning he asked to see the 'Pastor' and seemed anxious to thank me for the little I had been able to do for him.

It was nearly four when I got back to my cellar, tired enough I must confess, and sad at heart after the scenes I had just witnessed, but happy and thankful to God that I had the chance of speeding many a brave fellow on his way to eternity.

If the limit of your patience is not reached by this time, my time is, and hence I must take my bow and retire. The weather at present is very fine, though much on the warm side, to which few, I think, object. Where the days go to I cannot tell, but there is big consolation in the thought that every day that passes brings one nearer home and all the loved ones there.[27]

According to Lt Col. Watson's report of the raid, nearly all the casualties sustained by the left party of the 8th RIF were caused by machine-gun fire from the south side of Harrison's crater. Two weeks earlier, on 27 June, a raid in the area of the same crater had been undertaken by battalions of other Irish regiments. Lieutenant J.F.B. O'Sullivan, 6th Connaught Rangers, has left a fascinating account of the raid and the details of this raid seem more in keeping with some of Fr Doyle's account. [FN1]

Lieutenant O'Sullivan's 6th Connaught Rangers were in the same rotation scheme as the 8th RIF and on 31 July the latter relieved the former in the right sub-section of 14 BIS sector. That same day Willie Doyle wrote to Mai:

A wee line to thank you for your welcome letter and to greet you as you emerge from 'the desert', overflowing of course with spiritual delight. How I wish I had a bit of a desert here, at least the well and palm tree part with its cooling shade, for we are just frizzling at present, with I don't know how many degrees 'frying heat' as the old Brother in Clongowes called it, and frying heat it certainly is, buried in the chalk trenches. All the same I am thriving and if not exactly 'waxing fat' since nearly all the wax and fat have melted off, the bill of health is A1.

I sleep about 40 hours a day when I get the chance (at the present moment there are two huge 12 inch guns just beside me and even 40 winks are difficult.) I have ten meals regular, never thought I could face ten meals a day till I tried, wonderful what one can do, while my poor orderly has nearly emptied the well, leaving of course the six dead Germans behind, in his efforts to make tea. In a word I am doing well as far, at least, as the body is concerned, though the poor soul is in a bad way I fear.²⁸

Contrary to this light-hearted appraisal of his recent activities, Willie had been kept busy in at least one endeavour, attending to the needs of the wounded Captain Galvin. A few years after the war ended Barry Galvin's brother Daniel wrote to Professor Alfred O'Rahilly:

My brother and myself were great friends of Father Doyle's and between us we were with him the whole time he was in France, as he was first with my brother's regiment, then with mine. He gave my brother the last sacraments when he was badly wounded in a raid at Loos, and wrote to my father every day, until the doctor at the C.C.S. reported him out of danger.²⁹

Fr Doyle first wrote to Mr Galvin on 11 July 1917:

I am sorry to have to tell you that your son Barry was wounded last night while most gallantly leading an attack on the German lines ... you would feel proud of your son if you knew how splendidly he did his work; he was wounded trying to protect his men.³⁰

Captain Barry Galvin was eventually evacuated to base hospital at St Omer and then to the Kitchener Hospital in Brighton. The 8th RIF was notified on 16 August 1916 that Captain Galvin had been granted the Military Cross. He returned to duty in November 1916.[FN2]

Willie's letter continues and he comments about one of his pet mission projects in the Congo where he wanted to be a missionary. Although the language may seem insensitive for enlightened 21st Century susceptibilities, there is no doubting that earnest philanthropy is Willie's intention. His comment about Mai's conversion is intriguing, which would no doubt be explained if we had the other side of Willie's correspondence:

I am ever so glad the dear Father had a pleasant time with you and fine weather, he always enjoys a trip to Queenstown as indeed does another person whom I know, everyone is always so kind.

I do not know if I told you that the 'Black Baby Crusade', though now partly suspended, proved a great success. I got well over 1,000 half crowns, and as in some places a poor child can be bought for six pence there should be a goodly army of woolly black souls before the throne of God now. In addition, two priests, one in Scotland the other in Australia, have taken up my card scheme and are working it well. The idea of buying a little 'God-child' from the slavery of the devil, and packing it off safe to Heaven, appeals to many.

I gave you a secondary intention in my Mass each morning during the retreat, so Fr Keane need not take all the credit of your conversion to himself (I presume you are converted this time). Heaps of love, dearest Mai, and every blessing…[31]

Given his love of horses, it is surprising that Willie didn't mention in this letter, or the one to follow to his father, the brigade horse show. This took place on Friday 28 July at Noeux-les-Mines while the 8th RIF were in divisional reserve at Mazingarbe, when the battalion transport of 7th Royal Inniskilling Fusiliers captured many of the important prizes.

It was Hugh's turn next to receive a letter from Willie dated 10 August, starting with disappointing news:

We are all, officers and men alike, in a sweet humour at the present moment: Listen to our 'tale of woe'. It is customary when a Division has been in the Line for three months to get back to the base for a month's rest. Goodness knows the poor fellows want it, for practically during all that time they have not had a decent night's sleep, none of course while actually in the trenches. We have seen the other Divisions round us go back and return again, but we, like the Grandfather clock kept on all the time, 3 months, 5 months nearly now without a break! However when going up to the firing line a fortnight ago the good news came that this was our last round, and the long promised rest, away from the sound even of the guns, was before us. Then like a bolt from the blue came the cheerful information that there was to be no month's rest, that the ordinary week's break between each spell in the firing line was done away with, and that with the exception of four days in sixteen spent 'in reserve' amid the ruins of a shattered village behind the lines, we were doomed for the rest of our lives apparently to the trenches. I suppose it is a compliment to the fighting qualities of the 16th Division, for we are holding the most critical sector of the line, but it is a compliment to all of us would willingly forgo. As a matter of fact the very night we handed over a certain portion of the Front to another regiment, the Germans (how did they know of the change) came over and captured the trenches, so we had to go back again.[32]

Turning a negative into a positive, Willie continues:

One result at least of this strenuous life is that I have become as hard as nails, in really tip top health, and I am quite convinced that when I get back home, I shall want to give three missions at the same time, one would never satisfy me now. When the home-coming will be is not easy to tell, for I should have said to crown our misfortunes 'all leave of absence' has been stopped a few days after I returned, so I was very lucky to have got over to Ireland.[33]

Willie evidently had time to spare to write a detailed letter despite news being at a premium:

As news is scarce I wonder would you care to have some idea of my daily life in the trenches. Let me introduce you to my house and home. It is nothing very grand, just a hole in the side of the trench, the entrance made as small as possible to keep out stray splinters of shells, not to speak of the cool night breezes, for my house does not boast of a door or windows. I am fortunate, however, that I am just able to stand upright, though at times I forget my surroundings and bang my head against the beams of the roof: at present I have 972 bruises on various parts of my skull, but am hoping to have more later on.

The German officer who lived here before my arrival was evidently a man of taste: he put planks on the floor and lined the walls with boards, making it very dry and comfortable, for which I bless the dear Hun, but it makes my 'appy 'ome look like a respectable packing case. I am living in fear and trembling that some day Bob and Jennie may pay me a visit: they <u>might</u> squeeze in, but they certainly would never get out again, even I have to be careful about the size and extent of my meals.[34]

The question marks in the next sentence are Willie's sardonic comment on the nature of his sleeping arrangements:

> In one corner is my bed ??, just a couple of planks raised off the ground, not too soft, but welcome as any couch of down to a dead-tired man. I am never lonely at night for I have many visitors: a stray dog, a trench cat or two, who stroll in to say 'bon jour' and of course my never failing friends the mice and rats. I never knew till I came out here that rats sing!! It is a fact. They have built their nests behind the boards of my mansion walls, which I may tell you does not add to the sweetness of the abode, and many a time I have heard them singing to one another for ever so long, quite a sweet, musical note. From time to time they poke their heads out and look at me as much as to say 'You are a queer sort of rat you are'.
>
> At a certain hour of the morning, which we shall not mention, I tumble out. I am quite free to arrange my day's programme, and often the morning light is breaking before I get the chance of lying down. For example the other night I had to bury one man at 11.30, a second some time after 2am and had barely turned in when word came that one of my poor boys had had his leg shot off in a distant part of the trench. I was directed the wrong way which added an extra half hour to my walk, and a great deal to my anxiety lest the lad should be dead, but thank God he was alive when I reached him, a comfort surely to us both.
>
> Every morning I have the happiness, and it is a big one, of offering the Holy Sacrifice of the Mass, and a dug-out is a poor place to ask the good God to come to, but He lived in a stable once and can sympathise, I know, with my poverty.
>
> Breakfast is quite a banquet: tea with condensed milk, fried bacon, bread and butter, with jam or marmalade to follow. No wonder we are all praying the war may last centuries. You must not examine the breakfast set too closely, but it is wonderful all the things a knife can do, spoons and forks are quite unnecessary, while tea seems to taste doubly sweet out of a bully can, provided you do not burn your lips too often.
>
> The morning slips by in visits to the dressing stations (I have five to look after in various parts of the trenches) and saying a few prayers, and as much of my office as I can (sometimes none) and confessions or chats with

the men. Quite often an officer will drop in for a friendly controversial talk, resulting thank God, in much good. There is no doubt that the faith and sincere piety of our men have made an immense impression on non-Catholics and have made them anxious to know more about the true Church.*³⁵*

Fr Doyle's next comment is interesting. He confirms official War Office policy that chaplains are not supposed to go into the front line trenches, but that he does so, and claims his immediate colleagues do not:

In the afternoon I make a tour of the front line trenches. To be candid it is part of my work which I do <u>not</u> like. We chaplains are not bound to go into the firing line, in fact we are not supposed to do so, but the officers welcome us warmly, as a chat and a cheery word bucks the men up so much. I look on it as a big act of charity, more especially as my colleagues won't take the risk, so the burden falls on me. It is not that the danger is very great, in fact I think it is much less than in other parts of the trenches, because the trench being built in this way …³⁶

At this point Willie has drawn a rough sketch of a trench system and then continues his explanation:

You are perfectly safe in a 'Bay', owing to the walls of clay on either side, unless a shell fell on the very spot you were standing. But it is the uncanny feeling which comes over one knowing that the enemy, in parts, are only 30 yards away which makes the trip unpleasant. I have often come to a 'bay' blown in shortly before by a shell from a mortar, a little gentleman weighing 200lbs, you can see him coming in the air and when you do – well you slip into the next 'bay' and try and feel as small as you can. I have had to crawl on my tummy past a gap in the trench, but I can honestly say I have never had anything approaching a close shave, the Lord does not forget His goats when He is minding His sheep.

Thus the days and weeks slip past rapidly by and happily. The life, in spite of all its deadly monotony, is full of interest and the spice of excitement is never wanting, more especially while you are waiting to see where this shell is going to drop. Our glorious weather still continues, brilliant sunshine and great heat, but for all that very enjoyable. Whether it is the heat or the good feeding the conduct of the rats is becoming outrageous, they simply won't get out of your way in the trenches, there is not the slightest difficulty in catching them by the tail as they climb leisurely up the bank. What is to be done? Send out Tiger Tim for a week. When you see Jennie please thank her for her nice card, the words were very beautiful. I am glad they are going to do their 'bit' in Harrogate.[37]

One wonders what Willie's sister-in-law Jennie was up to in Harrogate, and if it had anything to do with the war effort, as he has couched the enquiry in his last sentence in war slang. Or possibly the observation relates to Willie's widowed brother-in-law Frank, who used to live with Lil in another part of Yorkshire, in Sheffield. Once again Willie is writing to Hugh on 21 August, starting with a startling revelation:

The receipt of a letter from Ireland saying how sorry they were to hear I had been wounded gave me quite a start, for you know men have gone through a charge with bullets sticking in them without knowing they had been hit. A careful examination revealed the fact that with the exception of one leg and an arm which are missing (probably left behind in frantic haste to avoid a coming shell) I have not received a scratch, thank God, and have not even been on the sick list. This does not include the scratches, many and deep, made by the loving embrace of the 'Misskittles' who are absolutely shameless in this part of the world: I don't mind sharing my midnight couch with a respectable old rat, or a few stray mice, but I draw the line at these hussies. Like all other feminine creatures, give them a chance and they will scratch you. (N.B. for goodness sake don't let this go the round of the holy convent.)

Since I wrote last nothing of very great interest has taken place except one rather curious thing. We have fitted up a room in a deserted house as a small chapel, where we celebrate Mass for the men from time to time: a privilege which the poor fellows appreciate. In one corner are the cellar steps, down which priest and congregation vanish with marvellous celerity when occasion requires, for the Bosch has a particular love for this village. Yesterday when no one was near, a shell came through the wall and fell on the floor without bursting, covering the little altar with bricks and plaster in such a way as to make one think it must have been the Old Boy who directed the shell in his fury. He has got a few shrapnel shells himself lately, and I suppose he wants to get his own back.

The bill of health is excellent and now that the intense heat has passed somewhat, life is more liveable, for the weather keeps beautifully fine. I want this letter to catch the post, as you may possibly be uneasy about me, though I know you have too much common-sense and trust in Our Lord's protection for that. Au revoir for the present: my next letter will be longer.[38]

The 16th (Irish) Division finally received welcome orders to vacate the Loos sector towards the end of August 1916 and:

On the 24th the divisional artillery fired off their surplus ammunition as a farewell present from Ireland before going down south ...[39]

Four days later Willie writes to Hugh, Monday 28 August:

A line in haste to tell you we are on the move to the rear to enjoy a well-earned rest after our continuous month in the trenches. This order reached us suddenly and I need not say was most welcome. We marched here last night and are off again immediately to some destination unknown, but miles away from the sound even of the guns, hence for the next month or so you will know I am in no danger whatever, except sleeping so long I may never awaken! Shall write again in a few days: much love Will

P.S. Many thanks to Mai and Lena for welcome letters. Neither I nor Fr Kelly have been wounded, thank God.[40]

Two days later, 30 August 1916, whilst en-route, Willie found time to hastily scribble a post-card to his niece Nora; a comic coloured picture on the front depicting three infants eating biscuits with the caption 'Preparing for a Siege'. His barely legible scrawl says:

*Many thanks to you and Mother for your welcome letters. We have gone back for a rest which so far has meant long marches. We left at 3am yesterday and got here last night. Much Love Willie.*⁴¹

Footnote 1: *At Rest in Philosophe, 6th Connaught Rangers, June 1916,* Lieutenant J.F.B. O'Sullivan, papers in Imperial War Museum.

Footnote 2: Barry St John Galvin personal file, WO 95/338 and 8th Battalion Royal Irish Fusiliers War Diary entry 16 August 1916, WO 95/1978.

CHAPTER 19
FROM LOOS TO THE SOMME:
DEAD MAN TALKING

*'In the end of ends, infantry is the deciding factor in every battle …
(it) bears the heaviest burden of a battle and requires
the greatest sacrifice…'*
Erich Ludendorff

Willie commenced his next letter to the grand old man of Melrose on 2 September 1916, and adds to it a light-hearted postscript. It appears that erroneous reports of Fr Doyle and Fr Kelly having been wounded had escalated to rumours of the former's death, prompting Willie to comment: *I am glad to hear I am dead, it will save much letter writing.*[1] The letter had also started in an upbeat vein:

You should have had a letter from me some days ago but since I wrote last we have been constantly on the move, which has left me with little opportunity of doing so. Even now letter writing is not easy. I am living out in the open on top of a hill, real 'red injun' style, except that the wigwam is wanting and I live out and sleep under the blue sky of heaven and the wings of my guardian angel. Fortunately now the weather is delightful, fine and warm, so that life is quite enjoyable, but I am just wondering what we shall do when the rain begins to fall again.[2]

Willie then reveals the toll taken on the 16th (Irish) Division since it had embarked for France at the beginning of the year. No doubt Fr Doyle was speaking in round figures and perhaps there was some slight embellishment on his part:

To pick up the thread of my narrative. The sudden order to leave Loos came as a welcome and unexpected surprise, more especially as this move to the rear meant the long hoped for rest. We have had a hard six months of it in the trenches, holding one of the most dangerous bits of the line. Our men have done their work well, which you will realise when I say that over 15,000 men, including of course many sick and slightly wounded, have passed through the doctors' hands, not a bad total for a division of 20,000 men. To their credit be it said, they have not lost a trench or yard of ground in the six months. Sudden and secret as our orders were the Germans knew all about it, as we were leaving the trenches they put a board up with 'Good bye to the 16th Division we shall give it hot to the English when they come!' It is a mystery how they know all we do.[3]

The Reverend Father William Doyle S.J. had joined the Army in November 1915, and spent the ensuing months with his brigade, enduring the miseries of life in Loos; coping with the gas, the shelling, the rats and the fleas, and suffering the loss of men he regarded as 'his own flock'. Unabated, his letters home have underlined the high points, and the low points, of this life but now, at the beginning of September 1916, he was about to embark on a venture for which nothing could have prepared him. Perhaps he thought: Anywhere but Loos:

I left Loos without a tear, though not without many drops of sweat, for the rats and the flies had been making things uncommonly lively recently. My last dug-out was evidently their council chamber and, resenting my intrusion, literally danced on me. I woke up the first night to find King Rat calmly sleeping at my feet. Before I quite realised it, he calmly ran along my legs and across my face, a procedure which is about the limit I think. I am not exaggerating or dreaming, for as I jerked my head I heard their ladyships go 'plop' against the wall. I hope the King lost a couple of his wives that night, for without being uncharitable he seems to be a regular King Solomon who had a warm corner in his heart for the ladies. I know Our Lord tells us 'to turn the other cheek' but I do not know any text saying we should be walked on by rats.

We got the first night to a village in the rear, where I had the good fortune to have a billet with a luxurious bed: was strongly tempted to resign my commission and stay in it for a year. Next morning on again about 14 miles of a march, the men in fine humour as word had gone round that this was to be our resting place for a month. It was not to be however, as after one day's repose we heard that we were to move once more, this time at 2.30am in the morning.[4]

His thoughts turning towards a Promised Land:

After a couple of hours steady tramp we entrained and jogged along for seven hours till Amiens was reached. We had an oil store in our carriage and so were able to make tea for breakfast, which was fortunate as subsequent events will show. At last I thought we have reached our destination and I was not sorry to be near such an historic spot as the famous old town of Amiens, but it was Dame Disappointment once more, a march and a big one lay before us.

I shall not easily forget that afternoon; it was sweltering, the heat terrific as we tramped out of the station up the side of an endless hill. The officers, from Captains upwards, have horses but I prefer to shoulder my pack and foot it with the boys for I know they like it, and besides I don't see why I should not share a little of their hardships. We had just halted for a rest when a terrific thunder storm, or rather three of them burst upon us and in a few moments every man was wet to the skin: I was wise in time and again in luck by coming across an old tarpaulin under which I lay snug and happy and dry 'till the clouds rolled by.' The rest of the march I shall leave you to picture, through the thick mud and floods in some parts. The men stuck it well, many of them plodding on till they fell by the roadside.

To give you an idea of the good form I am in, though foot sore, I was quite fresh when we reached our destination at eleven that night, though I had been carrying a young lad's equipment (about 60lbs) in addition to my own. No dinner, no supper, no tea, but I saw an inviting well in a courtyard. The good woman offered me a cup, but at the moment a bucket was more in my line, so I drank till the well was dry, a few prayers, one roll in a blanket and I was fast asleep in a cosy corner.

Next day a delicious rest: surely this is the Promised Land we all thought, when at the end of dinner in came a telegram from Headquarters 'Division will march in the morning at seven.' I wish you could see one division on the road, a mere trifle of 20,000 men, but from head to tail we cover 35 miles of road with transport, guns etc.[5]

Hope springs eternal:

We reached this 'Green Hill Far Away' two days ago, quite a lovely spot as long as the rain holds off, for there is not even a dug-out to shelter in. It makes little difference for as I write word has come in that we are to march in the morning: no rest for the wicked! I must keep other scraps of news for my next letter as I have many little things to do.

Thousands of thanks for your dear welcome letter, you never forget me and even if you did not say so I know I have your holy prayers. A little story to close. One of the men not too famous himself for piety brought in a black sheep for confession: he was a brawny boy and I fancy helped out his arguments by a little physical force. Seeing a good opportunity for landing another fish I said to him: 'What about yourself, were you with the priest recently?' 'Oh! Father' he answered 'I am all right. I was at my duty three years ago!!' I believe the poor chap was really sincere but am glad to say he is 'righter' now.[6]

The 'Green Hill Far Away' proved a very short respite, as explained in Willie's next letter of 11 September 1916:

In my last letter I left you under the impression that we were making our way steadily towards the place appointed for our well deserved rest, and indeed we all thought so, but as a matter of fact many, very many, alas! of our brave fellows were never to enjoy that promised time of quiet on this earth, for our road was leading us to the battlefield of the Somme.[7]

The plans for the 1916 summer campaign had been agreed at an Allied planning conference in December 1915, when a proposal was made for a large-scale attack in the Picardy sector, involving both British and French troops in a massed attack, intended to achieve the long hoped-for breakout through the German defences. The nature of such plans meant they were subject to change and the German commander Erich von Falkenhayn forced a revision when, on 21 February 1916, he launched

Operation Gericht ['Operation Judgement']. A massive attack by massed German divisions struck the French Army's positions around the city of Verdun, resulting in a protracted battle during which increasingly large numbers of French troops were drawn into the struggle. As a result, plans for the Allied offensive on the Somme had to be drastically revised, and the summer campaign became a largely British affair, supported by a much-reduced French army on the southern flank.

The campaign, which became known as the Battles of the Somme, lasted from 1 July 1916 until 18 November 1916. It is, of course, the First Day of the battle that is etched in the annals of history; the day, in popular legend, that the men of the British Army were sent walking into killing fields of slaughter, after the British artillery bombardment of the German wire and lines failed to have its desired effect. Saturday 1 July 1916 is often referred to as the blackest day in the history of the British Army, when some 60,000 casualties accrued, two for every yard of the British front line; almost exactly half of the men in the 143 battalions who had attacked were either wounded, reported missing or were killed, with the infantry sustaining the overwhelming majority of the casualties. Nine Victoria Crosses were awarded, six posthumously; four were awarded to men in battalions of Irish regiments serving in the 36th (Ulster) Division[8] (other battalions of the same regiments were attached to the 16th (Irish) Division at Loos).

Willie Doyle and the 16th (Irish) Division arrived on the Somme just about the mid-point of the battle and, instead of having their prolonged, scheduled rest completely away from the line, the 16th (Irish) Division was now assigned to participate in a later stage of the Somme battle. Preceding them had been battalions from Irish regiments, who had featured throughout the battle serving with one or other of a dozen or so divisions from across the spectrum; Regular, Territorial, and New Army divisions, who had been shattered on the Somme battlefield.

An anecdote that would have appealed to Willie Doyle's sense of humour, before it was temporarily blunted by the scenes he was to witness on the Somme, concerns the 2nd Leinsters, serving with 24th Division, some of whom, on being relieved on 25 August 1916 in the front line at Guillemont by a Bantam unit ...*very kindly stayed to lower the parapets to a height fit for the little men* ...[9] Newly arrived at the Somme, the brigades of 16th (Irish) Division came under the authority of the existing commanders of XIV Corps already in-situ. At the end of August 1916 the divisions of XIV Corps were consolidated before their objective, a German strongpoint formed in the ruined village of Guillemont.

Guillemont, September 1916

Guillemont, situated on high ground, had been pounded to a heap of discoloured rubble, but underneath it lay deep-mined dug-outs which remained intact, with tunnels to access the village wells. In front of the heavily fortified remains was a wide, open plain, nick-named 'Death Valley' because of the ease with which the Germans were able to defend it. Guillemont, and the neighbouring village of Ginchy, had been fortified with reinforced concrete machine-gun positions, which now stood in the way of the British advance. The forward movement of the British line had ground to a halt at Guillemont railway station, a few hundred yards from the outskirts of what was once human habitation. Like the village, the station was unrecognisable, except for the railway line, and such was the devastation at Guillemont that the historian of the Leinster regiment observed:

> *Guillemont, except as a name, or a tactical position, had long ceased to be, and on all sides one heard the muttered query 'Where is the _____ village?*[10]

To the south of Guillemont lay an infamous sunken road, which by this time was a series of huge shell holes filled with detritus.

The Germans had also had to bring up reinforcements, to scenes they had never before witnessed. Ernst Jünger had a premonition of what lay in store for him when, en-route to Guillemont on 23 August 1916:

A runner from a Württemberg regiment reported to me to guide my platoon to the famous town of Combles, where we were to be held in reserve for the time being. He was the first German soldier I saw in a steel helmet, and he straightaway struck me as the denizen of a new and far harsher world.[11]

The next day Lt Jünger and his platoon from 73rd Hanoverian Fusiliers were issued with their own steel helmets. They arrived several days later at Guillemont, exhausted, confused and disorientated after their guide had taken a wrong turn under heavy shrapnel fire, during which journey two platoons vanished. He records:

On, on! Men collapsed while running, we had to threaten them to use the last energy from their exhausted bodies. Wounded men went down left and right in craters – we disregarded their cries for help ... At last we reached the front line, which was occupied by men huddled together in little holes. Their dull voices trembled with joy when they learned that we were come to relieve them ...My platoon's sector was on the right flank of the regiment's position, and consisted of a defile hammered by constant shelling into little more than a dip ... When morning paled, the strange surroundings gradually revealed themselves to our disbelieving eyes ... The defile proved to be little more than a series of enormous craters full of pieces of uniform, weapons and dead bodies; the country around, so far as the eye could see, had been completely ploughed by heavy shells. Not a single blade of grass showed itself. The churned up field was gruesome. In among the living defenders lay the dead. When we dug foxholes, we realised that they were stacked in layers... The village of Guillemont seemed to have disappeared without trace; just a whitish stain on the cratered field indicated where one of the limestone houses had been pulverised. In front of us lay the station, crumpled like a child's toy; further to the rear the woods of Delville, ripped to splinters.[12]

Another British attempt to take Guillemont was scheduled for 3 September 1916, in which the 47th Brigade of 16th (Irish) Division was to fight. Whilst 48th Brigade and Willie Doyle's 49th Brigade remained briefly in a rest camp, 47th Brigade was sent to make up the numbers for this next offensive. The brigade was temporarily transferred to 20th Division, which had been weakened by exhaustion and general ill–health. The history of the 20th Division notes that at the end of August 1916:

> ... the state of the whole line was foul. The men, too, were given little rest; on the night of the 28th/29th all available men of all three brigades were working in the forward area. These very severe conditions told on the health of the troops, who were becoming so exhausted that it seemed doubtful whether they would be fit for the severe fighting which the capture of Guillemont would probably involve... The 60th Brigade had suffered so severely, and the strength of the units had been so seriously reduced, that on the 1 September the Corps Commander decided that the 47th Brigade of the 16th Division should be used on the attack on Guillemont and that the 60th Brigade should be withdrawn into reserve.[13]

Prior to the attack there was the usual hustle and bustle of planning: Commanding Officers and their Adjutants attended conferences; Quartermasters ensured there were adequate supplies; Regimental Aid Posts were set up; and so on. Despite such attention to detail, once the 'push' got underway the Irishmen were to be hampered by unfamiliar terrain whilst moving to their jumping-off points under cover of darkness. The men of 7th Leinsters and 6th Connaught Rangers had to depend on guides who, like the German guide a few days previously, managed to get lost! Fortunately, with luck playing a major role, both battalions were able to get to their destinations in time. In a letter to his mother afterwards, Lt J.F.B. O'Sullivan of 6th Connaughts described the wait at their front line starting position:

> There we all lay, sprawled in a rough mass; snatching mouthfuls from the pieces of loaf and bully beef that had been in our packs all day, and trying to ease tired feet and shoulders.[14]

The Connaughts were also afflicted by the universal problem, suffered by all combatants, of the difficulty of obtaining fresh water. O'Sullivan continued:

> The area where we now found ourselves had been recently fought over – in

fact it was very close to the limit gained by the original 1 July push – and the ground had been churned into a lather of mud. The roadside was littered with discarded equipment; rifles, ammunition boxes, shell cases, grenades and reels of unused barbed wire. The stench from bloated horse carcasses overwhelmed one to the point of vomiting.[15]

Following their arrival at assembly positions, the Commanding Officer of 6th Connaughts', Lt Col Lenox-Coynham, briefed his officers on the plan of attack and issued the Orders of the Day. But then:

The session was barely over and the CO about to make a few extra comments when a blinding flash and shattering blast wrecked the doorway. Simultaneously a jet of wet dust spattered over us.' An orderly had been pulverised by the blast: 'I glanced at my notes and saw the 'wetness' to be nothing less than blood and bits of brains...[16]

The shell had terminated both the meeting and the life of one of O'Sullivan's colleagues:

Feeling very shaken and upset I stepped over poor Crowley's remains and, turning into the sap found myself surrounded by a group of maniacs. The same explosion had shocked the four runners into a state of utter delirium, and they sprawled about as if in the throes of tetany.[17]

On 2 September 1916, Major General W.B. Hickie, GOC 16th (Irish) Division, considered it important to send a message of support to the battalions of his 47th Brigade who had been brought temporarily under the command of 20th Division, and who, for this assault, was working in conjunction with battalions of that Division:

The divisional commander sends his best wishes to the officers and men of the Brigade and knows that their action tomorrow will go down in history.[18]

At noon on 3 September the British artillery intensified its shelling of the German lines, which had already been going on for several hours. Many shells were 'unders' falling short to such a degree that, in combination with German replies, the 6th Connaughts took 200 casualties even before they went over the top, and the Commanding Officer had to bring forward two reserves companies as reinforcements. The 6th Connaught Rangers assembled in Rim Trench and were to attack towards the quarries. Three British Divisions were involved in the attack in the area of Guillemont. The 5th Division was disposed to the south; 20th Division held the centre; and to the north, 7th Division were concentrating on the neighbouring village of Ginchy.

The 20th (Light) Division had some 8,000 men in four brigades available for their sector of the attack, although of these, the depleted 60th Infantry Brigade were in reserve with only 1,045 men in 3 battalions. The 59th Infantry Brigade had 2,300 men in five battalions; 61st Infantry Brigade had 2,253 men in four battalions and the Irishmen of the seconded 47th Infantry Brigade had 2,400 men in four battalions. The Connaught Rangers were immediately to the west of the quarries; to their left were the 7th Leinsters in the Gridiron trenches north of the railway. In support were the 8th Royal Munster Fusiliers in Knott and Mike trenches, and in reserve east of Trônes Wood were the 6th Royal Irish Regiment.[19]

At zero hour, as the Connaught Rangers stormed out of Rim trench their C.O., Lt Col Lenox-Conyngham, fell dead in the act of pointing his cane to direct his men. Another casualty was Lt O'Sullivan, who was wounded in the shoulder in front of a concrete strongpoint. As he fell to the ground, the men of his platoon, not having realised that their leader was injured, interpreted the action to mean they should also go to ground. O'Sullivan was frantic:

In a frenzy I got up and shrieked myself hoarse to no purpose. To signal with my arms was painful and slow, but by dragging the rifle by its muzzle and going forward at least indicated that the advance should go on. Moments later they were all up and going again. The unrehearsed breather was a lucky chance, because once on their feet the men recovered the wild abandon of the charge just at the moment when Germans began to emerge from shell holes and wrecked trenches. Behind the strong point a scuffle and scramble developed as a group put up a hectic resistance that was overwhelmed by the bayonet stabbing onslaught; a vortex of shrieking; of yells and brutish grunting – then rushing ahead leaving the crumpled bodies in a stink of blood and high explosive.[20]

Having managed to stagger on, catch up with his re-focused men, take the surrender of several dazed Germans and enter Guillemont, Lt O'Sullivan was amazed by the number of dead Germans: *it was not a matter of walking round the bodies but of having to step over them.*[21] Private Tom Hughes of the Connaughts was awarded the Victoria Cross for his bravery when, despite being injured and after having the wound dressed, he returned to the front line and single-handedly captured a German machine-gun. In doing so he was wounded a second time but he still managed to bring back three prisoners.

For their part in the assault the 7th Leinsters assembled before dawn in a system of trenches known as the Gridiron, some three hundred yards due north of the northern outskirts of the village. The three prongs of the Gridiron were so shallow the men could only sit in the bottom, keeping their heads well down. For hours on end they: *squatted cramped and motionless never showing a hair but 'lying like lions in their lines thirsting for blood'*[22]. They were without any rations, none having come up because of the intensity of the German artillery bombardment. The 7th Leinsters attacked south and a party of twenty-six bombers led by Lt John Vincent Holland advanced through their own barrage to clear a substantial part of the village, bombing enemy dug-outs and forcing out the occupants. In doing so they took twenty-one casualties, seven of whom were killed. Lieutenant Holland was later awarded the Victoria Cross; Sergeant Michael Kelly received the Distinguished Conduct Medal, as did Lance Corporal Arthur Lee who was wounded. Military Medals were awarded to Corporal Patrick Colgan, Lance Corporal Edward Dowling, Private Timothy Coughlin and their wounded colleagues Privates Daniel Synnott, Bernard Moore and Michael Clarkin; Private John Ford was recommended for a battlefield commission.[23]

These short snap-shots of the derring-do of the 6th Connaughts and 7th Leinsters can give only a flavour of the actions of all the infantry battalions on 3 September at Guillemont. But it is the deeds of all the attacking Irishmen which impressed the *Daily Chronicle,* reporting:

> ...*the charge of the Irish troops through Guillemont was one of the most astonishing feats of the war – almost too fast in its impetuosity ... a wild and irresistible assault.*[24]

On the other hand, Captain J.M.H. Staniforth of the 7th Leinsters commented in a letter home dated 12 September 1916:

> *Of course there was none of the 'wild, cheering rush' one imagines. We stopped outside the parapet to straighten the line, and then moved forward at an ordinary walk. I remember noticing the air was just one loud noise – like moving in a kind of sound-box. And the machine-gun bullets snapped about your head rather like a swarm of angry hornets: all hissing and crackling; it was rather curious; I don't quite know how to describe it.*[25]

The apparent over-enthusiastic onslaught of some of the Connaught Rangers, however, almost compromised one zone of the assault, which the 10th King's Royal Rifle Corps had to mop up. The history of that unit records the Germans: *...shooting into the backs of the Irish who had overrun them. This, however, was remedied by despatching the Reserve Company and one platoon of A Company to deal with the trouble.*[26] The Twentieth Division history expands further:

> *In their impetuous advance the Connaught Rangers on the right passed the Quarries without completely clearing them, and the left flank of the 10th K.R.R.C., attacking on the left of 59th Brigade, was placed for a time in a difficult position. Lieut.-Colonel Blacklock, commanding this battalion, at once grasped the situation, and by detaching his reserve company and a platoon from one of the companies in the line to clean up the Quarries averted what might have been a very awkward state of affairs.*[27]

There are many other stories, such as that of the Field Company of Royal Engineers and Pioneers from 11th Hampshires, who had:

> *...the inglorious but essential work of consolidating the captured ground – digging new trenches, often simply by connecting a string of shell holes and revetting, or strengthening their sides and wiring the front.*[28]

Signallers laid cables and Regimental Aid Posts worked flat out in the most trying and stressful of conditions. Captain Watkins, Royal Army Medical Corps attached to 7th Leinsters, had only landed in France on 1 September. His actions were described as follows:

*This officer's first aid dressing station was in a shell hole just outside Battalion headquarters. Here he worked continuously for the next twenty-four hours, regardless of danger, coping with the stream of wounded, friend and foe alike. It must be remembered that he was under heavy shell fire for many hours but he might have been in England so little effect had it on him.*²⁹

Another chaplain, like Fr Doyle, stayed with his battalion even in the front line. The Reverend Fr Wrafter remained with 8th Royal Munster Fusiliers throughout, while they carried out the unenviable task of mopping up as far as the sunken road. The list goes on.

Somme Sunken Road, September 1916

More than seven hundred German prisoners were taken, many of them wounded, while: *the enemy dead lay thick on the captured ground.*³⁰ The Irish battalions of 47th Infantry Brigade alone had 1,147 men wounded or killed (from a total of 2,400). Unfortunately, there were insufficient stretchers to cope with the stream of wounded from both sides and prisoners were pressed into service to help evacuate them. One German officer, in a mistaken breach of protocol, was instructed to help out with a stretcher:

> *Vigorous expostulation of course followed but this was not the time to conform to any punctilio of military etiquette. The fiery Hun was ordered to do what he was told, and he did it.*[31]

Lt Holland displayed great chivalry as well as the bravery which won him the VC. He and another soldier from the 6th Royal Irish Regiment, carried a wounded German, whom they seated on a rifle, from one of the places Lt Holland had bombed, back to an aid post. Stretcher cases were taken after treatment in the R.A.P.s to the field ambulances in Trônes Wood, which necessitated a tortuous journey of five hundred yards across Death Valley.

After the main battle, reliefs of the exhausted battalions took place. Those of 47th Brigade were relieved by 48th Brigade, although men from the Connaught Rangers had one last duty to perform. They recovered the body of Lt Col J.S.M. Lenox-Conyngham, who was born of an Ulster Protestant family, but who died devoted to his southern Irish nationalist battalion. He was buried:

> *...in a little churchyard just behind the lines, amidst every possible manifestation of grief and respect, deeply lamented by all the battalion he had raised and led for just two years.*[32]

One of Lenox-Coyngham's subalterns, Lt O'Sullivan, after initially coping with his injured shoulder to continue leading his men in the attack, subsequently sought treatment. Then pain and nausea overcame him and he returned to battalion headquarters where he learned of the toll taken on the Connaught Rangers. Not only was the commanding officer killed, but the second-in-command, Major Campbell, was wounded and dying, and the battalion was down to less than 400 men.

Wallace Lyon of the 7th Leinsters remembers the period after the taking of Guillemont, the last attempts at reclaiming it by the enemy, and his men holding on until they were relieved:

> *We had no food but our iron rations, and what we could scrounge from the*

dead. No water but what we carried in our water bottles, and what rain we could catch in ground sheets and no contact with anyone but the enemy who seemed to appear on every side. On the third night a captain of the third Battalion of the Grenadier Guards came along with his troops and told me his battalion was taking over the position from what was left of our Brigade. By that time I could have kissed him. I wasn't even certain of the best way back, but he told me not to wait on formalities but go. I limped off with about 40 odd men, many of them wounded, all that was left of the 150 that started out.[33]

Elsewhere, other Irish battalions, the 7th Irish Rifles and 1st Munsters, together with a battalion from the King's Liverpool Regiment, helped repel three German counter-attacks, whilst the remnants of all the original attacking battalions slogged back to camp. Lt Charles Weld of the 7th Leinsters noted in his diary:

... we were all so tired I thought we would never reach the place, having had no rest or sleep since the night before the attack. Quite a number of men dropped from sheer exhaustion and lack of sleep ... Many familiar faces are absent.[34]

There was to be no rest and relaxation in billets. The battalions of 47th Brigade found themselves bivouacking in the rain in the camp at Carnoy. Replacement drafts for all attacking battalions occurred where possible, in other cases battalions remained at reduced strength. Nevertheless, Irish morale remained high and: *it was difficult to say whether the camp was German or Irish; nearly everyone sported a German helmet and a German greatcoat.*[35] The historian of the 7th Leinsters noted ironically that:

Previous to leaving the line 'officer commanding carrying party' was given charge of one jar of rum, which was left over, with strict orders to take particular care of and to land it safely in Carnoy. The carrying party arrived safely but not the jar of rum. The adjutant was informed that it had unfortunately been broken, which was no doubt the case.[36]

'Accidents' notwithstanding, Brigadier General Pereira, O.C. 47th Brigade, addressed 7th Leinsters on 6th September at Carnoy, complimenting them on the fine work they had done in the capture of Guillemont.[37]

Another commanding officer was appointed to the 6th Connaught Rangers, an English Major by the name of Rowland Feilding, who was transferred from the Coldstream Guards and later confirmed in his appointment as Lieutenant Colonel. Feilding immediately noted the fine work his new battalion had carried out at Guillemont, writing to his wife on 7 September 1916:

> *My new battalion is one of the two which captured Guillemont four days ago:- as hard a nut to crack as there has been in this battle, so far... the remnant of it, was bivouacking when I joined it, on a slope alongside the ruins of Carnoy, amid a plague of flies, reduced (apart from officers) to 365 other ranks, and very tired after the capture of Guillemont, in which it had taken a prominent and successful part, though the toll had been so heavy.[38]*

This, then, is the scene into which Fr Doyle and 49th Brigade arrived. They too were soon into action. To pick up the early narrative of Willie's letter of 11th September, he reassures his father of his safety, but prepares him for the shocking descriptions to follow:

> *I have been through the most terrible experience of my whole life, in comparison with which all that I have witnessed or suffered since my arrival in France seems of little consequence: a time of such awful horror that I believe if the good God had not helped me powerfully by his grace, I could never have endured it. To sum all up in one word – for the past week I have been living literally in hell, amid sights and scenes and dangers enough to test the courage of the bravest, but through it all my confidence and trust in our Blessed Lord's protection never wavered, for I felt that somehow even if it needed a miracle, He would bring me safely through the furnace of tribulation. I was hit three times: on the last occasion by a piece of shell big enough to have taken off half my leg, but wonderful to relate I did not receive a wound or a scratch – there is some advantage you see in having a good thick skin![39]*

Like Fr Wrafter during the battle of Guillemont, Fr Doyle was to be in the thick of the action during the storming of the neighbouring village of Ginchy a week later. Willie's letter in which he prepares to relate those events continues:

> *As you can imagine, I am pretty well worn out and exhausted, rather shaken by the terrific strain of these days and nights without any real sleep or repose, with nerves tingling, ever on the jump, like the rest of us, but it is all over now, we are well behind the firing line, on our way at last for a good long rest, which report says will be enjoyed close to the sea. The 16th Division weak in numbers as it was has covered itself with glory: our boys fought as only Irish lads can do, took two villages by a splendid dashing charge, which had beaten off all previous attacks, and made an opening for the big things which are soon to follow now.*
>
> *The price was a heavy one and I am left to mourn the loss of many a good friend and scores of my poor boys with just this consolation that I know my presence was a help and a comfort and every man was well prepared to meet his maker where he fell.*
>
> *So many things have happened since I wrote, all seems part of one big dream, but I shall try to give you an outline at least of my doings, though I do not know when this letter will reach you, as I expect we have many a long march to face again before we settle down. I shall have to write at odd moments, as best I can, so you must excuse all defects.*[40]

Willie's letter of 2 September started on a light-hearted note of 'dead man talking', the continuation of his letter of 11 September was more a case of 'dead man walking.'

CHAPTER 20
GUILLEMONT TO GINCHY:
DEAD MAN WALKING

'Guillemont was easy enough and that was the first battle that we fought there. But Ginchy was tough, there was no doubt about that.'[1]

PRELUDE

After the Battle of Guillemont, the seconded units of 16th (Irish) Division were finally restored to the command of Major General Hickie. Prior to that happening, the objectives for seconded 47th Infantry Brigade were the same as those noted in the War Diary of 61st Infantry Brigade (20th Division) dated 29 August 1916, which stated:

The 20th Division will capture Guillemont, clear it and then establish itself on the Wedge Wood – Ginchy Road from T.26.a.1.7 on the right to T.20.a.1.5 on the left where touch will be established with the 5th and 7th Divisions respectively.'[2]

(The letter and number combinations are trench map grid references).

Unfortunately, whilst during 3 and 4 September 1916 the British 20th and 5th Divisions achieved their objective of securing Guillemont, the 7th Division was unable to take Ginchy.

When the Somme offensive opened two months previously, the initial axis ran roughly south-west to north-east, along the line of the old Roman road between Albert and Bapaume. However, despite successes on the right flank of the offensive, the failures on the left necessitated a progressive re-alignment of the main axis of the attack, toward the relatively high ground of the le Transloy Ridge. The villages of Guillemont and Ginchy started to dominate the battlefield in late July 1916.

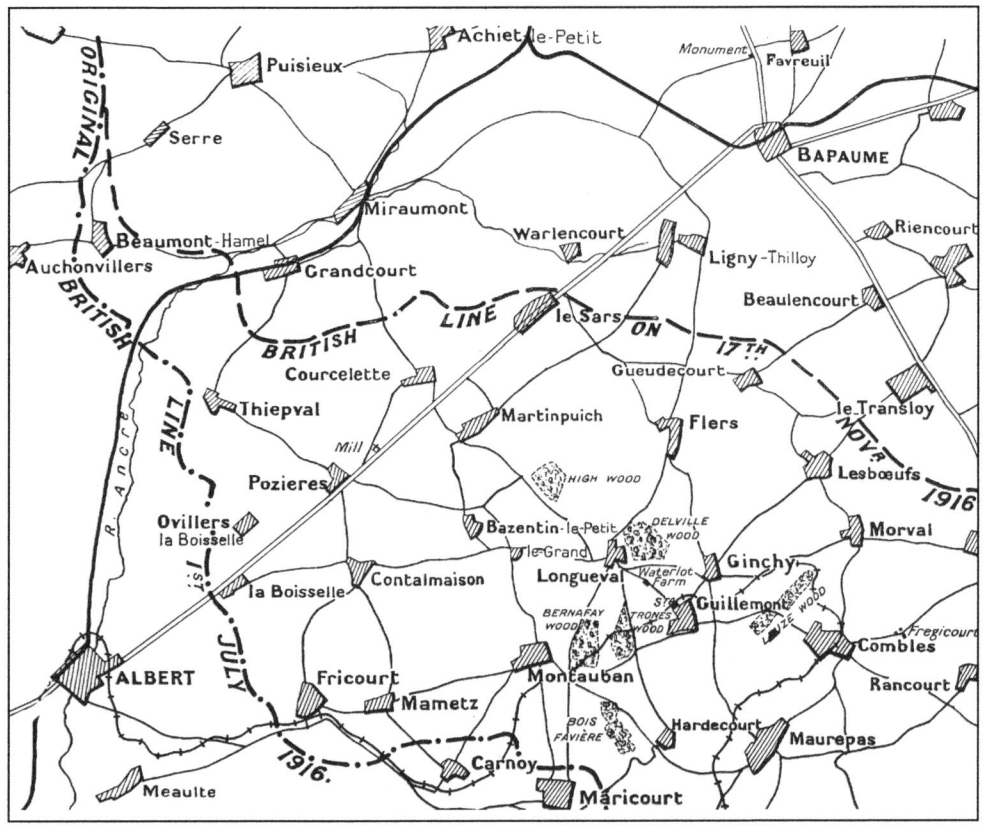

MAP Albert-Bapaume referencing Guillemont and Ginchy

On the far right flank of the 1 July attack the British 30th Division and the French XX Corps had succeeded in capturing the German First and Second Line positions, but did not advance further to the Third Line for fear of out-running the artillery support. Bernafay and Trônes Wood were eventually captured on the 14 July, but stubborn resistance within Delville Wood prevented the securing of the ridge beyond, which was known as the Le Transloy Ridge.

After the situation was reassessed, Guillemont was first attacked on the 22 July by the British 30th Division. This attack failed, as did successive attacks during the remainder of July and throughout August, at great cost to that division and those that followed. However, the British line did progressively inch forward towards Guillemont and, to the north, Delville Wood had all but been secured by the end of

August. When Guillemont was finally taken early in September, attention turned to a second attempt at securing the neighbouring village of Ginchy, which the Germans had thus far successfully defended.

SUNDAY 3 TO TUESDAY 5 SEPTEMBER 1916

As their comrades in the 47th Brigade were in the thick of the action in the assault on Guillemont on 3 September, the 48th and 49th Brigades of 16th (Irish) Division had been camped throughout that bloody Sunday behind the front line in Happy Valley. Willie Doyle's letter of 11 September describes waiting there:

On Sunday 3 September definite news came that we were destined for the front. We had reached the spot from where I last wrote a few days previously, which strange to say bore the familiar name of Bray.[3]

The familiar name of Bray for the Doyle family was the seaside town in County Wicklow, four miles south of Dalkey on the east coast. Bray-sur-Somme, where Willie was camped, is at the heart of the Upper Somme valley where, pre-war, the river and its ponds and tributaries made it a paradise for fishermen, boating trips and messing about in the water. The historian of the 7th Royal Inniskilling Fusiliers recalls marching along the main Amiens to Bray road on 31 August 1916, down to their camping area in Happy Valley, where:

On reaching the camp we soon discovered that the tent accommodation was not going to be sufficient for the battalion. This was of little or no consequence, as the weather was so hot that it was preferable to sleep in the open…Bathing parades in the Somme (just south of Bray) afforded most delightful recreation after the hot and dusty march all day.[4]

Willie continues to recount his experience of the same area:

This is part of one huge camp, which stretches for miles and miles, the French on one side, ourselves on the other. I had never seen such a scene of life and animation before. Picture to yourself the whole of the Three Rock Mountain, the Vale of Shanganagh, Killiney, Bray Head and far beyond Greystones covered with a dense mass of men, horses, guns and wagons with piles of stores all round. Tents are few as I soon discovered, but then one does not look for comfort in the midst of war. Multiply that camp tenfold, crowd every road with columns of marching troops, with an endless stream of motor wagons, gun teams and ammunition carts, and you will have some faint idea of my surroundings. We were camped on a high hill, at the foot of which flowed the river Somme which gave me a chance of a welcome scrub.

Each morning I said Mass in the open and gave Holy Communion to hundreds of the men. I wish you could have seen them kneeling there before the whole camp, recollected and prayerful, a grand profession surely of 'the faith that is in them.' More than one non-Catholic was moved by it and it made many a one I am sure turn to God in the hour of need.[5]

Happy Valley, Somme, September 1916

At 7.30 p.m. on 3 September, as the remaining men of the Connaughts and Leinsters of 47th Brigade were making their way back to camp following their part in the taking of Guillemont, the Officer Commanding 8th Royal Irish Fusiliers, 49th

Brigade (under the temporary command of 5th Division) received verbal orders to move to Billon Farm to the south of Guillemont. Here, a portion of the battalion was to remain whilst others pushed further forward. The War Diary noted:

> *That place was reached about 11pm when instructions were given for the Battalion to move on to take up a position in CASEMENT TRENCH about 300ˣ S. of BERNAFAY WOOD on the MARICOURT-LONGUEVAL road. All packs were left behind and only the trench strength of the Battalion moved on, 20 officers only were taken. The remainder of the Battalion remained at BILLON FARM.*[6]

Fr Doyle was evidently one of those who continued the journey. He obviously realised that they were destined for the sharp end and that his ministrations would be required. Presumably, he could have remained behind, but he would not have entertained the thought. Willie continues recounting his experiences:

> *That evening just as we were sitting down for dinner, spread on a pile of empty shell boxes, urgent orders reached us to march in ten minutes. There was only time to grab a slice of bread, and hack off a piece of meat before rushing to get one's kit. As luck would have it, I had had nothing to eat since the morning, and was famished, but there was nothing for it but to tighten one's belt and look happy.*
>
> *After a couple of hours tramp a halt was called. 'All impediments, kits, packs, blankets to be stacked by the side of the road' came the order. This meant business evidently as we set off again with nothing but our arms and the clothes we stood in. If it rained we got wet, and when it got dry we got dry too, jolly prospect, but 'c'est la guerre,' war is war. I held on to my Mass things, but to my great sorrow, for five days I was not able to offer the Holy Sacrifice, the biggest privation of the whole campaign. One good result at least came from this trial: it showed me in a way I never realised before, what a help daily Mass is in one's life.*[7]

Up to this point, since their move from Loos, both battalions of 49th Infantry Brigade's Royal Irish Fusiliers had come under the temporary command of 5th Division. As Tom Johnstone notes:

> *Unlike the 36th (Division) at Thiepval, the brigades of 16th Division were thrust piecemeal into a continuing battle under command of other divisional commanders... It can only have been galling for Gen. Hickie to watch, helplessly, as his brigades were used in this way.*[8]

Willie and his flock obeyed orders from whatever official source; his story to his father continues:

> *The greater part of that night I spent humming Moore's famous song 'My lodging is the cold, cold ground.' The Head Quarters' officers found shelter in a narrow trench under the road, open at both ends, so fresh air and ventilation were not wanting. There was no room to stretch one's legs, or lie down, but we sat on 'the cold, cold ground' (Mother Earth's kitchen fires must have been out that night) and slept or pretended to do so. Without covering or blankets any sleep was impossible, but the hours crept on between short dozes and long spells of shivering, till at last the welcome sun sprang out of bed to warm us up.*[9]

The character of the Somme operations was entirely different from Loos, as Willie records:

> *Morning brought another surprise. Though the country round about Loos was full of guns, one scarcely ever saw one so carefully were they hidden, but here were our cannon, scores, hundreds of them of all sizes and shapes standing out boldly in the fields and roaring as if they had swallowed a dish of uncooked shells. That never ending roar and crash of bursting shells was one of the most trying things of the past seven days.*
>
> *Our guns, some at least of them, are never silent; day and night without a moment's break they hammer the enemy's lines, at times to such a degree that it is almost useless to try and talk with the infernal roar. It is meant to shake the morale of the foe and judging by the dazed look on the faces of the captured Germans, whom I have seen, the work is being well done.*[10]

At 1 p.m. on the 4 September the battalion received orders to move up in close support of 95th Infantry Brigade, to be available in case of a hostile attack near

Leuze Wood, south east of Ginchy. To the east of Ginchy and north of Leuze Wood was a German strong-point trench known as the Quadrilateral, which was manned by German Machine-Gunners. Ginchy (at 45°) the Quadrilateral (at 90°) and Leuze Wood (at 45°) formed the three points of a triangle. The Quadrilateral, unlike a trench that ran from point A to point B, looped round on itself to form an irregular circular route. It was covered by wide belts of barbed wire, some of which were sixty yards wide, much of it buried under patchy vegetation. Unfortunately, this gave the appearance that the wire had been successfully cut by the British bombardment. Combles, diagonally south-east of Ginchy, was located on a road that passed along the northern perimeter of Leuze Wood. The road was strongly held by the Germans, exposing the British-held east and north flanks of Leuze Wood and making them vulnerable to attack.

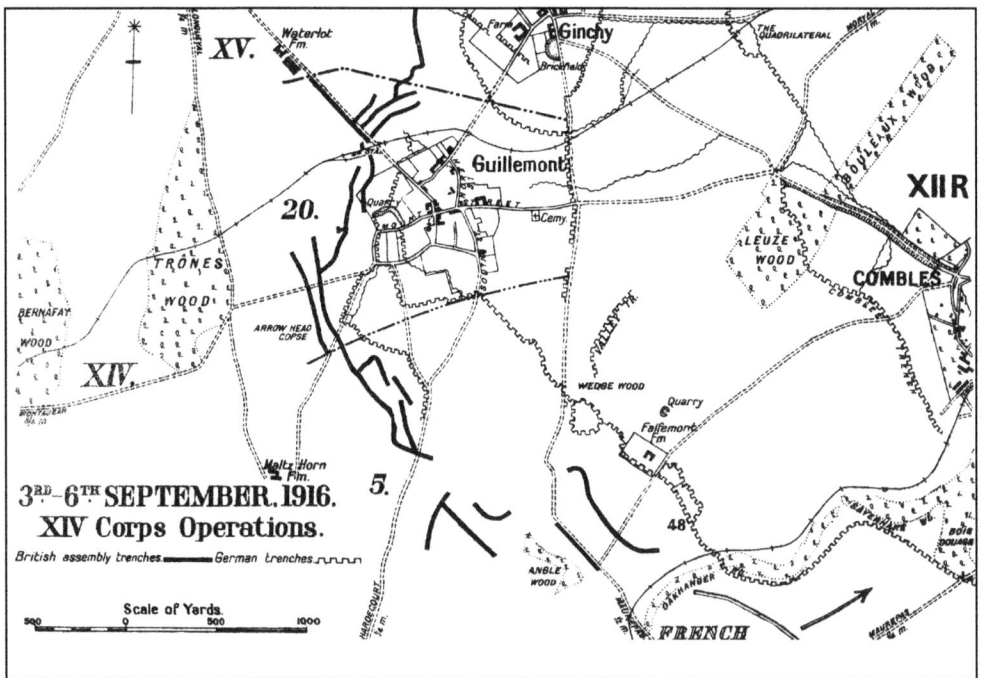

MAP of Leuze Wood referencing Guillemont, Ginchy and Quadrilateral and Combles

The guide from 95th Brigade provided to lead the 8th Royal Irish Fusiliers took them to the wrong place, a familiar occurrence! To illuminate that point, the historian of the 56th Division, whose brigades fought alongside the Irish at Ginchy, stated:

The Somme field of battle was a most hideous place and absolutely bewildering. A guide was a treacherous person to trust, or perhaps we should say he was a broken reed to lean on; for the poor fellow had no treacherous intent in his heart, he was anxious enough to lead troops in the right direction, but nine times out of ten was completely lost a few minutes after he started. And there were, perhaps, more mistakes made in attempting to trace the front line in that great battle than any other.[11]

The intended position was not reached until 7pm. Willie Doyle, perhaps, was not aware of being lost, so busy was he observing the astonishing transformation compared to the situation at Loos:

Our next track was a short one, over the brow of the hill and down into the valley, nearer still to the front line and the attention of the Boche shells. Another arsenal of guns was stationed here, with little or no attempt at concealment, the reason being that they must push on with the advancing troops. What a change this is from the trench life of the past six months, where for days one never saw a soul over-ground. Here, though quite close to the enemy's guns, as we know to our cost, men and horses move about as calmly as if there was no such thing as war.[12]

No sooner was the battalion approaching its position than the enemy shelled the trenches, inflicting between 20 and 30 casualties. So, one aspect at least of Willie's experience of war hadn't changed: his ability to escape a close shave, this time from the shell fire which accounted for the casualties recorded in the War Diary. He says:

In this valley of life and death we had our first casualties and it was here that your poor Will also nearly left his old bones. I was standing about a hundred yards away watching a party of my men crossing the valley, when I saw the earth under their feet open, and then instantly men disappeared in a cloud of smoke, while a column of stones and clay was shot a couple of hundred foot into the air. A big German shell, by the merest chance, had landed in the middle of the party. I rushed down the slope, getting a most unmerciful whack between the shoulders, probably from a falling stone, as it did not wound me, but it was no time to think of one's safety. I gave them all a general Absolution, scraped the clay from the faces of a couple of buried men who were not wounded, and then anointed as many of the poor lads as I could reach. Two of them had no faces to anoint and others were ten feet under clay, but a few were living still.

By this time half a dozen volunteers had run up and were digging the buried men out. War may be horrible, but it certainly brings out the best side of a man's character. Over and over again I have seen men risking their lives to save or help a comrade, and these brave fellows knew the risk they were taking, for when a Boche shell falls in a certain place, you clear as quickly as you can, since several more are pretty certain to land close. It was a case of duty for me, but real courage for them.[13]

One of those injured was Major Uniacke, who had played such a prominent role during the gas attacks at Loos and was singled out for particular praise in his Commanding Officer's report, although not recommended at the time for immediate reward. However, since then he had gained the DSO, in recognition of cumulative actions of gallantry. Willie's account continues:

We dug like demons for our lads' lives, and our own, to tell the truth, for every few minutes another 'iron pill' from a Krupp gun would come tearing down the valley, making our very hearts leap into our mouths. More than once we were well sprinkled with clay and stones, but the 'cup of cold water' promise was well kept, and not one of the party received a scratch. We got three buried men out alive, not much the worse for their trying experience, but so thoroughly had the shell done its work that there was not a single wounded man in the rest of the party; all had gone to a better land. As I walked back I nearly shared the fate of my boys, but somehow escaped again, and pulled out two more lads who were only buried up to the waist and uninjured.[14]

At this stage permission was obtained to relocate the battalion, whilst awaiting further orders, and in a downpour of rain about 9.30 p.m. they reached a relatively more secure place, albeit not a particularly pleasant one. Willie continues:

Meanwhile the regiment had been ordered back to a safer position on the hill and were able to breathe once more. Our resting place that night was a fine luxurious shell hole open to all the blasts of heaven. To make matters worse, we were posted fifteen yards in front of two batteries of field guns, 12 in number, while on the right a little further off were half a dozen huge 60 pounders. Not once during the whole night did those guns cease firing, making the ground tremble and rock like a small earthquake, till I thought my head would surely crack in two with the ear-splitting crashes. Shells, as one very soon learns, have an unpleasant trick of bursting prematurely as they leave the muzzle of the gun. In the next shell hole lay the body of one of my men who had been killed in this way, so the prospect of a night spent in this dangerous position was not a pleasant one. A soldier has to go and stay where he is sent, but to move would have made little difference, for dodge as you might you could never get out of the line of fire of the innumerable batteries all round: many a time have I seen the earth open in front and around me, ploughed up by the bits of our own shells, which helped to make things more lively still.

Rain was falling in torrents as we prepared to go to bed in our shell holes. Seated on a box in the bottom of the hole for protection against our guns, huddled together for warmth, our feet in a pool, we watched the water trickle down the sides and wondered how long it would take to wash us out. I have spent many more pleasant nights in my life, but never a more uncomfortable one, drenched by the falling rain, which would persist in running down my neck, ravenous enough to eat a live German and so tired and weary that the roar of the guns failed to keep me awake. I could not help thinking of Him, who often 'had not where to lay His Head' and it helped me to resemble Him a little. Providence was good to us, for after some time a tarpaulin was found (I am afraid stolen) which we stretched over our cave, bailed out the water and settled down for a night of 'shivery o.' Strange to say I am not one bit the worse for this trying experience, and others like it, nor did I even get a cold.[15]

By now it was 5 September and finally the Officer Commanding 16th (Irish) Division, Major General William Hickie, was allotted a divisional front line at the Somme that he could prepare to take charge of. This was in front of Ginchy and the

Quadrilateral. That morning, two of Major General Hickie's battalions were making their way to the new divisional front, but six more were still under the command of 5th and 20th Divisions, whilst those of the shattered 47th Brigade were regrouping in Carnoy. Willie Doyle would have been unaware of these logistical niceties, and continues his account, following his battalion's orders to relieve the first battalion of the Devons in Leuze Wood:

> *At last came the expected order to advance at once, and hold the front line, the part assigned to us being Leuze Wood, the scene of so much desperate fighting. The first part of our journey lay through a narrow trench, the floor of which consisted of deep, thick mud and the bodies of dead men trodden under foot. It was horrible beyond description, but there was no help for it, and on the half rotten corpses of our own brave men we marched in silence, everyone busy with his own thoughts. I shall spare you the gruesome details, but you can picture one's sensations as one felt the ground yield under one's feet and one sank down through the body of some poor fellow.*[16]

Although Willie tells his father that he will spare him the gruesome details, his description is, nevertheless, grisly and even more shocking in its immediacy than any memoirs written post-war:

> *Half an hour of this brought us out on the open, into the middle of the battlefield of some days previously. The wounded, at least I hope so, had all been removed, but the dead lay there stiff and stark, with open staring eyes, just as they had fallen. Good God! Such a sight! I had tried to prepare myself for this, but all I had read or pictured gave me little idea of the reality. Some lay as if they were sleeping quietly, others had died in agony, or had the life crushed out of them by mortal fear, while the whole ground, every foot of it, was littered with heads or limbs or pieces of torn human bodies. In the bottom of one hole lay a British and a German soldier locked in a deadly embrace; neither had any weapon, but they had fought on to the bitter end. Another couple seemed to have realised that the horrible struggle was none of their making and that they were both children of the same God; they had died hand in hand, praying for*

and forgiving one another. A third face caught my eye, a tall, strikingly handsome young German, not more I should say than eighteen. He lay there calm and peaceful, with a smile of happiness on his fair face, as if he had had a glimpse of Heaven before he died. Ah! If only his poor mother could have seen her boy. It would have soothed the pain of her broken heart.

We pushed on rapidly through that charnel house, for the stench was fearful, till we stumbled across a sunken road. Here the retreating Germans had evidently made a last desperate stand, but had been caught by our artillery fire. The dead lay in piles, the blue grey uniforms broken by many a khaki clad body. I saw the ruins of what was evidently the dressing station, judging by the number of bandaged men about, but a shell had found them out even there and swept them all into the net of death.

A halt of a few minutes gave me the opportunity I was waiting for. I hurried along from group to group and as I did the men fell on their knees to receive Absolution. A few words to give them courage, for no one knew if he would return alive, a 'God bless and protect you boys', and I hurried on to the next company. As I did a soldier stepped out of the ranks, caught me by the hand and said: 'I am not a Catholic, Sir, but I want to thank you for that beautiful prayer. [17]

Once the relief of the 1st Devons had taken place the 8th RIF established their line in Leuze Wood according to orders, digging new trenches where necessary during the night. Small parties of personnel from other British units also occupied the wood, or its fringes, including half a platoon of the Duke of Cornwall's Light Infantry one company of London Scottish and a platoon of 7th Royal Inniskilling Fusiliers. The 8th RIF War Diary notes:

The position held by the Battalion was far from secure owing to it being a salient with the flanks very insecure ... In front of the woods the enemy's line was about 100^x north and parallel to our front line.[18]

Fr Doyle continues his account:

The regiment moved on to the wood, while the doctor and I took up our position in the dressing station to wait for the wounded. This was a dug-out on the hill facing Leuze Wood. The previous afternoon it had been occupied by the Germans, before our men drove them out. Some poor chap must have taken refuge there and have been bombed out, for the sides and roof were stained all over with fresh blood. At one end was a suspicious looking mound of fresh earth, which I did not investigate too closely, but as I said a prayer for the repose of the soul, the dead German will forgive me I trust for walking on his grave. To give you an idea of my position. From where I stood the ground sloped down steeply into a narrow valley, while on the opposite hill lay the wood, half of which the fusiliers were holding, the Germans occupying the rest, the distance across being so short I could easily follow the movements of our men without a glass. Fighting was going on all around, so that I was kept busy, but all the time my thoughts and my heart were with my boys in the wood opposite. They had reached it safely, but the Germans somehow had worked round the sides and temporarily cut them off. No food or water could be sent up, while ten slightly wounded men who tried to come back were shot down one after another.[19]

WEDNESDAY 6 TO THURSDAY 7 SEPTEMBER 1916

At 2.30am on the morning of the 6 September the 8th RIF War Diary notes:

During the night our heavies directed their fire on the wood causing considerable casualties to the Battalion. This took place during the whole of the 6th and four messages were sent for them to lengthen their range.[20]

The proliferation of 'unders' had not also escaped Willie's attention:

To make matters worse, our own artillery began to shell them, inflicting heavy losses, and though repeated messages were sent back, continued doing so for a long time. It appears the guns had fired so much they were becoming worn out, making the shells fall 300 yards short. Under these circumstances it would have been madness to try and reach the wood, but my heart bled for the wounded and dying lying there alone.[21]

Not only would it have been folly for Fr Doyle to venture forward, it was also decided not to: *move Battalion Headquarters forward into the wood owing to the insecure state of the position and the difficulty of maintaining communications with Brigade from that forward position.*[22]

This decision was made by the Officer Commanding 8th RIF, Lt Col S. Watson, who inspected the wood at 8.30 a.m. on the 6 September and noted: *it was found that the S.W. end of the wood was being shelled and that the approach to the wood was under constant sniper fire which caused numerous casualties.*[23] Half an hour later, as Willie Doyle also mentioned, rations had arrived from behind the lines but, owing to the hostile barrage and sniper fire, it was found impossible to get these up to the companies, adding to the misery of the men in the wood.

There followed a full and difficult day of operations for the 8th RIF. They were engaged in holding posts in trenches in Leuze Wood; these operations being framed on orders issued by 95th Brigade, but passed on to them by the London Scottish, when it became evident that those from the brigade had failed to arrive. The Operational Orders were, indeed, somewhat confusing and it later transpired that one order in the original, to reconnoitre ground for an advance by an unnamed battalion coming up from 15th Brigade, was not passed on by the London Scottish. In the event, up until the time the 8th RIF was relieved, the anonymous unit had not arrived.

The general picture showed that, on the right of the Front Line, the French had reached the railway in Combles and the 95th Brigade was understood to be through Leuze Wood. Germans with machine-guns were holding up other attacks. Had everything gone to plan, two companies of 8th RIF were supposed to cover the advance of the unnamed battalion from 15th Brigade through the wood, with rifle and Lewis gunfire; the other two companies of fusiliers were to provide patrols into neighbouring Bouleaux Wood, reconnoitring ground in order to secure a good jumping off point for the 15th Brigade's battalion.

Before being relieved, signallers from 8th RIF had established a signalling post at the south west edge of Leuze Wood, to transmit messages to battalion H.Q. and establish communications with the French at Combles railway. This was set up by Sergeant Holton, assisted by Privates Gavaghan and Jones, under heavy fire, until the daylight signalling lamp was broken by shellfire. Touch was obtained with batteries in the rear, but not with the French.

Apart from the fact that the battalion from 15th Brigade didn't arrive during 8th

RIF's watch, the Germans, of course, had their own ideas. The 8th RIF War Diary records that the enemy was active during the whole morning and a hostile patrol entering the wood from the east side was driven off, leaving two fusiliers dead and two wounded. By 7.30 p.m. the enemy had made an organised counter-attack, again from the east side of Leuze Wood, and also from the direction of Bouleaux Wood. The 8th RIF War Diary notes:

> *Our front line trench was driven in on the second line running diagonally through the wood and that trench was attacked from the east. The second line held the enemy back and finally drove him out of the wood and the front trench was re-occupied by patrols by 10pm. Owing to the darkness it was difficult to estimate his numbers and his casualties, but they must have been numerous as many dead and wounded were seen inside the wood, whereas these must have been more on the front edge where hand-to-hand fighting was heavy. The total prisoners left in our hands was one warrant officer and twenty other ranks.*[24]

The 7th Royal Inniskilling Fusiliers were on the western fringes of Leuze Wood. Earlier in the day the battalion's Commanding Officer, Colonel H.N. Young, had been severely wounded by a sniper and was sent down the line to be evacuated to England. Their historian describes the situation at 8pm, as it was getting dusk:

> *...a hurricane bombardment descended over the whole battalion area. 'A' Company (Captain Parr) was submitted to concentrated fire of the most intense nature. Machine-guns played on their flank from the direction of Ginchy Telegraph. Under cover of this sweeping barrage the Boche attempted to regain a footing in the wood but was unsuccessful ... Our artillery, when they saw the S.O.S. rockets, put down a most effective barrage on the enemy's lines ... The position after the attack was that we were in possession of the entire wood, with posts established on the reverse slope to the east.*[25]

Fortunately, the 7th Inniskillings only suffered twenty-five wounded during the forty-five minute attack. At about the same time Willie Doyle had decided:

> *When dusk came I made up my mind to try and creep through the valley, more especially as the fire had slackened very much, but once again the Providence of God watched over me. As I was setting out I met a Sergeant, who argued the point with me – 'You can do little good, Father,' he said, 'down there in the wood, and will only run a great risk. Wait till night comes, and then we shall be able to bring all the wounded up here. Don't forget that though we have plenty of officers and to spare, we have only one priest to look after us.' The poor fellow was so much in earnest I decided to wait a little at least. It was well I did so, for shortly afterwards the Germans opened a terrific bombardment and launched a counter attack on the wood. Some of the Cornwalls who were holding a corner of the wood broke and ran, jumping right on top of the fusiliers. Brave Paddy from the Green Isle stood his ground and rose to the occasion, first shooting the men from Cornwall and then hunted the Bosches with cold steel.*[26]

Willie's comment about shooting the men from Cornwall can be taken with a very large pinch of salt. He evidently got carried away in his story telling which, as so often, was jokingly embellished for dramatic effect. The historian of the Duke of Cornwall's Light Infantry merely comments:

> *The platoon under Lieut. Lee had an adventurous time in Leuze Wood: they disappeared for two days. Everyone thought they had been killed or captured, but they turned up on 7 September quite safe and sound.*[27]

Willie continues with disconcerting news, which luckily proved to be false:

> *Meanwhile, we on the opposite hill were having a most unpleasant time. A wounded man had reported that the enemy had captured the wood; communication was broken and Headquarters had no information of what was going on. At that moment an orderly dashed in with the startling news that the Germans were in the valley and actually climbing our hill! Jerusalem! We non-combatants might easily escape to the rear, but who would protect the wounded? They could not be abandoned. If it were daylight the Red Cross would give us protection, but in the darkness of the night the enemy would not think twice about flinging a dozen bombs*

down the steps of the dug-out. I looked round at the blood-stained walls and shivered. A nice coward, am I not? Thank God the situation was not quite as bad as reported, our men got the upper hand and drove back the attack, but that half hour will live long in my memory.[28]

The 8th Bn Royal Irish Fusiliers was relieved at 10.30 p.m. on 6 September by the London Scottish, after suffering heavy casualties of officers, two of whom had been commended for sterling work at Loos. Four officers were killed that day, including Captain G.W. Eaton who had won the Military Cross and five officers were wounded; 36 other ranks had been killed, 95 wounded and 40 missing; and two others were posted as missing but believed to have been taken prisoner. (The total of 173 casualties included 21 casualties from the previous two days.)[29]

After being relieved the battalion marched to trenches west of Arrow Head Copse, west of Guillemont, where they went into reserve. Their Officer Commanding submitted twenty-three names for gallantry awards for actions on the 6 September, including the Military Cross for one of the wounded officers, Second Lieutenant A.L. Dobbyn. The two signallers, Private Gavaghan and Private Jones were recommended for the DCM. However, at the end of September it was noted that Military Medals only were granted to Sergeant Rafferty, Sergeant Dougan and Private Beecher, all instead of the DCM.[30]

SATURDAY 9 AND SUNDAY 10 SEPTEMBER 1916

On 9 September a renewed attack on Ginchy was launched at 4.45 p.m. XIV Corps was to secure the line: Ginchy – Quadrilateral – Leuze Wood – Combles; whilst XV Corps and III Corps had other objectives. Thus far Ginchy had withstood all attempts to take it and the Quadrilateral had not been tested. Major General Hickie had all his division restored to his command, but it was a division that was physically exhausted, mentally shattered and greatly reduced in numbers after six days of action. Willie Doyle continues his account of his period on the Somme:

I fear you must be weary of this letter, so I shall try and finish up. I have given you an outline of my doings and little remains to be said except the last day's experience at the Front, Saturday 9th. It was arranged that the 16th Division were to storm Ginchy, a strong village against which previous attacks had failed. By good fortune, or rather because we had lost so many officers, the 8th Fusiliers were held in reserve. At seven in the morning our heavy guns opened fire, and till five in the evening rained a storm of bullets and shells on the defenders.[31]

The left attack of XIV Corps was delivered by the 16th (Irish) Division and Major General Hickie tasked 48th Brigade with the capture of Ginchy; 47th Brigade (by now down to the numerical strength only of a single battalion) was allocated the seizure of the Quadrilateral, and 49th Brigade was in support. The remains of 8th RIF were restored to the command of 49th Brigade some hours after the attack was launched, but in reserve. Their brigade comrades, 7th Royal Inniskilling Fusiliers, went into action commanded by a captain, as did 48th Brigade's 9th Royal Dublin Fusiliers. Many 16th Division companies were now led by second lieutenants, who would normally have only have been in charge of platoons, and many platoons were led by sergeants; some of the Other Ranks were new drafts to replace previous casualties.

Indeed, Brigadier General Ramsey of 48th Brigade: *reported that his men would require to be relieved as soon as they had taken the village, and he was assured that this would be done.*[32] Their exhaustion (as telegraphed by the Press Association Special Correspondent at British Headquarters in the Field, France) was reported in *The Irish Times,* on 10 September: *The outstanding feat of the past twenty-four hours has been the taking of Ginchy... The spirit of the Irish troops who, fresh from the heavy fighting which resulted in the capture of Guillemont ... was simply amazing.* The report goes on to relate an amusing anecdote of several Irishmen, who were fresh in another sense, and particularly up for the battle of Ginchy:

On the night before the attack ... three men employed as servants of the brigade staff mess 'deserted.' They left a note saying that they had not been in the last 'scrap,' but that they meant to have a hand in the taking of Ginchy, ending with the words; 'If all right, back tomorrow.'

Zero Hour was, unusually, set for late afternoon in preference to an early morning start, intended to catch the Germans by surprise and limit their chances of a successful counter-attack in fading light. However, it also meant that if areas of the British assault didn't progress as quickly as planned, their troops would also be hampered by loss of light. Added to which a: *...thick autumn mist which arose as the sun set prevented observation from the air, so that brigade and divisional headquarters received little information.*[33] Stirred into this mix were belated orders, to wait two minutes until after zero hour, which some units received and others appeared not to, plus inevitable rumour and false reports once the assault got under way. All these factors seemed set to create a potential recipe for disaster.

Men waited for Zero Hour, in trenches that were little more than ditches, for hours on end, some for almost two days. The British shelled, the Germans counter-shelled, the British plague of 'unders' continued with devastating consequences: more loss of life. Despite such horrendous conditions Willie Doyle recounts a nonchalant anecdote, albeit three months later, which he heard from the first-hand experience of the 8th Royal Dublin Fusiliers:

> *During the bombardment of Ginchy – the most intense artillery preparation, it is said, of the whole war – one Paddy was seen sitting calmly in a shell hole, smoking his pipe and sewing a button on his trousers, regardless of the fact that bullets and shells were falling like hail all round him! Another lad was half way through a tin of bully beef, when the order came to 'go over the top' and take the town. As he charged up the slope of that awful inferno – I saw it and even now cannot understand how anyone got through alive – he wired into that beef till the last scrap was gone, then flung away the tin, unslung his rifle and bayonet and made for Berlin in track of the fleeing Germans.*[34]

Unfortunately, the British barrage completely missed whole sections of the German front line. Nevertheless, 48th Brigade succeeded in taking Ginchy, the swiftness of their assault catching the German machine-gunners by surprise. Despite being with his battalion in reserve, Fr Doyle was not to be deterred from observing the action from a distance:

> *Shortly before five I went up on the hill, in front of the town, and just in time to see our men leap from their trenches and dart up the slope, only to be met by a storm of bullets from concealed machine guns. It was my first real view of a battle at close quarters, an experience not easily forgotten. Almost simultaneously all our guns, big and little, opened a*

terrific 'barrage' behind the village, to prevent the enemy bringing up reinforcements, and in half a minute the scene was hidden by the smoke of thousands of bursting shells, British and German.

The wild rush of our Irish lads swept the Bosche away like chaff. The first line went clean through the village and out the other side and, if it were not for the officers acting under orders, would certainly be in Berlin by this time. Meanwhile the supports had cleared the cellars and dug-outs of their defenders: the town was ours and all well.[35]

Ginchy, September 1916

Willie refers to experiencing a battle at close quarters, although he would not have been as near as he implies. From his battalion's reserve position in the vicinity of Arrow Head Copse, Willie would have made his way not quite a mile north to the ridge at Waterlot Farm, north-west of Guillemont and overlooking Ginchy to the east. He would have seen the barrage quite clearly, but no doubt his narrative about sweeping the enemy away and clearing cellars etc. would have been gleaned from first-hand accounts afterwards.

The 1st Royal Munster Fusiliers led the attack on 48th Brigade's right flank. This Regular Army battalion had been transferred to the 16th Division from 29th Division, and contained a rump of men who had survived the bloody landings on V beach at Gallipoli in April 1915. Their assault on Ginchy was equally bloody, sustaining severe losses in return for no gains. Success was achieved from the right, with the 7th Royal Irish Rifles, reinforced by 7th Royal Irish Fusiliers, sweeping into Ginchy. Taking over from them, the 8th and 9th Royal Dublin Fusiliers carried the attack further forward, advancing to the second objective at 5.25pm. In doing so their Commanding Officer, Captain W.J. Murphy, was killed as the battalion reached Ginchy. To make matters worse, their progress had been hampered by wreckage of the village:

We had to clamber over all manner of obstacle – fallen trees, beams, great mounds of brick and rubble – in fact, over the ruins of Ginchy.'[36]

But, Ginchy was taken, and German prisoners too. The Press Association Special Correspondent reported:

At one place I saw upwards of fifty prisoners, most of them either slightly wounded or suffering from shell-shock, and I was very much impressed by the manner in which the doctor and his attendants went over them, dressing every injury and doing their utmost to make them comfortable.

A trench of 200 Bavarian soldiers was described elsewhere:

Some of them had their hands up. Others were kneeling and holding their arms out to us. Still others were running up and down the trench, distracted, as if they didn't know which way to go, but as we got closer they were down on their knees too.[37]

An 18-year-old subaltern, Lt Emmet Dalton, and his sergeant, also took prisoners. Dalton won the Military Cross for action at Ginchy with 'A' company of the 9th Royal Dublin Fusiliers, his citation reading:

When, owing to the loss of officers, the men of two companies were left without leaders, he took command and led these companies to their final objective ... After dark whilst going about supervising the consolidation of the position he, with only one sergeant escorting, found himself confronted by a party of the enemy, consisting of one officer and twenty men. By his prompt determination the party were overawed and, after a few shots, threw up their arms and surrendered.[38]

Emmet Dalton also took over 'B' company when they lost their officer in command, Tom Kettle, early in the advance on Ginchy. Like Willie Doyle, who often referred in his letters home to how grand 'his' Irish lads were, Lieutenant Kettle of 9th Royal Dublin Fusiliers felt exactly the same:

I have never seen anything in my life so beautiful as the clean and so to say radiant valour of my Dublin Fusiliers.[39]

The thirty-six year old former nationalist M.P. for East Tyrone had left Dublin on the evening of 14 July 1916 to take up his commission in France with the 9th Royal Dublin Fusiliers. Kettle's health was not good, undermined for many years by an over indulgence in alcohol. Nonetheless, Fr Felix Burke, the battalion's chaplain, found Lt Kettle to be an ideal officer:

Needless to say the men loved him and we all looked up to him as a towering genius and storehouse of information.[40]

By the middle of August, Lt Tom Kettle's health had deteriorated and he was offered a staff appointment, which he turned down and he also refused to go on sick leave. As Zero Hour approached on the 9 September 1916, he was in charge of 'B' Company, mingling among his men, offering cheerful and encouraging words. As he advanced forward in the assault on Ginchy he took a rifle bullet to the upper chest, killing him within minutes. The young Lt Dalton of 'A' Company pressed a crucifix into his hand, before leaving his friend, and resuming the attack.[41]

Continuing with what is only a snap-shot of the actions that day, amongst the 8th Royal Dublin Fusiliers was Captain John Patrick Hunt, who won a DSO for his actions at Ginchy. He and his company mounted a ten hour rear-guard action, during which they kept the enemy from turning the flank of the 16th (Irish) Division attack.

Despite their own losses, the inexorable rush of 48th Brigade's onslaught reaped its rewards; men of the 47th Brigade were not so lucky. They attacked the Quadrilateral in accordance with the changed orders, whilst 48th Brigade had not. Major (but soon to be confirmed Lieutenant Colonel) Rowland Feilding, the new Commanding Offcier of 47th Brigade's 6th Connaught Rangers, wrote to his wife on 10 September 1916:

> *It is over. After a wait of forty-two hours, the leading Companies of the Brigade went over the parapet yesterday after noon at forty-seven minutes past four o'clock.*
>
> *The scheduled moment of 'Zero', as a matter of fact, was two minutes earlier, but at the last moment orders came to postpone the assault two minutes, to give time for a final intensive bombardment of the German lines.*
>
> *Perhaps there were good reasons for this, though it might be thought by the critical, that a bombardment would be as effective during the two minutes preceding, as those following Zero; and, having regard to the difficulty of ensuring the delivery of messages to the front line at such times as these, that it would have been wiser to avoid interference with the Infantry Timetable.*
>
> *The prearranged plan was that the 6th Royal Irish Regiment on the right and the 8th Royal Munster Fusiliers on the left should lead the attack for 47th Brigade, in four waves, at distances of 50 paces, and that they should be followed, at 15 paces, by two more waves, composed of the 6th Connaught Rangers, with one Company of the 7th Leinster Regiment and two of the 11th Hampshire (Pioneers). The 168th Brigade was to be on our right.*
>
> *The right battalion of the 48th Brigade – which like ourselves belongs to the Irish Division – to our immediate left, moved forward at 4.45, having, presumably, failed to hear of the postponement.*
>
> *I cannot say whether this influenced our artillery, and caused them to abandon or to modify the intended last two minutes of 'intensive' bombardment, though it certainly had the effect of bringing on the enemy's counter-barrage before its time. I can say that on my immediate front our artillery fire continued to be ineffective, and it is a fact that the Germans seemed very little disturbed by it, their snipers coolly continuing their operations even after the attack had been launched.*[42]

Such is the fine line between triumph and tragedy, the action was a veritable slaughter. Feilding continues with a long description of ensuing events, but, sadly, those events are all too neatly summed up in his next paragraph:

The leading wave of the 47th Brigade, as I have said, left the trench at 4.47. It was immediately mown down, as it crossed the parapet, by a terrific machine-gun and rifle fire, directed from the trench in front and numerous fortified shell-holes. The succeeding waves, or such as tried it, suffered similarly.[43]

Captain Staniforth of the 7th Leinsters, in his letter home of 12 September, gives a long account of his part in the assault to take Ginchy; men dropping like flies after going 'up and over'; sheltering in shell-holes; of being knocked unconscious by a shell fragment; waking on a stretcher and insisting on returning to the line; crouching once again in shell-holes at Midnight 'waiting and watching.' He then describes:

I saw fifty men wiped out in ten seconds by a machine-gun at one point; they simply melted away and dropped before you could realise where they had gone. Of course we were cut off from all communication, so we could do nothing but wait and watch for the lines of running, tumbling German figures to top the ridge and come at us. We lay there until two in the morning; but I don't remember much because I got a bit light-headed then ... At two o'clock, however, shadowy figures loomed up out of the dark and materialised as our relief, and we gathered our handful together and began to pick our way out ... Excepting headquarters, myself and one other were the only officers who came back of those that went over. All my old friends – all those who were with the battalion at Fermoy and Kilworth – gone. I am commanding the Company now, and giving myself orders in default of anyone else to give them to.[44]

Scottish units of 56th Division, in the line next to 16th (Irish) Division, and believing that the Quadrilateral had been captured, had advanced in six waves about 12.15 a.m. on the 10th, but darkness and mist caused a loss of direction. The historian of that division, in his preamble to the start of the attack on the 9th writes, perhaps in vindication of what was to come:

A study of the battle of the Somme will show that at some time or other every unit lost direction. It was exceedingly difficult to recognise an objective; even the heaps of ruins which marked the sites of villages were frequently mistaken. It is a rolling, featureless country. But perhaps the chief cause of loss of direction was the shape of the jumping off line. The German defence was very obstinate and the fighting severe. Troops, having made an advance, had to hang on anywhere, facing the enemy where he opposed them most fiercely. The result was a zig-zag line, a crazy front, where troops frequently faced east and west and were told to attack north. On an ordinary practice field-day, a platoon commander can get his men out of a trench and make them wheel in the desired direction, but in action attacking troops will always be drawn towards the nearest firing. Men getting out of a trench and hearing or seeing an enemy in front of them will go towards him, no matter how much orders to the contrary have been dinned into their heads.[45] (This explanation, in hindsight, might also provide some mitigation for the failure of the Irishmen to properly mop up Guillemont six days previously!)

The 56th Divisional history continues:

The battle on the 9th has always seemed like a wild rush in fast-fading light. It was opened at 4.45pm, but on the left of the Corps it seems to have been delayed. Nowhere was it entirely successful in the assault. The situation remained obscure and fighting continued for several days.[46]

Willie Doyle's account of the fighting on the 9th, written on 11 September, reflects such confusion, which resulted in his battalion being ordered forward into close support:

At the same time a feeling of uneasiness was about. Rumour said some other part of the line had failed to advance, the Germans were breaking through etc. etc. One thing was certain, the guns had not ceased, something was not going well.

About nine, just as we were getting ready to be relieved by another regiment, an urgent order reached us to hurry up to the Front. To my dying day I shall never forget that half hour, as we pushed across the open, our only light the flash of bursting shells, tripping over barbed wire; stumbling and walking on the dead, expecting every moment to be blown into Eternity. We were halted in a trench in the rear of the village and there till four in the morning we lay on the wet ground, listening to the roar of the guns and the scream of the shells flying overhead, not knowing if the next moment might not be our last.[47]

Fr Doyle's commanding officer, Lt Col Watson, had moved the battalion from their support position at Arrow Head copse, west of Guillemont, to trenches at a crossroads east of Guillemont and south of Ginchy, in order to consult with higher authority. Here was located the Headquarters of the Royal Irish Regiment and Colonel Curzon, under whose orders Watson had been placed at 8.30 p.m. Unfortunately, Curzon had been killed a short time before the arrival of the 8th RIF and the new commander, Colonel Brown of the Royal Munster Fusiliers, had taken over a confused and chaotic situation. At first Watson was under the impression that he needed to move some of his men up to fill a gap in the line. But on leaving Colonel Brown to go and reconnoitre, he found that battalions of the Royal Inniskilling Fusiliers, Royal Irish Regiment and London Scottish had the line covered: *It was then about midnight. I therefore decided to keep the Battalion where it was and to strengthen the trenches in case of hostile counter attack.*[48]

Willie's narrative resumes:

Fortunately we were not called upon to attack and our casualties were very slight, but probably because the terrible strain of the past week was beginning to tell, or the Lord wished to give me a little merit by suffering more, the agony and fear and suspense of those six hours seemed to surpass the whole of the seven days.[49]

Eventually, in the early hours of 10 September, whilst the fighting continued, the depleted 8th Royal Irish Fusiliers marched back to Billon Farm without coming into action again at Ginchy, a relief for Fr Doyle in more ways than one:

We were relieved on Sunday morning the 10th at four o'clock and crawled back (I can use no other word) to the camp in the rear. My feet perhaps are the most painful of all, as we were not allowed to remove our boots even at night, but otherwise I am really well, thank God, and a few days good rest will make me better than ever. At present we march one day and rest the next, but I do not know where our final halt will be.[50]

Rowland Feilding and the remnants of his 6th Connaught Rangers endured a nervous wait under shell fire, having been forced back to the jumping-off trench, before being relieved by 4th Grenadier Guards, and marching back to Carnoy Craters. He doesn't mention whether he was one of the men who glimpsed peculiar looking objects hidden in the woods, which turned out to be prototype tanks. Much more relevant to Feilding was the poignancy that:

The scene was very weird as we picked our way back this morning, through the waste of shell-holes with their mournful contents, accompanied by our wounded, and preceded by a stretcher on which lay the body of Colonel Curzon, who had commanded the Royal Irish, and who dined opposite me with the Brigadier four nights ago – on the night I joined this Brigade. I found myself following immediately behind his body.[51]

Another depleted battalion to stagger away from the carnage as best they could was the 7th Leinsters. When they arrived in the vicinity of Carnoy about 6 a.m. on 10 September, their first mortifying task was to send a messenger to the 4th Grenadier Guards: *...asking them to collect our dead. It had been utterly impossible for us to do this ourselves for the first time in the history of the Battalion ...*[52] Captain Staniforth noted the visit of a General, presumably Hickie, who made a speech referring to fresh battle honours and heroes: *But that doesn't make up for empty chairs, shreds of companies, scraps of platoons.*[53]

IMMEDIATE AFTERMATH

The actual losses of the 16th (Irish) Division on the Somme are difficult to quantify conclusively. Myles Dungan advises a ten per cent death rate; also stating that out of a starting strength of 11,000 officers and men of the infantry, engineers and pioneers, almost half became casualties. [54] Tom Johnstone gives total casualties of 224 officers, and 4,090 men, amongst whom deaths totalled 1,167; this analysis ties in with Dungan's figures. Johnstone also suggests that: *In a successful assault there are no 'missing' – or prisoners.*[55] However, the official monthly return of casualties made by the 16th (Irish) Division for September 1916 was 643 killed, 2,851 wounded and 859 missing, so adding these killed and missing together makes 1,502.[56] Undisputedly, most deaths occurred amongst the infantry.

As well as the two Victoria Crosses awarded for Guillemont, the Division had six Distinguished Service Orders and nearly three hundred other decorations for the Somme as a whole. Fr Doyle was to discover some months later that his name was amongst New Year's Honours, the Military Cross being awarded for cumulative actions since his arrival at the Front. In the meantime, his missive to his father written on 11 September ends on a positive note:

> *What a relief to be away from the guns and the roar and noise of battle. All is going well out here. We are preparing a big surprise for Brother Fritz, which I am not allowed to mention, and the general feeling is that Xmas, if not before, will see the end of this terrible struggle, God grant it!* [57]

Here ends a selective look at the Battles of Guillemont and Ginchy, seen from the point of view of Willie Doyle and a small supporting cast. This account does not presume to have provided an in-depth analysis covering this stage of the Somme battles; there are many academic studies fulfilling that need, and some of these are listed in the bibliography. The War Diaries for all the assaulting units are available for inspection at the National Archives in Kew. Although Fr Doyle could never have been prepared for the experiences he was called upon to endure in Picardy, his letters around this time all bear witness to the undiminished strength of his faith, his belief in his own survival, and the optimism with which he now looked forward.

CHAPTER 21
NOT MUCH REST WITH THE DEVILS:
DAWN BREAKING

'Passion of Christ comfort me as I fight my way up the path of life safe to the haven of Thy Sacred Heart.'[1]

Willie Doyle closed his letter dated 11 September 1916 by indicating to his father that a big surprise was being prepared for the Germans and telling of his hope that the war might come to a close by Christmas. Whilst many men wrote home with encouraging sentiments, mostly without foundation, Willie's hopes were justified following the twin triumphs of Guillemont and Ginchy. Perhaps he also knew of the plan to bring into action, for the first time, the latest technological development, the use of tanks.

The 16th (Irish) Division saw no further action on the Somme, the Guards Division having taken over from them and they finished the job at Ginchy and the Quadrilateral. The reason it was so important to take Ginchy was because that rubble of remains, which was a former enemy stronghold, formed a salient into British territory, where the proposed jumping-off positions were located for a major tank offensive. This assault was planned to take place on 15 September between Courcellete on the left flank and Flers, where the tanks were to come into action, on the right flank. On their way back to the safe haven of the appropriately named Happy Valley, men of the 16th (Irish) Division had a: *first glimpse of strange objects apparently trying to secrete themselves in the wood;* the: *new pattern armoured machines.*[2] The Germans had considered Ginchy well-nigh impregnable and a German officer was quoted as saying to an Irish officer: *you attacked us with devils, not men – no one could withstand them.*[3] Having been beaten by devils in the guise of soldiers, the next obstacle the Germans had to contend with were the new mechanical iron-clad fiends.

The battle of the Somme raged for another two months, until the 18 November

1916. Bad weather, the on-set of winter, and the exhaustion of the troops made further campaigning impractical, despite Douglas Haig's initial desire to continue the campaign in the (largely correct) belief that Germany's army reserves had now been almost totally exhausted. In terms of ground captured, the five-month battle had failed to achieve even the original objectives of the first week of the battle. The line ultimately stabilised through the Butte de Warlencourt, two thirds of the way from Albert to Bapaume, which remained in German hands. However, the success or otherwise of the campaign was not measured purely in terms of ground won or lost. Most importantly, through the engagement of German troops on the Somme, enemy pressure on Verdun had been relieved, and with it the danger that France would militarily be brought to its knees. Additionally, although the British had suffered massive casualties, the new divisions of Kitchener's Army had learnt how to fight a war, along with many lessons which were to prove invaluable in 1917 and 1918.

Germany, whilst having had the tactical success of holding the British and French on the Somme, had taken tremendous losses which had destroyed the remaining experienced core of the German infantry. The Germans came to the realisation that ground held was less important than strategic advantage, and even whilst the final stages of the battles of the Somme were being played out, the Germans had begun preparing to give up territory and establish a new, shorter, defensive line some twenty miles further to the east of their present occupation. This fortified line, which became known to the British as the Hindenburg Line, was to be progressively assaulted in 1917.

After less than a week of rest in a peaceful back area of the Somme region, the Irish Division was relocated to the Ypres Salient. On 23 September 1916 when Willie started his next letter home, he was blissfully unaware of the evolution of the Hindenburg Line. Having previously whetted his father's curiosity, Willie reverts to the ordinary details of life away from the front line:

Life in the army I find is a life of delightful and unexpected surprises. You are told that you are going to some large town and at once visions of comfortable quarters, with perhaps the luxury of a real bed loom up before you; you reach the town only to find you do not stay there but have to tramp out into the open country and fight for a corner in some ancient barn. You hear that the journey is to be done by rail, but nothing is said after ten miles march before and after reaching the station, while the crowning joy of all is to count on a month's rest and then find yourself back in the trenches within a week.[4]

The 8th Royal Irish Fusiliers had marched via Morlancourt to Sailly-le-Sec, arriving at 9.30 p.m. on 11 September, where they remained in billets for the next six days. Their brigade comrades in 7th Royal Inniskillings Fusiliers had made a similar journey and their historian comments:

Marching back from Billon Farm to Sailly-le-Sec, the battalion was ordered to keep to the tracks across country as much as possible; this was done in order to keep the main roads clear for the fresh divisions coming down into the battle area, and also to prevent the roads getting blocked up with unnecessary traffic. Most of the main roads in the back areas were choc-a-bloc with transport of every description passing to and from the line all day and all night.

About 5pm we arrived at our new billeting area, where we found there was ample accommodation for all. Had the battalion been up to the same strength as when we came down from the Loos Salient, the job of getting the men fixed up comfortably would have been otherwise ... The work of reorganising the companies and platoons was sufficient in itself to keep the officers and NCO's busy. Deficiencies in our equipment and stores had to be made good, and more important at that moment was the state of the men's clothes after the past ten days of mud and shell holes up the line.[5]

On Wednesday 13 September a Special Order of the Day, signed by Brigadier General Leveson-Gower, commanding 49th Infantry Brigade, was sent to all Battalion Commanding Officers and conveyed to all ranks:

'The Brigadier wishes to express his admiration for the conduct and gallantry of all ranks of the 49th Infantry Brigade during the recent operations, during which they have added greatly to the honour of their Regiments and Corps and also their country. The discipline displayed and the bravery exhibited by all ranks was most marked. The following has been received from 16th Division:- General Wilson Commanding IV Corps wires

> *'Hearty congratulations to 16 Div from IV Corps.' South African Brigade wires to 16 Division 'Hearty congratulations on your success.' Ends.*[6]

Willie's narrative about the vicissitudes of his journey continues:

> *All these pleasant surprises have been mine recently. We had a few very restful days in the place I last wrote from, a delightful spot on the banks of a wooded river, but since then we have been on the move by rail and motor lorries, and 'Shank's Mare' till we found ourselves in Normandy where the boys had the time of their lives among the apple orchards.*[7]

Willie's reference to Normandy is curious because he and his battalion most certainly did not go anywhere near that region of France. The obvious explanation is that his hand-writing was misinterpreted.

Half-way through their period in billets at Sailly-le-Sec, and following on from his Special Order of the Day, the GOC 49th Infantry Brigade inspected the 8th Royal Irish Fusiliers at 11.30am on 15 September. Coincidentally, as well as lining up with his rallying message to the troops, his visit came five and a half hours after an unusual and unsettling occurrence for the battalion. Willie explains:

> *The enjoyment of the little holiday was somewhat spoiled by an experience which I trust may never be repeated – the execution of one of my own men. It was the one thing I dreaded most when coming out here, and it is strange this melancholy duty should have fallen to me, for the man did not belong to my regiment, but was transferred to us a short while ago from another. I did all I could to save the poor fellow's life, as I believe there was a strain of insanity in the family, but it was his third offence meriting the death penalty, so my efforts were unavailing.*[8]

The man Fr Doyle refers to was Private Joseph Carey. Willie says the executed man did not belong to 8th Royal Irish Fusiliers and, indeed, the war graves registration of his burial records him being in the 7th battalion. However, all the documents on the Court Martial file refer to Private J. Carey, 21373, 8th Royal Irish Fusiliers, and the comments made by his commanding officer were from Lt Col S. Watson of 8th Royal Irish Fusiliers. Perhaps Willie did not want to admit to his father that Carey was one of his flock, as it might amount to a sign of the padre's failure to inspire the man to do his duty!

Private Carey had first absented himself without leave even before embarking for France. This offence occurred at Southampton in March 1916, and for it he got fourteen days detention. Two months later in France, he was found wandering around a town behind the lines in the Loos Sector when his unit was in the Front Line, for which he received ninety days Field Punishment Number One (which meant being tethered to a fixed object, such as a cartwheel, for up to two hours a day.) He went missing again twice more in June; he claimed loss of memory and did not remember leaving his unit; he did not have any equipment with him when found but was wearing his steel helmet.

Private Carey was court martialed in August and sentenced to death. The delay between the dates of the offences and that of the trial was because, at different times, the principal witness and the accused were both in hospital. At his trial Private Carey didn't call any witnesses in his defence, but stated:

> *I lose my head in the trenches at times and I do not know what I am doing at all. My family is afflicted in the same way. My father committed suicide over it. My brother's death in the Phoenix Park, five years ago on 17 March 1916 [sic] was due to the same thing ... Though I am affected the way I am by the heavy shelling I try to do my best. I came up voluntarily to serve my King and Country.*[9]

It is strange that the obvious error relating to the date was left on the record. The Court obviously did not think any of this information about Carey's family relevant or try to follow it up. It was not established whether Joseph's father had committed suicide or how, why and when his brother died in Phoenix Park, Dublin. Either Carey made an error or the President of the Court, Major R. Ross White, made a mistake in recording the timing of the Phoenix Park incident, which no one thought important enough to correct, let alone investigate. Joseph Carey seemed to imply that these incidents, along with the shelling, unhinged him. Interestingly, and coincidentally, the leader of the Irish National Invincibles, the organisation responsible for stabbing the Chief Secretary for Ireland and the Permanent Undersecretary, in 1882 in Phoenix Park, was a James Carey. Perhaps this piece of information was lodged in the back of Joseph Carey's mind prompting him to concoct a story of his own; or perhaps there actually was a recent, genuine, incident in which his brother had died, and maybe Joseph really was unhinged. But if the shelling contributed to his state of mind, this doesn't account for him going A.W.O.L. in Southampton before he had heard the sound of the guns. Indeed, the doctor who examined him could find no evidence of mental instability. Carey's commanding officer commented that:-

His character from a fighting point of view was quite useless. His behaviour otherwise is quite ordinary but absence from the trenches is a common crime with him. In my opinion the crime was deliberately committed to avoid going into the Front Line. He always has enough intelligence to find himself out of the range of guns.[10]

It was proposed at brigade level that the sentence should be carried out, but higher up the GOC 16th (Irish) Division, Major General Hickie, recommended the sentence be commuted. He in turn was over-ruled at higher levels. The brigade comment (before going to Hickie) on 25 August 1916 was that: *I am of the opinion that the crimes were deliberately committed. The discipline at present in the huts is not good. I consider the sentence should be carried out.*[11] Major General Hickie stated on 26 August: *I recommend that the sentence be commuted and that the prisoner given a chance to redeem his character in the near future.*[12] The casting vote at First Army Headquarters was: *I recommend that the sentence be carried out as the crime was apparently deliberately committed.*[13]

The premeditation of Carey's actions appear indisputable, along with the repetition of the offence, but the issue of 'hut discipline' and setting an example may have assumed as much importance to the final outcome. An interesting observation was made by John Lucy, 2nd Bn Royal Irish Rifles, writing from a distance of time in 1936, on the subject of an execution carried out in October 1914 in the La Bassée sector:

With food came news that rather shocked us: a deserter from an English regiment had been executed by firing-squad that day. We were fed up about that, and would not look at it. An execution for cowardice or desertion hits us all too hard, and I doubt if it achieves the effect the authorities aim at. It disgusted the fighting troops, who perhaps are the most merciful of men.[14]

However, two months later, following the first Battle of Ypres, John Lucy comments:

> *At this time a good many men of other regiments were being executed for cowardice and desertion, and I think one or two were shot for rape. Their names, crimes, and punishments were read on parade ... The military authorities took every advantage on these occasions to enforce discipline, and firing parties were made up of bad or indifferent characters to show them what to expect themselves in certain contingincies. Thus cowardice was curtailed by fear of a greater horror.*[15]

As for Joseph Carey, the decision to execute him was made on 27 August 1916, but the sentence was not actually carried out until 15 September 1916. Somehow or other he got himself evacuated to Base Camp hospital at Boulogne via the 20th Ambulance Train, setting off a trail of embarrassing telegrams flying backwards and forwards to establish why, and on whose authority. The issue was also complicated by the transfer of 16th (Irish) Division from the command of First Army to Fourth Army. Eventually it was established that immediately after the trial, Dr Buchanan, who had testified that he could find no evidence of insanity, authorised Carey's removal to hospital due to inflammation in the area of his groin, on the site of a previous bubo. (A bubo is an inflamed large swelling or blister, characteristic of illnesses such as Gonorrhoea, Syphilis, Tuberculosis or Bubonic Plague.) The medical reports did not make it clear whether Carey was currently suffering from any illness, the implication being it was a localised flare-up from the earlier condition. As a consequence of the paper-chase to establish what had happened following the Court Martial, Fourth Army Headquarters sent a telegram to the Deputy Judge Advocate asking:

> *Pending the results which are being made as to the cause of this man's evacuation will you please advise as to the validity of the conviction in this case. The medical evidence contained some hearsay, but I doubt if it need be taken as invalidating the case.*[16]

The issue of possible doubt (relating to what was described as the 'hearsay' of Carey's account of the death of his father and brother) does not appear to have been given any further consideration. The Commander-in-Chief confirmed the decision and once Carey recovered he was sent back to his unit, to be executed at Corbie at 6.05 a.m. on Friday 15 September 1916. Fr Doyle continues his account of Private Carey's execution:

> *Somehow he had been left under the impression that the sentence would not be carried out, so I had to break the news to him that he would be shot at six the next morning. The poor chap took it well, though he felt for his young wife who lives in Dublin. I chatted with him for a while and cheered him up, getting him to accept his punishment, terrible as it was, from the hands of God, as a certain pledge of his salvation. As he wanted to sleep a while I left him, but returned early next morning, heard his Confession, gave him Holy Communion, and remained praying with him until the fatal moment came. It was a strange experience, to sit beside a man in the full vigour of life, knowing that in half an hour he would be in eternity. Honestly I believe it would have been easier for me to have been shot myself, than to go through that awful scene.*
>
> *My one consolation was that he could not be better prepared for death and that he faced the inevitable so calmly. 'Might I have a bit of a smoke, Father?' were almost his last words, for a moment or two after, the door of the stable where he was confined was thrown open, four soldiers blindfolded him and led him out to a tree,to which they bound him securely. Drawn up in front were a file of ten men with loaded rifles. At a signal from the officer they took aim: 'fire' came the order, and as the volley crashed out I raised my hand and gave him a last Absolution. The body quivered slightly and then the head dropped, the legs gave way and another victim of the war had gone to God.*[17]

Three days after the execution of Joseph Carey, on Monday 18 September 1916, the infantry of the 16th (Irish) Division were on the move once more. Their ultimate destination was the Ypres Salient, which had been occupied by the combatants of both sides since the opening phases of the war; two major battles had already been fought there in 1914 and 1915. The division was conveyed from Sailly-le-Sec by French motor busses to Hallencourt, near Abbeville, reaching there at about 9 p.m. to go into billets. The 8th Royal Irish Fusiliers' War Diary records that: *the embussment was very slowly carried out and the journey was also slow.*[18] On the

20th they marched to Pont Remy for entrainment at 10.50 p.m, arriving in Bailleul where they de-trained at about 7.30 p.m. on the 22 September. They resumed marching to the neighbourhood of Westoutre and billeted for the night. At 1.45 p.m. on 23 September the battalion paraded prior to marching to Kemmel in order to relieve battalions of the 4th Canadian Division. Preceding them was the 177th Brigade, Royal Field Artillery, attached to 16th (Irish) Division. One of the gunners of 'C' Battery, Richard Newman, noted in his diary:

> *When we took over, our infantry were not with us, but the Bavarians were in the opposite trenches with a notice put up. WELCOME 16TH IRISH. This was supposed to demoralise us. However, we knew that the Bavarians were never aggressive troops and it was not long before both sides were sitting on the top, swapping bully beef for cigars, as they had not time for black sausage or black bread, the Bavarians would give anything for a piece of white bread and would not believe that it was still standard issue. The authorities soon put a stop to all that by bringing the artillery into action. Then they took the Bavarians out and put the Prussians in and that was the end of our quiet interlude.[19]*

Willie also noted the striking contrast in this new part of the line:

> *On once more, over the frontier into a country not unknown to both of us and there we have settled down to work again, but in almost the quietest part of the line, a striking contrast to our stirring times at Loos. Though all this moving about is trying, more especially as much of it was done at night, with long stretches without any chance of a meal, in other respects it was very pleasant and an agreeable change. I was not too well for some days with a slight attack of dysentery, from which a great many were suffering, but that trouble is quite past now, and I am in my usual good form.[20]*

Willie starts another stage of a letter to his father on 24 September from brigade headquarters at Kemmel, where the battalion was in reserve:

> *I got this far last evening. While waiting for the final stage of our journey, little thinking of the pleasant surprise which was awaiting me. Your dear*

letter of the 13th was waiting to welcome me on my arrival, and hence I am glad to be able to send you in return the best of good news. I am writing in a magnificent chateau, the late residence of Mons Hennessy of brandy fame: quite a small palace, though somewhat the worse for two years military occupation, including a visit from the German Crown Prince and his staff. I have just been for a stroll round the park and gardens and lakes, doubly enjoyable for the glorious weather, which has come back to us again. This is to be our Head Quarters for some time to come, I believe. We are not very far from the Front Line, but there seems to be some kind of mutual understanding up here to lie low, like in the famous 'Brere Rabbit' and 'do nuffin' for I have not heard even a rifle shot for hours, in fact I am wondering has peace been signed![21]

Yet again there is a little mystery attached to Willie's comments. The 8th Royal Irish Fusiliers made their Headquarters in Kemmel Chateau, which was owned by Gustave Bruneel de Montpellier, who was not a member of the Mons Hennessy family although he could have had plenty of brandy in the cellar! So it appears Willie was misinformed, or has added another little bit of spice to season his narrative. Either way, the Chateau didn't last much longer because it went up in flames late in 1916, after Irish soldiers made fires in some of the rooms to warm up. Willie continues:

I need not say what a relief and what a rest this quiet change is to all of us, in fact I am hoping the war may last ten years yet, this is such a charming place, how it has escaped destruction is a mystery to me. To complete our good fortune, 'leave of absence' has been opened again for us. I do not expect to get away for some time, as there are many who have not had a holiday since we landed in France seven months ago, and naturally they are first on the list, but it cheers one up to look forward to seeing you all again in the near future. I hope you will lay in a good stock of 'Bully Beef and Biscuits' in anticipation of my visit, for I warn you beforehand that I want at least seven meals a day to keep me in fighting trim.[22]

The Book of the 7th Royal Inniskilling Fusiliers says of the same district:

The first impression of our new front – more especially after the desolation *of the Somme area – was one of comparative peace and quietness. For the next few months, with a few exceptions, this impression remained. To all intents and purposes there was nothing doing – it was typical stagnation trench warfare at its worst ... The best news at this time was the re-opening of leave to the United Kingdom.*²³

Returning to Willie Doyle, he describes a day out sight-seeing in France before arriving in Belgium:

*Before leaving the scene of our last fierce fighting I paid a visit to the town of Albert, to see one of the many wonders of the war. In the town stand the ruins of a once magnificent church, a famous shrine of our Blessed Lady, a huge statue of whom crowned the tower. This statue was struck by a German shell and knocked from its position many months ago. As it fell, the base caught somehow and the statue remains hanging over the street at right angles to the tower, apparently resting on air. Our Lady is holding the Divine Infant at arms-length over her head, as if calling to someone to catch Him before she falls. The whole thing is very curious: if I can I shall send you a photo later.*²⁴

LEFT: *Albert Basillica*

Willie ends his letter settled in Belgium at Kemmel, having also recently received news from his father:

You can be quite at ease about me now. Danger is reduced to a minimum, even if I had not ample reason to feel that Our Blessed Lord intends to bring me safely through this time of trial, as He has done in the past. I am a bit tired after so much moving about for the past month, but I mean to rest now that I have the chance combined: otherwise I am in the best of health and spirits too. The little trouble I spoke of has quite gone. Thousands of thanks again for your welcome letter: you are indeed good to write so often. Much love to everyone and heaps to your own dear self.[25]

The 8th Royal Irish Fusiliers remained in reserve at Kemmel until 27 September when they relieved the 7th Inniskillings in the right front line, their first experience of front line duties at Ypres Salient. Leaving their billets the men would access the front line from communication trenches, such as Watling Street, Fosse and Via Gellia, peeling-off York Road (Kemmel-Vierstraat Road). The history of the 7th R.Inn.F. describes the front line sector:

There was one thing obvious about the sector, and that was that it was a fool's paradise. Should the enemy contemplate a raid or try to worry us with artillery fire, his task was easy, and our position would be most uncomfortable. Another serious disadvantage to the area was the absence of proper dug-outs, or even shelters to provide protection, and above all the drainage question was acute. In wet weather it looked as though we should get flooded out. At the time we took over, the dry season of summer had left the trenches in a fair condition, but this state of luxury did not last long when the weather broke. Before our first tour in the line was over, plans were submitted by the C.O. to the brigade office for two new company headquarters and various other improvements ... On the 27th inst. The battalion was relieved by the 8th Royal Irish Fusiliers and moved back to brigade reserve in the hutments known as Kemmel Shelters. The camp was on the 'safe' side of Mont Kemmel, about two miles west of that village on the main Kemmel-Locre Road. Though the position was quiet from the shell point of view, it was most uninteresting and dull. Locre, a distance of about two miles and a half from the camp, was the only centre of attraction in the district ...[26]

As well as the usual estaminets, Locre had a cinema, and a hall where the Irishmen organised boxing competitions. Second Lieutenant Frank Laird wasn't overly impressed with the village:

Locre itself did not provide much in the way of entertainment. An officers' club, to wit, a small hut with a few papers and numerous drinks in it, a picture house, one or two shops, and a military barbers, about represents the extent of its resources.²⁷

A selection from Lt Col Rowland Feilding's (6th Connaught Rangers) impressions is also worth recording. Writing from the same area late in September 1916:

24 September 1916. We moved 6 miles this morning to this place (Locre), where I hear we are likely to remain undisturbed for a week or eight days; after which we are due to go into the trenches in front which are reputed to be very peaceful:- a theory which is certainly supported by the absence of the 'angrier' sounds of war. There is a big convent here, where the nuns provide meals for British officers, and we lunched and dined there today, very comfortably.

25 September 1916. The men are living in wooden huts, and so should I be, except that I must have a table to write at and something to sit upon, and the huts are devoid of furniture. So I have procured a bedroom at a little convent in the village.

*26 September 1916. Today I have been to reconnoitre the trenches, or rather breastworks, which we are to take over. They cross the swampy ground below the Wytschaete Ridge, which, crowned by the ruins of the Hospice and a red pile of brick, or what looks like brick, frowns down upon them. Some 5 miles to the left stands up the skeleton of Ypres, where the ruined Cathedral can from our trenches be seen, towering into the sky. All was very quiet. The line will be wet and nasty in winter, but today the sun was shining, and the whole country seemed smiling. The silence was quite extraordinary. There was no shelling. Moreover trees were standing, and many of the buildings are only slightly damaged. The fields are green and coloured with wild flowers; and today I saw two cows grazing not so very far behind the firing line, while as I walked along the communication trench, two cackling cock-pheasants flew overhead.*²⁸

Willie Doyle's long narratives home had taken their toll on his writing materials, as he acknowledges in a postcard to his sister Lena on 2 October:

*I am afraid I did not thank you for the box of pencils which are very useful. Weather fine and warm here. All well.*²⁹

The chaplain's next missive to his father was dated 11 October 1916. By this time the Officer Commanding 8th Royal Irish Fusiliers had submitted Fr Doyle's name, along with eight of his battalion colleagues (three posthumously), for the New Year's Honours List. Shortly before, Lt Col Watson had also recently been awarded the DSO; not long afterwards, he was transferred out. On 5th October his last entry in the 8th Royal Irish Fusiliers' War Diary reads:

> *'The battalion was amalgamated with 7th Battalion Royal Irish Fusiliers under the title 7/8th Royal Irish Fusiliers and under the temporary command of Captain T.F. O'Donnoll 7th Battalion. Lt-Col Watson was ordered to proceed to take over command of 1st battalion The Queens.*[30]

The amalgamation of the two battalions was necessary because it was no longer possible to replace casualties suffered by the 16th (Irish) Division with sufficient new drafts of Irish soldiers. Recruitment in Ireland could not keep up to speed, and the rate of enlistment had been dealt a fatal blow by the events in Dublin since the Easter Rising in April 1916. Upon amalgamation, the English Lieutenant-Colonel, Sidney Twells Watson, thirty-seven years old, returned to his former regiment, Royal West Surrey (The Queens), with whom he had served since March 1900.

Recruitment had, actually, fallen off considerably all over the British Isles, hence conscription had started on 2 March 1916, under the provision of the *Military Service Act* of January 1916. However, this did not apply in Ireland due to the delicate political situation. The 16th (Irish) Division was now under the command of IX Corps and General Sir Herbert Plumer's Second Army, along with 36th (Ulster) Division. Moreover, the southern and northern Irish divisions were located in close proximity, and the men came into frequent contact in and around the billeting villages of Locre, Dranouter and Kemmel. The French town of Bailleul (referred to by the Irish as Ballyhooly) was safe behind the lines, but close enough to get to for leisure activities, and another place where north and south would rendezvous. Frank Laird described 'Ballyhooly':

> *Here were some passable shops, a British Ordnance stores, a few hotels and restaurants, a Pierrot show supplied by Army troops, and a most excellent officers' club ...*[31]

Willie commences the letter of 11 October 1916 to Hugh Doyle:

Your more than welcome letter reached me a few days ago. I should have answered it at once, only I have been more than usually busy as my confrere Father Kelly has gone away on leave and I have the four battalions, all in different places, to look after.[32]

After the two 'New Army' service battalions of the Royal Irish Fusiliers had been amalgamated, the vacancy left in 49th Brigade was filled by a Regular Army battalion, 2nd Royal Irish Regiment. Willie continues:

When he comes back I shall try and get away, though it is possible there may be some delay, as we cannot go when we wish, however I hope to have the pleasure of seeing you towards the end of the month. As your report about the prospect of my usual seven meals per diem was not very promising I intend to bring a few tins of 'bully beef' to fall back on in case of shortage. Our happy days in the grand chateau passed all too quickly and we are back again at the old round of trench work. But what a difference! If Loos was hell this place is paradise. To begin with, there is scarcely any shelling even in the front line, with the result that for days we have not a single casualty. Then the country is extremely pretty, well wooded and undulating, so that even close up to the firing line one can walk in the fields with perfect safety.[33]

The district in Flanders that Willie describes is to the south of the city of Ypres. By this time Ypres had been bombed to smithereens by the Germans, who dominated the ridges outside, although they had never been able to secure a foothold in the city. Hence a salient had been formed, the Germans having a perfect field of fire from their concealed positions on high ground, from Hill 60 through to Messines. They were able to fire on their opponents from three sides, putting all servicemen in danger, not just the soldiers, but also the support services, who would not normally be exposed to such peril.

To the naked eye much of the Flanders region looks flat. In terms of domination, any ten-foot rise is of immense strategic value to an army, out of all proportion to the actual elevation. Leon Wolff, the author of one of the first modern studies of the Flanders campaign of 1917, describes the terrain thus:

The one major exception to the flatness is the famous Ridge, an arc of feeble hills and highlands running from some miles north of Passchedaele southward to Messines and then west towards Hazebrouck. Its average elevation is about 150 feet. Yet the German holders of these modest heights enjoyed a great military advantage not only in observation but in the placement of guns and defensive fortifications.[34]

One of the few hills in the district, and the highest peak, is the Kemmelberg, approximately 350 feet above sea level, which stands some seven miles to the southwest of Ypres city. Here the British army built hut encampments to provide rest facilities behind the front line, although a rogue German shell or two occasionally found their way to the lofty heights of Kemmel. To the east of Mont Kemmel (and south of Ypres) runs the Messines-Wytschaete Ridge, part of the ridge system held by the Germans. As already described by Willie and his contemporaries, the countryside here had thus far remained relatively unscathed; farmland was dotted between woods of larch and oak. All the action so far in the Ypres area had taken place further north. Things were soon to change.

On 16 October 1916, the 7/8th battalion Royal Irish Fusiliers moved to Kemmel Shelters where they relieved the 2nd Royal Irish Regiment in brigade reserve. This was followed by two days of drill training. On the 20 October they swapped with the 2nd R.I.R. again, in front line duty before the Messines-Wytschaete Ridge. During their spell there the Battalion War Diary records the, by now, usual round of daily shelling, sniping and firing of Lewis guns, all of which was returned in kind by the enemy. And so the rotations continued, along with regular exercises when in reserve at Kemmel; fatigues, training in bombing, sniping and the Lewis gun, and close order drills. The history of the 7th R.Inn.F. provides an insight into battalion routine here, when earlier in the month they had been rotating with 7/8th Royal Irish Fusiliers:

On the 9 October we were relieved in the front system by the 8th Royal Irish Fusiliers, and then moved back into brigade support at Kemmel Shelters ... In support, a certain amount of training was carried out by companies, but, as usual, the working parties rather interfered with this. Besides this, one company always remained forward in Kemmel Chateau in closer support. As a general rule, after the morning drill parades were finished, the men were free more or less for a few hours to do as they liked. This programme, of course, did not apply to the company in Kemmel, who, being under tactical notice to move at a moment's notice, devoted nearly all their time to improving and maintaining the defences in their own immediate vicinity. Time passed quickly ... back again in the front system, taking over the same sector from the 8th Royal Irish Fusiliers ... As the weather got worse later on, the number of sick increased ... Activity had considerably increased since our arrival in Kemmel, and it was now the common practice of the Boche to send over a considerable amount of heavy trench mortars at frequent intervals during the day ... The constant damage to these linking trenches and boyeaux made the drainage problem more difficult. Although the weather was still favourable, it was easily apparent that unless some action was taken we should soon be flooded out.[35]

Returning to Willie Doyle, his billets continued to be at the chateau, although he had also been moving up to the line when it was the turn of his battalion. He continues:

This house of security and freedom, with green hedges and trees all round, makes life quite a different thing. At Loos, and more so at the Somme, scarce a vestige of vegetation remains. Long ago every leaf and twig was torn from the trees by the rush of passing shells, the wind of which would carry you off your legs. What once were woods are now gaunt naked poles still standing in the midst of smashed boughs and trees torn to splinters, while the smoke and poisonous fumes from millions of gun shells have killed and blasted the grass and shrubs, the result being a vast arid plain of decimation. You can imagine our relief to find ourselves walking through green fields and along hedgerows covered with blackberries, trying to persuade ourselves that a war is really going on and the enemy just behind the neighbouring hill.

The first night I came up to the trenches I found a very comfortable dug-out, where I slept the sleep, if not of the just, at least of a tired man. That night I dreamt a dream, not like Joseph of seven years of plenty, nor even of seven years of war: God forbid! but a dream of Killiney Strand. I could hear the ripple of the waves and the splash of disporting mermaids (mermen might sound better). I awoke feeling rather stiff and decidedly dampish and as I did I heard the swish, swish of a swimming rat apparently under my feet. I lifted a piece of tin on the ground and found I had been sleeping over a pool of two feet of water, the bathroom evidently of Mr. and Mrs. Rat and Co. Being a man of peace I did not stay to argue the point, whether they should remain or I, and now I am happy in another little den, like the foxes whom Our Lord complained of, and am able to offer the Holy Sacrifice every morning provided I don't try to stand too straight. On Sundays I am able to get a good number of the men together for Mass, under cover of the trees, as there is a danger otherwise of a bomb or two from a passing enemy aeroplane. I need not tell you what a pleasure it is for them.[36]

Despite the relative calm and peace of this new area, Willie's thoughts were, naturally enough, sometimes preoccupied by the carnage he left behind at the Somme. He shared his reflections of that time with his father:

This Mass in the green fields reminded me of another Mass I said at the Somme. By cutting a piece out of the side of a trench I was just able to stand in front of my tiny altar, a biscuit tin supported by two German bayonets. God's angels no doubt were hovering overhead, but so were the shells, hundreds of them, and I was a little afraid that when the earth shook with the crash of the guns the chalice might be overturned. Round about me, on every side, was the biggest congregation I ever had: behind the altar, on every side, and in front, row after row, sometimes crowding on one another but all quiet and silent as if they were straining their ears to catch every syllable of that tremendous act of sacrifice – but every man was dead. Some had lain there a week and were foul and horrible to look at, with faces black and green. Others had only just fallen and seemed rather sleeping than dead, but there they lay for none had time to bury them; brave fellows every one a friend and foe alike, while I held in my unworthy hands the God of Battles, their creator and their judge and prayed Him to give rest to their souls. Surely that Mass for the dead in the midst of and surrounded by the dead was an experience not easily to be forgotten.[37]

Returning to a lighter note he continues:

> *I have at last been able, after much difficulty, in getting you a photo of Our Lady holding the Divine Child in her out-stretched arms, face downwards. The French say when it falls the war will end, which will be quite true for the unfortunate Tommy who happens to get that few tons of metal on his head.*
>
> *I don't think I told you of the magnificent present I received from the 'Mother Bountiful', otherwise the Provincial of the Good Shepherd, in the shape of a beautiful, hand-made flag. On one side is a large picture of the Sacred Heart and on the other the name of the Brigade and regiment with O'Neil's war cry: 'Ave Maria.' The men are immensely proud of it, and feel it is a sign of God and His Blessed Mother's protection, for at the Somme the 8th Fusiliers had by far the smallest casualties. The flag arrived the very night we left for the Front.*[38]

Despite his burden of heavy responsibilities as Military Chaplain, Fr Doyle also kept up to date with pre-war projects close to his heart, as he explains:

> *Another bit of news that may interest you and which makes me think my poor boys are not forgetting my intentions now they are happy in heaven. For some time before the war my heart was nearly broken trying to get three ex-nuns received into some convent, one had been ten years professed and was out nearly as long, regretting every day more and more her foolishness. A short time ago all three were quite unexpectedly received in three different convents within a few days of each other and have written letters telling of their great happiness and gratitude. Now, don't all speak together, but if anyone wants a hubby, or a £1,000 or any trifle like that, just let me know – now's your chance (commission charged only on successful deals.)*[39]

This last sentence was a portent of events to come. Long after the end of the Great War devout devotees of Fr Doyle continued, and continue still in the 21st Century, to direct prayers to him to intercede on their behalf. Back in 1916, Willie ends his letter:

> *Time, paper and light are all failing, so I shall end right here as the Yanks*

say. I may not write again since I hope to see you so soon but will send a card or two to let you know my movements. God be with you dearest Father, till we meet again in the dear old home. I often think that the good God is letting darling Mother continue still the watchful, loving care she ever had of her children and that is why I have escaped all harm. If that is so, poor Mother had a busy time of it lately.[40]

CHAPTER 22
TRANSFERRED TO THE 'DUBS':
A CATHOLIC CHAPLAIN'S CHEERY CHAT

Then lift the flag of the last crusade,
And fill the ranks of the last brigade,
March on to the fields where the world's remade
And the ancient dreams come true.

A Song of the Irish Armies, Lieutenant T.M. Kettle,
9th Royal Dublin Fusiliers, K.I.A. 9 August 1916

The idyllic life Willie had described in his last letter quickly turned into a mucky existence, as Autumn tip-toed towards Winter. Writing to Hugh on 26th October 1916 he says:

As I have only the tips of my nose and two fingers sticking out of a sea of mud, I must ask you to excuse all short-comings in this letter written under such difficulties.

You said in your last welcome despatch to me that 'you hoped I would soon be shaking the dust of Belgium off my feet' as a matter of fact a small earthquake would be needed at the present moment to free me from the affectionate embraces of 'Mother Earth.'

However that is a trifle, as I have good news for you – Fr Kelly's attack of 'strong weakness' has passed, and he is back again, leaving me free to get away. Better still I have been promised the next vacancy on the 'leave boat,' which may be any day now, so I shall be with you soon, please God.

I intend to go to Cork first, as before, to spend a couple of days there, and one in Limerick before going on to Dublin, but I shall let you know when to expect me.[1]

Willie's sister Mai was in a convent at Cork and his brother Charlie in the Jesuit Province of Limerick.

Hugh Doyle by this time had reached the venerable age of 84 and Willie's concern for him is evident when he requests that his father should not venture into Dublin city centre to meet him off the train:

> *Please do not meet me at Kingsbridge; November is not May and you might easily catch cold. I think I shall be able to find my way as far as Dalkey.*
>
> *Mai's fear that I shall come back a 'Bag of Bones' (Nuns can be very complimentary) will receive a rude shock, for I am really in the best of form, though a bit tired after 18 continuous days in the trenches.*[2]

Fr Doyle's long stint of duty in the various grades of trenches was obviously attributable to Fr Kelly having been indisposed, while Willie covered for him. Fr Wrafter, of 8th Royal Munster Fusiliers, refers to his fellow chaplain in a letter written on 8th November 1916, saying that Fr Doyle was badly in need of a break. Unfortunately Willie's plans to get away, once Fr Kelly returned to duty, suffered a setback; writing the day before, he informs his father:

> *They say 'there's many a slip', before one gets off for a holiday out here, and this has been my case.*
>
> *I was hoping to leave today or tomorrow, when a telegram arrived last night from 'Head Quarters' – 'All leave stopped for the present.' This may hold for a few days or may be for some time, so there is nothing for it but sit down and wait patiently till the German Torpedo Boat, or whatever is blocking the Channel, goes home. I should have been with you before this only a couple of weeks ago leave was stopped in the same way, for a little while, which put us all back. I shall report progress later on. No news of any kind, except perpetual rain, which never fails to visit us daily.*[3]

Following the Battle of Jutland earlier in the year, there had been a renewed German campaign against enemy ships in the North Sea, resulting in the sinking of 1.4 million tons of shipping between October 1916 and January 1917.

It wasn't too much longer before Fr Doyle got away on leave. Before doing so he may well have performed what would be his last burial for the 7/8th Royal Irish Fusiliers, that of 2/Lt William Mary Augustine Keane. The son of Thomas Keane of Galway was killed in action on 4 November 1916 and is now buried in Kemmel Chateau Military Cemetery.

Authorisation for Willie's leave eventually came through and he returned home to Ireland some time in mid-November. The next information from him is dated Thursday 30 November 1916, written from back at battalion base, describing his typically unconventional journey there. The second stage of his return journey was preceded by a Zeppelin raid. During the night of 27 November through to the 28th, seven Zeppelins dropped more than 200 bombs over England, largely avoiding London for targets in the Midlands. Twenty-three such raids occurred in 1916, during which 125 tons of ordnance were dropped, killing 293 people and injuring 691. Naturally enough the raids caused near hysteria in the civilian population. Back at the front, simultaneous with the November air-raids, Private Henry Brown, son of Edward and Mary Brown of Rockfort Avenue, Dalkey, was added to the roll of, what had now become routine, casualties. Willie was aware of the raids, even if he got the geographical details wrong:

> *My postcard will have told you of my safe arrival in London to be welcomed by bombs from a Bosche aeroplane, which missed their mark as I was away at Harrow. I crossed over on Wednesday, reaching Boulogne at 5.30 only to learn that our train did not start till the ghastly hour of 1 a.m., a little military joke no doubt.*
>
> *Having refreshed the inner-man and got Benediction for the poor soul, I spent most of the long wait in the Officers' Club where there is a good library.*
>
> *The journey was a cold one, as you may imagine, in a carriage without heating of any kind, with hard frost outside, but I fell asleep in spite of the fact that my two feet were nearly lumps of ice.*
>
> *We got to our railroad at 7 o'clock; I said Mass in the Convent, having first duly impressed on the good nuns that if man 'does not live on bread alone' he likes a little now and then. The hint bore fruit in the shape of boiling coffee with a hay-stack of bread and butter after Mass. The haystack I am sorry to say vanished like corn before the Germans.*
>
> *My only adventure was a roll off my bicycle, head over heels, into the mud, of which Belgium has a specialité. No harm was done, but my*

orderly will have a job to dig my clothes out of the clay.

The weather has been very cold here while I was away; however a change seems coming, which means less frost and more rain. 'Let them all come' say I, the more the merrier.

I am feeling all the better for my little trip and have begun to count the days till the next one, which, please God, will not be long coming round.

Much love to everybody and heaps to your own dear self.[4]

On 1 December 1916, the day after his return, Fr William Doyle was transferred from his duties with 49th Brigade to 48th Brigade; he was nominally attached to 8th Bn Royal Dublin Fusiliers. He writes home with his news five days later:

You will see by the headline of my letter that I have been changed from the Irish Fusiliers to the 8th Dublins, and now belong to the 48th Brigade which is also part of 16th Division.[5]

The 16th (Irish) Division formed one of three divisions of IX Corps, which was now one of three Corps of British Second Army.

Naturally I am very sorry to part with my own men, some of whom cried when I told them I was going, but on the other hand I am really glad to be with the 'Dubs' as we have a good deal in common. In addition, my Colonel, the son of Sir Henry Bellingham, is an excellent Catholic and an extremely kind man; we are great friends already.[6]

Sir Henry Bellingham was the 4th Baronet of Castle Bellingham, and was born in 1846 on the family's large country estate, Castlebellingham, in County Louth, in Ireland. [Hereditary Baronetcies had been introduced by King James I of England in 1611, as a means of raising funds for the settlement of Ireland.] Henry Bellingham was educated in England, and was called to the Bar by Lincoln's Inn in 1875; he served in the British Army, and as a Member of Parliament for County Louth. He succeeded his father Sir Alan Bellingham in the Baronetcy, in 1889, and he inherited the Castlebellingham estate from his uncle in 1900. After serving the county of his birth in various legal capacities, Henry became Lord Lieutenant of Louth in 1911. He was a devout Catholic, having also found the time, in an extremely full career, to serve as Private Chamberlain to three Popes, Pius IX, Leo XIII and Pius X.

Sir Henry Bellingham's two sons followed him into the army. The eldest, Edward, whom Willie Doyle was so pleased to have as his new Commanding Officer, had been educated at Sandhurst College and served in the Second Boer War. Many men from County Louth, and Castlebellingham in particular, had already given their lives, or were currently serving with Edward Bellingham's 8th Bn Royal Dublin Fusiliers.

By the time Fr Doyle joined him, Edward was approaching his 38th birthday, six years younger than the padre. Lieutenant Colonel Bellingham had already received several accolades by this time, being commended for leading his men by example during the gas attacks at Loos in April 1916 and actions at Ginchy in September. The *Dundalk Democrat* of 23 September 1916 recorded:

> *Though no public announcement of the fact has yet been made, we learn from a relative of one of the officers serving with the battalion that Colonel Bellingham has been accorded the D.S.O. in recognition of the gallant part recently taken by his battalion in the Somme fighting. Colonel Bellingham both before and since the battalion went to the front had won the repute of a most capable officer, and by the officers and men of his battalion he is held in the warmest affection and esteem. It is their opinion – and there are no better judges – that their Colonel well deserves the distinction that has been awarded him.*

On Tuesday 10 October 1916, Lieutenant Colonel Bellingham received the DSO during a private audience with the King at Buckingham Palace. His citation in the Supplement to the *London Gazette* on 20 October read:

> *For conspicuous gallantry in action. He took command of the two leading battalions when the situation was critical, and displayed the greatest determination under shell and machine gun fire. The success of the operation was largely due to his quick appreciation of the situation, and his rapid consolidation of the position.*

Serving alongside Edward Bellingham was really just a bonus for Willie Doyle (in addition to having billets at the Sisters of Mercy convent at Locre) as he explains:

Besides, the change makes very little difference as I am quite close to my old Battalion in the line, so that on the whole I am rather pleased than otherwise with the change, which has some advantages.

My present dug-out is not too luxurious; to use an Irishism. When I want to stand up straight, I must sit down, and the rats are simply shameless, but if the roof is low my spirits are high and I feel in the very best of form.

I fancy we are in for a hard winter; we have had a good deal of frost, which I rather enjoy, though it is not too warm in the trenches. However, every six days we get back to billets in the village, where I have a comfortable room in the Convent, with a luxurious bed.

Recently I discovered in one corner of the room a large box of raisins, another of apple-chips, and a third full of prunes; I am having the time of my life, and am counting the hours till my spell in the trenches is over!

There is really nothing to report, everything being very quiet on both sides. Though you know how glad I am to get your welcome letters, I do not expect you to write often, as you are kept very busy with the V. de P. work.[7]

Willie had not previously mentioned his father's role in The Saint Vincent de Paul Society. Whether this was a new venture, the Society needing extra help due to the effects of the war, or whether Hugh had a long-time commitment to the organisation is not known, but probably the latter. A week later Willie writes on 13 December:

As the clerk of the weather evidently knows this is the last winter he will find us in the trenches, he is determined not to lose the chance of being particularly nasty and unkind; fog, sleet, rain and yesterday a heavy snow-storm, have been our daily programme, so that conditions of life at present are none too pleasant.

However, as I told you in my last letter, I have a very comfortable billet in the Convent where I come when my six days' spell in the trenches is done, where I spend six days more trying to dig some of the mud out of my clothes, my hair, in fact every bit of me. I hope the Kaiser gets his mud bath too!

I am becoming quite at home in my new battalion and making friends with the men. One of the first I came across was Willie Doyle from Dalkey Hill, a grandson of old Sil's, proving once more this is a very small world after all.[8]

(Sil Doyle (unrelated) had been the general handy-man at *Melrose* when Willie was growing up. The following reference to Lady Jane is his sister-in-law, Jenny.)

When I have told you that I am well, with the exception of a slight cold (quite a novelty) nearly gone, and that things are very quiet, no casualties, I have exhausted my stock of news.

As I write, a huge plum pudding sent by the thoughtful Lady Jane has just walked in the door. A hundred thousand welcomes! The Lord grant I don't get killed till after Xmas at least, it would be a fearful disaster to leave that treasure behind, to be devoured by the holy nuns.

With heaps of love, dearest Father, and every blessing for the coming Christmas.[9]

One of the subaltern's of 8th Bn Royal Dublin Fusiliers, 2/Lt Frank Laird had fond memories of the nuns and the convent near Locre:

Locre Convent, crosses at window show Fr Willie's room.

Outside it [Locre] was a goodly array of army huts, where the men on rest resided, and the Convent, where the officers of a couple of battalions messed well on very reasonable terms, tended by J_ and X_, two kindly Belgian maidens, whose knowledge of the movements of the local British battalions was unequalled by any common officer of the line. The hall with its glass roof, long tables, its pious aphorisms hung on the walls, 'To work is to pray,' and so forth, its piano at one end, and, most important of all, its iron stove standing in the middle, was a home from home. Here we breakfasted, lunched, teaed, (sic) and dined, toasted muffins on the lid of the stove, read, wrote, and talked in our off hours, and generally had a sing-song in the evening... The resources of this beneficent establishment even extended to hot baths in the basement, a very present help to gentlemen just arrived from the trenches. The sister in charge dished out a few buckets of hot water strongly coloured with the red mud through which it came. With these the officers retired behind a partition, filled one of several baths in a row, and got a surprisingly good clean down in spite of the colour of the cleansing fluid.[10]

As Christmas approached, so did an important anniversary. On 18 December 1916, Major General W.B. Hickie, Officer Commanding 16th (Irish) Division, sent out a message to be conveyed to all personnel of the division. The sentiments of the message harked back to a bygone era (which Fr Doyle went on to incorporate into a sermon later in 1917). Hickie's message was:

Today is the anniversary of the landing of the 16th Division in FRANCE.[FN1] *The Divisional Commander wishes to express his appreciation of the spirit which has been shown by all ranks during the past year.*

He feels that the Division has earned the right to adopt the motto which was granted by the King of FRANCE to the Irish Brigade which served in this country for a hundred years:-

'Everywhere and always faithful.'

With the record of the past, with the memory of our gallant dead, with this motto to live up to, and with our Trust in God, we can face the Future with confidence.

GOD SAVE THE KING[11]

Three days later, the 8th Royal Dublin Fusiliers' War Diary noted that 116 men arrived to join the battalion; all were Royal Dublin Fusiliers; whereas a day later 93 more men, who were all reserve cavalrymen, were taken on the strength. On 24 December it was noted that 2nd Lieutenant C.D. Marlow qualified as very good, being very keen and interested in work at bayonet and physical training held at 16th Divisional School.

Indeed, an examination of the 8th Royal Dublin Fusiliers' War Diary for December reveals a hive of activity; men coming and going for one reason or another; rotations to and behind the front line; and the weather changing from one vile condition to another. When not in the line, fit men spruced up with baths or attended a variety of training courses; unfit men were admitted to and discharged from hospitals; and drafts of men from elsewhere moved in to replace those men who had been killed, or who were evacuated as long-term casualties through injury. On 19 December Willie wrote to his sister Mai, beginning:

I want to have a little chat with you, but you must promise to keep to yourself what I write to you.[12]

He goes on to open out about his revulsion for his situation in a way that he would not dream of burdening his father with. He often confided in the nun of the family in this way and continues his letter:

Did I ever tell you that my present life was just the one I dreaded most, being from a natural point of view repugnant to me in every way? So when our Blessed Lord sent me to the Front I felt 'angry' with Him for taking me away from a sphere of work where the possibilities, at least, of doing good were so enormous, and giving me a task others could perform so much better. It was only after a time that I began to understand that 'God's ways are not our ways, nor His thoughts our thoughts', and the meaning of it all began to dawn on me. In the first place my life, especially here in the trenches, has become a real hermit's one, cave and all, a mixture of solitude with a touch of the hardships of a foreign mission. The result has been that God has come into my life in a way He never did before. He has put strange thoughts into my head and given me many lights which I feel have changed my whole outlook upon life. Then I feel, oh, so strongly, that I am going through a kind of noviceship, a sort of spiritual training, for some big work He wants me to do in the future. I feel every day as if a spiritual strength and power were growing in my soul. This thought of being trained or fitted for God's work (if I may use the comparison with all reverence) like St. John the Baptist, has filled me with extraordinary joy and made me delight in a life which could not well be much harder.[13]

In a repetition of similar sketches sent to his father, Willie goes on to describe the conditions he lives and works in whilst at the front; he then ends his letter to Mai:

Through all this, and much in addition, the one thought ever in my mind is the goodness and love of God in choosing me to lead this life, and thus preparing me without a chance of refusal for the work He wants doing. No amount of reading or meditating could have proved to me so convincingly that a life of privation, suffering and sacrifice, accepted loving for the love of Jesus, is a life of great joy, and surely of great graces. You see, therefore, that I have reasons in abundance for being happy, and I am truly so. Hence you ought to be glad that I have been counted worthy to suffer something for our dear Lord, the better to be prepared to do His work.[14]

Having now, somewhat contrarily, changed his position from repugnance to great joy he asks for Mai's prayers:

Ask Him, won't you, that I may not lose this golden opportunity, but may profit to the full by the graces He is giving me. Every loving wish from my heart for a holy and happy Xmas. Let our gift to the divine Babe be the absolute sacrifice of even our desires, so that His Will alone may be done.[15]

At the end of December Willie started composing another of his long budgets to Hugh, which he despatched home with a covering letter. By this time the recommendation of his previous Commanding Officer, Lt Col Watson, had been acted upon and Fr Doyle was informed that he was awarded the Military Cross. This award was published on 1 January 1917 in that day's Supplement to the

London Gazette, page 33. There was no citation, as this was a New Year's Honours List award for services rendered beyond the usual call of duty, rather than for one specific act, but he was Mentioned in Dispatches on 4 January for his work during the gas attack.

Willie sends his budget with his letter of 9 January 1917, giving his thanks for the compliments he had received from home.

> *Herewith the promised tin of 'Bully Beef' which I trust will not give you indigestion! Ever so many thanks for all your kind congratulations on the Military Cross, which came as a bit of a surprise to me.*
>
> *I know Mai, Lena and all others who have written will not expect a letter as I am kept pretty well on the run just now. I am ever so well with not even a cold. P.S. You will be glad to know, as we are, that 'the Pig' has been removed (see book). We shall have peace again.*[16]

And so Hugh receives Willie's diary of events [the 'book' to which Willie refers], which doesn't spare any unsavoury details, but is written in a light-hearted tone once again to try and allay Hugh's concerns.

> **20 December 1916**: *It has occurred to me that there are many little things in my daily life, trivial in themselves, of little interest to myself from their frequency, but which might prove of great interest to the 'Old Folks at Home.' On the off chance then of pleasing someone who may care to read these hasty 'Jottings by the Way' I venture to begin this diary, making no apology for style or writing, since I must write under all conditions and in all sorts of places, and sitting on a wet sandbag, with one's feet in four inches of mud, are not ideal conditions for composition.*
>
> *My first difficulty is what name to christen the beast, otherwise this production 'Round the Camp Fire' will do nicely, but unfortunately there ain't none, so I can't get round it, though I should very much like to. 'A Catholic Chaplain's Cheery Chat' sounds well, but how can even a Chaplain be cheery when he has just discovered that a rat has made a big 'dug-out' in his Xmas pudding and some kind friend has appropriated – nice word – his stock of candles.*
>
> *'Job' says holy Scripture 'cursed the day he was born' he certainly lost*

no time in beginning! The 'Cheery Chaplain' under much provocation began later in life but is making good progress now.

'Sparks from the anvil' (not Mt. Anville) would be very suitable if 'German Shells' were substituted for the hammering place, but I think myself that 'Meditations in a Belgian Ditch' will meet the case, as it describes my mode of life perfectly.

Picture a good respectable deep Irish ditch with plenty of water and mud in the bottom; scrape a fair-sized hole in the bank, cover the top with some sheets of iron, pile sand-bags on top and you have my dwelling, otherwise 'Mud Pie Castle.' N.B. Since writing this the child has been christened 'Bully Beef' a bully child anyhow.

It is only a trifling inconvenience that you cannot stand up right, or that you must step outside if you want to pull your trouser on with comfort, but then you don't want to because you don't get the chance of taking them off, being against regulation to undress in the trenches; 'be you always ready' is the motto there.

The door serves as a window as well and lets in, not only light and air, but stray cats, rats galore and many creepy-crawly beasties, not to mention rain, snow and at times a breeze which must have been hatched in the North Pole. There I live like Diogenes in the tub, sometimes pretty well frozen, especially at night, but as happy as any mortal man can be on this earth, for if human comforts are wanting, the abiding presence of Him, Who was born in a stable, makes up for all else and supplies the want of everything. What does it matter if your piece of meat is cold (it always is) or your tea is well smoked and tastes of petrol; what does it matter if your loaf of bread is often sodden with the rain, or the rations almost vanish on their way up the trenches?

One can very humbly echo the words of Master – 'I have meat to eat which you know not of'.[17]

It was in this dug-out that Fr Doyle rotated with Fr Francis Patrick Mary Browne, the other chaplain serving with 48th Brigade. On the evening of Saturday 23 December 1916 they met for the first time in the dug-out when Fr Browne came up with his battalions, 2nd and 9th Royal Dublin Fusiliers, who were relieving the 8th Royal Dublin Fusiliers and 7th Royal Irish Rifles.

Frank Browne was seven years younger than Willie Doyle and had followed in Willie's educational footsteps into the Society of Jesus. Like Willie, Frank had gone to St Stanislaus College, Tullabeg; Belvedere College, Dublin; and to Milltown College, Dublin; he now found himself in the front line with Fr Doyle. Just as Willie was new to the Dubs, so too was Frank Browne, who had seen earlier service with the Irish Guards from the beginning of March 1916 until he was wounded on 23 September, sustaining a gun-shot wound to his lower jaw while visiting a gun battery. After surgery to remove the steel casing, and a period of convalescence, Frank had only just returned to his duties and been posted to 2nd Royal Dublin Fusiliers. Fr Browne recalled later:

During our whole time there we relieved each other in this way every eight days. I remember how decent Fr Willie used to be, coming up early on the relief days, before his Battalion came up, in order that I might get away. He knew how I hated it – and I did not hate it half as much as he did. We used generally to confess to each other before leaving. We were very exact about waiting for each other, so that I do not think the (48th) Brigade was ever without a priest in the line.[18]

Willie's budget continued as from two days before the relief took place:

21 December: *A day I always like because the turning point of the year and from this on the evenings will be longer, the mornings brighter and, best of all, the sun hotter. I can quite understand now why the missioners when preaching to the Eskimos tell them that Hell is the devil and all of a cold place, otherwise every man Jack would just be longing to get there as soon as possible.*

I wonder does Brother Fritz know I am writing this diary? There is precious little he does not seem to know – to furnish us with 'copy' he has just sent over several shells, a thing he has not done for a long time, which have landed uncomfortably near. Probably the real reason is because close beside us we have installed a 'Flying Pig' and they are searching for his sty. A 'Flying Pig' let me explain is the pet name for a huge trench mortar shell weighing 250lbs.

The first one we sent over to the Bosch line landed near two big trees, which were lifted out of the ground root and branch and pitched yards away. Fritz does not like the Pig and is thirsting for his blood.

The men have a regular vocabulary for the various kinds of shell. 'Crump' is quite a recognisable English word now and if you roll the 'r' well expresses perfectly the rending, tearing sound of a high explosive. 'Crumps' are gentlemen to be avoided, for splinters fly for hundreds of yards and hurt. I came across a tiny (?) fragment which I was barely able to lift with both hands.

Then we have the famous 'Whiz-Bang', so called because they come with lightning speed, faster than the report of a gun; you hear a sudden whiz, then a crash and you thank your good Angel you were where you were. There is no dodging a 'Whiz Bang.'

A 'Rum Jar' describes itself, the only difference being that the place of the liquid is taken by a fuse and a couple of hundred lbs of high explosive. When a R.J. hits the ground don't be too near, for the roar will easily break the drum of your ears, or bury you under a ton or two of clay. Fortunately the men can see them coming high in the air, and strange to say, no one ever waits to notice if they burst. A 'Rum Jar' will get the laziest man out of bed in part of a second. Try one and see!!

I must not forget an old friend 'Weary Willie' one of our big shells, which comes along slowly through the air, grunting and groaning, in such a way as to make you almost believe he was about to fall down on you through sheer exhaustion. You could not help loving 'W.W.' but the Hun prisoners say he is a beast and simply explodes with rage.[19]

Willie's breadth of detail, of the kind that would be worrying to his family, is really quite astonishing, as he continues:

But to return to my visitor – I had just finished breakfast when I heard Miss Krupp come singing overhead with that peculiar note which warns of her proximity. I ran to the door (the running consisted of one step) and saw the explosion at the bottom of the little hill about 200 yards away. A moment later another scream and the earth is flying sky-high, this time 50 yards nearer. I waited anxiously for the next shot. Again the range was shorter, the third shell bursting half the distance from the first and then I realised that at this rate of progression I should very soon have an unwelcome visitor landing at my very door, for my dug-out was in direct line of fire. There was no time to adopt the Dublin lad's advice when faced with a difficulty and 'send for the polis', nor was there any use trying to get out of the way, for as likely as not another shell would land in the trench itself, while my dug-out afforded some protection.

Holy Scripture says 'Some put their trust in chariots and horses but our hope is in the Lord.' I knew there was nothing to fear while His powerful protection was over me, and it never failed me yet, but I confess I shook with fear as another shell came crashing down and the stones and the clay rattled in a shower outside and on the roof.

It is a curious thing I have never had a moment's hesitation, nor ever felt fear in going into the greatest danger when duty called and some poor chap needed help, but to sit 'in cold blood', so to speak, and wait to be blown to pieces or buried by a 'crump' is an experience which tests one's nerves to the limit. Thank God I have been able to conceal my feelings and so help others to despise the danger when I was just longing to take to my heels.

An officer said to me at the Somme: 'I have often envied you your coolness and cheerfulness in hot corners.' I rather surprised him by saying that my real feeling was abject fear and I often shook like a leaf. Once more God was good and stopped the guns, much to the relief of us all. ------ Mother of Mercy that last one was near![20]

Willie evidently stopped for a break following the close encounter. He continues his description later:

I am writing the same afternoon and the Bosch has begun again his old game, quite spoiling my lunch. It was all so quiet and peaceful when suddenly a biggish shell came plump down close to where I was writing, sitting. Three of my lads came tearing in to my dug-out, they had nearly been sent to glory and felt they were safe with the priest. The poor priest cracks a joke or two, makes them forget their terror, and goes on with his lunch while every morsel sticks in his throat from fear and dread of the next shell. A moment passes, two – 'here he comes' – dead silence and anxious faces for a second and then we all laugh, for it is one of our own shells going over to Fritz, a sort of polite 'leaving cards.' Five minutes more and we know all danger has passed, but it has been a memorable day for me, though only one of many such in the past.[21]

The days were hastening towards Christmas, and Willie had taken delivery of many letters and parcels:

22 December: *Though there is snow on the ground and a frosty snap enough to take one's nose off I find it hard to bring home to myself that Xmas, the season of peace and good will, is so near. However, good friends are evidently determined I shall not, for letters and parcels are pouring in. First came Jennie's 'Rum Jar' (apologies to the generous donor) which had great holding out, till a villain of a rat worked his way into the middle of the pudding and built itself a home there. There was not much of the P.P. left after that but the remainder was all the sweeter. My genius of an orderly fried meat and pudding all together and brought both on the same plate to my dug-out with a smile of triumph on his face. He is a good poor chap but I would not recommend him as a cook. I think I shall suggest to the General to fire a large number of these new 'R.J.'s' across to the enemy. The Bosch would certainly surrender then in hope of getting more, or explode from sheer delight – or other causes.*
Lena and Willie's gift of 'smokes' was a God-send.[22]

Willie's sister Lena, like her older sister Elizabeth, had married an older man, who was also called Willie. One assumes Fr Doyle smoked, hence the gift of cigarettes, or maybe Lena and her husband Willie had simply responded to the padre's request to send 'smokes' for the men. Willie Doyle doesn't say whether he kept any cigarettes for himself, whilst he also uses the collective 'we' when having a good time tucking into edible goodies, which he has evidently shared out:

The parcel arrived in the midst of pelting rain which had been going on all day. I put on my big boots and coat and trotted up, or should I rather say waded up, to the front line and gave each man a handful. You would not believe how it bucked them up or how welcome that smoke was to the brave fellows as they stood there in mud and water, soaked through and through, hungry and sleepless. 'Sure Father, it's little enough to bear for our sins', is the way the rough lads look at their hardships. Almighty God would be a queer God if He did not forgive and forget whatever they may have done with such a spirit as this.

An account of the disappointment I got, when I found a piece of bacon in my parcel some time ago, moved another generous soul to send me a glorious Xmas cake. This is all very well, but I see I must take immediate steps to widen the door of my dug-out else I shall become a regular Prisoner of Chilon – I mean of over feasting. Another admirer (sex not to be divulged) contributed a box of biscuits and chocolates; what a time we are going to have!! I wish it were Xmas every day and twice on Sundays!![23]

The covering letter sent with this budget, which ran to the end of the year, was dated 9 January 1917, but in the meantime Willie had fired off a separate letter dated 28 December 1916, describing the holy days of Christmas. This letter is inserted here in two chunks, in the middle of the budget, to maintain the chronology of the events of the Christmas period. Willie starts the letter with New Year wishes before proceeding with an account of church services and Midnight Mass on the:

24 December: *Before we 'sod' the old year – a wretched old fellow he was too – I must send you and all the dear ones at home my best wishes for the new. For every one of us may it be a holy and a happy year with the blessing of peace, which I think is fairly certain now? We had a quiet, if not a very merry Xmas, which I had the good luck to spend in billets. I got permission from General Hickie to have Midnight Mass for my men in the convent, a privilege which they showed their appreciation of by turning out in a way I never expected.*

The chapel is a fine large one; in ordinary times there are over 300 boarders and orphans in the convent. At the end of the chapel is the refectory separated by folding doors, so that by opening these we had double the space.[24]

The convent may no longer have taken in school-boarders, but it still functioned as an orphanage. Fr Doyle continues:

An hour before Mass every inch of space was filled, even inside the altar rails and in the corridor, while numbers had to remain outside in the open, for word had gone round about our Mass and men from other battalions came to join us, some walking several miles from another village.

We were kept hard at work hearing confessions all the evening till nine o'clock, the sort of confessions you would like, real serious business, no nonsense and no 'trimmings'. As I was leaving the village church, a big soldier stopped me to know, like our Gardiner Street friend, 'if the Fathers would be 'sittin' any more that night.' He was soon polished off poor fellow and then insisted on escorting me home.[25]

This is a bit confusing as Willie had already stated that Midnight Mass was held in the convent at Locre, therefore it appears that he had also heard confessions earlier in the evening in the village church. This back area of the Ypres Salient still managed to function as normal. The big soldier Willie referred to obviously bore some resemblance to someone Willie and Hugh knew from the Jesuit Church, St Francis Xavier, in Gardiner Street in Dublin city, north side. The identity of Dolphin's Barn (which follows) is a suburb of Dublin to the south of the city centre.

He was one of my old boys and having had a couple of glasses of beer 'it wouldn't scratch the back of your throat, Father, that French stuff' – was in the mood to be complimentary. 'We miss you sorely, Father, in the battalion,' he said 'we do be always talking about you.' Then in a time of great confidence; 'Look, Father, there isn't a man who wouldn't give the whole of the world, if he had it, for your little toe! That's the truth.' The poor fellow meant well, but 'the stuff that would not scratch his throat' certainly helped his imagination and his eloquence.

I reached the convent a bit tired, intending to have a rest before Mass, but found a string of the 'boys' awaiting my arrival, determined that they at least would not be left out in the cold.

I was kept hard at it hearing confessions, till the stroke of twelve and seldom had a more fruitful or consoling couple of hours' work: the love of the little 'Babe of Bethlehem' softening hearts which all the terrors of war had failed to touch.

I sang the Mass, the girls' choir doing the needful. One of the Tommies, from Dolphin's Barn, sang the Adeste beautifully, with just a touch of the sweet Dublin accent to remind us of 'home sweet home', the whole congregation joining the chorus. It was a curious contrast:- the chapel packed with men and officers, all most strangely quiet and reverent (the nuns were particularly struck by this) praying and singing most devoutly, while the big tears ran down many a rough cheek; outside the cannon boomed and the machine-guns spat out a hail of lead – peace and good will – hatred and bloodshed!

It was a Midnight Mass none of us will ever forget and will certainly live in our memories for many a year. A good 500 men came to Holy Communion, so that I was more than rewarded for my work.

We were fortunate too in the weather, which had been very bad for months; however at Xmas it was beautifully fine and frosty, and Christmas a good day also, which helped to make things more pleasant.[26]

Reverting to the separate budget, Willie records extra details which he did not include in the letter he sent on 28 December.

25 December: *I have already sent you an account of our Midnight Mass, so there is no need to go over the same ground. I found Canon Arthur Ryan of Tipperary occupying my room when I got back from the trenches, however, there was plenty of space for both of us and seeing I have slept with eight other officers in a room one fifth of the size, I have no reason to grumble. It was a strange Xmas. Masses in the morning, a good dinner for the men in the afternoon, which they thoroughly enjoyed, and the burial of six poor fellows in the afternoon, killed by a chance shell as they lay asleep. Up at the Front Line all was quiet. The Germans hung white flags all along their barbed wire and did not fire a shot all day, neither did we, so there was a slight attempt at least at 'peace on earth to all men.' Every mind, I fancy, was full of the same desire and thought, 'Well, please God this will be the last Christmas away from the old land.' And so say we all.*[27]

The 8th Royal Dublin Fusiliers' War Diary reveals that Lt Col Bellingham wasn't with his battalion for Christmas; he had been wounded on duty and sent to 2nd Army Central School at Wisqúes. The entry for Christmas Day read:

> *The men were given a holiday today and their Xmas dinner was eaten in a large marquee put up in the convent grounds. The dinner went off very well and the men seemed to enjoy the day very much. Major Gen. W.B. Hickie and Brig. Gen. F.W. Ramsay visited the men at dinner.*[28]

Returning to Willie's correspondence, his separate letter has extra information over and above that in the budget:

> *One sad incident marred what was otherwise a pleasant time. On St. Stephen's Day the men were engaged in a football match, when the Germans saw them, sent over a lovely shot at long range, which carried away the goal post – the umpire gave a 'foul' and bursting in the middle of the men, killed three and wounded seven. The wounded were bandaged up and hurried off to hospital, the dead carried away for burial, and then the ball was kicked off once more and the game went on as if nothing had happened. The Bosch must have admired the cool pluck of players for they did not fire any more.*[29]

Willie doesn't indicate from which battalion the dead and injured were from. The 8th Dubs' War Diary for that day noted:

> *A little colder today. Six men to hospital today and two rejoined from hospital. The officers Xmas dinner was held tonight at the convent and passed off very pleasantly. NCO's Xmas dinner took place.*[30]

Willie continues:

> *This is just one little incident of the war, showing how little is thought of human life out here; it sounds callous, but there is no room for sentiment in warfare, and I suppose it is better so.*
>
> *We are having a visit at present from Canon Arthur Ryan of Tipperary. As it was in his parish the 'Irish Brigade' was started the General Commanding Officer invited him to come over and see the 16th Division. He is a fine speaker and has given the men several stirring addresses. He has been immensely impressed by all he has seen and heard of the men, as*

well as by the novelty of the surroundings, which to say the least of it, are full of interest to a stranger. Brother Fritz rose to the occasion and sent in half a dozen shells, close enough to where he was staying – he shared my room in the convent – a thing they never did before. I think it made him realise there was no place like home, and wish it was not such 'a long way to Tipperary.'' Yesterday he was speaking to me of the battalions in a field, when a battery of our guns suddenly opened fire, a short distance behind, the shells screaming over his head. The poor Canon thought his last hour had come and ducked for all he was worth. The boys yelled with delight and cheered madly when another salvo followed, bringing the venerable Canon down for a second time. No one enjoyed the incident more than the Canon himself, who had to confess that not every 'Canon can stand up to a British gun.'

St. Ignatius concluded one of his epistles thus: 'Where my letter began there let it also end.' I echo those famous words by wishing you and everyone, down to the puss cat, and 'Tiger Tim', the happiest of Happy New Years and many of them.[31]

Thus ends the letter of 28 December 1916, despatched before the year ended. On 31 December Lt Col Bellingham returned to the battalion. His month-end summary provides an interesting snap-shot of the battalion's relatively new posting:

There has been a marked increase of enemy artillery activity on this front during the month of December. Enemy mennenwerfer and T.M. (trench mortar) activity fluctuates and it is believed he moves his trench armament to different positions by means of light railways. The enemy (Saxons) do not patrol much on our front. Our nightly patrols have not encountered one. It is doubtful if the enemy occupy their front line. All Very lights are sent up by the Hun from their support line. Sounds of mining opposite N.24.10 [trench map grid identification] were once reported but no confirmation has been received. The RIGHT of the line is not occupied being too badly blown in. Our right bombing post is however within 50x of the battalion on our RIGHT (the 7/RIRRIF). The LEFT of our line does not communicate with that of the battalion on our LEFT. There is an interval of 30x. Communication is kept up on both flanks by means of nightly patrols. It is very difficult to keep the front line trenches in a proper state of repair. They are continually falling in owing to weather effects or being blown in by the enemy in retaliation to our tri-weekly T.M. and Stoke bombardments. There appear to be no enemy snipers. This is surprising as parts of our front and support lines are enfiladed from NORTH and SOUTH.[32]

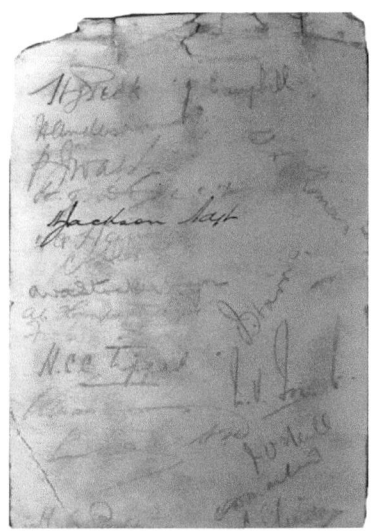

Front and reverse of 8th RDF Christmas 1916 Menu

Meanwhile, Willie continued to compose his overlapping budget, which wasn't sent until several days into 1917. This resumes with an entry for 26 December, which concentrates more on his own experiences of that day, having already told his father about the unfortunate football match.

> **26 December:** *The only thing of interest to chronicle today is a gallant but unsuccessful attempt to get a couple of months' vacation by means of a 'Blighty.' I was riding on my bicycle past a waggon when the machine slipped, throwing me between the front and back wheels of the limber.*[33]

A 'Blighty' was an injury which was bad enough for the casualty be sent back home, but not sufficiently serious to cause disability or be life-threatening. Willie continues:

> *Fortunately the horses were going very slowly and I was able, how I cannot*

tell, to roll out before the wheel went over my legs. I have no luck, you see, else I should be home now with a couple of broken legs, not to speak of a crushed head. The only commiseration I received was the remark of some passing officers that 'the Christmas champagne must have been very strong.'[34]

Whether Willie had partaken of champagne is not known, but he did have Christmas dinner with fellow officers of 8th Royal Dublin Fusiliers, the menu offering choices such as tomato soup, fillet of pork, vegetables and pastries, followed by coffee. Twenty-one of those present signed their names on the reverse of the menu card, including Second in Command of the battalion, Major A.C. Thompson and his brother, Captain F.S. Thompson, MC.

Frank Laird remembered the Thompson brothers:

Captain Thompson and his elder brother, Major Thompson, who became Colonel of the Battalion soon after my arrival, on the departure of Colonel Bellingham to become a Brigadier, both hailed from Nicaragua. The Major was even a bigger man than my skipper, quiet, sarcastic, with an eye that seemed to penetrate one's vitals, a splendid seat on a horse, and an equally secure one at the head of his battalion. With ample powers of making himself unpleasant to shirkers and ill doers, he was the decentest (sic) and fairest of men to officer and man whom he conceived to be honestly endeavouring to do his duty. In the line he had the disagreeable habit of wandering along to some point where the parapet was deficient and snipers active, and standing there with half his long body exposed, keeping some unhappy lieutenant dancing unwilling attendance, while he pointed out where he wanted wiring done or the defences otherwise improved.[35]

So, it would appear that Willie Doyle was not the only one to walk tall in defiance of the hot steel sent over by the enemy! Willie continues with his narrative:

Our artillery, not having fired at the Bosch for a whole day, are simply bursting for a 'strafe.' The unfortunate infantry in the 'Front Line' on both sides curse these same gunners loud and deep. All is calm and peaceful when for no reason apparently they suddenly start a terrific bombardment for half an hour or so, and then retire to their comfortable farm house safe in the rear. Presently Fritz, who had been well behaved up to this, opens his retaliation and for another half hour or so, while our men crouch in their trenches, 'Whiz Bangs', 'Crumps', 'Rum Jars' and 'Rifle Grenades' come flying over, smashing in the parapet and communication trenches, all of which means increased work to repair.

It is said that the troops who held this part of the line before us had a sort of mutual understanding with the enemy, neither side fired much so that life was quite enjoyable, in fact it seemed a perfect Paradise when we came first, but you could not keep Paddy Whack quiet, he must trail his coat and have a belt at someone, with the result that things are lively at times, even in Paradise.

Our artillery, then, having mortified themselves for twenty-four hours, gave our Teuton friends a most unmerciful hammering, sending over on our Divisional Front, which is relatively very short, no less than 9,000 shells of all kinds. The material damage done must have been enormous, for we could see planks and trench boards flying in the air like straws, the accuracy of our guns being really marvellous.[36]

The next paragraph illustrates Fr Doyle's concern for all men caught up in the conflict, and the sort of information gleaned by raids into enemy territory and interrogation of prisoners:

'The Pig' was busy also, confining herself chiefly to a couple of trees a time. I wonder what Dr. Lennon would think if he saw our two elms sailing over into his garden! 'The Pig' would do it with the greatest of ease and pleasure, but I fear would include the best part of Melrose and Linton in its bite as well, while the lady in the lodge would need no funeral! The material damage and no doubt the moral effect was very great, but one cannot help wondering were there many casualties. Some poor devils were caught in the inferno, we could see then running like hares across the open, peppered by our machine guns and followed by our shells, and let me tell you that you <u>can</u> run when you have a few H.E.'s hopping on your heels. The majority, however, I expect were stowed away safely in the bottom of their dug-outs, some of them 30 feet underground, but how they

keep the water out in this land of rain and wet is a mystery.

I have come across two more Dalkey men, in addition to Sil Doyle's grandson, in the battalion, Nolan and Rooney. Cheers for the Royal Dalkey Fusiliers!![37]

At times one wonders whether Willie planned his descriptions with the intention of making the situation seem less squalid, almost homely, or was the references to Melrose and the doctor's house next door merely spontaneous? No doubt Hugh would be pleased to learn of the presence of the two Dalkey men in the battalion, in addition to Sil's grandson. Willie continues:

28 December: *We are back again to the trenches to end the old year and begin the new one there. Before we go in I try to get as many men as possible to Confession the previous evening and then Mass and Holy Communion in the morning. As one battalion is some miles away from the other this means an early start and ride or walk, often through pelting rain, slush and snow. I have celebrated Mass in some strange places and under extraordinary conditions, but somehow I was more than usually impressed this morning. The men had gathered in what was once a small convent, for with all their faults, their devil-may-care recklessness, they love the Mass and regret when they cannot come. It was a poor, miserable place, cold and wet, the only light two small candles, yet they knelt there and prayed as only our own Irish poor can pray, with a fervour and faith which would touch the heart of any unbeliever. They are as shy as children, and men of few words, but I know they are grateful when one tries to be kind to them and warmly appreciate all that is done for their souls' interest.*

I heard two stories today about our Irish lads at the Somme, both 'true bills' as Bob would say, which prove once again there are no soldiers in the world like them. They have all the dash and go of the hot-blooded Celtic race, the courage of lions and then that strong, deep Faith which makes them see the hand of God in everything, even their own death to fall back on.[38]

[The anecdote which Fr Doyle relates in his letter is not included here, because it has already been referred to in the preceding chapter, *Guillemont to Ginchy*.]

They are just grand, these brave boys of mine, it would be hard indeed to not to love them. One of them told me yesterday, in great confidence, that he was not sixteen yet and he has been through a year already of hard fighting. No wonder the angry German officer called the 16th Division 'a pack of devils.

29 December: *To vary the monotony of this record of blood and carnage I shall quote a letter to hand by this post, all the way from India. It is only one of many which I receive from all parts of the English-speaking world, telling of the impression made on the writers by reading the life of Fr Ginhac.*

'St. Aloysius' College, Bangalore, India, 30 November 1916
Dear Rev. Father
Ever since I read the life of Fr Paul Ginhac, S.J. translated so well by you, I feel a great devotion towards him. Nothing has increased more the love of God in me in the course of this year than this Life of the saintly Father. I, yet a student, from far off India beg of you, therefore, to send me a picture and a relic of Fr Paul Ginhac. If I receive any favour through his intercession I shall let you know. Yours most obediently. Boniface D'Sousa.'

Not a bad English letter for an Indian and consoling to me to know that the book is doing good so far anyway, a reward, too, for the labour expended on it which was not small.

One of the last letters on the same subject came to me all the way from Alaska and a previous one from Rhodesia, South Africa. I wish the holy man would put the 'comether' on the war.[39]

The word 'comether' is as transcribed by Lena and the meaning seems to be - to get under one's influence. Therefore, Willie is wishing for the intercession of Fr Paul Ginhac to bring about an end to the war (and no doubt he prayed for this also). Willie's sentiments about the English skills of an Indian must be taken in the context of the time and, in any case, his goodness of heart towards humankind in general has already been well documented. However, his (light-hearted) prejudice in favour of one particular branch of the human race (Irish nuns) follows!

31 December: *Last day of 1916 and what a year it has been for us all. A little sermon here would do everyone good, no doubt, but like the Huns I shall store up my ammunition for a more favourable occasion and fill up the last pages with the following little incident.*

On one of my rambles recently I came across a small and evidently very old chapel, which I found afterwards was built about the year 800. Round the walls were hung a number of quaint paintings from which I learned the following story.

This chapel was built in honour of three Irish (of course) 'virgins' who were martyred on this spot about the year A.D. 800. It appears that one day these three holy nuns of 'surpassing beauty' (this remark was quite unnecessary since all nuns are that) and in addition of 'royal blood' (Irish convents are full of it) doubtless finding convent life at home a bit slow and monotonous, took it into their heads to make a pilgrimage on foot to Rome. So tucking up their skirts, or whatever else you call them, they 'up's and they off's' for the Holy City, followed by the cheers – I mean prayers – of the whole community, for one was the Lady Abbess.

All went well, so the picture said, till they reached the forest in France where the chapel now stands. They were just sitting down to a frugal meal – a very high tea I would call it, for one can see a ham, a loaf of bread, several bottles of wine, and a melon – 'the knife was in the melon' to use a famous phrase, when the blood-thirsty robbers fell upon them and whipped off their 'blooming 'eads.'

Nearby in his castle lived a blind nobleman, who was much alarmed to hear flocks of birds pecking at his windows. He and his retainers go out and are led by the birds to the spot where the three beautiful virgins lay weltering in their blood. (By some means they have stuck on their heads again, looking better that way, but this is a mere trifle for they are really dead!) The blind nobleman is told what has taken place; he orders the bodies to be buried and a chapel built to their memory, and as he prays and weeps God restores his sight and all ends well.

I trust this sad story will be an eloquent warning to any nun 'of surpassing beauty' who may be thinking of gallivanting to Rome, or elsewhere. Even a memorial chapel is a poor recompense for the loss of one's 'blooming 'ead!' [40]

This anecdote adds nothing to our sum of knowledge about Fr Doyle or his experiences in the Great War, but is a diversion (albeit somewhat grotesque) from the grim reality of it all, exactly as Willie intended.

Here endeth Willie's *'Meditations in a Belgian Ditch'* and the year of Our Lord, 1916, now comes to an end.

Footnote 1: Although Fr Doyle arrived in France with 49th Infantry Brigade in February 1916, the 47th and 48th Brigades had preceded them in December 1915. Recruiting fit men had been a particular problem for 49th Brigade and so they were given a few months more to recruit further.

CHAPTER 23
PORK AND BEANS:
AND MACONOCHIE RATIONS!

'Let the stoics say what they please, we do not eat for the good of living, but because the meat is savoury and the appetite is keen.'
Ralph Waldo Emerson (1803–1882)

Willie Doyle starts the New Year recording in his private notebook:

The conviction is steadily growing stronger that I am doing what God wants specially from me by making the 100,000 aspirations. I have not experienced much trouble in doing so for the past twelve days.[1]

The exclamation of spiritual aspirations – short heartfelt prayers which remind the faithful that they are in the presence of God – were an extremely important part of Fr Doyle's spiritual life. His diary entries record how, at certain points in his life, he repeated tens of thousands of aspirations each day. Nobody quite knows how he managed to say (and count!) so many.[2] Obviously, the number is estimated rather than an individual count and Professor Alfred O'Rahilly refers to Fr Doyle's feat as a psychological mystery. The figure of 100,000 aspirations was the highest number recorded (10,000 the lowest according to his notebook entry on 22 April 1912.)

As for his correspondence, the Reverend Father William Doyle's letters home do not appear to have been censored, presumably because he was an officer (Captain.) As for communications coming the other way, newspaper reports were freely circulated, as indicated by Willie's postcard to one of his nieces dated 4 January 1917:

Many thanks for the 'Daily Sketch' which comes regularly and passes through many hands as you can well imagine. All well.[3]

One of Willie Doyle's New Year's resolutions for 1917 must have been to write even more extensive budgets (diary) than previously. Other memoirs of chaplains reveal them getting involved in setting up canteens and entertainments, but by this stage in the war, coupled with the location of the 16th (Irish) Division close to Locre and Bailleul, there may not have been the same pressures on Fr Doyle and so he spent any spare time writing home. It was a task he evidently enjoyed, as he makes clear in his next letter home dated 16 January 1917:

> *A line just to report a 'clean bill of health' and all well on board the good ship 'Saucy William.' I am scraping up another tin of 'Bully' which I hope to send you by the time you have digested the first one.*
>
> *If you find the jottings sufficiently interesting to wade through I shall go on with them, as it is only a pleasure to me to write and these trivial incidents give you some idea of my life.*
>
> *Following very heavy rain, floods and general misery, we are now having a spell of snow and hard frost. Fine healthy weather, no doubt, but bad for the poor nose and toes.*[4]

Willie's weather report, and those which follow, confirm that the winter of 1916 to 1917 in this region was cold in the extreme. Indeed, many military hospital admissions resulted from ailments caused by the severe weather conditions. Willie finishes his letter:

> *Current rumour says we are going back directly to the rear, for our long promised Divisional rest. There have been so many promises and disappointments we feel inclined to believe it only when it comes, but the prospect is cheering.*
>
> *I am off now to look for a dead man, as my supply of soap is growing small and he, poor chap, won't want his now.*[5]

Second Lieutenant Frank Laird had arrived in the sector, via 16th Infantry Base Depot at Étaples, France, to take up his appointment with 8th Bn Royal Dublin Fusiliers early in the New Year. His observations about the cold conditions were:

> *My first experience of France was frosty in the extreme. The ice was half a foot thick, fields and roads were iron bound. A breeze which blew over*

the snowy flats around Locre served to rub the fact of a hard winter into the dullest apprehension. When we left the warm quarters of the Convent hall, and retired to the wooden hut which four of us used as our sleeping apartment, we found that even with the help of a stove the problem of keeping warm in our 'fleabags' was not an easy one to solve; while rising in the bitter morning, shaving and dressing with fingers almost too numb to button our clothes, was an ordeal which made the hot coffee and boiled eggs of breakfast doubly agreeable.[6]

On 27 January Willie writes to his father again enclosing a budget which runs from 1 to 13 January. The covering letter says:

As you confess in your most welcome letter to have made a regular glutton of yourself over the tin of 'Bully' I won't risk another, but send instead some 'Maconochie Ration' which I hope you will enjoy.

I have just had long, interesting letters from Lena, Mai and Charles, with the regular 'Cheer-O' from Jennie, enclosing a big box of rosaries. You are all good to the poor, old man here who is in the best of form, though more or less frozen in parts. Still, the hard frosty weather is a most welcome change from perpetual rain and mud.

I enclose a very kind letter from Dr. Browne, as I told his Lordship in my reply I felt more proud of it than the M.C.

If not too much trouble would you send these two parts of the diary to Fr Brennan to read, as it will save me writing. I enclose his address to remind you.[7]

Willie has now started to regularly refer to his budgets in military culinary terms, the humour of which his family no doubt found easy to digest! However, this next budget (Maconochie Ration) starts on a more philosophical note:

1 January 1917: Whatever may be said of the birth and life of the Old Year it certainly died in a glorious burst of noise.

All last evening, with intervals for refreshment, our gunners were hard at it – 'worrying the Boche' they call it, not caring of course whether they worry or not the man of peace who would dearly love a sleep. Then when midnight struck a tremendous cannonade to usher in the New Year and duly impress the Hun that the last year of his military power has come.

Fritz was strangely quiet, no retaliation, drinking our health probably in the depths of his safe dug-out, all except the unfortunate sentries who had to face the music in the opposite trenches and kept sending up 'verey lights' or star shells to make sure we were not coming over to raid him. It was a fine display of artillery work, but we shall pay for it, of that I am certain, the 'we' being the poor infantry holding the trench and not the good gunners.

Same night: *I was right: we did pay for our fun and the particular spot selected for the scourging was the place where I have the honour to live.*

This morning again our guns opened up and the 'Flying Pig' joined in with gusto. Oh! That someone would slay that beasty pig, make him into sausage or blow him (I should say her) to Dalkey. If not friend Fritz will soon blow us to Kingdom Come.

Again the Germans were almost silent and then about one o'clock just as our artillery had ceased they gave it to us back and for two hours and a quarter pasted us with shells till I thought not a man would be left alive to tell the tale. How little the expression 'we were shelled for two hours' conveys to you! People read in their papers some mornings 'The enemy fiercely attacked our trenches but were driven back again' and never give a thought to the brave fellows who lie in heaps mangled and bleeding, nor to the moans of pain, nor the broken hearts in many a home. Not many at home care much, I fear, otherwise we should hear less of these brave speeches about 'no peace at any price' from men who will never have to fight. If only the world, Allied and German, could see and hear what we see and hear daily there would soon be a shout for 'peace <u>at any</u> price'.[8]

The 8th Royal Dublin Fusiliers' War Diary for 2 January 1917 confirms a number of injuries from enemy shelling. Willie continues:

Words could never convey the pent up agony (it is the only word to use) of those two hours, waiting, waiting, always waiting for something to happen, without being able to fire even a bullet in return. I do not think the feelings of a condemned man on the scaffold, waiting for the bolt to be drawn, could be much worse. You know your chances of being hit are relatively small, but there is always the chance that you may and as shell followed shell in quick succession, sometimes two or three together, even the bravest seemed to shrink up as if they were struck and faces grew long and drawn.

For the moment there was nothing to be done so I went on with my Office, but all the time I was torn with anxiety for the safety of my poor boys. It seemed to drive all anxiety and fear for my own safety out of my head. Even when one shell burst very near and the smoke and fumes drifted in through the door of my 'Castle' nearly smothering me, my chief thought was for them and my prayers for their safety.

The prophet of old never called on the good God more earnestly than I did then: 'Spare, O Lord, spare Thy people' for humanly speaking the casualties were bound to be heavy, as the whole German fire was concentrated on this one spot, with the object evidently of knocking out I nearly said the 'bloody' Pig!

At last I could stand it no longer; I felt I must go round and see what damage had been done, though I knew I should be called if really wanted. The fire had slackened considerably, not more than four or five shells coming over each minute, so out I went and started down the trench. I had only taken six paces when I heard the scream of a coming shell right for me. Every shell has a special 'note.' You hear some and do not even look up, for you know by their sound they are safe overhead and will burst far away. A second makes you a wee bit anxious for a moment, till you locate its direction and you know all is well, for you at least, but there is a third kind of 'note' which when you hear you don't even stop to think but dive straight for the first rat hole or gooseberry bush, anything, no matter what, which might give cover, or failing that you dig your nose as deep as you can into the ground and try to feel small.

Here the value of practical experience comes in and many an old campaigner will save himself where a novice would come to serious harm. I flung myself on my face and as I did the ground took a jump and the sky came tumbling down from the crash that followed. With the beautiful logic of an Irishman, or rather want of it, I heard myself exclaiming: 'Good

Lord, I'm killed,' which was so obviously untrue that I burst out laughing.

There is some consolation in the thought that if you do get hit or buried by a kindly 'crump' you hear nothing about it till someone pulls you out by the legs, so the fact that I heard the crash told me I was safe. I looked up and saw my unwelcome visitor had fallen two feet from my own door! Had I been five seconds later I probably would have been converted into a beautiful specimen of a cabbage strainer and at last made really hol(e)y!' [9]

Windows and crockery obviously being in short supply, Willie continues:

*I did **not** go back to see how many panes of glass were broken, or how much of my crockery was left. I knew that was safe, but sped me on thanking some good souls for their good prayers. A few yards further on a substantial sod of earth weighing it seemed to me a ton and a half, though it was probably less, nearly knocked all the breath out of my body, but that was a trifle seeing it might have been a similar lump of Rhineland iron.*

I found three of my boys, who had been sheltering together, wounded, two of them slightly, the third rather badly. He was only a lad and was moaning in great pain. When I had anointed him I put my arms round the poor boy, he could not lie down, being hit in the back in several places and he rested his head on my breast like a little child. It seemed to ease the pain for he ceased moaning and possibly felt safer, for the shells were bursting round us and he was trembling with fear.

We then got him under cover of the dressing station and I was able to enquire about the rest. Marvellous to relate, not another man had been hit, nor was there a single other casualty at the end of the two and a half hours bombardment, though hundreds of shells had rained down on all sides of us, in fact lead and iron enough to have put half the British army out of action, if they only stood in the right place.

This is one of the mysteries of the present war. Here were the Germans 'strafing' us for a solid two hours, at the cost of thousands of pounds, pouring shells over a small space crowded with men who had very little protection, except from splinters, and at the end of it all could only put one direct hit to their credit. They were of course firing by the map only and without observation balloons, and for accuracy and range were simply wonderful, but one shot was a few feet too far and the next six feet inches too short which just made all the difference.

In addition the harmless 'duds' helped to save our lives. A 'dud' is a shell which fails to explode, dear, kindly, creature and 'duds' fortunately are plentiful on both sides. I watched one of our guns firing 19 'duds' in succession, but that was probably some of the American ammunition made by German workmen, who obligingly left out the fuse, or filled the shell with sand, and so helped the Vaderland. Wily old Boche![10]

Willie is no doubt reflecting trench humour. The background to his reference to 'duds' was the shell scandal of 1915, when there were inadequate supplies of all calibres of shell to meet the needs at the front, and a high proportion of shells fired which failed to explode. This was generally a result of the fuse on the shell (the graze fuse) requiring a hard impact to set off the firing mechanism. The soft soil of the churned up battlefield, combined with inherent design weaknesses in the fuse, resulted in many shells exploding harmlessly deep in the ground and, on occasion, as many as one in four fuses failing to explode at all. Consequently, the Ministry of Munitions was formed in May 1915, which was tasked with increasing the quantity of shells produced and ensuring quality of manufacture. As the UK industrial capacity for this type of work had already been exceeded, significant contracts were placed in Canada via the Imperial Munitions Board. The introduction of a new design of fuse, the No 106, in early 1917 largely alleviated the problem of fuses failing to set off the firing mechanism. Returning to Willie, he continues:

One good result came from this attack, the 'Pig,' the cause of all our trouble, was removed next day since when we have been left in peace.

4 January: *I did not get my work finished till rather late tonight and as I had to <u>turn out</u> again shortly it was not worth while <u>turning in</u>. Some of my men were to make a raid on the enemy trenches in the early hours of the morning, dangerous work and heavy casualties often, so I make it a point to go round the line and give each man Absolution before he 'goes over the top.' It is a hard and anxious time and a big strain waiting for the word to be given and I know it is a comfort to them to see the priest come round and a cheery word bucks them up.*

As I was walking along the Front Line trench, 2.30 a.m., in the morning I met a group of officers who began to congratulate me. I was rather mystified till one of them asked me had I not seen my name on the Honours' List for the Military Cross. It was the first I had heard of it and was about the last thing in my mind, for I certainly never expected it. I felt very much like a soldier in a recent picture of Punch. A lady is visiting a wounded Tommy: 'And you tell me, my poor man, that a huge German shell fell beside you and buried you 20ft deep, when a second one came and dug you up again unhurt. How <u>did</u> you feel?' 'Never more surprised in my life, ma'am!'[11]

Willie did, of course, know that he had been awarded the Military Cross, but perhaps he was not aware that the award would be gazetted with the New Year's Honours List. He then goes on to make a curious comment, indicating that he had written a letter about the award. This is another mystery which might be solved if the other side of the correspondence were available:

'I am sorry these rewards are given to chaplains, for surely he would be a poor specimen of the Lord's Anointed who would do his work for such a thing, but seeing that they are going I must say I am really glad because I know it will give pleasure to an 'old soldier' at home, who ought long ago to have had all the medals and distinctions ever conferred.

Writing later I have learned a curious thing. I have reason to believe that the famous letter, which at one time I feared would have caused serious trouble, had not a little to say to the awarding of the Military Cross. It brought the little bit of good I was able to do for the men in a prominent and certainly unintended way under the General's notice, so that once again 'the Lord disposeth all things sweetly' according to His own wise plans and everything happens for the best, even when Tim runs away with the leg of mutton!

One thing has been really gratifying, viz the very warm and sincere congratulations I have received from the General down, everyone seemed more pleased than if they had received it themselves, while I need not say the poor men are just delighted. The Dubs taking all the credit to themselves.

All went well with the raid. We should have had more prisoners only a hot-blooded Irishman is a dangerous customer when he gets behind a bayonet and wants to let daylight through everybody.

I got back to my bunk at six and slept like a top till seven, not too long you will say, but if you come out here you will find all the old-fashioned ideas about food and sleep and wet clothes and the rest of it rapidly vanishing. It is wonderful what you can do with a cup of tea and one hours' sleep in the twenty-four. (Personally I would vote for two hours, and two cups of tea with a wee bit of bread.)[12]

Fr Doyle never forgot his purpose in being with his men in the front line, as he explains on 5 January that:

Confessions this cold weather are rather trying. You must get the men where and when you can. Sometimes in the trench to the accompaniment of the 'thud, thud' of stray bullets into the sandbags behind or in front of you; sometimes walking along the road, or squeezed into a hole called a dug-out. The place counts for nothing since one can anywhere pour the Precious Blood of Jesus over the sinful soul and give back peace and happiness to many hearts.

As a rule the men come to some old barn as often as not without a roof, or to a room which has no window or door; it is a trifle breezy at times, but there would be no fun in the campaign if it were all 'beer and skittles'.[13]

Willie is also ever mindful of giving an account of the actions he saw taking place above him in the sky, as on 8 January:

Our airmen, very justly, have earned a big reputation for their skill and daring, but the 'Allyman' can still give them points in cuteness. The word 'Allyman' is probably new to you, but is the word used by our Irish boys for the enemy. They picked it up in France and it is simply a corruption of Les Allemands, the Germans.

Time after time I have seen our air squadrons sailing up and down, looking in vain for some Boche to devour and then the moment they went back to the rear for lunch out came the cautious Hun, took all the photos he wanted, noted positions of guns etc. and returned safely to his lines in peace, without a nasty air fight, in which he generally comes off second best.

This afternoon I saw a very clever bit of work. One of our planes was going along on its usual beat when literally, like a bolt from the blue, a German airman shot down on him from the sky. He had crept up at such a height that even our vigilant observers had not noticed him, then fixing his bearings by means of a powerful telescope he dived straight for our man before the latter realised what was taking place. There was a loud rattle of machine gun fire and the enemy was off as fast as he had come. I saw a thick column of black smoke rising from our aeroplane – a bullet had struck the petrol tank and the next instant it burst into flames.

Wherever the pilot was he was certainly a brave, cool fellow. To dive at once for safety would have meant destruction, for the rush of the wind would have carried the flames to the wings of the machine, and so with the petrol tank blazing fiercely behind him, he brought his plane slowly to the ground and saved his own and his observer's life, though he was badly burnt in doing so.[14]

Frank Laird was also enthralled with similar, unfamiliar, sights:

An interesting sight to my unaccustomed eyes on these first days, was the arrival of a Boche aeroplane flying very high overhead and our gunners trying to demolish him. The little white clouds, appearing as the 'Archies' burst round him, showed up very prettily against the frosty blue sky. They served, I presume, to keep him high, but as to hitting him, that seemed rather a pious hope than an active expectation.[15]

Willie continues with his budget, still on the same theme:

9 January: *Our visitor from the sky was back again today repeating his old trick, with the same success, this time against one of our captive balloons. It was a thrilling sight to see the huge bag of fire gas burst into fire as the bullets hit it, and more thrilling still to watch the two unfortunate occupants of the car jump for their lives, fall like stones through the air, more rapidly each second till, with an intense gasp of relief, we saw the* *parachute open and both men land unhurt in safety.*

The Boche airman, well satisfied with his double coup, was well away before our men could take up the chase. If he has any respect for his skin he would be well advised not to come near this part of the line again, as more than one is thirsting for his blood.[16]

The next segment of Fr Doyle's budget moves away from daylight observations to night-time activity:

13 January: *'Two men badly wounded in the firing line, Sir.' I was fast asleep, snugly tucked up in my blankets, dreaming a pleasant dream of something 'hot.' One always dreams of lovely hot things at night in the trenches, sitting at a warm fire at home, or of huge piles of food and drink, but always steaming hot.*

'You will need to be quick, Father, to find them alive.' By this time I had grasped the fact that someone was calling me, that some poor dying man needed help, that perhaps a soul was in danger. In a few seconds I had pulled on my big boots, I know I should want them in the mud and wet, jumped into my waterproof and darted down the trench.

It was just 2a.m., bitterly cold and snowing hard. God help the poor fellows holding the tumbled in ditch which is called the Front Line, standing there wet and more than frozen, hour after hour; but more than all God help and strengthen the victims of this war, the wounded soldier with his torn and bleeding body lying out in this awful biting cold, praying for the help that seems so slow in coming.

The first part of my journey was easy enough, except that the snow made it difficult to keep one's feet, and I began to realise that one cannot run as easily at 44 as one could at 24, a fact which is probably more true at 84, as you will have discovered.

All went well till I reached a certain part of the trench, which rejoices in the attractive name of 'Suicide Corner,' from the fact that the Germans have a machine gun trained on it and at intervals during the night pump a shower of lead on that spot in the hope of knocking out some chance passer-by.

It was just my luck that as I came near this place I heard the 'Rat-tat-

tat' of the beastly gun and the whiz of the passing bullets. It was not a pleasant prospect to run the gauntlet and skip through the bullets 'made in Germany' but what priest would hesitate for a second with two dying men at the end of the trench. I ducked my head - en passant might I remark that Darwin's theory of our descent from apes is quite wrong, I am certain we must come from ostriches, since the first thing every man does in danger is to hide his head and then he feels quite 'comfy.' I ducked my venerable head, as I have said, and 'chivvied' down that trench. (I do not know what this word means, but I believe it implies terrific speed and breathless excitement.)

In the dark and at that distance I was quite invisible to the Boche gunner, but I think the Old Boy himself was turning the handle that night, but luckily for me was out of practice; the cold I expect upset his aim. Away on my left as I ran I could hear in the stillness of the night the grinding 'Rat-tat-tat' of the machine gun, for all the world as if a hundred German carpenters were driving nails into my coffin, while overhead 'crack, crack, whiz, whiz' went the bullets tearing one after another for fear they would be too late.

It was a novel experience to have a whole machine gun all to yourself, but it is a pleasure I am not particularly anxious to repeat. At the same time I do not think I was really in any great danger as judging by the sound the leaden shower was going too high.[17]

Despite what appears to be very great danger, Fr Doyle takes it all in his stride. Indeed, he is quite nonchalant about the routine exchange of fire which was a fact of every-night life, despite the fact that on this occasion it had found its deadly target:

The guns make all movement by night very unpleasant. Both sides have any number of them firing all night, from time to time at fixed points, for example cross-roads, 'dumps,' light railways etc., everywhere in fact where men are likely to be. Yet in spite of the fact that each fires about 10,000 rounds each night and bullets are flying about like mosquitos, it is very rare indeed that anyone is hit, weeks at a time without a casualty and scarcely never if one takes the ordinary precautions.

The first man was 'in extremis' when I reached him. I did all I could

> *for him, commended his soul to the merciful God as he had only a few minutes to live, and hurried on to find the other wounded boy.*
>
> *A journey along the Firing Line in the day time is not an easy matter, but in the darkness of the night it baffles description. A star shell from time to time gave me light and I made good progress, only to end in blackness and a pool or a shell hole full of mud and water.*
>
> *I found the dying lad, he was not much more, so tightly jammed into a corner of the trench it was almost impossible to get him out. Both legs were smashed, one in two or three places, so his chances of life were small as there were other injuries as well. What a harrowing picture that scene would have made. A splendid young soldier, married only a month they told me, lying there pale and motionless in the mud and water with the life crushed out of him by a cruel shell. The stretcher bearers hard at work binding up as well as they may his broken limbs; round about a group of silent Tommies looking on and wondering when will their turn come. Peace for a moment seems to have taken possession of the battlefield; not a sound save the deep boom of some far off gun and the stifled moans of the dying boy, while as if anxious to hide the scene, nature drops her soft mantle of snow on the living and dead alike. Then while every head is bared come the solemn words of absolution, 'Ego te absolve,' I absolve thee from thy sins. Depart Christian soul and may the Lord Jesus Christ receive thee with a smiling and benign countenance. Amen.*
>
> *Oh! surely the gentle Saviour did receive with open arms the brave lad who had laid down his life for Him, and as I turned away I felt happy in the thought that his soul was already safe in that land where 'God will wipe away all sorrow from our eyes, for weeping and mourning shall be no more'.*[18]

The 8th Royal Dublin Fusiliers' War Diary records for that day:

> *At 9.30pm during a raid by 49 Brigade three casualties occurred in our right front company from T.M. fire. Our parapet was also blown in – 28219 Taggete E and 28223 Watts C killed, 25205 Justin T wounded. Heavy frost.*[19]

Charles Cumming Watt was 19 years old, the son of Alexander and Isobel Watt of

Cecil Road, Seaforth, Liverpool. Pre-war, he had been an employee of the shipping line Ellerman Hall in Liverpool. He is buried with his colleague and fellow private soldier E. Taggett in Kemmal Chateau Military Cemetery (note the spelling variations, a common problem for researchers!) Willie's account continues:

I was slightly damp by the time I reached my dug out, but it was not the first time my clothes had dried on my back and I suppose it will not be the last.

I must give due notice here not to expect another budget for some time, as with all the good will in the world, news cannot be made to order. Most days are uneventful with nothing of interest to record, unless it be a 'tramp up the trenches and back' which like the famous 'walk on the Nanpanton Road', in days of old would soon begin to tire. I have a few scraps of news to relate and one little incident which might have had a different ending but I shall keep them till 'our next' and conclude by wishing everyone goodnight, for I am going to tumble into bed, save the mark! to try and warm my old bones.

Much love to everyone, not forgetting the lion's share for your own dear self.[20]

Willie's next budget commences on 16 January and runs through until 5 February; it is sent with a covering letter dated 6 February 1917, which says:

The 'ration tin' is filled up quicker than I expected so I send it along herewith. I am glad you find the little diary sufficiently interesting. Since last I wrote the weather instead of changing as I thought has become even colder. However I have finished seventeen days in the trenches and jolly cold they were too and am back now in my billet in the convent for a week.

Lena kindly asks in her letter if I want anything. A good, rapid thaw would be most welcome, but apart from that I really have all I want. Hard as the weather is I enjoy it and certainly have nothing to complain of in the way of health or fitness.

I am really sorry to hear poor Frank has had such a nasty attack. I hope you will keep him as long as you can, the rest and change will do him good.[21]

The person Willie refers to is, in all probability, his brother-in-law Frank Whelan, aged about 68, who had evidently had some kind of health scare, serious enough to warrant him being kept at *Melrose* for recuperation. Frank had outlived both his much younger wife, Willie's sister Elizabeth, who died in 1914, and their only child, Eileen who died in 1915, when the family were living in Sheffield. Willie continues:

> **16 January:** *Fearing you may grow tired of a constant diet of 'Bully' I am sending you some new rations. 'Pork & Beans' is quite a standing joke, though not a pleasant one, at the Front.*
>
> *A committee of food experts, having discovered that lentil beans contain one and a half times more nourishment and flesh forming properties, than a corresponding weight of meat, promptly decided that, from time to time, Tommy should be fed on this delicious product of Mother Earth, and thereupon, I am sure, promptly sat themselves down to a roast leg of mutton, to show that if they were experts they were no means faddists.*
>
> *This directly hails from Canada. The method of procedure is this: fill a can with a pound of small beans; on top place a piece of fat, not larger than a shilling; seal up carefully and wrap in a coloured label on which is printed (and so must be true) the startling intelligence that 'five beans are of more value than a piece of meat.' Then allow a pig to rub his sides against the packing case, and vóila, you have a sustaining dinner ration of 'Pork & Beans.'*
>
> *The first time you sit down to this repast you experience the most frightful temptation to vain-glory and pride as being the equals of the ancient hermits, and then you feel 'orrible empty, so that even granting that a tin of beans is of greater value than a rib of beef, we are all ready to vote, and vote solid every time, for the old fashioned steak.*[22]

Willie now goes into reminiscent mode. He had always been able to get by on very little sleep, which would account for the energy he was able to muster in writing such long accounts to home:

> **17 January:** *We have been comparing experiences at the Somme today. One officer told me that he and some others took their meals and slept as*

best they could in a dug-out containing fourteen corpses. They had no means of burying them, were probably too worn out to try, and as some had been there a long time, it was wiser to leave them alone. It would be hard to beat that for horror.

I thought our dug-out in one of the trenches at Loos was bad enough. One end of it had been blown in by a big shell, burying two men, whom it was impossible to get out, and we lived at the other. They, poor chaps, were covered with clay, but not deep enough to keep out the smell of decaying bodies, which did not help one's appetite at meal time, and then when your nerves were more jumpy than usual, you could swear you saw the dead man's boot moving, as if he were still alive. I am thinking Glasnevin cemetery will be quite a favourite place to live after the war.[23]

Glasnevin Cemetery in Dublin was (and still is) the largest non-denominational cemetery in Ireland, which was consecrated on 21 February 1832 and the first burial took place the following day. Fr Doyle continues his narrative:

18 January: *'The world is a small place' goes the old saying. Here is another proof of it. Some six months ago one of my officers, Captain Galvin of Cork, was badly wounded in a raid and was left lying near the German trenches. When his loss was discovered, a couple of men, with great bravery, crawled out and carried him in to our lines, thereby saving his life. Quite recently Captain Galvin was presiding over a court-martial in Dublin and before passing sentence on the prisoner asked him had he anything to say in his defence: 'Only this, Sir,' was the reply, 'I was one of the two men who fetched you in, when you were left lying in NO MAN'S LAND, and was wounded myself doing so.'*

I need not add that extenuating circumstances in the prisoner's favour were quickly found and he left the court a happier and doubtless wiser man.[24]

Four officers of the 8th Royal Irish Fusiliers were recorded as having retrieved a badly wounded Captain Barry Galvin from No Man's Land, in the Loos sector in July 1916, two of whom subsequently died in September at Guillemont. The other two were 2/Lt E.E. Sergint and 2/Lt J.E. Rea. Willie may have received this information via a letter directly from Barry Galvin, or more likely from his brother Daniel who was a newly arrived officer of the 9th Royal Dublin Fusiliers. Barry Galvin had recuperated from his wounds and was carrying out duties at Portobello Barracks, Dublin, awaiting a new posting back to the Front. Willie's narrative continues:

> *This incident has made me set about polishing up my German, for I quite expect some morning to meet the Kaiser strolling down our trench. 'Gooden Tag' will do nicely to start with, and wish him 'good morning' and then I can fall back on our old friends 'Grose Mudder' and 'der Hund.' I guess Kaiser Bill will be surprised.*
>
> **20 January:** *This afternoon occurred one of those little incidents, insignificant in itself, which have proved to me over and over again the wonderful protective power of prayer, and at the same time the loving care of the good God. Though sometimes I feel I may unnecessarily alarm you by recounting my 'escapes', on the other hand gratitude for so manifest goodness on God's part impels me to recount them, since the effect upon myself has been to give me a wonderful trust and confidence that, that protection will not fail me to the end.*
>
> *It had been an unusually long and exciting day, for the Boche took it into his head to pound the front line trenches rather heavily. There had been some casualties, surprisingly few considering the amount and weight of stuff sent over, but it was only natural that the men should be a bit shaken – in every sense – by such a fierce bombardment.*[25]

The War Diary recorded seven men wounded. Willie's story continues:

> *A visit from the Padre at such a moment is quite a tonic to the poor chaps and bucks them up wonderfully. When the shelling had ceased, (not before) I made the round of the trenches. You see I am not fool-hardy, for I quite appreciate the truth of the statement, that no matter how beautiful a dead donkey may be, a living ass is more useful, and this poor ass is going to keep wagging his 'tailor-wailer' (with apologies to Tim) as long as he can.*

I got back to my dug-out, which is a couple of hundred yards behind the firing line, tired and hungry, and sat me down to dinner. Owing to some mistake or other, the soup, fish, entré, roast and sweets did <u>not</u> turn up, but bread and 'Bully' washed down by copious libations of tea made a repast fit for a king, or even a Kaiser. Don't ask me where the water came from, I certainly am not anxious to learn, for the men hold that if you boil the water you need not bother about its source, or how many dead beasties it has washed on its journey. I have had tea of the most wonderful shades of brown and black, but barring the taste at times I am not a whit worse for this mysterious beverage.

The Germans must have had some very bad coffee today, for again in the evening they opened a most lively fire, which occasioned the incident I alluded to.

Some shells, when they explode, have a most unpleasant trick of sending their 'nose-cap' flying through the air, making a horrible noise. I have seen these gentlemen land fully a mile from the point the shell struck, and it is strongly recommended not to get in their way, unless you are qualifying for a 'Wooden Cross.'

I was coming up the communication trench, quite a long way back from the danger zone, and had reached a point where the trench bends at right angles, so that I was facing the embankment or side, when I heard the whizzing hum of a 'nose cap.' I had heard this noise hundreds of times, but there was something about this particular visitor which beckoned danger. Instinctively I stopped dead, but before I had time to think what I should do, there was a dull thud and the clay of the bank was splashed up in my face. I clambered over the side of the trench and found a sweet creature of a 'nose cap' weighing between four and six pounds buried two feet in the ground.

The greater part of this particular trench is very low, but fortunately for me, the spot where I was at the moment was higher than my head, otherwise, judging by the direction of the flying cap it must have caught me fair in the chest, and made a two foot hole in poor me, instead of the bank. It was another case, surely, of 'Thus far shalt thou go and no farther', much to the comfort and satisfaction of the younger Abbot.[26]

The shells Willie refers to were shrapnel shells, which exploded like shot-gun cartridges several feet above the ground and sprayed close to four hundred lead balls. His narrative continues the next day:

> **21 January and following days:** *Much too busy rubbing whale oil into my all but frozen feet to think of writing, even if there were any news, or to be more strictly truthful, impossible to hold the pencil with fingers which have no feeling. I do not know how many degrees 'frying heat' of frost we have had, but it must be something very near the Lower Regions. Certainly the Lord is 'scourging us with scorpions.' The cold, bitter, biting cold is indescribable, impossible to get warm, or remain so long, but there is a good time coming soon, very soon and 'we are not down-hearted.'*
>
> *The guns on both sides are not frozen, it is quite evident, and keep thundering away, night and day, the grim tragedy of war never ceases and the grave-yards of France and Belgium, not to speak of other nations, grow larger and fuller.*
>
> *Now and again some amusing episode breaks the monotony of everyday life, which the following is a sample.*
>
> *The men, during cold weather, get a tot of rum in the early morning, which must not be confused with our friend the 'Rum Jar', a very different thing I need not say. Sometimes, through the carelessness of an officer some of it is left lying about, a temptation which even Saint Michael himself could not resist on a frosty morning. On this particular occasion a certain man was found decidedly merry beside an empty jar, just as the General was reported to be coming along the trench. To save the poor chap, his pals persuaded him, not without much difficulty, to pretend he was dead and they placed him on a stretcher well covered over with a blanket, and then carried him rapidly away.*
>
> *As the body passed by the General stood to attention and exclaimed: 'Salute the gallant dead', when to the horror of those concerned the 'corpse' sat up and a muffled voice called out, 'Who the b----- H--- is that?'*[27]

Fr Doyle moves seamlessly from this amusing incident to his description of a raid undertaken by the Division to the left of 16th (Irish) Division. His estimate of the distance being that the action was about a mile away:

26 January: *I wish I were able to give you a description of the most awe-inspiring spectacle possible to witness – a battle at night, such as we had in the early hours of this morning. I call it a battle for in any other war it certainly would be so, though probably all you will read about it in the official despatch will be: 'We raided the enemy's trenches last night', to which I might add, 'Enemies' casualties very severe, ours insignificant,' as usual.*

I was sleeping the sleep of a just, but decidedly cold, man when the sudden crash of artillery told me something serious was on hand. To my relief I saw that the engagement, though close at hand, was not on our front, though these 'stunts' have an unpleasant trick of spreading along the line. From the intensity of the fire I concluded that the Division on our left were about to make a raid and the guns were hacking their way through the German wire, as otherwise, the infantry could not advance. Before uncut wire entanglements the efforts of the bravest are useless, and it is a horrible sight to see a row of dead bodies hanging on the wire, like so many scare-crows, shot before they had time to use their wire-cutters.

'No Man's Land', the space between the opposing trenches, ought really to be called 'Dead Man's Land', for piles of brave fellows lie there unburied, and will lie there till their bones are bleached. I tried to get permission to go out and give some of them Christian burial, but the Colonel would not hear of it, adding that he 'thought there were corpses enough there already.' Perhaps he was right, but of all the good works of holy Tobias singled out for praise by the Angel Raphael as most pleasing to Almighty God, was 'his burial of the dead by night.' I wish Holy Toby was with me here, he would have the time of his life and dead bodies galore for his zeal.

The night was very dark, though the flashes of the guns were so continuous one could almost read a book by their light – the noise and the roar you can best imagine yourself!

One battery fascinated me! Every few seconds a long tongue of flame, sometimes two or three together, would spring out of the inky blackness, as if some fiery dragon had made a spring at the enemy, and was then hauled back by his chain. Another spring, a longer forked tongue, another roar –

two, five, a dozen – and I could see the shells bursting high over the heads of the Boches, waiting for the coming attack.

The fight was by no means one-sided. In a wonderful short space of time the German gunners got to work and flash answered flash, and shell replied to shell, till it seemed as if a hundred terrific thunderstorms had broken loose on the world.

From where I stood I had a magnificent view of the action, about half a mile away. One could follow the line of trenches quite easily by the roar of bursting shells, while at intervals the earth itself seemed to split with a terrifying roar and crash, liberating its imprisoned fires and the whole countryside was lit up as a huge 'Rum Jar' burst apparently right on top of our men.

Then came the quick rattle of the machine guns, the roll of rapid fire musketry; the white puffs of smoke from exploding bombs telling the tale of a charge, which would end in death for many a gallant lad.

It was hard to stand there watching souls being launched into eternity and not be able to do anything except pray for God's mercy on those who needed it most. Perhaps, after all, that help was better than any other, for God's ways are not our ways and there is no limit to his mercy.[28]

Willie conveys the continuing intensity of the freezing weather, quite simply but graphically, in the next few lines of his budget:

27 January: *Cold!*
28 January: *Colder!!*
29 January: *More colder!!!*
30 January: *!!!!!!!!!!!!!!'*
31 January: *Language not fit for publication. Thank God there is nice warm Purgatory to look forward to.*[29]

The 8th Royal Dublin Fusiliers' War Diary records admissions to and discharges from hospital on a daily basis and although the reasons are not stated the bitterly cold weather must have been a big factor. The entry for 29 January from Battalion Headquarters at York House reads:

Eleven to hospital, two from hospital, five wounded. Very cold and freezing. Impossible to use picks or shovels in front lines.[30]

Frank Laird recalls the best part of the day was the distribution of a warming rum ration first thing in the morning:

Attended by the Company Sergeant-Major, the officer proceeded along the trench with the rum jar, filling out a small dose in the measure and handing it to each man in turn, occasionally putting in an extra drop for the older hands, whose wellseasoned [sic]throats required an extra warming. The potent fluid spread a general air of joviality over the scene. To men who had stood the biting frost, or worse still, the rain and mud of a winter's night in the trenches, it was a godsend.[31]

Willie's budget continued for another few days, but in the meantime he penned a quick letter to Hugh dated 30 January 1917:

I have nothing of great importance to report this week, except the frost which, like you at home, we are enjoying in this severe weather. For the past three weeks we have had the most intense cold I have ever experienced, snow and hard continuous frost both day and night. Even the natives say they never remember the like and I can quite believe them.

As a rule I enjoy nothing better than a good walk in frosty weather but the wind is so penetrating and cutting that unless obliged to do so no one is keen about going out.

To give you an idea of our present atmospheric conditions, before I have finished dressing in the mornings, not a very long process, the water in which I washed is frozen again. One has to be very careful, too, of one's feet, keeping them well rubbed with whale oil, if not you would find yourself unable to walk with half a dozen frozen toes and in for a very unpleasant time. The dug out is not the warmest of spots just at present, but even if I felt inclined to growl I would be ashamed to do so seeing what the poor men are suffering in the trenches. My life is a Paradise compared to theirs, though I hope sincerely the real 'Happy Land' will be a trifle warmer when we get there. There have been several deaths from exposure, but speaking for myself I find the cold invigorating and it seems to suit me in every way. Appetite? Hush not a word. In strict confidence, very poor, but the barometer is rising.[32]

The last comments about his appetite indicate that Willie Doyle continued to struggle with the digestive problems which plagued him throughout his adult life. The letter continues:

A little story which I read some time ago has helped me along not a little during these hard days. The Blessed Curé d'Ars was visiting an invalid boy who had been bed-ridden for years. 'Father' he said 'I really have very little to bear. I don't feel now my sufferings of yesterday and our Lord has not yet sent me those of tomorrow, so that my pain is really only for a moment.' That lad was a philosopher, but he never lived in a trench I bet.

This morning a change has taken place, the wind has shifted round, and if I mistake not a thaw is not far away. Then we shall have the real fun, slush and wet, floods in all the trenches and the parapet tumbling in after the prolonged frost.

Everything loving and kind to everyone, your own dear self especially. I am ever so sorry to hear of Frank's illness but glad to learn he is on the mend. Feed him up on 'BULLY BEEF' there is nothing better.[33]

Back to the budget, entitled Pork and Beans, which continues (Willie evidently did not have use of either a bicycle or horse at this time):

2 February: *As I am not allowed to have Mass for my men up near the firing line on account of the danger of having many gathered together I go back each morning to where the reserve company is stationed, about twenty minutes' walk, which gives those who are free a chance of coming often to Holy Communion. Today, however, I was able to offer the Holy Sacrifice in the trenches, my chapel being a dug-out capable of holding ten or a dozen comfortably, but as my congregation numbered forty-six the vacant space was small. How they all managed to squeeze in I cannot say; our Blessed Lady must have worked a miracle, being her feast day.*

There was no question of kneeling down, the men simply stood, silently and reverently round the little improvised altar of ammunition boxes; glad as one of them quaintly expressed it – 'glad to have a say in it.' Surely Our Lord must have been glad also, for every one of the forty-six received Holy Communion and went back to their posts happy at heart and strengthened to face the hardships of these days and nights of cold.

The same afternoon, as I was coming back from my round of the Front Line trench I was caught in a rather heavy 'strafe' of the Germans. The point they were shelling was some little distance further on, but quite close to my way home and as splinters were flying about rather abundantly I thought it well to get under cover.

Accordingly, I crawled into a hole in which there were already six men and judging by the look on their faces no one could have been more welcome. 'Come in Father', one of them cried, 'we're safe now, anyhow.'

Poor fellows, they have such simple, strong faith and reverence for the priest that they would not mind, I think, if all the shells in Prussialand came tumbling into the trench; 'Isn't the priest of God with us, what more do you want?'

Though we were safe enough where we were, in another sense our position was not too secure, as the shells were flying over our heads and now and then one would fall short, making the ground quiver like a small earthquake.

A few minutes later one of the men came running round the corner of the trench and tumbled on top of us, simply shaking with laughter. A 'dud' shell (one which does not explode) had landed on top of his dug-out, the next one to ours, half burying him and two others in clay and debris, but without causing further damage. With the thoughtlessness of youth he looked upon it as a capital joke, though only for someone's last prayers his last hour had come.[34]

It is safe to assume that Fr Doyle was experienced enough by now to be able to distinguish between joviality and hysteria, and that this was not a case of shell-shock. He continues:

When the storm had died down I made my way home, not a little amused to see one man kneeling, with his head shoved into a small hole in the side of the trench, the rest of his body being quite exposed to anything that came along, a new method I suppose of fighting a rear guard action and another proof of my ostrich theory. I had almost reached my 'appy, 'appy, 'ome when the Boche sent over a big parting shot, but quite a good distance away. Far as it was, bits of shrapnel came flying through the air and pattered all around me like so many hail stones. I was congratulating myself on being in a place of comparative safety when I heard the hum of a shell fragment coming spinning apparently in my direction. Nearer and nearer it came; I could not see it of course, but every second the noise grew louder. There was no use running to the right or left, the best chance was to remain quite still and trust to Providence and Mary's protection.

For once I felt my name was written on this messenger from Krupp and I found myself wondering where it would hit me. Would it fall down on my poor head, or would it just come ripping along my arm or down my leg? Would it catch me plump in the back, and if it were a jagged piece of iron would it tear my coat in such a way that I should have to trouble Conan for a new one? If I were badly hit how long would I lie there in the snow till someone found me, and best of all, how many weeks would it take to patch up the old 'oss before he could take to the field again? What strange thoughts surge through one's mind at such a moment!

I stood there feeling very much as the early Martyrs must have done in the prisons of the Coliseum, listening to the roaring of the wild beasts which were to devour them; or the human victim, bound and laid on the altar of sacrifice of the old pagan rites. They must have said, as I did interiorly, 'I wish you would hurry up and get it over.'

Nearer and nearer came the spinning instrument of torture, making me cringe as a dog does before the up-raised whip, then a sudden whizz, a dull thud in the ground beside me and I knew I was safe once more.

My visitor was a most respectable, stout gentleman, quite friendly though inclined to be a little too familiar. Nice as he was I left him lying on the ground and went away thanking God he had not hit me.[35]

Willie next has cause to thank an anonymous nun, but despite his witty attempt at disguise it is obvious it must be Mai:

5 February: *I was just finishing up this for the post when a large envelope was handed to me from a holy nun, whom you do not know, though Mai does. She is none of your ordinary, common or garden Holy Nuns, but a real out and outer. Inside the envelope I found a cake of carbolic soap, nothing more!*

Sister dear, I love you for your motherly gift, but you have made me feel very much like the tramp to whom the good lady offered a shirt button; 'Thank you kindly lady I have buttons in plenty but I have ne'er a shirt to put them on.'

If your gift had included a little hot water you would have made me as happy as a king, but when you have tried for a few mornings to wash your face with black ice, you give it up in despair and glory in your dirt!

Let us hope, when we next meet, that if the colour of sanctity is wanting when one returns from the trenches, at least there will be the delicate aroma of carbolic soap.[36]

Willie had previously alluded to the shortage of soap and Mai had obviously responded as quickly as she could, without even having time to enclose a note! Here the budget ends, sent with the good news that he is due leave. First, though, on 7th February Willie wrote to his Jesuit Province about finances and seeking permission to visit Mai at the convent on his way home on leave:

I enclose a cheque for £150 and hope to send you another £50 when certain allowances are paid. I have also paid for my outfitter. As I am due for leave shortly may I pay a visit to my sister at Queenstown and the convent on my way to Dublin? I can get a free ticket for this. Thank God your Province is sending us some help, it is badly needed.[37]

Willie sent his budget home five days later, when he also enclosed a covering note, plus another letter from an un-named woman for his father's attention. Unfortunately we do not know the contents of the latter, although we get the general gist:

This is only a line to give you the best of news that I hope to see you very soon. I am due a fortnight's leave on the 19th and as soon as ever I can after that date I shall get away.

Today at least there is a welcome change in the weather, after 40 days of hard continuous frost. We may not be quite out of the wood yet, but there are hopeful signs of better things. I think the limit was reached when the wine froze in the Chalice at Mass and a lamp had to be procured to melt it before going on with the Consecration. I am thinking it will take fifty lamps to thaw out the poor Chaplain.

The enclosed may interest you; I was not aware I gave anybody courage for I have felt many a time the need of a big dose myself, but perhaps this good lady, whom I have never met, has an eye for future business.

Your most welcome and always interesting letter just arrived, thousands of thanks. You are really wonderful to write so often, with so much on your hands.

A bientôt as the French say; I hope my next letter will be myself.[38]

Willie's next contact with his father does, indeed, appear to have been in the flesh! When Fr Doyle wrote on the 12 February 1917 enclosing the budget, he did not mention the unpleasant duty he performed on 10–11 February; perhaps he was too exhausted and maybe he preferred to tell his father in person when he arrived home. This relates to the few lines in the 8th Royal Dublin Fusiliers' War Diary for 11 February, reporting the death of 19207 Private M.B. Byrne of the battalion's 'B' Company. Fr Doyle administered the last rites and the service for the burial of the 19-year-old Dubliner, son of Patrick and Mary Anne Byrne. The Irish military historian Tom Burke researched this incident and found that, on the evening of 10 February 'B' Company were on wiring duty in freezing conditions along the Vierstraat Switch. The Germans had been shelling in the area during the day and recommenced in the evening when Michael was hit whilst bringing up rations for his platoon. When he did not arrive with the rations, his friend Private Hanlon went to look for him about 10 p.m. He found Michael unconscious and bleeding profusely from a back wound and so he sent for the chaplain. Fr Doyle and Pte Hanlon remained with Pte Byrne until he died just before Midnight. The body was taken back down the line and buried in the cemetery on the site of a former creamery, La Laiterie.[39]

Seven days after this stressful evening, Fr Doyle had no hesitation about signing a renewal of his contract with the Expeditionary Force. About this time the Chaplains' Department had opened up a School of Instruction near St Omer and was to run its first course for twenty-five chaplains. Whether Willie would have accepted an invitation to attend, had one been extended, is doubtful, especially as it was so close to his scheduled leave.

Willie's leave home early in March 1917 was his last. Again, we do not have any details about his holiday other than the fact he went to visit his brother Charles at the Jesuit Province in Limerick. Charlie particularly remembered one incident of his brother's visit:

> *During the last time he was at home on leave from the Front, he came down to Limerick where I was stationed. We went out for a walk together. Coming home, we met a number of people walking out towards Ballinacurra as they often do on a Sunday evening. As each couple or party came near us, I noticed all eyes became fixed on Willie with a curiously interested and reverential expression. I stole a glance at him. His eyes were cast down, and upon his face was that same unearthly look of sweetness and radiance I had seen on it that evening years before in Melrose.*[40]

There is also testimony of Fr Doyle's visit to his Province at Rathfarnham Castle; a Scholastic of the Province of Sicily, quoted by Fr Charles Doyle, wrote:

> *I shall never forget the last time I saw Fr Willie. It was the morning he was returning to the Front after his last leave home. We Juniors at the Castle had gathered in the hall to give him a rousing send-off. As he had not yet come down, I slipped into the chapel for a visit. There I found him. He was in uniform, standing at the altar, and knocking at the Tabernacle Door most gently. It was his loving farewell to his Eucharist Lord. I was greatly moved and edified at his simplicity and at his love for Jesus.*[41]

Back at the front, Willie wrote home on 15 March 1917, describing a journey of many misadventures:

> *My first postcard will have told you of my safe arrival in London after one of the roughest passages I have ever had. I have been across the Channel dozens of times and never yet broke my resolution of not feeding the fishes, but as the good ship would insist on trying to stand on her head, even the*

resolve of years broke down, though I was only sick for about half a minute.

Wednesday I spent in London as I had some few things to do, including a call to my banker, and then on enquiry I found I should have the best part of the next day free as my train did not leave till 2 o'clock. On reaching the station I found, not a little to my annoyance, that the boat train had left at 11.50. There was nothing for it but to spend a third night in London.

Determined not to be late a second time I went down to Charing Cross very early, walked about outside for a while and then entered the station. In response to my query, the porter replied; 'Yes Sir, the boat train left punctually at 11.50.' I must have been dreaming for somehow I had got it in my head that 11.50 was ten minutes to one. I knew something terrible would happen as a result of Jennie's two chickens, boiled by five cooks and that is the best excuse I can make, for I am not drinking during Lent, but it meant I had to stay another night in London.[42]

This last comment is interesting in view of his pre-war work with an abstinence society, which tends to support his position of being one of temperance rather than abstinence (except during Lent) - or it was one of his little jokes! Willie continues:

I made up my mind to wait 24 hours before getting into a temper, and one would see St. Paul's come true; 'To those who love God all things work together quite good' for I was puzzled why both coming and going I had been held up in this way, when I was so anxious to get back. When I read the war news next morning all seemed clear, for the day before, the very day in which I should have been in the trenches, had I not been delayed, the Germans had made a fierce attack, five times indeed, on the part of the Line held by my men; had broken through to some depth before being driven back and who knows I might have been singing the 'Watch on the Rhine' now, only for the fog and my stupid mistake. I was sorry to have missed the 'fun' but not a little thankful that I had escaped a very hot time.[43]

One of those caught in the attack Willie refers to was Private G. Sagar, who had been badly wounded on 6 March and died the following day despite being evacuated to hospital. The 8th Royal Dublin Fusiliers' War Diary for 8 March recorded:

Heavy bombardment of Divisional Front began 3.50pm very heavy on right Battalion of left Brigade where enemy penetrated line causing casualties and leaving some dead and wounded in battalion's hands. Front of 8th RDF heavily shelled but not attacked by infantry.[44]

As far as the 8th Royal Dublin Fusiliers were concerned, this attack had left Privates Chittendon, Chambers and McClory, together with Company Sergeant Major Mangan, all wounded, on duty; another five men, Haines, Donohoe, Boyce, McArdle and Kenny, were injured and one, Seaver, reported missing. Willie continues:

My train from Boulogne on Sunday morning brought me within ten miles of my destination, so there was nothing for it but to tramp the rest of the way. It was a beautiful evening and I swung along the road in great form, in spite of my great-coat and heavy pack, for I knew at any time I could get a lift on one of the many water lorries passing by. I had gone a few miles when an unpleasant fact dawned upon me: all the cars were coming towards me and none behind. In other words, I was on the <u>return</u> line, for to avoid confusion, all traffic runs in a circle, up one road and back the other. There I was toiling along mile after mile with 'cars, cars everywhere and never a drop to drink', which is a bit mixed but explains my position.

Fr Browne has gone on leave, which means I shall have my hands full, though at present things are very quiet, probably on account of the wet weather and inexhaustible mud.

I have a good deal of correspondence to make up, but I will report progress in due course. I am feeling in every way all the better for my enjoyable time at home, which everyone tried to make so pleasant, but I am pained to learn from Bob's letter that Tim funked the trenches at the end, in spite of his grand Red Cross. All the same I must admit he is a wise old dog.

Heaps of love to your own dear self, and to each one.[45]

Two days later, Saturday 17 March 1917, the men of the 8th Royal Dublin Fusiliers attended Divine Services for St Patrick's Day. Fr Doyle's 'hands' did double the work in Fr Browne's absence, and doubled up again, offering the sacraments on both Saturday and Sunday.

CHAPTER 24
REHEARSING PLUMER'S PLAN:
AIDED BY GABRIEL

'Your Majesty will be pleased to hear that I found the troops everywhere in the most splendid spirits and looking the picture of health.'
Field-Marshal Sir Douglas Haig, letter to King George V,
Monday 9 April 1917

On Monday 19 March 1917 the 8th Royal Dublin Fusiliers were relieved at Butterfly Farm and proceeded to Birr Barracks, Locre, to go into reserve. They were congratulated by General Officer Commanding 48th Infantry Brigade on the clean and excellent handing over of the camp. The following day Willie resumed diary entries, addressed to the folks at *Melrose*, in a ponderous mood. Reminiscing and philosophic, he writes:

In resuming this diary after my little holiday I cannot help thinking of the thirteen months which I have spent on active service, a time so full of thrilling incidents, providential escapes from serious injury and sights and scenes too horrible to dwell on, that I often wonder have they really taken place, or is it only part of some strange dream.

It is hard to describe the life or sum up the feelings of one who can never say he is perfectly safe. The danger may be very great, it is often remote, but it is ever there, hanging over one's head like the sword of Damocles and at times rudely breaking in on the peace of fancied security.

You may remember my telling you, when we were on the other front, and were resting in a town a good eight miles back, how a shell came through the wall of my bedroom, missing my bed by an inch, and then out the other side, without exploding! Fortunately, or otherwise I was out at the time, but though I put the head of my bed in the hole on the principle that no two shells ever land on the same spot, it was not easy to copy the Psalmist and sign 'in peace shall I sleep and take my rest', for I had constant visions of the poor chaplain landing some night, bed and all, in the neighbouring courtyard, amid a shower of tiles and bricks.

It would be idle to say that I have not suffered, though far less than many others, Old Shylock's remark has often come back to me 'Suffering is the badge of our tribe;' it is certainly the lot of the soldier in this campaign. We have had it in countless forms – extremes of heat and unsoundable depths of cold; water above and below you, wading through it knee deep for days, and then a burning sun 'with never a drop to drink.' There have been long tramps by day. With pack and equipment growing heavier each hour, till the sweat rolled down one's face in streams and a plunge in the mud would have made little difference to the condition of one's clothes. Nights without sleep, burying the happy dead under cover of darkness, hurrying along the trench with the music of screaming bullets to speed some poor soul into eternity and be well rewarded by the gratified cry: 'Thank God, the priest.'[1]

One assumes the dead are 'happy' because they have escaped the carnage, as well as having the priest's blessing which sends them on their way safely to their maker on high! Willie resumes:

There have been nights, too, of stern marching in the cold and rain and long cheerless journeys in a crawling train, where the only active thing was a ravenous appetite; nights of mortal fear when slumbering men, roused by the cry of 'gas' sprang from the ground and seized their helmets as they saw the hideous green vapour rolling towards them, or tried to snatch a few moments of rest, in spite of the crash of bursting shells.

We have had millions of rats who quietly eat up what you hoped to eat and other unwelcome visitors who preferred to eat you. We have had good billets and bad billets and no billets at all, till at last one ceased to care very much where the sleep was to be, whether on a bed, on the stairs or floor, or in the open field, provided only they let you sleep.

We have been wearied and foot sore and worn out; famished with hunger at times, sick and tired of the whole wretched business, wishing for a peace so long in coming, but never once down-hearted.

Speaking for myself, I can say with all truth I have never spent a happier year, for though I have occasionally felt as if the limit of endurance was reached, I have never lost my good spirits, which have helped me over many a rough road.[2]

Willie confirms the sentiments expressed in many post-war testimonies, of men experiencing a strange kind of serenity amidst the horrors of war. The reliability of military routine; conviction, if not in the cause certainly in your comrades; the camaraderie of the group and faith (for some) was the gel which enabled the servicemen to stick it out. Willie continues:

Yet these things are little compared to what I may call 'moral suffering.' Pain and privation are only momentary, quickly pass and become delightfully sweet, if only borne in the spirit with which many of my grand boys take these things: 'Shure, Father, it's not worth talking about, after all is it not well to have some little thing to suffer for God and His Blessed Mother.' But the craven fear which at times clutches the heart, the involuntary shrinking and dread of human nature, of danger and even death are things which cannot be expressed in words.

An officer, who had gone through a good deal himself, said to me recently 'I never realised before what Our Lord must have suffered in the Garden of Gethsemene when 'He began to fear and grow sorrowful.' Yet His grace is always there to help one when most needed, and though the life is hard and trying at times, I have never ceased to thank Him for the privilege (I call it nothing else) of sharing in this glorious work.'

Let me give you just one illustration of what I mean. We reap a good harvest with Confessions every day at any time the men care to come, but there are many who, for one reason or another, cannot get away before going into the trenches, which nearly always means death for some poor fellows, we give them a General Absolution. I do not think there can be a more touching or soul inspiring sight than to see a whole regiment go down upon their knees to hear that wave of prayer go up to Heaven, as hundreds of voices repeat the Act of Contrition in unison, 'My God, I am heartily sorry that I have ever offended you.' There is an earnestness and a depth of feeling in their voices which tells of real sorrow, even if one did not see the tears gather in the eyes of more than one brave man – and then the deep reverent silence as the priest raises his hand over the bowed heads and pronounces the words of forgiveness. Human nature is ever human nature, and even Irish soldiers commit sins; you can picture then the feelings of the priest standing before that kneeling throng knowing that, by the power of God, his words have washed every soul pure and white at the words of Absolution and to watch the look of peace and happiness on the men's faces as they lift their rifles and fall into rank, ready for anything, even 'to meet the devil himself' as my friend of long ago shouted out as he marched by me. Don't you agree with me that the consolations and real joys of my life far outweigh the hard things and privations, even if there were no 'little nest egg' being laid up in a better and happier world?[3]

These thoughts were penned by Willie whilst the 8th Royal Dublin Fusiliers were in reserve and billeted around the Locre area. Willie interrupts his budget to send a quick letter back to his father, dated 21 March 1917, the same day the battalion were sent for bathing at the Divisional Baths at Westoutre. Lt P.J. Gueret was also sent that day to Terdeghem to attend a French speaking course, always an asset when it comes to finding billets or food. Willie's letter indicates how lucky he was in being able to smooth over his 'accidental' absence without leave, no doubt one of the little privileges of being a man of the cloth under the uniform! He continues:

Your welcome letter reached me about the same time as mine got to Dalkey, giving you an explanation of my delay in getting back. I was able to manage about an extension of leave, so no unpleasantness followed, and I had the benefit of a couple of extra days in London. I took Fr Browne's place in the trenches, but was only there a week when the 48th Brigade got orders to move back for a rest.

At present I am staying in the Convent, where I have been billeted, but after a little while we are to go further away for some weeks, a pleasant and

> *welcome change from the muddy trenches, not to speak of the persistent attention of the Boche shells.*[4]

As March marched towards April 'showers' the condition of the trenches would not have improved and Willie would be even more appreciative of his comfortable billet with the nuns. The 8th Royal Dublin Fusiliers' War Diary notes, on 28 March:

> *Heavy rain prevailed during the day and later in the day weather became intensely cold.*[5]

The one and only advantage of the previous frosty conditions was that it kept the trenches dry. Frank Laird remembers:

> *The front line trenches were not what we had been taught to expect in the text books and lectures of the Cadet Battalion. They had traverses and fire-bays all right, but, in place of being six or seven good feet underground, they were mainly a breast-work towards the enemy, of sandbags with a parados of a rather so so kind marked by gaps here and there. There were spots where the breastwork itself was on the low side, and it was necessary to proceed in a humble and undignified stoop to avoid the attentions of snipers. On our left in particular there was a gap between ourselves and the next battalion only held by a bombing post. With the hard frost, however, the trenches were pleasantly dry, and owing to the protection from the wind, warmer than the open country.*[6]

Willie's letter continues:

> *We return to the same part of the line after our rest, though no one can say how long we shall be there, or indeed what is going to happen. The general impression is that the German retirement at the Somme has delayed plans somewhat, but probably the weather is the real cause of this present spell of quietude. The last few days have been particularly bitter and cold, with some snow and hail, the last kick of winter before it leaves us I suppose.*
>
> *I shall let you know how things go on, though news at present is very scarce. It is no news to say I am thriving and if not 'waxing fat' at least able 'to kick' well.*

Au revoir for the present. Heaps of love to everyone and your own self in particular.[7]

The battalion did, indeed, leave the Locre area on Saturday 31 March to go back behind the lines for a period of training and recreation. Prior to this, though, Willie returns to his separate daily budget, continuing on March 22:

I am gradually acquiring a great devotion to Moses and Aaron (including of course Mrs Moses and Madame Aaron) as well as all the other holy Israelites of the land of Egypt. I have a wondrous feeling of compassion and sympathy for them, since they were once in a deuce of a fix trying to make bricks without straw. En passant, might I ask you, what they wanted the straw for? We don't make our bricks with straw, as far as I know. Was it to wipe their hands on when they had finished mixing the clay? Or to clean their pipes or what? Perhaps Monsieur William, Balbriggan could throw some light on this most interesting question.[8]

Monsieur William was Willie's brother-in-law and one assumes he smoked a pipe. Willie continues:

Here am I, like the Jews of old, trying to do the impossible and fill a diary without any news! Life, even at the Front, soon settles down into a humdrum monotony. There is little of much interest to distinguish one day from another, and if rumours are plentiful, real news is scarce. From time to time something out of the ordinary crops up, is spoken about for an hour and is then forgotten.

For example, this morning an officer was sitting in the barber's shop having his hair cut, not a thousand miles from where I am sitting now. Everything had been very quiet for days, when suddenly the scream of a shell was heard from the enemy's lines. The officer had just remarked 'That beastly shell is coming jolly near' when he was flung to the other side of the hut and saw the barber's head lying on the ground beside him; the shell had come smashing through the wall, killing the unfortunate man, taking his head off, and only slightly wounding the officer. Only another example among thousands in this war of the old saying, 'Two women shall be grinding corn, one shall be taken and the other shall be left'.[9]

The battalion War Diary for that day, 22 March 1917, had recorded:

> *About 20–30 5.9s were sent into Locre during the afternoon between 2 and 3 p.m.*[10]

The timing is a bit later than Willie indicates but nevertheless confirms Willie's story, as did Frank Laird who, referring to the barbers wrote:

> *Two officers were there, one waiting and one having his hair cut by the private who officiated as barber, when a stray shell fell just outside the window, through which a piece came and took the barber's head off. Some days later I met the two officers who had a few days in hospital to recover from shell shock. The one who was being barbered said he put his hand up, and finding his head covered with blood and brains, concluded they were his own, a fact which he found difficult to reconcile with his being able to stagger out from the hut.*[11]

Willie's narrative continues:

> *Later on in the day, I was walking down the road behind an ammunition cart piled up with 'rum jars' when, to my horror, I saw three of them roll off and crash upon the road. I knew they had no 'detonators' or caps, which make them explode, but all the same you do not care to have 60lb high explosive shells hopping about you, especially if labelled 'handle carefully.' Had these gentlemen gone off in a rage, as they might easily have done, I should by this time be a long way past the moon and still travelling rapidly!*[12]

Willie next tells another anecdote about the war in the air, which seemed to hold a particular fascination for him as he had relayed similar stories in the past. On 24 March he records:

> *Here is my little contribution to the vexed question so hotly discussed at the present time 'Have we supremacy in the air?' It was a beautiful clear morning, such a morning as would tempt the laziest aviator to have a sail,*

so many eyes were on the watch out for visitors. We had not long to wait. Away in the distance a solitary Boche aeroplane was seen approaching, flying very fast towards where we are. With that love for fair play and a good even fight, for which the British navy is so justly famous, three of our machines together made for the adventurous Hun, probably thinking he would fly for his life back to where he came from. On the contrary, the rude fellow made for them; in a brace of shakes, had sent two of our machines crashing to the ground, and the third limping home, evidently badly mauled, and then seeing there was no one else 'having any', continued on his journey.

I have seen (in the newspapers) one of our men taking on eight Germans at a time, but they cannot have been the same stuff as our visitor, who is evidently 'a topper'.[13]

Two days later, 26 March, Willie reports a narrow escape by his brigade colleague Fr Browne, who was in the Front Line with his battalion, and the demise of:

My dear little dug out up in the trenches, which sheltered Fr Browne and myself alternatively, has vanished. It did not fall gloriously in battle, pierced through with a shell, or blown sky-high by a cunningly driven mine shaft; it did not even crumble away slowly, worn out by old age and labours (like its venerable owner) but was laid low, ignominiously, by a common pick and shovel! 'Sic transit Gloria dug-out' (sorry I don't know the Latin word) but then the Romans were soldiers not moles as we are. I loved my tiny sand-bag hut, even though the roof was wondrous low. And you had almost to put your legs outside the door if you wanted to stretch them. It would have given about as much protection as a cardboard box, had a shell hit it plump; but once inside I felt quite 'comfy' even when falling 'crumps' made its poor sides quiver and shake again, and many a time, during the long winter, have I crept in with a sigh of relief out of the bitter cold, happy in the thought that the snow at least could not reach me there. St. William in his mountain cave was not in it, with your poor hermit, for if he had a swarm of devils round him, he was not tormented by a legion of rats (I vote for the devils) and he had nothing more dangerous than some undigested cockleshells to bother him.

> *However, by an unlucky chance this house on the hill stood, apparently, in the direct line of a German battery. They landed four shells in front of the hall-door, (the kitchen door is not used), fortunately dropping them over the sand-bag wall in front, which saved the homestead considerably. They bashed in a trench a foot behind the house, much to the consternation of Fr Browne, who was inside at the time, and who, like a wise man, cleared out for safer quarters.*[14]

Frank Laird confirms Fr Doyle's account and at the same time provides an insight into the fortitude and courage of Fr Browne.

> *On the left of S.P. 13* [Strong Point 13] *as we looked towards the front line, a row of jagged stumps of trees stood up, and midway down them was the hut occupied by the Padre, generally Father Doyle, but during one of our tours another Padre who had been with the Irish Guards. One evening as we were being gently strafed, he came down to the Doctor's hut where we were assembled, and said if we did not mind he would remain with us for a while, as he felt uneasy about being alone under shell fire. The same man soon after, when a message came in that a man had been wounded, set off through the shell fire in the dark refusing to take a runner with him as it was too dangerous!*[15]

Willie continued to lament the loss of the sand-bag hut:

> *Twice they smashed the trench a few yards in front, and once one biggish shell cut our beautiful tree which spread its arms over the roof, clean in two, before tearing the back out of the patient dug-out. As the tree was a good eight inches or more in diameter it was just as well it got the first attack.*
>
> *Shortly after, the General came along and seeing the state of affairs told the Padre to get him gone out of the danger zone, which I am sorry to say the disobedient Padre did not do, and then gave orders for his house to be pulled down, even though he had to admit not a penny of rent was owing.*
>
> *I felt there was little use my trying to prove to M. le General that his fears were quite unfounded and that there was absolutely no danger, but I do not mind telling you the cause of my security. I have a first class*

Guardian Angel, which is not to be wondered at, since you and darling Mother baptised me 'Gabriel'. 'The Strength of God.' Whoever he is, he is a real decent chap and had done his work well. When the shelling begins I send him out to sit on the top of the roof. He does not like it a bit, nor can I blame him, for things are hot at times, but he goes all the same, and then takes it out of me. Sometimes I hear him give a whistle or whatever Angels do in that way and he shouts down: 'Look out Bill, there's a big one coming.' I know he only does that to frighten me, to try and 'get the wind up', as they say, so I shout back 'Go to HEAVEN!' for I suppose you can't send a respectable Angel any place else, and we remain the best of friends. He is the best 'backstop' I ever met, but then he has the advantage of a big pair of wings to flick off the nasty dangerous ones to a safe distance.

I am sorry to say he has lost his job now, though he did his work well, and through many an anxious hour kept the flag flying, and the roof over my head. The morning I came out of the trenches the homestead was laid low, so I have sent my Angel Guardian back to Heaven, to get a few patches in his breeches – I mean his wings – he was quite unpresentable – but have promised to take him on again and give him plenty to do before the Summer is over!!!![16]

Willie's latest budget comes to an end and he posts it home with a letter dated Thursday 29 March. He evidently has procured bound notebooks in order to record his diary entries, no doubt to make the documents more robust, to withstand being circulated around various members of the family and colleagues at Rathfarnham:

I thought I should have been able to fill up this book before posting it to you, but as we are moving off tomorrow and also my stock of news being exhausted, I think it better to send it on now.

You will see I have little of any importance to report, but as you told me these scraps of news are interesting to you I just keep jotting them down, as it is a real pleasure to me to have a little talk with my dear father, even though only on paper.

We are only going back to the rear for some days to continue our 'rest cure', which as far as the poor men are concerned has consisted so far of extra drill. Then to finish the cure, we tackle a week's march, eating when you can get the chance and sleeping as best you can.[17]

Fr Doyle confirms the testimony of so many of his contemporaries, that the word 'rest', used in the context of moving away from front line duties, is a bit of a misnomer! He continues:

Fortunately the weather, which up to this has been very wet and cold, with much snow and rain, has mended at last so I think we shall not have a bad time during our march, a pleasant change in any case after the monotony of trench warfare. We come back here about April 21st as we are now supposed to be training for a rapid pursuit of the terrified fleeing Boche, that is as soon as he begins to flee, which I am thinking is just not yet. I shall send you card at least, from time to time, for I know you will not expect me to write much. Bill of health remains excellent, but I shall want a new pair of legs by the time we limp home.[18]

Willie's optimism about the weather was misplaced. The next day was showery and whilst the battalion was away for nineteen days there were only half a dozen instances recorded in the War Diary where the weather was stated to be fine; although, on Friday 13 April it was actually mild with sunshine! For the remainder of the time it was at best dull and other times cold rain, sleet, snow and high winds were the order of the day. On the day of departure, 31 March 1917, the War Diary for 8th Royal Dublin Fusiliers records:

Battalion left Locre at 8.55am and proceeded to Les Ciscaux 2½ miles NW Hazebrouck arriving there at 3.30pm. Dinners were taken en route. Battalion marched out from Locre 30 Officers 573 OR, 9 men fell out on line of march. This was the first stage of march into 2nd army training area.[19]

The battalion strength speaks for itself: whilst a full complement would be roughly thirty Officers, they would have expected to be in charge of about a thousand Other Ranks. Replacements for men who had been killed, those temporarily wounded and sick in hospital and others invalided home permanently were hard to come by. The foul weather conditions took a toll on the battalion's strength almost on a daily basis. In addition to the nine men who struggled during the march the first day, another eight men 'fell out on line of march' on cold, showery 1 April, and seven men on 2 April. On 1 April twenty-two men with bad feet were sent ahead of the battalion, starting half an hour earlier in the morning at 8.30 a.m., under 2/Lt J.F. Johnson of 'C' Company. Whereas the bulk of the battalion arrived at St Martin-au-Laërt, north-west of St Omer, at 3.50 p.m., Johnson's contingent didn't get there until 7 p.m. and four men were instantly admitted to hospital. The march was completed at Nordesques, on the road between St Omer and Calais, on 2 April. Frank Laird recorded that the three days tramp consisted of seventeen miles the first day, fifteen the next and ten on the last.[20]

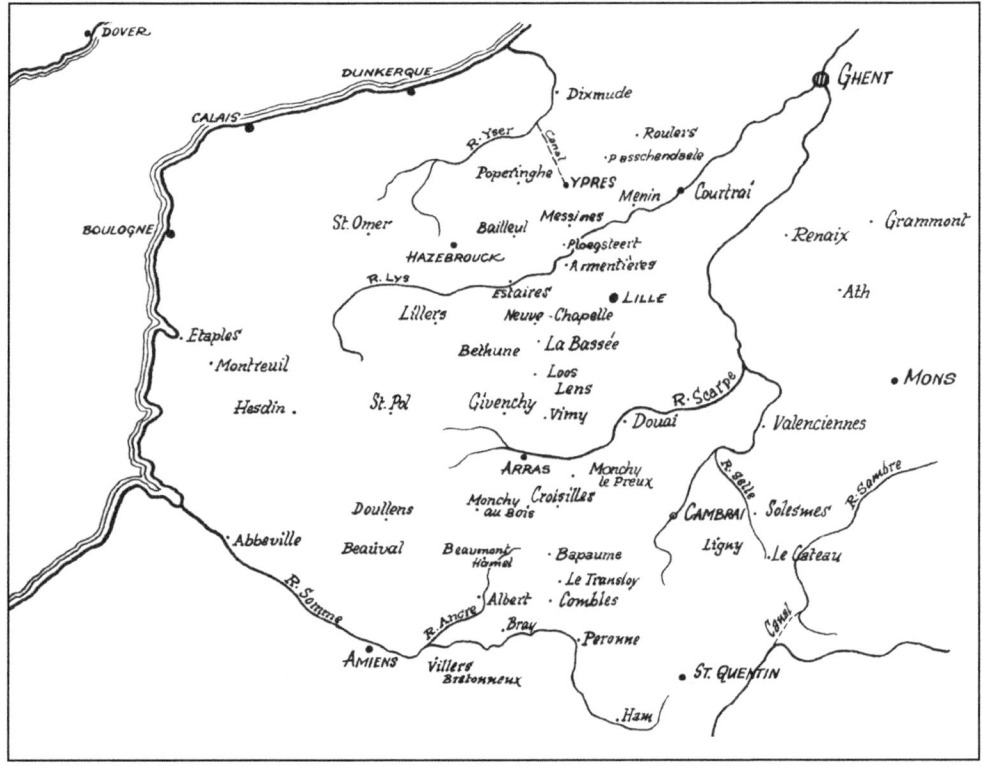

Map of Pas de Calais and adjoining areas

The battalion was in billets in the Nordesques area by 12.40 p.m.; another six men were admitted to hospital; the remainder of the day for everyone else was spent resting. Two days later 2/Lt Johnson was granted ten days leave because his father was dangerously ill. Frank Laird remembered:

At the end of our journey we were comfortably fixed up in divers French farmhouses ... The house was on one side and the barns etc., as a rule, on the other two ... The colossal manure pit in the middle was always a source of great interest, and sometimes of amusement, as when one of our sergeants, rashly trying to walk over the hardened crust, went through to his waist.[21]

On the 3rd April training commenced. Primarily, the purpose of this period of training for the whole brigade was to rehearse their part in an attack being planned by General Plumer, which was scheduled for that summer on the Wytschaete/Messines front. Replica trenches were specially constructed for this purpose and the men of 48th Infantry Brigade were allocated to Second Army Training Area, marked 'W' on the reams of Operational Orders, and other paperwork, meticulously generated by the Staff Officers. [Staff Officers were those officers attached to Headquarters, whose primary function was to undertake research, and to liaise with Commanding Officers, in the planning and coordination of logistics in preparation for forthcoming operations.]

The strenuous march of 8th Dubs notwithstanding, reveille on 3 April was at 6 a.m., followed by cleaning of arms for an hour, then company officers' inspections and, from 9 a.m. until 1 p.m., a programme of intense training. Because of heavy snowfall, the men had to be instructed inside their billets until 10.30 a.m. when the snow cleared, and they then proceeded to the training ground. The afternoon was supposed to be for organised recreation, but the ground conditions would not allow this.

Over the course of the next eleven days the men took part in a range of activities, as well as being sent for bathing at Tournehem. There was bayonet training and musketry training, including a brigade competition for which the 8th Royal Dublin Fusiliers gained first place. Physical training activities took place suited to the harsh weather, such as running, cross-country running and route marches. There was a brigade football competition, won by a team of Fr Doyle's lads, initially drawing 2–2 against the 9th RDF on 12 April, beating them in a replay a day later 1–0 and then going on to defeat the Royal Irish Rifles 2–0 the following day.

The most important activities, however, were those listed with such headings as 'Attack in Open Warfare' and 'Attack in new formation; advancing under fire and use of ground.' Various devices were used to simulate battle conditions, such as:

> *The Brigade will carry out an attack practice over the trench system marked out with tracing tape ... In trench to trench attack creeping barrage will be indicated by men carrying flags.*[22]

The 8th RDF War Diary records Divine Services taking place on the three Sundays the men were away, the second of which was Easter Sunday, 8 April 1917. Fr Doyle, however, had a lot more work on his hands than just these services. Just over halfway through this period of extended exercises, he wrote home on Tuesday 10 April 1917:

> *Here I am for the past week or more and have not had an opportunity of sending you a letter of Easter greetings. Drink? Over feasting? Laziness? The whole bunch, perhaps, but the real reason is I have had very little time to myself. The 'here' is a spot, and a beautiful one, some fifteen miles from the sea, where we have come to rest and go through a course of training.*
>
> *The morning is given up to various exercises, one of which is the storming of a dummy German trench, to the accompaniment of fearful, blood-curdling yells, enough to terrify the bravest Hun. The afternoon is spent at football and athletic sports, so that the men are having a good, if a strenuous, time. So is the poor Padre. My two regiments are quartered in two villages some miles apart. The four Companies of each Regiment in different hamlets and to make things more inconvenient still, the two Platoons of each Company, thirty-two in all, are distributed in as many farmhouses. You can imagine I have no easy task to get round to see all my men, which I am anxious to do, so as to make sure that every man, if possible, gets to his Easter Duty.'*[23]

Not all the Royal Dublin Fusiliers were Catholic. Frank Laird had to rise at 7.40 a.m. on Easter Sunday to take charge of a group attending a Church of England service in a barn: *'where we sat around on bundles of hay agricultural implements.'*[24] Willie continues:

> *I have Mass every morning for them, with many Communions daily, seventy today in one church, and then in the evening, having finished*

Devotions in one village, and heard the men's Confessions, I ride over to the other for Rosary and Benediction, with more Confessions. In addition to this, there are stray 'units' scattered about in various places; machine gunners, trench mortar battery men, etc. etc., who, with the instruction of converts, prevent me from feeling time hanging on my hands.

However I am enjoying the rest here immensely. It is such a relief to be out of sound, even, of the guns, to be sure of a quiet night's rest, without the possibility of waking up with a Boche bayonet sticking into your ribs, and in addition the country is very pretty, undulating and well wooded, though too early in the year to look its best.

Like you we have had, and are having, very cold and wet weather with much snow. From time to time we get a beautiful warm day and then back again into winter shivers. But on the whole things are not too bad.[25]

Willie then retraces his steps to give an account of the movements which had been so succinctly summed up in the 8th Bn Royal Dublin Fusiliers' War Diary, starting from their departure from Locre. He says:

Perhaps it will be best to take up events as they occurred. We left Belgium on the Saturday before Palm Sunday, a glorious morning, dry under foot with brilliant sunshine. The Brigade of four regiments made a gallant show, each headed by their band of pipers and followed by the transport etc. We were the first to move off and so came in for an extra share of greetings from the villagers, who turned out to see us pass. As fine a lot of sturdy lads as you could wish to gaze on, not to mention the gallant chaplain.

Our march for the first day was not a very long one, something about 20 miles, but as every pace took us further and further from the trenches, the march was a labour of love. At mid-day a halt was called for dinner, which had been cooking slowly in the travelling kitchens which accompanied us, and in a few minutes every man was sitting by the roadside negotiating a big supply of hot meat and potatoes, with a substantial chunk of bread. We poor officers were left to hunt for ourselves, a hunt which did not promise well at first, as the people in the 'estaminets' were anything but friendly and said they had nothing to give us to eat. The reason I discovered later was that some British officers had gone away without paying their bill, a not uncommon thing I am sorry to say.[26]

Frank Laird's experience was a little different:

I was also surprised to find that the smallest and poorest looking French cottages could generally be relied on for a good cup of coffee and a first-class omelette. The number of eggs consumed by the British officer in France must have been colossal.[27]

Continuing this theme, Willie continues:

Eventually, with the help of a little palaver and my bad French, our party secured some excellent bread and butter, coffee and a basket of fresh eggs. When I left the table the officer next to me was attacking his sixth egg, at which stage I deemed it prudent to retire, fearing an explosion which I dislike.

On again after an hour's rest. Marching with a heavy rifle and full kit is no joke, hence our pace is slow. I often wonder how the poor men 'stick it' and stick it they do, most of them at least, till I have seen them drop senseless by the road from sheer exhaustion.[28]

Willie's narrative is somewhat more descriptive and enlightening than the War Diary phrase *'fell out on line of march'*. He continues:

As a rule they are left there to follow the column as best they can. For if they knew that falling out meant a lift, not many of the regiment would reach their destination on foot. To make matters worse we had to tramp along over the rough, paved roads which must be an invention of the Old Boy to torture people. At first the road feels like this $_{mmmm}$, then after ten miles mmmm, till at last you are positive that they have paved the way with spikes instead of stones, something in this fashion ^^^^. My poor feet!

At last the town we were bound for came in sight and hopes of a good rest were high, when word came along that we were not to stay in that haven of peace and plenty, but trudge on another three miles. The camel is supposed to be a patient animal, but Tommy can give him points every day.

> *Our lodging was a mutilated country farmhouse, dirty and uncomfortable, the less said about it the better, but everyone was too tired to care much, even though we officers, snoring on the floor, felt inclined to envy the sardines in their comfortable box.*[29]

The place was Les Ciscaux and with so many men to find billets for, many found themselves some way out of town. The next day was a Sunday and although the War Diary indicates that there was a Divine Service, there was no time for Mass for the men. However, Fr Doyle managed to say Mass as usual, as he describes:

> *It was impossible to have Mass for the men in the morning, even though it was Palm Sunday, as there was much work to be done and we had to be off early. I got away to the little village and offered up the Holy Sacrifice for them, bolted down a couple of eggs, congratulating myself it was not a Friday, emptied a coffee pot and fell into my place as the regiment marched off.*[30]

Fr Doyle's religion, of course, dictated that he does not consume meat on Fridays. One wonders how easy it was for him to stick to this at all times during his military career. Knowing him he probably went without completely, fasting, rather than eat meat on a Friday. He continues:

> *That was a hard day. We were all stiff and sore for want of previous exercise and in addition were well scourged by sleet and rain and snow, though at times the sun did its best to brighten things up a bit.*
>
> *Our luck turned as we reached our night's halting place and a good sized town* [St. Martin-au-Laërt] *with comfortable billets. A big party of my men were quartered in the public ballroom, which contained an automatic organ. The last I saw of them was a score of 'couples' waltzing round quite gaily, without a sign of having the best part of a forty mile march to their credit. Headquarters were billeted with one of the nicest families I have met for a long time, every one of the family doing its best in the real French style to make us comfortable and feel at home. Whether it was the excitement of our coming, or the polite attentions of the officers, or their heroic, if barbarous, attempts to speak French, or all of these together, the eldest girl suddenly*

> *went off into hysterics, but was soon brought to her senses by the doctor, who was present, and the evening ended merrily as a marriage bell.*
>
> *Monday saw us early afoot. Nothing of great interest except that the country was becoming more hilly and prettier, the stones harder, our feet and shoulders sorer and quite a longing for the repose of the trenches springing up in many a heart.*
>
> *That evening ended our tramp and here we have been ever since and are to remain for some time longer, much to our joy. Probably we shall return to the same place we came from, but no one really knows our future movements.*[31]

The following Sunday was Easter Day and Fr Doyle's flock attended Easter Mass at the church in Nordesques, when he reminded them of a particular 'duty!' He says:

> *I am very comfortable with the good curé, a very excellent priest, who has been really kind. I gave the men a hint on Easter Sunday to make his collection a good one and the dear old man tottered off to his home hugging a sack of copper and silver coins, with a liberal sprinkling of five franc notes and, I expect, a varied assortment of trouser buttons!! He has gone away today probably on a 'big bust'.*[32]

The turn-out the previous Wednesday for another service and devotional duty is a strong indicator of the faith of Fr Doyle's flock, trouser buttons notwithstanding! This 'Spy' Wednesday (more properly, 'Holy Wednesday', the Wednesday of Holy Week, before Easter) is said to have acquired the name because of the betrayal of Jesus Christ that day by Judas Iscariot. Willie says:

> *I must finish up if you are ever to get this. One little incident before I close. On Spy Wednesday evening, after Benediction, I told the men I wanted nine volunteers to watch an hour during the following night before the Altar of Repose. I had barely finished speaking when the whole church made a rush up to the altar rails and were keenly disappointed when I told them I could only take the first nine, though I could have had thirty an hour if I wanted them. I was touched by the poor fellows' generosity, for they had just finished a long, hard day's work with more before them. I got*

the nine men to bring their blankets into the little sacristy and while one watched the others slept. Surely our Lord must have been pleased with His Guard of Honour and will bless them as only He can.

I'm done. Bill of health perfect. I strained my leg a bit mounting my horse the other day, it was rather painful at first but practically all right now. Would send you an Easter Egg if I had one but enclose an extra packet of love instead.

Ever dearest Father, your own loving Will. Your long most interesting letter just received. You are very good to write.[33]

Willie's last comment was made in all seriousness because he knew how little time Hugh Doyle had with all his various commitments, such as the St Vincent de Paul Society and his grand-children's penny bank. However, the largest chunk of his time was taken up with his continued employment as a civil servant at the Court of Bankruptcy in Dublin, in spite of reaching the grand age of four score years and five.

Willie's next letter was written on Wednesday 18 April 1917. The Irishmen had left the Nordesques area on Sunday 15 April, after Divine Service, to trudge the journey in reverse. Willie continues his narrative of the last few miles and advising that the 8th Dubs were about to go into the front line:

We got back to our old quarters yesterday evening after a hard march of three days and I am writing from my comfortable convent billet which I exchange tomorrow for a spell in the trenches.

The final stage of our journey was a very trying one. The weather has got bad again – it is snowing heavily as I write – and we had to face the cobble stones at six in the morning with a hurricane of rain and sleet, which slashed like a whip. However, even the long French roads have an end and we finally reached our destination pretty well worn out, sore of foot, not to speak of shoulders, with tongues hanging out for a bite and a sup, a thing not to be wondered at, seeing as we had tramped for over eight hours without a morsel of food.

The change has done us all an amount of good, though as I explained in my last letter, the 'rest' was not much of a rest for me, the men being so much scattered about the country. In fact I spent most of the time on my bicycle, or riding around on my horse like a second Napoleon, one morning covering a good twelve miles, without drawing rein, so that I have had my share of exercise and fresh air, which has left me as fit as a fiddle.[34]

The battalion had marched out of St Martin-au-Laërt to go to Les Ciscaux on 16 April and on arrival that afternoon the Medical Officer inspected the men's feet. There had not been as many fall-outs during the return leg, perhaps indicating that the time away from the harshness of the front line had been beneficial to the men. Also that day, the adjutant, Lt Jackson proceeded on a three-day course to Royal Flying Corps (56th Squadron) at Bailleul, an indication of the increasing importance of that service.

On Tuesday 17 April the battalion started out at 6.30 a.m., arriving back in Kemmel Shelters at 1.30 p.m., where another foot inspection took place. The billets were cleaned and inspections were also made of arms and equipment, and deficiencies were made up where possible. The Lewis Gun Officer and Signalling Officer reconnoitred the left sub-section (Vierstraat–Wytschaete Road on the left to Lark Corner on the right) in preparation for the next tour of trench duty by the 8th Royal Dublin Fusiliers.

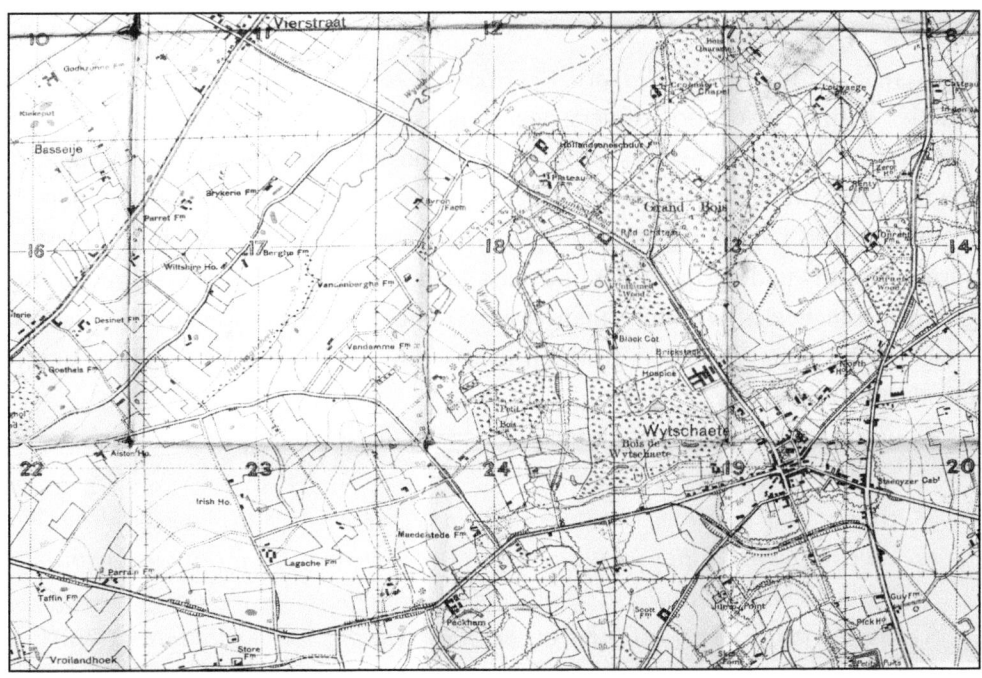

A section of Trench MAP, Messines area

The relief took place during the evening of the 19th, replacing the 7th Leinster Regiment, and was completed by 9.30 p.m. Frank Laird remembered marching to one such relief, although it is not clear whether it was this one or not, but the story is amusing and would have appealed to Willie Doyle. The issue of camouflage is also interesting:

> *Next evening we set out for the front line, timing it to arrive at the danger zone about dusk. I had the honour of marching beside Captain Thompson, with the platoon behind and a piper playing Irish airs on an Irish bagpipes just under our noses. The intention doubtless was kindly, but we both heaved a sigh of relief when he abandoned his tuneful labours a little way out and permitted us to proceed in peace. We passed some genuine and some dummy houses by the wayside; the latter looked innocent enough until we came abreast of them and saw the muzzle of a big gun sticking out. Then we topped a rise, and on the slope towards the enemy, marched under a series of screen hung from side to side of the road so as to break the view from the other side.*[35]

The remainder of night of 19 April 1917 passed very quickly; the enemy was quite inactive with the exception of very occasional sniping and machine-gun fire along the parapet, but no casualties were taken to hospital. Of greater significance to the battalion strength was that 50 Other Ranks were attached to 250th Tunnelling Company. The tunnelling companies of the Royal Engineers had been working surreptitiously underground for the past year, cautiously burrowing under the German trenches to lay more than twenty mines in preparation for the planned attack in this area. Engineers from all over the Empire lent their expertise to this clandestine operation.

Willie next compares the relative quietness of the sector to events elsewhere:

> *Though things are lively enough elsewhere, all is very quiet on our front, the Boche having quite enough to think of I expect. We do not know our future movements, but it is likely we shall remain as we are for some weeks at least, though just now events move rapidly and well, thank God.*[36]

This is probably the British attack on German defences in and around the French town of Arras, which started on Easter Monday, 9 April and continuing until 16 May 1917. Frank Laird recorded:

Easter Monday was a slight day and the Captain, Hastings, and I went for a walk, which ended in a visit to a house in the hamlet of La Panne ... Many bottles of champagne were produced ... Harris of D Company, who was with us, introduced Thompson as 'Un millionaire Espagnol' ... A heavy snow shower being abated, we set out for our billets, some in a zig-zag fashion, and on the way called in on D Company. There the news of the capture of Vimy Ridge had just arrived, which caused Thompson to waltz round the room with the fat old Frenchman of the house; and so home to dinner.[37]

Willie ends his missive home on a customary homely note:

Little of interest happened during the stay in the rear, which passed all too quickly for all of us. I shall send you a few jottings later on, as I want to post you this and I have many little things to do and several letters to write.

I hope Bob and Jennie had a good time in Queenstown and found the old Missioner well and fit with an appetite for the glorious cake, sharpened by a forty days fast. I expect the said cake has been honourably buried long since.[38]

Fr Doyle's battalion spent nine days in the Front Line. The War Diary records the usual round of hospital returns, personnel struck off (or taken back on) battalion strength, men and officers departing and returning from training courses, fatigues and trench maintenance, enemy activity and the ubiquitous weather reports.

On 21 April it was recorded that a dug-out was built at SP13 and another was in the course of construction. SP13 was to assume a great significance for the padres and would be etched in the memories of the Reverend Fathers Browne and Doyle less than two months later. On 23 April it was noted that 2nd Lieutenant F.M. Laird, together with one Other Rank, had proceeded to Terdeghem to attend a grenade course. He commented:

The course was highly compressed to get it inside a week, and between lectures and practice we had not much spare time. The first parade was at 7.45, and from that till dinner at 7.30 we were mostly at work ... At the end of our week we had a grand night attack by bombing on some trenches dug in the school grounds. This was a most realistic affair, with Verey lights, etc., etc., and bags of sand for bombs, of which the Commandent was very proud ... I managed to secure the degree of G.Q.I. or 'Good Qualified Instructor'...[39]

While the 8th Royal Dublin Fusiliers were on Front Line duty their brigade colleagues, 2nd Dubs, were in reserve at Locre. While the 8th Dubs were constructing SP13, the 2nd Dubs were engaged in a football match versus the 9th Royal Irish Fusiliers, a battalion from 108th Brigade of 36th (Ulster) Division. The northern battalion prevailed, beating the southerners seven goals to nil.[40]

The 8th Royal Dublin Fusiliers were relieved by the 2nd Royal Dublin Fusiliers on 27 April 1917, going into brigade support in the hutments at Butterfly Farm. Two days later Willie writes a short letter enclosing another budget. He advises:

As I shall be away for two or three days I send on the budget as it is. The last few pages you can use for writing down your good resolutions if you feel tempted that way.

I have nothing to add to my last postcard. Everything very quiet and peaceful here. We are not to return to the trenches for some time, I am at this moment trying to forget that there is such a thing as a war, listening to our Divisional band playing under my window – 'The Mikado'![41]

This next general Budget is headed Easter 1917 and covers some of the topics Willie had already written to Hugh about, but also new information and musings, especially on the status of religion and the church in France. Despite spending so much time over the Easter period at his Easter duties, the Padre evidently had enough time to put pen to paper also:

There is very little of interest to record about our fortnight's stay at Nordasque [sic]*, a village you will have some difficulty in finding even on a large map, but after the ceaseless roar of the guns and too frequent crash of bursting shells it was a perfect paradise of peace to war-worn men.*

Had the weather been less wintry, without snow, sleet and storms of wind, our rest would have been more pleasant, nestling in the midst of well wooded hills, surrounded by orchards of pines trees and boasting of as neat a church as I have seen for a long time.

The village was doubly blest by the presence of a holy, zealous curé, who seemed more anxious even than I that the men should profit spiritually by their stay in his parish and not only gave me every facility for my work, but helped himself as far as he could.

I am convinced the French clergy will benefit very much by this war. All over the country, as you know, there are a multitude of tiny parishes numbering often less than 200 souls, including children (I have seen the actual figures.) Even if all there were practical Catholics, that would never give work for a priest with two wooden legs, the result being that a man with little to do often does less than he has to do, for abundance of work creates a spirit of zeal.

Now that the ranks of the clergy have been sorely decimated, some 3,000 French priests have been killed already, the survivors will have to multiply their efforts and take charge of perhaps two or three parishes, much to their own personal advantage I think.

Easter Sunday was quite a red letter day in the annals of the town. The regiment turned out in full strength, headed by the pipers – not the original ones who played before Moses, they are long since turned into margarine by the resourceful Germans – and crowded the sanctuary, every inch of church and beyond. I had eight stalwart sergeants standing guard with fixed bayonets round the altar.

At the Consecration and also the Communion of the Mass the buglers sounded the Royal Salute, which is only given to the Monarchy; the guard at the word of command presented arms and in our poor humble way we tried to do honour to the Almighty King of Kings on His glorious triumph. I must not forget to add that the lassies and maidens did us the honour of coming to sing during the Mass, casting many an envious glance (so rumour says) down on the handsome Irish lads praying so devoutly below. What a grand matrimonial market we might have had were it not for the blessed old tower of Babel!

My only adventure, if I may call it so, was furnished by a horse lent me one day. The beast was a good goer, with plenty of pace, but had one little failing which I was not long in discovering – he had a passionate love for convoys and insisted on following every one he met. He would go along quite nicely till the last waggon passed and then round he'd go too and off with him after the caravan.

After liberal use of whip and spur he would at last give up his own will and go the way I wanted, but 50 yards down the road suddenly a dead stop, which the first time nearly sent me flying over his head, as I was not expecting this manoeuvre, and he was round and off again.

Right triumphed over might in the end, but the 'old 'oss' showed me what he <u>could</u> do if he liked, by backing to the edge of a deep ditch full of mud and water, as much as to say 'I'll land you there if you don't keep quiet.' I have made this useful discovery, however, that there are more obstinate things in the world than holy nuns!!

Low Sunday saw us on the homeward march once more to the tune of cold pelting rain. If you ever want to do a bit of extra penance try a 20 mile march over a muddy French road with wind and rain doing their worst; it is an experience to look back on rather than wish to repeat. Towards the afternoon the sun came out to cheer us up and dry our clothes, so things were not as bad as they might have been.

We stayed that night close to St. Omer, which gave me the chance of visiting the old Jesuit College – the beginning of Stonyhurst – and the famous cathedral begun about 1100. It was a magnificent building, though not one of the first class cathedrals of France, and rich in historic memories. It certainly made one reflect on the rapidity of time, to read on the walls words like the following: 'King Louis of France (St. Louis) and his pious Mother Queen Blanche visited this church in 1219,' a little trifle of 700 years!!

I was just in time for Benediction, sung by the whole congregation, a large one too. I could not help thinking, as the volume of music rolled through the vast cathedral, how many prayers and petitions had ascended to God from that spot in the past 800 years and how many graces and benedictions had poured from that same altar, where the Almighty, who never changes was blessing us as He blessed the generations who had gone. The words of the great French novelist, M. Huysemans, came back to my mind 'The walls of our old churches are petrified prayer.'

The more I see of France the more I am puzzled what to think of the religious state of the country. It is quite apparent that indifference is very widespread, though the Curés say the people as a whole they do not lose the Faith and are anxious to be reconciled with the church before they die, a sort of a back door way into Heaven, trying to have the best of both worlds. On the other hand, I have been amazed by the number of new churches erected in recent years, chiefly at private expense, at the costly way in which they are furnished and above all by the crowds attending Vespers on Sunday.

If there were a little more of Fr O'Flynn's gentle argument of 'coaxing the lazy ones on with the stick' France might easily be a different country! The Faith and fervour of our Irish lads have made a great impression everywhere and I was quite delighted once to hear the French Curé rubbing it into his congregation, drawing a contrast between them and the Irish soldiers, much to the disadvantage of the former.[42]

Willie now changes tack:

As I write, a curious little bit of news has reached me. Before we left the Loos district our Divisional General Hickie suggested that all ranks should subscribe towards a memorial of our stay there and a monument to the memory of the men who had fallen in action. This was to take the form of a life size statue of Our Lady of Victories to be carved in white marble by the best Paris sculptor and erected in the church of Nouex-les-Mines, where the Divisional Headquarters were, with the names of the fallen inscribed on the pedestal. We are all to receive a small book containing a photo of the statue, names of subscribers etc., which will be a pleasing memento of the 16th Irish Division.

A few days ago the statue arrived from Paris and a party of men were despatched from here to erect it in Noeux-les-Mines. They had barely reached the town when a huge German shell, the only one fired that day, came through the roof of the church and practically blew it to bits! This is all the more remarkable as the town had often been shelled but the church was never hit. Fortunately the statue had not been erected and was *uninjured and our Blessed Lady is only waiting for the Boche to be driven back to occupy the site prepared for her.*

I see by the papers that since this happened Loos has been the centre of fierce fighting, being just in front of Lens, so I expect not much remains of Nouex-les-Mines by this, but Mary's statue is safe.[43]

The statue had left Paris on Friday 16 March but the lorry carrying it had been delayed en-route, so did not arrive at its intended destination until Sunday 18 March. It was stored in the Curé's house at Bruay until 2 October 1921, when it was blessed by Mgr. Julien and placed on a side altar in the restored and rebuilt Church of St Martin at Noeux-les-Mines.[44] There it remains.

Willie's narrative continues but gets a bit confusing. He starts reminiscing; narrating incidents which took place the previous year in August and, indeed, in February 1916:

It will not be out of place here to put on record a striking instance of our Blessed Lady's protection of myself, which I have not mentioned before, though it took place on the feast of her Assumption.

15 August has always been a day of many graces for me. It is the anniversary of my consecration to Mary, of my Vows to the Society, and was very nearly making me surpass our Lady herself by ending me higher up than she ever got in her life.

We were out of the trenches at the time staying in a village called Mazingarbe, not far from Noeux-les-Mines. It was here that the previous February I received my 'baptism of fire' and the shelling stopped in a wonderful way as I rode along the road. You may remember the account I gave you at the time. That afternoon most of the men were in a field outside the town engaged in athletic sports............[45]

Then he switches, in mid-narrative, indicated by the dotted line, to an actual occurrence which took place as he is writing:

May I interrupt this narrative to give you a sample of the delights of my life? I am writing in my little dug-out and a shell has just plumped down outside giving us a good shake, falling about as near as the tennis court at home. I am waiting for the next one. If he be a small shell the sandbags will probably burst and no great harm will result, except a few holes in my blankets or my old skin. If my visitor happens to be a fat gentleman and catches the roof fair, he will walk through without stopping to knock and, well, I'm afraid you won't have the trouble of reading this, but you can say a few prayers for me instead. I often marvel how God gives His graces as they are wanted and so the hard and impossible thing becomes easy. Here I am, as all are, face to face with eternity waiting for this shell to come crashing through as it may any moment and yet writing away as calmly as if the danger were a million miles away. I know Our Lord is faithful to His promises and 'not a hair of our head will be touched without His permission,' and I have also a double assurance of protection because Gabriel is back again, sitting out on the roof (in a grand new pair of 'trousyousers') so I can rest in peace. No other shell has come, hence I can resume the thread of my narrative of 15 August ……….[46]

The dotted line again indicated that Fr Doyle had put this incident behind him and has reverted back to reflections about August 1916:

I was at the men's sports that afternoon when the Germans began to shell the town and for a while made things quite lively. Knowing there were a good many of my boys about I hurried back as quickly as I could and made my way up the long narrow street. The shells were all coming in one direction, across the road, not down it, so that by keeping close to the houses on the 'shady' side there was little danger, though occasional thrills of excitement, enough to satisfy Don Quixote himself.

I reached the village crossroads in time to lift up the poor sentry who had been badly hit and with the help of a couple of men carried him to the side of the road. He was unconscious but I gave him absolution and was halfway through the anointing when, with a scream and a roar which made our hearts jump, a shell whizzed over our heads and crashed into the wall directly opposite on the other side of the street, covering us with brick dust and dirt. Bits of shrapnel came thud, thud on the ground and walls around us, but neither I nor the men were touched. 'Begorra, Father, that was a near one anyhow' said one of them, as he brushed the dirt off his tunic and started to fill his pipe 'it was well we had your reverence with us when Jerry (a pet name for the Boche) sent that one across.' 'You must not thank me boys' I said 'don't you know it is our Lady's feast and Mary had her mantle spread over us to save us from all harm.' 'True for you, Father' came the answer, but I could see by their faces that they were by no means convinced that I had not worked the miracle and I fear, for once, our dear Mother was robbed of much of the glory and thanks which were her due. I don't think she will be very angry, do you?

Though it was the 15 August I was taking no risks, especially with this reputation to maintain, so the poor boy being dead I bundled the rest of them down a cellar out of harm's way and started off again.

Heavy as the shelling was, little damage was done, thanks to the fact that the sports had emptied the town. One man was beyond my aid, a few slightly wounded and that was all.

As I came round the corner of the church I met four of my boys calmly strolling along in the middle of the street as if they were walking on Kingstown Pier 'with their hands in their breeches coat like cucumbers' (to quote a famous saying of dear old Fr Lentaigne.) I won't record what I said but my words, helped by the opportune arrival of an unpleasantly near 'H.E.' (high explosive) had the desired effect and we all took cover in the church.

It was only then I realised my mistake, for it soon became evident the Boche were firing at the church itself. One after another the shells came in rapid succession, first on one side, then on the other, dropping in front and behind the building, which was a target with its tall white tower. It was madness to go out and I do not think the men, some score of them, know their danger, nor did I tell them but 'man of little faith' as I was, I cast anxious eyes at the roof and wished it were stronger, even though Mary's mantle was stretched over it, for I thought perhaps there might be a hole in the garment which she had forgotten to patch.

All's well that ends well, they say. Not a shot hit the church, though the houses and road got it hot. Our fiery ordeal ended at last, safely and happily for all of us and 15 August 1916 went down on my list as another day of special grace and favour at Mary's hands.

I often congratulate myself on my good fortune in being appointed to the 'Irish Brigade' more especially as the last vacancy fell to me.[47]

The last vacancy Willie mentions was at divisional level rather than brigade, evidenced by Willie's quotation marks, and in any event there were three brigades in the 16th (Irish) Division. Willie is alluding to the Seventeenth Century 'Wild Geese', an 'Irish Brigade' which served in continental armies. He continues, possibly somewhat smugly but definitely with more than a hint of pride:

> *The vast majority of the chaplains at the Front seldom see anything more dangerous than the shell of an egg of doubtful age. They are doing splendid work along the lines of communication, in the hospitals or at the base. Even those who are attached to non-Catholic Divisions have little time to get to the trenches, their men are so scattered, but we in the Irish Brigade live in the thick of it. We share the hardships and dangers with our men and if we have less polish on our boots and belts than other spruce padres let us hope we have something more to our bank account in a better world.[48]*

On 27 April there is another, long budget entry which commences:

> *I have spent most of this day in thinking of God's wonderful goodness to me twelve months ago – the anniversary of the awful gas attack at Loos, when, if you remember, some invisible, almost physical, force turned me back to get my helmet, which I had thrown aside leaving my dug-out that morning, an act which saved my life.[49]*

The description which follows, as written by Willie in April 1917, but referring to April 1916, has been included out of sequence in chapter 16, because it seemed more appropriate and brought more clarity to the overall story of the gas attack. Therefore, it is not repeated in this chapter. Willie's budget now ends, as does this chapter.

CHAPTER 25
APPROACHING THE BATTLE OF MESSINES:
'WHAT HO! SHE BUMPS!'

*'General Plumer came to lunch today.
Afterwards he explained his plan of attack and received my approval'*
Field-Marshal Sir Douglas Haig, diary entry of Thursday 10 May 1917

The weather continued to improve and in typical fashion, Willie's next letter to his father, dated 7 May 1917, commences with a weather report. He writes:

> *I had to finish my last letter rather hurriedly as I wanted to take advantage of a few free days to make a little excursion and pay a visit to the good, dear nuns at Amettes, who were so kind to me on my first arrival in France. It was a trifle of some 80 kilometres (about 50 miles) of a journey, but the weather being glorious, not too hot, and dry, I thought little of it as I mounted my bicycle and started to trundle my 20 odd stone of flesh, bones and blood along the roads of France.[1]*

Fr Doyle certainly was not 20 odd stone, but maybe that's how it felt after covering so many miles on his bicycle! It isn't clear why he had a few free days. The 8th Royal Dublin Fusiliers' War Diary for the end of April indicates that things were very quiet. So quiet in fact that on 28 April, a programme of sports was arranged for the afternoon, which included football, route marches and cross country runs. Despite the upturn in the weather, and consequent improvement in the state of the men's feet, it was still thought expedient to send one 'Other Rank' on a course in chiropody on 1 May. Three days previously Frank Laird returned from Army Grenade School:

On April 29 I travelled back (by a London bus!) to my own folk near Kemmel. We were now stationed in a camp of wooden huts, in glorious hot weather which lasted all May. For the good of the men's health and morale inter-company sports were the order of the day. Needless to say C Company won that day. We were first in the cross country race, and in the shooting our four platoons took the first four places, mine being second, and though D Company beat us at football our aggregate of points put us on top... The officers had a rifle competition ... though near the line here we suffered no harm, in spite of one stray shell which went right through the roof of a hut but buried itself in the floor without exploding.[2]

When the battalion was relieved by 6th Connaught Rangers, they proceeded to Doncaster Huts at Locre. Frank Laird remembered:

On 6 May we were back in Locre, and working parties formed our chief employ. They were not, on whole, too unpleasant. At least they had the advantage of preventing any other parades. Half the Company went one day and half the next. We usually started for the line in the late evening, or at night, and did not return until 4,5 or 6 in the morning. Two Lieutenants went in charge, and when we returned we ate anything that was to be had, and tumbled into bed till mid-day or so. The days off were very 'cushy' as there was no duty to be done on most of them.[3]

Lieutenant Arthur Glanville of 2nd Royal Dublin Fusiliers recalled a slightly different state of affairs. After he was taken a Prisoner of War and interned at Rastratt in Germany in May 1918, he commenced a diary and reflected retrospectively on 'my life since I joined the army.' He wrote:

April 1917. We had a good time training and came back to the same front to find it very much livelier. Things were pretty nearly ready for the attack on the Wytschaete-Messines Ridge. The 'dirty' work fell to our Brigade. We were put into the line and kept there, while the other Brigades resting and training for the attack. Constant raids and shelling – and even in Support Reserve and Billets we had to spend most of our time working in the line.[4]

Reverting to Willie's letter of 7 May, he continues his description of his few days furlough:

> *I went along leisurely, having plenty of time, for I knew the Sisters would put me up for the night and so made many little detours to visit some of the Churches, which are always interesting. I was rather amused in one to see behind the altar a very handsome stained glass window of the Nativity. The shepherds stand grouped at the back, Our Lady and St. Joseph kneel on one side of the Crib, while on the other, dwarfing every other figure is the Curé himself, in an attitude of prayer, looking as if he had swallowed a pound of butter. The worthy man is evidently determined not to be forgotten when he books his passage to another world, or to leave to posterity the task of erecting a monument to his memory, a hint which might be taken by our Rev Clerical friends – Fr Tom for example – would look really well as the Impenitent Thief on Calvary.*[5]

Father Tom Murphy – he of 'The Mighty Murphy Monster Monstrance Memorial'[6] was Willie's cousin from Newry Cathedral, where they both officiated at periodic missions – Willie's letter continues:

> *At the bottom of the same church is a mortuary slab, which reads as follows: 'Erected by Monsieur X in honour of his dear wife Marie who lived 79 years, 4 months, 6 days. They were married 55 years, 9 months, 2 days, 7 hours, R.I.P.' There is nothing like being accurate, but possibly this unfortunate man wanted to record that he had so much of his Purgatory already done!*
>
> *I reached the Convent late in the evening, after a most enjoyable and restful ride through the country, away from the din and roar of war. The Sister who opened the door looked at me with all her eyes in a dazed, frightened sort of way. 'I remember you perfectly, Father,' she said, 'but I think I had better let the Mother know first,' and she vanished like a flash, leaving me rather mystified. In a few moments old Mother Hen and all her Chicks came swarming in: 'Mais, mon père, you are dead! We saw in the paper that you were killed by a shell – Fr Doyle, S.J., n'est ce pas?' 'The same old 'oss, Madame, but as far as I know still very much alive ' and*

then I told her about Fr Denis Doyle S.J. who, God rest his soul, has got me so many Masses and prayers by mistake. Thereupon all fell on each other's neck and wept; the weeping on the necks of the more elderly dames being of short duration to prevent jealousy alone. The convent larder was next emptied and, for a dead man, I did remarkably well, ending with a glorious sleep.

I spent most of the next day wondering round the country, with a visit to the home and shrine of the 'beggar man saint' John Baptist Labré. FN1 *I often think he must be nearly mad with envy, watching us in the trenches, surrounded and walked on and sat upon by his 'pets,' but from the same 'pets' deliver us O Lord, as speedily as may be, this coming hot weather.*[7]

Willie next proceeded to Noeux-les-Mines, shocking someone else of his acquaintance in the same way that he had astonished the nuns:

On the way home I took in Nouex-les-Mines and heard from the Curé (who, by the way, looks very uncomfortable and made a grab for the Holy Water when I appeared from the dead) the whole story of his church and Our Lady's statue, which I mentioned in my last letter.[8]

Having returned from his excursion, things obviously remained quiet for Willie because he repeats news he has already written about, but this time in more detail. He continues with the saga of the statue of Our Lady of Victories:

On Passion Sunday, as I told you, the men arrived with the box and asked him where he wished the statue of Our Lady of Victories to be erected. As it was only a quarter of an hour before High Mass he told them to come back later and then turned into his own garden a few yards away to finish his office. The Mass servers were playing outside the church, which at that moment, was empty, the sacristan having finished his preparations had lately left, when a 15 inch shell fired from a German naval gun about the distance of Skerries from where you are crashed through the wall and exploded in the Sanctuary. As a rule shells burst on impact, but this being an armour piercing shell, came through the wall like paper and exploded inside, with results impossible to describe.[9]

Skerries is a coastal town in the northern part of County Dublin, about twelve miles from Hugh's home in Dalkey. The gun was undoubtedly a large calibre weapon, but would not have been a naval gun. Willie continues:

When I went into the ruin I exclaimed to Mons le Curé 'surely you have had fifty shells in here!' 'No', he answered, 'only one. The havoc you see is the work of a single shot.' Not a trace of the beautiful altar where I so often offered the Holy Sacrifice remains. The carved stalls, the altar rails, benches and chairs are smashed into splinters, the roof and parts of the walls are stripped of plaster. I have never seen such a scene of desolation and destruction, the explanation being that the explosion took place inside the church and the liberated gases rushed round like ten thousand mad animals, rending and tearing all they met, seeking for an exit.

Our Lady of Victories in church at Noeux-Les-Mines

The building was nearly as large as Kingstown church, but from end to end it is a perfect ruin. Pictures, organ, statues, all are gone, the door of the sacristy blown in and the vestments torn to ribbons, while not a particle of the beautiful stained glass, which filled the twenty large windows, remains now.

There is just one ray of comfort in this sad destruction, not a life was lost. Ten minutes later the church would have been crowded with civilians and soldiers; few of them, probably, would have been touched by bits of the shell, but not a soul could have been left alive by the shock. I have seen on the battlefield men, sometimes a row at a time, standing or leaning against a trench, untouched by bullet or shrapnel, simply killed by the force of an exploding shell. You can picture the result in a strong enclosed building.

Here, as in so many other places, God again showed His power in a wonderful way. Quite near the altar stood a magnificent Calvary; one arm of the Crucified is torn off, but otherwise neither the figure nor the cross is injured. Poor St John got badly smashed up and Saint Mary Magdalen has a bullet through her heart, the very thing she would have asked for, but our Blessed Lady, with the exception of a slight scratch on one hand 'stands by the cross' absolutely untouched, in the midst of all the havoc and ruin.

The shell you will remember fell in the sanctuary, blowing the altar to bits. After much search and digging among the debris the tabernacle was found, whole and entire; inside the ciborium,or sacred vessel containing the Blessed Sacrament, was standing upright, not even the cover having been knocked off and the Consecrated particles in perfect order, though the tabernacle must have been blown to the ceiling.[10]

It seems strange that Willie has included an explanation of a ciborium, as Hugh Doyle must surely have known this. Perhaps he did it because he knew that copies of his letters were circulated elsewhere, with the possibility that some readers may not be au fait with such technical terms. Indeed, it may even be the case that it was not Willie that included the explanation in his hand-written letter, but Lena who transcribed it and circulated the typescript. Willie continues:

This bit of news ought to make you quite happy. If, for example, you hear one day that I was last seen rapidly making for the moon, don't be uneasy, for I shall certainly come down again safely with the pious ejaculation on my lips: 'What Ho! She bumps!' Or should I vanish under fifty tons of bricks, possess your soul in patience for a week as it takes some time to lift a house or two off one's chest and you will find that, like Lazarus of old, I am none the worse for a few days rest in a tomb.

That ends my little stock of news. The weather, thoroughly ashamed of its bad conduct, has put on its best face and is pouring sunshine on us for the last ten days, so that one timid green leaf has actually put out its head. The Boche is extremely good and well behaved, causing us no trouble worth speaking of, in fact seems anxious to meet our wishes in every way. Yesterday he erected a notice board on his front line: 'You can have a present of these trenches on 8 May.' Whether this is his little joke, or he means to retire, we do not know, but we have not had such a quiet time for the past fifteen months.[11]

Tuesday, 8 May 1917 came and went with the enemy still ensconced and Willie's battalion of 8th Royal Dublin Fusiliers still in reserve. That night the battalion provided 320 Other Ranks for working parties with the Royal Engineers and also for the pioneers of the Hampshire Regiment, having already supplied 245 men two nights previously. A typical working party would be digging six-foot trenches for telephone wires to run up to the front line, the depth of the conduit attesting to the level of planning, and to the attitude that nothing should be left to chance. Frank Laird did not have fond memories of that job:

The job most disliked by the men was burying a telephone cable all the way up to the front line at a depth of six feet. When the party arrived on the ground the portion for the night was marked off in lengths for each man. The slow workers were sometimes only half way down when the quick ones had finished. The little R.E. officer had provided himself with a six foot pole which he ran about with testing the depth, and meticulously insisting that it should be the same everywhere. The result was that sometimes the sodden earth of Flanders fell in in spots, and had to be dug again with much profanity.... This digging in the open up to the reserve lines was eerie work at night, and not without its danger. We were fortunate enough to have no casualties.[12]

On 9 May all available officers and men attended a gas shell demonstration and the following day was set aside for bathing at Westoutre, so that everyone was spick and span for Church Parade on Sunday 12 May 1917.

Before these events Willie had ended his letter with what appears to be a reference to his father's sense of humour, followed by a bit of banter of his own. Hugh Doyle's latest letter to Willie informed him of food shortages in Ireland, probably making some remark about maybe having to resort to eating the family's pet dog. Willie's riposte was:

I am sorry to hear that, owing to shortage of meat in Ireland, poor Tim is to perform the 'Happy Dispatch' at an early date. It is a sad ending to the life of a faithful hound, who served his master well, but I should like to suggest that he be boiled for many hours before eating for, if I mistake not, the said Tim is a tough old dog. What about the parrot? And have you ever tried 'devilled rat a la tranche'?[13]

Willie writes to Hugh again on 15 May 1917:

Thank you ever so much for your most welcome letter just received. I cannot tell you how eagerly I look forward to their arrival, but at the same time I should be much more content if you did not write so often, for I know you have a good deal of correspondence (not to speak of the Penny Bank) and – though you might not believe it – you are not as young as you were!

I have absolutely no news to send you this week. As far as we are concerned there might be no war going on, things are so quiet. Even the gunners on both sides seem to have caught the epidemic of peace and for the past few days have scarcely fired a shot, to which state of affairs no one objects!

Father Browne and I have taken advantage of our whole Brigade being out of the trenches for the past fortnight to organise month of May devotions for the men. We have rosary, hymns, short sermon and Benediction every evening, followed by more hymns, as the 'boys' like to hear their own voices.

Unfortunately, 'working parties' are the order of the day and night at present, so many cannot come, but all the same we have had a big church full each evening.[14]

Frank Laird describes another duty of the working parties:

As a variant from the telephone wire we had the 'Chinese Wall' to operate on – a huge wall of sandbags with dugouts here and there in it, which was constructed along behind the second line to serve as an assembly place when the attack came off .... Besides these works the preparations for June 7th included a water supply laid on in pipes to the front line, a tunnel, with large dug-outs, which ran from the entrance to the communication trenches to the front line also, and various new roads cut out from the back areas to the line, so as to distribute the enemy shell fire when it came.[15]

Returning to Fr Doyle and the May devotions:

One result of the devotions has been the conversion of the only really black sheep in the regiment, a man very many years away from his duty, a hard, morose character upon whom I had failed many times to make any impression. I saw it was useless to argue with him, so at the beginning of the month I handed him over to the Blessed Virgin as a hopeless case with which she alone could deal. Last evening I met him and thought I would try once more to make him see the awful danger he was running of losing his soul. It was all no use, the devil had his prey too tightly held to shake him off like that. Then a thought struck me: 'Look' I said, 'this is the month of May, you surely won't refuse our Blessed Lady.' The poor fellow fell on his knees and there and then made his confession. I gave him Holy Communion and now he is a changed man, as happy as a lark.

After that I think there is some hope of Mai's conversion, judging by her own account she is in a bad way! Being like George Washington, incapable of a lie, I must admit that I have failed utterly to get drunk – I mean sick – and the bill of health continues A.1.[16]

More news follows on 22 May 1917, Willie's letter to his father commencing in a familiar vein:

I have long suspected and am now quite convinced of the fact that you are in league with the 'Clock Man.' How you manage it I do not know, but somehow you get him to slip over a few days in the week – at least so it seems to me – for barely have I despatched one letter to you than it is time to begin another. I do not mean this as a grumble, for it is a real pleasure to write to my dear old father, but the trouble is to find something fresh to say. When I have told you that the weather is roasting hot and that I am browned and bronzed and bonny, I have exhausted my slender stock of news, or nearly so.[17]

A few days previously Fr Doyle's flock had relieved the 7th Royal Inniskilling Fusiliers at Vierstraat, in the right sub-sector of the front line, on Friday 18 May. Things were now beginning to liven up, both in front and behind the lines. The history of the latter battalion records:

On 17 May we were relieved in this sector by 8th Royal Dublin Fusiliers, and on completion proceeded to Birr Barracks (Locre) where we remained in Divisional Reserve until 3 June.

During this period the battalion supplied many fatigue parties to work in the forward zone ....

The ensuing fortnight at Birr Barracks was spent in preparation for the forthcoming offensive. The activity along the whole of the 2nd Army front was enormous. Every day saw fresh arrivals of field artillery and heavy guns. Dumps of ammunition, observation balloon sections, new aerodromes, etc., sprang up all over the country with astounding rapidity. From St. Eloi to Armentiéres the countryside was undergoing a metamorphosis – the essential arrangements were being completed before 'zero' day'.[18]

Returning to Willie's letter, he confirms the increase in artillery activity:

We have been back in the trenches for some little time, which I always enjoy, though it may seem strange to you. Things have been more lively, especially yesterday when the Boche gave us a most unmerciful hammering in return for a fierce bombardment from our guns. I think he is sorry he did so, for he got back more than he bargained for, as we seem to have ten guns to his one.[19]

The 8th Dubs' War Diary for this period indicated that the artillery on both sides was very active, leaving wounded, death and destruction in the wake of the shelling. For the first couple of days of this tour of front line duty, the War Diary recorded *our artillery active throughout the day*. Then, from Monday 21 May onwards, the Germans returned heavy bombardments right up until the battalion was relieved on Saturday 26 May. Frank Laird recalled:

During these months of preparation the British shell fire was unceasing, and grew in volume week by week as more guns were mounted. At last they became so plentiful that all idea of hiding them was abandoned, and we saw the unusual spectacle of guns lying wheel by wheel in the open.[20]

Frank Laird got a brief respite from it all when he was sent on a Young Officers' course at Camp Locre on the day the heavy shelling began, 21 May. The ever practical British Army also required the attendance of four other officers on a cookery demonstration course at Hazebrouck three days later, including 21-year-old Northern Irishman Arthur Vivian Green, who went on to play a significant role in Fr Doyle's story. Frank Laird recorded:

The school was chiefly taken up with map making, and reading, and with a study of the elaborate model of the German position on Wytschaete, which had been constructed by an engineer near Locre. This covered a considerable piece of ground, and was an exact model of the hill and all the systems of trenches with their respective names. It was altered as new trenches were spotted by the aeroplanes, or old ones smashed up by our fire. A high wooden platform ran round it from which a bird's eye view could be obtained. This open advertisement of our intentions struck a good many officers with surprise.[21]

Oblivious to all this, Willie continues:

Brother Fritz for once did me a good turn. I had arranged to hear the men's Confessions, shortly before he opened fire and a couple of well-directed shells helped my work immensely by putting the fear of God into the hearts of a few careless boys who might not have troubled about coming near me otherwise. I wonder whether the Sacraments were ever administered under stranger circumstances. Picture my little dug-out (none too big at any time) packed with men who had dashed in for shelter from the splinters and shrapnel coming down like hail. In one corner is kneeling a poor fellow, recently joined who has not 'knelt to the priest', as the men quaintly say, for many a day, trying to make his confession. I make short work of that for a shower of clay and stones falling at the door is a gentle hint that the 'crumps' are getting uncomfortably near and I want to give him absolution in case an unwelcome visitor should walk in. Then, while outside, the ground rocks and seems to split with the crash of the shells – big chaps some of them – I give them all Holy Communion, say a short prayer and perform the wonderful feat of packing a few more men into our sardine tin of a house.

As soon as I got the chance I slipped round to see how many casualties there were, for I thought not a mouse could survive the bombardment. Thank God no one was killed, or even badly hit, and the firing having ceased, we should breathe again. I was walking up the trench from the dressing station when I heard the scream of another shell. To vary the old proverb 'He who hides and runs away will live to hide another day.' I could not hide so I ran, like sixteen hares, up one trench, down another, and round every corner I met, followed so I would have sworn, by that beastly shell, up and down the trench and round the corners. Failing to catch me, he burst in rage and later on I danced a jig on his (or her) ignoble grave and then made my way home.[22]

This is another instance of the lucky escapes for which Willie was famed, even though the battalion War Diary indicates that trench damage was actually more significant than deaths or woundings. Willie continues:

It was then I realised my good fortune. There were two ways to my dug-out and naturally I choose the shorter. This time, without any special reason, I went by the longer way and it was well I did for the shell pitched in the other trench and probably would have caught me nicely as I went by, but instead of that it wreaked its vengeance on my unfortunate orderly, who was close by in his dug-out, sending him spinning on his head, but otherwise not injuring him. He is a 'Paddy from Cork' and has got a hard head.

I found another string of men awaiting my return for Confession and Holy Communion, in fact quite a busy evening, thanks once more to Fritz's 'H.E.' or High Explosive, which has a wonderful persuasive effect of its own. I am wondering, when I give my next retreat, how many pounds of H.E. will it take to move 14 stone of 'H.N.' (what this stands for I shall leave you to guess, but it has something to do with the inmates of a convent.)[23]

Here Willie draws this letter to a close:

> *I hear Michael, my orderly, hard at work frying onions for my dinner, what a time we are going to have, so I must put up my shutters and say au revoir. Now that he has had a good blowing up I am hoping for great things and that he won't wash my socks again in the water with which he makes the tea. After all as the farmer says 'Pigs is pigs and war is war' and fresh water is scarce, so hurrah for the laundry tea!*
>
> *God bless you all. Please stick me into the back of a Hail Mary. P.S. I know Fr J. Brennan S.J. Rathfarnham Castle would be glad to read some of my old letters if you could send him a bundle some time.*[24]

Shortly after completing this letter, Willie dropped a few humorous lines on a postcard to his sister, dated 25 May 1917. Lena had obviously recently written to him and enquired whether there was anything he wanted which she could send:

> *Many thanks for your most welcome letter and thoughtful offer. You might send some 2lbs of (I forget the name) and half a stone of (I don't know how to spell the word) but nothing else. No news of any consequence. The same old Bill – still blooming and busting. Love to everyone. Will.*[25]

Willie's May narratives continue on Tuesday 29th, three days after leaving the front line, when he wrote home in sweltering conditions:

> *I was half afraid I should not be able to get a letter off to you this week, as I have had a good deal of running about to do, exhausting work in this intensely hot weather, under a blazing sun, which has almost made us long for the frost and snow of the past winter. Then at night we have been busy with raids and things of that sort, so that one has to try and snatch an hour's sleep whenever one can. However I keep well through it all, thank God; a bit tired, perhaps, from time to time, but we are moving back from support to reserve which will give a chance of at least 40 winks with a few over.*[26]

The 8th Bn Royal Dublin Fusiliers War Diary refers to a raid ('things of that sort'!)

carried out by the enemy on Saturday 19 May, which was repaid in kind on 25 May. The raid on 19th was recorded thus:

> *At 2am a small enemy party entered our trenches and attacked two sentries killing one and wounding the other. On a LG [Lewis Gun] opening fire on them the hostile party hurriedly withdrew leaving behind a steel helmet, large wire cutters and some bombs.*[27]

The 8th Dubs' raid on the 25th was somewhat different, but equally unproductive:

> *At 10.30pm a minor offensive operation was carried out against the enemy lines. The object being to obtain prisoners and identifications under cover of our artillery barrage. Our party consisting of 2 officers (2/Lt's J. Doherty and G.D. Philippe) and 20 OR moved across to the enemy front lines which were found practically obliterated. Party was unable to proceed beyond the front line owing to the barrage put up by the enemy in response to his S.O.S. signal which was sent up within two minutes of our artillery opening fire. Party returned to our lines safely suffering one slight casualty.*[28]

Willie's tongue-in-cheek 'take' on raids in general, as recorded in his latest letter, was:

> *As you might like to know how the 'game of raiding your neighbour' is played, a sort of novelty for your next garden party, I shall give you a few particulars. You dig two trenches about 100 yards apart and fill one with the enemy, who are well provided with hand bombs, machine guns etc. Some night when you think they won't expect your coming, a party of your men climb over the top of their parapet and start to crawl a là Red Indian towards the foe. It is exciting work for star shells are going up every few minutes and lighting up No Man's Land, during which time your men lie on their faces motionless, probably cursing the inventor of the said star-shells, or Very Lights, and praying for Egyptian darkness. It is part of the game that if the enemy see you, they promptly paste you with bombs (which hurt) or give you a shower bath of leaden bullets. For this reason, when the game is played at garden parties it is recommended to*

place husbands in one trench and wives in the other and to oppose P.P.'s or Rev. Mothers by their curates and communities; in this way accuracy of aim is wonderfully improved and the casualties delightfully high, which is a desideratum in these days, when the supper hour arrives.[29]

Reverting to a serious tone he continues:

Having reached a certain distance the raiders wait for the artillery barrage to open. That is a sight never to be forgotten. At a fixed moment every gun opens fire simultaneously with a crash that shakes the Heavens and for five minutes the enemy's trench, from end to end, is a line of fire lit up by the hundreds of bursting shells. Then the barrage lifts like a curtain to the second trench, to keep back reinforcements, while the attackers dash through the cut barbed wire, over into the trench, sometimes to meet a stout opposition in spite of the awful shelling, sometimes only finding the bleeding remains of what was once a brave man. Dug-outs are bombed if their occupants won't come out, papers and maps secured, prisoners captured if possible, to be questioned later for information, which seems to be freely and foolishly given, and then the raiders, carrying their own dead and wounded get back as quickly as they can to their own lines, for by this time the enemy artillery have opened fire and things are warm and lively.[30]

Willie then describes a particular raid:

A few nights ago I had been along the Front Line as usual to give the men a General Absolution, which they are almost as anxious to receive for the comfort it will be for their friends at home, should they fall, as for themselves. I was coming down to the advanced dressing station when I learned that a small party had 'gone over the top' on our right, though I had been told the raid was only from the left. When I got to the spot I found they had all gone and were lying well out in No Man's Land. It was a case of Mahomet and the mountain once more. The poor 'mountain' could not come back, though they were just longing to, but the Prophet could not go out, could he not? So Mahomet rolled over the top of the sandbags into a friendly shell hole and started to crawl on his hands and knees and tummy towards the Boche trenches. Mahomet only being a prophet was allowed to use bad language of which privilege he availed himself, so report goes, to the full, for the ground was covered with bits of broken barbed wire, shell splinters, nettles etc. etc. and the poor Prophet on his penitential pilgrimage left behind him much honest sweat and not a few drops of blood.

That was a strange scene! A group of men lying on their faces, waiting for certain death to come to them, whispering a fervent act of contrition and God's priest, feeling mighty uncomfortable wishing he were safely in bed a thousand miles away, raising his head in Absolution over the prostrate figures. One boy, some little distance off, thinking the absolution had not reached him, knelt bolt upright and made an act of contrition you could have heard in Berlin, nearly giving the whole show away and drawing the enemy's fire.

There was really little danger, as shell holes were plentiful, but not a little consolation when I buried the dead the next day, to think that none of them had died without absolution. I was more afraid getting back into our own trenches, for sentries seeing a man coming from the direction of Hun-Land do not bother much about asking questions and object to nocturnal visitors.[31]

The sequence of the events described in Willie's narrative, and their timings, seem at this point to have become somewhat confused. He refers to burying the dead, but if this was, in fact, the story of the raid on 25 May, then the 8th Dubs War Diary for that day refers only to one slight casualty. It may be the case that the small party that *had 'gone over the top' on our right* were the 8th Dubs, but that it was actually another unit on the left who suffered more casualties, including the dead buried by Willie the next day. Just to add to the confusion, his letter continues with the statement: *The following night, 24 May, my own Dubs made another attack* but this date does not tie in with the War Diary date of 25 May. Nevertheless, the letter continues:

Nothing of great interest happened except this. I told them it was a lucky night for such dangerous work as it was the feast of 'Our Lady of Christians' and Mary would surely help and protect them. Our Blessed

Lady's mantle must be well mended by this, for not only did the raiding party return without a scratch, but there was not a <u>single</u> casualty, either in the front or rear trenches, in spite of the heaviest shelling I have seen for a long time. I fancy Mary and all the Blessed in Heaven will be very glad when the war is over, as they must be working overtime to safeguard us from danger.[32]

The letter next makes reference to a German prisoner, but none were recorded as having been taken during the raid on 25 May. Perhaps Willie, who was writing four days later, had become muddled from several hectic days of raiding in the front line, and it may be that he has jumbled events together, because there was, indeed, another raid, which took place on 27 May, and which did result in the capture of German prisoners. This raid was undertaken by twelve officers, three hundred men and ten sappers from 2nd Bn Royal Dublin Fusiliers, who Fr Doyle would, of course, have considered his own Dubs just as much as the 8th Dubs. Willie says:

One German prisoner, badly wounded in the leg, was brought in. He knew only a few words of English, but spoke French fluently. I try to do all I can for the unfortunate prisoners, as sometimes not much sympathy is shown them and they have evidently been drilled into believing that we promptly roast and eat them alive. I gave him a drink, made him as comfortable as possible, and then seeing a rosary in his pocket, asked him was he a Catholic. 'I am a Catholic priest' I said 'and you need not have any fear.' 'Ah monsieur' he replied 'vous êtes un vrai prêtre' (you are a true priest.) I suppose he was thinking of the gentlemen in the Gospel who left the bleeding man lying on the road and went on his way, which shows that even the maligned Hun can be grateful too. He gave me his home address in Germany and asked me to write to his parents. 'Poor father and mother will be uneasy' he said as his eyes filled with tears. 'O mon Dieu, how I am suffering, but I offer it all up to You.' I hope to get a letter through by means of the Swiss Red Cross, which will be a comfort to his anxious parents who seem good, pious souls.

I am going to take time by the forelock and get in an hour's sleep now while I have the chance. Much love to everyone and may God bless you all. P.S. Please thank Lena and Jennie for their letters.[33]

The 2nd Dubs did sustain casualties, so this must have been the raid that Willie was referring to earlier. In contrast to Willie's narrative, the official version of the raid on 27 May was somewhat shorter, and resolutely concise. The Diary entry for 48th Infantry Brigade recorded that, at 10pm:

> *A Strong Raiding Part of the 2nd Royal Dublin Fusiliers entered the enemy's trenches in N.24.b penetrating as far as NANCY SUPPORT and effecting the capture of 1 Officer (a Company Commander) and 30 other ranks. In addition to these 1 Officer and about 50 other ranks are suspected to have been killed. Our casualties consisted of (a) Officers – 4 wounded (very slightly) and 2 missing (b) Other Ranks:- 2 killed, 31 wounded (mainly extremely slightly) and 8 missing. Many of those reported as missing have since been found. The information procured from the prisoners has proved extremely valuable.[34]*

This raid was engraved in the memories of two Officers with 2nd Royal Dublin Fusiliers, Lieutenant Arthur Glanville and Captain Noel Drury who both made a brief reference to it in memoirs written later. Their recollection of numbers of prisoners taken is at slight variance with each other and the War Diary. Arthur Glanville recorded briefly:

> *May 27. We did a Battalion Raid on Petis Bois – most successful – took 27 prisoners.[35]*

Whilst Noel Drury recalled:

> *May 27. Big raid carried out by 12 Officers and 300 Other Ranks captured 1 German Officer and 29 Huns and many maps, photos and paper.[36]*

The 2nd Bn Royal Dublin Fusilier's War Diary said:

> *1st and 2nd Objectives were reached with practically no opposition, and prisoners were taken there. At 10.8.p.m. 2nd and 3rd Objective and bombing combats ensued. Enemy's trenches were found to be very badly knocked about. Dug-outs poor and barely splinter-proof, 30 prisoners including one*

> *Officer were taken and much valuable information gained from Maps, Aero Photos and papers brought back. At least 50 of the enemy were killed. At 11.24.p.m. raiders returned.*[37]

The 27 May was also significant, being the date that Major G.W. Kenny was appointed Second–in-Command of 8th Bn Royal Dublin Fusiliers, having transferred from 7th Bn Royal Innsikilling Fusiliers back in February. He took over from Major A.C. Thompson who had been promoted to Officer Commanding. His brother, Captain F.S. Thompson had also been promoted, but transferred to 9th Bn Royal Dublin Fusiliers, as ruefully described by Frank Laird:

> *On 28 May I had a working party up the line, and visited 'Major' Thompson, of the 9th, in his dugout. Our good skipper had received the promotion he so well deserved shortly before, and, to our great regret, was transferred, as second in command under Colonel Hunt, to the 9th Dublins.*[38]

The next week-and-a-bit was described by Captain Arthur Glanville, 2nd Royal Dublin Fusiliers, thus:

> *We had a dreadful tour in trenches after this lost 50 per cent of the Battalion in killed and wounded – constant shelling.*[39]

Willie Doyle's next letter to Hugh was written on Saturday 3 June 1917, four days before the opening of the defining battle of 1917 for the British forces; defining in that innovatory tactics were used, and that it was a hugely successful battle for the British. Officially, the operation is known as the Battle of Messines, named after the main village in the area, but the Irish objective was the smaller hamlet of Wytschaete. Willie starts his letter:

> *We came back to 'reserve' on Sunday morning, the 3rd, after a rather strenuous time of sixteen days at the Front, more than usually trying for want of sleep. As Mass for the men was not till mid-day I had planned a glorious 'soak' in the convent, an unblushing, gluttonous feast of blankets for the poor old tired 'oss.*
>
> *Once again le Bon Dieu was good to me, this time in the best of all*

ways by quietly upsetting all my little plans. By some misunderstanding my orderly did not meet me as arranged and I had to walk home, with my heavy pack (of sins) on my back instead of riding. I reached my billet at 2am only to find that someone had locked the door of my room and there was no way of getting in. I had not the heart to waken up the poor nuns and after all when one is fast asleep is not a hard plank just as soft as a feather bed? You see I am becoming a bit of a philosopher![40]

Fr Doyle's sentiments are undoubtedly sincere. Following the initial disappointment, he genuinely viewed the cancellation of his planned ablutions and recuperation as providential. Here was yet another opportunity to offer a small sacrifice and make reparation for his sins. His letter continues:

The next morning I had Mass in a field close to the camp. I wish you could have seen the men as they knelt in a hollow square round the improvised altar, brilliant sunshine overhead and the soft of green of Spring about them. They looked so happy, poor lads, as I went down one line and up the other giving them the 'Bread of the Strong' and I could not help thinking of another scene long ago when our Lord made the multitude sit down upon the grass and fed them miraculously with the seven loaves. Before I got to the end of my 700 communions I felt wondrous pity for the twelve Apostles, for they must have been jolly tired also.[41]

Their position was Clare Camp, a couple of miles west of Locre. The seven hundred communions was a heavy work-load, but what is even more interesting is that it indicates how under-strength his two battalions were, even taking into account the absence of non-Catholics. If three or more battalions were present then the ratio was even worse.

In addition, the large number of consecrated Hosts distributed by Fr Doyle during his celebration of this Mass highlights an issue that it may be easy to overlook, namely the requirement for the supply of altar breads and other necessaries to the chaplains working in front line areas. In the myriad complexities of keeping an army supplied with all its wants, including food for the troops, ammunition, fuel, medical supplies and animal fodder, provision had still to be made for the supply of what would have amounted to vast quantities of the small breads, to be delivered right up to the front line areas in which the chaplains were working. Supplies may have been obtainable locally from convents or perhaps parish priests, and each chaplain would doubtless have taken responsibility for ensuring the safe storage of his 'provisions' at suitable locations close to where he was likely to be holding services; but for priests like Willie Doyle, who would have wished to celebrate Mass daily, and perhaps several times each day in order to bring the Eucharist to scattered groups of their men, the problem of ensuring the continued and timely supply of this essential element of their work must have been a formidable consideration.

Willie continues with his letter:

> *At present I am living in the camp, which is further back even than the convent, out in the green fields of the country, most peaceful and restful. I have a little tent to myself, but have rosary, Mass, confessions etc. out in the open. The men have absolutely no human respect, and kneel in rows waiting for their turn 'to scrape', as if they were in the church at home, paying no heed to the endless stream of traffic. I am sure non-Catholics must wonder what on earth we are at.*[42]

Willie did not mean the men were disrespectful, but was referring to the fact that they had no privacy and no sense of individuality. They were no doubt grateful in their prayers that, thus far, they had evaded a much worse fate, as he continues:

> *As the war goes on I am getting a taste of new horrors. I am pretty well accustomed now to burying <u>in a handkerchief</u> all that is left of some unfortunate man, or to pick up, as I did yesterday a helmet containing the brains of another, as complete as if someone had cracked an egg and poured the contents into a cup, but not a trace of his body could be found.*[43]

Willie's fascination for aeroplanes continued, as did describing their movements to his father. He continues:

> *The work of a shell is rapid and merciful, but to watch a man falling from the sky and see him dashed to pieces at your feet tries the nerves of the strongest. A few evenings ago I saw five of our aeroplanes come*

down in an hour. The first victim was a light scouting machine which was attacked from behind by a Boche who was hiding in a bank of clouds. From the first he had not a chance against the heavier and faster enemy. I watched him diving and twisting to escape the machine gun bullets, then suddenly the plane crumpled and fell like a stone to the ground and crashed into the trench not far from where I stood. I gave the poor boy – he was only eighteen – absolution as he rushed to his death, for you may imagine there was not much left of either of them, man or machine, after the awful impact.

The others fell further away, one at least coming down safely. Next morning a squadron of six of our big battle-planes passed over our heads. One of them dropped behind a little and, as he did, like a hawk on its prey a German airman, so high up that we did not see him, dived straight down on top of him. There was a rattle of machine guns, our aeroplane burst into flames while the enemy made off in safety as fast as he could. We watched the blazing ship come slowly down, still under perfect control, but then, some 5,000 feet from the ground, two figures burning also jumped from the plane and disappeared behind the German lines. The papers may say what they like, but there is no denying the cleverness and cunning of the enemy which compels the admiration of even those who hate them.[44]

Whatever, and however painful the subject Willie writes about, it's not long before he returns to a teasing tone with his father, as he continues:

Are you a Hun? Well in any case you are a bold, bad old man!!! In spite of all I said I have just received another long letter from you. Seeing I was hungering for news of your own dear self I suppose I must only forgive you this once and hope (in secret) you <u>will</u> do it again.

Thank you ever so much for sending the letters to Father Brennan, he has always been a good, kind friend to me and I know is anxious to hear of my doings. I am grateful, too, for your friend's criticism and words of praise. As I said to Mai recently I often wonder what you can find interesting in these hastily scrawled letters, so that you have given me so much encouragement to continue in the hope that they will give you all pleasure.

I have no further news to give you, nor do we know anything about our future movements. We may remain here a considerable time, or possibly receive orders to march elsewhere, in which case I shall send a postcard as often as I can, even if it is only an official, printed one, to let you know I am well 'as this leaves me at present'.[45]

The last few lines of the above sentence illustrate how lucky Willie Doyle was, both to be sufficiently educated, and to have the opportunity, to send such long letters home. The 'Other Ranks' letters, of course, were censored and more often than not they sent postcards instead, scribbling standard one-liners such as 'hope you are well as this leaves me at present.' In addition to his regular correspondence and diaries Willie also found time to make his opinions felt in publications, as he notes in a postscript:

There is a letter of mine in the 'Irish Catholic' about 'Masses for our Dead Soldiers.' It is on the inside leader page and may interest you. I think the date is 26 May.[46]

The text of that letter, under the pseudonym Nemo, is:

One is often struck, on glancing over the papers, at the numerous appeals made to provide 'comforts for our troops,' but no one ever seems to think that the souls of those who have fallen in battle may possibly be in need of much greater comfort than the bodies of their comrades who survive.

With all the spiritual help now at their disposal, even in the very firing line, we may be fairly confident that few, if any, of our Catholic men are unprepared to meet Almighty God. That does not mean they are fit for Heaven. God's justice must be fully satisfied, and the debt of forgiven sin fully atoned for in Purgatory. Hence I venture to appeal to the great charity of your readers to provide 'comforts for our dead soldiers' by having Masses offered for their souls. Remembrance of our dead and gratitude are virtues dear to every Irish heart. Our brave lads have suffered and fought and died for us. They have nobly given their lives for God and country. It is now our turn to make some slight sacrifice, so that they may soon enter into the joy of eternal rest.[47]

Shortly after, Willie reveals to a friend another glimpse into his inner life, in a letter dated Tuesday 5 June:

> *'... we have had a terrible time for the last three weeks, constant and increasing shelling, with many wonderful escapes. We are on the eve of a tremendous battle and the danger will be very great. Sometimes I think God wishes the actual sacrifice of my life – the offering of it was made a long time ago. But if so, that almost useless life will be given most joyfully. I feel wonderful peace and confidence in leaving myself absolutely in God's Hands. Only I know it would not be right, I would like never to take shelter from bursting shells; and up to a few days ago, till ordered by the Colonel, I never wore a steel helmet. I want to give myself absolutely to Him to do with me just as He pleases, to strike or kill me, looking up into His loving Face, for surely He knows best. On the other hand I have the conviction growing stronger every day that nothing serious will befall me; a wound would be joy 'to shed one's blood for Jesus', when I would gladly empty my veins for Him. Otherwise why would He impress so strongly on my mind that this 'novitiate' out here is only the preparation for my real life's work? ... I am very calm and trustful in face of the awful storm so soon to burst. But could it be otherwise, when He is ever with me and when I know that should I fall, it would only be into His arms of love?*[48]

Two days later Willie witnessed much bloodshed but his veins remained full. That day was to be a landmark for the British Army, the 16th (Irish) Division and also Fr William Doyle.

Footnote 1: St John Baptist Labré was born in Amettes in 1748, dying thirty-five years later in Rome, after spending much of his adult life applying unsuccessfully for admittance to different religious communities, which involved hundreds of miles of walking. He ended up a homeless tramp on the streets of Rome for the last decade of his life. Despite all this, or maybe because of his persistence, the working of God's grace was recognised in him; after Labré's death 136 miraculous cures were attributed to his intercession.

CHAPTER 26
THE BATTLE FOR THE RIDGE:
BITE AND HOLD!

Oh! for the peace of a perfect trust
A heart with thee at rest.

Willie next wrote to Hugh on 11 June 1917, eight days after the previous letter he had sent to *Melrose*, during which time momentous events had intervened. The battle for which 16th (Irish) Division, and all their counterparts in Second Army, had been so meticulously prepared for by the Staff, under the guidance of General Sir Herbert Plumer, had opened on 7 June 1917. Second Army's success was spectacular and they quickly achieved their objective; to defeat the German garrison occupying the Messines – Wytschaete Ridge. An advance of two miles was achieved in one day.

General Herbert Charles Onslow Plumer belied his sixty years, his appearance was that of a much older man, with his shock of white hair and large moustache, and his watery blue eyes evocative of a comfortable old grandfather in his dotage. Nothing could have been further from the truth. Plumer had taken on the brief of planning for the assault against the southern ridge of the Ypres Salient with robust vigour, developing and applying new methods, for which the men under his command were thoroughly organised. Created 1ˢᵗ Viscount Plumer of Messines at the end of the War, he was universally and affectionately known by his men as 'Daddy' Plumer.

It was characteristic of the thoroughness of Plumer's preparations that the Staff of Second Army had even built a replica model of the German defences that were to be attacked. However, some reacted with a degree of scepticism, as Frank Laird described:

The model was open to anyone, and Captain Thompson was highly disgusted when he went to inspect it and was elbowed by a fat Belgian civilian. Some held the opinion that the whole thing was a blind for the spies, and that we were not going to attack there at all, but the event proved them wrong.[1]

Lt Col Rowland Feilding, 6th Connaught Rangers, described it to his wife after the battle, which is generally referred to as the Battle of Messines:

We even had a large-scale model, covering about an acre, which represented, to scale, Wytschaete, the woods, and the villages beyond. This latter – which I believe was made by the engineers – was a triumph of skill. It looked like a huge toy village, and would have delighted the children.[2]

Every man knew what was expected of him and his colleagues, which was achieved through detailed orders, briefings and rehearsing attacks in various formations, as well as working with the large-scale models.

Mock attacks were organised on the scale model, with flag-waving soldiers representing the 'creeping barrage'. It was normal, before a major assault, to put down a heavy bombardment of the enemy positions, and the technique of providing a creeping barrage, to give additional protection to the attacking troops, had been developed. The fire from artillery guns, or machine guns, directed initially against the enemy's front-line position, was timed to lift and move, or 'creep' forward just before arrival of the assaulting infantry. The barrage moved forward in pre-determined stages, providing a protective curtain of fire behind which the attacking infantry would advance. The infantry in turn used the same leap-frogging technique, as described by the historian of the Royal Inniskilling Fusiliers:

The manoeuvre of attack was by 'leap-frogging.' Within the Battalion, one or more Companies had a certain immediate objective, and having achieved that end, waited at the position until the rest of the Battalion moved forward through them to win the next step. When a Battalion had finished its immediate task it waited there to consolidate until another Battalion moved up and passed through to carry the good work a further step. Finally, a Division, having reached the limit of advance set for it, rested there to consolidate and a fresh Division moved through its ranks to extend the attack further.[3]

The model, at Scherpenberg, a few miles north of Locre, was too big to be disguised and in any case there was no need to do so. It did not matter that the Germans were aware that an attack was planned, as Plumer had a surprise weapon that he did manage to keep largely under wraps. This was the twenty-five enormous mines constructed beneath the German front line. Although, in the event, only nineteen mines, for one reason or another, were actually exploded, the Germans remained blissfully unaware of what was in store for them.

The mine explosions may have been the highlight of Plumer's plan, but he also realised that, in order for the infantry to be able to capitalise on the mayhem caused by the explosions, the close co-operation of all other arms of service was vital. Therefore, engineers, artillery, machine-guns, tanks and aircraft were utilised as never before.

The opening entry of the War Diary for 16th (Irish) Division, 7 June, states:

At 3.10a.m., Zero hour, the division, in co-operation with the 36th Division on the right and the 19th Division on the left, attacked and captured the WYTSCHAETE-MESSINES RIDGE and the enemy trenches east of it as far as the Mauve Line. In a subsequent phase the 33rd Infantry Brigade, attached to this Division, attacked and captured the OOSTTAVERNE LINE.
At Zero hour the MAEDELSTEDE, PETIT BOIS AND PECKHAM mines were exploded, causing considerable damage to the enemy's trenches and inflicting many casualties on him. At the same time an intense Artillery and Machine Gun barrage (from 44 machine guns) was opened. Under cover of this combined barrage our assaulting waves left their trenches and advanced against the enemy.[4]

Plumer's bite and hold tactics were successful across the whole front line; exemplified by the attack of the 16th (Irish) Division (their infantry advancing under cover of a meticulously timed creeping barrage from their machine-gunners) to reach and hold the Mauve Line, whilst the 33rd Infantry Brigade followed on through to a farther objective. Each brigade had four clear objective lines, which were colour coded on their maps as Red, Blue, Green and Black. However, there was also a further, 'final' objective, the Mauve Line, to which, if possible, they should push out strong outposts to assist the fresh brigade coming from behind. The sector of the Mauve Line which formed 8th Dubs' objective ran from Sonen Farm to Leg Copse, east of Wytschaete village.

So, Willie's letter to Hugh on Monday 11 June was just a quick update to let his father know he was OK following the battle for the Ridge, reports of which would have been all over the newspapers. He explains:

> *To save unnecessary anxiety I told you in my last note that we were again on the march, which was quite true, but the march was not backwards but towards the enemy.*
>
> *When I wrote we were on the eve of one of the biggest battles of the war, details of which you will have read on the morning papers. I was with our gallant Irish boys in the capture of the famous Wytschaete (Witch Cat, as they call it) ridge, all through the hard fighting of the past few days and am now back in safety in the rear, without a scratch, thank God!*
>
> *We are all in tremendous fettle over the grand victory but, to be candid, dead beat. When I have had a wash (which will take some time as the dirt is thick) half a dozen square meals at the same sitting and a little sleep of 56 hours, I shall send you a long letter. This is only a line to let you know I am well and safe.*
>
> *We are camping in a wood, green and fresh after the ploughed battle field. I am trying to scribble this sitting on a pile of sandbags with the Colonel beside me (a good friend and extremely kind.) I hope he won't fall asleep before I do and roll over on his back as he is a tidy weight to pick up.*[5]

The Colonel to whom Willie refers was Lt Col A.C. Thompson, commanding 8th Bn Royal Dublin Fusiliers. Willie's brief post-battle update ends:

> *We do not know as yet where we are going. Possibly we may have a good tramp before us, but it will be towards rest and quiet, away from danger and the never ceasing roar of the guns. I did not lose my head in the past battle, but I left my hat behind me and many pounds of superfluous flesh, the heat was terrific.*
>
> *Our blessed Lord has been good to me has he not? But it is all due to your united prayers. One eye is asleep already, I must stop. Ever your loving Willie. P.S. thank Chas and Lena for their welcome letters.*[6]

The following day, Tuesday 12 June 1917, Willie settled down to write a long account of his observation and involvement in the build up to and during the actual Battle of Messines. As on previous occasions he commences by covering old ground, but goes into more details. He begins his account:

> *Now that I am myself washed, as our French friends say, have demolished the fatted calf and slept the sleep of the weary just, I shall try and jot down my personal experience of the trying time we have gone through, as I know this will be of more interest to you than anything else I could write.*
>
> *Let me say first of all that I am really well, though naturally still very tired, or rather dazed from the noise and strain of the past month. I have suffered a good deal too, from blood blisters on my feet, the result of having to wear one's boots so constantly, which made climbing up and down the shell-holes, mile after mile of it, quite a delightful torture. Otherwise I am fit and well, deeply thankful I need not say to the good God for having brought me safely through this record big battle, without hurt or harm while the reaper death was so busy on all sides.*
>
> *Though our big attack and the consolidating the positions won occupied us only three days, we had a most exciting three weeks previously, a time of so much danger that I did not mention it in my previous letters.*[7]

He continues this letter, retracing the period Friday 18 May to Saturday 26 May. It should be noted that although Willie enthusiastically says the Germans knew every detail, in fact there were two crucial details they did not know. The first was the date of the planned attack; the second was the extent and size of the mining operation, and the number and spread of the mines that would be detonated under them:

> *For months past preparation on a gigantic scale were being made for the coming attack, every detail of which the Germans knew. For some reason or another he left us in comparative peace for a long time and then suddenly started to shell us day and night. We had just gone into the line for our eight days and a lively week it was. How we escaped uninjured from the rain of shells which fell round about us I do not know. The men had practically no shelter, as their dug-outs would scarcely keep out a respectable fat bullet, not to speak of a nine or twelve inch shell*

(this the diameter of the shell base, not its length) and used to run to us for protection, like so many big children, with a confidence I was far from feeling, that 'the priest' was a far better protection than yards of reinforced concrete. I have come back to my little home more than once in the early hours of the morning to find it packed with two legged smoking 'sardines' quite happy and content in spite of Fritz's crumps, to be greeted with the remark: 'we were just saying, Father, that this is a lucky dug-out and it is well for us that we have your Reverence with us.' God bless them for their simple faith and trust in Him, for I feel I owe it to my brave boys that we were not blown sky-high twenty times. In fact the 'Padre's Dug-Out' was quite a standing joke among the officers, who used to come after a 'strafe' to see how much of it was left. Never once did Gabriel fail me, though he did annoy me by whistling: 'We'll have a hot time of it tonight.'

Our next eight days in support were even worse, as the Boche had brought up more guns and used them freely. Our Headquarters was a good sized house which had never been touched since the war began, being well screened by a wood behind.[8]

Willie is referring here to the Rossignol Estaminet and once again he starts to retrace his footsteps, adding more flesh to the bone! It's not clear whether the officer he mentions next was one of the 8th Dubs or from another unit:

We were in the middle of dinner the first evening when in quick succession half a dozen shells burst close round. It was only later on we learned the reason of this unexpected attack. One of the officers, in spite of strict orders to the contrary, had gone on a raid with a map in his pocket on which he marked various positions, our H.Q. amongst others. He was captured and 'the fat was in the fire.' Owing to someone's carelessness no provision had been made for protection against a bombardment and we had to stand in the open with our backs against a brick wall watching the shells pitch left and right and in front, wondering when would our turn come.

Three or four times each night, at a couple of hours interval, the torture began afresh, just as one was nodding off to sleep, sending men and officers flying for safety to the 'shady side' of the house. Shelling in the open or in a trench is not pleasant, but this was horrible, for we knew the guns were searching for the spot so obligingly marked on our map.[9]

Frank Laird's recollections after his course at Brigade School, Locre, were:

On 27 May I rejoined our battalion. We were now billeted on 'York Road,' which ran just behind the communication trenches from the line. Our mess was in the Doctor's House, the remnants of a comfortable country doctor's residence when the occupant had departed to make room for a more deadly class of practitioner. The men lived in some buildings hard by.

Our house had a decent cellar which was most welcome at times... In the evenings, however, when the munitions and supplies were coming up, we were generally strafed for a while, and when it got particularly lively there was a general meeting in the cellar ... One night in the cellar I noticed a stranger beside me who looked somewhat rattled. I asked where he came from, and he said he had been beside the driver of a motor lorry which was coming up, loaded with gas cylinders. Our road was the main route to the line. As the lorry came opposite the Doctor's House the front was struck with a shell and the driver killed, and my friend had legged it into my cellar ...

I left that unhealthy neighbourhood without regret. At the end of our period the Boche put two 'five nines' into the house where the Colonel and Adjutant were stopping, and killed one of the Colonel's runners. He and the Adjutant escaped almost by a miracle and came down to our shanty for the rest of the night.[10]

The Colonel's Headquarters was in Rossignol Estaminet and Fr Doyle had just left it when the latter incident, related by Frank Laird, occurred. Willie's letter continues:

One morning about 2am I had gone down the road to look after some men when two shells smashed in the roof of the house I had left, killing five of our staff and nearly knocking out the Colonel and two other officers. We got shelter in another Mess, only to find that this was a marked spot too, though the aim was not so accurate.[11]

In fact the War Diary indicates that four were killed instantly on that occasion, but it may be that someone else died later of wounds. The 8th Royal Dublin Fusiliers' War Diary records the incident in some detail:

2 June, Rossignol Estaminet. At 1.15a.m. hostile shelling commenced in and around Headquarters area. The first shell short, another going overhead and setting alight to camouflage screening heavy artillery which were in position in front of Battalion H.Q. The third shell obtained a direct hit on Bn Headquarters blowing in the side of the wall and demolishing the upper rooms. A second direct hit was also obtained exploding in the mess kitchen wrecking the mess room.[12]

The arbitrary nature of the effects of such shelling is succintly illustrated by the Diary. Ironically:

1894 CSM Doyle who was entering the cellar for safety was killed. 11716 Pte Downes was also killed and two OR, one from RE and one from RIRifles, who were seeking cover, were also killed by the same shell. For twenty minutes the area around Headquarters was heavily bombarded and several casualties inflicted...[13 FN1]

The War Diary confirms Frank Laird's account that the senior officers joined him and the other occupants of the Doctor's House, and the entry for that day ends with a completely unrelated, but interesting, aside:

HQ evacuated the Estaminet and were accommodated for the night at Doctor's House with D & C Coys ... 23787 Pte G. Rifland being found underage is transferred to England and struck off the strength.[14]

Willie's narrative of 12 June moves on:

All during this time our guns were keeping up the bombardment of the Wytschaete Village and Ridge, which the 16th Irish Division was to storm. I think I am accurate in saying that not for ten minutes at any time during these sixteen days did the roar of our guns cease. At times one or two batteries would keep the ball rolling and then, with a majestic crash, every gun, from the rasping field piece to the giant 15 inch Howitzer would answer to the call of battle, till not only the walls of the ruined house shook and swayed, but the very ground quivered.

You may fancy the amount of rest and sleep we got during that period, seeing that we lived in front of the cannon, many of them only a few yards away, while the Boche, with clock-like regularity, pelted us with shells from behind!

If you want to know what a real headache is like, or to experience the pleasure of feeling every nerve in your body jumping about like so many mad cats, take the shilling and spend a week or two near the next position we hope to capture.

All things, even Jennie's famous three ton plum pudding, come to an end and at last we finished our sixteen days 'Limbo' (Purgatory is not near enough to Hell!) and marched back to the rest camp with tongues, to vary the metaphor, hanging out for sleep. That night a villainous enemy airman dropped bombs close to our tents and the following day the guns shelled us, far back as we were. We must be a bad lot for 'there is no rest for the wicked' they say. For once my heart stood still with fear, not so much for myself as for the poor men. There we were on the side of a hill, four regiments crowded together, our only protection the canvas walls of the tents, with big shells creeping nearer and nearer.[15]

Willie's memory was spot on. His battalion had been relieved on the night of 2/3 June by 1st Bn Royal Munster Fusiliers; shortly afterwards 2/Lt C.D. Marlow, along with two Other Ranks, proceeded to a course of instruction in Lewis Guns at IX Corps School. Second Lieutenant Marlow is the second significant subaltern who went on to play a large role in the fate of Fr Doyle.

At Clare Camp, that Sunday commenced with Mass, for Willie at least, but it was not to be a day of rest. All supplies had to be checked and replenished and a general clean up, prior to preparations being made for the coming attack. The hustle and bustle was interrupted at 11.15am when two shells fell directly on the camp, causing it to be evacuated but luckily there were no casualties or significant damage. Willie's 12 June letter continues with his colourful memories:

Orders had been given to scatter, but it takes time to disperse some 4,000 men and one well-aimed shell would play havoc in such a crowd. Forgive me for mentioning this little incident. I want to do so in gratitude and to bring out the wonderful love and tenderness of our Divine Lord for His own Irish soldiers, not to claim the smallest credit for myself.

I had brought the Ciborium to my tent after Mass as the men were coming to Confession and Holy Communion all day. Human Beings could not help us then, but He who 'stilled the tempest' could do so easily. There was only time for one earnest 'Lord save my poor boys' for at any moment the camp might be a shambles, full of dead and dying, before I rushed out into the open. As I did a shell landed a few feet behind an officer sending him spinning, but he jumped up unhurt. A moment more down came a second right into the middle of a group of men and, miracle of miracles, failed to explode. A third burst so close to another party I was sure half were killed, though I must confess I never saw dead men run so fast before, and so it went on, first on one side, then on another, but at the end of the half hour's bombardment not a single man of the four regiments had been hit, even slightly.

I remember long ago dear old Fr Nicholas Walsh used to say 'don't forget that after all Almighty God is a <u>gentleman</u> who won't take a mean advantage of you.' I think He proved Himself to be something more that day – a kind and loving Father to His children – like your own dear self, though I fear you won't admit the comparison.

The chances of a good night's rest were at an end, for we had to turn out and sleep as best we could, under the hedges and trees of the surrounding country. It was a big loss to the men, as once the attack, which was due in three days, began there was little chance of closing an eye.[16]

Frank Laird also recorded these events in a bit more detail:

On 2 June we left the Doctor's House and gladly betook ourselves a few miles further back. We left, of course, by night and reached our destination, tents pitched in a field some way outside Bailleul, by daylight, when we retired to bed and slept till 10 a.m. This location was a distinct improvement. The weather was delightfully fine and warm, ideal for being under canvas. The camp was clean and green and fresh, and there was little to do in the daytime.

However, there was one fly in the ointment. Some Boche gunner, who

> was reported to have his weapon on a barge on a canal, used to open fire on our camp at intervals, dropping a shell every few minutes for a while, and imparting an air of uneasiness to the place. By day we had to retire out of the camp to the next field farther on, where we moved a hundred yards or so each time he lengthened his trajectory, and so kept out of his way. By night we had to leave our tents a few times, and take to sleeping along the hedgerows of adjoining fields.[17]

The War Diary confirms that the weather was fine, so that was at least one consolation for the men sleeping in fields adjoining the camp. The balmy weather also aided Fr Doyle and Fr Browne as they went about their ministry. Willie's 12 June letter continues:

> We priests say a prayer at the end of our Office asking the Lord to grant 'noctem quietem' 'a peaceful night.' I never fully appreciated this prayer till now and have said it more than once lately with heart-felt earnestness.[18]

The enemy shelling of the camp was, of course, just one side of the coin, because the men of the British Divisional Artillery Columns had been hard at work feeding their guns, aimed in the other direction, since late April. Immediately prior to the Battle of Messines, they had laid their lives on the line every bit as much as the infantry during the actual attack:

> Heavy work fell on the 16th DAC. For more than a fortnight the personnel were constantly at work by day and night. They were often under heavy shell-fire and suffered many casualties, but the manner in which they carried out their duties was beyond all praise.[19]

Willie continues:

> Those few days were busy ones for us, Fr Browne and myself. The men knew they were preparing for death and availed themselves fully of the opportunities we were able to give them. Fortunately the weather was gloriously fine, so there was no difficulty about Mass in the open. There was a general cleaning up and polishing of souls, some of them not quite

too shiny, a general Communion on two days for all the men and officers, with the usual rosary and prayers each evening, consoling for us because we felt the men had done their best and the future might be safely left in the hands of the great and merciful Judge.

I fancy the feelings of most of us were the same: awe, not a little fear and a big longing to have it all over. We knew the seriousness of the task before us, for Wytschaete Hill, the key of the whole position, was regarded even by the General Staff as almost impregnable and the German boast was that it would never be taken.[20]

Frank Laird was not a Catholic, so there is no record from him about consulting either Fr Doyle or Fr Browne. His memories were more worldly:

Bailleul was visited in force by officers a night or so before the big event, as a last flutter. We had a gay time in the restaurant where I supped, and the fun, as usual on these occasions, was led by Irish officers.[21]

On Wednesday 6 June 1917 Major General W.B. Hickie, Commanding 16th (Irish) Division, issued an Order of the Day:

'The Big Day is very near. All our preparations are complete, and the Divisional Commander wishes to express his appreciation and his thanks to all the officers and men who have worked so cheerfully and so well. The 16th Division is fortunate in having had assigned to it the capture of the stronghold of Wytschaete. Every officer and man – Gunners, Sappers, Pioneers, RAMC, ASC and infantry of historic Irish regiments – knows what he has to do.

Let all do their best, as they have always done, continuing to show the same courage and devotion to duty which has characterised the 16th (Irish) Division since it landed in France, and it will be our proud privilege to restore to Little Belgium, the 'White village,' which has been in German hands for nearly three years.[22]

With this rallying cry the 16th (Irish) Division moved into battle assembly positions in the early hours of the next day. Plumer's Second Army attack had been deployed on a broad front from Mount Sorrel to St Yves by the three corps; X Corps, IX

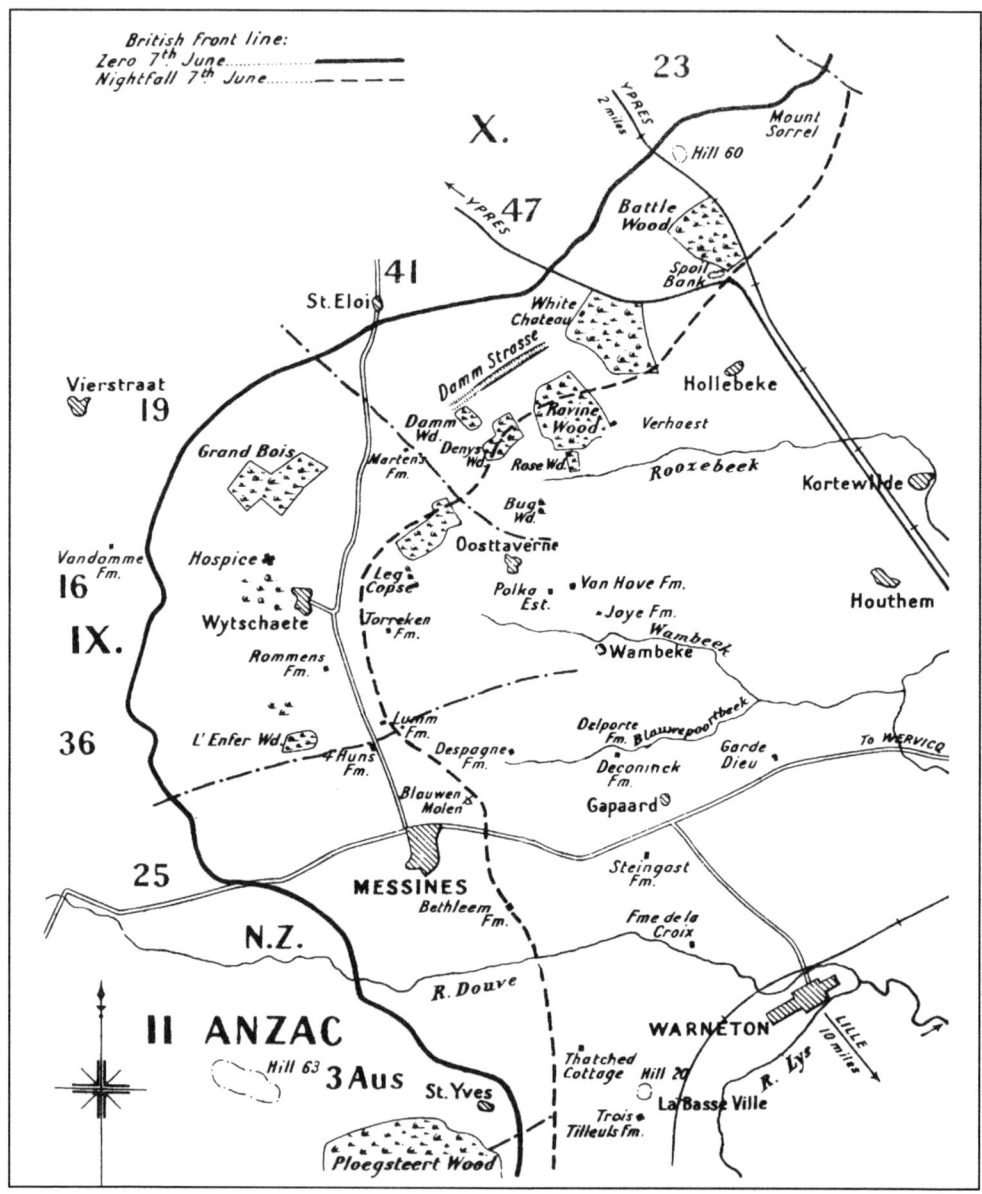

A map of the Battle of Messines

Corps and II ANZAC Corps. 16th (Irish) Division formed the centre division of their IX Corps, in the Vierstraat – Petit Bois sector, with 19th Division on their left and 36th (Ulster) Division on their right. Their IX Corps held the centre of Second Army's position, with X Corps to the left (to the north, in the Mount Sorrel - St Eloi sector) and II ANZAC Corps to the right (further to the south, around Messines – St Yves.) This was the first occasion the two divisions from Ireland, broadly representing opposite ends of the political and religious spectrum, had lined up together – the first time they would fight side by side.

The formation within each corps in their own sector of the line was that: from each of their divisions, two out of the three brigades attacked, whilst the third stayed in reserve in case of enemy counter-attack, and then helped to consolidate the positions captured. The four battalions of each attacking brigade were deployed using two in the first wave of attack, and a third in the second wave; whilst the fourth battalion acted as moppers-up and provided carrying-parties. A few personnel from each battalion also remained in reserve, as explained by Second Lieutenant Frank Laird:

When orders came in for the push a ballot was taken to see what officers would be left out to remain behind and act as reserve in case those who went over the top suffered heavily. To Sheridan, Johnston and myself the lot fell to 'only stand and wait'.[23]

In addition to his rifle, each man in the attacking waves had to carry 170 rounds of ammunition, two Mills bombs, and a pair of wire cutters; one man in every two carried a shovel with which to dig in and consolidate objectives. Two machine-guns and two Stokes mortars protected the flanks, whilst not forgetting the role of the artillery in pounding the German lines, as Willie again acknowledges in his letter of 12 June:

Without detracting one bit from the dash and bravery of our Irish lads, which won unstinted praise from everyone: 'The best show I have seen since I came to France,' said Sir D Haig, full credit must be given to the artillery for pounding the defences to dust, without which our troops would still be on this side of the 300 foot hill instead of a couple of miles the other side. Everyone felt the losses would be severe, if not colossal, and as we sat on our hill and gazed down into the valley beyond, crammed with roaring guns and watched the shells bursting in hundreds, knowing the

moment was near for us to march down into that hell of fire and smoke, it was small wonder if many a stout heart quaked and thoughts flew to the dear ones at home, whom one hardly hoped to see again.[24]

There are numerous German accounts of the trauma of the British bombardment, as provided by Jack Sheldon. For example, one of the German observers of Field Artillery Regiment 32 of 40th Infantry Division remembered the rude awakening towards the end of May which spoiled what had previously been a fairly agreeable job of manning an observation post. The OP was in a monastery and initially the British had directed their heavy calibre shells elsewhere on Messines Ridge, leaving the monastery alone. Then:

Suddenly, one day a shell landed right in front of us. It was only light calibre, so it had very little effect on our concrete pillbox.... Gradually the light calibre rounds gave way to 280mm shells, which crashed down with massive detonations, sending up huge pillars of earth and dust. Initially they landed beyond us, but gradually they crept closer.... Our concrete pillbox heaved and swayed with each close impact by the shells. Thick powder smoke filled the room whenever a shell exploded really close, windows shattered, tiles and chunks of concrete rained down; the interior of our post often looked very rough indeed.... Not until the very last day before the attack did they manage to crush half of it with a direct hit.[25]

Willie's letter continues:

There were many little touching incidents during these days, one especially I shall not easily forget. When the men had left the field after the evening devotions I noticed a group of three young boys, brothers I think, still kneeling saying another rosary. They knew it was probably their last meeting on earth and they seemed to cling to one another for mutual comfort and strength and instinctively turned to the Blessed Mother to help them in their hour of need. There they knelt as if they were alone and unobserved, their hands clasped and faces turned towards Heaven, with such a look of beseeching earnestness that the 'Mother of Mercy' must have heard their prayer 'Holy Mary pray for us now at the hour of our death. Amen.'

> *On Wednesday night, 6 June, we moved off so as to be in position for the attack at 3.10a.m. on Thursday morning, the feast of Corpus Christi. I got to the little temporary chapel at the rear of our trenches soon after twelve and tried to get a few moments sleep before beginning Mass at one, a hopeless task you may imagine as the guns had gone raging mad.*[26]

The companies of 8th Royal Dublin Fusiliers, commanded by Lt Col A.C. Thompson, had moved off at 8.30 p.m., on a fine clear evening, to take up assembly positions. The War Diary notes that the men were in great spirits, also confirmed by 2/Lt Frank Laird, who recorded:

> *On the night of 6 June everything was in readiness. Officers had donned, in most cases, Tommies' uniforms to make them less conspicuous. All the paraphernalia had been overhauled and examined, and at dusk the Battalion moved out to march to the assembly point. I felt rather mean when I said 'good-bye' to my friends and my platoon, and saw the crowd depart in the height of good spirits. Father Doyle went with them. I saw the Colonel take him aside for a private talk before they left, perhaps giving him some last commissions in case he was knocked out.*[27]

Battalion Headquarters was at SP13 (Strong Point 13 being a trench map reference) located in the ruins of Vandamme Farm, situated on the reverse slope of the ridge running along the valley between Wytschaete and Kemmel Hill. This was where Fr Doyle and Fr Browne set up their temporary chapel. It was 11.50 p.m. when the two Padres reached the little chapel constructed of sandbags, where they had an hour's rest on two stretchers borrowed from the huge pile nearby. Leaving their servant asleep, they got up at 1 a.m. to prepare the altar for Mass and put on vestments. Fr Doyle said Mass first and was served by Fr Browne, who, not having yet made his Last Vows, renewed his Vows at the Mass, as he always did at home on Corpus Christi. Then they changed back into uniform, had breakfast at 2.30 a.m. and made for their respective Aid Posts.[28]

Willie's 12 June letter continues:

> *I could not help thinking would this be my last Mass, though I never*

really had any doubt the good God would continue to protect me in the future as He had done in the past and I was quite content to leave myself in His hands, since he knows what is best for us all.

Mother Francis sent me these lines when I came up first, they have been such a help to me I think you will like them as much as I do.

A Perfect Trust

Oh! for the peace of a perfect trust
My Loving God, in Thee
Unwavering faith that never doubts
Thou choosest best for me.
Best though my plans be all upset
Best though the way be rough
Best though my earthly store be scant
In Thee I have enough.
Best though my health and strength be gone
Though weary days be mine
Shut out from much that others have
Not my will, Lord, but Thine!
Oh! for the peace of a perfect trust
That looks away from all
That sees Thy hand in everything
In great events or small.
That hears Thy voice, a Father's voice
Directing for the best
Oh! for the peace of a perfect trust
A heart with thee at rest.

As I walked up to my post at the advanced dressing station I prayed for the 'peace of a perfect trust' which seems to be so pleasing to our Lord. He must have heard my prayer for the prophet Daniel never skipped about among his lions with greater confidence and feeling of security than your own Will did that day among the shells, though to tell the truth I would almost sooner face a lion (a stuffed one especially) than half a dozen German 'crumps'.[29]

Meanwhile, Frank Laird had set out to get a view of the opening engagement of the battle:

With Sheridan and Johnston I started in the small hours for Mont Rouge, a hill which commanded a good view of the surrounding country, and got there before 3 a.m. Just then a calm before the storm appeared to have settled on the hostile lines, which were marked by the arcs of the ascending Verey lights. The shelling gradually died away, and there was almost a dead silence when, at 3.9 a.m., an old friend who used to harry us in camp pooped off a single shot. He got 'some' retaliation.[30]

Twenty minutes previously, Fr Doyle was waiting:

It wanted half an hour to 'zero time' (the phrase used for the moment of the attack.) The guns had ceased firing to give their crews a breathing space before the storm of battle broke; for a moment at least there was peace on earth and calm, which was almost more trying than the previous roar, to us who knew what was coming.

A prisoner told us that the enemy knew we were about to attack, but did not expect it for another couple of days. I pictured to myself our men, row upon row, waiting in the darkness for the word to charge and on the other side the Germans in their trenches and dug-outs, little thinking that seven huge mines were laid under their feet needing only a spark to blow them into eternity. The tension of waiting was terrific and the strain almost unbearable. One felt inclined to scream out and send them warning, but all I could do was to stand on top of the trench and give them Absolution, trusting to God's good mercy to speed it so far.[31]

The German strong points in this sector of the line had been mined with charges, two each of 30,000 lbs. under Petit Bois, and a single charge of 34,000lbs under Maedelstaede Farm. To the north, just beyond the boundary with the Irishmen's Corps colleagues of 19th Division, was the Nags Nose at Hollandscheschuur Farm, which was mined with three charges of 14,900 lbs., 18,500 lbs. and 34,200 lbs. To the south, in the 36th Division's area was the Spanbroekmolen mine, packed with 91,000 lbs. of explosive. (The other mines elsewhere were located at Hill 60, St

Eloi, Peckham, Kruisstraat, Ontario Farm, Trench 127 and Trench 122).[32]

These mines were the result of the work of the Royal Engineers' Tunnelling Companies, who had been carrying out deep mining operations since mid-December 1915, and to whom infantry battalions such as the 8th Dubs had supplied details of men as temporary help. Operations continued throughout 1916 and early 1917, with the final two mines, at Maedelstede Farm and Ontario Farm only completed in early June, just days before the attack. A total of twenty-five mines had been constructed, but only nineteen were detonated for varying reasons. The Germans had detected just one, the mine at La Petit Douve, but they clearly did not know this was only one of so many. [FN2]

The mine shafts and tunnels had been sunk, incredibly, in conditions of great secrecy, to depths in places of a hundred feet, through to blue clay underneath saturated sub-soil; the machinery and supplies needed were transported via purpose-built railways, and strenuous efforts were made to conceal the heaps of spoil brought up from the blue clay areas, thus avoiding their detection by enemy aeroplanes. Thousands of men had worked, eaten and slept in chilly, artificially lit underground tunnels for weeks, straining nerves to breaking point. As well as those that carried out the tunnelling, others had the equally nerve-wracking task of listening for possible German activity.

In the event, at 3.10 a.m. on Thursday 7 June 1917, the nineteen operational mines, packed with a total of nearly a million pounds of highly explosive ammonal, were detonated directly underneath the German positions on the Messines Ridge. The fact that the Germans were not expecting any kind of attack early that morning, let alone huge mine explosions, is illustrated by the instance of troops of the 40th (Saxon) Division being in the process of handing over their line to 3rd (Bavarian) Division at Zero Hour. As the mines exploded the effect, for many miles around, was like that of an earthquake. In Lille, fifteen miles away, terrified people rushed panic-stricken into the streets, and the shock and noise of the explosions were felt in London and in various parts of south-eastern England. Frank Laird reported his experience viewing from Mont Rouge:

> *Just a minute later the surprise packet we had prepared for the Boche was revealed – the first mine went off in a cloud of dust lit by a fiery glow, and was followed by its eighteen brethren all along the front. We heard no noise of their explosion where we were five miles off, but the hill on which we*

stood shook under our feet like a mass of jelly. The debris thrown upwards by the mines still hung in the air when our tremendous barrage opened. Terrifying as the mines appeared, the barrage looked worse. The whole line was enveloped in clouds of smoke and dust and flashing flame, and the roar of the artillery and rattle of machine-guns combined in one continuous deadly thunder.[33]

The explosions were not all simultaneous – the last coming nineteen seconds after the first – which caused even worse panic amongst the German garrison, and the shattering effect on German morale far exceeded even Plumer's expectations. The effect on the attacking troops was, in places, equally spectacular. In an attempt to maintain security over the planned attack, the Allied troops, although to some extent aware of the mining activities, if not exactly the scale of the operation, had not been forewarned about the plan to detonate the mines at the same Zero Hour as the infantry advance, and in places troops were caught by the dust and toxic fumes thrown up by the explosions. Some men were physically violently sick, units became mixed up with each other in the confusion, and some troops started the attack by moving in the wrong direction! For the most part, though, Plumer's plan worked perfectly, and the attack met with astonishing success.

Willie continues, in the narrative of his letter of 12 June:

Even now I can scarcely think of the scene which followed without trembling with horror. Punctually to the second at 3.10 a.m. there was a deep muffled roar; the ground in front of where I stood rose up as if some giant had wakened from his sleep and was bursting his way through the earth's crust, and then I saw seven huge columns of smoke and flames shoot hundreds of feet in the air, while masses of clay and stone, tons in weight, were hurled about like pebbles. I never before realised what an earthquake was like, for not only did the ground quiver and shake, but actually rocked backwards and forwards so that I kept on my feet with difficulty.

Later on I examined one of the mine craters, an appalling sight, for I knew many a brave man torn and burnt by the explosion, lay buried there. If you expand the old Dalkey quarry near the railway very considerably and dig it twice as deep you will have some idea of the huge size of one of our mine craters, twenty of which were blown along the front of our attack.[34]

Although most witnesses testify to the power of the mines, the 2nd Dubs' Lieutenant Arthur Glanville was more over-awed by the force of the artillery barrage:

June 6/7 Marched up to line. Great attack starts at dawn by the exploding of the famous mines (which it is claimed were heard in England) but which to us were like a chestnut bursting in a fire in comparison to the war of the artillery which were laying down the biggest barrage in the war. Saw our tanks for the first time in action. We followed up the attack for a distance of 1000 yards when we saw our forward troops had completely broken through. Same night we went up and & took over the line 4 or 5 miles in front.[35]

Lt Col Rowland Feilding's 6th Bn Connaught Rangers did not go into battle as a composite unit; his troops had been distributed amongst other units. Feilding was at Battalion HQ, and described the scene from his position:

Yesterday morning (the great day) I got up and went out at three o'clock. The exact moment of the assault (known to us as 'Zero'; by the French as 'l'heure 'H'') which had been withheld by the Higher Command, as is usual, till as late as possible, had been disclosed to us as 3.10a.m.

I climbed on to the bank of the communication trench, known as Rossignol Avenue, and waited. Dawn had not yet broken. The night was very still. Our artillery was lobbing over an occasional shell; the enemy – oblivious of the doom descending upon him – was leisurely putting back gas shells, which burst in and around my wood with little dull pops, adding to the smell but doing no injury.

The minute hand of my watch crept on to the fatal moment. Then followed a 'tableau' so sudden and dramatic that I cannot hope to describe it. Out of the silence and darkness, along the front, twenty mines – some of them having waited two years and more for this occasion – containing hundreds of tons of explosive, almost simultaneously, and with a roar to wake the dead, burst into the sky in great sheets of flame, developing into mountainous clouds of dust and earth and stones and trees.

For some seconds the earth trembled and swayed. Then the guns and howitzers in their thousands spoke: the machine gun barrage opened; and the infantry on a 10 mile front left the trenches and advanced behind the barrage against the enemy.[36]

The timing of Zero Hour was another example of Plumer's scrupulous planning. At that time of year dawn would just be breaking over the German lines, so that they would be highlighted against the horizon, whilst the British forces remained shaded and had visibility of about a hundred yards in front of them as they assaulted. The thought that must have gone into the planning of the attack shows the extent to which lessons had been learnt after the disaster on the opening day of the Somme offensive in July 1916. Then Zero Hour was set for 7.30 a.m., because it was believed that the infantry advance had to be timed to take place in full daylight, to give the attacking troops chance to see their objectives.

Continuing with Willie Doyle's account:

> *Before the debris of the mines had begun to fall to earth the 'Wild Irish' were over the top of the trenches and on the enemy, though it seemed certain they must be killed to a man by the falling avalanche of clay. Even a stolid old English Colonel standing near was moved to enthusiasm 'My God' he said 'what soldiers! They fear neither man nor devil!' Why should they? They had made their peace with God. He had given them His own Sacred Body to eat that morning and they were going out now to face death as only Irish Catholic lads can do, confident of victory and cheered by the thought that the reward of Heaven was theirs.*
>
> *Nothing could stop such a rush and it was the old game of the Irish footballers at Rugby and so fast was the advance that the leading files actually ran into the barrage of our guns and had to retire.*[37]

This happened to 1st Bn Royal Munster Fusiliers. They were in the second wave of 47th Infantry Brigade's attack. Their Brigade colleagues, 6th Royal Irish and 7th Leinsters, had reached their objective, the Blue Line, when the Munsters, coming from behind, went through, supported by a tank, and continued to their Black Line objective. In doing so, one company overtook the barrage. (Although the Munsters had a tank in support, in the event many of the tanks that were lined up for action were actually hampered by the success of the mines.)

Willie's letter of 12 June continues:

> *Meanwhile, hell itself seemed to have been let loose. With the roar of the mines came the deafening crash of our guns, hundreds of them. This much I can say; never before, even in this war, have as many batteries, especially of heavy pieces, been concentrated on one objective and how the Germans were able to put up the resistance they did was a marvel for everyone, for our shells fell like hail stones.*[38]

The war correspondent Sir Philip Gibbs recorded:

> *I saw the ... mines go up and earth and flame gush out of them as though the fires of hell had risen. A terrible sight, as the work of men against their fellow creatures ... It was a signal for 750 of our heavy guns and 2,000 of our field guns to open fire; and behind a moving wall of bursting shells, English, Irish and New Zealand soldiers moved forward in dense waves.*[39]

The men of the infantry, many laying down to ride the shock of the explosions, some wearing gas masks, then had to struggle forward in the lingering glare of the blasts, in blinding, choking dust, gaseous fumes, falling debris and ear-splitting din, to navigate round gigantic craters. In such circumstances it is hardly surprising that some were disorientated, including those that lost the creeping barrage. In addition, as Willie pointed out, it was amazing that the Germans who survived the blasts were able to mount any kind of opposition. The men of 47th Brigade had to get past enemy machine-gunners in concrete gun posts in the Bois de Wytschaete, as did those of 49th Brigade, who also encountered the same problem coming from Leg Copse, Unnamed Wood and L'Hospice.

The charge for one of the mines in the Irish zone, at Spanbroekmolen, activated seconds after the others, but unfortunately sufficient seconds had passed to cause the deaths of some of the men of 36th (Ulster) Division, who had started their attack exactly on time. A survivor, Lt T. Witherow, of 8th Bn Royal Irish Rifles, remembered:

We'd made it through the machine-gun fire and almost got to the German positions, when a terrible thing happened that nearly put an end to my fighting days. All of a sudden the earth seemed to open and belch forth a great mass of flame. There was a deafening noise and the whole thing went up in the air, a huge mass of earth and stone. We were all thrown violently to the ground and debris began to rain down on us. Luckily only soft earth fell on me, but the Lance-Corporal, one of my best Section Commanders, was killed by a brick. It struck him square on the head as he lay at my side. A few more seconds and we would have gone up with the mine.[40]

Willie's account continues:

In a few moments Fritz took up the challenge and soon things on our side became warm and lively. In a short time the wounded began to come in and a number of German prisoners, many of them wounded also. You may think I am a pro-German, but I must confess my heart goes out to those unfortunate soldiers whose sufferings have been terrific. I can't share the general sentiment that 'they deserve what they get and one better' for, after all, are they not children of the same loving Saviour who said 'Whatever you do to one of these My least ones you do it to me.' I try to show them any little kindness I can, getting them a drink, taking off the boots from smashed and bleeding feet, or helping to dress their wounds and more than once I have seen the eyes of those rough men fill with tears as I bent over them, or felt my hand squeezed in gratitude.

My men did not go over in the first wave, they were held in reserve to move up as soon as the first objective was taken, hold the position and resist any counter attack. Most of them were waiting behind a thick sand-bag wall, not far from the advanced dressing station where I was, which enabled me to keep an eye on them.[41]

The thick sand-bag wall was the Chinese Trench and was where the Munsters had earlier assembled. As Willie explained, the 8th Bn Royal Dublin Fusiliers and their 48th Infantry Brigade colleagues were in reserve, waiting to cope with whatever eventualities came their way.

The dispositions of the 8th Dubs were: 'A' Company along Chinese Trench;

'B' Company at Haringbeek; 'C' Company on the West Side of Fort Halifax; and 'D' Company and H.Q. near Wiltshire House, with one section of a Trench Mortar Battery attached. Four hours after 'Zero' one section of 48th Machine Gun Company reported for duty with the battalion and was attached to 'D' Company. Despite all that had been thrown at them, the Germans still managed to return a barrage. As Frank Laird watched from afar, one shell scored a direct hit on Chinese Trench, causing mayhem. The chaplain was on the scene as Willie's narrative, written on 12 June, explains:

> *The shells were coming over thick and fast now and at last what I expected and feared happened. A big 'crump' hit the wall fair and square, blew three men into the field fifty yards away and buried five others who were in a small dug-out. For a moment I hesitated, for the horrible sight fairly knocked the 'starch' out of me and a couple more 'crumps' did not help to restore my courage. I climbed over the trench and ran across the open, as abject a coward as ever walked on two legs, till I reached the three dying men and then the 'Perfect Trust' came back to me and I felt no fear. A few seconds sufficed to absolve and anoint my poor boys and I jumped to my feet, only to go down on my face faster than I got up, as an 'express train' from Berlin roared by.*
>
> *The five buried men were calling for help but the others standing around seemed paralysed with fear, all save one sergeant whose language was worthy of the occasion and rose to a noble height of sublimity. He was working like a Trojan tearing the sand-bags aside and welcomed my help with a mingled blessing and curse. The others joined in with pick and shovel, digging and pulling till the sweat streamed from our faces and the blood from our hands, but we got the three buried men out alive, the other two had been killed in the explosion.*[42]

The sergeant was Company Sergeant Major Tait, described by Frank Laird as:

> *... small, stout, active, and a natural born soldier. A cooper in Guinness's before the war, he had come out with the 16th Division, and he had made such good use of his time that he had become the most expert of men-at-arms.... Always fertile in expedients, and full of energy and the capacity for*

getting things done, he was simply invaluable to our Captain in keeping the Company in first-class trim ... He was as good a soldier in action as out of it, and richly deserved the D.C.M. and M.M. which came his way.[43]

Fr Doyle's account continued:

Once again I had evidence of the immense confidence our men have in the priest. It was quite evident they were rapidly becoming demoralised, as the best of troops will who have to remain inactive under heavy shell fire. Little groups were running from place to place for greater shelter and the officers seemed to have lost control. I walked along the line of men crouching behind the sand-bag wall and was amused to see the ripple of smiles light up the terrified lads' faces (so many were mere boys) as I went by. By the time I got back again the men were laughing and chatting as if all danger was miles away for, quite unintentionally, I had given them courage by walking along without my gas mask or steel helmet, both of which I had forgotten in my hurry.[44]

Reading this last paragraph on its own out of context, one might be inclined to the view that the writer had rather a high opinion of himself, and was prone to exaggeration. However, there are many personal testimonies to back up Fr Doyle's accounts. One such was from Captain C. F. Healy who, himself, had won the Military Cross. He visited the Doyle family and told Charlie the following anecdote, which illustrates both Willie's disdain for his own safety and his infectious good humour:

On one occasion I had to arrest him because he had neither his steel helmet nor his respirator. A few days afterwards he came to where I was. He had one gas respirator round his neck, another round his waist and a third on his back; he had a knapsack on his right shoulder and one on his left shoulder; he had a steel helmet on his head and one in each hand. 'Now Captain,' he said, 'do you think I am complying with regulations?'[45]

Frank Laird's knowledge of the 'Chinese Wall' incident was second hand, but nevertheless he confirms the details and then asserts:

> *After this, as some of the troops were getting unsteady under the heavy fire in their exposed position, the good Padre restored their confidence by walking along the line without his tin hat or gas mask, which, as frequently happened him* [sic], *he had forgotten.*[46]

Finally, at 11.30 a.m. orders to advance were received from 48th Brigade H.Q. At 11.55 a.m. under the scorching mid-day sun and heat of battle, the 8th Dubs moved forward. Captain G. E. Cowley advanced on the left with his 'B' Company; 'C' Company were on the right under 2/Lt B.W. Hughes, whilst 'A' Company were at centre under 2/Lt F. M. Kiernan (minus two platoons who had been allotted to the Trench Mortar and Machine Gun sections, for carrying ammunition.) In reserve were 'D' Company commanded by Captain C. F. Healy. Good progress was made despite heavy shelling from 4.2's and 5.9's and casualties were slight. At 2 p.m. 'A' Company reached its objective on the Mauve Line and established a post in front. Several prisoners were captured in dug-outs, four 77mm field guns and two machine-guns taken. Ten minutes later 'B' and 'C' Companies also reached the objective and started consolidating. At 6 p.m. the 33rd Infantry Brigade followed up and passed through on to their position. Willie's account continues:

> *When the regiment moved forward the Doctor and I went with them. By this time the impregnable (!!) ridge was in our hands and the enemy retreating down the far side. I spent the rest of that memorable day wondering over the battlefield looking for the wounded and had the happiness of helping many a poor chap, for shells were flying about on all sides.*[47]

Lt Col Feilding succinctly summarised the events across the 16th (Irish) Division's front thus:

> *The battle once launched, all was oblivion. No news came through for several hours: there was just the roar of the artillery; – such a roar and such a barrage has never been before. Our men advanced almost without a check. The enemy – such of them as were not killed – were paralysed and surrendered. In Wytshaete Village they rushed forward with their hands up, waving handkerchiefs and things. And no one can blame them. The ordeal through which they have been passing the last fortnight must have surpassed the torments of hell itself.*[48]

British Front Line, Wytschaete, June 1917

Despite the chaos, Fr Doyle, as ever, was mindful of his religion no matter the circumstances, and had not forgotten it was the Feast of Corpus Christi, which celebrates the Body and Blood of Christ really present in the Eucharist. (It is customary in many places for a procession to take place at the end of Mass on this feast day, which is followed by a Benediction of the Blessed Sacrament). Willie's 12 June letter continues:

> *I knew there was no chance of Mass in the morning, but I had taken the precaution of bringing several Consecrated Particles with me so that I should not be deprived of Holy Communion. It was the feast of Corpus Christi and I thought of the many processions of the Blessed Sacrament being held at that moment all over the world.*

> *Surely there never was a stranger one than mine that day as I carried the 'God of Consolation' in my unworthy arms over the blood-stained battlefield. There was no music to welcome His coming, save the scream of a passing shell; the flowers that strewed His path were the broken bleeding bodies of those for whom He had once died and the only 'Altar of Repose' He could find was the heart of one who was working for Him alone, striving in a feeble way to make Him some return for all His Love and Goodness.*
>
> *I shall make no attempt to describe the battlefield. Thank God our casualties were extraordinarily light, but there was not a yard of ground on which a shell had not pitched, which made getting about very laborious, sliding down one crater and climbing up the next, and also increased the difficulty of finding the wounded. Providence certainly directed my steps on two occasions at least.*[49]

Although the Battle of Messines was a great success, there were still British casualties. The 16th (Irish) Division War Diary recorded at 11 p.m. on 7 June that 50 Officers were casualties, along with 971 Other Ranks.[50] Willie, as ever, was bent on helping and giving absolution to all within his power:

> *I came across one young soldier horribly mutilated, all his intestines hanging out, but quite conscious and able to speak to me. He lived long enough to receive the Last Sacraments and died in peace. Later on in the evening I was going in a certain direction when something made me turn back, when I saw in the distance a man being carried on a stretcher. He belonged to the artillery and had no chance of seeing a priest for a long time, but he must have been a good lad for Mary did not forget him 'at the hour of his death'.*
>
> *The thing I remember best of that day of 24 hours' work are: the sweltering heat, a devouring thirst (which comes from the excitement of battle), physical weakness from want of food and a weariness and footsoreness which I trust will pay a little at least of St Peter's heavy score against me.*
>
> *Friday was a repetition of the previous day. I made a glorious breakfast in a shell-hole, off a piece of chocolate, a couple of biscuits picked up on*

the ground (I wiped the clay off first as the Belgians may want it again) and washed the lot down with a draught of water from my bottle. I am certain you did not enjoy your bacon and eggs one half as much as I did my 'hard tack' and chocolate. Later on I came in for a cup of tea – without milk, which really spoils good tea – so I did not do too badly.[51]

The 8th Bn Royal Dublin Fusiliers spent Friday 9 June 1917 holding their position on the Mauve Line at Sonen Farm. They came under enemy fire, but it did not cause too much of a problem, although Fr Doyle had one of his usual lucky escapes. Willie's 12 June letter continues:

Fighting was over for the moment, as we were hard at work bringing up the guns to support the infantry in their advanced positions. Nothing of very great interest happened during the next two days and I had only one fairly narrow escape from an eight inch shell, which got so terrified at the sight of a Jesuit in khaki that it exploded. I threw my 'tin hat', as the Tommies call the helmet, on the ground and tried to crawl under it, evidently without complete success judging by the clods of earth which came whacking on my back till I was pretty well black and blue. Brother Fritz certainly hammered some breath out of me but failed miserably to damp my good spirits or diminish my trust in the Sacred Heart.[52]

Late on Saturday 9 June, the 8th Dubs were relieved at 11 p.m. by the 5th Dorsets of 33rd Brigade, moving back to a new position adjoining VC and York Roads, west of Wytschaete. The officers who had been balloted out of the action caught up with their colleagues and Frank Laird recalled:

Having held the line on the 7th and 8th, the battalion came back to York Road on the 9 June, where we rejoined them and found them in great fettle. In spite of the tremendous shelling they had been through, the casualties were very slight. We only lost one officer, Hastings, who was badly hit in the left shoulder.

The men slept in an open field behind the 'Doctor's House' on the night of the 9th. It was a much healthier locality now than during our last stay there, the Boche having been pushed some miles farther off. A few stray shells did drop round, but no one was hurt. One youth had a narrow escape as a shell fell right beside him. By some miracle he escaped unhurt and was able to get up and run like a hare.[53]

The *Irish Times* for that date reported that:

Over 6,400 prisoners, including 132 officers, have passed through the collecting stations to date as a result of yesterday's operations. More than twenty guns are reported so far as being collected.

The 8th Bn Royal Dublin Fusiliers War Diary for Sunday 11 June 1917 reported:

Day spent in packing and clearing up. Casualties during offensive operations were eight killed and 2nd Lt. J.L. Hastings and 44 OR wounded, 3 OR missing. Weather fine but inclined to rain.[54]

The 8th Dubs then moved to Clare Camp, reaching there about 10a.m. Frank Laird recalled that: *The men of my platoon were decked with German helmets and caps, and had improvised a band of mouth organs and tin cans which discoursed martial music by the way.*[55] On Monday 11th an official photographer arrived from G.H.Q. and took photos of the men with the souvenirs they had picked up during, and in the aftermath of, the battle. Lt Col Feilding of 6th Connaughts noted to his wife: *A large number of the men of the battalion are now the proud possessors of wrist watches – trophies of war.*[56] Captain Arthur Glanville, 2nd Dubs, remembered:

I got a Mauser pistol as a souvenir. We go out for a rest. Splendid time at Rubrouck and Bollezeele. Captain Webb goes home. Captain Jameson joins us also Wolfe and Humphrey. Went to tank administration and I had a ride in a tank.[57]

Before the 16th (Irish) Division departed to the rear area, many messages of congratulation were received following the taking of Wytschaete, such as that from IX Corps' Commander, General Hamilton Gordon:

The Army Commander wishes me to convey to all ranks his warmest congratulations and his appreciation of the splendid work done on the 7th inst. Well done 16th Division. Heartiest congratulations on capture of Wytschaete. I fully realise what a magnificent effort by each individual has been.[58]

In the meantime Willie had fired off his quick letter on Monday 11 June assuring his father of his safety, followed by the longer, detailed letter on Tuesday 12 June, which he continues as follows:

We were relieved early on Sunday morning, not a bit too soon, as both men and officers were quite worn out and the strain was beginning to tell. We spent last night (Monday) in the camp, which I have spoken of earlier, this time in peace and quiet. Tomorrow morning we march further back in company with the other Brigades and probably will move on further for a good rest.[59]

The 7th Royal Inniskilling Fusiliers were at Locre at the same time; their historian observed:

Our stay in Locre was a brief one and was occupied most of the time by supplying enormous fatigue parties up the line for work on making the roads and tracks which had been so damaged by artillery fire in the battle area. In many ways these working parties were interesting, as they gave us ample opportunity of studying the visibility from the ridge which the Germans had enjoyed for so many months. Great interest was taken by all ranks in examining the colossal craters made by our mine explosions. In many cases a couple of houses could have been nicely hidden in the cavities.[60]

Captain Arthur Glanville, 2nd Royal Dublin Fusiliers remembered:

We spent three days making a new line. Never will I forget the smells and sights. The dug outs were all blown in even those 30ft below the ground level.[61]

Lt Col Feilding of 6th Connaughts was also interested in the topography:

I picked up Brett, who was the Company Commander on duty, and we explored together the ruins of Wytschaete;- the abomination of desolation;- almost another Guillemont! You can just distinguish where the roads were. You can recognise what was the chief outstanding feature – the church – only by tracing its position from the map. It should be in the middle of the square. All is dust and rubble. We visited the famous Hospice, which caps the ridge, and used to be the most prominent landmark during the long months when we occupied the breastworks in the swamp below. The highest bit of wall remaining is 8 or 10 feet high. The only structures that have resisted our bombardments are the steel and concrete emplacements built by the enemy among the foundations of the village, several of which withstood the racket fairly well; and if the garrisons had stood their ground they could have given a lot of trouble.[62]

Willie finally finishes his letter of 12 June 1917:

I am quite ashamed of this letter it is so egotistical, all about myself, but then, dearest Father, you know I write for you and you want to know all about your boy and his doings – good and bad. If you send it on to Mai ask her to 'devour it' (to use her own phrase) so that it will not fall into other hands. I hope you will be able to read it as I have had to scribble it off in all positions, sometimes standing, and my writing is never of the best.

Much love to everybody and God bless and keep us all. P.S. Your welcome letter just to hand. I should have written to Mrs Kelly before, but one must wait for the official notification to be sent from the War Office. I shall write at once. Please thank Jennie also for her letter and tell her I am quite satisfied with the arrangement.[63]

There is no explanation for either of these last two postscript remarks, as we only have Willie's side of the correspondence, so there is no clue as to the arrangement with his sister-in-law Jennie. As for Mrs Kelly, she was probably the mother of Lance Corporal Christopher Kelly who had perished, aged 27, on 21 May and was buried at La Laiterie Cemetery. He was the son of Thomas and Mary Kelly of Deans Grange, Blackrock, a few miles from Dalkey. (Ten days after Christopher Kelly was laid to rest at La Laiterie Military Cemetery, an NCO of 'A' Company,

9th Battlion Royal Dublin Fusiliers, was killed and buried in the same cemetery. Lance Corporal D. Hayes from Dublin was just 16 years old, although obviously the authorites at the time were not aware of the fact. The boy must have displayed a maturity far beyond his years, both in appearance and ability, to have been an NCO.) [FN3]

One other mystery, which will be addressed in the next chapter, is the fact that Willie does not mention the death of Major William Redmond, 6th Royal Irish Regiment, even though this letter to his father had been written the day after he paid his respects at the grave. The Reverend Fathers Willie Doyle and Frank Browne were two of the first visitors to Willie Redmond's grave at Locre on Sunday 10th June, where he had been laid to rest two days previously in the grounds of the convent.

Here ends a selective account of the Battle of Messines, seen from the point of view of Willie Doyle and a small supporting cast. There are available many academic studies providing an in-depth analysis of the whole battle, of which some are listed in the bibliography. War Diaries for all the assaulting units are available for inspection at the National Archives, Kew.

Footnote 1: CSM D. Doyle 8th Battalion Royal Dublin Fusiliers was the husband of M. Doyle of Summerhill, Dublin. Pte J. Downes also 8th RDF was the son of Mr J. Downes of Ballinascorney, Tallaght, County Dublin.

Footnote 2: Kruisstraat No. 1 mine became flooded and was abandoned. The mine at La Petit Douve Farm was discovered by the Germans in August 1916 and, being badly damaged, was abandoned. Four further mines, on the extreme right (south) flank of Plumer's positions, had been set under the Birdcage Trench, but in the event, Plumer decided that these were too far to the right to make any significant contribution to his main attack, and the four mines were, accordingly, left undetonated. Subsequent efforts to clear these mines were frustrated by the German Spring Offensive in March 1918, and over time, they became forgotten.

Forgotten, that is, until Sunday 17 July 1955, when one of the Birdcage mines, triggered it is believed by an electrical storm, suddenly detonated, causing a massive explosion and leaving a huge crater. No loss of life was reported, although local newspapers recorded that the milk yield from local cattle was seriously diminished in the ensuing weeks! It is a tribute to the skill and expertise of Plumer's miners and engineers that, having lain under the ground, neglected for thirty-eight years, the mine was still viable, and capable of detonating to such devastating effect.

Footnote 3: Daniel Hayes, son of Patrick Hayes, 2 Cottage, back of High Street, Dublin.

CHAPTER 27
PEACEFUL DAYS IN THE PAS DE CALAIS:
AND A TALE OF TWO WILLIAMS

'With all my heart I am going to give my blessing to you, officers and men of the British Army, children of our sister-nation, Catholic Ireland ... May God, by a just compensation for sacrifices accepted in common, bring to an end the interior conflicts which rend the nations. And if there still remain legitimate aspirations of the Irish people to be satisfied, I bless your hopes and ask of God their realisation.'

Mgr. Julien, Bishop of Arras, Boulogne and St Omer, 15 July 1917

Willie Doyle's next letter home to his father, Hugh, is dated 24 June 1917. Perhaps there was an earlier one which mentioned the death of Willie Redmond, but if so it was overlooked and was not transcribed by Lena, or it has been mislaid. However, Professor Alfred O'Rahilly does not allude to the matter either, even though he was in possession of Fr Doyle's hand-written letters. Certainly the gap between the 12th of the month and 24th is quite a large one for such a prolific writer, and one would expect that a short letter might have been sent in-between-times.

If, therefore, no other letter was sent to Hugh Doyle between 12 and 24 June, it seems odd that Willie did not mention the grave at Locre in either letter, even if he had omitted the details of Redmond's death because it had been widely covered in the newspapers: local, national and international. Willie and Frank Browne's signatures were the second and third (Major General Hickie being the first) recorded in the visitors' book for Major Redmond's grave in the grounds of Locre Convent.

On the other hand, Lt Col Rowland Feilding of 6th Connaughts did write to his wife about the loss of the Major on 7 June 1917:

> *Willie Redmond is also dead. Aged fifty-four, he asked to be allowed to go over with his regiment. He should not have been there at all. His duties latterly were far from the firing line. But, as I say, he asked and was allowed to go – on the condition he came back directly the first objective was reached; and fate decreed that he should come back on a stretcher ... Willie Redmond is buried in the nuns' garden, on almost the very spot I had chosen for myself.[1]*

Willie Redmond was actually 56, the oldest man with the 16th (Irish) Division (by four years – 2/Lt Maloney of 1st Munsters, aged 52, was also in action during the Battle of Messines.) Willie Redmond, like his younger namesake Willie Doyle, was a most charismatic public figure. An army man before going into politics, he was a Member of Parliament with the Irish Parliamentary Party for three decades and brother of the party leader John Redmond. Returning to the army, Captain Willie Redmond re-joined his unit, 6th Bn Royal Irish Regiment, and served in the front line at Loos in 1916, but in June that year was invalided home seriously ill. When he returned, because of the deterioration in his health, he was pressed into duty on the Divisional Staff and promoted to Major. Consequently, he was kept out of the action at Guillemont and Ginchy in September 1916 by Major General Hickie.

Redmond realised the inevitability of becoming a permanent 'staffer' but wanted one more taste of action with his men. He was partly motivated by the fact that he and his brother had made stirring speeches, urging their fellow southern Irishmen to join with their northern brethren in serving the old enemy's cause; but he was also badly stung by anonymous criticism from Ireland following his enforced non-combatant role. Therefore, he desperately wanted to lead by example at Wytschaete/Messines.

Major Redmond managed to persuade Major General Hickie to allow him into action on condition that he retire once his men achieved their first objective, such was his and the confidence of senior officers in the plan. Even so, his Commanding Officer Lt Col Roche-Kelly made one final attempt to keep him at Battalion Headquarters. Instead, Major Redmond led his 'A' Company into battle, having previously spoken the night before to every man in the battalion, many of whom came from his parliamentary constituency in the city of Waterford. During the advance, he was struck by shell splinters and although his injuries were minor, with only slight wounds to the left leg and arm, ultimately he did not survive the shock to his system.

Major Redmond was rescued and transported by stretcher bearers of the 36th (Ulster) Division, and it was to their Aid Post he was first taken. The symbolism would not have been lost on Willie Redmond or on Willie Doyle. He was initially found by Private John Meeke of the 11th Royal Inniskilling Fusiliers, who tried to carry the Major on his shoulder, but was hampered when he was subsequently wounded himself. Eventually Willie Redmond reached the 36th Division's Casualty Clearing Station at Dranoutre, but he died that evening at 6.30 p.m., receiving the Sacraments from Fr Barrett, a Catholic Chaplain of 36th (Ulster) Division.

Exactly twenty-four hours later he was laid to rest in the garden at the convent at Locre. Major General Hickie had managed to procure a coffin and Major Redmond was first laid out in the convent chapel while Mass was said. Troops from battalions of 36th and 16th Divisions provided a Guard of Honour and officers from both divisions, together with men from his regiment, were present. Four Generals, and officers from other units, also attended the funeral.

There was universal sadness at Willie Redmond's death which transcended political and religious barriers. His wife and brother received over 400 messages of sympathy; from the Pope, from royalty and other heads of state or their representatives, from prominent political and religious figures; and from ordinary Joe Public in Ireland, the British Isles and across the world.

Lt Col Rowland Feilding was an English Tory who would have been instinctively opposed to Willie Redmond's nationalist ambitions. But he wrote to his wife:

> *How one's ideas change! And how war makes one loathe the party politics that condone and even approve when his opponents revile such a man as this! ... The extent of our advance you will have learnt from the newspapers, and I hope you and all the world will have learnt also that the South Irish Division and the Ulster Division went forward side by side; - that they opened the battle.*[2]

General Sir Alex Godley commanded the II Anzac Corps, who attacked to the right of the two Irish divisions, and had many friends in both, including Willie Redmond. Godley had hosted a dinner on New Year's Eve 1916 for Redmond and three others from both Irish divisions. He recorded:

> *On the last day of the year, we had the first of several most interesting*

and amusing dinners, when we got the four of them together. The talk and arguments between the two Unionist Orangemen of the black north, and the Southern Home Rulers, egged on by Charles Gwynn and myself, would become rather heated; but I need hardly say that they always finished by falling on each other's necks, and were in reality the best of friends.[3]

On hearing of the death of Major Redmond, General Godley commented:

We are all very sorry about Willie Redmond having been killed. He was a very charming personality, and I only hope that it may at any rate help to compose the Irish differences.[4]

The senior Chaplain of 49th Infantry Brigade, Fr Edmund Kelly wrote:

He received every possible kindness from the Ulster soldiers. In fact, an Englishman attached to the Ulster Division expressed some surprise at the extreme care which was taken of the poor Major, though no Irish soldier expected anything else, for after all, the Ulstermen are Irish too.[5]

Leaving one Irish William and turning back to the other, Fr Willie Doyle advises Hugh Doyle, on 24 June 1917:

Your two welcome letters have just reached me, for which many thanks. I am glad you found my last budget interesting for it was written so hurriedly, in bits and scraps, and all sorts of place, I was half afraid you might not be bothered wading through it.

To pick up the broad thread of my last account, we marched back to the rear after the battle by easy stages, bidding goodbye to Locre and the convent where we had spent nine months, not unpleasant ones in the beginning, though lively towards the end.

Looking back on that terrible winter we went through I often wonder what I should have done were it not for the room the good Sisters put at my disposal when I got back from the trenches and which gave me a chance of a decent rest and sleep. I don't suppose we shall ever see the convent again, but the memory of the kindness shown us all, myself especially, as

I was part of the community will not easily be forgotten.

We spent the rest of the week billeted in farm houses, the weather ideal if on the hot side and the peaceful country seeming a paradise after the din of battle. It was only when the strain was taken off that we realised how utterly tired we were, but rest had come at long last and we took it night and day.[6]

These sentiments were echoed by G. A. Cooper Walker, the historian of the 7th Royal Inniskilling Fusiliers, who noted:

The 20 June saw us once more on trek – this time quite a short march to the village of Eeke, about five miles N.W. of Caestre. In favourable weather, such as we had at that time, we thoroughly enjoyed moving about the back areas. The change from the routine life in the trenches was highly appreciated by all ranks. The day's work was generally finished by lunch time, and for the rest of the day the men were quite content to remain in billets and enjoy a good rest.[7]

On Monday 11 June 1917 Willie Doyle's 8th Royal Dublin Fusiliers had marched out of Clare Camp bound for billets in the Merris area, on the road towards Hazebrouck. The 8th Royal Dublin Fusiliers spent around six weeks in Pas de Calais area well behind the Front Lines, moving within a triangular area denoted, approximately, by a line from St Omer to Hazebrouck and up to Wormhout.

A month later, Captain Staniforth of the 7th Leinsters, about to do the journey in reverse, drew to the attention of his folks back home the logistics of transporting essentials while moving from place to place:

Your parcel arrived yesterday ... most of it had to be consigned at once to storage, where I probably won't see it again for some months: for the 35 pound limit is most rigidly enforced these days. When the division is always 'en état de patir' at an hour or so's notice ... you have to cut down superfluities with a very unsparing hand – for a heavy larger sleeping-bag, a pair of field boots, and the cowhide kit-bag itself make a very big hole in the 35lb, to start with![8]

As the crow flies it is about seven miles from Locre to Merris, but marching via roads added to the distance and time taken, especially if they were subject to strict traffic control regulations. Captain Staniforth ruefully continued:

Moreover they have a nasty way of stopping the battalion suddenly at midday on the road, weighing it, and ordering each piece over the regulation weight to be pitched then and there by the roadside.[9]

The passage of troops, vehicles, supplies and artillery along what were essentially rural roads, which were not particularly wide, had to be carefully planned and monitored. Severe problems could arise if, for example, a full battalion marching in one direction encountered other major traffic moving towards them on the same road. Complex one-way systems were often enforced and the direct consequence was that troops had very circuitous routes by which to cover what appear on maps to be only short distances.[FN1]

Two days en-route the 8th Bn Royal Dublin Fusiliers' War Diary remarked:

The IX Corps Commander watched the Battalion march past at Metterin and congratulated it on its smart appearance and turn out. He also expressed his appreciation of its work in the advance at Wytschaete.[10]

By Saturday 16 June the 8th Dubs were sufficiently organised, rested and refreshed to arrange a sports programme during the afternoon. This welcome break came to a sudden end when the battalion was ordered to back-track to Westoutre, just a mile and a half west of Locre. On Sunday morning the leading company moved off at 8.15am to march to their destination. The battalion arrived at 12.30 p.m., following, what the 8th Dubs' War Diary refers to as, 'a warm march', which saw five men fall out. This pressing return march had taken just four hours, compared to the leisurely two days during the outward journey. Willie's letter of 24 June explains how this came about:

Then just as we were settling down to enjoy a well-earned repose, urgent orders reached us to return at once to the trenches. I shall not easily forget that day's march (Sunday 17th.) The heat was terrific and the road long and hilly. The men 'stuck it' magnificently, in fact too much so, for several of them fainted from exhaustion and were fairly well done up by the time camp was reached.[11]

Worse was to come. After cleaning up and preparing for bed, orders were received at 10.45 p.m. to return to their original billets in the Merris area! At 5 a.m. the following morning the battalion paraded to march off, during the course of which seven men fell out of the line of the march. Lt Col Rowland Feilding of 6th Connaught Rangers throws some light on the problem of men falling out, describing his battalion's march back behind the lines during the same period:

Yesterday, we marched back here – to safety – in grilling heat. What with their box respirators with extensions, steel helmets, P.H. gas helmets, rifles, ammunition, packs, etc. there is little doubt but that the infantry soldier is getting over-loaded for marching. His equipment grows as the inventions for killing grow. Already, he must carry between 70 and 80lbs. And after a bout of inactivity in the trenches (I refer only to the lack of exercise), you can well understand that he is not in condition for weight carrying.[12]

Willie's letter of 24 June continues:

That night at one a.m. word was received that the order was cancelled and that we were to return to the place we had come from! Someone had blundered, or perhaps it had dawned upon the minds of those in power that the endurance even of the Irish soldiers has a limit. The next few days we spent marching back further and further to the rear and now we are settled down in quite a nice part of France, very comfortable in fine farm houses and, best of all, here we stay for some weeks at least, resting and training. It is delightfully peaceful and quiet and if the weather did give us a good drenching on the march, it is on its best behaviour now, plenty of sun with a cool breeze.[13]

The 8th Bn Royal Dublin Fusiliers eventually found themselves north-west of Hazebrouck at Rubrouck, arriving there via Merris and Eke, on Friday 22 June 1917, Rubrouck being approximately fourteen miles directly from Merris. The men were billeted in farms dotted in the countryside around Rubrouck. Fr Doyle was billeted near Zeggers-Cappel.

Three days previously, the War Diary recorded that punishments for two Other Ranks of 'B' Company had been cancelled. Private 14487 C. Dougan and 9970 Pte T. Malloy had been court-martialled in May and sentenced to Field Punishment Number 1, the latter man for 60 days effective from 16 May and the former for three months effective from 9 May. Their offences were not recorded, but the remainder of their sentences (being bound in restraints and attached to a fixed object, such as a gun wheel, for up to two hours a day) would have been interrupted by the battle anyway. Their punishments were rescinded for gallant conduct on the night of 29 May; unfortunately no details were given of their actions.

Willie continues his letter of 24 June written from billets in the Rubrouck area:

There are many little incidents in the last battle which I suppose would be of interest to you, if I could only recall them. Two horrible sights are photographed on my mind: one a convoy of waggons which had been caught by our own artillery and every horse killed. The poor beasts had evidently gone mad with fear and made frantic efforts to break the traces, judging by the extraordinary positions in which we found them lying. It was a sad and pathetic sight to see the fearful wounds on these poor beasts and the look of terror on their faces.[14]

Frank Laird reported the same incident:

Some strange sights were seen by the 8th as they went over the hill to consolidate the position and hold it against counter attacks. In one spot a train of transport waggons and horses were lying completely smashed up, having been apparently caught by the barrage.[15]

The second sight Fr Doyle refers to is very intriguing. If his description had not followed immediately on from that about the waggon and horses, one would feel inclined to believe that this was another example of the light-hearted banter he and Hugh Doyle often engaged in. Willie says:

The other was a corpse 'dump' of German dead, the bodies tied in bundles and some of them with heads cut off and hands and legs amputated below the knee, <u>run through the body with a pole,</u> so that three could be carried *at the same time. I must confess I did not believe the stories of the 'Corpse Factory' but here was evident proof of its existence, for the heads, hands and feet of the dead had been chopped off by the Boches themselves. The sight was too horrible for words, but it will give you an idea of the grim earnestness with which the war is being waged.*[16]

This sounds a very fanciful scenario, but at the same time the question of the existence of a 'corpse factory' was not new. What is immediately questionable here is whether Willie is retelling rumours, or whether, indeed, he is repeating someone else's authentic first-hand experience or, incredibly, actually relaying a personal experience . Whether the underlined words were from Willie's hand, to emphasise the horror of what he was conveying, or whether Lena did so whilst transcribing, is not known. It is such a fantastical scenario that one would think it would have come to the attention of Frank Laird also and he would have included it in his memoirs. However, his only comment about dead Germans was:

In a regimental head-quarters dugout the adjutant was found lying dead at the top of the stairs, and the colonel had been killed as he was getting out of his bunk when the mines went off.[17]

Frank Laird's memoirs were written some years after the war, but during the war the story of a 'corpse factory' had been reported by *The Times* on 16 April 1917, which claimed the Germans were distilling glycerine from the bodies of their dead. The report caused such outrage that it was discussed in the House of Commons on 30 April and was vigorously denied by the German government; they claimed they were rendering dead animals from the battlefield. There were many instances of propaganda during the war with both sides accusing the other of atrocities. Had any of the allied soldiers witnessed such a dump of mutilated corpses during their advance, or during the consolidation of their gains at Wytschaete/Messines, one would expect that reports would have appeared in contemporary accounts, later memoirs and/or official papers; this author has been unable to trace any such evidence. On the other hand, the tone of Willie's account indicates his belief in the event. Indeed, the issue did not go away. Writing later about events in January and November 1918, Captain J.C. Dunn of the Royal Welch Fusiliers stated:

Fantastic stories circulated, with circumstantial detail, of the German dead being collected that the fat and other useful derivatives might be extracted for the making of munitions, and of nutriment. (On Armistice day Kent and the Brigade Interpreter were told the current story by the Municipal Engineer at Aulnoye. He pointed to one of the factories, and declared that he had seen the naked German dead, wired in threes, lying in trucks in its railway siding.) [18]

Back in September 1914, John Lucy heard what he considered to be a weird tale about an officer who completely vanished during the Battle of the Aisne. His wry comment being:

Following my own experience of hearing that my dead brother was alive and only slightly wounded, I found it hard to believe many of the stories bandied about. The troops, I am sure, did not lie deliberately, but their imagination, in the stress of battle, often played strange tricks on them. [19]

Lt Col Rowland Feilding, 6th Connaughts, records in his letter home a disquieting sight following the Battle of Messines, which he was confident was not a trick of the imagination:

My men found a dead German machine-gunner chained to his gun. This is authentic. We have the gun, and the fact is vouched for by my men who took the gun, and is confirmed by their officer, who saw it. I do not understand the meaning of this:- whether it was done under orders, or was a voluntary act on the part of the gunner to insure his sticking to his gun. [20]

Willie ends his own letter with another enigmatic comment, this time about his father. Hugh Doyle was at that time staying with his daughter, Lena; one assumes from what Willie says it may be following a misadventure:

I shall not promise to send a letter for some little time, chiefly for want of news, but I shall keep in touch with you by an odd post card, that is if I do not become too lazy to write that much.
  I am ever so pleased to learn you are with dear Lena (whom please

thank for her letter) and the chicks in Balbriggan. The next bit of news probably will be that you are taking headers off the top of the light-house, or some other feat worthy of your venerable grey hairs!!!

I have pretty much got over the efforts of the last month's hard work, but these days in the country are doing wonders for us all.[21]

The business of the 8th Bn Royal Dublin Fusiliers in the Pas de Calais is revealed by the unit's War Diary written up by Major G.W. Kenny. There were Sunday church parades, such as on 24 June at Zeggars Cappel, where Fr Doyle was billeted. Obviously, there were no trench duties, but the diary records the usual to-and-from hospital (sickness being a common reason for being hospitalised) and the opportunity was taken to disinfect the underclothing of the men. New drafts of men arrived and some personnel were granted leave. Men and officers were sent away on training courses, but there was also training en-masse in-situ by companies carrying out their own schemes. Time was allowed for sports competitions and inter-company arms competitions; recreation also, although on 7 July the village of Bollezeele was placed out of bounds to all troops of the brigade. Disciplinary issues, unfortunately, reared its ugly head in the form of a Field General Court Martial, when 40901 Private Letley was sentenced to two years' imprisonment with hard labour for 'Absence without Leave,' one year of which was commuted by GOC 48th Infantry Brigade. There were also instances of NCOs and acting NCOs being deprived of their appointments for irregular conduct.

Inspections took place, including visits by GOC to the Battalion Headquarters. On 25 June there was a practice march-past, which then took place for real two days later before the XIX Corps Commander; the 16th (Irish) Division having been transferred to XIX Corps, Fifth Army. It was inclined to rain on Wednesday 27 June, nevertheless at 11.30 a.m. the companies paraded for the march, led by H.Q. staff, followed by Companies in the order 'A', 'D', 'C' and 'B', with the Company Transport bringing up the rear.

Mundane administration had to be attended to; for example an Audit Board was convened on Wednesday 4 July, consisting of Major G.W. Kenny, Capt G.E. Cowley and Capt C.F. Healy, to examine the Regimental account. The next day Major H.R. Stirke from 9th Bn Royal Dublin Fusiliers, was attached to 8th Bn as acting Second-in-Command. Three days later Major Kenny was authorised to wear the badges of his new rank, Lieutenant Colonel; the previous Officer Commanding,

Lt Col A.C. Thompson, having been sick for some time, was transferred to England and struck off the strength of the battalion.

The same day as Lt Col Kenny was confirmed in his post, Sunday 8 July 1917, his battalion set off to march to Tatinghem for intense training in a specially prepared area, where the men were accommodated in a tented camp nearby, whilst a few officers and H.Q. staff were in billets. The day before, Mass had been celebrated for all companies in a field of the farm where 'D' Company had been billeted, before leaving for their new accommodation in tents. Once again the battalion marched in heavy rain, but this time it was a long march rather than a march-past. The rain commenced at three o'clock in the morning on 8 July and continued for some hours following their departure two hours later. They arrived at Tatinghem at 10.52 a.m., the men spending the remainder of the day in drying clothes and equipment, whilst Lt Col Kenny inspected the Tilques Training Area allotted to the battalion for training.

The period of intensive special training began the next day with Reveille at 6 a.m., breakfast at 7 a.m., and sick parade at 7.45 a.m., followed by the march to the training area. Training covered issues such as trench attacks, time control and management and movements in artillery formation by sections and platoons. On Thursday 12 July the battalion carried out an attack against two objectives on the training area and practiced advanced phases of assault in open warfare. Two days later a 'Brigade Scheme' was scheduled; Reveille was at 5 a.m. so that the battalion could get to the training area by 6.15 a.m. Unfortunately, at 8.15 a.m. heavy rain began to fall resulting in cancellation of the scheme, so they trudged back to camp to try and dry clothes, clean equipment and arms. For those that had the energy the afternoon was devoted to recreation; not so for Private J. Mahoney, who had been transferred to Base the day before on being discovered under age and so was struck off the strength.

The weather was fine on Sunday 15 July, which was lucky for the Church of England members of the battalion, such as Second Lieutenants Charles Marlow, Arthur Green and Frank Laird, for whom a service was held in the Transport Field at 9.30 a.m. The Roman Catholics, on the other hand, paraded at 10.30 a.m. and marched the few miles to St Omer for a brigade service at the Cathedral, including a march past the Divisional Commander, Major General Hickie. Willie Doyle describes this in a letter six days later.

Prior to the writing of that letter, on the morning of Monday 16 July at 5.10 a.m., the battalion moved from the camp to march approximately ten miles north to billets in the Eringhem area, via St Martin-au-Laërt, St Omer, St Momelin, Lederzeele and Broxeele. Whilst on the move, Willie wrote a short note in haste on Tuesday 17 July 1917:

> *As I may not have an opportunity for some time of writing to you, now that we are on the move again, I send just a line to let you know that all is well. If you slipped in an 'H' before the last word you would be nearer the mark, for some of these recent days have been warm enough to make the stay of his Satanic Majesty on earth quite comfortable. You may guess it is no joke marching, all the same we had a good time, very restful in one sense, though the old legs give a groan now and again. We are not due for our turn in the trenches for a bit longer and perhaps before we get there the war will be over. In haste Will.[22]*

The following five days were filled with more training of the conventional kind – arms drill, bayonet fighting, musketry and so on, together with the usual kind of routine already noted, before the battalion was on the move again. Two days before setting off Fr Doyle played a practical joke on his Mess colleagues, as described by Professor O'Rahilly, who presumably was told the anecdote by one of those present:

> *One day Fr Doyle chanced upon a fresh unsoiled copy of the 'Daily Mail' for a Friday in October 1914, describing the German capture of Roulers. A glance at the scare headings on its front page suggested a hoax on the mess of the 2nd Dublins. Next day, which was a Friday (probably July 20) he managed to get into the mess before the others. He substituted the old copy and abstracted the new one, which he proceeded to read while waiting the turn of events. The first to come in was Major Smithwick who, seeing the heading, called out: 'They've begun the big advance. Roulers is captured.' At once there was great excitement, and all crowded round to get a peep at the stirring news. But after some moments there were puzzled exclamations. 'Why, it's the Germans who have taken Roulers.' 'It's not Friday's paper'; 'yes it is'. Then the fraud was discovered, and its author was discovered behind the authentic paper.[23]*

PEACEFUL DAYS IN THE PAS DE CALAIS

On Sunday 22 July the battalion had another long march, south-east to the Winnezeele area, closing back in on the Ypres Salient. Two weeks earlier the 7th Royal Inniskilling Fusiliers had preceded them :

By the 9 July we had moved canvas in the Winizeele [sic] area. Here we remained for a few days over the fortnight, when the division was concentrated in reserve before the opening of the third battle of Ypres. Nothing of interest remains to be said of our stay in Winizeele [sic] except that the weather treated us most favourably.[24]

There was also nothing of particular interest to remark about the few days the 8th Dubs spent at Winnezeele. The day before arriving there Willie Doyle had written a long letter home to Hugh, dated 21 July 1917:

They are giving us a few days breathing space on the road, so I take advantage of our temporary halt in our pilgrimage to send you my usual scribble. My present habitation is a tiny room in an equally tiny cottage, the only thing in it (barring the f---s) being the bed, which occupies 9/10 of the space. A beautiful dung-heap under my window sends me, alternately, odoriferous whiffs and savage mosquitos, but one can cheerfully put up with these small inconveniences instead of German shot and shell.

Our week of special training contained nothing of interest except that my battalions were again very far apart and much scattered. However I did not object to this as riding about the country in this beautiful weather was quite enjoyable and I could arrange my hours as I pleased.

An amusing incident took place the first morning we arrived. One old French lady was horrified on looking out of the window to see a column of soldiers in extended order advancing calmly through her field of oats. Arming herself with a stout stick she rushed out and started to wallop the leading files, declaring they might trample on her but not on her precious corn. Hearing a noise behind her, Madame turned round only to see six huge tanks walking up the hill literally 'making hay' of her cornfield. With a scream of rage the old lady made for the tanks, waving her stick and defying them to come further at their peril. It was only when two of them made for her (in fun) that she realised the battle was a one-sided affair and retreated to her fort. The English Government had warned the people that this ground would be needed for manoeuvres, had given them full compensation and told them they would sow their crops at their own risk. However, like true French people they wanted to get the money and the corn as well.

On Sunday last we had a very impressive ceremony in the cathedral of ------ The new Bishop had just been consecrated and the suggestion was made to have a Church Parade of the whole Brigade in his honour. The Brigadier-General, though not a Catholic, very kindly offered to command them himself and General Hickie with his Staff promised to be present.[25]

This reference is, of course, to the service for Roman Catholics of the 48th Infantry Brigade which took place on Sunday 15 July 1917 in St Omer Cathedral. Had all four battalions of the brigade been at full strength and all Catholic, then some four thousand men would have been squeezed into the cathedral. As it was, the Catholics of the three Royal Dublin Fusilier battalions amounted to approximately two thousand troops, so the Cathedral must have been packed to the rafters. The new Bishop was Mgr Julien, Bishop of Arras, Boulogne and St Omer. Fr Browne said Mass and Fr Doyle preached. Willie continues:

It was a splendid sight to see the magnificent old Cathedral filled with men, as devout a congregation as ever gathered within its walls. The most famous preacher in France, who does not wish his name mentioned, preached an eloquent, thrilling, soul-inspiring (and some other adjectives which I have forgotten) sermon and at the end of the Mass, the Bishop in a neat little speech thanked the men for the great honour they had paid him. He was specially struck, he said, by the fact that most of them had marched a long way to be present (some nearly 10 kilometres) and asked his flock, who were present, to learn a lesson from the grand spirit and deep Faith of the Irish soldiers. The ceremony concluded by a march past, with bands playing, in front of the Episcopal Palace, the Bishop taking the salute.[26]

Willie received many compliments for his sermon and probably felt somewhat embarrassed, hence his flippant comments about the anonymity of the most famous preacher in France. His letter continues:

> *The whole thing made a great impression and people could not help contrasting the respect and honour shown by the British Army with the narrow-minded persecution of the French Government.*[27]

Professor Alfred O'Rahilly noted [the Irish Brigade he refers to was the 'Wild Geese' of the Seventeenth Century]:

> *The sermon appealed to the men by its more or less historical reference to the Irish Brigade that had come there three hundred years before. The men of the 8th Dublins declared that Fr Doyle 'ought to get into Jim Larkin's shoes!' It appealed to others for a different reason. General Ramsay (a Protestant) stated afterwards that it was one of the most tactful and impressive sermons he had ever heard and General Hickie said that he was intensely pleased with the way in which 'dangerous' topics had been handled without offending anyone. It certainly required some diplomatic skill to appeal to Irish regiments in the British Army by evoking memories of the Irish Brigade which fought against England. Nor was it easy, without hurting English susceptibilities, to convey the fact that the Irish soldiers who were listening were fighting for what they believed was Ireland's cause as well as Belgium's. Fr Doyle succeeded.*[28]

Fr Browne also wrote a descriptive letter about this momentous sermon:

> *I arrived at the Cathedral about 11 o'clock and was in despair to find that the Pontifical High Mass was not yet finished. Our people are so punctual and the French so regardless of time-tables that I was sure there would be confusion and delay when our 2,000 Catholics would begin to arrive. But it was not to be. Quietly and wonderfully quickly the Mass ended, and the people went out to watch the Bishop go back in procession to his house close by. I was relieved to see that neither he nor any of the priests unvested. Then Fr Doyle and I had to try and clear away the hundred or so people who came wandering in for the last Mass – which for the day was to be ours. 'Donnez place, s'il vous plaît, aux soldats qui vont arriver,' I went round saying to everyone. They moved from the great aisle and got into the side-chapels, leaving the transepts and the aisles free. Many refused to do this,*

when with pious exaggeration I said, 'Presque 3,000 soldats irlandais vont arriver tout à l'heure.' And lo! They were coming. Through all the various doors they came, the 9th Dubs marching in by the great western door, the 8th Dubs through the beautiful southern door, through which St. Louis was the first to pass just 700 years ago, the 2nd Dubs coming into the northern aisle and making their way up to the northern transept. Rank after rank the men poured in until the vast nave was one solid mass of khaki with the red caps of General Hickie and his staff and the Brigadiers in front. Then up the long nave in quick clanking march came the Guard of Honour. Every button of its men, every badge, shone and shone again; their belts were scrubbed till not even the strictest inspection could reveal the slightest stain, and their fixed bayonets only wanted the sun to show how they could flash. Up they came, and with magnificent precision took their places on either side of the altar. I was just leaving the sacristy to begin Mass when I saw the Bishop's procession arriving. He had promised to come only after the sermon, but here he was at the beginning of the ceremony, making everything complete. Of course, I saw nothing, being engaged in saying Mass, but those who did said it was a wonderful sight. The beautiful altar, standing at the crossing of the transepts and backed by the long arches of the apse and choir, was for the feast surrounded by a lofty throne bearing the statue of our Lady of Miracles. The sides were banked up high with palms; then the Guard of Honour standing rigidly in two lines on either side; lastly the Bishop in his beautiful purple robes on his throne. From the pulpit Fr Doyle directed the singing of the hymns and then, after the Gospel, he preached. I knew he <u>could</u> preach, but I had hardly expected that anyone could speak as he spoke then. First of all he referred to the Bishop's coming, and very, very tactfully spoke of the terrible circumstances of the time. Next he went on to speak of our Lady and the Shrine to which we had come. Gradually the story was unfolded; he spoke wonderfully of the Old Irish Brigade in their wanderings over the Low Countries. It was here that he touched daringly, but ever so cleverly, on Ireland's part in the war. Fighting for Ireland and not fighting for Ireland, or rather fighting for Ireland through another. Then he passed on to Daniel O'Connell's time as a schoolboy at St. Omer and his visit to the Shrine. It certainly was very eloquent. Everyone spoke most highly of it afterwards, the men particularly, they were delighted.

After the sermon Mass went on. At the Sanctus I heard the subdued order, 'Guard of Honour, 'shun!' There was a click as rifles and feet came to position together as the Bishop came from his throne to kneel before the altar, twelve little boys in scarlet soutanes, with scarlet sashes over their lace surplices, appeared with lighted torches and knelt before his Lordship. At the second bell came the command, 'Guard of Honour, slope rifles!' And then as I bent over the Host, I heard, 'Present arms!' There was the quick click, click, click, and silence, till, as I genuflected, from the organ-gallery rang out the loud clear notes of the buglers sounding the General's Salute.[29]

Willie's own letter (21 July) which omits nearly all of this detail, continues:

You may be interested to hear that the Sergeant whom I spoke of in my long letter, him 'of the ruddy language', has been awarded the D.C.M. (Distinguished Conduct Medal) the private's equivalent of the M.C. I told the Colonel of his coolness and fine work in digging out the five buried men and recommended him for a decoration, which I am glad to say was accepted at H.Q. The poor chap is very proud of his medal, which I told him he won by his eloquent language![30]

The 8th Bn RDF's War Diary noted on 17 July the award by the Commander-in-Chief of seven gallantry awards to the 8th Dubs; four Military Medals, one bar to an MM, one Military Cross and one Distinguished Conduct Medal awarded to 14613 CSM Tait, whom Willie had assisted in dragging men out of the rubble of the collapsed Chinese Trench. On 19 July it was noted that 16725 Sergeant P. Kavanagh had been honoured by the French and awarded the Medaille Militaire. Willie's letter continues:

Another item of news will also please you. Our Division will not take part in the coming big offensive, as we are being held in reserve, so you need not be uneasy about me when the storm bursts. I expect this will decide whether we shall have to face another winter or not, though at present the end seems as far off as ever.

Many thanks for enclosures which I was glad to see. I am afraid I was the only one who did not send you congratulations on the '85 not out' score, but do so now --- ad multos annos --- limited however to 1,000.[31]

Unfortunately, Willie's assertion proved to be incorrect, unsurprisingly in view of the special training the 16th (Irish) Division had just undergone. Major General Hickie remembered post-war:

> *The 16th Division which had made a great and glorious name for itself both at Wytschaete and on the Somme, was specially applied for by the Commander of the Fifth Army in view of the impending third battle of Ypres. We were withdrawn from the line and given three weeks special training. The whole Division was in splendid order and as smart and full of military ardour as it was possible for any body of men to be. Brigades took it in turn to work in an area which we had laid out as a model of the German trenches to be attacked. The other Brigades carried on ordinary training and were in billets near St. Omer.*[32]

On Wednesday 25 July the battalion was marching back over the border into Belgium, to another camp, Watou Number 2, just west of Poperinghe. The 8th Dubs paraded to march off at 4.50 a.m. in fine weather, reaching the new camp at 9.30 a.m., the weather having turned wet; one man fell out. The weather was fine for the next three days, then on the fourth day, Sunday 29 July, Divine Services for Church of England and Roman Catholics had to be abandoned owing to violent thunderstorms and heavy rain. The Roman Catholic Divine Service took place, instead, the following day at 9 a.m. in a field adjacent to the camp, prior to the battalion preparing to move on yet again.

An item of interest in the War Diary was that 21889 Private J. Mahoney had been granted a £20 bounty. This would have been under the terms of Army Order 209 of 1916, relating to men who had been in the army pre-war and, on the termination of their original enlistment period, had been compulsorily required to remain with the colours. Private Mahoney, presumably, was one of the dwindling number of 'Old Contemptibles' and had obviously been transferred out of his original Regular Army battalion. (Possibly he had been injured and on recovery sent to the New Army battalion he now found himself in.) He and his colleagues in 8th Bn Royal Dublin Fusiliers were gradually edging their way towards the front line of the Ypres Salient to participate in a new offensive. In preparation for this their Medical

Officer had inspected the men, and twenty-five Other Ranks had been attached for duty to 166th Field Company of Royal Engineers.

The next stop for the battalion was Brandhoek, the other side of Poperinghe and west of Ypres. They moved off Monday evening at 9.25 p.m., arriving just into Tuesday 31 July at half past midnight, the opening day of Third Battles of Ypres. About 10.30 a.m. the area of their assembly positions in reserve at Brandhoek was shelled, but there were no casualties. The weather was fine but turned to rain towards evening. At 6.15 p.m. orders were received to prepare to move forward and the battalion was ready thirty minutes later, when they were temporarily attached to 164th Brigade of 50th Division. At the Menin Gate they met their guides who led them to position in Reserve Trench, Congreve Walk, north-east of the Vinery, which was reached at 10.15 p.m. Battalion Headquarters was located at the mound of the Chateau attached to Potijze cross-roads.

The 8th Royal Dublin Fusiliers' inspirational Chaplain, Captain the Reverend Father Willie Doyle was, as ever, at their side; whilst the 6th Royal Irish Regiment had to do without their equally charismatic officer, Major Willie Redmond.

Footnote 1: The Quartermaster General's branch of the General Staff was responsible for determining the formations to which specified roads in an area should be allocated, and it was then the responsibility of the Provost Marshal of each formation to ensure that the QMG's instructions were followed. For each separate Army area, road circuit maps were produced, to cover 'normal' traffic and 'operations' traffic, and generally, roads coloured red might be used in both directions by all traffic. Roads coloured blue might be used in both directions by cars and motor cycles, but by all other traffic the blue roads could be used only in the directions indicated by arrows drawn on them. During the preparations leading up to major operations, traffic was strictly controlled by the military police under the Assistant Provost Marshal, and the entrances and exits to and from villages and towns was strictly controlled, with police patrols at major junctions, and so on.

CHAPTER 28
INTERLUDE:
BITS AND SCRAPS FOR AN OLD MAN'S BREAKFAST

*'This is the day which the Lord hath made;
we will rejoice and be glad in it'*

Psalm 118

Before the 8th Battalion Royal Dublin Fusiliers moved off on Monday 29 July 1917, to its assembly point at Brandhoek, Willie Doyle had already started his next letter home. The letter, written as the battalion was marching over the Belgian border to Watou, was dated 25 July 1917, and concentrates as much on personal news as on what was happening in the war zone. His opening remarks give an insight into why his sister Lena transcribed his letters using a typewriter:

> *These little scrapings are just for yourself, small items not of sufficient interest to go in a letter, scarcely worth reading in fact, but since 'love looks not at the value of the gift but the intention of the giver' they may receive a warmer welcome than they deserve.*
>
> *I often wonder how you manage to decipher my 'spider scrawls', which do duty for hand-writing, for I seldom have the chance of using a table and nearly always scribble away on my knee, sometimes even standing and, in the past, so bothered by the never ceasing crash and bang of the guns, often scarce knowing what I am jotting down. My correspondence bureau at the present moment is a comfortable bank by the side of the road under a leafy hedge, for though I am as brown as a berry the sun is a bit too hot for my liking.*[1]

Although the 8th Dubs had set off in fine weather from their peaceful haven in France at 4.50 a.m. on 25 July, by the time they arrived across the border at Watou

INTERLUDE

at 9.30 a.m. that same morning, it was raining. Willie must have started his letter during a break in the march, but it would still have been early in the morning before the sun became too strong; hence his remark about the sun must relate to the weather up to that point. He continues:

> *Nearby is a good-sized wood, 'Bois de Rossignol' the map calls it and the name is apt, for it is full of nightingales who just at present are at their best. It is wonderful how little the birds mind the din of war: they have been born in noise and sing away quite merrily and build their nests up in the very front line, in spite of the shells bursting so near. I watched one nightingale about 3.30 a.m. on the morning of the last big battle, perched on the stump of a tree, singing away as if he thought the roar of the thousands of guns was a challenge to him; I am sorry to say the guns beat him in the end, but he put up a good fight. Another gentleman, or rather lady this time, has just gone down the road, running like one o'clock as if all the Germans in Hunland were after her --- a big sow who had got her head into a biscuit tin and could not get it off, the lid having caught behind her ears. Some gallant knight rescued the lady from her too attentive lover, but my sides are still sore from laughing.[2]*

How long the break from marching lasted isn't known, but Willie also found time to drink coffee as well as penning a few lines by the roadside. He changes the tense when he continues the letter, suggesting that he finished it later that day. Certainly, there seems to be too much text for it to be consistent with having been written during a short break en-route:

> *While I was writing one of my men, belonging to the Irish Rifles, of which I have charge also, passed by. We chatted for a few minutes and then he went on, but came back shortly with a steaming bowl of coffee, which he had bought for me. 'I am not of your flock, Father', he said 'but we have all a great liking for you.' And then added 'If all the officers treated us as you do our lives would be different.' I was greatly touched by the poor lad's thoughtfulness and impressed by what he said; a kind word often goes further than one thinks and one loses nothing by remembering that even soldiers are human beings and have feelings like anyone else. Was it*

not John Boyle O'Reilly who wrote:

*'A kindly word is a kernel sown
Which will grow to a goodly tree
Shedding its fruit when time is flown
Down the gulf of Eternity'*³

John Boyle O'Reilly [1844–1890],^(FN1) was an Irish writer and lecturer who turned *The Pilot,* a local Boston newspaper started by a Jesuit, into one of America's most-read newspapers. His story was of the kind of romantic nationalism which would have appealed to a young Willie Doyle. Willie's memory of the O'Reilly verse is imperfect; several words are incorrect, the most significant one being in the first line, where Willie writes 'a kindly word' when, in fact, O'Reilly's script was 'a kindly act.' Nevertheless, the sentiments were the same and Willie continues with some good news:

*You will be glad to know, as I was, that the 9th edition (90,000 copies) of my little book 'Vocations' is rapidly being exhausted. After my ordination when I began to be consulted on this important subject, I was struck by the fact that there was nothing one could put into the hands of boys and girls to help them to a decision, except ponderous volumes that they would scarcely read. Even the little treatise by St. Liguori which Fr Charles gave me during my first visit to Tullabeg, and which changed the whole current of my thought, was out of print. I realised the want for some time, but one evening as I walked back to the train after dining with you, the thought of the absolute necessity for such a book seized me so strongly (I could almost point out the exact spot on the road) that there and then I made up my mind <u>to persuade someone to write it</u> for I never dreamt of even attempting the task myself.*⁴

The manager of *The Messenger* must have been taken aback by the success of these pamphlets, as Willie continues:

I soon found out that the shortest way to get a thing done is to do it yourself, or rather God in in his goodness had determined to make use of me, because I was lacking in the necessary qualifications to get His work done, for I am firmly convinced that both in 'Vocations' and 'Shall I be a Priest', my part consisted in the correction of the proof sheets and in the clawing-in of the shower of 'bawbees.' I remember well when the M.S.S (which does not stand for 'Mrs', as Brother Hegarty read out once in Clongowes ... 'St Jerome went off to Palestine carrying his Missus') having passed the censors to my great surprise, the venerable manager of the 'Messenger' office, shaking his head over the prospect of its selling, for he said with truth 'It is a subject which appeals to a limited few.' He decided to print 5,000 and hinted I might buy them all myself.[5]

The Sacred Heart Messenger, was (and still is) a Jesuit magazine published monthly in Dublin, the first issue of which appeared in January 1888. It was started by Fr James Cullen, the founder of the *Pioneer Total Abstinence Association of the Sacred Heart,* with whom Willie had worked. Fr Cullen's idea for a magazine was approved by his rector at Belvedere College and he was given a pound note and the use of a room to start up. That first year the magazine achieved a circulation of 9,000, rising by 1904 to 73,000 copies being sold each month. Pamphlets were also printed, such as Willie's one entitled *Vocations,* which achieved the same rapid selling success as *The Messenger* itself. Willie continues:

Then when the pamphlet began to sell, and orders came in fast, I began to entertain the wild hope that by the time I reached the stage of two crutches and a long white beard I might possibly see the 100,000 mark reached. We are nearly at that now without any pushing or advertising and hope the crutches and flowing beard are still a long way off. God is good is he not? As the second edition came out only in the beginning of 1914 the sale has been extraordinarily rapid.[6]

Willie continues on a humorous note, bringing in other members of the family to share in his narrative:

It is consoling, from time to time, to receive letters from convents and religious houses saying that some novice has come to them chiefly through reading 'Vocations' for undoubtedly there are many splendid soldiers lost

> to Christ's army for the want of a little help and encouragement. Does not even the great Judge Robert Doyle admit that once for 15 seconds during a retreat he had thoughts of being a Trappist? Perhaps if he had read this famous book then, at the present moment, instead of administering sundry punishment to poor Tim's 'Tailer-Wailer' or scourging his long suffering spouse, Lady Jane, he might be now sitting on a good solid plank bed scourging himself.
>
> However, we need not despair. Holy Mother of the Church makes provision for such cases and, if both agree, husband and wife may enter a monastery. I know a score of convents which would take Jennie and make her Lady Abbess on the spot, for her great culinary skill, the only 'dot' asked being the materials of a gigantic cake which would stand the attacks of the whole community for twelve months (I'm thinking it would need to be a mighty big one.) Fitzwilliam St mansion and the Judge's pension could be handed over to Alice and Tim, everyone would be happy – at least the last named – and the world still go merrily on.[7]

Willie's efforts had borne fruit in more ways than one; not only had the sales of his pamphlet exceeded expectations but:

> A welcome gift from a benefactor, not a benefactress this time, has just reached us in the shape of a donation of £8 to distribute 1,000 free copies of 'Vocations'. The donor believes that if one cannot volunteer for the War himself, the next best thing is to try and get someone else to do so. One can never tell into what generous heart the good seed may fall, or the number of souls that possibly may be saved by this distribution. May God bless him and send along 1,000 more imitators for 'the harvest is great and labourers few' said our Blessed Lord and He ought to know.[8]

At this point Willie interjects yet more humour, and shows off his arithmetical skills, to carry his point:

> N.B. As I fancy I hear the fluttering of cheque books, may I say that £2-17-9 will do the trick (9d. per 18 copies) and put 1,000 happy girls (or boys) into as many happy convents. Please don't _all_ speak together.

> *I am cogitating another little book, which will bring untold blessings on my head. As you are a special friend I shall whisper its title <u>as a profound secret</u>: Hints to Maidens, Old Maids and Widdies, How to Get Married Soon … And …. Find the Right Sort of Boy with moneybags. The first copy to go to cook as I think she is all three. When this comes out, hot cakes will not be in it with the selling. I wonder would Sarah like a copy?*[9]

Willie's next comment confirms that he must have continued writing the letter dated 25 July over a period of the five days the battalion was at Watou. The post being delivered at the camp, Willie advises not only another literary success but also the negotiation of a profitable business deal! He says:

> *Just as I write this the post brings a most welcome and agreeable surprise in the shape of a cheque for £17-4-0 from Messrs Washbourne, London being my 1/- royalty on 344 copies of the 'Life of Fr Ginhac, S.J.' sold between Jan: 15 and Jan: 17. The terms they arranged for publication of the book were that they should bear the full cost (and risk) of the printing, binding, advertising and circulation: I was to receive a dozen free copies or more if I wanted them, a special reduction of 2/- for any copy I ordered myself and, when 600 copies were disposed of, an additional royalty 1/- per copy sold afterwards. As 1500 copies were printed this would mean a clear gain on my part of £45 without any risk. When the publishers fixed the price at 8/6 I thought the sale was killed and told them so, for I did not think many people would care to invest such a sum in the life of a man no one had ever heard of. Hence my astonishment when some 900 copies went in the first year and now, greater wonder still, an additional 344 copies, not including those sold since the beginning of this year, have gone to swell the total.*
>
> *I am glad Messrs Washbourne have made handsomely on the sale, as printer after printer refused to have anything to do with the book, though I staked Fr Ginhac's reputation that it would prove a financial success. He has certainly worked this miracle if he never did anything else and I am beginning to think he is not a bad sort of old chap, even though he looks so desperately in need of a square meal. I have a pile of letters from all parts of the world, Alaska, Ceylon, South Africa etc. etc. asking for*

relics and mentioning many favours received through the Holy Father's intercession, so that the labour of getting out the volume, and it was not light, has brought its own reward. If the £17 would be useful to anyone you might let me know, but you need to write quickly before the Gardiner Street Shylock sweeps it into his moneybags.[10]

Fr Doyle, of course, had taken a vow of poverty and so any money he had, over and above what had to be used for necessary expenses, was given away to deserving causes. The reference to Gardiner Street is the office of the Jesuits in Dublin, to whom the money would go unless Willie directed it elsewhere. His letter continues, referring to the Battle of Messines/Wytschaete:

Before our last big battle I gave the men a few 'talks' on Sunday about heaven, where I hope many of them are now. I have the satisfaction of knowing that what I said helped the poor fellows a great deal and made them face the coming dangers with a stouter heart. The man of whom I told you last year, who said he 'did not care a damn for all the bloody German shells,' (please excuse the language) 'because he was with a priest that morning,' expressed in a forcible manner what many another felt, that when all is said and done a man's religion is the biggest (and only true) consolation and the source of real courage.

I reminded them of the famous saying of the B. Curé d'Ars: 'when we get to Heaven and see all the happiness which is to be ours for ever, we shall wonder why we wished to remain even one day on earth.' God hides these things from our eyes, for if we saw now 'the things God has prepared for those that love Him,' life on earth would be absolutely unliveable, and as I said, the man who falls in the charge is not the loser but the gainer immensely, is not the unlucky one but the fortunate and blessed.

You should have seen how the poor chaps drunk in every word, for rough and ignorant as they are they are, they are full of Faith, though I fear their conception of an ideal Heaven, for some at least, would be a place of unlimited drinks and no closing time. There was a broad smile when I told them so.[11]

Returning to the subject of vocations:

INTERLUDE

I do not know if I have told you of a scheme which I have in my mind to help poor boys who are anxious to be priests. Before the war I was in contact with a number of very respectable lads and young men whose one desire was to work for God and the salvation of souls but who, for want of means, were not able to pursue their studies. I was able to help some of them and get them free places in America or England with a couple at Mungret but the number of applicants was far in excess of the resources.[12]

Mungret College was a Jesuit establishment situated near the village of Mungret, some three miles west of Limerick. Willie develops his theme:

One day, having successfully negotiated or missed a couple of shells, I was struck by a happy idea which did not hurt half as much as the Boche 'crump' would have done. I was coming home on leave and made up my mind to make an experiment with my idea, which was this. I gave a little talk to the Sodality of the Children of Mary in a certain convent in Dublin, on the need for priests at the present time and what a glorious work it was to help even a single lad to become one of the 'Lord's Anointed.' I told them how many were longing for this honour and suggested that they should <u>adopt</u> some poor boy and pay for his education until he was ordained. Two hundred girls subscribing 5/- a year would provide £50, more than enough for the purpose. I suggested that this money ought to be the result of some personal sacrifice, working overtime, making a hat or dress last longer etc., but as a last resource they might collect the 5/- or some of it.

The idea was taken up most warmly; nearly all the money for this year is paid in, though the girls are nearly all factory hands, and the lucky boy, Paddy Dunne from Wicklow, a fine lad of nineteen, clever and refined though a poor orphan, will begin his college course in September. I am hoping 'when the cruel war is o'er' to get the other convents to follow suit, for the scheme is simple and no great burden on any one and is a ready solution of the financial difficulty and should bring joy to many a boy's heart. Certain difficulties naturally suggest themselves, but I think we may safely count, a little at least, on our blessed Lord's help, since the work is being done for Him, and go on with confidence.[13]

Having exhausted his stock of news and updated Hugh Doyle on his pet projects, Willie goes into reminiscing and instructive mode, then his thoughts turning back to the gas attack at Loos. He obviously had a bit of time on his hands and wanted to extend the written connection with his father. His letter continues in a light-hearted fashion:

> *What would you say to a little trip with me this morning up to the Front Line trench? If you have drops of sweat to shed prepare to shed them now, for if you come back with a glorious thirst which any old toper might envy, you will have to carry a well moistened jacket as well. You are game? I need not ask that for I am wondering what would stop you 'going over the top' and having a whack at the Boche if you once got to the Firing Line: not a mere trifle of 85 Summers certainly.*
>
> *Unless you want to be turned back by the first sentry you will have to carry your gas helmet and crown your venerable head with a heavy steel hat, the weight of which is apt to make even a saint swear, until you hear bits of shrapnel hopping off it, when you sing a Te Deum instead. You will need a stout heart too, for it is an uncanny feeling to walk deliberately into the danger zone, knowing that at any moment you may meet a shell taking its morning stroll down the trench and that before the day is many hours older you may be rubbing noses with St. Peter. You have a good long tramp before you, for this communication trench with all its twists and turns may be two or three miles long. See diagram.*[14]

At this point Willie has included a drawing of Front, Support and Reserve trenches criss-crossed by a Communication trench, with the chaplain's dug-out at the end of the Support trench.

He next refers to that angel, Gabriel, who he believed watched over William Joseph Gabriel Doyle:

> *A monotonous time it is, as the 'ditch' with banks of earth on either side is 10ft deep, just broad enough to allow men to walk in single file, but completely shutting out view of everything. If you want to lead a contemplative life, now is your chance.*
>
> *Gabriel and I have settled this trench-trotting between us. He walks*

below, while I trudge along on top until he begins to smell danger (he has a wonderful nose for bullets) when he calls out: 'Down with your dust' and I roll on top of him and continue the journey in safety.

You may be surprised to find a solid wooden flooring all the way, which secures dry feet all the way, though in Winter as a rule the heavy rains turn the trenches into young rivers of mud and water, making the going very laborious. During this part of the journey there is little danger for though you may hear the scream of passing shells, or the ear-splitting crash of an explosion nearby, you know that the pieces will fly over your head and the chance of anything falling into the trench is remote indeed.

I wish I could say the same of the anti-aircraft shells, which are constantly bursting overhead. Many a time I have walked along with small bits hopping round like so many hail stones, but it is very rare that anyone is hit – don't move for your life! You are going to have your first real thrill and ten seconds concentrated agony. That peculiar whistling noise is a 'dud' anti-aircraft shell which has failed to explode and is coming rushing down straight for us. There is no use running, it is safer to remain still and hug the side of the trench. It can't be feet away. Instinctively one shuts one's eyes and clenches one's fists waiting for something to happen, a something that seems hours in coming. At last a thud, followed by an explosion which sends the clay in a shower over our heads and we can breathe again in safety. A near thing, certainly, just a yard to the right of the trench, so there is some excuse for one's heart going thump, thump and for that sickening sensation in the presence of great danger. I am rather glad this little adventure took place (as it really did) for it shows how safe a man is in a good trench unless the shells burst in.

There is a party coming towards us down the trench and as they have 'the right of way' we must squeeze into a corner to let them pass. A poor wounded fellow on a stretcher with death already stamped on his face. The bearers lay their burden gently down - these rough men have the tender heart of a woman for the wounded – reverently uncover their heads and withdraw a little as the priest kneels behind the dying man's head. A glance at the 'Identity Disk' on his wrist, stamped with his name, regiment and religion show that he is a R.C., for there are few men, no matter what their belief, who do not carry a rosary or a Catholic medal round their necks. I wonder what the non-Catholic Padres think of this fearful increase of 'Idolatry'?

'Ah, Father, is that you? Thanks be to God for His goodness in sending you – my heart was sure to die without the priest. Father (the voice was weak and came in gasps) Father, oh, I am glad now I always tried to live a good life, it makes death so easy.'

The Rites of the Church were quickly administered, though it was hard to find a sound spot on that poor smashed face for the Holy Oils and my hands were covered with his blood; the moaning stopped. I have noticed that a score of times, as if the very touch of the anointing brought relief. I present the crucifix to his lips as he murmured after me 'My Jesus mercy' and then as I gave him the Last Blessing his head fell back and the loving arms of Jesus were pressing to His Sacred Heart the soul of another of His friends, who I trust will not forget amid the joys of Heaven him who was sent across his path to help him in his last moments.

It is little things like this which help one over the hard days and sweeten a life which has little in it naturally attractive. If you had come up the trench with me twelve months ago, on the morning of the gas attack, and watched that same scene repeated hour after hour, I think you would have thanked God for the big share you have in the salvation of so many souls.

Word has just reached me that breakfast tomorrow morning will be at 3 a.m. and I must have Mass over first, so if you <u>don't</u> mind we shall trot back down our trench and get a few hours' sleep before the march begins.

N.B. Please ask Lena to put on the top of the typed letters 'PRIVATE, NOT TO BE COPIED'. Unauthorised copies have been sent to undesirable places lately.[15]

On Sunday 29 July, the day thunderstorms caused the abandonment of Divine Services, Willie closes his letter, so as to be up early on the Monday ready for Mass, and for a successful attempt to hold the Catholic Service in the field adjoining the camp at Watou, before preparing for yet another move that evening.

The history of the 7th Bn Royal Inniskilling Fusiliers noted about that Monday, 30 July 1917:

It was on the 30 July, after four days in the camp near Watou, that we moved into the shell zone once again. Marching through Poperinghe that evening we got some idea of the scale of the new offensive. As usual, the roads were choc-â-bloc with transport vehicles and motor lorries. Everything seemed to be moving in one direction only – to the salient.[16]

The 16th (Irish) Division were on the march again, back to the hot-spots of the Front Line and a new battle scheduled for 31 July 1917.

Footnote 1: John Boyle O'Reilly came from a comfortable home near Drogheda, County Meath and his life started very conventionally. Aged fifteen, he became an apprentice on a newspaper in Ireland, before moving to the north of England to live with relatives for two years, where he pursued his career on a different newspaper. His life then took a more adventurous turn, when he enlisted with the local volunteer regiment, 11th Lancashire Rifles. Then, when he returned to Ireland in 1863, the nineteen-year old joined the 10th Hussars in Dublin. He also became a member of the Irish Republican Brotherhood and recruited more members from the Regiment. He was convicted of conspiracy and transported to Western Australia on the last convict transport ship to sail; *The Hougoumont* reached Freemantle on 9th January 1868. A little over a year later, with the help of a Catholic priest, Father Patrick McCabe, O'Reilly managed to escape, eventually arriving in Philadelphia, via Liverpool, in November 1869. From there he found his way to Boston, settling in the suburb of Charlestown where there was a large Irish community. Employment with *The Pilot,* marriage, children and a successful writing career followed. His verses and poetry became very popular and he used *The Pilot* and lecture tours to promote Irish issues and culture.

CHAPTER 29
THE START OF ANOTHER BATTLE:
THIRD YPRES – RUIN AND DESOLATION, DESOLATION AND RUIN

I am still alive though at present I am more likely to die from drowning than from hostile fire. It has rained solidly for three days and the place is knee deep in mud. It is extraordinary weather for August.

R. Macleod, 241st Brigade, Royal Field Artillery, 3 August 1917.[1]

When the Catholics of 49th Infantry Brigade assembled in St Omer Cathedral on 15 July 1917, the weather in the Flanders region that summer had been largely balmy and remained mostly so for the next two weeks. But as August began the rain started to fall; and fall; and fall. Willie Doyle was, by now, composing one of his long budgets, which would cover a period of several weeks. In the meantime, he fired off a couple of quick communications home. His brief letter to his father dated 2 August 1917 starts thus:

We got back to camp in the early hours of this morning, having been in reserve during the big fight, of which you would have read in the papers. We were not in action and had no casualties but had a rather trying time from the rain and mud which were appalling.[2]

Despite Second Army's and 'Daddy' Plumer's huge success in masterminding the Battle of Messines, responsibility for the next offensive was transferred to General Hubert Gough and his Fifth Army. As a consequence, there was an inevitable delay between the success of the June battle and the launch of the next one on 31 July 1917, by which time the unseasonably bad weather had set in. In any case:

THE START OF ANOTHER BATTLE

The eternal verities of warfare mean that artillery and troops cannot be effortlessly switched between battlefields; defences do not necessarily crumble by some process of osmosis and a successful frontal assault in one part of the line does not predicate success in another frontal assault a few miles away in different tactical circumstances.[3]

After months of wrangling following the Chantilly Conference of 15 November 1916, and following completion of British operations at Arras and Vimy Ridge (undertaken in co-operation with the ill-fated French offensive in Champagne) the British forces' Commander-in-Chief, Sir Douglas Haig, was finally able to get his plans for the long awaited 'Third Ypres' operation sanctioned by the politicians and the French. Haig had progressed from the rank of Lieutenant General, commanding I Corps with the BEF in August 1914, to the rank of General in December 1915, when he was appointed Commander-in-Chief of the British Army. A little over a year later, in January 1917, he became a Field Marshal. He had made a statement of his intentions to a meeting of his Army commanders at Doullens on 7 May 1917:

The objective of the French and British will now be to wear down and exhaust the enemy's resistance by systematically attacking him by surprise. When this end has been achieved the main blow will be struck by the British forces operating from the Ypres front, with the eventual object of securing the Belgian coast and connecting with the Dutch frontier.[4]

A month to the day later, the Field Marshal had overseen the achievement of one element of the surprise he referred to, with the success at Messines. The successful capture of the Messines Ridge had been a vital prerequisite to Haig's proposal for a larger offensive on the Ypres Salient, which was aimed at pushing forward from Ypres and driving the enemy back and away from their positions on top of the Passchendaele Ridge. Haig fully understood that the denial of the Ridge to the enemy, with its commanding views westwards towards the coast, was an essential preliminary to his plans for a land-based operation against the German submarine bases at Bruges, Ostend and Zeebrugge. Now, on Tuesday 31 July 1917, his hour had arrived.

Following the Battle of Messines, the enemy could no longer overlook Ypres from the south, but they still dominated from the north, east and north-east. The

Germans were by now in no doubt of the Allied intentions and, in any event (unlike at Messines) preparations for the new attack could not be concealed. The historian of the 2nd Bn The Prince of Wales's Leinster Regiment noted:

> *Fully forewarned the Germans had taken every step to meet the assault. They had by now realised that the continuous trenches afforded poor protection against the terrific bombardments of the Allies, unless abundant underground cover could be provided, for which the waterlogged terrain of Flanders was unsuited. Accordingly they introduced what was almost a revolution in the tactics of the defence, namely the substitution of depth for breadth; that is to say they held their ground by a series of rows of disjointed trenches and strong points, while scattered about were small concrete blockhouses with walls of great thickness each garrisoned by about twenty men with two or three machine guns. These were the famous 'pill boxes' now to be tested for the first time.[5]*

By September 1916 the German Fourth Army had formulated six lines of defence in the Ypres Salient, although the rearmost positions were still under construction in 1917. The first stage was the lightly-held Front Line, followed by five named stages: Albrecht-Stellung, Wilhelm-Stellung, Flandern I, Flandern II and Flandern III. All lines were interconnected and scattered in between were hundreds of camouflaged pill-boxes, which were often built into existing structures (or their ruins) such as farm buildings. Along Flandern I previous trenches were almost entirely replaced by concrete bunkers. These bunkers were strong enough to withstand the heaviest of artillery bombardments and manned with machine-gunners, ready to curb the advance of Allied Infantry. This scheme was overseen by Colonel von Lossberg, Germany's top defensive expert, reporting to General Sixt von Armin.

> *The crux of von Lossberg's formula ... was counter-attack. Bodies of troops for this purpose were staggered in depth throughout the rear, with the strongest ones furthest back. In this way, he hoped, his retaliatory blows would get successively more powerful, should the need arise.[6]*

Despite these innovations to the fortifications, the actual front line had remained static. Regular Army man John Lucy of the Royal Irish Rifles first served in the

THE START OF ANOTHER BATTLE

Ypres Salient at the end of 1914; when he returned in July 1917 he observed:

Before we covered the first mile to Hell-Fire Corner I had all the information I wanted ... From my knowledge of the place I knew the line was practically in the same position as it was over two and a half years ago.[7]

More recent arrivals of the New Armies, 7th Bn Royal Inniskilling Fusiliers was in 'B' Camp, two miles south-west of Vlamertinghe, on the night of 30–31 July, awaiting further orders. Their historian remembers:

Before dawn the attack had been launched from Woesten to Ypres, and before 11 o'clock that morning we heard some scraps of news from the line. One report said all objectives had been captured and our troops had broken through; another, that the French Army was advancing through Houlthoust Forest – all equally untrue. Later in the day we got word, officially, that the attack was successful along the army front, and that in nearly every case the final objectives had been reached. This was good news, but our spirits sank considerably at the change in the weather. Our worst enemy in this stage of an attack was rain, and down it came, as it often had done before, on zero day. The result of the bad weather setting in was to hold up the attack for a week, which was all in favour of the enemy. Within a few hours the forward zone was little better than a quagmire of water-logged shell holes, a sea of mud and water in a land of absolute desolation.[8]

Whilst the French lined up for the attack on 31 July with two divisions of their First Army's I Corps, this was an offensive played out mainly by British and Empire forces. A measure of success had been achieved before the onset of rain, but not in the crucial areas. Willie Doyle's short letter of Thursday 2 August continued, and finished, confirming the state of the ground:

The weather has unfortunately broken, very cold, with unceasing rain, more like December than August. If we can manage to dig ourselves out of the clay in which we are firmly planted we march somewhere else tomorrow, but from what I hear there is little chance of our crossing bayonets with the Boche for a good while, so there is no need to be uneasy except about my vanishing in the sweet Belgian mud. I wish you could have seen us last night floundering knee deep through slush and mud, but happy at the prospect of a warm meal and a glorious sleep (on the ground) when we reached our destination. Hope you are all well 'as this leaves me at present.' P.S. many thanks to dear Mai for her letter, with enclosure, just received.[9]

On the day this letter was written, the 8th Dubs had returned to Erie Camp from their reserve position on the Frezenberg line. One of their subalterns, 2/Lt M.F. O'Donnell, had been wounded and men from the battalion, and from 16th (Irish) Division generally, had been engaged in burying dead for their XIX Corps colleagues, the 55th Division, who had been in the front line attack of 31 July.

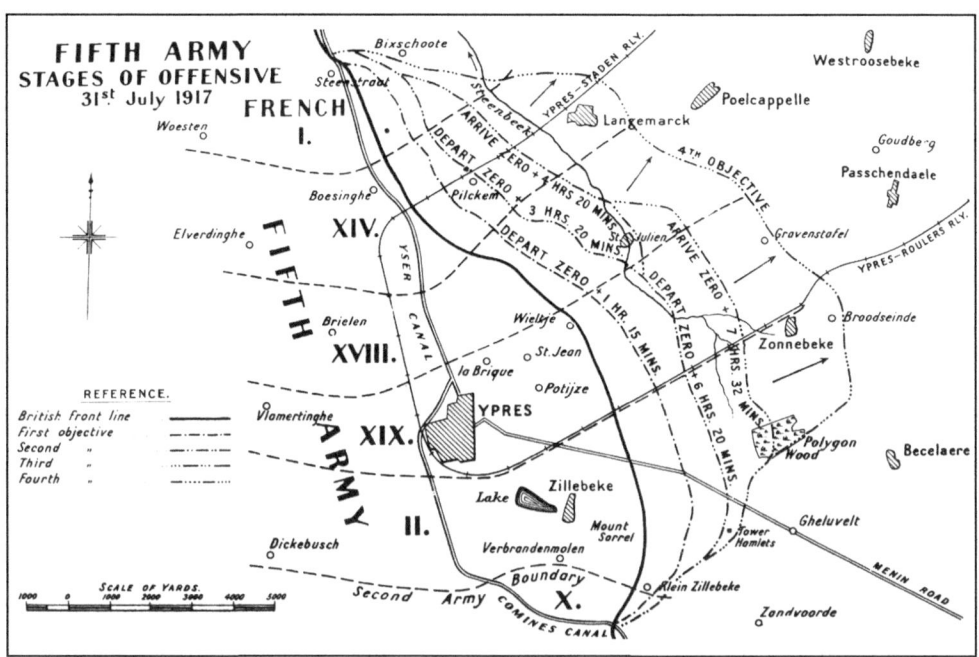

Map of the Front Line, 31 July 1917

Two divisions of XIX Corps, 15th on the right and 55th on the left, attacked on 31 July, whilst the other two divisions, 16th and 36th (the two Irish divisions once more side by side) were in reserve. The two offensive divisions of XIX Corps attacked from positions just right of centre of the whole fifteen-mile line. To their immediate left were other Fifth Army divisions; first came those from XVIII Corps;

beyond them came divisions from XIV Corps; then, the Guards Division; and on the extreme left the two French divisions. To the right of the divisions of XIX Corps were divisions from II Corps, and, from Second Army, divisions of X Corps, IX Corps and II Anzac Corps. The total number of troops in the seventeen divisions actually assigned to the assault amounted to about 100,000 men. Behind them, were seventeen more divisions, ready to move forward if required. The German Fourth Army's front-line units consisted of three groups of nine divisions; in reserve were six divisions and behind came two more, then another two and finally a further three divisions completing their deployment. Although numerically weaker at this stage, the German force was being supplemented by the arrival of additional divisions of troops released from the Eastern Front following the collapse of the Russian military effort in the wake of Tsar Nicholas II's abdication, and the onset of the revolution.

The infantry attack of 31 July was, of course, preceded by an artillery barrage. The Germans had 1,556 light and heavy guns in place, compared to the British total of 2,299. Oberstleutnant Freiherr von Forstner, Commander Infantry Regiment 164, was stationed opposite the left of 55th Division's position on that awful night of 30/31 July 1917, which he remembered as the:

> ... *worst I ever experienced. The fire increased to an intensity that was simply beyond our power to comprehend. Our blockhouse and nearby mortar battery received more than 1,000 large calibre shells. The earth trembled, the air shimmered. My pillbox heaved and rocked as though it was going to collapse. Almost by a miracle it received no direct hits. Everyone who dared to go out was wounded. Stabsarzt Katte resorted to issuing opium.*[10]

As well as terrorising those men (of both sides) who were not protected by concrete bunkers, the artillery barrage (and counter-barrage) was to have a secondary effect, to churn up ground that did not drain well, and destroy the ditches and underlying dykes which channelled the water away. This damage to the drainage system was exacerbated by the heavy rain which would fall during August.

The writer of the History of 55th Division (published in March 1919) was the Senior Chaplain of the Division, The Rev J. O. Coop. This Padre acknowledges assistance for his account from Lieutenant Colonel R.T. Lee and his report echoes so many others with regard to the weather. He commented:

The weather during the whole of June and during the greater part of July had been ideal weather for campaigning purposes. Unfortunately, on Sunday, 29 July, a particularly heavy thunderstorm filled up the shell holes and turned roads and tracks into a morass. The succeeding days were dull and hazy, making the completion of the artillery preparation peculiarly difficult, and typical Flanders weather conditions prevailed on the morning of the 31st – the moment chosen for the attack. Low lying clouds which made aerial observation and co-operation as difficult as could be imagined; a dampness of atmosphere, threatening rain at any moment; a half sodden ground, greasy and depressing; such was the luck of the weather at 3.50 a.m. on the 31 July 1917, when the artillery barrage opened …Shortly after eight o'clock in the evening the rain, which had been threatening all day, came down steady and remorseless, and continued with varying intensity for weeks. The weather conditions, indeed, could not have been worse and the elements seemed to be throwing in all their weight on the side of the enemy. Shell holes became feet deep in water; mud changed from dough to slime; everything was discouraging, disappointing and depressing enough to break the spirit of any but the British soldier.[11]

There were four objectives for the men of the attacking infantry waiting along the line; the Blue Line was the first objective, corresponding to the German front line and immediate support works, which were only lightly manned. Next was the Black Line, which was the enemy's second line. After that the objectives became tougher; the Green Line was the German system of trenches linking into pill boxes. Finally the Red Line, which was only to be attempted that day if everything was going to plan and working well.

The infantry of XIX Corps attacked across the Pilkem Ridge towards the German defensive positions on the Langemarck-Gheluvelt Line. Initially, the 55th Division was successful, reaching their Third Objective on the Green Line, before having to pull back to the Black Line, which Rev Coop noted had to be held at all costs; he adds:

The Division had fought well… All objectives had been taken and the subsequent withdrawal from the Green Line to the Black Line was forced upon it by circumstances for which it was not responsible.[12]

THE START OF ANOTHER BATTLE

This was to become a common theme of contemporary accounts i.e. taking objectives but being forced back through no fault of their own. Even this achievement came at a cost and the division suffered 70 per cent casualties. It may be that one of the bodies, buried by Willie Doyle's men, was that of the runner for Captain Thomas Owtram, 1/5th Bn, King's Own Royal Lancaster Regiment. Owtram remembered reaching the German front line and:

> *In the trench just in front of us a number of Germans could be seen in the faint light. They appeared to be throwing things at us. There was a sound of bursting hand grenades. Then the Germans got out of the trench and ran back. As quickly as I could, I got my men over the trench and moved forward again (leaving the so-called mopping up parties to deal with any of the enemy who might be skulking in their dug-outs). I could only see about twenty yards in either direction, so hoped that the platoon commanders on my right and left were doing likewise. We resumed the advance. To the best of my knowledge it was only as we were getting near the reserve line that constituted our final objective that we ran into the curtain of machine gun fire that caused us such heavy casualties. I saw my runner who was close beside me fall apparently lifeless without a sound and at that same moment I received a blow where my left leg joined my body that knocked me over as though a horse had kicked me. Bullets were flicking the earth all around me. The parapet of the trench at which our advance was to terminate was about five yards in front of me. I got up and made a dash for it. As I was crossing the parapet, another bullet hit me, piercing my right knee joint.*[13]

Captain Owtram could no longer continue and crawled into a captured enemy trench to shelter and hope to be rescued. Already both the other officers of his company had been killed and all NCOs, bar one, who now assumed command. Owtram was lucky enough to be rescued from the trench in which he lay wounded by stretcher bearers brought to him by the Medical Officer of the Liverpool Scottish, Captain Noel Chavasse VC, operating under heavy shell fire. This scenario resonates with events still awaiting Willie Doyle.

On the right of Captain Owtram's battalion were their brigade colleagues 1/6th King's Liverpool Regiment, who captured about 100 prisoners. Had he been around, no doubt Fr Doyle would have been concerned for the spiritual welfare of these prisoners. Taking into consideration they were safe, and had a lot to be thankful for, he would have been less impressed with the enemy's complaint:

> *A number of prisoners were captured especially near Jasper Farm, one German officer actually complained to Captain Tyson that our men spoke roughly to him.*[14]

The night of the 31 July and the following day was spent by XIX Corps in consolidating gains on the Black Line. On 2 August, the day Willie Doyle's men completed their grave-digging detail for 55th Division and returned to Erie Camp, the Germans launched a counter-attack at one of the 55th Division's positions, Pommern Redoubt, which was repulsed, before the 55th was relieved by the 36th Division. The relief was completed between 4 and 7 August and the remnants of the 55th Division proceeded to the Recques area, near St Omer to rest, recuperate and recover their strength.

Whilst the 36th Division was now in the Front Line, their fellow Irishmen of 16th Division were waiting for further orders. Willie sent a postcard home dated 6 August and says:

> *A hasty line to let you know all is well. Unceasing rain for five days has made the country a quagmire and hinders any serious operation except marching, which is unending. We go first to one spot then another, spend 48 hours in the trenches and come out like so many drowned rats, rest a day or two and off again – I am waiting for a big tramp at the present moment. Don't expect much writing from me for a while till we settle down, but I shall keep in touch (if I can) by a postcard.*[15]

Despite the dire conditions Willie continued scribbling details of his activities and completed another budget, which turned out to be his penultimate one. This he prefaced with a note:

> *As I fear my card from the battlefield may not have reached you and you will be on the lookout for news of me, I send you on the enclosed, though I have a good deal more to add. I shall only say I am well, thank God, and*

once more have come safely through all dangers and there were many.

When you read part 2 of my letter to follow in a few days you will understand better why I feel a bit fagged out and knocked about in more senses than one. We are out of the line at present and I do not know our future movements, but you may depend on it that I shall secure leave at the very first opportunity and congratulate you on your 68th birthday!

A bundle of letters is waiting for me somewhere; probably there is one from your dear self among them for which loving thanks. Please thank Lena for her kind gift of cigarettes and Jennie for her letter. My mail bag will be a bit full for some days. Hoping the enclosed will be another 'on the knees of my heart' letter.[16]

The birthday for which Willie sent congratulations was, of course, Hugh Doyle's 86th birthday, but Willie has deliberately transposed the numerals, which not only to flattered his father, but is an acknowledgement of the old man's vigour and energy.

Willie's long narrative, musings and reflections now begin from yet another new Front Line location. His budget, as transcribed by his sister, commenced on 30th July 1917 and was headed:

Private: Not to Be Copied
The Battle of Ypres Part 1 30 July 1917

This budget, like previous ones which had gone before, retraces previous days and old ground Willie has already mentioned in shorter correspondence. He starts:

For the past week we have been moving steadily up to the Front once more to face the hardships and horrors of another big 'push' which report says is to be the biggest effort since the War began. The blood-stained Ypres battlefield is to be the centre of the fight, with our left wing running down to the Belgian coast, from which it is hoped to drive the enemy, and perhaps force him by a turning movement, to fall back very far.

The preparations are on a colossal scale, the mass of men and guns enormous. 'Success is certain' our Generals tells us, but I cannot help wondering what are the plans of the Great Leader and what the result will be when He has issued His orders. This much is certain: the fight will be a desperate one, for our foe is not only brave, but clever and cunning as we have learned to our cost.

Mass in the open this morning under a drizzling rain was a trying if edifying experience. Colonel, officers and men knelt on the grass with the water trickling off them, while a happy if somewhat damp chaplain moved from rank to rank giving every man Holy Communion. Poor fellows! With all their faults God must love them dearly for their simple faith and love of their religion and for the confident way in which they turn to Him for help in the hour of trial.[17]

Divine Service was, of course, held on the Monday because the bad weather had prevented it taking place on Sunday 29 July 1917. Willie continues:

One of my converts, received into the Church last night, made his first Holy Communion this morning under circumstances he will not easily forget. I see in the paper that 13,000 soldiers and officers have become Catholic since the war began, but I should say this number is much below the mark. Ireland's missionaries, the light-hearted lads who shoulder a rifle and swing along the muddy roads have taught many a man more religion by their silent example than he ever dreamed of before.

Many a time one's heart grows sick to think how few will ever see home and country again, for their pluck and daring have marked them down for the positions which only the Celtic dash can take; a post of honour, no doubt, but it means slaughter as well.

We moved off at 10 p.m. a welcome hour in one way, as it means marching in the cool of the night, instead of sweating under a blazing sun, still when one has to put in a long day of hard work and legs and body are pretty well tired out already, the prospect of a stiff march is not too pleasant.[18]

The War Diary actually recorded that the battalion moved off from the camp at Watou on Monday 30 July 1917 at 9.25 p.m, but no doubt it took more than half an hour for such a large number of men to exit the camp. The budget continues with Willie wandering off track a bit to relate a religious parable:

Help comes to one in strange ways and the remembrance of a quaint old story has lightened for me the weight of a heavy pair of boots over many a mile of muddy road. The story may interest you:-

In the good old days of yore a holy hermit built him a cell in a spot a few miles from the well so that he might have a little act of penance to offer to Almighty God each day by tramping across the hot sand and back again with his pitcher. All went gaily for a while and if the holy man did lose many a drop of honest sweat he knew he was piling up sacks of treasure in Heaven and his heart was light. But – oh! that little 'but' which spoils so many things – but though the spirit was willing, the sun was very hot, the sand most provokingly hot, the pitcher the divil and all of a weight and the road seemingly longer each day. 'It is a little bit too much of a good joke' thought the Man of God to tramp these miles day in day out, with me old bones clanking like a traction engine. Why not move the cell to the edge of the well save time (and much bad language probably) and have cold water in abundance and a dry hair shirt on me back?

Away home he faced for the last time with his brimming water jar, kicking the sand about in sheer delight, for the morrow would see him on the track and an end to his weary trudging, when suddenly he heard a voice, an angel's voice he knew it must be, counting slowly 'One, two, three, four.' The hermit stopped in wonder and so did the voice but the next step he took the counting began again 'Five, six, seven.' Falling on his knees the old man prayed that he might know the meaning of this wonder. 'I am the Angel of God' came the answer 'counting up each step which long ago you offered up to my Lord and Master, so that not a single one may lose its reward. Don't be so foolish as to throw away the immense merit you are gaining by moving your cell to the water's edge, for know that in the eyes of the Heavenly Court nothing is small, which is done or borne for the love of God.' That very night down came the hermit's hut and before morning broke he had built it again five miles <u>further</u> from the well and for all I know he is merrily tramping still backwards and forwards across the burning sand, very hot and tired no doubt, but happy in the thought that the Recording Angel is busy counting each step.[18a]

The relevance of this story becomes clear later in Willie's account. He continues:

> *I do not think I need point the moral, but I hope and pray that my good angel is strong at arithmetic and won't get mixed when he starts his long tot! It was 1.30 a.m. when our first halting place was reached and as we march off again at 3 a.m. little time was wasted getting to sleep. It was the morning of 31 July, the feast of St. Ignatius, a day dear to every Jesuit, but doubly so to the soldier sons of the soldier saint. Was it to be Mass or sleep? Nature said sleep, but grace won the day and while the weary soldiers slumbered the Adorable Sacrifice was offered for them, that God would bless them in the coming fight and, if it were His Holy Will bring them safely through it.*[19]

The Catholic Church celebrates the feast days of Saints on virtually every day of the year. The number of canonised Saints is greater than the number of days in the calendar, so two or more Saints could share the same day, which is usually assigned to them on the date of their death or, if this is unknown, the date of canonisation. St Ignatius Loyola's Feast Day of 31 July, the day he died in 1556, is unique to him. Willie continues:

> *Mass and thanksgiving over, a few precious minutes of rest on the floor of the hut and we have fallen into line once more. As we do the dark clouds are lit up with red and golden flashes of light, the earth quivers with the simultaneous crash of thousands of guns and, in imagination, we can picture the miles of our trenches spring to life as the living stream of men pour over the top and the Fourth Battle of Ypres has begun.*[20]

Willie refers to the Fourth Battle of Ypres, whereas the campaign became known as *Third Ypres*; possibly Willie has added the extra number by counting the Battle of Messines as a separate 'battle of Ypres'. He continues:

> *Mens' hearts beat faster and nerves seem to stretch and vibrate like harp strings as we march steadily on, ever nearer and nearer towards the raging fight, on past battery after battery of huge guns and howitzers belching forth shells which ten men could scarcely lift, on past the growing stream of motor ambulances, which with its red burden of broken bodies the first drops of that torrent of wounded which will soon pour along the road.*

THE START OF ANOTHER BATTLE

> *I fancy not a few were wondering how long would it be till they were carried past in the same way, or was this the last march they would ever make till the final Roll Call on the great Review Day.*
>
> *As I said in a previous letter we were to be held in reserve for the opening stages of the battle, so we lay all that day (the 31st) in the open fields, ready to march at a moment's notice should things go bad at the Front.*[21]

The War Diary for the 8th Royal Dublin Fusiliers states its location on 31 July as Brandhoek, north-west of Ypres, moving that evening nearer to the Front Line north-east of Ypres. The 7th Royal Inniskilling Fusiliers had a similar wait close by:

> *A more disagreeable march it would be difficult to imagine. Rain came down steadily all night and the darkness was intense. It was only with difficulty that we found our location, and when we did the disappointment was very great. Soaked to the skin and thoroughly worn out, we discovered a bare field was our reward. Not even a trench or a hut to shelter in for the night. More by good luck than by good staff work the men fixed up bivouacs out of their mackintosh sheets, but these hastily improvised shelters gave little or no protection against the elements.*[22]

Willie continues his narrative:

> *A curious incident happened close by while we were waiting. One of our aeroplanes, flying rather low, dashed into the cable which was holding an observation balloon overhead. The steel wire snapped like a thread, the balloon with its two occupants shot up into the air disappearing in the clouds, while the aeroplane crashed to the ground, both pilot and observer were killed. A few moments later we saw the two balloners come dropping down attached to their parachutes and land safely, none the worse for their trying experience.*
>
> *Bit by bit news of the fight came trickling in: the Jocks (15th Scottish Division) in front of us had taken the first and second objective with little opposition and were pushing on to their final goal. All was going well and the steady stream of prisoners showed that for once Dame Rumour was*

not playing false. Our spirits rose rapidly, in spite of the falling rain, for word reached us that we were to return to the camp for the night as our services would not be required. Then the sun of good news began to set and ugly rumours to float about.[23]

The 15th Scottish Division was disposed immediately to the right of the Rev Coop's 55th Division, the two offensive divisions of XIX Corps, whilst the two in reserve were, of course, 16th Irish and 36th Ulster. One of the objectives of the 'Jocks' was Frezenberg village and this locality was to play a pivotal role in Willie Doyle's story. The history of the 15th (Scottish) Division states:

On the right the 44th Brigade found that the wire round North Station Buildings and Frezenberg had been well cut by the preliminary bombardment, and, in face of heavy fire from these places, the leading companies of the Black Watch and Gordons fought their way through the village and on to the Black Line. One of the tanks, 'Challenger,' was of the greatest assistance in the capture of Frezenberg. Under command of 2nd Lieutenant C.S. Walker, she entered the village, and dealt with many fortified houses that were holding up the advance. It was an exceedingly fine performance to get a tank over such bad ground, and the assistance it gave us was of immense value to the brigade. Unfortunately most of the remaining tanks had been put out of action by this time through either being bogged in shell-holes and marshy ground, or hit by artillery before reaching the Blue Line.

On the left serious opposition was encountered by the 46th Brigade in the attack on the Frezenberg redoubt, on the Ypres-Zonnebeke road. This work lay just behind the crest-line, and directly they reached it the leading waves of the K.O.S.B. were met with machine-gun fire from concrete emplacements on either side of the road, suffering heavy casualties. The advance on this part of the line was momentarily checked, but the Borderers were not to be denied. Finding that it was impossible to get forward in the face of such heavy fire, a party from the left company, under 2nd Lieutenant Causley, worked round to the north of the Redoubt. 'Here Causley and another company officer, 2nd Lieutenant Connachie, were killed, and it was under the command of 2nd Lieutenant Houston that the gallant little party finally captured the strong-point.[24]

THE START OF ANOTHER BATTLE

So, a measure of success for 15th Scottish Division, as well as 55th Division, but elsewhere along the front line things had not gone so well. To the right of XIX Corps, the objective of II Corps, the Gheluvelt Plateau, was not taken; only the Blue Line had been reached. The starting positions of the British centre divisions were from a slight salient in the line, so that the deeper they penetrated the enemy's positions, the deeper the bulge. When men to the right of the 15th Division could not keep up, the Scots in the bulge were enfiladed with machine gun fire, mortars, and shells from 77mm field guns. Willie continues:

The wily Boche was at his tricks again. Knowing that all his artillery positions were noted by our airmen and 'registered' for shelling, he had quietly withdrawn the guns to new positions, leaving one behind to keep up a rapid fire and so deceive our gunners. Whether it was the impetuous Celtic dash that won the ground, or part of German strategy, the enemy centre gave way while the wings held firm. This trick has been played so often and so successfully one would imagine we should not have been caught napping again, but the temptation for victorious troops to rush into an opening is almost too strong to be resisted and probably the real state of affairs on the wings was not known. The Scotties reached their objective only to find they were the centre of a murderous fire from three sides and having beaten off repeated counter-attacks of the 'demoralised enemy' were obliged to retire some distance. Old Man Hun so far had not done too badly.[25]

Thus, the attacking men of XIX Corps had to retreat from their furthest gains, but not before their 16th (Irish) Division colleagues in reserve were mustered. For them, it was to be a continuation of the long tramp which started twenty-four hours previously when they left Watou. The first stage of their march to Brandhoek had taken them three hours, reaching there just after midnight, where they had come under shell-fire and had to wait in fields all day for further orders. According to the 8th Royal Dublin Fusiliers' War Diary orders to move were received at 6.15 p.m., whereas it was later by the time word reached Willie:

It was nearly eight o'clock and our dinner was simmering in the pot with a tempting odour, when the fatal telegram came 'the battalion will move forward in support at once'.

I was quite prepared for this little change of plans, having experienced such surprises before and had taken the precaution of laying in a solid lunch early in the day. I did not hear a single growl from anyone, though it meant we had to set out for another march hungry and dinnerless with the prospect of going a second night without sleep. When I give my next nuns' retreat I think I shall try the experiment of a few supperless and bedless nights on them, just to see what they would say and compare notes with the soldiers. The only disadvantage would be that I should be inundated with applications to give similar retreats in other convents, everyone being so delighted with the experiment, especially the good Mother Bursar who would simply coin money!

On the road once more in strict fighting kit, the clothes we stood in, a rain coat and a stout heart. A miserable night with a cold wind driving the drizzling rain in our faces and the ground underfoot being rapidly churned into a quagmire of slush and mud. I hope the Recording Angel will not be afraid of the weather and will not get tired of counting the steps as I did: 'Ten thousand and one, ten thousand and two' – a bit monotonous even with the story of the old hermit to help one.

The road was a sight never to be forgotten. On one side marched our columns in close formation, on the other galloped by an endless line of ammunition waggons, extra guns hurrying up to the Front, and motor lorries packed with stores of all kinds, while between the two flowed back the stream of empties and ambulance after ambulance filled with wounded and dying.

In silence save for the never ceasing roar of the guns and the rumble of cart wheels we marched on through the city of the dead – Ypres, not a little anxious for a shower of shells might come at any minute. Ruin and desolation, desolation and ruin is the only description I can give of a spot once the pride and glory of Belgium. The hand of war has fallen heavy on the city of Ypres: scarce a stone remains of the glorious cathedral and equally famous Cloth Hall; the churches, a dozen of them, are piles of rubbish: gone are the convents, the hospitals and public buildings and though many of the inhabitants are still there, their bodies lie buried in the ruins of their homes and the smell of rotting corpses poisons the air. I have seen strange sights in the last two years, but this was the worst of all.

THE START OF ANOTHER BATTLE

Ruins of Ypres

Out again by the opposite gate of this stricken spot, which people say was not undeserving of God's chastisement, across the moat and along the road, pitted all over with half filled shell holes. Broken carts and dead horses, with human bodies too if one looked, lie on all sides, but one is too weary to think of anything except how many more miles must be covered.[26]

Hence Willie Doyle and his men found themselves at the Menin Gate to meet their guides from 164th Brigade (50th Division), to whom they were temporarily attached. His narrative continues:

A welcome halt at last with, perhaps, an hour or more delay. The men were already stretched by the side of the road and I was not slow to follow their *example. I often used to wonder how anyone can sleep lying in mud or water, but at that moment the <u>place</u> for sleep, as far as I was concerned, did not matter two straws, anywhere would do to satisfy the longing for even a few moments slumber after nearly two days and nights of marching without sleep.*

I picked out a soft spot on the ruins of a home, lay me down with a sigh of relief and then, for all I cared, all the King's guns and the Kaiser combined might roar till they were hoarse and all the rain in Heaven might fall as it was falling then, I was too tired and happy to bother.[27]

The 8th Dubs eventually set off, reaching Reserve Trench at Congreve Walk, north-east of the Vinery, at 10.15 p.m. Battalion Headquarters was close by at the mound of the chateau attached to Potijze cross-roads. The transcription of Willie's budget continues dated 1 August and here the timeline becomes confusing. He refers to the morning (1 August) as if he had only just arrived at headquarters, whereas the 8th Dubs' War Diary recorded the staff reaching there at 10.15 p.m. the previous night. Willie says:

It required a big effort to believe that this raw, bleak morning was the first of the hottest summer month, glorious August! The rain had made the clay as slippery as ice and the semi-darkness added a spice of excitement to the adventure.

I was chuckling over the disappearance of an officer in front of me into a friendly trench, from which he emerged, if possible, a little more muddy than he was, when I felt my two legs shoot from under me and I vanished down the side of a shell-hole which I had not noticed. As I am not making a confession of my whole life I shall not tell you what I said, but it was something different from the exclamation of the pious old gentleman who used to mutter: 'Tut, tut' every time he missed the golf ball.

The Head Quarters Staff found shelter in an old mine shaft, dark, foul-smelling and dripping water which promised soon to flood us out. Still, it was some protection from the down-pour outside and I slept like a top for some hours in a dry corner, sitting on a coil of wire (no, not barbed wire! I get enough pin-pricks without that.)[28]

Given the circumstances, it's not really surprising that Willie became a little confused in his haste, later, to write up the account. He continues:

Morning brought a leaden sky, more rain and no breakfast! Our cook with the rations had got lost during the night, so there was nothing for it but to tighten one's belt and bless the man (backwards) who invented eating. He who feeds the 'birds of the air' would not forget us and by mid-day we were sitting down before a steaming tin of tea, bully beef and biscuits, a banquet fit to set before the Emperor of China himself, after nearly 24 hours' fast.

Not for a moment during the whole of that day did the merciless rain cease. The men, soaked to the skin and beyond it, were standing up to their knees in a river of mud and water and like ourselves were unable to get any hot food till the afternoon. Our only consolation was that our trenches were sheltered and we had no casualties. Someone must have had compassion on our plight, for when night fell a new Brigade came in to relieve us, much to our relief and joy.[29]

Men from 8th Dubs had formed a working party for burying the dead of 55th Division, along with their brigade colleagues 2nd Royal Dublin Fusiliers. (Presumably 55th Division's own chaplains officiated if, indeed, they were able to conduct any sort of funeral services.) As gruesome a duty as this was, they may have regarded themselves lucky, compared to remaining with the rest of the battalion, standing up to their knees in filthy water, just waiting. Willie continues:

Back to the camp we had left the previous night, one of the hardest marches I ever put in, but cheered at the thought of a rest. Once again we got through Ypres without a shell, though they fell before and after our passing, good luck was on our side for once. Here we remain for a couple of days busy with pick and shovel, digging the mud out of clothes and here I must close this diary, for the present, until our next operations are over.[30]

On Wednesday 1 August 1917, *The Times* newspaper in Britain proclaimed:

Great Allied Attack. Ypres Salient Widened. Two Miles' Advance.

In fact, the Salient had not been widened and at the most important point the advance was only a third of a mile; the average gain was nowhere near two miles and the centre of the line remained exposed in an uncomfortable salient. No ridges were captured and the main German line was not reached, let alone broken.

> *The human cost of this limited achievement had been staggering. The Fifth Army had suffered 27,000 casualties killed wounded and missing and the Second Army some 4,500, whilst the relatively fortunate French had lost under 2,000. Battalions full of strong fit men, forged by their training and previous battle experiences, had been reduced to husks. Even the strongest could not help but be moved by the scale of the losses and the suffering etched on the faces of those who had survived.[31]*

Company Sergeant-Major John Handley, 1/6th Bn King's Liverpool Regiment, 165th Brigade, 55th Division remembered:

> *On marching back behind Ypres, Brigadier Duncan, that hard stern soldier whom we feared, stood by the roadside taking the salute. 'March to attention!' rang out the order; then 'Eyes right!' and as we turned our heads we saw him standing erect, his right arm raised in the 'salute' and tears streaming down his face. It was indeed a sorry brigade he saluted that day – the remnants of battle – for barely a quarter of his men returned.[32]*

Thus General Gough's plans for a quick advance had been thwarted, and an already exhausted 16th (Irish) Division were about to enter the fray, to play a significant part in the continuation of the Third Battles of Ypres.

CHAPTER 30
FATEFUL AUGUST:
MUCK, MUD AND MIRE

'July 31 to Aug 12: In and out of line on Frezenberg sector. Hell all the time! Mud awful, no trenches, no shelters, no landmarks. All movement by night, shellfire all the time and everywhere casualties enormous! Several killed every day and wounded every hour. Aug 13: Rotten time in bivouacs near Vlamertinghe. Bombing every night, rain every day and shelling all the time. Iron rations. Aug 14: Move up line to our fates.'
Captain Arthur Glanville, 2nd Bn Royal Dublin Fusiliers[1]

Willie's next entry in his budget commenced on Sunday 5 August, continuing the narrative he described as 'Part 1 of *The Battle of Ypres;*' a gap of four days had elapsed since his last entry. Willie continues with this diary type narrative for his father until 12 August, when he sends it with a covering letter. Having read Fr Doyle's experiences since arriving in the Ypres area to date, and those events to follow, it really is quite extraordinary that he managed to summon up the energy to write home at such length. Captain Staniforth of 7th Leinsters also wrote home on 5 August 1917:

This is the first time I have managed to get a line through to you. The battle still goes on – haven't had a wash since Tuesday (this is Sunday!) or a bite of hot food, and been soaked through all the time! The state of the ground between rain and shell-fire is absolutely indescribable.[2] [FN1]

Lieutenant Colonel R.G.B. Jeffreys, 2nd Royal Dublin Fusiliers, recorded in his diary three days previously:

I think I have just got through the worst 24 hours I have put in in this country. We were under a great deal of shell fire down in a filthy mine shaft, *dead all around us and so wet, that no matter where one walked, one was well over the ankles. The task of collecting the dead was terrible and the men slipping about in all directions.*³ ᶠᴺ²

In addition to men of Willie's 8th Royal Dublin Fusiliers having been engaged in burial duties, others were attached for various other divisional duties. Although 16th (Irish) Division was in Corps Reserve, many of its men were used in forward areas to make up carrying parties and to perform fatigue duties (some, indeed, were front-line reinforcements) toiling in the swamps of the Steenbeek and Hanebeek valleys where they were vulnerable to German fire.

On Saturday 4 August a party of 8th RDF was sent out from Erie Camp to reconnoitre the line of the battalion's forthcoming move to the firing line, during which 2nd Lieutenant S. Morris was injured at the appropriately named Hell Fire Corner. This formed a junction on the Menin Road running eastwards from Ypres to the Front Line, following the route along which all troop and supply movements were made. The busy supply routes were under constant observation and fire by Germans on the high ground. Consequently, all movements took place under cover of darkness and at Hell Fire Corner canvas screens had been erected beside the road to camouflage the route and to give troop and traffic movements some shelter from direct observation by the enemy. The battalion was to move into a front-line position on the Sunday evening. Willie writes earlier in the day, before setting off:

> **All day I have been busy hearing the mens' confessions and giving batch after batch Holy Communion. A consolation, surely, to see them crowding to the Sacraments, but a sad one too because I know for many of them it is the last Absolution they will ever receive and the next time they meet Our Blessed Lord will be when they see Him face to face in Heaven.**
>
> **My poor brave boys! They are lying now out on the battlefield, some in a little grave, dug and blessed by the chaplain who loves them all as if they were his own children, others stiff and stark with staring eyes, hidden in a shell-hole where they had crept to die while, perhaps, in some far off thatched cabin an anxious mother sits listening for the well-known steps and voice which will never gladden her ear again. Do you wonder, in spite of the joy that fills my heart, that many a time the tears gather in my eyes as I think of those who are gone?**⁴

Whilst Willie refers to 'his' boys lying out on the battlefield, the 8th Bn Royal Dublin Fusiliers had not yet been in actual fighting action during this opening phase of the Third Ypres campaign. However, they had been working close to the front lines, under shell-fire, to keep the line occupied and supplied, taking casualties from ordnance and gas; it is important also to remember that Willie regarded all Irishmen as his 'boys', including the 36th (Ulster) Division, whom Willie had taken to his heart (and vice versa). The 36th Division's War Diary report for early August commented:

To cope with the work in the forward area – principally in making of tracks, roads and gun emplacements, etc. large working parties – running into close on 1,000 men a day – had to be furnished.[5]

The War Diary entry for 6th Connaught Rangers of 2 August 1917 paints a similar picture:

A stretcher bearing party of 200 men (50 from each company) under 2nd Lt. J.J. Pope was out working for the 55th Division from 2am to 11am searching for and bringing in wounded from the area covered by the old German front system ... Their task was very arduous and under the most trying conditions and the way in which it was carried out was acknowledged in the attached letter from the G.O.C.'s 16th and 55th Divisions.[6]

Two days later, the 8th Dubs were preparing to relieve another 16th (Irish) Division battalion in the Front Line. Willie continues:

As the men stand lined up on parade I go from Company to Company giving a General Absolution, which I know is a big comfort to them, and then I shoulder my pack and make for the train which this time is to carry us part of our journey. 'Top end for Blighty, boys, bottom end Berlin,' I tell them as they clamber in, for they like a cheery word. 'If you are for Jerryland, Father, we're with you too' shouts a big giant, which is greeted with a roar of approval and Berlin wins the day hands down.[7]

The War Diary recorded that at 6 p.m. on 5 August the battalion started their journey from Erie Camp by train to a location called Asylum in the centre of Ypres; thence they marched out of the city, initially along the Menin Road, before branching off at Hellfire Corner to relieve the 1st Bn Royal Munster Fusiliers on their section of the Blue Line. Willie continues his narrative:

Though we are in fighting kit there is no small load to carry. A haversack containing little things and three days' rations which consist of tinned corn-beef hard biscuits, tea and sugar with usually some solidified methylated spirit for boiling water when a fire cannot be lighted. The full water bottles, a couple of gas helmets, the new one weighing nine pounds, but guaranteed to keep out the Old Boy himself, then a water-proof trench coat and, in addition, my Mass kit strapped on my back on the off-chance that some days at least I may be able to offer the Holy Sacrifice on the spot where so many men have fallen. My orderly should carry this but I prefer to leave him behind when we go into action, to which he does not object.

On a roasting hot day tramping along a dusty road, or scrambling up and down shell-holes, the extra weight tells, but then I think of my friend the hermit and the pack grows light and easy. As I marched through Ypres at the head of the column an officer ran across the road and stopped me. 'Are you a Catholic priest' he asked 'I should like to go to Confession.' There and then, by the side of the road, while the men marched by, he made his peace with God and went away let us hope as happy as I felt at that moment. It was a trivial incident but it brought home vividly to me what a priest was and the wondrous power given him by God.

All the time we were pushing on steadily towards our goal, across the battlefield of the previous week. Five days almost continuously, rain had made the bare ground worse than any ploughed field, but none seemed to care, as so far not a shot had fallen here. We were congratulating ourselves on our good luck when suddenly the storm burst. Away along the front trenches we saw the 'S.O.S.' alarm signal shoot into the air, two red and two green rockets telling the artillery behind that the Boche were attacking and calling for support. There was little need to send any signal as the enemy's guns had opened fire with a crash and in a moment Pandemonium, in fact fifty of them, were let loose.[8]

This section of the Blue Line, which the 8th Dubs were approaching to take over from the 1st Munsters, was at Frezenberg. Willie continues his narrative:

I can but describe the din by asking you to start together fifty first class thunder storms, though even then the swish and scream, the deafening crash of the shells would be wanting. On we hurried in the hope of reaching cover which was close at hand, when right before us the Hun started to put down a heavy barrage, literally a curtain of shells, to prevent reinforcements coming up. There was no getting through that alive and, to make matters worse, the barrage was creeping nearer, only fifty yards away, while shell fragments hummed by like 'a woman with her dander up!

Old shell holes there were in abundance but every one of them was brim full of water and one would only float on top. Here was a fix! Yet somehow I felt that though the boat seemed in a bad way, the Master was watching even while He seemed to sleep and help would surely come. In the darkness I stumbled across a huge shell-crater recently made, with no water. Into it we rolled and lay on our faces while the tempest howled around, and angry shells hissed overhead and burst on every side.

For a few moments I shivered with fear for we were now right in the middle of the barrage and the danger was very great, but my courage came back when I remembered how easily He, Who had raised the tempest, saved His apostles from it and I never doubted He would do the same for us. Not a man was touched, though one had his rifle smashed to bits.[9]

Not a man was touched in Willie's immediate vicinity, but there were casualties. The War Diary dryly noted that:

Relief impeded by barrage brought down by SOS on way up. 2/2 T. Roberts and 6 men wounded. 1 missing.[10]

When the relief was finally completed, the disposition of the individual companies of 8th Dubs was: 'A' Company on the right by the railway line, 'B' in the centre and 'C' on the left. Behind them in support was 'D' Company in the ruins of Bill Cottage, and Battalion Headquarters had been set up in an old German dug-out in Wilde Wood. In front of them were fearsome concrete German strongpoints and camouflaged battery positions: the immediate obstacles to be contended with were Borry Farm, Vampir and Potsdam.

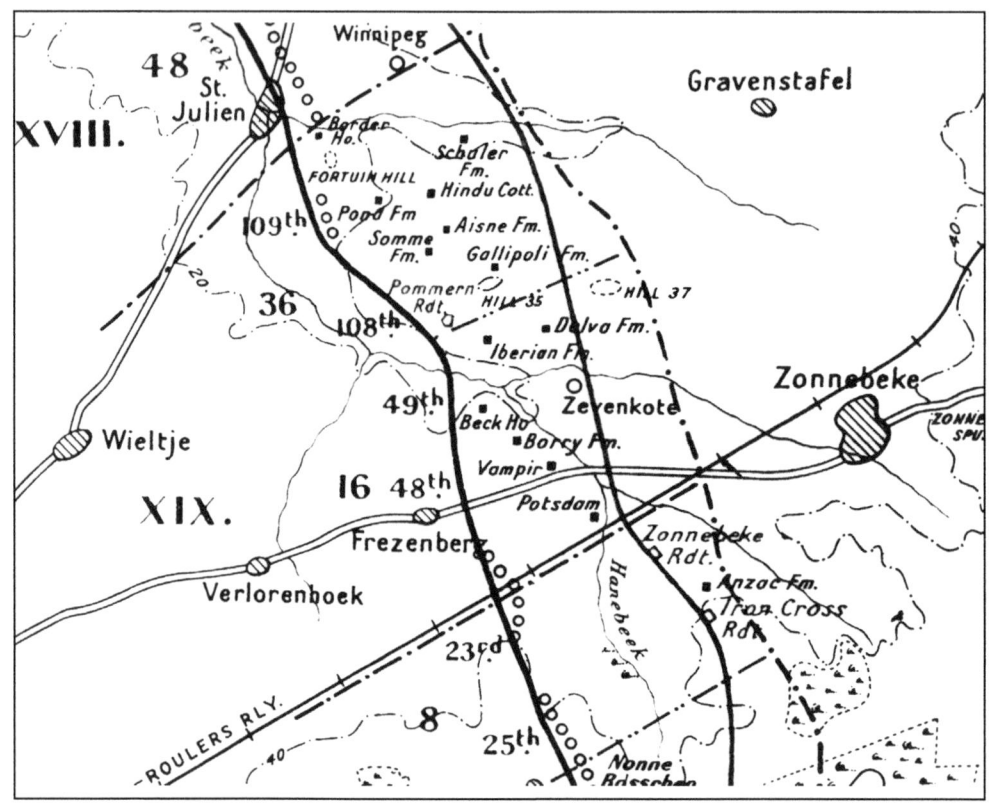

A map of Frezenberg area, August 1917

Major Stirke, Captains Cowley and Healy, and Second Lieutenants Wilmore, Mallan and Anderson, with eighty men, were kept back as 'battle surplus' at detail camp,[FN3] so that a nucleus of the battalion would remain available in the event of some catastrophic incident. Major Stirke was soon called upon. Willie continues:

> *We reached Head Quarters, a strong block-house made of concrete and iron rails, a masterpiece of German cleverness. From time to time, all during the night, the enemy gunners kept firing at our shelter, having the range to a nicety. Scores exploded within a few feet of it, shaking us till our bones rattled: a few went smash against the walls and roof and one*

burst at the entrance nearly blowing us over, but doing no harm, thanks to the scientific construction of the passage.[11]

The staff at Battalion HQ came to no harm, on this occasion, but the following day the battalion came under very severe shelling resulting in two soldiers being killed, and twenty-three wounded. A day later, on Tuesday 7 August, the H.Q. staff had a different experience, and the War Diary recorded:

3 am HQ staff asphyxiated by explosions of several boxes of Verrey lights by a German shell which landed in entrance to dug-out. Captain Sheridan took command. Lt Col Kenny, 2 Lt Jackson (adjt) 2/Lts Walsh & Manley wounded at Hqs. 2/Lt Marlow wounded at duty. 9 am 2/Lt Hughes wounded by accidental explosion of a bomb. 10 am Major Stirke arrived from detail camp and took command: 2/Lt Anderson came up later as Adjutant. K 10, W31, Missing 1: mostly shell fire.[12]

Willie mentions this incident at Headquarters in passing, but keeps the details for another time as he had obviously tired of writing his budget and wanted to get it in the post. He ends thus:

Here I had my second marvellous escape, which I shall relate in due course. I tried to get a few winks of sleep on a stool, there was no room to lie down with sixteen men in a small hut and I came to the conclusion that so far we had not done badly and there was every prospect of an exciting time.[13]

This portion of the budget was posted to *Melrose* with a covering note dated 12 August:

Dearest Father, when I finished writing the last line I could not help asking myself should I ever continue this little narrative of my adventures and experiences, for we were under marching orders to make our way that night to the front Line, a series of shell-holes in the ground won from the enemy. To hold this we knew would be no easy task, but I little thought of what lay before us, or of the hardships and sufferings which were to be crowded into the next few days.

It is Sunday morning, 12 August. We have just got back to camp after (for me at least) six days and seven nights on the battlefield. There was no chance last night of a moment's rest and you may imagine there was little sleep the previous nights either, sitting on a box with one's feet in twelve inches of water! For the past forty-eight hours we have lived, eat and slept in a flooded dug-out which you left at the peril of your life, so you may fancy what a relief it was to change one's sodden, muddy clothes.

Tired as I am I cannot rest till I try to give you some account of what has happened, for I know you must be on the look-out for news of your boy, and also because my heart is bursting to tell you of God's love and protection, never so manifest as during this week. He has shielded me from almost countless dangers with more than the tender care of an earthly mother – what I have to say sounds in parts almost like a fairy tale – and if He has tried my endurance, once at least almost to breaking point, it was only to fill me with joy at the thought that I 'was deemed worthy to suffer (a little) for Him'.

I shall give you, as simply as I can, the principal events of those exciting days, as I jotted them down in my little notebook.[14]

With the first part of his budget safely despatched, Willie picked up the thread again in the next part of his detailed narrative, which takes up the story from Monday 6 August 1917. As before, he provided a specific heading for this part of his budget:

Private: Not to Be Copied
The Battle of Ypres Part 2

If you look up the daily papers of these days you will find little recorded. There were a few attacks and counter-attacks and we pushed forward our line a little on the flank, but the state of the ground from the constant rain made movement impossible. Incidentally it added much to our bodily discomfort and spiritual joy à la Hermit!

We lived in water; we revelled (and rolled many a time) in mud, thick, yellow, sticky mud and horrible, foul smelling, black slime. Once I indulged in the luxury of a clean pair of socks and five minutes after trying to get to a wounded man fell into a pool up to my knees, so gave up trying to keep dry in despair. There being no Good Shepherd laundry on the battlefield, at which I wonder! – we dried our socks and clothes (or to be truthful tried to) by sleeping in them, then the first thing in the morning gave them a good wash in the rain, or by slipping into an obliging shell-hole.

Trying to wash your face and hands was the one unforgiveable sin, as water is more precious than diamonds. Some had courage, if they got the chance, which did not always offer, to perform their ablutions in the ditch, though it meant you smelt like a walking Glasnevin for hours afterwards. I spent the first night, as I said, at Battalion Head-Quarters, but the following morning, though the Colonel and other officers pressed me very much to remain with them on the grounds that I would be more comfortable, I felt I could do better work at the advanced dressing station, or rather aid post, and went and joined the Doctor.[15]

The doctor and the dressing station would have been located just behind the supporting company at Bill Cottage. Willie describes his location later, but for the moment he continues with the story of the explosion at Headquarters in Wilde Wood (see colour photo of trench map):

It was a providential step and saved me from being the victim of an extraordinary accident. The following night a shell again burst at the entrance to the block-house, as it had done our first night there, but this time exploded several boxes of 'Very Lights' (or rockets) which had been left at the door. A mass of flame and dense smoke rushed into the dug-out, severely burning some, and almost suffocating all the officers and men, fifteen in number, with poisonous fumes before they made their escape. Had I been there I should have shared the same fate, so you can imagine what I felt as I saw all my friends carried to hospital, possibly to suffer ill effects for life, while I, by the merest chance, was left behind, well and strong to carry on God's work.[16]

Following this narrow escape, Willie's first priority was, as ever, to improvise as necessary in order to be able to celebrate Mass:

I'm afraid you will think me ungrateful, but more than once I almost regretted my escape so great has been the strain of these past days, now happily over. For once getting out of bed (save the mark) was easy, in fact a delightful task for I was stiff and sore from my night's rest. My first task was to look round and see what were the possibilities for Mass. As all the dug-outs were occupied, if not destroyed or flooded, I was delighted to discover a tiny ammunition store which I speedily converted into a chapel, building an altar with the boxes. The fact that it barely held myself did not signify, as I had no server, and had to be both priest and acolyte and in a way I was not sorry I could not stand up as I was able, for once, to offer the Holy Sacrifice on my knees. It is strange that out here a desire I have long cherished should be gratified, viz to be able to celebrate alone, taking as much time as I wished and not inconveniencing anyone.

I read long ago, in the acts of the Martyrs, of a captive priest chained to the floor of the Coliseum (sic) prison offering up Mass on the altar of his own bared breast, but apart from that, my Mass that morning must have been a strange one in the eyes of God's angels and, I trust, not unacceptable to Him.[17]

Willie goes on to describe a typical dressing station and, in particular, the current one he was operating from:

Returning to the dressing station I refreshed the inner man in preparation for a hard day's work. You may be curious to know what an 'Aid Post' is like. Get out of your mind all ideas of a clean hospital ward, for our First Aid dressing-station is any place, as near as possible to the fighting line, which will afford a little shelter – a cellar, a coal-hole, sometimes even a shell-hole. Here the wounded, who have been roughly bandaged on the battlefield, are brought by the stretcher bearers to be dressed by the doctor.

Our Aid Post was a rough tin shed built beside a concrete dug-out, which we christened the 'Pig Sty'. You could just crawl in on hands and knees to the solitary chamber which served as a dressing room, recreation hall, sleeping apartment and anything else you cared to use it for. One could not very well sit up, much less stand in our chateau, but you could stretch your legs and get a snooze if the Boche shells and wounded men let you. On the floor were some wood-shavings, kept well moistened in damp weather by a steady drip from the ceiling and which gave cover to a host of curious little creatures, all most friendly and affectionate. There was room for three, but as a rule we slept six or seven, officers side by side. I had the post of honour next to the wall, which had the double advantage of keeping me cool and damp and of offering a stout resistance if anyone wanted to pinch more space, not an easy task you may well conclude. I spent a good part of the day, when not occupied with the wounded, wandering around the battlefield with a spade to bury stray dead. Though, as I said, there was not much infantry fighting owing to the state of the ground, not for a moment during the week did the artillery duel cease, reaching at times a pitch of unimaginable intensity. I have been through some hot stuff at Loos, and the Somme was warm enough for most of us, but neither of them could be compared to the fierceness of the German fire here.

For example, we counted once some 50 shells, big chaps too, whistling over our little nest in 60 seconds not counting those which burst close by: in fact one became so accustomed to it all that one ceased to bother about them, unless some battery started strafing your particular position, when you began to feel a little personal interest in every newcomer. I have walked about for hours at a time getting through my work with 'crumps' of all sizes bursting in dozens on every side. More than once my heart has nearly jumped out of my mouth from sudden terror, but not once during all these days have I had what I could call a 'narrow escape', and ever a strange, confident feeling of trust and security in the all powerful protection of Our Blessed Lord.

You will see before the end that my trust was not misplaced. All the same I am not fool-hardy, nor do I expose myself to danger unnecessarily, the coward is too strong in me for that, but <u>when</u> duty calls I know I can count on the help of One who has never failed as yet.[18]

Willie's next entry has been transcribed as 7 August, but actually must have been 8 August. The battalion War Diary for that day recorded that the 8th Dubs was relieved by the 9th Dubs at 3.30 a.m. A counter-attack during the relief and heavy bombardment by gas shells caused casualties to both the incoming and the departing battalions. Four and a half hours later the weary 8th Dubs passed Ecole on the way to Vlamertinghe Number 3 camp. Willie, however, was not with them. He continues his narrative:

> *No Mass this morning thanks, I suppose, to the kindly attention of the Evil One. I reached my chapel of the previous morning only to find that a big 9.5 inch shell had landed on the top of it during the day; I went away feeling very grateful I had not been inside at the time, but had to abandon thought of Mass as no shelter could be found from the heavy rain.*
>
> *The battalion went out today for three days' rest, but I remained behind. Father Browne has gone back to the Irish Guards. He is a tremendous loss not only to myself generally, but to the whole Brigade, where he did magnificent work and made the best of friends, and so I was left alone. Another chaplain was appointed, but for reasons best known to himself, he did not take over his battalion and let them go into the fight alone. There was nothing else for it but to remain on and do his work, and glad I was I did so, for many a man went down that night, the majority of whom I was able to assist.*[19]

Instead of the three days rest Willie refers to, the 8th Dubs only benefitted from one day back behind the lines at Vlamertinghe. At 6pm on Thursday 9 August they set off once more to relieve the 9th Dubs, following heavy losses by their colleagues. The men of the 9th Dubs, who Fr Doyle had remained with, were at a more advanced position on the Black Line. They had been subject to an intense enemy bombardment and suffered severe casualties, especially in their 'C' Company; from which the Officer Commanding, plus two other Second Lieutenants, were killed, and:

> *2/Lt. J. McGrath was the only officer left in C Coy and did valuable work in keeping the coy together under most distressing circumstances.*[20]

Willie continues the narrative of his extended spell in the front line with the 9th Royal Dublin Fusiliers:

> *Word reached me about Midnight that a party of men had been caught by shell-fire nearly a mile away. I dashed off in the darkness, this time*

hugging my helmet, as the Boche was firing gas-shells. A moment's pause to absolve a couple of dying men and then I reached the group of smashed and bleeding bodies, most of them still breathing. The first thing I saw almost unnerved me, a young soldier lying on his back, his hands and face a mass of blue phosphorous flame, smoking horribly in the darkness. He was the first victim I had seen of the new gas which the Germans are using, a fresh horror in this awful war. The poor lad recognised me as I anointed him on a little spot of unburnt flesh, not a little nervously, as the place was reeking with gas, gave him a drink which he begged for so earnestly and then hastened to the others.[21]

The new gas Willie refers to was mustard gas, as described in the 6th Connaught Rangers' War Diary:

During the night (3 August) *shelling was again heavy and the battalion had its first experience of the new mustard gas employed by the enemy, the shells being cleverly mixed with whizz-bangs.*[22]

Willie was less enamoured with the ingenuity of the delivery of the gas, as he continues:

Back again to the Aid Post for stretchers to help to carry in the wounded, while all the time the shells are coming down like hail. Good God! How can any human being live in this?

As I hurry back I hear that two men have been hit twenty yards away. I am with them in a moment, splashing through mud and water, a quick Absolution, the last Rites of the Church, and a flash from a gun shows me that the poor boy in my arms is my own servant, or rather one who took the place of my orderly while he was away. His name is Corporal Threfall a wonderfully good and pious lad who had an aunt in New Hall convent where Frank's sister is (could you please send me the correct address as I should like to write to her.)'

By the time we reach the first party all were dead, most of them with charred hands and faces. One man with a pulverised leg was still living. I saw him off to hospital, made as comfortable as could be, but could not help thinking of the torture as the stretcher jolted over the rough road ground, up and down the shell-holes.

Little rest that night for the Boche simply pelted us with gas-shells of every description, which thanks to our new helmets did no harm. Fritz is an expert in gas torture. He has long treated us to weeping shells and many an unrepentant tear have I shed; now he has some stuff which tickles your throat and nose like pepper, making you sneeze like a soda water bottle; a gas which burns your hands and face and a beast of a thing which gives you all the delights of a rough sea voyage; hence you can have quite a lively time if you wish to.[23]

Having relieved, without incident, the battered battalion of 9th RDF, the company dispositions of 8th RDF now found 'C' on the right, 'D' on the left, 'B' in right support and 'A' in left support. Battalion Headquarters was at Frezenberg Redoubt. Captain Cowley was the only officer left at detail camp with about sixty men.

Captain Staniforth of 7th Leinsters describes the Frezenberg Redoubt around about this time, thus:

It was the German brigade-head-quarters, and consisted of an underground concrete fortress on the highest point in the neighbourhood, just beside the cross-roads that marks the site of FREZENBERG VILLAGE – now more utterly destroyed even than Guillemont and Ginchy. Inside were five compartments; living rooms, sleeping rooms, servants and orderlies' quarters, etc. In all it had about the accommodation of a large-sized flat.[24]

Willie continues, bringing a lighter tone to his narrative:

There is little to record during the next couple of days, except the discovery of a new cathedral and the happiness of daily Mass. This time I was not quite so well off, as I could not kneel upright and my feet were in the water, which helped to keep the fires of devotion from growing too warm. Having carefully removed an ancient German leg I managed to rest by sitting on the ground, a new rubric I had to introduce also at the Communion, otherwise I could not have emptied the Chalice. I feel that when I get home again I shall be absolutely miserable because everything will be so clean and dry and comfortable. Perhaps some kind friend will pour a bucket or two of water over my head occasionally to keep me in good spirits.[25]

Frezenberg

The 8th RDF had set off from Vlamertinghe at 6pm on 9 August and remained in the front line until 3am on Sunday 12 August, when they were relieved by 1st Royal Munster Fusiliers. Prior to that, Willie had more work to do in the most dangerous zone, as he describes:

When night fell I made my way up to a part of the line which could not be approached in daylight to bury an officer and some men. A couple of grimy unwashed figures emerged from the bowels of the earth to help me, but first knelt down and asked for Absolution. Then leisurely set to work to fill in the grave. 'Hurry up boys', I said, 'I don't want to have to bury you as well', for the spot was a hot one. They both stopped working much to my disgust, for I was just longing to get away. 'Be gobs, Father', replied one, 'I haven't the divil a bit of fear in me now after the holy Absolution.' 'Nor I', chimed in the other, 'I am as happy as a king.' The poor Padre, who had been keeping his eye on a row of 'crumps' which were coming unpleasantly near, felt anything but happy; however, there was nothing for it but to stick it out as the men were in a pious mood and he escaped at last, grateful he was not asked to say the rosary.

 10 August: *A sad morning as casualties were heavy and many men came in dreadfully wounded.*[26]

The 8th RDF War Diary for that morning recorded heavy casualties caused by a barrage attack on the right, which killed nine and wounded twenty-three, including three Second Lieutenants, two severely. Willie continues his narrative:

One man was the bravest I ever met. He was in dreadful agony, for both legs had been blown off at the knee, but never a complaint fell from his lips even while they dressed his wounds and he tried to make light of his injuries. 'Thank God Father,' he said 'I am able to stick it out to the end. Is it not all for little Belgium?' The Extreme Unction, as I have noticed time and again eased his bodily pain. 'I am so much better now and easier, God Bless You,' as I left him to attend a dying man.

 He opened his eyes as I knelt beside him: 'Ah! Father Doyle, Father Doyle', he whispered faintly and then motioned me to bend lower, as if he had some message to give. As I did so, he got his two arms round my neck and hugged me. It was all the great fellow could do to show his gratitude that he had not been left to die alone and that he would have the consolation of receiving the last Sacraments before he went to God.

 Sitting a little way off I saw a hideous bleeding object, a man with his face smashed by a shell with one, if not both, eyes torn out. He raised his head as I spoke: 'Is that the priest? Thank God I am all right now.' I took his blood-covered hands in mine as I searched his face for some whole spot on which to anoint him and I think I know better now why Pilate said: 'Behold the Man' when he showed Our Lord to the people.

 In the afternoon while going my rounds I was forced to take shelter in the dug-out of a young officer belonging to another regiment. For nearly two hours I was a prisoner and found out he was a Catholic, come from

Dublin, and had been married just a month. Was this a chance visit or did God send me there to prepare him death, for I had not long left the spot when a shell burst and killed him. I carried his body out the next day and buried him in a shell-hole and once again I blessed that Protecting Hand which had shielded me from his fate.[27]

The bombardment continued into the early hours of Saturday 11 August, wounding four Second Lieutenants, including Frank Laird, [FN4] plus Major Stirke. Five Other Ranks were killed, seventeen wounded and one man was missing. Communications were impossible. Willie continues:

That night we moved Head Quarters and Aid Post to a more advanced position, a strong concrete emplacement but a splendid target for German gunners. For the 40 hours we were there they hammered us almost constantly, day and night, till I thought our last hour had come. There we lived with a foot, sometimes more, of water on the floor, pretty well soaked through for it was raining hard at times. Sleep was almost impossible - fifty shells a minute made some noise - and to venture out without necessity was foolishness. We were well provided with tinned food and a spirit lamp for making hot tea, so that we were not too badly off and rather enjoyed hearing the Hun shells hopping off the roof, or bursting on the walls of his own strong fort.'

Close beside us I had found the remains of a dug-out which had been blown in the previous day and three men killed. I made up my mind to offer up Mass there for the repose of their souls, in any case 'I did not know a better hole to go to' and to this little act of charity I attribute the saving of my life later in the day. I had barely fitted up my altar when a couple of shells burst overhead sending the clay tumbling down. For a moment I felt very tempted not to continue, as the place was far from safe, but I was glad later I went on, as the Holy Souls certainly came to my aid, as I did to theirs.

I had finished breakfast and had ventured a bit down the trench to find a spot to bury some bodies left lying there. I had reached a sheltered corner when I heard the scream of a shell coming towards me rapidly and, judging by the sound, straight for the spot where I stood. Instinctively I crouched down, and well I did so, for the shell whizzed past my head – I felt my hair blown about by the hot air, and burst in front of me with a deafening crash. It seemed to me as if a heavy wooden hammer had hit me on the top of the head and I reeled like a drunken man, my ears ringing with the explosion. For a moment I stood wondering how many pieces of shrapnel had hit me, or how many legs and arms I had left and then dashed through the thick smoke to save myself from being buried alive by the shower of falling clay which was rapidly covering me. I hardly knew how I reached the dug-out for I was speechless and so badly shaken that it was only by a tremendous effort I was able to protect myself from collapsing utterly, as I had seen so many do from shell-shock.[28]

Shell-shock is a controversial subject in relation to the Great War and it is interesting that Fr Doyle refers to it. His narrative continues:

Then a strange thing happened, something seemed to whisper in my ear, one of those sudden thoughts which flash through the mind: 'Did not that shell come from the hand of God? He willed it should be so? Is it not a proof that He can protect you no matter what the danger?' The thought that it was all God's doing acted like a tonic, my nerves calmed down and shortly after I was out again to see could I meet another iron friend. As a matter of fact I wanted to see exactly what had happened, for the report of the H.E. shell is so terrific that one is apt to exaggerate distances. An officer recently assured me he was only one foot from a bursting shell, when in reality he was a good 40 yards away!

You may find it hard to believe, as I do myself, what I saw. I had been standing in a corner made by a trellis work of thin sticks. By stretching out my hand I could touch the screen and the shell fell <u>smashing the woodwork!</u> My escape last year at Loos was wonderful, but then I was some yards away and partly protected by a bend in the trench; here the shell fell, I might say, at my very feet, there was no bank, no protection except the wall of your good prayers and the protecting arm of God.[29]

In the early hours of Sunday 12 August the relief took place. Once again an enemy bombardment started as the battalions made their change-over. One Other Rank of the 8th RDF was killed, four men were wounded and seven men were missing. Eventually, they arrived at Erie camp after a tortuous journey, which Willie describes:

That night we were relieved, or rather it was very early morning 4.30 a.m. when the last Company marched out. I went with them so that I might leave no casualties behind. We hurried over the open as fast as we could, floundering in the thick mud, tripping over wire in the darkness and, I hope some of the lay members cursing the Hun gunners for disturbing us by an odd shot. We had nearly reached the road, not knowing it was a marked spot, when like a hurricane a shower of shells came smashing down upon us. We were fairly caught and for once I almost lost hope of getting through in safety.

For five minutes or more we pushed on in desperation; we could not stop to shelter, for dawn was breaking and we should have been seen by the enemy. Right and left, in front and behind, some far away, many very close, the shells kept falling. Crash! One has pitched in the middle of the Line wounding five men, none of them seriously. Surely God is good to us, for it seems impossible a single man will escape unhurt and then, just when the end seemed at hand, our batteries opened fire with a roar to support an attack which was beginning. The German guns ceased like magic, or turned their attention elsewhere, we scrambled on to the road and reached home without further loss.[30]

At Erie camp it was established that sixty-six men needed to go to hospital and a draft of twenty-three other ranks, with Second Lieutenant C.J. Doyle, joined from 16th Divisional Depot. On the following day, unlucky thirteen, 2/Lt Doyle had to be taken to hospital.[FN5] Before the evening of Tuesday 14th, Willie Doyle had written his last words home. He completed his budget after arriving back at Erie Camp on the 12 August, which was received at *Melrose* with a covering note dated 14 August 1917. He ends, quite unwittingly and ironically, with the encouraging words:

I have told you all my escapes, dearest Father, because I think what I have written will give you the same confidence which I feel that my old armchair up in Heaven is not ready yet and I do not want you to be uneasy about me. I am all the better for those couple of days' rest and am quite on my fighting legs again. Leave will be possible very shortly I think, so I shall only say au revoir in view of an early meeting. Heaps of love to everyone. As ever dearest Father, Your loving son Willie.[31]

Typically, his last words were designed to put his father's mind at rest, even to the extent of leading Hugh to believe that he had been resting himself, which was highly unlikely. Sadly, he was soon to go to his final rest.

Willie's last letter home

Footnote 1: Captain Staniforth was transferred on 13 August 1917, back behind the lines somewhere in the Pas de Calais, to take command of a company of reinforcements, and so was not involved in the Battle of Langemarck.

Footnote 2: Lieutenant Colonel Jeffreys was sent to Casualty Clearing Station No.12 on 5 August 1917 to be treated for bad sciatica. He remained there until 20 August, then went home for three weeks leave and returned to France on 19 September 1917.

Footnote 3: The War Diary does not offer any further identification of detail camp. This author assumes it would have been at Erie Camp where the majority of the battalion started out from and then returned to.

Footnote 4: Second Lieutenant Frank Laird was returned to 'Blighty' where he recovered and went back to duty. In March 1918 when the Germans launched a major offensive on the Somme front, 2/Lt Laird was temporarily attached to an Entrenching Battalion. When the counter attack started 2/Lt Laird returned to the Royal Dublin Fusiliers, was wounded in action again and was taken prisoner. He was in a Prisoner of War camp until 19 December 1918 and arrived back on friendly soil, at Leith in Scotland, on Christmas Day. Some time between then and 1925 he was asked to give a lecture about his experiences as a POW, for which he wrote up the narrative which formed the last ten chapters of the volume *Personal Experiences of the Great War (an unfinished manuscript)*. He then started writing up his experiences from the outbreak of war onwards, but did not finish before dying some time in 1925. Nevertheless, May G. Laird decided to privately publish the unfinished manuscript, which omits his service between marching back to Locre on 11 June 1917 and March 1918.

Footnote 5: As reported in the War Diary, 2/Lt C.J. Doyle subsequently died, apparently on the same day as Willie, although his name does not appear on the CWGC Debt of Honour Register.

PART 3

FINALE – BUT NOT THE END!

CHAPTER 31
THE OLD ARMCHAIR:
EVERYWHERE AND ALWAYS FAITHFUL

'The soft chimes of the angelus bell mark the fall of evening. Another day is gone. Another precious day, our measurement of God's most precious gift, time, has passed away and is swallowed up in the vast gulf of the irrevocable past. Another day has passed! Another stage of our journey towards our final end is traversed. Nearer still than yesterday to that solemn moment of our lives, its end; nearer still to heaven with its joys unknown, untasted; nearer still to Him for Whom we labour now and strive to serve. How many more days are left? Too few alas! for all we have to do, but not so few that we cannot heap them high with noble deeds and victories bravely won.'

Fr William Doyle, 13 July 1917.[1]

Willie Doyle recorded these words in his diary two days before preaching his last sermon in St Omer Cathedral on 15 July 1917. A little over a month later he was dead. Now, as we approach the end of Willie Doyle's life on this earth, his personal testimony has ended. His final budget had been sent to *Melrose*, and he would write no more to his 'dearest Father'. But, his story continued for a few days longer, and the details can be put together using the unit War Diaries of his beloved Royal Dublin Fusiliers.

From the moment Fr Doyle went into the Front Line near Frezenberg on Sunday 5 August, his final days were largely spent in expending great physical effort to get to and from, and to work in, the firing line; existing in muck, mud and water; under constant, nerve-jangling enemy bombardment; witnessing sights to turn the strongest of stomachs; conscientiously remaining in the front line above and beyond the call of duty; assisting with the injured; burying the dead; performing his sacramental ministry and, above all, easing the passage of the mortally wounded to their maker.

As for the 8th Royal Dublin Fusiliers, they had been decimated in holding the line and could no longer function as a discrete unit. During the period in August in which the 48th Infantry Brigade were in the line prior to going into battle on 16 August, they suffered severe casualties from sickness (mainly owing to the adverse weather conditions), shell fire and gas, which accounted for no fewer than 27 Officers and 678 Other Ranks. (For the three brigades of 16th (Irish) Division as a whole the losses totalled 107 Officers and 1,957 Other Ranks).

The 8th RDF had started to march out of Erie camp at 6 p.m. on 5 August 1917; between then and 3 a.m. on 12 August, they had one spell of 38½ hours away from the Front Line, which including marching time – and another march back in front of them! Fr Doyle remained in the Line for the whole 7½ days under constant bombardment. They had just one full day, 13 August, to regroup at Erie Camp before being mustered for the next stage of the battle.

The 8th Royal Dublin Fusiliers was now divided. Two companies (plus an extra platoon) were attached as carrying parties to the also depleted 9th Royal Dublin Fusiliers and 7th Royal Irish Rifles. Details from the other two companies were sent to Ecole under 2/Lt Kiernan as Reserve Carrying Party and the remainder were formed into a composite company. When the men met their guides at the Menin Gate at 4 p.m. on Tuesday 14 August 1917, to move once again up to the Front Line, only Captains Healy and Sheridan, plus 2/Lt Harris, were left behind at Erie Camp as battle surplus. Fr Doyle had no intention of remaining behind:

> *Major Cowley took in B & D Coys (less 7 Platoon still attached to Bde Carrying Coy) with 2/Lts Peacey, Warren, Marlow, Green, Mallen and Father Doyle as a composite company about eighty strong attached to 2 RDF. Lorries to Asylum: marched thence to line.'*[2]

The Asylum was in the middle of Ypres, north of the railway line. From there the troops made their way through the ruins of the city, moving out through the gateless Menin Gate to the bleak wastelands beyond.

Major Cowley, under whose command Willie now found himself, had been newly promoted because of injuries to senior officers. Two of the five subalterns, Second Lieutenants Peacey and Warren, were back on duty after sustaining minor wounds only three days earlier, whilst 2/Lt Marlow had recovered from an injury suffered seven days previously. Major Cowley's platoon, with eight Lewis Guns, relieved the 7th Leinsters about 8 p.m. on the 14th, while enemy aeroplanes attacked with bombs and machine guns, causing some casualties amongst the men leaving, but none amongst those arriving. The composite company went to Douglas Villa, just south of Frezenberg, with some men just behind in reserve in Ibex trench. The following day 2/Lt Warren had to go back with what the War Diary describes as 'bad neuralgia' and was replaced by 2/Lt Poulter, who had just returned from leave. The line was comparatively quiet. The following morning, Thursday 16 August, was 'Zero'.

Overall Picture

The first fighting during the opening phase of The Third Battles of Ypres, on 31 July 1917 (the Battle of Pilkem Ridge), had secured the Blue Line and had pushed forward on to the Black Line. The objectives for the next full-scale attack on 16 August 1917 (the opening of the Battle of Langemarck) were to advance to the Green Line, and on to the Red Line. General Gough had originally scheduled 14 August for the operation; however, the logistical conditions were not favourable, neither was the weather; yet the only concession Gough made was to delay the attack by two days. The same timescale, of two days on from Zero, was exactly how long it then took for the new assault to grind to a halt.

At dawn on the 16th, the front line from St Julien, on the left-hand (northern) flank of the XIX Corps sector, down to the Ypres-Roulers railway line south of Frezenberg, was held by the Irishmen of 36th (Ulster) and 16th (Irish) Divisions, waiting for the order to advance. The 8th RDF War Diary records great confusion among troops moving up to assembly positions in readiness for Zero Hour at 4.45 a.m., owing to the lack of direction posts; many troops stopped to check their bearings at 8th RDF Headquarters in Wilde Wood.

Logistically, the German defenders had the upper hand, although they too suffered from the appalling conditions in which they had to live and work, and from the dreadful state of the weather. The Company Commander of 3rd Company Reserve Infantry Regiment 263, Reserve Oberleutnant Sűssenberger, noted:

During the afternoon of 15 August we received the news that we were to be relieved that night by Infantry Regiment 184. We breathed a sigh of relief; we had given our all both physically and spiritually. The military expression for this degree of exhaustion was 'fought out'. It summed up our situation exactly. The relief arrived after midnight. The company commander of 3rd Company Regiment 184 arrived at my dugout, bathed in sweat and at the end of his strength. He explained to me that he still did not have his whole company; a large number were still floundering in the mud. In view of the extreme difficulty of the task before him, he did not feel that this chaotic relief was a good omen.[3]

The left flank of the Allied attack was held by Fifth Army's XVIII Corps with, to their left, the French I Corps further north around Bixschoote. To the right (south) of XVIII Corps, the line was held by their Fifth Army colleagues in XIX Corps; whilst to their right, facing the Gheluvelt Plateau, were II Corps.

In a reversal of XIX Corps' dispositions for the 31st July attack, the two Irish Divisions, that had been in reserve, now became the attacking Divisions; the 36th on the left and 16th on the right, the latter concentrated around Frezenberg. 16th Division attacked towards the Zonnebeke Ridge, with 49th Brigade on the left (next to the northern Irishmen) and 48th Brigade on the right; 47th Brigade were in reserve. The Official History states:

To reach its objective, the original German Third Line on Anzac and Zonnebeke spurs, the XIX Corps (Lieut.-General H.E. Watts) had to cross a mile of open ground, chequered with pillboxes and strongpoints. The two divisions selected to lead, the 16th (South Irish) [sic] and the 36th (Ulster), were hardly in a fit state for such a task. They had taken over the line only on the 4 August; but, whilst in corps reserve, at least half of their infantry had been continuously employed in the forward area as carrying parties and other duties since the last week in July; they had lived and worked throughout the most trying fortnight in the quagmire of the Hanebeek and Steenbeek valleys, overlooked by German machine-gunners and artillery observers on the opposite spurs, and subjected to a shelling almost as intense as that on the II Corps sector. Casualties and sickness had consequently reduced the battle-strength of the two divisions by one-third, some of the battalions, indeed, being down to half their establishment. The loss of efficiency had been cumulative, and, owing to the need for frequent inter-battalion reliefs, all units had been equally affected.[4]

Some front-line personnel believed that this state of affairs had been exacerbated by an act of treachery by which the Germans had been given advance warning of the attack. G.E. Mackenzie of 153rd Brigade, Royal Horse Artillery, remembered:

> *I was shown a report captured from a German dug-out in the front line which had been translated and circulated by our GHQ. The night before* (15 August) *a sergeant of the Welsh Fusiliers who had been employed as a clerk at GHQ and had been returned to the line for disciplinary purposes had treacherously deserted to the enemy taking with him not only information of tomorrow's attack, but also a copy of a map on which was indicated the position of every battery on that section of the British front.*[5]

This betrayal was also noted by Captain Arthur Glanville of 2nd Bn Royal Dublin Fusiliers, to whom Willie Doyle's unit was attached:

> **15 August:** *Day of misery for all and anxiety for officers who do not know what time attack starts until late at night. Impossible to get into position in dark under hellish shelling.*
> **16 August:** *Attack at dawn – given away by Sergeant Phillips. Boche puts up terrible barrage before zero as we are moving into position.*[6]

Dispositions of 48th Infantry Brigade on 16 August 1917

The front-line assaulting battalions of 48th Infantry Brigade were: 9th Royal Dublin Fusiliers (on the left) and 7th Royal Irish Rifles (on the right), who had been allotted the task of advancing through the Green Line, moving forward to capture and consolidate objectives on the Red Line. The strength of both of the attacking battalions was down to less than fifty per cent: the 9th RDF had 21 Officers and 423 Other Ranks, whilst the 7th RIR had just 17 Officers and 353 Other Ranks.

    Behind the assaulting battalions and following in support was Captain Glanville's 2nd Royal Dublin Fusiliers, whose task was to mop up and consolidate, but their 'C' Company was to remain behind on the Black Line ready to meet any enemy counter-attack. Major Cowley's Composite Company of 8th Royal Dublin Fusiliers came under orders of the Officer Commanding 2nd Royal Dublin Fusiliers, with remaining men of the battalion either attached to the assaulting battalions for carrying duties, or attached to the Royal Engineers for other work. The assaulting strength of the 2nd Dublins was 14 Officers and 293 Other Ranks (compared to November 1916 when Noel Drury recorded in his diary 32 Officers and 957 Other Ranks.)[7] The Composite Company of 8th Dublins had 6 Officers and between 80 and 90 Other Ranks (the total number varies in differing accounts in the War Diary.)

The reserve battalion for 48th Brigade was 1st Royal Munster Fusiliers (seconded from 47th Brigade) who were to send one company forward to occupy Douglas Villa south of Frezenberg, as soon as the Composite Company of 8th Royal Dublin Fusiliers had vacated it; the remaining men of 1st Munsters were to stay behind on the Blue Line, to await further orders.

Zero 4.45 a.m.

At the start of the attack, British heavy artillery from a range of 6,000 to 8,000 yards behind the lines launched short, concentrated bombardments on German strongpoints and the troops assaulted under a creeping barrage of machine gun fire. Unfortunately the artillery failed, for the most part, to find their targets in front of the Irish and as German machine-guns, located in impregnable concrete dug-outs, were largely unaffected by the fire, the creeping barrage afforded no protection to the attacking troops. Two of the twelve gun teams of 48th Machine Gun Company tried to move to Potsdam, on the right, at 5.40 a.m. to open a new barrage, but were destroyed by shell fire. Similar scenarios played out elsewhere along the Irish front. The Official History states that:

> *The waves of assaulting troops were so thin that, in the words of one participant, the operation looked more like a raid than a major operation. Although resistance was met at once from the German strongpoints, two to eight hundred yards ahead, the leading companies, torn and raked by bullets from front and flanks, continued on up the bare shell-pitted slope... the 48th [Infantry Brigade] (Br.-General F.W. Ramsay) was badly cut up by machine guns in Potsdam, Vampir and Borry Farms. Mopping-up parties were so scarce and strung out that the Germans were able to bring out machine guns from these shelters, and fire into the backs of the leading men. Even so, observers saw isolated parties arrive within a hundred yards of the German Third Line, their objective.*[8]

Given the appalling conditions under which the Irishmen were operating and what is known of Fr Doyle's character, his grim resolve to stay with his 'boys' (those of his own battalion and others) was unsurprising.

Situation on the left of 48th Infantry Brigade's front

The 9th Royal Dublin Fusiliers had, indeed, made it beyond the Potsdam-Vampir-Borry Farm line, as far as one hundred yards west of the next strongpoint, Bremen Redoubt (behind Vampir Farm), where their attack stalled. The German bombardment had taken such a toll, that the pursuing 'moppers-up', provided from 'B' Company 2nd RDF, were reduced to two officers and three other ranks. Shell-fire had rained down on them even before they cleared the Black Line and German machine-gunners emerged from pill-boxes to fire into the back of them. At 7.30 a.m. a message timed almost two hours earlier brought the dreadful news that nearly every officer and man had been killed or wounded:

> *An Officer was at once sent from Battalion Headquarters with three orderlies to investigate the situation. The 3 orderlies were killed on leaving Battalion Headquarters and the Officer also immediately on his return. No communication was subsequently again established with the assaulting Companies.*[9]

Orders were sent out from 48th Infantry Brigade Headquarters which resulted, at 9 a.m., in 'C' Company of the 2nd Royal Dublin Fusiliers moving up in support of 9th RDF. They got to within a hundred yards of Bit Work, between Potsdam and Vampir, but only two officers and ten men remained.

Situation on the right of 48th Infantry Brigade's front

The 7th Royal Irish Rifles on the right did not fare much better, their left and centre companies being raked by enfilade fire from Borry Farm. Nevertheless, they reached the Green Line at 5.16 a.m., but nearly every Officer had been hit and the two companies had suffered so heavily that they ceased to exist as fighting units. The right company, however, did manage to clear the huts and dug-outs by the Ypres-Roulers railway line in front of Potsdam, capturing 30 prisoners, before moving down the railway and across the Hanebeek. Dodging the hot steel of the

Germans, a few remnants managed to reach the Red Line, but couldn't hold their position because the 'moppers-up' of 'A' Company, 2nd Royal Dublin Fusiliers, had not succeeded in knocking out enemy machine-guns. These Dubs had reached the Support Company of 7th Royal Irish Rifles and dug in along the line, to the huts on the south side of the railway, but all officers were casualties. Nearly twelve hours after 'Zero', at 4.10 p.m., owing to the withdrawal of the 2nd Middlesex on the right (23rd Brigade of 8th Division of II Corps), the remainder of 'A' Company, 2nd RDF, consisting of one NCO and six men, were compelled to move back to their starting position on the Black Line.

Captain Glanville, 2nd Royal Dublin Fusiliers, recorded in his diary:

A and B Companies in front wave completely wiped out. I get order from Battalion to reinforce in full daylight over shell holes full of water. Under hellish fire I collect as many of the Company as possible and give the signal to advance but one after the other is shot down. I was nearly buried by shellfire but remained untouched. We reach front wave – mostly dead about 50 yards from Boche front line of pillboxes. There is one other officer, completely exhausted I place myself and about 10 men who have survived in his hands. We remain all day and night and next day in shell holes. It is death to move – to raise oneself an inch out of the mud.[10]

Some German testimony

On the German side, Leutnant Hans Bromm, Commander 12th Company, Infantry Regiment 84, tells how they had linked up with other units early on 16 August, establishing a right flank on the railway embankment. Their right flank was on the 16th (Irish) Division's right flank, where the 16th joined the 8th Division, and from where the 12th Middlesex were forced to withdraw, leaving the Irish exposed. Leutnant Bromm remembered being in the Front Line behind the Hanebeek stream, which by this time was a swamp resulting from sustained shelling. The quagmire was a major obstacle for the attacking troops and the Germans also had the advantage of the shelter provided by:

... a relatively undamaged block house in our area which was used as an aid post for the wounded. During the hours which followed we were involved

in a permanent fire fight. When, as a result of a counter-stroke mounted by Reserve Infantry Regiment 90, the British were flooding to the rear in large numbers, we engaged them from our position off on the flank with rifle and machine gun fire, causing them considerable numbers of casualties. By 4.00 pm the weather was clearing and our positions began to be engaged by an increasing amount of enemy artillery fire. There were several men killed in the platoons of Reserve Leutnant Schlüter and Vizelfeldwebel Schnibben, but we waited in vain for an enemy attack. At this point our reserves, who had been left out of the battle in the morning, came forward. As far as the eye could see, away to the left and right and emerging over the railway embankment, was one line of infantrymen after another – all of them endeavouring to get forward to our lines.[11]

Composite Company, 8th Royal Dublin Fusiliers

Major Cowley and the Composite Company of 8th RDF, including Fr Doyle, had been attached to 2nd Royal Dublin Fusiliers. Their orders were to move up to their assembly position on the Black Line, immediately after 'B' Company of 2nd RDF vacated it at 'Zero' to mop up for their 9th battalion colleagues. The Composite Company were to wait for further orders, along with 'C' Company of 2nd RDF. The 8th Royal Dublin Fusiliers' War Diary narrative pin-points Major Cowley's Company moving at 4 a.m.:

> *As we came down the ridge the enemy started a heavy bombardment, gradually increasing in intensity as our guns accelerated. Wounded began to appear, apparently from the assaulting Battalions who were forming up in front of us.*[12]

The six officers and eighty-five men found shelter in good dug-outs and gun pits to the north of the railway line and a railway dump (Trench Map reference D.25.d.2.2)[FN1], about five hundred yards forward from Douglas Villa.

Here they avoided the brunt of the German barrage, much of which fell behind and to the right of them along the railway line and also to the left at Frezenberg. The narrative states that the barrage consisted of 4.2s and H.E., low bursting shrapnel with a few 5.9s and appeared to be working back from West to East. However, although they escaped the worst of the shelling for the time being:

At least two machine guns sprayed the parapet of our dug-outs at frequent intervals. At 6am the Medical Officer of the R.I. Rifles established a Dressing Station in one of the gun pits near us; this attracted fire, which caused us 2 Officers and about 6 men casualties.[13]

The two wounded Officers were Second Lieutenants Poulter and Peacey. It was subsequently reported that Fr Doyle set to in assisting the Medical Officer inside the gun pits and making forays outside to fallen soldiers. The gun pits would have been little more than shallow scrapes and would not have afforded a lot of protection. The Composite Company 8th RDF waited for further orders and at 9 a.m. received cautiously optimistic news, which was to prove a false dawn:

At about 9am we heard that the R.I. Rifles and 9th R. Dub. Fus., had captured all their objectives. I heard also from O.C., 2nd R.D.F., that the 9th were held up near Bremen Redoubt.[14]

Shortly after, confusion ensued when waves of counter-attacking German soldiers suddenly came into view, over the crest of the Zonnebeke-St Julien spur, in the vicinity of Bostin Farm. No warning of this counter-attack was given, as explained in the history of the 8th Division, adjoining 16th (Irish) Division:

... at about 9.30 a.m. the enemy launched along the whole front of the division a series of powerful and determined counter-attacks in which he employed large numbers of fresh troops, brought up in buses from the direction of Passchedaele. The masses of low cloud which had rendered the night so dark and made the forming up of our troops for the assault so difficult, now impeded our aeroplanes in their work of indicating targets to our guns. Though the de-bussing of the German reinforcement could be clearly seen by our forward troops, the thickness of the weather made it impossible for ground artillery observers to discern or answer the 'S.O.S.' signals which the infantry sent up. Deprived of the protection of their artillery, exhausted and thinned in numbers by a difficult advance and by five hours' continuous fighting under heavy flanking fire, and with their rifles in many cases clogged and useless with mud, the men were unable to hold their ground against the enemy's counter-attack divisions. Our front was driven in and there was a general retirement.[15]

On the adjacent Irish front, as soon as the counter-attack was spotted, Major Cowley decided it was time to move out of the dug–outs, and go up in support of the Royal Irish Rifles. It is also likely that it was at this point, as the fighting was becoming more intense, he decided non-combatants should retire. Consequently, the Doctor and the Chaplain retreated to Headquarters in Wilde Wood. Fr Doyle refused to rest or even eat (as reported by the official war correspondent Sir Philip Gibbs) before deciding to return to the firing line.

Meanwhile, Major Cowley, having made the decision to move forward:

> ...informed O.C. 2nd R.D.F. to this effect. On trying to inform 'C' Company, 2nd RDF, and to get them to move up with me, I found they had already gone up somewhere without telling me.[16]

Major Cowley's narrative (written up on 18 August after the attack) does not indicate how he established contact with the Officer Commanding 2nd Royal Dublin Fusiliers at Douglas Villa or how long it took. It is hardly surprising that he would have been unaware of the fact that 'C' Company 2nd RDF had followed their 'B' Company colleagues in trying to mop up after 9th RDF on the left of the 48th Brigade frontage, which had proved a hopeless task for all the Dubs involved on the left of the attack. Major Cowley's narrative continues:

> *I therefore ordered half the composite Company (original 'D' Company) being 2 Officers and 40 strong to move up in rear of the R.I.R., whilst I myself took up the other half (original 'B' Company) 2 Officers and 40 men astride the dividing line between the original frontages of the R.I.R.'s and 9th R.D.F. echeloned to the front of 'D' Company. This to repair as far as possible the absence of 'C' Company, 2nd R.D.F., who as said had gone off, I did not know where. I moved in eight parallel echelons in file, each with a Lewis Gun. On the way up I called at Colonel Francis' Headquarters. He told me that he did not think the 9th R.D.F. had got past the Green Line ... I was to move up, elucidate situation, support the 9th on the Green Line and report to him.*[17]

Major Cowley's narrative goes on to tell how he, and his forty men of the original 'B' Company, only got 200 yards beyond the gun pits on the Black Line when they came under heavy rifle and machine gun fire on both flanks, from Borry Farm and Vampir Farm to the left, and Potsdam and high ground to the south of the railway on the right. They took cover in a shell hole in the neighbourhood of Bit Work to regroup. Then they rushed in stages straight ahead towards Vampir Farm, to join up with 9th and 2nd Royal Dublin Fusilier colleagues, whom the major had spotted through binoculars laying on the ground, only to find most of them dead or wounded. By this time, his men had sustained twenty-two casualties and 2nd Lieutenant Mallen was mortally wounded.

Major Cowley and Captain Glanville

Major Cowley found Captain Glanville and 2/Lt Wolf, together with twelve men, of 'C' Company 2nd RDF in shell holes. The remnants of Major Cowley's Company took cover with them, linking up the shell holes into a strongpoint. They were surrounded by wounded and dead, the rain of steel never ceasing:

> *Opposite us were a line of square apparently intact concrete dug-outs extending with intervals ... to Vampir. I could see none but wounded and dead to my North and none of our men at all to the South. The enemy had a machine gun in front of us ... in addition to those on our flanks ... Their Snipers and Machine Guns were active, firing at us from 3 sides and from dug-out loop-holes. We succeeded in keeping our end up especially with the Lewis Guns but latter* [sic] *I had to stop as we were running through too much S.A.A.* [small arms ammunition] *and I expected a counter-attack.*[18]

In the afternoon they managed to get in several wounded, including an officer, from in front of Vampir Farm. The officers could no longer contemplate advancing any further and they consolidated their position. After dark they managed to gather up more stragglers of the 2nd and 9th RDF; the Germans allowed several wounded to walk back at 9 p.m. One of the wounded of the 9th RDF, Lt Daniel Galvin, managed to drag himself to the Dressing Station via a series of shell holes, remaining in the first one from 5 a.m. to 3 p.m. with shells raining all around.

Early on Friday morning 17 August, Major Cowley observed the enemy in the dug-outs at Vampir Farm, about three hundred yards away, being relieved, and estimated the numbers manning that strongpoint as fifty. He had been trying to get runners through to (and back from) Colonel Hunt, 9th RDF, at HQ, and finally succeeded late in the afternoon. Major Cowley's instructions were:

> *Relief Division takes place tonight. Not certain whether they will take our advanced posts in front of Black Line. Would advise you to withdraw another 100 yards at least as soon as it gets dark. Meanwhile should you be counter attacked withdraw as best you can and send runners to inform me.*[19]

Major Cowley together with Captain Glanville and their shattered rag-tag collection of men and officers withdrew at dusk, over marshy ground which was so bad that all holes and ditches were full of water, and they could find no form of shelter, let alone dig in. They therefore had to return all the way back to the Black Line to await relief in the early hours of Saturday 18 August.

What of Father Doyle?

Major Cowley does not mention Fr Doyle in his narrative. Perhaps Willie initially went back as far as Douglas Villas or H.Q. at Wilde Wood. But something Major Cowley does say gives an indication of Willie's next movement. The major said he quickly lost touch with 2nd Lieutenants Marlow and Green, in charge of the forty men of the original 'D' Company, 8th RDF. These two subalterns were subsequently reported dead in the same location as Willie. So it would seem the padre subsequently returned from HQ to the Dressing Station in the gun pits, then made his own decision to move forward from there, into the same locality as Marlow and Green.

Whilst Major Cowley and his team had edged to the left towards Vampir Farm, 2nd Lieutenants Marlow and Green moved right towards Potsdam, under fire from both sides of the railway line. The gun pits housing the Dressing Station were left in charge of Corporal Raitt. The platoons worked up the railway, but their movements could not be traced accurately because the officers (who had the compasses, maps, watches etc.) had died.

The account of the 2nd Royal Dublin Fusiliers stated that Marlow and Green's platoons succeeded in reaching a position west of Potsdam, but further advance was impossible due to machine-gun fire. Surviving NCOs reported afterwards, to Major Cowley, that they dug in, at a position less than 100 yards north of the railway, and about 300 yards from Potsdam (trench map position D.25.d.10.5). This was approximately 800 yards forward from the Black Line and about 400 yards forward from the Dressing Station in the gun pits.

The War Diary of 8th Royal Dublin Fusiliers records:

2/Lts Marlow and Green & Fr Doyle (chaplain) were killed in a dug-out in front of the Black Line near the railway.[20 and FN2]

This sentence is the only official War Office documentary evidence that Fr William Doyle did not remain at the Dressing Station, but that he advanced into the firing line. The fact that he went forward is the only indisputable fact of Willie's death. The 'Old Armchair' was ready for him after all.

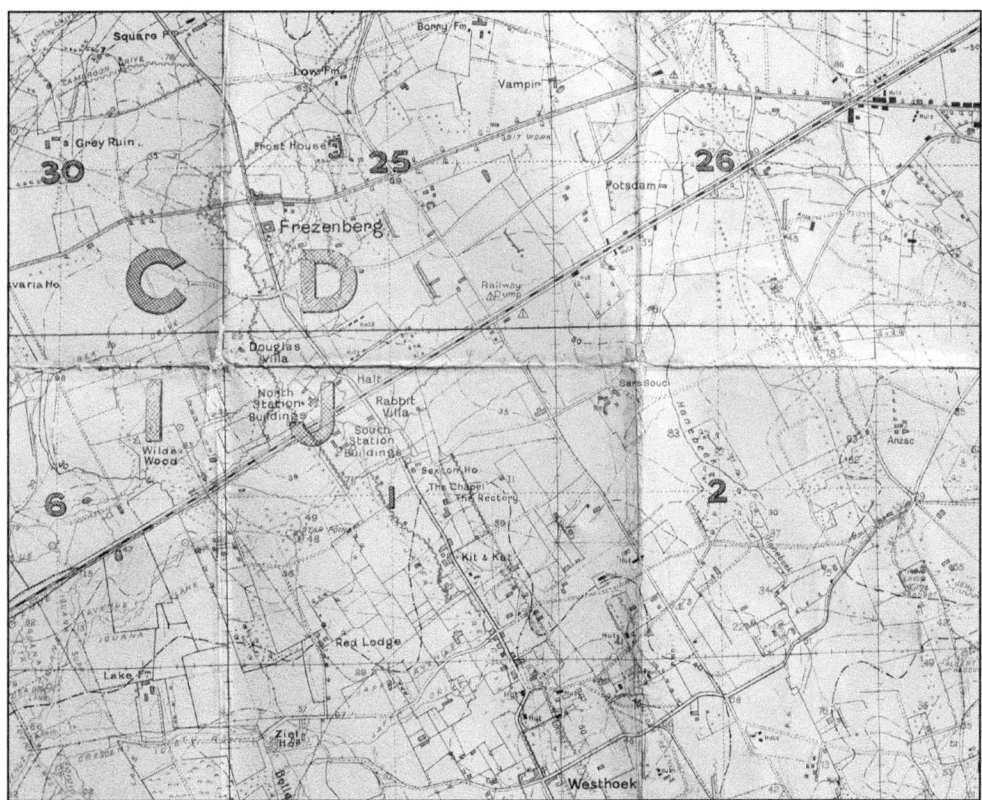

Frezenburgh Trench map

Footnote 1: See photo of Hooge trench map in photo illustrations. To identify a reference on the trench map: first locate on the map the upper case letter at the beginning of the reference string. This capital letter (in the string) is followed by a number, which on the map is placed in the middle of where four squares connect. The top left square associated with that number equates to lower case 'a' in any trench reference string, the top right equates to 'b', the lower left square is 'c' and lower right is 'd'. The next part of the trench reference string is a number, between 1-10, which refers to the gradations along the bottom of each square, and the final number in the string refers to the gradations going up the side of the square. So, for example, the trench map reference, on the Hooge trench map, where the gun pits were, is D.25.d.2.2 i.e. block D25, lower right square, at the intersection of two gradations along and two gradations up.

Footnote 2: In this context, and in most instances of military parlance, 'in front' means beyond i.e. Fr Doyle was killed past the Black Line in a forward position.

CHAPTER 32
LOST AT YPRES:
THE CONFOUNDING CIRCUMSTANCES OF WILLIE'S DEATH

*Greater love hath no man than this,
that a man lay down his life for his friends.*

John 15:13 King James Bible

The news of Willie's death was a huge blow to 16th (Irish) Division, coming a month almost to the day after the memorable service at St Omer Cathedral on Sunday 15 July 1917. In the congregation then was Thomas B. Sheridan, whose battalion of 6th Connaught Rangers was elsewhere on the Front Line in August, and he observed later:

> *If the Ypres battle had been next morning* [16 July] *and the weather was as clement as it then was, we should not have had the dismal adventure of the end of the month and Fr Doyle would not have preached this as his last sermon, or died assisting wounded in the swamps round Frezenberg.*[1]

Fr William Doyle's body was lost on the Ypres battlefield. No more precise details are known of his fate. When examining the evidence from the narratives in the various War Diaries, plus personal testimony, the possible time and scene of his death was most likely to have been late afternoon on 16 August, in the vicinity of where some men from the 8th Royal Dublin Fusiliers had dug-in, west of Potsdam.

Eleven hours after Zero on 16 August (about 4pm) the Germans had mounted another counter-attack; as they advanced the quantity of artillery fire directed on their opponents increased, forcing them to try and withdraw. The testimony of Private McInespie, Willie Doyle's runner, is recorded by Professor O'Rahilly; some editions of his book start this testimony with the assertion:

'The best substantiated account is this.' Then continues: *'Fr Doyle had been engaged from early morning in the front line, cheering and consoling his men, and attending to the many wounded. Soon after 3p.m. he made his way back to the Regimental Aid Post which was in charge of a Corporal Raitt, the doctor having gone back to the rear some hours before. Whilst here word came in that an officer of the Dublins had been badly hit, and was lying out in an exposed position. Fr Doyle at once decided to go out to him, and left the Aid Post with his runner, Private McInespie, and a Lieutenant Grant. Some twenty minutes' later, at about a quarter to four, McInespie staggered into the Aid Post and fell down in a state of collapse and shock. Corporal Raitt went to his assistance and after considerable difficulty managed to revive him. His first words on coming back to consciousness were: 'Fr Doyle has been killed!' Then bit by bit the whole story was told. Fr Doyle had found the wounded officer lying far out in a shell crater. He crawled out to him, absolved and anointed him, and then, half dragging, half carrying the dying man, managed to get him within the line. Three officers came up at that moment, and McInespie was sent for some water. This he got and was handing it to Fr Doyle when a shell burst in the midst of the group, killing Fr Doyle and the three officers instantaneously, and hurling McInespie violently to the ground.'*²

Professor O'Rahilly does not state to whom McInespie and Raitt reported these proceedings, or how he was alerted to them. In other editions of his biography, O'Rahilly records a slightly different version of events, which he attributes to Lieutenant-Colonel Stirke, Captain Healy, Lieutenant Kiernan and Father Browne. Once again, O'Rahilly does not say how he came by the testimony of these officers and in at least two cases the alternative testimony could not have come from eye-witnesses.[FN1] Nevertheless, it is stated that, whilst rescuing the wounded officer, Fr Doyle encountered three more officers whilst they were sheltering in a German pill-box (the entrance, of course, facing the enemy attack) when a shell struck just as the padre was entering. Although this version does concur with the War Diary, which states that the men were killed in a dug-out, there is no clue in the diary as to the source of that information. [FN2]

Some versions of the O'Rahilly biography contain a post-war photograph of a concrete blockhouse, described as near Frezenberg, and state that it is possibly the scene of Father Doyle's death. This blockhouse was actually located at Potsdam and no longer exists. (On the relevant trench map it is shown as a rectangle to the right of the word Potsdam i.e. to the east, trench map reference D.26.c.6.9.) [FN3]

However, the available evidence suggests that the dug-out referred to in the 8th Royal Dublin Fusiliers' War Diary was more likely to have been west of Potsdam. Any assertion about the location of such places is fraught with difficulties. War Diaries and narratives were written up after the event using trench map locations. However, it must be remembered that the state of the terrain may have distorted the perception of the men on the ground at the time and the pin-pointing of some locations may not be absolutely precise.

What is clear is that the location of the dug-out in which Fr Doyle and Second Lieutenants Marlow and Green were killed was in the 7th Royal Irish Rifles' frontage. The account of the day's action on 16 August 1917 in their War Diary gives several trench map references. They were the battalion which attacked on the right of 48th Infantry Brigade's front, and this was the area into which Second Lieutenants Marlow and Green led their half of the Composite Company of 8th Royal Dublin Fusiliers. The diary identifies concrete dug-outs at D.26.c.3.7, (below the P of the word Potsdam on the map) where German machine guns were able to keep in action, because the early morning artillery barrage by the British passed over them. Fire from this machine gun post caused many casualties. However, a few men of the right company 7th RIR managed to get past it, even capturing 30 prisoners at D26.c.4.5. alongside the Ypres-Roulers railway, and sending them back to the British lines. Some 7th RIRs then forged forward along the railway and crossed the Hanebeke stream, but by the time the Germans launched another counter-attack late that afternoon, the men who had crossed the Hanebeke had not been seen or heard of. The War Diary states:

The line on the west of Potsdam Dugouts gradually dwindled away in casualties and the last six men with some 2nd Dublins came back to the Black Line under cover of darkness.[3]

It would appear that, apart from the party which crossed the Hanebeke early in the morning and then disappeared, the furthest forward the right flank men of 48th Infantry Brigade progressed was just west and south of Potsdam. Father Doyle was still alive late morning, as he temporarily returned to HQ in Wilde Wood, so he could not have been killed going to the aid of anyone who had progressed east of Potsdam that morning i.e. in the vicinity of the bunker shown in the O'Rahilly biography. In any event, subsequent testimony says Willie was alive later that afternoon.

Meanwhile, an attempt had been made by Lieutenant Kingston, 7th Royal Irish Rifles, approaching from the huts on the railway, to *turn the flank* ⁴ at the dug outs D.26.c.3.7 and take out the German machine gunners. These are the dugouts immediately west of the blockhouse pictured in the O'Rahilly book. Lt Kingston made this gallant attempt using just his revolver, but was killed and what was left of his platoon was wiped out by a shell. The German machine gunners remained firmly in place, indicating that the place where Fr Doyle died was west of even this location.

The history of the 8th Division records the 2nd Middlesex, immediately to the right of the Irish, getting only temporary respite from enfilade machine gun fire, as a result of the Irish efforts:

> *The approach of 48th Infantry Brigade towards Potsdam Redoubt eased the situation temporarily and enabled the left of the Middlesex to resume its advance; but having reached a line running due South from the railway at a point approximately opposite Potsdam, its progress was again held up by the same cause. There seems, indeed, little doubt that few, if any, of the British troops North of the railway were able to pass East of Potsdam, with the result that the German garrisons there were left free to command the situation South of the railway with machine guns posted in the Redoubt and on the higher ground beyond it.*⁵

The history of the 15th (Scottish) Division also confirmed this view:

> *On the 17th the move to the front line began, and that night the 46th Brigade took over the whole of the right sector ... from the 16th Division, the ground it had occupied a fortnight earlier. The position of the front line had not changed greatly ... The fortified farm buildings still defied capture ...*⁶

It therefore seems that Willie met his fate in an unnamed dug-out or, indeed, outside it, to the west of both the Potsdam bunker and the next set of machine gun-dug-outs to the west again. It seems likely that Willie's place of death would have been close to where the surviving NCOs of Marlow and Green's platoons dug in, at a position 100 yards north of the railway at trench map position D.25.d.10.5.

The issues of the circumstances of Willie Doyle's death and the bunker are not the only anomalies in this story. His death was reported in the 8th Royal Dublin Fusiliers' War Diary, written up on the 18 August, but no date was assigned to the event. However, the earlier entry for 16 August stated that:

> *The D coy half worked up the railway: cannot trace their movements accurately as all the officers with them are dead.*[7]

This implies that Fr Doyle had, indeed, already met his fate on Thursday 16 August 1917. Yet all the official documents on his War Office personal file refer to the date of death as the day after; a few even state 18 August, whilst the Commonwealth War Graves Commission's record is 17 August. One assumes that this was resultant upon Fr Doyle's demise appearing in the War Diary entry for the 18 August and not the 16th. As for the 17th, this flies in the face of the claim that later in the 'day' some men from Royal Dublin Fusiliers, retiring from a more forward position, came across Willie's body. The remnants of both 2nd and 8th Royal Dublin Fusiliers on the right started to withdraw around 4pm on the 16th when it would still have been daylight; other troops on the left did so in darkness at 10 p.m. on the 17th – none of the accounts indicate that Fr Doyle died at night.[FN4]

Writing three months later to a friend, Brigadier General H.F. Kays, Major General Hickie says of Fr Doyle:

> *On the day of his death – 16 August he had worked in the front line and even in front of that line and appeared to know no fatigue ... He was killed by a shell towards the close of day and was buried on the Frezenberg Ridge.*[8]

Professor Alfred O'Rahilly refers to Willie's exertions during 16 August thus:

> *Fr Doyle was speeding all day hither and thither over the battlefield like an angel of mercy; his words of Absolution were the last words heard on earth by many an Irish lad that day, the stooping figure of priest and father, seen through blinding blood, filled the glance of many in their agony.*[9]

O'Rahilly's assertion must have been based on subsequent eye-witness testimony, and it supports the fact that Willie's exertions took place over the course of one day rather than two. Fr Doyle's efforts also made the British press. Sir Philip Gibbs, writing in the *Daily Chronicle*, 22 August 1917, said:

> *All through the worst hours an Irish padre went about among the dead and dying giving Absolution to his boys. Once he came back to head quarters, but he would not take a bite of food or stay, though his friends urged him. He went back to the field to minister to those who were glad to see him bending over them in their last agony. Four men were killed by shell fire as he knelt beside them, and he was not touched – not touched until his own turn came. A shell burst close by, and the padre fell dead.*[10]

Both these descriptions come from the pens of men writing in a style designed to awe their readers, but there can be no doubt of the truthful essence of the narratives. The fact that Willie had disobeyed orders even to be as far forward as the Dressing Station, let alone beyond it, was confirmed by Lt Col H.R. Stirke, temporary Officer Commanding, 8th Royal Dublin Fusiliers, who wrote:

> *I know that he had been sent back by the O.C. of one of the regiments, together with some other non-combatants, as the fighting was very severe and it was not necessary to risk more lives. He only remained behind a few hours and then returned to the firing line, like the brave man he was.*[11]

Another mystery in this conundrum is that Willie may, initially, have been given a hasty burial. There was a report that:

> *Later in the day some of the retiring Dublins came across the bodies of all four. Recognising Fr Doyle, they placed him and a Private Meehan, whom they were carrying back dead, behind a portion of the Frezenberg Redoubt and covered the bodies with sods and stones.*[12]

Two hundred and eighty bodies of the 16th (Irish) Division's dead were recovered, but another seven hundred and eighteen were subsequently identified as missing, including that of Willie Doyle. Unfortunately, although the Frezenberg Redoubt afforded those inside its concrete dugouts protection, the land around was in a very exposed position. Battalions of 15th (Scottish) Division relieved the Irish on 17 August and the 7/8th King's Own Scottish Borderers Headquarters was located at Frezenberg Redoubt. Their War Diary said:

> *Frezenberg Redoubt was shelled night and day intermittently with 18 pdrs and 5.9s. Battalion HQ received a great amount of attention from the enemy artillery because of it being situated on the forward slope and in full view of the enemy.*[13]

Any bodies, whether given a hasty burial, or those which were just left exposed as they had fallen, would inevitably have been churned up and hit by the unrelenting shell fire, the mortal remains slowly sinking into mud and water.

The KOSB's War Diary reveals the difficult conditions in which their companies tried to work over the next few days, just carrying out absolutely essential tasks supplying the front line troops, and incurring heavy losses. Eventually, on the 19 August:

> *During the day, Battalion Headquarters at Frezenberg was subjected to a violent bombardment, and at dusk HQ were moved back to Bill Cottage, which was on the other slope of the Redoubt.*[14]

No mention is made in their War Diary about any attempts to retrieve and send back the dead for burial. However, those few officers left in command of the Royal Dublin Fusiliers were initially confident of recovering Willie Doyle's body. Captain C. Healy visited Charles Doyle very soon after Willie died (although the exact date is unknown), and Charlie remembered:

> *Captain Healy also mentioned that the exact place of burial is known and efforts would be made to remove the remains to Locre.*[15]

The nuns at Locre Convent were anxious to have Fr Doyle's remains for burial. The Superioress wrote to Fr Browne on 21 August 1917:

> *What very sad news I have received! Our good brave holy Fr Doyle has been*

killed! Compassionate Lord Jesus give him eternal rest! Rev. Fr Browne will accept my condolence, my feelings of sympathy in the great loss of our good Fr Doyle, your confrère. Notre petit saint, he has now received his recompense for his holy life, his great love for God and neighbour. Oh! he was so much loved by everybody and never will we forget him. We are all very glad to have had him with us in the convent and to have made his life as comfortable as possible. Were it not possible, Rev. Fr, to bring his holy body to the convent? It were a great honour to us to have it.[16]

Indeed, Father Achiel Van Walleghem, the parish priest of Dickebusch, recorded in his diary on 11 September 1917:

Next to Major Redmond's grave, another burial place has been prepared for the chaplain Father Doyle, a very exemplary priest and brave man, who was killed two weeks ago between Frezenberg and Zonnebeke, and whose remains still lie unburied in the first enemy line ...[17]

But it was to prove a forlorn hope, even though Hickie was still holding on to that prospect in his letter to his friend Kays, dated 18 November 1917, which stated:

I hope to be allowed when things settle down and we can get a party to do it, to move his remains to the Convent Garden at Locre and to put these in a grave beside that of Willie Redmond.[18]

The names of both Father Doyle and Private Meehan, along with countless others, are now commemorated on the Memorial to the Missing at Tyne Cot.

The names of the two Second Lieutenants recorded as having died alongside Willie, are also engraved on this memorial. Charles Dwyer Marlow was aged 22, the son of Arthur and Amelia Frances Marlow of Clonlyne, Penrhyn Bay, Llandudno, Carnarvonshire. Arthur Vivian Green was aged 21, the son of Herbert Percy and Jessie Green of Limehurst, Holland Park, Knock, Co. Down. He was educated at the Methodist College and Royal Academical Institution, Belfast.

Rewinding to the immediate aftermath of the battle, the remnants (mostly Other Ranks) of the 8th Royal Dublin Fusiliers hauled themselves back to Vlamertinghe Number 3 camp, arriving to bivouac about 3 a.m. on Saturday 18 August 1917. A similar scene played out for their comrades in the Front Line in the other units of 16th (Irish) Division, as recorded by Captain Arthur Glanville, 2nd Royal Dublin Fusiliers:

We march or rather drag ourselves back to Ypres, heedless of shell fire.[19]

It was the same to their left where 36th (Ulster) Division also suffered grievously in the fighting. Indeed, several battalions in both of the Irish divisions had losses so great that they ceased to be fighting units and were subsequently amalgamated.

An exhausted Major Cowley had the onerous task of writing up the narrative of the attack by the platoons of his composite Company of 8th Royal Dublin Fusiliers. The War Diary notes casualties of Other Ranks, including those attached to carrying parties etc., as being forty-seven: killed 5, wounded 30, missing 12. The full number of Officer casualties are not noted, but what is known is that, in addition to the death of Father Doyle, Second Lieutenants Doherty, Doyle, Green, Mallen and Marlow were killed (the first two on Carrying Party duties); 2/Lt Peacey was wounded and 2/Lt Poulter was injured seriously enough to be evacuated to hospital early on Saturday 18 August.

The War Diary does not note whether church parades were held on Sunday, 19 August behind the lines, but if they were they must have been muted affairs in view of the large losses, especially that of one of the 16 (Irish) Division's padres. The loss of Willie Doyle was profoundly felt throughout both the 16th and 36th Divisions, as revealed by the tributes recorded in a later chapter. A report of his death was recorded in the *Liverpool Echo,* dated 25 August 1917:

The special correspondent of The Times *on the British front in the west described recently the heroism of an Irish Roman Catholic chaplain who, in the recent advance by Irish regiments, 'went up with the men, sustained and cheered them until the last, till he was killed.' The news has now reached Dublin of the death in action on August 17 of the Rev. William J. Gabriel Doyle M.C., Chaplain to the Royal Dublin Fusiliers.*

Suffice to repeat here, two short sentences from tributes from both sides of the spectrum. From an un-named Belfast Orangeman, reported in the *Glasgow Weekly News* of 1 September 1917:

Fr Doyle was a great deal amongst us. We couldn't possibly agree with his religious opinions, but we simply worshipped him for other things.[20]

And the opening sentence of Major General W.B. Hickie's letter of 18 November 1917 to Brigadier General Kays stated:

Father Doyle was one of the best priests I have ever met, and one of the bravest men who fought or worked out here.[21]

Footnote 1: O'Rahilly says[22] that the account of Fr Doyle entering the German pill-box when the shell struck him was given by Lieutenant Colonel Stirke, Captain Healy, Lieutenant Kiernan and Father Browne. However, it is doubtful whether at least two of these men could have been eye witnesses and so must have related second-hand accounts which were reported to them. In this version Pte McInespie also continues as an eye-witness, but as for the others, Fr Browne had, by this time, transferred to the Irish Guards, Lt Col Stirke presumably would not have been in the front line and Captain Healy was one of the officers balloted out of the action and remained at Erie Camp; he may have been brought up from reserve later, but there is nothing in the War Diary to indicate this. Perhaps Lt Kiernan was nearby, he had been in charge of a carrying party, but it is not clear whether that was on the left of the attack, or on the right where Willie died. Lt Daniel Galvin, 9th Royal Dublin Fusiliers, wrote to Professor O'Rahilly after the publication of the latter's book. Galvin asserted that *the dates and places in the book are very accurate,*[23] but, again, he was not an eye-witness to Willie's death, having been wounded during the attack to the left of Fr Doyle's movements. However, Lt Galvin would have heard the reports of all the exploits of the rest of 48th Brigade personnel that day, including Fr Doyle's.

Footnote 2: Myles Dungan points out that, such was Willie Doyle's fame post-war, ex-soldiers were anxious to become retrospective 'witnesses' to his death. He cited the case of 76-year-old Jimmy O'Brien who served with the Royal Dublin Fusiliers during Third Ypres when he was aged 20, who insisted when interviewed that *I was with Father Willie Doyle, the Jesuit, he was shot down beside me and I was wounded in the shoulder.* [Then] *I lay in a shell hole up to my neck in water.*[24]

Footnote 3: See photo of Hooge trench map in photo illustrations section. See Footnote 1 at the end of Chapter 31 to identify a trench map reference. The approximate trench map reference relating to the photo of the Potsdam bunker in the O'Rahilly biography is: D.26.c.6.9 i.e. in the D section, number 26, lower left square, the intersection of six gradations along and nine gradations up.

Footnote 4: Later editions of the O'Rahilly biography also state that McInespie and Raitt thought that Fr Doyle died on 17 August, which contradicts the earlier edition and adds to the general confusion of the exact details of Willie's death. As they were both in the Front Line, however, they could easily have been disorientated with regard to the timeline.

CHAPTER 33
AFTERMATH:
CAST ASIDE LIKE OLD SHOES

If they had the power to dry up miles and miles of waist deep mud there would have been some sense to it. As it was the Ypres battlefield just represented one gigantic slough of despond into which floundered battalions, brigades and divisions of infantry without end, to be shot to pieces or drowned, until at last and with immeasurable slaughter, we had gained a few miles of liquid mud which were of no use to anyone.[1]

The battle of 16 August 1917, fought in the beleaguered Ypres Salient, is now named after the only area of the action in which a small measure of success was achieved. Ultimately, it was only on the extreme left flank of the Allied attack, to the north around Langemarck itself, that any progress was made. Success was counted in hundreds of yards and the depth of the advance in this sector varied between 1,000 to 1,500 yards, but this came at a cost, across the whole front line, of some 15,000 casualties. The Official History commented on the depressing failure of the Battle of Langemark:

It was an ill-conceived attempt that, from the very start, was almost bound to fail. Artillery superiority had not been established, nor had there been any concentration of resources opposite the Gheluvelt Plateau. Finally, the unspeakably muddy conditions overwhelmed the efforts of the infantry and rendered tanks useless.... In many ways the events of 16 August mirrored the events of 31 July.[2]

Men of the Royal Dublin Fusiliers, like Captain Cowley and Captain Glanville, who had spent hours sheltering as best they could, before retreating back to the Black Line on 17/18 August, had stories to tell; that of Willie Doyle's friend Lieutenant Daniel Galvin of the 9th Bn RDF was brief but harrowing:

> *I was wounded four times that day* [16 August] *and then spent 24 hours in a shell hole up to my chest in water. That ended my conversation with the army.*³

Temporary Lieutenant Galvin sustained gunshot wounds to the left loin and left arm. On 22nd November 1917 he was still on the dangerously ill list at 2nd Southern General Hospital Bristol, but recovered, though never fit enough to return to action. Whilst Lt Galvin and other wounded were evacuated to base hospitals, the rest of the battered 16th (Irish) Division moved in stages to join Third Army in France, their services no longer being required by Fifth Army. The first destination of 8th Royal Dublin Fusiliers was Esk Camp, west of Poperinghe, where a draft of fifty-eight men joined from divisional base, and then on to billets near Wormhout. On Tuesday 21 August the battalion entrained early morning at Esquelbec, detraining at Bapaume at 1 p.m. and marched to billets at Courcelles-Le-Comte. Following the departure of 16th (Irish) Division, their former Officer Commanding XIX Corps, Lt Gen Sir H.E. Watts, commended the departing troops, saying they had fought well, but that the hardships they had suffered in the fortnight before had not helped during:

> *...an attack over very difficult country against the best troops in the German army and against an hitherto untried system of defence.*⁴

When you add to this praise the previous acclaim of Lt Gen Sir Alexander Hamilton-Gordon, IX Corps Commander at Messines, it is difficult to reconcile the attitude of General Gough of Fifth Army following the Battle of Langemarck. He tried to apportion blame on 16th (Irish) Division for the failure of the attack when Field-Marshal Sir Douglas Haig visited Fifth Army Headquarters on Friday 17 August. Fortunately, Haig had his own view that all attacking divisions had been through extremely trying conditions prior to zero and: *consequently, they could have had no sleep, and must have been dead tired* ⁵ and that the 16th (Irish) Division had fought well. Gough persisted with his view and after the war crassly stated: *I was aware the division was not of the highest standard* ⁶ but he produced no credible evidence for this.

Casualties from the Battle of Langemarck for the 36th (Ulster) Division were 81 Officers; 1,955 Other Ranks. The 36th (Ulster) Division's losses meant that the 7th and 8th battalions of Royal Inniskilling Fusiliers had to be merged, with effect from 23 August, followed by the 8th and 9th Royal Irish Rifles on 29 August 1917.

AFTERMATH

The 16th (Irish) Division lost 115 Officers, 2,042 Other Ranks; over the longer timeframe of 1 to 20 August, their losses were 221 Officers and 4,064 Other Ranks. Eventually, the two battalions Willie Doyle had worked most closely with, 8th and 9th Royal Dublin Fusiliers, were amalgamated as from 24 October 1917.

Within days of Gough's interview with Haig, the tone of the initial optimistic, jingoistic newspaper reports had started to change. Phillip Gibbs' despatches had reached the newspapers, including the *Irish Times*. On the day his description appeared in *The Daily Chronicle*, of the Irish padre falling dead delivering his ministry on the battlefield, a telegram was received at the War Office. On Wednesday 22 August 1917 a scribbled scrawl asked:

> *Have you any information respecting Captain the Revd Wm J Doyle Chaplain to the Forces 8th Royal Irish Fusrs reported killed on 17 August reply Doyle Melrose Dalkey.*[7]

Followed the next day by another telegram:

> *Hugh Doyle Melrose Dalkey Dublin wishes to know whether the rumour that his son Revd William Doyle Chaplain to the Forces attached to 8th Royal Dublin Fusiliers was killed on 17 August is true or false.*[8]

A reply was sent to Willie Doyle's father the same day:

> *Deeply regret to inform you report just received Rev. W.J. Doyle M.C. A.C.D. was killed in action on August Seventeenth a.a.a. The Army Council express their sympathy.*[9]

Eighty-six-year-old Hugh Doyle now had the unpalatable task of informing the rest of his family about the loss of their loved one, along with telling Willie's Jesuit superiors at the Province at Rathfarnham. In fact, Hugh's other Jesuit son Charles, performed this task, which he described in a letter:

> *When I went up to Dublin, some days after Willie's death was announced, the Provincial asked me to go to Rathfarnham, go through Willie's papers etc., and take what I wished.*[10]

A telegram from the War Office to Doyle at Melrose

Post war picture of Tank C47 Conqueror which embedded in a ditch south of the Frezenberg Redoubt, 16 August 1917

Presumably Charles' letter was addressed to Professor Alfred O'Rahilly; certainly most of Willie's personal papers were loaned to him in order to write the biography, following some wrangling of conscience by Charles Doyle about whether Willie's instructions to burn them should be observed or not. Within a few weeks, Dublin solicitors Maxwell, Weldon and Co. had been appointed to sort out Willie's affairs, by which time it had become clear that Gough's plan had gone wrong; so much so that, by the 25 August, General Plumer and Second Army had assumed authority for the continuation of the offensive, as instructed by Field-Marshal Haig.

As the 16th (Irish) Division was to play no further part in the Ypres offensive, they had been relocated to the Bapaume-Miraumont sector of the front, the scene of the Battle of Arras in the spring. Large numbers of Irish Non-Commissioned Officers and men from Regular army units were transferred in. September was a fairly quiet affair, although the German artillery in that sector was sporadically active. Regular raids were organised, mirroring the activity of the division at their first posting in Loos.

Whilst Maxwell, Weldon and Co. was corresponding with the War Office about Fr Doyle's effects during September and early October, a measure of success was finally achieved back in the Ypres sector in the Battle of the Menin Road, followed by Polygon Wood and Broodseinde, during a period of dry weather. Dull, windless, rainy August was replaced by a sunnier September, during which the ground dried quickly. Ominously, rain returned in October, when 4.2 inches of rain fell, compared to 1.6 inches of rainfall in September, and nearly as much as the five inches which had pelted down in August.

The omens were not good when the next offensive, the Battle of Poelcapelle, started on 9 October, after the assault troops had laboured to their starting lines in drenching rain the previous evening. Three days later, the opening phase of the Battle of Passchendaele commenced. Again, the heavy rain and mud made movement difficult and little artillery could be brought closer to the front. Meanwhile, on that same day, 12 October 1917, probate of Willie Doyle's will was granted. An extract from the will read:

I leave all the property of which I may be possessed to John G. Byrne, John O'Connor and Francis Browne, or the survivors or survivor of them.[11]

The Reverend John Gabriel Byrne, the first of the three executors to the will dated

30 January 1909, was employed at Belvedere College, and Francis Browne was Willie's chaplaincy comrade from the Front. Presumably John O'Connor was also a Jesuit priest; all the money would be moved on to their Province. The gross value of Willie's estate was £99-14s-1d (ninety-nine pounds, fourteen shillings and one penny). A sum of £38-10s-0d was owed by the War Office, as confirmed in their letter of 22 October, although it is not clear whether this had already been included in the gross valuation, or was to be added to it. There ensued a stream of correspondence between the solicitors and the War Office. Writing on 24 October, Maxwell, Weldon and Co. queried:

> *We are in receipt of your letter of the 22 Octr. Herein, and note the amount of balance in your hands. Is it not usual for compensation to be awarded in these cases? The Deceased was a member of the Jesuit Order and the education of each of the members of that Order would at all events cost £1000, as we have been informed by the Head of the Order in Ireland.*[12]

The reply of 8 November stated:

> *Gentlemen, In reply to your letter of 24 October 1917, relative to the late Reverend W.J. Doyle, Chaplain to the Forces, I am directed to acquaint you that there is no compensation in the case of officers killed in action. Officers who serve under a contract, as did the late Chaplain, are entitled to an annual gratuity for each year of service and this has been duly credited to his estate.*[13]

This prompted the solicitors to send another letter ten days later in which they state they were aware that compensation was allowed for the late Rev J. Gwynne, which the War Office refuted in their letter of 22 November. An exchange then took place in which the solicitors were adamant that compensation had been paid for Fr Gwynne, with the War Office equally insistent to the contrary.

Whilst this flurry of correspondence was taking place, the final phase of Third Ypres, the Battle of Passchendaele, had ground to a halt with Allied troops taking what remained of that village. On 6 November the offensive was called off. Some of the iconic photographs of the Great War are of Canadian soldiers fighting against liquid mud and heavy sludge, in order to progress the attack against their human enemies holding the village. Passchendaele lay a mere five miles beyond the original starting point of 31 July; instead of the quick strike originally envisaged it had taken three months to capture and any thoughts of advancing further, to seize the original objective of the railhead at Roulers, was out of the question. During the whole offensive the Allies had lost 325,000 men, and the Germans 260,000. Nevertheless, the overall offensive known as The Third Battle of Ypres was deemed to be a relative success, because the Germans could ill-afford such heavy losses compared to the Allies, whose numbers were to be bolstered by the anticipated arrival of troops from America, following their entry into the war.

Later in the month, 20 November, the 16th (Irish) Division, now part of VI Corps in France, launched a full-scale assault on a formidable section of the Hindenburg Line opposite them, known as Tunnel Trench. This constituted a diversionary attack to the great tank offensive against Cambrai on the same day. Cambrai had become one of the most important railheads and location for Headquarters behind the German lines. Here, German divisions devastated during the Third Ypres battles were sent to rest, recuperate and refit.

Apart from a scare on the right flank of 16th (Irish) Division, where the Officer Commanding and twenty-six men out of twenty-eight of the right platoon, 6th Bn Connaught Rangers, became casualties, the attack went well. Nearly 3,000 yards of Tunnel Trench was taken along with seven hundred and eighteen prisoners, the bulk of them by 16th (Irish) Division, leaving five hundred German dead. Three days later 7th Leinsters captured the portion of the line still held by the Germans on the right flank.[14] Lt Col Rowland Feilding of the 6th Connaughts sent a long description of the attack on Tunnel Trench to his wife, finding room for an amusing anecdote which Willie Doyle would have been proud to have included in one of his letters:

> *The semi-darkness of the early morning was illuminated by the bursts of the shells, trench-mortar bombs, smoke bombs, and the flares and excited S.O.S. rockets of the enemy. The air vibrated with the hurricane of our machine-gun barrage whistling from behind and that of the enemy from the front. The enemy shrapnel was bursting angrily overhead. I met one of my men wandering slowly along the trench, with a hot-food container on his back, oblivious of the frenzy around him, but he clearly had something weighing on his mind. So I asked him what was the matter. I had to shout*

*to make myself heard. Said he: 'I've lost two men for their breakfasts, sorr.'
I felt sorry for the two men then sailing over Noman's Land, but I could
not help smiling at the predicament of the orderly man thus wandering
disconsolate!*[15]

The 16th (Irish) Division left VI Corps in December 1917; the Corps Commander, Lt Gen Aylmer Haldane, observed that:

> *I desire to place on record the good service of the 16th (Irish) Division which is about to leave the VI Corps after serving with it for 3½ months.*
>
> *The work of the division, both in the trenches and behind the Line, had been admirable and might well serve as a model of how such duties should be performed.*
>
> *In carrying out the capture of the German trenches on the 20 November and their rapid consolidation – an exploit which had defeated the efforts of the other Divisions – the Division showed once again what a splendid fighting machine it is.*
>
> *It is with great regret I am forced to part with the Irish Division. I desire to express to Major-General Hickie and all ranks under him my warmest wishes for their future welfare and the hope that I may be another time so fortunate as to have the Irish Division under my command.*[16]

One of the soldiers the Corps Commander referred to was nineteen-year-old Royal Dublin Fusilier Paul Smith, who had spent nearly a year on the Western Front. He remembered always feeling safe whenever Fr Willie Doyle was near and the padre's favourite saying when in heavy shellfire:

> *It is quite alright boys, it is not for us.*[17]

Following the loss of the protective presence of the padre in August, Paul Smith was invalided out of the army, after sustaining gunshot wounds to his arm and neck, possibly during the attack on Tunnel Trench in November. Two days before that attack, the General Officer Commanding 16th (Irish) Division, Major General Hickie, wrote a letter, on Sunday 18 November, to his friend Brigadier General H.F. Kays in Dublin. It referred almost exclusively to Willie Doyle; one sentence stated:

> *He was recommended for the Victoria Cross by his C.O. by his Brigadier and by myself. Superior authority however has not granted it.*[18]

The subject of the award of the VC is covered in the next chapter of this book.

On 6 December 1917 the War Office file for Fr William Doyle was annotated:

> *If the deceased officer's father applied for a pension this Dept would consider the case, but no application has yet been received.*[19]

The War Office evidently did not seem to consider it part of their brief to advise Hugh Doyle that this was the case!

In February 1918 Major General Hickie was invalided home on temporary sick leave. The division now, ironically, came under the command of General Hubert Gough. That same month the War Office finally issued a cheque to Willie Doyle's estate which, taking into account Willie's outstanding pay, allowances and the appropriate gratuity, amounted to £45-1s-10d. Whilst Hickie was in hospital, the German Spring Offensive began on 21 March and his division was decimated; but that is another story.

Southern Irishmen of the 36th (Ulster) Division did not fare much better. Fr Willie Doyle's friend, Captain Barry Galvin from Cork, who had been with 16th (Irish) Division and was seriously wounded at Loos in the summer of 1916, later went on to serve with 1st Bn Royal Irish Fusiliers, of 109th Brigade, 36th (Ulster) Division. He was captured at Andechy on 27 March 1918. His subsequent statement regarding the circumstances that led to his capture reads:

> *'D' Coy with Bn. Headquarters were in a redoubt in the Battle zone near St. Quentin on the 21 March. The other three Companies were captured the first day, and at 11pm we got orders to return. On the subsequent 2 days we fought rearguard actions at Hamel, Sommette- Eaucourt and Villeselve, and were then withdrawn from the line and billeted at Erches on the night of the 25th. On the morning of the 26th we found that the enemy had overtaken us. My company occupied a trench near Andechy, and the C.O. went back in a motor with the G.S.O.I. of the division to try and get news of the situation. They were, I learnt afterwards, captured on the way back. On the morning of the 26th I found that we were completely surrounded. About mid-day*

on the 27th, being without food, water, or ammunition, we split up into 2 parties and tried to get back to Erches. We got about half-way and found our way blocked. Parties of prisoners marching back from Erches passed over our trench, and a German Officer came up and told us that we might as well come along as the line had now gone several miles beyond us. Being completely out of ammunition by now, we had no option but to obey.[20]

April 1918 saw the remnant of the 16th (Irish) Division attached to XIII Corps, First Army, and they proceeded to reorganise and refit; what remained of its infantry was formed into a composite brigade. In June they moved to England and reconstituted, but the majority of its Irishmen were transferred to 36th (Ulster) Division. The most likely explanation for the demise of the 'Irishness' of the Division is that it was a political act of policy. In 1918 the Irish had few friends at Whitehall, especially Sir Henry Wilson, Chief of the Imperial General Staff, who, like Gough, was an obdurate adversary of Irish Catholic Nationalism. Even before this, following the Battle of Langemarck the previous summer, the feeling in the 16th (Irish) Division was:

...that they were cast aside like old shoes, no care being taken of the men who had survived.[21]

At the end of July the new-look division, now consisting of five English battalions, one Welsh, two Scottish and only one Irish (5th Royal Irish Fusiliers), returned to France and took part in the final advance to victory in Artois and Flanders.

Second Lieutenant Frank Laird, one of Fr Willie Doyle's flock of Royal Dublin Fusiliers, did not participate in the fighting which eventually led to the Armistice. He had previously been taken prisoner of war during the Spring fighting. He was repatriated and disembarked in Scotland on Christmas Day 1918, along with Barry Galvin. The last word of this chapter will be his:

Hats off to the British Infantry Tommy! – the man who bore the real brunt of the war, the hardest worked, worst housed, and worst paid man in the army, who for a shilling a day fought like a lion, worked like a ------ [horse,[FN1]*] carried himself everywhere like a cheerful gentleman, and laid down his life without complaint on every front for the freedom of the world.*[22]

AFTERMATH

Footnote 1: Frank Laird did not actually use the word 'horse' but that would be the accepted word we would use now in this context. The word he used is now, rightly, universally considered to be unacceptable, but that would not always have been the case in 1918.

CHAPTER 34
VC OR NO VC:
THAT IS A GOOD QUESTION!

'Be who God meant you to be and you will set the world on fire.'
St Catherine of Siena

INTRODUCTION

Fr William Doyle, S.J. was recommended for the Victoria Cross by Major General William Hickie, General Officer Commanding 16th (Irish) Division. The award was not made. However, many recommendations for gallantry awards were made during the course of the Great War and a good proportion of them were not granted.

Professor Alfred O'Rahilly, without using the actual word, suggested that there was some sort of conspiracy to prevent the award being made. He said:

> *Though Fr. Doyle cared nothing for human decorations – it was another Commander-in-Chief under Whom he served – it seems right to chronicle this judgement of others and to record the fact that he was recommended for the D.S.O. at Wytschaete and the VC at Frezenberg. However the triple disqualification of being an Irishman, a Catholic and a Jesuit, proved insuperable.*[1]

In an ironic and poignant twist of fate, Fr Francis Browne wrote about Fr Doyle on 15 August 1917, the day before Willie's death:

> *May God preserve him and keep him. He doesn't want VCs or anything else, but it would be the proudest moment of my life, if I could only call him VC So rooted is the prejudice against such as he, that one of the men here [Irish Guards] said to me – knowing what Fr. Knapp and Fr. Gwynn had done – 'Aren't our priests, Father, forbidden to take the VC!!!'*[2]

The author, military historian and ex-army officer Major Gordon Corrigan examined the Fr Doyle and VC issue in his book *Mud, Blood and Poppycock* and concluded that there was no evidence pointing to any chicanery at work. One of the points he makes is that, due to a number of political factors at play in Ireland when the O'Rahilly biography was published: *Professor O'Rahilly may not have been altogether detached in his opinions.*[3] Major Corrigan consulted the relevant sources at the National Archives before reaching his conclusion. He also consulted the archivist of the Irish Jesuit Province, who confirmed that their predecessors had no influence over the matter and would not have sought any such influence. Gordon Corrigan concludes that:

> *Although we may never know for sure, it seems that Father Doyle was never recommended for the Victoria Cross; not as any criticism of the man or of his actions, but simply because the criteria for an award were incredibly high.*[4]

What this statement overlooks is that Major General Hickie **did** write to a friend asserting that he had made a recommendation for the Victoria Cross. However, Gordon Corrigan's book was published in 2003 and his research was carried out prior to that. The letter in question from Hickie was nestling, at that time, in a family archive in Ireland, where it lay, undiscovered to anyone with an interest in military history, until 2009. Therefore, the only evidence Major Corrigan had of this was what was written in the O'Rahilly biography.

On the face of it, it does seem strange that Major General Hickie's recommendation was not acted upon. A transcript of the letter can be found in Appendix A, and photos in the photo section, along with the envelope in which it was sent. This bore the post mark 'Field Post Office D7', dated 19 November 1917 and stamped 'Passed by Censor No. 1424', with Hickie's signature underneath the red stamp. It was addressed to Brig. Gen. H.F. Kays, Kildare Street Club, Dublin, Ireland.[FN1] The letter was written on paper embossed in the top right hand corner *HEADQUARTERS 16th (IRISH) DIVISION*. Major General Hickie, referring to Fr Doyle, asserted in that letter:

> *He was recommended for the Victoria Cross by his C.O. by his Brigadier and by myself.*[5]

There is no reason to disbelieve this statement; he had nothing to gain by inventing such a statement in a private letter to a friend. In any case, there is a precedent for a crucial recommendation from Hickie, relating to a man under his command, being over-ruled. The previous year he had recommended clemency for Joseph Carey, but the decision from First Army Headquarters was that the death penalty for desertion should stand, and was duly carried out.

Gordon Corrigan refers to incredibly high criteria for the award of the Victoria Cross. The fifth clause of the original Royal Warrant stated:

It is ordained that the Cross shall only be awarded to those officers and men who have served Us in the presence of the enemy, and shall have then performed some signal act of valour or devotion to their country.[6]

The award was instituted by Queen Victoria and her Royal Warrant dated 29 January 1856 contained fifteen clauses. The seventh clause allowed the decoration to be conferred on the spot if the act was committed under the eye and command of an admiral or general officer commanding the forces. The eighth clause made provision for circumstances other than the seventh clause, so that if the act is proved to the satisfaction of an appropriate officer, that officer could report to the admiral or general officer commanding, who could then:

... call for such description and attestation of the act as he may think requisite, and on approval shall recommend the grant of the Decoration.[7]

Several amendments were made to the original warrant, the first in 1858, covering such issues as pensions and eligibility. An amendment dated 23 April 1881 recognised that: *doubts have arisen as to the qualification required for the decoration of the Victoria Cross*[8] and went on to clarify that the qualification shall be for: *conspicuous bravery or devotion to the country in the presence of the enemy.*[9]

Despite these provisions and amendments, no formal administrative arrangements had been made for the recommendation to be processed. The British Army's solution was the creation of a form and, subsequently, a committee. On 3 October 1914 General Codrington, the Military Secretary, wrote to the Secretary at the War Office:

I put this scheme before the Secretary of State [Lord Kitchener] *yesterday.*

He preferred not to have any joint action with the Navy, and does not think a Committee such as I suggested would serve a useful purpose. But he thought a small committee should consider recommendations for the Victoria Cross.[10]

The committee started work the following month when it considered the award of twenty-four cases recommended by Field Marshal Sir John French. It was noted that:

They have compared these with the Statutes and they submit that the recommendations are in accordance therewith and that those shown on the attached schedule should be laid before the King forthwith.[11]

Army Form W3121 was used for the recommendations of all the available gallantry awards during World War One. The form was in triplicate and if the award was approved, the wording on the document was used as a basis for the entry in the London Gazette. One part of the form was often filed with the daily Routine Orders of the unit concerned. One assumes that in the case of VC recommendations, a copy went before the committee for consideration. The final copies of the completed forms were kept in a central file of War Office archives in London, which was destroyed by enemy bombing during World War Two.

Army Form W3121 records the unit, regimental number, rank and name, date, place and details of action for which the individual is commended. The battalion officer making the recommendation had to state which award was recommended and append his signature. There is nothing on the form to indicate who had provided eye witness testimony. The AF W3121 could be annotated to indicate the levels it had reached (Brigade, Division, Corps, Army) and once the outcome was known it was noted whether the award was approved or not, or if it had been down-graded. Any award that was made then had to be listed on a schedule and the schedule number was entered on AF W3121.

The original royal warrant made no provision for posthumous awards. However, of the six hundred plus Victoria Crosses bestowed during the Great War, a quarter of them were given posthumously. It is impossible to say whether AF W3121 was used in all of the cases, which might depend on whether the recipient was wounded and subsequently died of wounds, or was killed outright. It is not known if an AF W3121 was completed on behalf of the Reverend Father William Doyle, but

Major General Hickie's comments imply such a possibility. Certainly he says a recommendation in some format was made and that it originated at the level of commanding officer of the battalion, through brigade and on to Hickie at division (which would imply the chain of command which is often seen annotated on an AF3121) but that:

> *Superior authority however has not granted it, and as no other posthumous award is given, his name will I believe be mentioned in the Commander-in-Chief's despatch.*[12]

And, indeed, the supplement to the *London Gazette* dated 24 December 1917 records 13490 Mentioned in Despatch:

> *Doyle Rev W.J., M.C., temporary Chaplain to the Forces, 4th Class (killed).*

The citations for all the Great War VC's generally start with "*For most conspicuous bravery*". 'Conspicuous' being the operative word in more ways than one, for not only did the courageousness of the act need to be obvious, it also needed to be witnessed. Any recommendation could only proceed through the system if the actions were sworn and attested to by three persons who had actually seen the event. It is reasonable to conclude, therefore, that there must have been many feats of bravery which were not so well witnessed, or where the witnesses were killed before being able to testify. Equally, there may have been cases where the witness testimony was not acted upon.

One such example is the case of Fr Ted McGrath, an Australian Roman Catholic Chaplain and a Missionary of the Sacred Heart, who served with 1st Battalion Cheshire Regiment, and who was awarded the Military Cross for actions in France in August 1918. Then, on 28 September 1918, when his unit was again engaged with the enemy, he saw one of the battalion officers take a shot to the stomach and immediately went 300 yards into no-man's-land, under heavy shell and machine-gun fire, to rescue him. This saved the life of Lt Attewell, as testified by the doctor: *He undoubtedly saved the Officer's life, owing to the very exposed position in which he lay, and the severity of his abdominal wound* [13] and Lt Attewell who said: *There is no doubt that this heroic act of the Chaplain saved my life tho' at very great risk to his own.*[14] Three officers provided witness testimony for the recommendation of the Victoria Cross; Lt Attewell, Doctor Jeremiah Holland and Lt Arthur Legh. Lt Legh referred to the chaplain making his way forward coolly and collectedly through the barrage to the assistance of the wounded officer. He also said:

Capt McGrath's coolness and prompt action are the more noteworthy when it is understood that this was the third day that the Battn had been in action almost continuously without sleep.[15]

Throughout the war, the final decision on the award of the Victoria Cross was made by King George V, who would, if at all possible, personally invest the award to the winner or, in the case of a posthumous award, to a close relative. But the recommendation had to reach him first. Presumably the case of Fr McGrath would have appealed to him, based on Douglas Haig's diary entry for Friday 4 December 1914:

In the evening I motored to St. Omer and dined with the King ... He expressed the opinion that the grant of the Victoria Cross for carrying a wounded man out of action was justified and was beneficial. I replied that each case must be judged on its merits ...[16]

But no award was made to Fr McGrath.

The subject of the award of this highest recognition for heroism is highly emotive. A whole book could be devoted to the theme of who was awarded the VC, who wasn't and who should have been, and the same is true of other gallantry awards. Often recommendations for a specific award was unsuccessful, but then down-graded so that, for example, the Distinguished Service Order was awarded instead of the Victoria Cross.

Father William Doyle quite obviously was not unique in being a brave chaplain. He won the Military Cross in 1916, one of five hundred and seventy-two others (including five Bars to the Military Cross) awarded to chaplains across the board during the Great War, along with ninety-six Distinguished Service Orders awarded to chaplains. By the end of the war there were 3,500 chaplains in post and during the course of the war over a hundred had died as a result of enemy action, and yet more scores of others had been wounded. The Military Cross was instituted on 31 December 1914. Howard Williamson, an author and authority on Great War medals, specifies the criteria for the award, amongst which:

> *The award was designed as a lesser award than the VC or DSO. It was to be awarded to: Captains, a commissioned officer of a lower grade, or a warrant officer in the Army. 'Periodic Awards' are those for acts of gallantry performed over a period of time, normally around six months. These awards are often underrated as they do not refer to a specific act of courage. Careful research of War Diaries and the Regimental Histories will often reveal these as hard won awards performed over a number of actions rather than the one. Their names were published in special gazettes e.g. Birthday, New Year Honours.*[17]

Willie Doyle's MC was one such 'periodic award', following his work in the front lines at Loos and the Somme. He had already received the 16th (Irish) Division's Parchment of Merit and obviously his actions then, and subsequently, had been noted and his cause promoted by senior officers.

Chaplain VCs and Fr Doyle

Three chaplains were awarded the Victoria Cross during the Great War, all ordained in the Church of England. The first was the Reverend Edward Noel Mellish, for actions during 27 to 29 March 1916 at St Eloi, Belgium. His award was published in the *London Gazette* on 20 April 2016 and read:

> *For most conspicuous bravery. During heavy fighting on three consecutive days he repeatedly went backwards and forwards, under continuous and heavy shell and machine-gun fire, between our original trenches and those captured from the enemy, in order to tend and rescue wounded men. He brought in ten badly wounded men on the first day from ground swept by machine-gun fire, and three were actually killed as he was dressing their wounds.*
>
> *The battalion to which he was attached was relieved on the second day, but he went back and brought in twelve more wounded men.*
>
> *On the night of the third day he took charge of a party of volunteers and once more returned to the trenches to rescue the remaining wounded.*
>
> *This splendid work was quite voluntary on his part and outside the scope of his ordinary duties.*[FN2]

Shortly before the publication of the April *London Gazette*, another courageous chaplain risked his life on 9 April 1916 at Sanaiyal in Mesopotamia and was subsequently awarded the Victoria Cross. The award for the Reverend William Robert Fountaine Addison appeared in the *London Gazette* on 20 September 1916:

For most conspicuous bravery. He carried a wounded man to the cover of a trench, and assisted several others to the same cover, after binding up their wounds under heavy rifle and machine gun fire.

In addition to these unaided efforts, by his splendid example and utter disregard of personal danger, he encouraged stretcher-bearers to go forward under heavy fire and collect the wounded.

This author has no knowledge of the local ground conditions at this site in Mesopotamia in April 1916 compared to St Eloi the month before, but would suggest, without taking anything away from the undoubted bravery of Rev Addison, that his actions do not have the same resonance as those of Rev Mellish. However, what both of these courageous chaplains evidently must have shared were sufficient, articulate and credible witnesses to their actions, as well as the recommendation of their commanding officer. On the other hand, Fr McGrath's actions appear similar to Rev Addison's, and there were three officers who provided eye-witness testimony, but Fr McGrath's recommendation was not even down-graded.

The third chaplain to receive the Victoria Cross was the Reverend Theodore Bayley Hardy VC, DSO, MC, the most decorated padre of the Great War and possibly the oldest to go anywhere near the Front Lines. He won the two latter awards within months towards the end of 1917 and was awarded the VC for three actions the following year; near Bucquoy on 5 April and east of Gommecourt on 25/26 April and 27 April 1918. He was gazetted on 11 July 1918 and the entry commenced thus:

For most conspicuous bravery and devotion to duty on many occasions. Although over fifty years of age, he has, by his fearlessness, devotion to men of his battalion, and quiet, unobtrusive manner, won the respect and admiration of the whole division.

His marvellous energy and endurance would be remarkable even in a very much younger man, and his valour and devotion are exemplified in the following incidents: ...[FN3]

There follows a very long citation, which not only breaks the guideline that it should be concise and clear, but also that it should not refer to previous service. Rev Hardy was quite clearly exceptional, not only for his acts of gallantry and devotion to duty, but also for his age and for the high esteem in which he was held. But the Victoria Cross is only awarded for acts of bravery in the presence of the enemy, not for being held in high regard or because of being a certain age whilst carrying out those courageous actions.

Rev Hardy was awarded the VC for cumulative actions; those on one day at the beginning of the month, followed by two days at the end of the same month in 1918. This author would argue that Fr William Doyle deserved the Victoria Cross for cumulative conspicuous bravery and dedication to duty over a continuous two week period the previous year, to which there were many witnesses, even if there was insufficient eye-witness testimony for the actions in which he was killed on 16 August 1917.

Many of Fr Willie Doyle's actions resonate with details of the citations for the three chaplains who were awarded the Victoria Cross. Of particular note was the fact that Rev Mellish stayed in the danger zone at St Eloi when his battalion was relieved in order to tend and rescue wounded men. Fr Willie Doyle's battalion was relieved early in August 1917, but he remained in the Front Line near Frezenberg, under heavy shell fire, in order to minister to the battalions previously looked after by Fr Browne, when the latter was recalled to the Irish Guards and his replacement refused to take up the appointment. In his own words:

> *There was nothing else for it but to remain on and do his work, and glad I was I did so, for many a man went down that night, the majority of whom I was able to assist.[18]*

Indeed, Fr Browne managed to slip away from the Irish Guards for a short time, in order to visit some of the Royal Dublin Fusiliers, about ten days after his transfer. In his letter of 15 August, written to his brother Rev W.F. Browne, C.C., he said:

> *Father Doyle is a marvel – you may talk of heroes and saints – they are hardly in it! I went back the other day to see the old Dubs, as I heard they were having – we'll say, a taste of the war. No one has yet been appointed to my place and Fr D has done double work. So unpleasant were the conditions*

that the men had to be relieved frequently. Fr. D had no one to relieve him and so he stuck to the mud and the shells, the gas and the terror.[19]

There is plenty of witness testimony of Fr Doyle performing similar actions to those of the three padres who were awarded the Victoria Cross, throughout his eighteen months on the Western Front.

Moreover, during the early fighting known as the Battle of Third Ypres, two VC's awarded bear points of comparison between the recipients and Willie Doyle. Both were awarded to non-combatants; the first for actions by a medical officer during the Battle of Pilkem Ridge, commencing 31 July 1917, the day when Fr Doyle was waiting in reserve with his men at Brandhoek Camp; the other was for a stretcher-bearer of 16th (Irish) Division on 16 August 1917, the day when Fr Willie Doyle was actually killed.

A Victoria Cross of 16 August 1917

Major General Hickie indicated that he had supported the unsuccessful VC recommendation made by both the Commanding Officer of Fr Doyle's battalion, 8th Royal Dublin Fusiliers, and the Brigadier of 48th Brigade. However, there was a successful recommendation for another battalion of 16th (Irish) Division. This was for twenty-two-year-old Frederick Room, 2nd Royal Irish Regiment, 49th Brigade, for whom the *London Gazette* of 17 October 1917 reported:

No 8614 Pte. (acting L.Cpl.) Frederick G. Room, R.Ir.Regt. (Bristol)
  For most conspicuous bravery when in charge of his company stretcher-bearers.
  During the day the company had many casualties, principally from enemy machine gun and snipers. The company was holding a line of shell-holes and short trenches. L./Cpl, Room worked continuously under intense fire, dressing the wounded and helping to evacuate them. Throughout this period, with complete disregard for his own life, he showed unremitting devotion to his duties.
  By his courage and fearlessness he was the means of saving many of his comrades lives.

One wonders why Frederick Room's case was approved but Willie Doyle's was not and at what stage did Fr Doyle's 'cause' come to an end? Although there is a file for the chaplain at the National Archives, the contents are purely administrative relating to Fr Doyle's appointment and the aftermath of his death. It contains nothing about the award of the Military Cross, let alone any recommendation for the Victoria Cross (or any recommendation for the DSO for Wytschaete as cited by Professor O'Rahilly and Lieutenant F.M. Kiernan.) [FN4] Did the Corps Commander turn it down, or the Army Commander, or the Commander-in-Chief, or influential voices on the VC committee, or the King?

Perhaps some clue can be gleaned from the diary of the Commander-in-Chief, Field-Marshal Sir Douglas Haig, who visited Lieutenant General Gough, Fifth Army Commander and Lieutenant General Watts XIX Corps Commander on Friday 17 August 1917. Haig recorded in his diary about the latter:

> *At XIX Corps I saw General Watts who gave a bad account of the two Irish Divisions (36th and 16th)*[20]

This is a somewhat ambiguous remark, because it could mean that General Watts was displeased with the two divisions, or it could mean that it was a shocking or difficult account to relay and listen to. Haig goes on to describe mitigating circumstances for the two divisions and, indeed, four days later Watts commended 16th (Irish) Division for fighting well, despite considerable hardships. When Haig saw Gough, however, it was clear that Gough was looking for a scapegoat. Haig recorded:

> *He was not pleased with the action of the Irish Divisions of XIX Corps (36th and 16th.) They seem to have gone forward, but failed to keep what they had won. These 2 divisions were in the Messines battle and had an easy victory. The men are Irish and did not like shelling, so Gough said.*[21]

Haig said:

> *But I gather the attacking troops had a long march up the evening before the battle through Ypres to the front line and then had to fight from zero 4.45 a.m. to nightfall. The men could have had no sleep and must have been dead*

tired. Here also a number of concrete buildings and dugouts were never really destroyed by artillery fire, and do not appear to have been taken. So the advances made here were small.... After Gough has got at the facts more fully I have arranged to talk the matter over with him.[22] [FN5]

Writing home to his wife on 20 September 1917, Lt Col Rowland Feilding of 6th Connaught Rangers commented about units of 16th (Irish) Division:

The battalion had a bad time in the fighting at Passchendaele while I was away ... The weather and fates fought against them ... In the case of some other battalions – to quote a description that has been given to me – after four or five days waiting in the trenches, the men were so exhausted with the shelling, and their feet so sore and swollen from the wet, that when the time came to attack they were so weak that they could scarcely have blown out a candle.[23]

Certainly, the opinion of Gough, as well as being at odds with Haig's and Feilding's comments, was not supported by General Officer Commanding 16th (Irish) Division. Even allowing for some natural bias, Major General William Hickie had nothing to gain from writing in his private letter to Brigadier General Kays in November 1917:

I can say without boasting that this is a Division of brave men – and even among them Father Doyle stood out.[24]

The VC recommendation for Acting Lance Corporal Room evidently did reach Gough. Was it approved because Room was English and had done his proper, allotted, job courageously well; whereas Fr Doyle was Irish and was associated with combat troops who, in Gough's opinion, had not performed their roles well? Moreover, although stretcher-bearer Room was a non-combatant, his role did take him into the forward lines, whereas the non-combatant padre had been ordered to retire behind the front line. Or was it just the luck of the draw? The Irish historian Tom Johnstone commented about the stretcher-bearers:

Without detracting from Cpl. Room's bravery, it is recorded by regimental historians that all stretcher-bearers behaved with the utmost gallantry in terrible conditions of rain and knee-deep mud, under heavy and unrelenting shell-fire.[25]

Stephen Snelling, author of a book in the series of *VCs of the Great War* indicates that the unit history only makes fleeting reference to Room's actions and that the only significant reference to be found anywhere is the VC citation. Indeed, this author would question whether, irrespective of Gough's opinion, Room was singled out further up the command chain.

On 26 August 1917, on notepaper headed Windsor Castle, Lord Sandfordham (Principal Private Secretary to King George V) wrote to General Sir W.R. Robertson (Chief of the Imperial General Staff) part of which states:

The King has read Lord Milner's Minute of the 23rd. in the War Cabinet papers, G.T. 1823. It confirms what His Majesty has heard for some time of the harm done by the repeated Press utterances in praise of the doings of the Dominion troops, while there is almost silence as to the British achievements and Losses... His Majesty asks whether you do not think that more information should be given as to the doings of the <u>British</u> units and their efforts and successes.[26]

By rewarding L/Cpl Room for his selfless bravery the powers-that-be highlighted the efforts of a <u>British</u> unit i.e. 16th (Irish) Division but decorated an Englishman (who was born and lived in Bristol) whose loyalty to Britain would be unquestionable, rather than the unknown allegiance of an equally deserving Irishman.

Another VC for the Medical Officer

Another VC of 'Third Ypres', which was actually a Bar to the Victoria Cross, was the famous case of Captain Noel Chavasse, who had already won a VC for actions at Guillemont on 9 August 1916. He had also been awarded a Military Cross in June 1915 and Mentioned in Despatches the following November. Captain Chavasse's Bar to the Victoria Cross was published in the *London Gazette* on Friday 14 September 1917:

For most conspicuous bravery and devotion to duty when in action.
   Though severely wounded early in the action whilst carrying a wounded

soldier to the Dressing Station, Capt. Chavasse refused to leave his post, and for two days not only continued to perform his duties, but in addition went out repeatedly under heavy fire to search for and attend to the wounded who were lying out.

During these searches, although practically without food during this period, worn with fatigue and faint with his wound, he assisted to carry in a number of badly wounded men, over heavy and difficult ground.

By his extraordinary energy and inspiring example, he was instrumental in rescuing many wounded who would have otherwise undoubtedly succumbed under the bad weather conditions.

This devoted and gallant officer subsequently died of his wounds."

The award of the Bar to Noel Chavasse's VC merits close examination in contrast to the case to be made for Willie Doyle. This author suggests that the citation has been overstated, either unwittingly due to the ambiguous nature of a certain comment, or deliberately. This citation echoes the first sentence of that for Rev Hardy, by the addition of the phrase 'devotion to duty' – a quality also more than self-evident in Fr Doyle's actions. Another extract from Fr Browne's letter of 15 August says:

I met the Adjutant of one of my two Battalions, who previously had only known Fr. D by sight. His first greeting to me was:- 'Little Fr Doyle' (they all call him that, more in affection than anything else) 'deserves the VC more than any man that ever wore it. We cannot get him away from the line while the men are there: he is in with his own and he is in with us. The men couldn't stick it half so well if he weren't there ...[27]

The fatal wound Noel Chavasse sustained whilst on duty in an advanced aid post coincided with the misgivings George V was starting to have, as expressed in the Stamfordham to Robertson letter written some weeks after the death of Chavasse, but before his award was gazetted. The King's view that more information was needed about the 'doings' and 'efforts' of British units was:

It certainly would be popular in the country and at the same time help to dissipate the erroneous ideas formed by our Allies as to the share we are taking in the war.[28]

Noel Chavasse was also a non-combatant, a medical officer of the Royal Army Medical Corps attached to a territorial unit, 10th (Scottish) Battalion, The King's (Liverpool) Regiment. The Liverpool Scottish did not take part in the Messines offensive and, during the six weeks prior to the launch of the Third Ypres campaign, they had been for a month of training in the Pas de Calais, followed by one four day spell in the trenches in the Wieltje area before being relieved. They then attacked on 31 July and during the ensuing Battle of Pilkem Ridge, Captain Chavasse was working in the advanced Regimental Aid Post, inside a captured German dug-out. From there he went outside that first night to help rescue a number of wounded men. On 4 August he died at the Casualty Clearing Station at Brandhoek.

Noel Chavasse's Commanding Officer Lieutenant Colonel F.R. Davidson wrote to the doctor's father on 2 August 1917:

> *I am sorry to say that Noel has been wounded today. He was hit early in the attack on 31 July., but stuck to the Battalion and carried out his duties. This morning at 3 a.m. he was caught by a shell and hit in several places.*[29]

But did Lt Col Davidson actually go on to recommend the Victoria Cross? There is nothing in the battalion war diary written up by him to indicate that such a recommendation had been made. It was noted on 8 August, four days after Noel died, that the Major General Commanding 55th Division made an inspection and congratulated all ranks on their splendid work during the attack on 31 July, but there is no special mention of individuals. Lt Col Davidson noted the casualty figures in the diary as at 31 August, including those for 31 July 1917, and the fact that four officers had been killed in action or died of wounds. No special note was made of the demise of Captain Chavasse or a gallantry recommendation. Lt Col Davidson did note gallantry awards for the "recent operations" as being five Military Crosses, two DCM's, one Bar to a Military Medal and seventeen Military Medals. Ribands [sic] for these awards were presented after church parade on 1 September, but there was no mention of a pending recommendation for posthumous award for Captain Chavasse. Nor were there any recommendations in the reports or war diaries of the R.A.M.C.

The 8th Royal Dublin Fusiliers' war diary also does not indicate that a VC recommendation had been made for Fr Doyle; neither were there any other gallantry recommendations listed, but then there was hardly anyone left in the battalion, even before the actions of 16 August 1917. However, the death of Fr Doyle was reported in the battalion war diary and the fact that he had died alongside two officers in an advanced combat position.

On 14 August 1917, Lieutenant Daniel Galvin of 9th Royal Dublin Fusiliers wrote home and made a telling comment. Galvin's battalion was one of the two ministered to by Fr Browne before his departure to the Irish Guards. He confirms the two padres' accounts of Fr Doyle taking over responsibility for the two extra battalions, and of Fr Doyle making himself constantly available in the front lines. Lt Galvin said about this devotion to duty in the presence of the enemy:

If ever a man earned the VC in this war, it is Father Doyle. He is simply splendid. He comes up every night under heavy shell-fire, burying the dead and binding the wounded and cheering the men. I wish to heavens we had a few doctors like him.[30]

Noel Chavasse was, indeed, one such doctor in the mould Lt Galvin would have liked. However, what is troubling about the Bar to the doctor's VC is that the citation for it conflicts with other available evidence. The 10th Liverpool Scottish's war diary, unfortunately, does not have any detailed accounts of the battalion's actions during the Battle of Pilkem Ridge, such as those which are contained in the war diaries of the battalions of Royal Dublin Fusiliers for the Battle of Langemarck two weeks later. The historian of the Liverpool Scottish, Major A.M. McGilchrist, whilst providing a bit more detail in his book published in 1930, basically just echoes the words of the VC citation. But the research done by Noel Chavasse's biographer, Ann Clayton, paints a different picture in a number of key areas.

Ann Clayton's research was extensive. Her primary sources included the personal letters and papers of the Chavasse family, plus diaries, recollections and reminiscences of five men who served with Noel Chavasse, including Private Edmund Herd who, from April 1916, had acted as Chavasse's orderly as well as stretcher-bearer. According to Ann Clayton's account, Captain Chavasse was standing outside the Regimental Aid Post and waving to soldiers to indicate its location, when he was hit by a shell splinter early in the attack of 31 July 1917. She records that Noel was well enough to walk back to the underground Wieltje dugout,[FN6] where he had his wound dressed; whereas the citation says he was severely wounded whilst carrying a wounded soldier.

After Noel had his wound dressed, he returned to the Regimental Aid Post in the more forward position, which was inside a captured German, two-storey, pill box situated by a farm. There are parallels with Fr Doyle. The first one being that Willie was sent back to battle Headquarters on the morning of 16 August (albeit he wasn't injured), but did not stay long, insisting on rejoining his men in the fighting zone. Secondly, Noel's final fatal injury occurred inside the RAP from a shell entering the doorway which faced, of course, towards the German lines. Likewise, Willie may have gone to his death in the same manner, but what is certain is that he was trying to get a wounded officer away from danger.

Ann Clayton continues with her account, that after returning from Wieltje to the Regimental Aid Post on 31 July 1917, Captain Chavasse made sorties that night into the open. He systematically combed the torn-up area vacated by the Germans only hours earlier, and helped to fetch in the wounded, including Captain Thomas Owtram who was retrieved by stretcher bearers under the direction of Captain Chavasse. Ann Clayton points out that the area concerned was not no-man's-land, as it was in possession of the Allied forces. However, it was under continual bombardment, both from the retreating Germans and any Allied shells that fell short.

Ann Clayton then deals with the final four days of Noel Chavasse's life, the first and second of August whilst he remained at his post, and the third and fourth at the Casualty Clearing Station where he died. She describes the early morning scene of 1 August 1917 when a queue of wounded had formed, standing in the rain, outside the RAP because there was no more room inside. Doctor Chavasse and his assistants worked desperately, cleaning and dressing wounds, before pointing out to the walking-wounded the safest way back to the dressing station at Wieltje.

Although Ann Clayton alludes to the historian of the Liverpool Scottish, whose account ties in with the citation, there is nothing in her narrative to support the statement in the citation that Chavasse left the RAP repeatedly during 1 and 2 August, to locate and attend to the wounded. In addition, according to the 10th Liverpool Scottish's war diary a total of 180 other ranks and officers were wounded for the period of 31 July to 31 August. It is safe to assume that these figures largely relate to the actions of the Battle of Pilkem Ridge, because the battalion started moving back well behind the lines on 4th August, and remained in the peaceful area of St Omer until mid-September. Therefore, it appears that Doctor Chavasse would have had his hands full with casualties coming into the RAP (walking wounded and stretcher cases) without being frequently out scouring for more. Certainly, the testimony which Ann Clayton has gathered points to the RAP being very busy; also that Captain Chavasse was particularly pleased with the assistance rendered by a captured German medical officer.

Ann Clayton draws attention to uncertainty about the number, and degree of severity, of the wounds suffered by Noel Chavasse in the lead up to his death. Pte Herd, who was there, did not record anything in his diary about the medical officer sustaining as many injuries as was later claimed by persons who were not there. Opinions also differed about the severity of the initial head wound suffered by Noel on 31 July.

This author suggests that the relevance of all these issues to Fr Doyle's story is that, in his case, the first-hand testimony of his orderly, Pte McInespie, seems to have been disregarded (or not sought) and that the first-hand testimony of Pte Herd about Dr. Chavasse was also deemed unimportant, but for crucially different reasons.

The citation for Noel Chavasse's Bar to the Victoria Cross appears in Ann Clayton's book at the end of her narrative, nearly twenty pages after her assessment of his actions for the relevant three day period commencing 31 July 1917. This provides a grand finale, but there is an intriguing symmetry to the fact that the citation is placed so far away from the narrative drawn from primary sources.

Seen from the perspective of Ann Clayton's research (albeit allowing that Chavasse did search outside of the RAP on the night of 31 July) it seems that the medical officer actually worked ceaselessly inside the aid post, before a shell found its way inside to inflict the lethal injury. This raises the question of how and why part of the citation came to be worded as it was: *... for two days not only continued to perform his duties, but in addition went out repeatedly under heavy fire to search for and attend to the wounded...*[31]

Perhaps the answer can be found in the letter written to Captain Chavasse's parents by Major General Jeudwine, Officer Commanding 55th Division, part of which, after paying tribute to Chavasse, made a somewhat ambiguous statement:

His death is a great loss to the Regiment, the Division, and the whole Army. We, his comrades, were proud of the distinction he had already won and for the noble deeds for which it was conferred by the King. His gallantry again on this occasion was magnificent ... many men who would probably have perished but for his self-sacrificing efforts were found, brought in and attended to by him before he received other wounds which proved fatal.[32][FN7]

Noel Chavasse's devotion to duty was unquestionable; his outstanding dedication in remaining at his post and working in appalling conditions with no rest, when also wounded, was unquestionable; his bravery in working thus in a location subject to shell-fire was unquestionable. What is open to doubt, however, is the interpretation of Jeudwine's words, which could be read to imply Chavasse had single-handedly rescued and treated many men and must have spent as much time working outside of the RAP as inside. The question this author asks is whether the citation for the Bar to the Victoria Cross was embellished, based on a false understanding (or deliberately exaggerated interpretation) of Jeudwine's words? This would fulfill the criteria of *bravery in the presence of the enemy* and be in line with the citation for his first Victoria Cross, which was much more detailed.

This author suspects that the opinions of King George V, as expressed in the letter of 26 August 1917 from Stamfordham to Robertson, along with the influence of Lord Derby, the Secretary of State for War, secured the Bar to the VC for Captain Chavasse and also may have put paid to the recommendation for Fr Doyle.

Lord Derby was a friend of Noel Chavasse's father, the Bishop of Liverpool. He also had strong connections to the city and was responsible for recruiting the Liverpool Pals Battalions in 1914. In October 1916, whilst still only Under-Secretary of State for War, he had infringed protocol by writing to the Bishop of Liverpool informing and congratulating him on the forthcoming award of Noel's first Victoria Cross:

> *I am doing something which is absolutely forbidden by War Office rules and yet I cannot resist the temptation to break the rules ... I want to congratulate you and him most sincerely on gaining the Victoria Cross.*[33]

In December 1916 Lord Derby was promoted to Secretary of State for War. In March 1917 he was involved in a consultation process between F.E.G. Ponsonby of the Privy Purse Office at Buckingham Palace, Lieutenant General J.S. Cowans at the War Office and the King, about the Victoria Cross ribbon. Cowans wrote to Ponsonby on 15 March 1917:

I have shown your letter to the Secretary of State, and we quite understand about the VC ribbon being by itself above other medals and decorations.

Lord Derby quite agrees that the best solution would be for a bronze VC to be attached to the VC ribbon in khaki, and in the event of the recipient receiving a bar to his VC he would then wear two miniature VCs on the ribbon. I quote your own words.

Would you kindly take His Majesty's orders on the subject, so we can get the matter settled?[34]

Also in that file is a typed transcript of the citation for the Bar to Noel Chavasse's Victoria Cross.

Seven days after Noel's death a letter, dated 11 August 1917, expressing sympathy from King George V (albeit signed by a Lady in Waiting) was sent to the Bishop of Liverpool. Then on 5 September Lord Derby again broke protocol, writing to the Bishop:

I signed something last night which gave me the most mixed feelings of deep regret and great pleasure and that was the submission to His Majesty that a Bar should be granted to the Victoria Cross gained by your son. There is no doubt whatever that this will be approved ...[35]

By this time, one assumes, the recommendation for the Victoria Cross for Willie Doyle must have been turned down. It is certain that his father did not receive a letter of sympathy from the King. Perhaps a recommendation had actually reached the desk of Lord Derby for consideration by the Victoria Cross committee; maybe it was considered by the committee; maybe someone considered the timing was all wrong because it would take away the gloss of the award to Noel Chavasse. Lord Derby commented in his letter to Noel's father:

In all the records of Victoria Crosses given I do not think there is one which will appeal to the British Public more than the record for which this Bar is to be given ...[36]

The deeds and death of Noel Chavasse were well documented in the Press and on 29 August a memorial service for him (and all the Liverpool Scottish deaths for the Battle of Pilkem Ridge) was held in the Parish Church of St Nicholas, on the Mersey waterfront. By this time also, Willie Doyle's deeds and death had been covered by the national Press, by newspapers in London, Liverpool, Glasgow and Dublin.

CONCLUSION

Fr Doyle may have been a non-combatant but, in his eyes at least, his role was in the front lines with the combat troops. His purpose was to attend to the Sacramental needs of his flock and to give them the comfort of religion and, in particular, the Last Rites of the Church to the dying and dead. A previous quote in an earlier chapter, from 2/Lt Frank Laird, referred to ordinary mortals taking cover under shell-fire, whereas Fr Doyle *made for them to see was he wanted*. As Fr Doyle once observed:

> *Over and over again I have seen men risking their lives to save or help a comrade, and these brave fellows knew the risk they were taking, for when a Boche shell falls in a certain place, you clear as quickly as you can, since several more are pretty certain to land close. It was a case of duty for me, but real courage for them.*[37]

And another telling comment after tending to a man whose legs had been blown off:

> *The Extreme Unction, as I have noticed time and again eased his bodily pain. 'I am so much better now and easier, God Bless You,' as I left him to attend a dying man.*[38]

One wonders what the citation for Fr Doyle would have been had the VC recommendation been granted, and whether it would have been solely for his deeds on 16 August, or if it would have included cumulative actions of the two weeks leading up to that day (in the same way that Rev Hardy was decorated for cumulative actions.) Major General Hickie's assessment (to Kays) was:

> *Fr. Doyle was one of the best priests I have ever met and one of the bravest*

men who have fought or worked out here. He did his duty **(and more than his duty)** most nobly and has left a memory and a name behind him that will never be forgotten. On the day of his death, 16 August, **he had worked in the front line and even in front of that line** and appeared to know no fatigue. (He never knew fear.) He was killed by a shell towards the close of the day and was buried on the Frezenberg Ridge.[39]

Hickie could not have witnessed Fr Doyle's actions on 16 August, but he must have been confident about the testimony of those who did. Whether there was sufficient eye-witness testimony for the grant of the Victoria Cross, in view of the large losses that day, is unknown. What is known is that there were a large number of eye-witnesses who testified to Fr Doyle's fearless actions in the presence of the enemy, whilst carrying out his duties as a priest, for two horrific weeks of August 1917 prior to his death on the battlefield. One such example is an extract from a letter written by Daniel Galvin to Professor O'Rahilly shortly after the publication of the biography:

... the extracts from Father Doyle's diary relating to the fortnight in August before he was killed are a very true description of a terrible time; and also gives those who wondered at his continuous contempt for death a small idea of what moral bravery means ... The dates and places in the book are very accurate ...[40]

Returning to Fr Browne, a further extract from his letter of 15 August stated:

Another Officer, also a Protestant, said 'Fr D. never rests. Night and Day he is with us. He finds a dying or dead man, does all, comes back smiling, makes a little cross and goes out to bury him, and then begins all over again.' I needn't say, that through all this, the conditions of the ground and air and discomfort surpass anything that I ever dreamt of in the worst days of the Somme.[41]

A report from Sir Philip Gibbs appeared in the *Daily Chronicle* and *Daily Telegraph*, in which he uses eye-witness testimony about Fr Doyle from soldiers of the 36th (Ulster) Division, who served and lined up next to the 16th (Irish) Division in August 1917:

The Orangemen will not forget a certain Roman Catholic chaplain who lies in a soldier's grave in that sinister plain beyond Ypres. He went forward and backward over the battlefield with bullets whining about him, seeking out the dying and kneeling in the mud beside them to give them Absolution ... Each time he came back across the field he was begged to remain in comparative safety. Smilingly he shook his head and went again into the storm.[42]

A letter in the *Glasgow Weekly News* of 1 September 1917 written by a Belfast man of the 36th (Ulster) Division echoed Sir Philip Gibb's report and contained the following statement about Fr Doyle:

He was as ready to risk his life to take a drop of water to a wounded Ulsterman as to assist men of his own faith and regiment. If he risked his life in looking after Ulster Protestant soldiers once, he did it a hundred times in the last few days ...[43]

The Royal Dublin Fusiliers were equally as effusive. Sergeant T. Flynn wrote to his mother on 18 August 1917 and the letter was published in the *Irish News* eleven days later, part of which said:

We had the misfortune to lose our chaplain, Fr. Doyle, the other day. He was a real saint and would never leave his men, and it was really marvellous to see him burying dead soldiers under terrible shell fire ... Everybody says that he has earned the VC many times over, and I can vouch for it myself from what I have seen him do many a time.[44]

The *Catholic News* of 15 September 1917 printed a letter from an officer of the 16th (Irish) Division, which was reproduced in *The Clongownian* magazine and identified only by the initials F.K. This was probably Lieutenant F.M. Kiernan, who was quoted in the O'Rahilly biography for providing testimony of how Fr Doyle died. Part of the letter said:

'God bless Father Doyle' is the heartfelt wish of all the men of the Irish Division today ... Ypres sounded the knell. Recommended for the D.S.O.

at Wytschaete, he did wonderful work at Ypres, and was recommended for the VC Many a dying soldier on that bloody field has flashed a last look of loving recognition as our brave padre rushed to his aid, braving the fearful barrage and whistling machine-gun bullets, to give his boys a last few words of hope.[45]

Other Royal Dublin Fusilier survivors of that bleak August were Captain Healy and Lt Col H.R. Stirke and tributes to Fr Doyle from them are contained in Appendix B, along with the full text of F.K.'s letter and other tributes.

Interestingly, the wording of the opening sentence of the Hickie to Kays letter suggests that Major General Hickie was responding to an enquiry about Fr Doyle. The fame of Willie Doyle's deeds had evidently reached the Brigadier General in Dublin and he wanted to know more from a reputable source.

Here is another interesting aside to finish this chapter. On 3 April 1920 someone signing himself as J.S. Fletcher, from an address near Emsworth in Hampshire, wrote to Professor O'Rahilly:

I have just had the privilege of reviewing your life of Fr. William Doyle for The Guardian; he was a singularly fine and noble man and one of whom Irish men of all creeds may well be proud. I can assure you that his splendid devotion was fully and widely appreciated in this country at the time of his heroic death. But there is one passage in your book to which I take strong exception, and I express it to you, though I have not mentioned it in my review. You say that in regard to Fr. Doyle and the Victoria Cross that 'the triple disqualification of being an Irishman, a Catholic and a Jesuit proved insuperable.' I think that upon closer reflection you will see that you cannot justify that remark.[46]

Mr Fletcher then goes on to explain his reasoning in some detail, pointing out that the VC has been awarded to a great many Irish Catholics; that Catholic chaplains had received gallantry awards; and that the Society of Jesus was the most popular of the religious orders in England. Professor O'Rahilly evidently replied, because Mr Fletcher again writes on 25 April 1920:

My dear Sir, I am very much obliged to you for your very courteous letter ...

> *I do not, of course, know what private information you may have as regards the War Office and the giving of the Victoria Cross. But as an old journalist of 30 years standing, with my ?^{FN8} knowledge of high official methods and practice in our Government departments, I can safely affirm that no considerations of creed or nationality is ever allowed to enter into the bestowal of place or honour. As I remarked, before, I think, the practice of bestowals of the Victoria Cross on Irishmen and Catholics is a very high one, as may easily be ascertained, since this list is printed in several works of repute.*[47]

So, did Professor O'Rahilly really have private information from within the War Office? And if he did, why did he not publicise it at some future date, before his death in 1969?

No doubt Mr Fletcher would have remained completely confident that no inside influences would ever be at work, based on connections and social standing, with regard to the bestowals of place or honours, even had he seen Lord Derby's letters to the Bishop of Liverpool!

Finally, this author hopes she has demonstrated that all the available evidence supports an award of the Victoria Cross to Fr Doyle. If retrospective awards could be made for exceptional cases that were overlooked at the time, a good case could be made for Father William Doyle. Whether retrospective awards per se are desirable or not is another matter.

Footnote 1: Horace Francis Kays was born on 15 May 1861. He was educated at Harrow and joined the Highland Light Infantry in December 1883. He took part in campaigns in the north west frontier of India in 1891 and was mentioned in despatches. He served in the South African war at the beginning of the century and was promoted to Major, October 1902. Further promotions followed: Lieutenant Colonel, December 1908, commanding 2nd Battalion, H.L.I.; Colonel, December 1912; Temporary Brigadier General, August 1914. He was created a CB on 3 June 1918, *'for services in connection with the war'*, and his name was *'brought to the notice of the Secretary of State for War for valuable services rendered in connection with the war'* (London Gazette 6 July 1918). However, he did not serve overseas during the war.[48]

Footnote 2: The Rev Mellish's Victoria Cross not only appeared in the London Gazette within a month after his actions, but a few days afterwards the VC ribbon was presented to him by General Haldane in front of the personnel Third Division, along with the ribbons for those who received the DSO, MC, DCM and MM, as described by the Rev Pat Leonard.[49] By contrast, Noel Chavasse's Bar to the VC was not noted in the Liverpool Scottish War Diary when it was recorded that other gallantry ribbons had been awarded.

Footnote 3: The rest of the citation reads: *An infantry patrol had gone out to attack a previously located enemy post in the ruins of a village, the Reverend Theodore Bayley Hardy (C.F.) being then at company headquarters. Hearing firing, he followed the patrol, and about four hundred yards beyond our front line of posts found an officer of the patrol dangerously wounded. He remained with the officer until he was able to get assistance to bring him in. During this time there was a great deal of firing, and an enemy patrol actually penetrated between the spot at which the officer was lying and our front line and captured three of our men.*

On a second occasion, when an enemy shell exploded in the middle of one of our posts, the Reverend T. B. Hardy at once made his way to the spot, despite the shell and trench mortar fire which was going on at the time, and set to work to extricate the buried men. He succeeded in getting out one man who had been completely buried. He then set to work to extricate a second man, who was found to be dead. During the whole of the time that he was digging out the men this chaplain was in great danger, not only from shell fire, but also because of the dangerous condition of the wall of the building which had been hit by the shell which buried the men.

On a third occasion he displayed the greatest devotion to duty when our infantry, after a successful attack, were gradually forced back to their starting trench. After it was believed that all our men had withdrawn from the wood, Chaplain Hardy came out of it, and on reaching an advanced post asked the men to help him to get in a wounded man. Accompanied by a serjeant, he made his way to the spot where the man lay, within ten yards of a pill-box which had been captured in the morning, but was subsequently recaptured and occupied by the enemy. The wounded man was too weak to stand, but between them the chaplain and the serjeant eventually succeeded in getting him to our lines. Throughout the day the enemy's artillery, machine-gun, and trench mortar fire was continuous, and caused many casualties. Notwithstanding, this very gallant chaplain was seen moving quietly amongst the men and tending the wounded, absolutely regardless of his personal safety."

Footnote 4: Lieutenant F.M. Kiernan, 8th Royal Dublin Fusiliers, stated in his letter published in *The Clongownian* (the magazine of Clongowes Wood College) that Fr Doyle was recommended for the DSO for Wytschaete. Perhaps this was for the same action for which Company Sergeant Major Tait won the DCM. Fr Doyle had assisted CSM Tait in digging men out of the rubble of the collapsed China Wall. Supporters of Fr Doyle would find it particularly galling that, earlier in the war, the DSO had been given to Officers who had not come under fire. The DSO was instituted in 1886:

The intention was to create an award for Officers in time of War for distinguished service where the award of the Victoria Cross was not appropriate. During 1914 to 1916, a number of awards were made to men who had not come under fire. Consequently, from 1ˢᵗ January 1917, instructions were given that the award should be restricted to 'The Fighting Services'.[50]

In contrast to Fr Doyle's case, the Rev Pat Leonard wrote home on 22 November 1916: *What on earth did (he) mean by giving me the DSO?*[51] He goes on to explain that quite a few chaplains were awarded Military Crosses for doing much more than him. Ironically, Noel Chavasse was quick to criticise some chaplains and was at odds with the senior chaplain of 55th Division, the Rev. J.O. Coop, DSO.

Footnote 5: This author could not find any further reference to Haig tackling Gough about his remarks. Lieutenant General Hubert Gough was born in Waterford, to an Anglo-Irish aristocratic family, and his father, uncle and brother had all been awarded the Victoria Cross. In March 1914 he took the lead at the Curragh Barracks in opposing the government's plans to use force, if necessary, to enforce Home Rule when the time came. Nevertheless, according to Major General Hickie, Gough specially applied for the 16th (Irish) Division to be transferred to Fifth Army following the Battle of Messines. Yet he was quick to "play the Irish card" when the "Third Ypres" offensive ground to a halt in mid-August 1917. It seems unlikely, therefore, that Gough would entertain the idea of a southern Irish, Jesuit priest (just three years his junior) being awarded the Victoria Cross.

Footnote 6: The deep dug-outs at Wieltje, lit by electric lights, stretched approximately 200 metres underground, under the main street of the ruined village. The network was so extensive it needed a "town major" to administer and supervise. Whilst troops were safe enough inside, the approach to the dug-outs was well known by the Germans and had been frequently shelled.)

Footnote 7: Ann Clayton has omitted some of the text of this letter. This author contacted the Bodleian Library to discover the full text, but the letter could not be found in the archives.

Footnote 8: the word denoted by the question mark is indecipherable, partly due to the tiny handwriting of the author and partly because the paper is fire damaged. Mr Fletcher's two letters are part of the archive of papers left by Professor O'Rahilly at Blackrock College, which were subsequently caught up in a fire. The edges of the pages of Mr Fletcher's letters were singed.

CHAPTER 35
MOPPING UP:
1918–2013

'He is not missing, he is here.'
Field Marshal Lord Plumer at the unveiling of the Menin Gate, July 1927

Following the Armistice on 11 November 1918, there was no 'land fit for heroes' to return to on the British mainland, let alone in Ireland. All hopes of any quick measure of independence had also expired with the silencing of the guns on the Continent. When southern Irishmen were eventually demobbed and returned to Ireland, they found the country embroiled in political turmoil. Some of them went on to take up arms in the cause of Irish independence, but most, like the majority of the population, were more concerned with trying to earn a living than with the concept of republicanism. Nevertheless, in the December 1918 General Election, the voters of southern Ireland turned against the traditional political caste of the UK government who had let them down so badly; Sinn Féin won 70 per cent of the seats, 73 out of 105. The new Members of Parliament refused to sit at Westminster; they set up the first Dáil Éireann and some Irish Volunteers reconstituted themselves as the Irish Republican Army. Nevertheless, the officialdom of the British government and its administration remained in place, along with its armed forces and army barracks throughout Ireland. In January 1919 these came under attack by the IRA and a guerrilla war ensued until a ceasefire was declared in July 1921.

Meanwhile, the *Treaty of Versailles* was signed on 28 June 1919, which dashed hopes in Ireland that the American government would take up Ireland's cause. As it was, the treaty concerned itself solely with deciding the future of the empires of the losers of the Great War, not of the victors.

Some Irish soldiers were still, at this late stage, waiting demobilisation. One such was Captain Barry Galvin, who, together with his brother Daniel, had served alongside Fr Willie Doyle. Both brothers had sustained serious injuries during the war; whilst Daniel was invalided permanently out of the army, Barry had returned to action. In February 1919 Daniel Galvin was found to be unfit for any further service, eighteen months after sustaining his injury and just two months after Barry had returned from spending nine months as a Prisoner of War in Germany.

Captain Barry Galvin was repatriated on Christmas Day 1918 and was sent for a short while to a concentration camp in Scarborough. He received a letter from the War Office a month later, addressed to him at a Cork address, with the request:

> *I am commanded by the Army Council to request that you will be good enough to forward direct to this Department, for the purpose of record, a statement in duplicate setting out the incidents which led to your capture by the enemy as a Prisoner of War.*[1]

He replied and eventually, on the 26 July 1919, he received another letter informing him that the circumstances of his capture had been investigated and no blame was attached to him. Following a period of leave, Captain Barry Galvin served with distinction for some months with the British Expeditionary Force providing aid in Russia. Then, on the closing day of 1919 the War Office wrote to him again about the demobilisation of the British Army and informed him that his services were no longer required, effective from 6 November 1919. The letter ended:

> *I am to take this opportunity of conveying the thanks of the Army Council for your services during the late war, and for having done all in your power to assist in bringing it to a successful conclusion.*[2]

On the same date as the letter exonerating Barry Galvin from blame for becoming a Prisoner of War, there was a government-sponsored Peace Day celebration, with mixed results. It sparked some demonstrations in favour of republicanism in Ireland, but Donal Hall comments in his study of nationalist politics in County Louth that:

> *The reality of Peace Day in Dundalk indicates a town which regarded the affair with widespread apathy, rather than one seething with republican fervour.*[3]

Apathy was not in evidence when one of the first memorials to the men who fought in the Great War had been unveiled some weeks earlier at St Nicholas' Church of Ireland, Dundalk; a brass tablet commemorating twenty-seven parishioners who had been killed in the war. That same church, together with the town's St Patrick's Roman Catholic Church, was the scene of annual ex-servicemen's parades on 11 November, from 1920, when poppies were widely sold and openly worn.

Sadly there were cases in Ireland of veterans of the Great War being threatened, intimidated and worse. Some estimates suggest that up to 200 ex-servicemen may have been murdered between 1919 and 1922. Nevertheless, this did not prevent memorials springing up throughout the country. In St Patrick's Church of Ireland Cathedral in Dublin there are nearly twenty memorials to individuals or groups who fell in the Great War. An ex-servicemen's association, the Comrades of the Great War, was also established; for example in Dundalk a branch was set up in September 1919 and by the end of the year had two hundred members. Staying in County Louth, Saint Fenian's Roman Catholic Church in Dromin has a stained glass window depicting the Assumption of Our Lady, which is *'dedicated to World War 1 Chaplain Fr William Doyle, SJ.'*

This paradox is illustrated by the case of Tom Barry, who had fought in Mesopotamia and who, on his return to Cork, was involved with ex-servicemen's organisations. Subsequently he became a prominent leader in the Irish Republican Army and took part in guerilla warfare during the Irish War of Independence. Another high profile participant was Emmet Dalton, who won the Military Cross at Ginchy, but who also followed in Tom Barry's footsteps into the IRA.

In February 1920, while the guerrilla war was still being played out, the first edition of Professor Alfred O'Rahilly's biography, *Father William Doyle, S.J., A Spiritual Study,* was published. Daniel Galvin wrote to thank Professor O'Rahilly for the copy of the life of Father Doyle:

> *... which is vividly interesting to anyone who had the good fortune to be intimate with him ... My brother and myself were great friends of Father Doyle's, and between us we were with him the whole time he was in France ...*[4]

Willie's sister Lena wrote to the Professor on 19 February 1920:

> *Although I have not had the pleasure of making your acquaintance, I cannot refrain from writing to you to tell you how delighted we all are with dear Fr Willie's 'Life' ...*[5]

In the summer of that year Hugh Doyle acquired a memento from the area where his son was killed; a small card dated 25 July 1920, adorned by a pressed wild flower and the title *Frezenberg Ridge.*

Souvenir card from Frezenberg Ridge

Some time that summer the town in which Willie's sister Lena lived underwent a terrifying experience as the war against the British continued. The ranks of the Royal Irish Constabulary had by now been increased by ex-Army officers, known as Auxiliaries, and also by temporary constables, largely veterans of the Great War recruited from Britain, who were referred to as the 'Black and Tans'. The nickname quickly became a pejorative expression, deservedly so, and was often used as a catch-all term for all police and army groups. Black and Tans were quick to take reprisals for IRA atrocities and were often indiscriminate and arbitrary in their choice of targets, many of whom were innocent bystanders, leading to even worse carnage. They were blamed for the sacking of Balbriggan, during which fifty-four houses and a hosiery factory were burned down and four Public Houses looted. Major General Hickie, a passionate pre-war supporter of Home Rule, and who had been hugely critical of its abandonment post-war, had absolutely no time for any of these paramilitary outfits.

Assassinations of British agents around the city of Dublin were, by now, a fact of life and a major operation took place on the morning of Sunday 21 November 1920, resulting in a dozen or more deaths and injuries. The war-weary people of Dublin were trying to lead normal lives and a crowd of ten thousand spectators was at Croke Park that same Sunday afternoon, watching a Gaelic Football match between the home team and Tipperary. British security forces were ordered to raid the match looking for suspects from the morning's mayhem. At 3.25 p.m., ten minutes after kick-off, unauthorised shots were fired and chaos ensued. Thirty-one people lost their lives, fourteen of whom were ordinary folk enjoying a football match.

Early in 1921 Alfred O'Rahilly, a staunch republican, was arrested and imprisoned for his political writing and then released in October. In-between, in July, a ceasefire had been declared, followed by, on 6 December, the signing of the Anglo-Irish Treaty. This sparked an even worse conflict in Ireland when family, friends and neighbours turned on one another, such was the vehemence of feeling either in support of the treaty or against. Those against the treaty wanted a fully autonomous republic. Many of those in favour of the treaty regarded it as an acceptable stepping-stone towards that outcome. The treaty provided for a self-governing Irish state in twenty-six of the thirty-two counties, with its own army and police, but with the same dominion status in the British Empire as Canada and Australia. However, those against the treaty could not contemplate swearing allegiance to the British Monarch, especially after so much struggle and bloodshed.

Given what we know of the Doyle family, it is safe to assume that Hugh Doyle may have been in favour of the treaty; Major General Hickie certainly was. Hugh, undoubtedly, would not have been in favour of the occupation, for the second time in six years, of his place of employment, Four Courts. On 14 April 1922 about two hundred anti-treaty militants, from the 1st and 2nd Battalions 1st Dublin Brigade of the IRA, occupied the Four Courts in Dublin. Hugh Doyle, incredibly in his ninetieth year, still commuted from Dalkey to work at Four Courts, until the siege took place. If his age had been no barrier to his continued employment, the siege might certainly have been the catalyst for his retirement! On 3 June 1922 a letter was sent out from Buckingham Palace, which read:

It has been brought to the notice of the King that you have just retired from your post of Chief Clerk in the Bankruptcy Court, Dublin, after completing 73 years of public service. His Majesty desires me to convey to you his congratulations on this unique record, coupled with the earnest hope that you may spend many years of well-earned rest in peace and happiness. Yours very truly A.H.L. Harding.[6]

A local newspaper held in the family archive reported the same event:

Mr Hugh Doyle, Chief Clerk in the Bankruptcy Court Dublin, retired yesterday after an unexampled service of 73 years. He was born on 7 July 1832 and entered the service in June, 1849 when he was only 17 years of age. He was a painstaking and courteous official, and was a regular and unfailing attendant at his office until the Four Courts were seized and occupied by forces of the I.R.A. some five or six weeks ago. He still enjoys good health, and is as active as a man of 90 years could expect to be. His son, Mr Robert Doyle, K.C. is Recorder and County Judge of Galway. The late Father William Doyle, S.J., the holiness and heroism of whose life, crowned by death while zealously discharging his duties as an Army Chaplain during the Great War, has been told in the biography by Professor O'Rahilly, was another son of Mr Hugh Doyle.[7]

A little over a week after the letter from George V was despatched to Hugh Doyle in Dalkey, the King was at Windsor Castle to perform the sad duty of overseeing the laying-up of the Colours of five historic Irish regiments. By now comprising of just two battalions each, 1st and 2nd Battalions the Leinster Regiment, Royal Irish Regiment, Connaught Rangers, Royal Munster Fusiliers and Royal Dublin Fusiliers were disbanded. The Colours of the regiments were passed into the safe-keeping of the Sovereign at St George's Hall on Monday 12 June 1922. This ceremony also marked the retirement of Major General William Hickie from the army.

The occupation of the Four Courts continued until 29 June 1922. The building was bombarded by Free State forces supplied with guns from the British, causing a fire and eventually a huge explosion. This, together with other damage at Custom House, resulted in the destruction of swathes of Irish historical records. Pitched street battles continued in the capital, until the Free State government exerted control on 5 July, and anti-treaty forces dispersed, mainly to the south and west. However, the country was by now firmly in the grip of the most dispiriting, destructive civil war, which petered out in a ceasefire on 24 May 1923; the pro-treaty side finishing on top. Hugh Doyle lived to see the end of the vicious internecine conflict, and nine days after the ceasefire was declared he received a package from the War Office, which contained two campaign medals, a letter and a form. The letter, dated 1 June 1923, said:

> *I am directed to transmit to you the accompanying British War & Victory Medals which would have been conferred upon The Reverend W.J. Doyle had he lived in memory of his services with the British Forces during the Great War. In forwarding the Decorations I am commanded by the King to assure you of His Majesty's high appreciation of the services rendered. I am to request that you will be so good as to acknowledge receipt of the Decorations in the attached form.*[8]

The two campaign medals were proudly preserved by the family alongside Willie's Military Cross and the bronze death plaque and scroll, which would have been received round about the same time.

The Galvin brothers in Cork also applied for and received their campaign medals. Sadly, by the end of 1923 Daniel was dead, aged thirty, having struggled with his health ever since sustaining wounds on the day Fr Doyle was killed.

Hugh Doyle died on 28 March 1924, three months before his ninety-second birthday. That year on Armistice Day eighteen thousand ex-servicemen, led by bands, paraded from College Green, Dublin in front of a crowd estimated at 50,000, who observed the two minutes silence at 11 a.m. Christopher Healy, from Blackrock, County Dublin was unlikely to have been in the crowd. Having joined the British Army in 1908 as a young Private, he was a Captain in Willie Doyle's Royal Dublin Fusiliers and ended the war as a Lieutenant Colonel with the Royal Innniskilling Fusiliers. He applied for his medals in 1924 and the medal index card shows his residence as 'Ginchy' at an address in north west London. Perhaps Christopher Healy had deemed it too dangerous to return to, or remain, in his home town.

Robert Doyle decided to retire from the judiciary round about this time. His duties as Recorder of Galway were becoming increasingly dangerous and he was provided with an armed guard whilst travelling round the court circuit. His great-niece (by marriage) Fay Castles remembered staying with Uncle Bob, who was now in residence at *Melrose,* in the nineteen-forties and:

He told me that after 1922 he didn't wish to work for the Government as he and his father before him had always worked for the British so he retired on a pension of £3,000 a year.[9]

In 1925 William Bernard Hickie was elected, with a record number of votes, as a member of the Seanad of the Irish Free State. That same year he became President of the Area Council (Southern Ireland) of the British Legion, in addition to already working tirelessly in the cause of old comrade associations. In 1926 Hickie oversaw the making of three memorial Celtic Crosses; one was erected at Messines; one at Guillemont; and one, dedicated to the men of the 10th (Irish) Division, was sent to Salonika. Crowds still filled the streets on Armistice Day 1925 and services were well attended.

In 1927 a new French translation, in paperback edition, of Alfred O'Rahilly's biography of Willie Doyle was printed in Paris by P. Lethielleux, 10 Rue Cassette, and by this time Longmans, Green and Co. had issued a third edition of the original work in English. The preceding years had seen translations issued in German and Italian and more were to come in Dutch, Spanish and Polish. The 1920's saw a number of essays written about Fr Doyle's spiritual life, and Catholic publishers such as the Jesuit *Irish Messenger Office* issued many pamphlets on the same theme, which were also translated into foreign languages and distributed on the Continent.

In December 1927 the Secretary of *British Sugar Developments Limited*, writing on behalf of one of the Company's Directors, sent a letter from their offices in London to the Chaplain General's Branch of the War Office:

I have been instructed by Mr. K.J. McKenna to write and ask you if you would be good enough to find out where the Rev. F. William Doyle was buried, and any other information you can obtain about him.[10]

The reply on the twelfth of the month, signed C.A. Lewis, was brief:

With reference to your recent letter, reference MB, asking for information as to the burial place of the Reverend F. William Doyle, I am directed to inform you that it is understood from the Imperial Graves Commission that his grave has not been located but that his name appears on the Tyne Cot memorial.[11]

Another note at the end of that month elaborated slightly:

Killed east of Frezenberg and was at the time buried just behind the front line in the Frezenberg Redoubt: Sheet 2F D.25. The grave however has not been located. Name appears on Tyne Cot mem. Entry in Tyne Cot Mem. Register Part VII.[12]

The Memorial to the Missing at Tyne Cot is located on the ridge east of Ypres that was reached by British Empire Forces on 4 October 1917, during the Battle of Broodseinde, and forms one of the boundary walls to the cemetery of the same name. It bears the names of almost 35,000 men whose last resting place is not known, who died on or after 16 August 1917. A further 54,000 names for the period prior to that date are recorded on the Menin Gate in Ypres.

Willie Doyle's name can be found on panel 160 of the wall, along with three other Chaplains, Fouth Class. Astonishingly, one of these is the Reverend John W. Eyre-Powell, whose family also had a home in Dalkey! He was an Anglican chaplain attached to 27th Labour Corps, who was killed by shell fire in April 1918, and his name is recorded on the war memorial in St Patrick's Church of Ireland, Dalkey.

Tyne Cot was designed by Sir Herbert Baker, one of three principal architects for the Imperial War Graves Commission (as it was then known). Another of the architects, Sir Edwin Lutyens, was later to produce a design for a large memorial park in Dublin. In March 1927 a debate in the Free State Senate failed to resolve the issue of progressing plans for such a memorial, which had been intermittently rumbling on since July 1919, when a trust fund had been established for the purpose. Mr W.T. Cosgrave, President of the Executive Council, appointed a lawyer, Cecil Lavery, to get the project up and running again. In December 1930 his War Memorial Council identified a site of sixty acres running along the River Liffey at Islandbridge and twelve months later the decision was ratified.

The General Election of March 1932 saw Cosgrave replaced by Éamon De Valera, whose radical manifesto included abolishing the oath to the British Monarchy. Nevertheless, although Remembrance Day commemorations were scaled back and the wearing of the poppy was seen to be provocative, the Islandbridge memorial project was continued. Once work commenced the workers were previously unemployed ex-army personnel; fifty percent were ex-British Army and the other half ex-Irish Army. Granite blocks of seven and eight tons from Ballyknocken and Barnaculla were man-handled into place, using tackles of poles and ropes, according to the design set out by Lutyens. The use of mechanical equipment was restricted so that the project provided a longer period of work for the labourers.

Whilst the early stages of the work at Islandbridge were taking place, Professor Alfred O'Rahilly gave a lecture on Father Willie Doyle, S.J., on Sunday 28 January 1934 at the Gaiety Theatre, Dublin. By this time an Austrian veteran soldier of the Great War was becoming increasingly powerful in Germany. When President Hindenburg died in August, Adolf Hitler announced a new *'Führer* law' to be voted on by the public in a plebiscite on 19 August 1934. He won with over 90 per cent of the vote and officially became the *Führer* of Germany.

Back in Dublin, work continued at Islandbridge and was completed in 1939. However, it was not to be officially opened for many years. Meanwhile, Cork man John Lucy had written his memoirs and these were first published in March 1938; he comments early in his book:

And today we southerners, who have fought side by side with the northern men in their own regiments, and who warmly remember their bravery and precious comradeship, heartily damn the righteous ones who earn haloes by fermenting ill blood.[13]

Three years later, another man of Cork, Barry Glavin, who had also served alongside Ulstermen, died at the relatively young age of forty-seven.

The *Irish Messenger* continued to produce biographical booklets about Father Willie Doyle, some of which proclaimed:

FATHER WILLIE, HIS WORLDWIDE APPEAL AND FAVOURS ATTRIBUTED TO HIS INTERCESSION.[14]

The booklets were sold for three or four pence a time and contained a disclaimer, which gives an indication of the contents of the pamphlets. It read:

It would be quite impossible, within the limits of this short pamphlet, to give even a short account of the thousands of cures and favours, spiritual and temporal, attributable to the life of Father Willie. The following list, however, is typical of the rest. It contains notifications of cures and favours from all the Continents of the world, from all the chief countries of Europe, from three-fourths of the shires in England, from every county of Ireland, and from every State of the United States of America. Where the communication has been received in a foreign language an English translation is given. Though, presumably, these notifications are genuine, and the actual experience of the writers, no guarantee of this is given here. Much less is any judgement passed upon the miraculous nature of the occurrences.[15]

One of the testimonies in the booklet would have delighted Willie Doyle, not only in view of his unfulfilled desire to go to the Congo Mission and his fund-raising activities, but also for the image of a money-box, which was a fond memory of his childhood. Headed *Australia*, it says:

This is the Sodality of St. Peter Claver for the African Missions. Funds were very low in January, so I named your holy brother 'Business Manager', and put a picture of him in an empty money-box, telling him how much he loved the negroes while on earth, and asking him to take the Australian Branch under his protection. From that day the box has never been empty: his picture is wrapped in cheques, notes, postal orders, etc. In a few weeks I was able to send £120 to Rome for Africa, and still the box was well filled.[16]

Such testimony followed on from the issue of a prayer for private devotion, written in the 1920's, which was printed in numerous languages on prayer cards and distributed world-wide:

O Jesus, who has given us the example of Your servant, Father William Doyle, graciously grant us the favours we ask You through his intercession ... [make petition] Teach us to imitate his love for You, his heroic devotion to Your service, his zeal for repairing the outrages done to Your glory and for the salvation of souls. Hear our prayer and show us the credit he now enjoys in Heaven so that we may soon be able to venerate him in public worship. Our Father, Hail Mary, Glory Be.[17]

It is hard to say when the last of the pamphlets and prayer cards were printed and distributed. One of the brief biographies, costing three pence, was in its 12th Edition in 1948, with sales up till then of 120,000. The inside front cover of the 12th Edition advertises other leaflets, one of which was four pages long, costing 7s 6d per 100 post free, or 7s 10d per dozen; the contents were a picture of Father Doyle accompanied by some of his sayings and a prayer.

By this time, Adolf Hitler and his cohorts had wreaked more havoc on the world: a Second World War had played out its course; Hitler had committed suicide and post-war trials of war criminals had taken place at Nuremberg. Ireland had remained neutral during this conflict, which was referred to as 'The Emergency.' In 1941, the Irish Secretary of the Department of External Affairs, Joe Walshe, defended his country's stance, explaining that as a small nation Ireland could not assume a role of defender other than of its own people. Back in 1915 the Lucy family from Cork expressed the same sentiment, despite brothers John and Denis serving with the British Army. John Lucy's first leave in April 1915 was painful when he returned home to Cork leaving the unrecovered body of Denis in France:

The ghost of my dead brother had come home with me. However willingly they tried, our family could not easily sacrifice for a cause not directly connected with Ireland.[18]

Nevertheless, during the Second World War, significant numbers of Irishmen had taken up arms against the menace of the *Third Reich* and volunteered to fight with British units, from Battle of Britain pilots to troops at the front. Despite the sentiments expressed twenty-four years previously, John Lucy returned to service with the B.E.F. in France in 1939 and 1940. There was also a large Irish Defence Force to protect their own island and to guard against invasion.

Following the conclusion of WWII, a young Fay Castles, just out of her teens, went to stay with her widowed 'Great-Uncle' Robert at *Melrose*. Fay's aunt Alice had been adopted as a young child by Robert and Jennie Doyle and Fay remembered:

When I was there a knock came on the door and it was some Americans who wanted to see the bedroom of Father Willie Doyle. I believe this was a regular occurrence.[19]

Fay visited several times in 1947 and after the death of her mother in 1948, which was the year Willie Doyle's brother-in-law, also named William, died. He had been preceded three years earlier by his wife. Lena's two sisters had long gone before her; Lil had died in 1914 and Mai in 1939. Lena was the only one of the Doyle siblings to have a typically large Irish family, one of whom died at only 7 months in 1900. Lil's only daughter survived her by just months, and died in 1915 aged 17. Bob Doyle out-lived his wife and siblings by decades; he and his wife Jennie appear to have had only one child, who also died in babyhood, although they adopted Alice Castles. Jennie Doyle, along with her brother, was also the guardian to Alice Castle's four brothers (one of whom was Fay Castle's father) and three sisters who were, evidently, welcome visitors to *Melrose*. As Fay said: *So the house has been well filled with children.*[20]

Up to 1948, small commemorations had been taking place at the War Memorial Gardens at Islandbridge, even though the site was slowly falling into disrepair. It is not known whether any members of the various branches of the Doyle family used to attend. By the following year all vestiges of British power over twenty-six counties of Ireland had been removed and the Free State became a Republic. Gradually, the Great War was air-brushed from its history, as the events of 1916 in Dublin flourished in the public consciousness; the War Memorial gardens at Islandbridge became almost derelict. During this year of 1949 Charlie Doyle followed Lena to the grave. Fay Castles remembers that on another visit:

> *One of Uncle Robert's brothers had lived not too far away I think as Aunt Alice and I would go to open the windows 'to air the house' as it was empty and it was up for sale as he had died.*[21]

William Hickie died in November 1950; he had left the political arena in 1936 and retired from the British Legion in 1948. A year younger than Bob Doyle, he preceded him to the grave by eleven years (aged eighty-five). Perhaps there was a toast to the memory of Hickie in April 1952, during a reunion dinner held by ex-Royal Dublin Fusiliers at the Kildare Street Club in Dublin. In attendance were several men whose names Willie Doyle would have recognised: G.H. Aylward, N. Drury, T.A. Glanville, E.A. Poulter, J.J. Carroll, S.J.M. Carroll, D.B. Gilmore. Telegrams were sent and received, when Her Majesty Queen Elizabeth II responded and sincerely thanked them for the following greeting:

> *The Officers the late RDF Dining Kildare Street Club Dublin. Tomorrow Saturday submit their humble duty to HM and at the same time assure her of their loyalty and affection to her and the Crown they had the honour to serve.*[22]

Perhaps this message from the ex-army officers was as much about making a private protest about feeling forgotten by their own Irish people, as the protocol behind the sentiment.

The following year a contemporary of the Doyle family's youngest nieces and nephews, Gerry McMahon, began a forty-five year career with the Irish Defence Forces, rising to the rank of Lieutenant General and becoming Chief of Staff. He later had this to say about his education and the existence of War Memorials commemorating the dead of the First World War:

> *Growing up I was never aware of the sacrifices of so many Irishmen in the Great War. It received little time in the history I learned in school except as a backdrop to the 1916 Rising and its aftermath. I was aware that there was a War Memorial in my native city but I never attended a service there. That was something British ex-servicemen sometimes did. Later on as an officer in the Defence Forces I studied the Great War from a military history perspective and although I was examining the conflict in order to extract lessons appropriate to my profession, I must admit that for the first time the enormous Irish involvement started to get through to me.*[23]

During the early military career of Gerry McMahon in the 1950's, the name of Fr Willie Doyle was still common currency. Indeed, by this time there is some suggestion that his 'cause' for beatification had been referred to the Vatican. Writing in *The Furrow* magazine, in March 1958, Kevin Smyth made an ironic, witty observation:

> *Dr. Samuel Johnson said that the Irish were a very fair-minded people: he never heard one Irishman speaking well of another. The same sentiment was echoed unconsciously by an Irish priest when he was asked was there any prospect of the beatification of Father Willie Doyle: 'No ... you'll never get one Irishman to swear to the sanctity of another.*[24]

It is not known whether Professor Alfred O'Rahilly had any input into such a cause, or indeed if there was/is one. Although most of his energies were devoted to an academic career, the professor also made contributions to his country's political and religious life. In 1954 Pope Pius XII conferred on him the Pontifical Order of Saint Gregory the Great, the highest distinction awarded by the Pope to a Catholic layman. In later years, following the death of his wife, he was ordained as a priest and died, aged 84, on 3 August 1969 whilst in residence at Blackrock College. As previously noted, Professor O'Rahilly never publically elaborated on his implication to Mr Fletcher back in 1920, that he had private sources in the War Office, who confirmed his own opinion *'the triple disqualification of being an Irishman, a Catholic and a Jesuit proved insuperable'* to the award of a Victoria Cross to Fr Willie Doyle.

By this time, John Lucy had been reunited in death with his brother Denis, when he passed on, aged sixtyt-eight, in Cork on 1 March 1962.

Robert Doyle saw out nearly forty years of retirement at *Melrose*; he was 97 when he died in December 1961. Before Bob died he had carried on Charlie Doyle's practice of responding to requests for relics of Father Willie, by cutting small squares from the padre's spare uniform and attaching them to a prayer card to send to applicants.

Ex-Royal Dublin Fusiliers were also given a warm welcome at *Melrose*. One such veteran, Lance Corporal Paul Smith, who lived in Manchester, England, often visited *Melrose* and referred to Bob Doyle as *'a grand Old Gentleman'* and remembered that Fr Willie's Military Cross was kept in a glass case in the entrance hall of the house. Mr Smith continued to keep in touch with the family after Bob died. He knew Willie Doyle well and writing on 26 April 1970 to Dr. Caenepeel in Ypres, whom he had recently met on a visit, Paul Smith says:

Fr Doyle's Uniform card

Well Doctor, I do know that the effects of 'Father Willie' are in possession of his two nieces who live in Balbriggan, County Dublin. It is his Sam Browne Belt, the Shawl, of which I send you a piece, and also they have his Military Cross. 'Father Willie' many a time was qualified for the Victoria Cross.[25]

Then again, a couple of weeks later on 19 May, he writes to the doctor:

I am in corresponding [sic] with relatives of 'Father Willie'. They live in Balbriggan, County Dublin, Ireland. I have recently received another piece of the shawl from them, 15 April 1970, and I am sending you another piece. This shawl was worn by a 'Saint' in and out of the trenches in very cold weather. I always pray to 'Blessed Father Willie' and I will say Doctor that my prayers have often been answered.[26 FN1]

 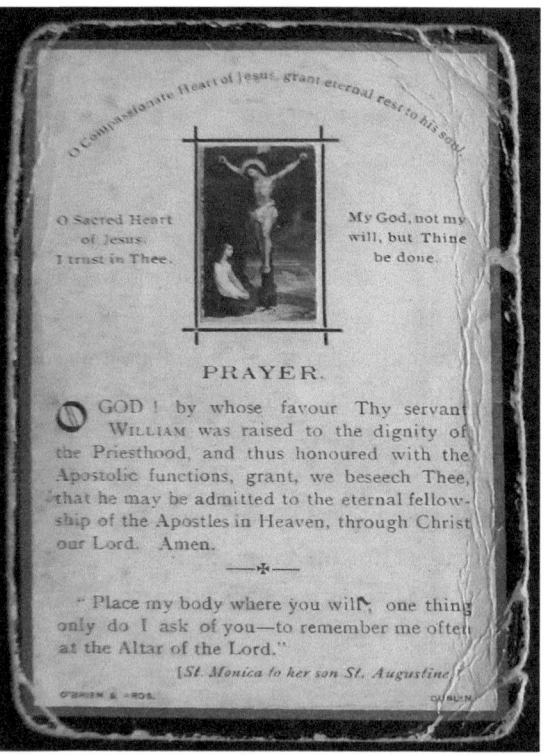

Fr Doyle's prayer card front and reverse

As an Irish veteran of the Great War living in England, it was easier, and more acceptable, for Paul Smith to visit battlefield sites in Belgium, than for ex-colleagues in Ireland. He travelled with the 19th Division's Old Comrades' Association and met Dr Caenepeel at a reception in the re-built Cloth Hall in Ypres. Unsurprisingly, he was the only traveller who had been in 16th (Irish) Division.

Dr Caenepeel was obviously very moved to receive the relic from Fr Willie's shawl; he expressed his appreciation in a note addressed to 'My Dear Paul Smith' dated 27 May 1970 and said:

> *I will always treasure this as a valuable token of your friendship and our common faith in Christ and his beloved son 'Father Willie'.*[27]

By this time the War Memorial Gardens at Islandbridge were derelict. The 'Troubles' in Northern Ireland had also broken out. Gerry McMahon remembered:

> *I of course now also know that my loyalist equivalents in Northern Ireland had a similarly flawed educational base. They concentrated on British History and largely ignored 'On Island' developments except where they affected the North such as the 1641 rebellion, the Jacobite Wars and 1798. As far as the Great War was concerned it was the sons of Ulster who fought on the Somme. The majority of those who fought there and who were Catholic nationalists were conveniently forgotten as they undermined the concept of the purely loyalist sacrifice.*[28]

In 1980, the issue of Remembrance still did not sit very comfortably with the Irish powers-that-be. The President of Ireland, Dr Patrick Hillery, was invited to attend the British Legion Remembrance Service for Ireland's war dead at St Patrick's Cathedral, Dublin. He declined the invitation. By the mid-1980's things started to move in a more positive direction when the Office of Public Works commenced restorations at Islandbridge; the reinstated gardens were formally dedicated by the representatives of the four main churches in Ireland and opened to the public on 10 September 1988. This took place ten months after the death and carnage wreaked by the IRA bombing of the war memorial at Enniskillen on Remembrance Day 1987.

When Mary Robinson became President in 1990 she opted to attend the British

Legion Remembrance Services in Dublin. There was still some way to go, however, as the Northern Irish peace process gathered momentum from 1994 onwards. The Irish writer and broadcaster Myles Dungan recalled this visit to France:

> *I first visited my 19-year-old grand-uncle Joe in Picardy, in France, on a sweet summer day in 1994. The conversation was one-sided as he'd been blown to pieces by a stray shell on the Somme in September, 1916. J.P. O'Reilly's grave was in a small cemetery in the middle of a cornfield. It was within sight of the huge Thiepval monument to the 70,000 missing-in-action of the Somme offensive. The well-kept graveyard held many Irish dead but there was not one southern Irish signature in the visitor's book provided by the Commonwealth War Graves Commission. Every second entry seemed to come from Northern Ireland but the log was unembarrassed by evidence of visitors from the Republic. This was part of a pattern that had endured for almost 80 years. Unionists honoured their Great War fallen while Nationalists paid homage to the dead of the Irish revolution. But where did that leave the thousands in between – the Nationalist dead of the 1914–1918 war? Precisely nowhere.*[29]

Within a few years of Myles Dungan's visit to his grand-uncle's grave, a force for peace and reconciliation, for the island of Ireland as a whole, started to gain momentum. In 1997 two Irishmen, Paddy Harte from the south and Glen Barr from the north, set up an organisation called *'A Journey of Reconciliation Trust'* to commemorate all those from the island of Ireland who died as a result of the Great War. It also had the wider aim to promote peace and reconciliation throughout Ireland. The year before they had issued a pledge at Thiepval on the Somme, part of which says:

> *From the steps of this war memorial – whose walls bear the names of thousands of young men from all parts of Ireland who fought tyranny and a common enemy, defended democracy and the rights of all nations, whose graves are in shockingly uncountable numbers and those who have no known graves – we condemn war and the futility of war. We repudiate and renounce violence, not just the bomb and the bullet, but all forms of violence, aggression, intimidation, threatening and unfriendly behaviour.*[30]

These two men greased wheels of change, which continued to turn and resulted in the construction of a Peace Tower, set in landscaped gardens near Messines in Belgium. This was opened on 11 November 1998 with King Albert II and Queen Paola of Belgium, President Mary McAleese and Queen Elizabeth II in attendance. In her speech, President McAleese said:

> *Today's ceremony at the Peace Park was not just another journey down a well-travelled path. For much of the past eight years the very idea of such a ceremony would probably have been unthinkable. Those whom we commemorate here were doubly tragic. They fell victim to a war against oppression in Europe. Their memory too fell victim to a war for independence at home in Ireland.*

Whilst Willie Doyle and his contemporaries were slowly gaining recognition throughout Ireland, Father Willie's memory had never dimmed for one Belgian woman. In 1999, Denise Dael, who would have been three years old when Fr Doyle died, claimed to know where the padre was buried. The British newspaper *The Guardian* reported on the claim of the 85 year old Ypres woman on Friday 12 November 1999:

> *I believe I know where he is buried and I think he should be exhumed because otherwise how could it be proved? It would be a very good thing for the church to make him a saint.*

Denise Dael had identified one of only two unnamed graves listed as being of an Irish officer at Potjze Chateau Military Cemetery; this assertion was arrived at with the help of a medium.[FN2] The Commonwealth War Graves Commission declined to exhume the remains; the decision would have been based on the balance of probabilities being extremely small that it was the padre's body.

The *Island of Ireland Peace Park* went through a period (albeit brief) of neglect following its inauguration. This resulted more from an issue of funding strategy, rather than disregard for the site. Lieutenant General (Retired) Gerry McMahon became responsible for over-seeing the project and he, together with another Limerick man, Michael O'Rahilly (who was distantly related to Professor Alfred O'Rahilly) lobbied vigorously to ensure it was properly funded and maintained.

The *Island of Ireland Peace Park* was overhauled and re-opened on 7 June 2004.

Speaking at the official re-opening, the Irish Minister for Foreign Affairs Dermot Ahern made a speech to advance the Northern Ireland peace process, commenting:

> *All those untold human stories that we lost in the First World War, and more recently in the conflict in Northern Ireland, must be remembered. And, in remembering, they must not be told for nothing. They must not be told to deepen divisions. They must be told to inspire us to overcome them.*

Willie Doyle's story is one such that has been told in times gone by, forgotten about and is now being told again. The telling re-started with references to Fr Doyle's military career in books coming out of Ireland in the 1990's, such as Myles Dungan's *Irish Voices From The Great War* and *They Shall Grow Not Old, Irish Soldiers and the Great War*. His assessment of Fr Willie:

> *In fact Doyle was recommended for the VC but it was not granted, an omission which reflected no credit whatever on those responsible for the decision.*[31]

In 2008 a biography about Mother Teresa was published, in which the author, Brian Kolodiejchuk, refers to her being inspired by the private vows made by the Irish Jesuit, Father William Doyle. The following year a traditional Catholic publisher, *Tradibooks* reprinted Professor O'Rahilly's biography, describing the publication as 'restored text and typography.' Then in June 2010, a citizen of County Dublin, Pat Kenny, set up the *Remembering Father William Doyle* website, with a link to purchase the *Tradibooks* publication. In February 2013 Pat Kenny announced:

> *It is with great satisfaction that we note that Fr Doyle has been announced as one of the patrons of the newly established Confraternity of Priest Adorers of the Eucharistic Face of Jesus ... The Confraternity is primarily aimed at the sanctification of its members and of the priesthood itself. This was a cause very dear to Fr Doyle's heart; indeed he offered his sufferings in the war, and even his very life itself, for the sanctification of priests and in reparation for the sins of priests. Anybody familiar with recent Irish history will know how important this intention is.*[32]

As for this book, it began in 2006 when the writer acquired a copy of Professor O'Rahilly's biography and was immediately gripped by the character of Willie Doyle. Having embarked on what has proved to be an enormous project in refreshing Willie's story, she also managed to trace descendants of Fr Doyle. In the Spring of 2012 two of his family retraced Fr Willie's steps with the author and her partner around a chilly France and Belgium. They visited a hushed Tyne Cot early one morning to see Fr William Doyle's name carved there, and the family later laid a wreath in his memory at the eight o'clock Last Post Ceremony at the Menin Gate. We were all enormously moved by these experiences.

The last note of this biography comes from an officer who knew Fr Willie Doyle, the full text of which can be found in Appendix B, Tributes:

> *Our gallant Jesuit chaplain has gone to the bourne from which no traveller returns, and he has taken with him the hearts of the Irish soldiers in France.*[33]

Footnote 1: Pieces of Fr Doyle's plaid shawl, sent by Paul Smith to Doctor Canaepeel, can be seen in the archives of the Research Centre, Historisch Centrum, Ieper.

Footnote 2: A file relating to Denise Dael's assertions is held at the archives of the Research Centre, In Flanders Fields Museum, Ieper.

APPENDIX A:
HICKIE LETTER

'For I know that my Redeemer liveth, and that he shall stand in the latter day upon the earth. And though after my skin worms destroy this body, yet in my flesh shall I see God: whom I shall see for myself and mine eyes shall behold.'
The Book of Job, Chapter 19, 25-27

See photos of pages and envelope in photo illustrations section.

18 November 1917

My dear Kays

Father Doyle was one of the best priests I have ever met and one of the bravest men who have fought or worked out here. He did his duty (and more than his duty) most nobly and has left a memory and a name behind that will never be forgotten. On the day of his death – August 16th – he had worked in the front line and even in front of that line and appeared to know no fatigue (he never knew fear.) He was killed by a shell towards the close of the day and was buried on the Frezenberg Ridge. I hope to be allowed when things settle down and we can get a party there to do it, to move his remains to the Convent Garden at Locre and to put them in a grave beside that of Willie Redmond.

He was recommended for the Victoria Cross by his C.O., by his Brigadier and by myself. Superior authority however has not granted it, and as no other posthumous award is given, his name I believe will be mentioned in the Commander in Chief's despatch. If I had known his father's address I would have written to him to congratulate him upon having had such a son, and in the name of the Division I would offer him my thanks for the work of the Priest, and in my own name as Commander I would offer my own for the spirit he infused into all he came in contact with – officers and men – and for his very glorious example. I can say without boasting that this is a Division of brave men – and even among these Father Doyle stood out.

All goes well. I am prouder than ever of my commands. I suppose we are half through the war now.

Yours ever

W.B. Hickie

APPENDIX B:
TRIBUTES

'May he rest in peace – it seems superfluous to pray for him.'
Fr Frank Browne, 20 August 1917

Letter published in the *Glasgow Weekly News*, 1 September 1917 from a Belfast man:

God never made a nobler soul. Father Doyle was a good deal amongst us. We could not possibly agree with his religious opinions, but we simply worshipped him for other things. He didn't know the meaning of fear, and he did not know what bigotry was. He was as ready to risk his life and take a drop of water to a wounded Ulsterman as to assist men of his own faith and regiment. If he risked his life in looking after Ulster Protestant soldiers once, he did it a hundred times in the last few days. They told him he was wanted in a more exposed part of the field to administer the last rites of the Church to a fusilier who had been badly hit. In spite of the danger to himself, Father Doyle went over. While he was doing what he could to comfort the poor chap at the very gates of death, the priest was struck down. He and the man he was ministering to passed out of life together. The Ulstermen felt his loss more keenly than anybody, and none more readier to show their marks of respect to the dead hero priest than were our Ulster Presbyterians. Father Doyle was a fine Christian in every sense of the word, and a credit to any religious faith. He never tried to get things easy. He was always sharing the risks of the men, and had to be kept in restraint by the staff for his own protection. Many a time have I seen him walk beside a stretcher trying to console a wounded man, with bullets flying around him, and shells bursting every few yards.[1]

Letter dated 15 August 1917 written from the Western Front by Fr Frank Browne to his brother in Ireland (transcribed by Fr Willie Doyle's sister Lena):

APPENDIX B

Father Doyle is a marvel – you may talk of heroes and saints – they are hardly in it! I went back the other day to see the old Dubs, as I heard they were having – we'll say, a taste of the war. No one has yet been appointed to my place and Fr D has done double work. So unpleasant were the conditions that the men had to be relieved frequently. Fr D had no one to relieve him and so he stuck to the mud and the shells, the gas and the terror. Day after day he stuck it out. I met the Adjutant of one of my two Battalions, who previously had only known Fr D by sight. His first greeting to me was:- 'Little Fr Doyle' (they all call him that, more in affection than anything else) 'deserves the VC more than any man that ever wore it. We cannot get him away from the line while the men are there: he is in with his own and he is in with us. The men couldn't stick it half so well if he weren't there: if we give him an orderly, he sends him back, he wears no tin hat and he is always so cheery.' Another Officer, also a Protestant, said 'Fr D. never rests. Night and Day he is with us. He finds a dying or dead man, does all, comes back smiling, makes a little cross and goes out to bury him, and then begins all over again.' I needn't say, that through all this, the conditions of the ground and air and discomfort surpass anything that I ever dreamt of in the worst days of the Somme. May God preserve him and keep him. He doesn't want VCs or anything else, but it would be the proudest moment of my life, if I could only call him VC. So rooted is the prejudice against such as he, that one of the men here [Irish Guards] said to me – knowing what Fr Knapp and Fr Gwynn [sic] had done – 'Aren't our priests, Father, forbidden to take the VC'!!![2]

Letter reproduced in *The Clongownian* from F.K. an Irish Officer of the Division (in all probability Lieutenant F.M. Kiernan, 8th Royal Dublin Fusiliers) and also printed in the *Catholic News* on 15 September 1917:

Do the boys who read this remember our share in the battle of the Somme last year? The winter of last year in Belgium? S.P. 13 and the little dugout of the brave padre rise up before me as I write. Liege Farm, and early Mass when our battalion was in reserve. Often have I knelt at the impromptu altar serving that Mass for the padre in the upper barn, hail, rain and snow blowing in gusts through the shell-torn roof. Then on all occasions his wonderful words of cheer during his little sermon to the 'boys.' 'God bless Father Doyle' is the heartfelt wish of all the men of the Irish Division today.

He knew no fear. As Company Officers, how many times have we accompanied him through the front line system to speak a word to the men. Well do we remember when at long last we went back for a rest and training, how our beloved padre did the three days' march at the head of the battalion with 'A' Company. Then, which of the men do not recall with a tear and a smile how he went 'over the top' at Wytschaete? He lived with us in our newly-won position, and endured our hardships with unfailing cheerfulness. In billets he was an ever welcome visitor to the companies, and our only trouble was that he could not always live with whatever company he might be visiting.

Ypres sounded the knell. Recommended for the D.S.O. for Wytschaete, he did wonderful work at Ypres, and was recommended for the VC Many a dying soldier on that bloody field has flashed a last look of loving recognition as our brave padre rushed to his aid, braving the fearful barrage and whistling machine-gun bullets, to give his boys a last few words of hope. Yes, we have lost a father and friend whose place we will find very hard to fill. Our gallant Jesuit chaplain has gone to the bourne from which no traveller returns, and he has taken with him the hearts of the Irish soldiers in France. A true Soggarth Aroon, may his soul rest in peace.[3]

Lieutenant Colonel H.R. Stirke, Officer Commanding 8th Royal Dublin Fusiliers, wrote in a letter dated 13 September 1917 to an unknown person, quoted by Professor O'Rahilly:

He was one of the finest fellows I ever met, utterly fearless, always with a cheery word on his lips, and ever ready to go out and attend the wounded and dying under the heaviest fire. He was genuinely loved by everyone, and thoroughly deserved the unstinted praise he got from all ranks for his rare pluck and devotion to duty ...I know that he had been sent back by the O.C. of one of the regiments, together with some other non-combatants, as the fighting was very severe and it was not necessary to risk more lives. He only remained behind a few hours and then returned to the fighting line, like the brave man he was.[4]

APPENDIX B

Sergeant T. Flynn, 8th Royal Dublin Fusiliers, in a letter written to his mother on 18 August 1917 and published in the *Irish News* on 29 August 1917:

We had the misfortune to lose our chaplain, Fr Doyle, the other day. He was a real saint and would never leave his men, and it was really marvellous to see him burying dead soldiers under terrible shell fire. He did not know what fear was, and everybody in the battalion, Catholic and Protestant alike, idolised him. I went to Confession to him and received Holy Communion from him a day or two before he was killed, and I feel terribly sorry after him.

He loved the men and spent every hour of his time looking after them, and when we were having a fairly hot time in the trenches he would bring us up boxes of cigarettes and cheer us up. The men would do anything he asked them, and I am sure we will never get another padre like him. Everybody says he has earned the VC many times over, and I can vouch for it myself from what I have seen him do many a time. He was asked not to go into action with the battalion, but he would not stop behind, and I am confident that no braver or holier man ever fell in battle than he.[5]

Extract from letter dated 20 August 1917 written by Fr Browne, to a person unknown, quoted by Professor O'Rahilly:

All during these last few months he was my greatest help, and to his saintly advice, and still more to his saintly example, I owe everything I felt and did. With him, as with others of us, his bravery was no mere physical show-off. He was afraid and felt fear deeply, how deeply few can realise. And yet the last word said of him to me by the Adjutant of the Royal Irish Rifles in answer to my question, 'I hope you are taking care of Fr Doyle?' was, 'He is as fond of the shells as ever.' His one idea was to do God's work with the men, to make them saints. How he worked and how he prayed for this! Fine weather and foul he was always thinking of them and what he could do for them. In the cold weather he would not use the stove I bought for our dug-out. He scoffed at the idea as making it 'stuffy' – and that when the thermometer was fifteen to twenty degrees below zero, the coldest ever known in living memory here. And how he loathed it all, the life and all it implied! And yet nobody suspected it. God's Will was his law. And to all who remonstrated, 'Must I not be about the Lord's business?' was his laughing answer in act and deed and not merely in word. May he rest in peace – it seems superfluous to pray for him.[6]

On 15 December 1917, having discovered Hugh Doyle's address, Major General Hickie wrote to *Melrose,* but there is only a short quote by O'Rahilly:

I could not say too much about your son. He was loved and reverenced by us all; his gallantry, self-sacrifice, and devotion to duty were all so well known and recognised. I think that his was the most wonderful character that I have ever known.[7]

Captain C.F. Healy, at an unknown date, but probably during his first leave following the events of 16 August 1917, called to see Charles Doyle to pay his respects and share his memories of Fr Willie. A transcript of his recollections was typed up:

Captain Healy told me that Willie was one of the bravest and most lovable men he had ever met. They were always great friends. He took from his pocket a leather case containing, I think, rosary beads and he said 'I wouldn't part with that for £1,000, he gave it to me not long before he was killed.' To give his own words as nearly as I can:- 'If I had gone through the one thousandth part of what your brother did, I would have been dead long ago. Wherever danger was, Fr D was and wherever Fr D was <u>there</u> was danger. Whenever I saw him coming towards me I told him to go away, as I knew the Boche would begin to shell that place at once. When shells were raining on us, Fr D used to wander about from dug-out to dug-out as if he were taking a walk for the good of his health and he was never hit. On one occasion when there was 'nothing doing' he wandered into a dug-out and at once the shelling began. One of the officers in the dug-out smilingly said 'Fr D you will have to get out of this, you are a regular Jonah, wherever you make your appearance the Huns seem to spot you and to fire at you.' The men would not believe the news that came through that he was dead, they said it was all wrong, that Fr D <u>could</u> not be killed, because they looked on him as a man whose life was miraculously preserved. When the bad news *proved to be only too true there was absolute consternation, you would think the Heavens had fallen in on the men. If a man was hit, you would think Fr D knew it by instinct, and he would be with the wounded man long before anyone else was, and did all he could for him. One day he rushed up to a wounded Ulster man and knelt down beside him 'Ah Father, he said, I don't belong to your Church. No, said Fr, but you belong to my God.' On one occasion I had to arrest him, because he had neither his steel helmet nor his respirator. A few days afterwards he came to where I was. He had one gas respirator round his neck, another round his waist, a third on his back; he had a knapsack on each shoulder, a steel helmet on his head and one in each hand. 'Now, he said, Captain do you think I am complying with the regulations?'!!! Whenever he came up to the men he always had his pockets stuffed with sweets or cigarettes, where he got them we never could make out, he had them when we officers had not.*

(Captain H also mentioned that exact place of burial is known and efforts would be made – as mentioned above – to remove the remains to Locre.) [8] This is a reference to Major General Hickie's letter to Brigadier General Kays, which was also transcribed and preceded the Healy transcription.

Letter from Daniel Galvin to Professor Alfred O'Rahilly, undated other than headed Saturday, but sent a short while after the publication in 1919 of the professor's biography about Willie Doyle. After greeting the professor, Daniel J. Galvin says:

Thank you very much for the copy of your life of Father Doyle, which I read last night, and which is vividly interesting to any one who had the good fortune to be intimate with him. Every page of the latter half recalled forgotten incidents and places, and the extracts from Father Doyle's diary relating to the fortnight in August before he was killed are a very true description of a terrible time, and also give those who wondered at his continuous contempt for death a small idea of what moral bravery means.

My brother and myself were great friends of Father Doyle's, and between us we were with him the whole time he was in France, as he was first with my brother's regiment, then with mine. He gave my brother the last Sacraments when he was badly wounded in a raid at Loos, and wrote to my father every day, until the doctor at the C.C.S. reported him out of danger. Though the part was foreign to his nature, Father Doyle was an ideal chaplain. The men all loved him, and even the protestant officers, when taking over a nasty piece of the line, would prefer to take Father Doyle up the line with their company than fifty additional men. I am sure that he must have made a tremendous number of converts to the Catholic faith in his two and a half years in France.

The dates and places in the book are very accurate. On the 16 August my regiment (9th Dublin Fusiliers) to which Father Doyle was attached went into the attack with twenty-one officers, and over five hundred men. Of these sixteen officers were killed and the other five wounded, and less than fifty men came out. I was wounded four times that day and then spent 24 hours in a shell hole up to my chest in water. That ended my conversation with the army. Out of evil etc.⁹

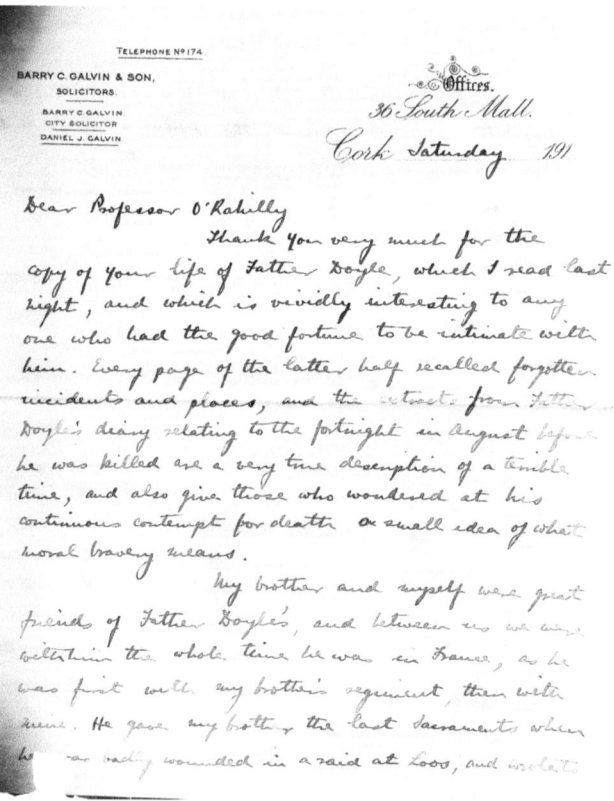

Galvin letter, circa 1919, page 1

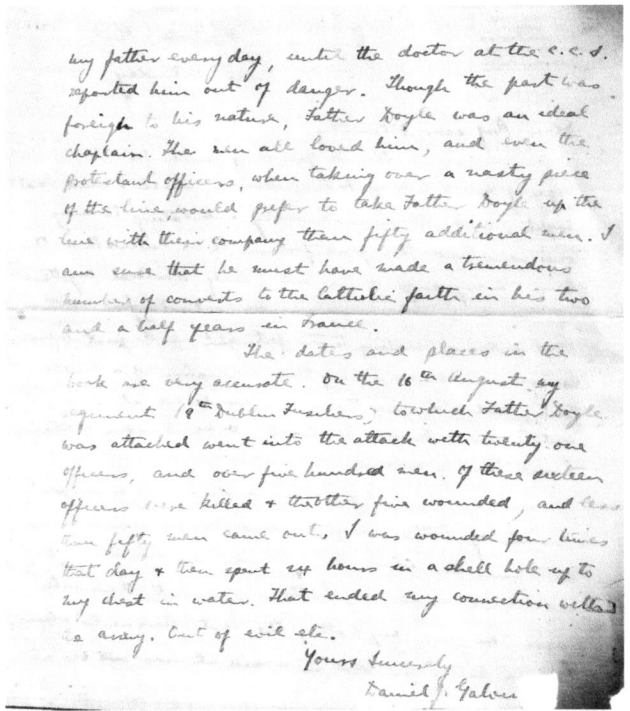

Galvin letter, circa 1919, page 2

Paul Smith, from the Harpurphey district in Manchester, travelled to Ypres in April 1970 as part of a tour party run by the Old Comrades' Association of 19th Division. Although he was born and lived in Manchester his mother was Irish, and as soon as he was 18 he went to Dublin and enlisted with 16th (Irish) Division in July 1916, serving with the Royal Dublin Fusiliers. He qualified as an instructor at a course for NCOs in November 1916 and was promoted to Lance Corporal. He was posted overseas in January 1917 and served for the best part of a year, before being invalided out after sustaining gun shot wounds to his arm and neck, for which he was awarded the Silver War Badge to denote his injury. He returned to the north of England to live and after his pilgrimage to Ypres in 1970 he wrote to one of the hosts. The full text of his letter dated 26 April 1970 addressed to My Dear Dr. Caenepeel says:

I have at last found the time to write, as promised. We all enjoyed our stay on your soil. Our reception in Ypres Cloth Hall was to say the least very inspiring. It was August 15 1917 that I first saw the Cloth Hall, absolutely down in ruins, also the whole town. What a great transformation scene I saw after nearly 53 years. 'VIVE LA BELGIUM.' Well Doctor my great disappointment was not visiting Locre Cemetery, time did not cater for the visit. I would very much have liked to have visited Major Willie Redmond's grave. I am sending you Doctor, as I promised, a memento of Father William Doyle. It is a piece of the Irish Plaid Shawl he wore in very cold weather when we were out from the trenches. I am also enclosing small pamphlets of Father Willie's own little prayers. I did promise you Doctor that I would let you have one of the leaflets with his photograph so sorry to disappoint you that I have none in my possession. If you write to this address, same will be sent on to you, and any reading you apply for. IRISH MESSENGER OFFICE, 5 GREAT DENMARK STREET, DUBLIN, EIRE. REFERENCE 'FATHER WILLIE'.

As you told me you have read 'Father Willie's life' by Father Rahilly (sic). He was Professor at Blackrock College, Dublin, was ordained at 70 years of age, a late vocation. Father Rahilly (sic) died about 10 years ago. I am anxiously waiting for the Photograph we had taken in the Cloth Hall. I gave my order to the Gentleman who took them, also my address. Well Doctor, I do know that the effects of 'Father Willie' are in possession of his two nieces who live in Balbriggan, County Dublin. It is his Sam Browne Belt, the Shawl, of which I send you a piece, and also they have his Military Cross. 'Father Willie' many a time was qualified for the Victoria Cross.

Our coach on our journey, Sunday 5th, brought us through Wychaate (sic) Village. The coach stopped outside a cottage, a lovely lady and her husband were at the door. Our interpreter done the speaking. The lady spoke good English. She asked if any 16th Division amongst us, I was the only one, I shown her my Cap Badge, Royal Dublin Fusiliers, it brought back memories to her, also myself. We advanced into Wychaate (sic) when the mines blew up on Messines. Memories. Well Doctor I will now close, hoping can (sic) understand my writing, all for now I remain Yours Most Respectfully Paul Smith.[10]

Paul Smith wrote to Doctor Caenepeel again on 19 May 1970 and this letter contains more detail about Fr Willie Doyle:

APPENDIX B

In answer to your most welcome letter of the 26 April, and please excuse my delay in answering same. First of all I will answer your queries in your letter. I am in corresponding (sic) with relatives of 'Father Willie.' They live in Balbriggan, County Dublin, Ireland. I have recently received another piece of the shawl from them, 15 April 1970, and I am sending you another piece. This shawl was <u>worn by a 'Saint'</u> in and out of the trenches in very cold weather. I always pray to 'Blessed Father Willie' and I will say Doctor that my prayers have often been answered. Your next query Doctor, 'Father Willie' belonged to the 8th Battalion of the Dublin Fusiliers, I myself belonged to the 9th Battalion of the Dublin Fusiliers. We had a Dublin Fusiliers Brigade, which conformed 3 Battalions, the 2nd, 8th and 9th Battalions, of which 'Father Willie' and a Father Browne attended to us all. Now 'Father Willie' Doctor was a very brave Priest. He was absolutely unconscious to all dangers around him. Whenever his presence was near, we always felt safe in heavy shell fire. I will tell you his favourite saying when we in heavy shell fire. <u>'It is quite alright boys, it is not for us'</u> of course he would be meaning the shells when they were getting too close. A braver man I have never met or been in the company of since.

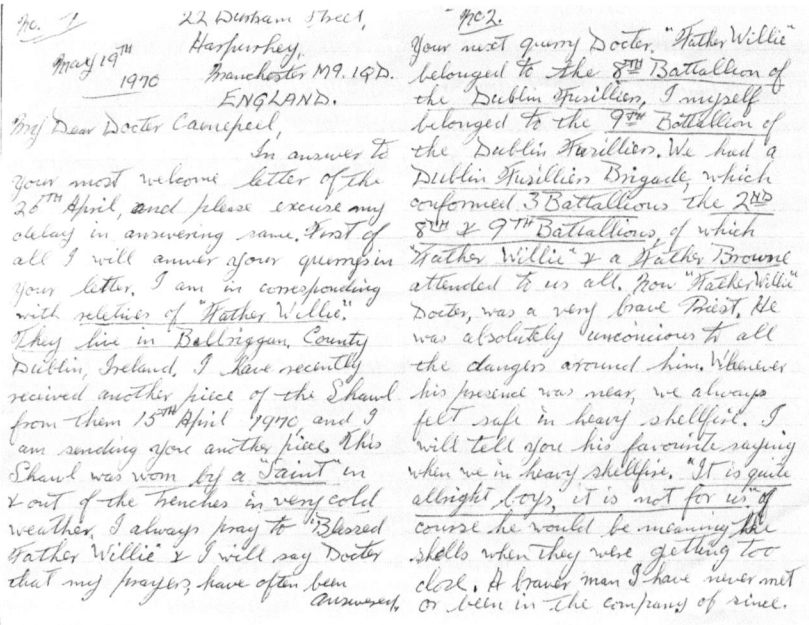

Page of Paul Smith's letter to Dr Caenepael on 19 May 1970, with text underlined

As you say in your letter, a visit to Major Willie Redmond's grave Locre, also a visit to monument of 16th Irish Division and Munster, Cork Co., it would be my great delight to visit same. I may later this year later on be able to stay in Ypres for a few days. The party I was with on our visit to the Cloth Hall, they are having another visit between 6–8 June. I will not be with them, I think it is a bit too much to ask so soon after, I could not be prepared financially in so short a time. The party stay in a hotel in Bethune, Hotel Commerse. When I come to Belgium I would have to stay in or around Ypres for us to visit the places you mention. I must tell you that 'Father Willie' was the recipient of the Military Cross for his very brave deeds in the firing zone. He deserved the Victoria Cross numerous times. When I have visited Ireland on holiday, at Dalkey his elder Brother lived there, Judge Robert Doyle who died in December 1961. I often visited him. He had me put on 'Father Willie's' Sam Browne Belt, and march up and down his study. 'Father Willie's' Military Cross was kept in a glass case in the entrance hall of Judge Doyle's house. He, Judge Doyle, was 97 years of age when he died, a grand old Gentleman. Now Doctor, to come back to dear 'Father Willie' again. As I promised you in Ypres I would send you a pamphlet of 'Father Willie.' Now the prayer on the back is for your private use, to him for his intercession, on your behalf. It informs you to write to Rev. C. Doyle, a brother of our 'Father Willie', but Father Charles Doyle is dead, as I was informed when I visited the church there. I am attaching to the leaflet another piece of 'Father Willie's' shawl, hoping you gain many favours asked for in your prayers to him. It would be very nice for you to be in the vicinity of Frieseburg (sic) [Frezenberg] to Pray to him, that is where he was killed. Also, please rember (sic) me in your prayers.

When I first joined the Dublin Fusiliers in Dublin I joined the 10th Battalion. The Battalion came to France in 1916, but I did not come with them. They suffered great losses at Maile Mailet [Mailly-Maillet] and when I come to Belgium on a visit you will please take me to there to visit some of their graves. Well Doctor I think I have explained a lot to you in my letter, hoping you understand my writing and wording in your leisure time. This small book I send to you is great interesting reading for all the Prayers answered from all over the world, through 'Our Father Willie's' Intercession. All for now, Good Night and God Bless till I hear from you again.[11]

It is not known whether Paul Smith ever returned to Ypres.

APPENDIX C:
THE CURIOUS CASE OF FANNY CRANBUSH

'Snatched from the Brink!'[FN1]

A rather unusual incident was recorded in *Merry in God*, the book probably compiled by Willie Doyle's brother, Father Charles Doyle. In April 1908, whilst giving a mission at Yarmouth, Fr Doyle was returning late one night to the presbytery, after hearing confessions in a church, when he came across a prostitute. He couldn't pass her by without stopping to ask her why she was out late and advising her to go home, saying: *'Don't hurt Jesus. He loves you.'*[1] Some years later he was finishing a retreat in a convent at Bray, County Wicklow, when he was handed a telegram from his provincial. He was to return to Dublin at once and there it was explained to him that his services were required at a prison in England. A telegram had requested: *'Please send Father William Doyle, S.J. ... Woman to be executed tomorrow and asks to see him.'*[2] A mystified Willie had been booked onto the night boat for Holyhead and arrived at 5am. He reached the prison in time to see the prisoner before her execution for her part in a poison case. When she had been asked about her religion on arrival at the prison, she originally said she had none and no need of a priest. A few days before the date set for her execution, however, she changed her mind. She asked to see a priest whose name and address she did not know, but that he was Irish and had been in Yarmouth about two years previously. The prison governor got in touch with the police at Yarmouth, who made enquiries at all the churches there. The Jesuits informed the police that a Father William Doyle from Dublin had given a mission at St Mary's a couple of years previously; the address of Willie's Superior was obtained and the telegram sent. When Willie was shown into the prisoner's cell it was to find the girl on the street that he had spoken to about Jesus' love in Yarmouth.

The prisoner's name was Fanny, still in her twenties and sitting, with bowed head and drawn, weary face, on the edge of a narrow bed: *...next instant her look was transformed as she sprang to her feet exclaiming: 'Oh, Father, thank God, you are come!' 'I'm glad I've come, my child!' said Father Doyle, as he took her by the hand and led her to a chair.*[3] Fanny told Fr Doyle her sad, sordid story. How his few words to her that evening resounded in her ears all through that night, how she discovered his identity by chance, how she kept off the streets for a number of weeks, but then hunger and want drove her out again and she sank lower and lower into degradation and crime. Fanny told Willie that she wanted to become a Catholic before she died and he quickly explained the essential articles of faith to her. He baptised her from her water jug and left her to reflect whilst he went to get permission and the necessary requisites to conduct Mass. He hurried off to the nearest Catholic Church where he obtained leave and articles for saying Mass. *A tiny altar was erected in the cell, and Fanny heard her first and last Mass, and received her God for the first and last time.*[4] The prisoner informed her confessor that she was happy in the love of Jesus and the knowledge that she had confessed and was sorry for her sins. *As she walked to the scaffold with Father Doyle, beside her, she whispered to him 'I am so happy Father! Jesus knows that I am sorry for having hurt Him, and I know that Jesus loves me.' A moment later and Fanny Cranbush, with her baptismal robe unspotted, was in the arms of Jesus.*[5]

Charles Doyle asserts in his book: *This true tale, which first appeared in print in the* Irish Messenger, *under the title of* Snatched from the Brink, *received confirmation soon after its publication from a Loreto nun in Australia. 'I have just finished reading* Snatched from the Brink *in the* Irish Messenger,' *she wrote. The facts of the story are quite familiar to me. I was stationed in our convent in Letterkenny when Father Doyle came to give the girls their retreat. In his opening talk he told them that he had just come from a prison in England, where the morning before he had been present at the execution of a young girl. He then told the story substantially as it appeared in the* Messenger. *It made a deep impression on me at the time, and, I am sure, on all who heard it.*[6]

This author spent some time researching this story and could find no record of a prisoner called Fanny Cranbush, although in all probability the name Fanny Cranbush is a pseudonym. However, there are probably other avenues still to be pursued. Yet the execution of a woman would have been high profile and this author can find no case of either an executed woman, or one who received a late reprieve, which matches the facts and timescale as relayed in *Merry in God*.

This story has been included because it forms part of the legend of Fr Doyle. This author thinks that there is every possibility he was asked to visit a jail in England; that there was a young girl, name unknown, who Fr Doyle met in Yarmouth in 1908 and who subsequently became a prisoner. But what her offence and sentence were is highly questionable. Perhaps the girl was on the brink of, and died, a natural death. No doubt Willie's version of events made a deep impression on the girls in the convent and gave them much cause for reflection. But the true facts of the case remain a mystery.

Footnote 1: The full account, reproduced from *Irish Messenger of the Sacred Heart, 1932,* can be read online at http://fatherdoyle.files.wordpress.com/2010/06/stories-of-fr-willie1.pdf

REFERENCES

Full details of sources are given in the Bibliography. For the purposes of the references, these are denoted by the surname authoring the source and the page number or date of letter. Four authors have multiple sources and are differentiated as follows:-

Quotes taken from the Longmans, Green and Co. edition of the Alfred O'Rahilly biography are denoted by 1925 and quotes taken from the Tradibooks edition are denoted by 2009.

Quotes taken from the Four Courts Press publication of Myles Dungan's *They Shall Grow Not Old* are denoted by 1995 and quotes taken from his Irish Academic Press *Irish Voices from the Great War* denoted by 1997. The article *Fighting Amnesia* is denoted by 'Dungan, article.'

Quotes taken from Terence Denman's *Ireland's Unknown Soldiers* are denoted by 1992 and those taken from his *A Lonely Grave, The Life and Death of William Redmond* are denoted by 1995.

Tom Johnstone is quoted in his own right and jointly with James Hegarty.

The author of *Merry in God, A Life of Father William Doyle, S.J.*, Roman Catholic Books, is unacknowledged – but was almost certainly Charles Doyle – and the references are shown as 'Merry in God'.

About this Book
1. O'Rahilly, 1925, page xi
2. *Merry in God*, page 5
3. O'Rahilly, 1925, page viii
4. *Merry in God*, 1939, Foreword
5. *Merry in God*, page 36
6. O'Rahilly, 1925, page xvi
7. Rosario, Blackrock College Archive

Prologue
1. Wolff, page 155
2. WD to HD 12/8/17, FAI
3. O'Rahilly, 1925, page 555

Chapter 1
1-9. *Merry In God*, pages 1, 17,22,21,8,11,16,22,4

Chapter 2
1. Ryan
2-18. *Merry In God*, pages 6, 25, 8, 18, 18, 16, 37, 14, 10, 9, 38, 39, 40, 21, 19, 20, 21

Chapter 3
1-13. *Merry In God*, pages 26, 33, 34, 34, 27, 29, 29, 30, 31, 39, 39, 36, 37

Chapter 4
1–20. *Merry In God,* pages 45, 45, 40, 44, 43, 44, 44, 44, 45, 45, 46, 46, 46, 48, 49, 48, 47, 49, 50, 51

Chapter 5
1. *Merry In God,* page 55
2. *Merry In God,* page 55
3. Bourke, page 18
4. Bourke, page 18
5. Cullen, page 6
6. Bourke, page 14
7. *Merry in God,* page 53
8. *Merry in God,* page 55
9. Bourke, page 14
10. Bourke, page 15
11–18. *Merry in God,* pages 59, 58, 56, 58, 62, 64, 63, 65
19. WD to Lena 27/8/00, FAI
20–27. *Merry in God,* pages 65, 69, 67, 67, 66, 59, 41, 69
28. O'Rahilly, 1925, page 38
29–31. *Merry in God,* pages 71, 70, 70
32. O'Rahilly, 1925, page 136
33–37. *Merry in God,* pages 136, 71, 72–73, 74, 73

Chapter 6
1–14. *Merry In God,* pages 75, 76, 76, 76, 77, 77, 78, 78, 79, 79, 79, 81, 81, 80
15–23. O'Rahilly, 1925 pages 62, 62, 63, 67, 76, 82, 84, 85 86
24–33. *Merry In God,* pages 79, 98, 82, 82, 83, 82 82, 84, 84, 85
34. O'Rahilly, 1925 page 52
35-47. *Merry In God,* pages 85, 86, 86, 90, 91, 91, 92, 93, 93, 93, 93, 61, 99
48. O'Rahilly, 1925 page 58

Chapter 7
1. *Merry In God,* page 107
2. O'Rahilly, 1925, page 111
3–8. *Merry In God,* pages: 101, 105, 114, 114, 102, 104
9–19. WD to Mai, Good Friday 1911, FAI
20–28. *Merry In God,* pages: 108, 108, 108, 109, 105, 105, 106, 106, 172
29. O'Rahilly, 1925 page 170
30–48. *Merry In God,* pages 149, 140, 153, 118, 154, 107, 115, 119, 121, 116, 116, 116, 119, 120, 120, 118, 122, 122, 122
49. O'Rahilly, 1925, footnote page 128
50. *Merry In God,* page 126,
51 and 52. WD from College of the Sacred Heart, 16 /2/12, FAI
53. WD sent some time in 1913 from St Patrick's College, Dundalk, FAI
54 and 55. *Merry In God,* pages 127 and 128
56. O'Rahilly, 1925, page 109
57 and 58. *Merry In God,* pages 128 and 129
59. O'Rahilly, 1925, page 113
60–66. *Merry In God,* pages 141, 131, 131, 130, 130, 130, 131

Chapter 8
1. *Merry In God,* page 181
2–4. Steinhauer, pages 262, 207–208, 208–209
5. Neillands, page 12

REFERENCES

6. Steinhauer, page 1
7. Keegan, Pimlico, page 70
8–9. Palmer and Wallis, page 44
10. Doudney, page 91
11. Hart, page 46
12, 13, 13a. Lucy, pages 79, 158, 73–75
14. Neillands, page 78
15. Molony, page 19
16–18. Lucy, pages 111-113, 114, 268-269
19–20. Hitchcock, pages 39, 40

Chapter 9

1. WO 339/123587, TNA
2. O'Rahilly, 1925, page 394
3–4. Spurr, page 116
5–6. Keeling, pages 192-193, 213
7–8. Lucy, pages 228, 342
9. Cooper-Walker, page 1
10. Starrett, pages 31 and 33
11–13. Cooper-Walker, pages 5, 16, 8
14. Hitchcock M.C., page 130
15. O'Rahilly, 1925, page 394
16. Spurr, page 131
17–18. Cooper-Walker, pages 14, 15
19. O'Rahilly, 1925, page 248
20. WD to HD 27/12/15, FAI
21–22. Keeling, pages 206-207, 218
23–24. Snape, 2008, page 204
25–28. *Merry In God*, pages 182, 184, 183, 183
29. WD to HD 17/2/16, FAI
30. O'Rahilly, 1925, page 398
31. *Merry In God*, page 184
32–33. WD to HD 17/2/16, FAI

Chapter 10

1–2. Snape, page 217
3–4. Johnstone and Hegarty, page 88
5. Rickard, page 14
6–7. Johnstone and Hegarty, pages 88, 105
8. Rickard, pages 53–54
9. Johnstone and Hegarty, page 111
10–11. Snape, pages 217, 228
12–14. Johnstone and Hegarty, pages 103, 103, 104
15. WD to HD 17/2/16, FAI
16–17. Spurr, pages 10, 19
18. Snape, page 254
19. Madigan, page 165
20. Leonard, page 32
21. Holmes, page 518
22–23. Snape, pages 190, 236
24. Leonard, page 3
25. O'Rahilly, 1925, page 438
26–28. Doudney, pages 139, 151, 159
29. Leonard, page 16
30. O'Rahilly, 1925, page 474
31. Blackburne, page 104
32. Hardy, page 21
33. O'Rahilly, 1925, footnote page 462
34. Laird, page 109

Chapter 11

1. O'Rahilly, 1925, page 399
2. O'Rahilly, 1925, page 399
3. WD to HD 21/2/16, FAI
4. Cooper-Walker, page 25
5–13. WD to HD 21/2/16, FAI
14. Cooper-Walker, page 26

15. Cooper-Walker, page 26
16. Johnstone, page 206
17. WD to HD 3/3/16, FAI
18. Graves, page 91
19. WD to Lena 2/3/16, FAI
20. WD to HD 3/3/16, FAI
21. WD to HD 3/3/16, FAI
22. WD to HD 3/3/16, FAI
23. Stewart and Buchan, page 63
24. WD to HD 3/3/16, FAI
25. Kipling, page 113

Chapter 12
1–2. Blackburne, pages 70, 66
3. Johnstone, page 209
4–5. Grieve and Newman, pages 69–0, 70
6. Kipling, page 113
7. WD to HD 10/3/16, FAI
8. Cooper-Walker, pages 27–28
9. WD to HD 10/3/16, FAI
10. Snape, page 204
11–12. May, page 176
13. Blackburne, pages 56 – 58
14–16. WD to HD 10 /3/16, FAI
17. O'Rahilly, 1925, page 400
18. WD to HD 10/3/16, FAI
19–20. WD to HD 17/3/16, FAI
21. WO 95/1978, TNA
22. Cooper-Walker, page 54
23. Johnstone, page 207
24. O'Sullivan, IWM
25–27. WD to HD 17/3/16, FAI
28. O'Sullivan, IWM
29–31. Staniforth, IWM
32–36. WD to HD 17/3/16, FAI

37. WD to HD 24 /3/16, FAI
38. Denman, 1992, page 183
39. WD to HD 24/3/16, FAI
40. WD to HD 31/3/16, FAI

Chapter 13
1. WD to HD 31/3/16, FAI
2. Denman, 1995, page 9
3–5. WD to HD 31/3/16, FAI
6. Lucy, page 14
7. Laird, pages 2–3
8–9. Dungan, 1997, pages 24, 19
10–11. Horne and Pennell, page 39
12–13. Lucy, pages 46, 294
14. Laird, page 2
15–16. Horne and Pennell, page 38
17. Lucy, page 345
18–19. Cooper, pages vii – xiii
20. Johnstone, page 10
21–22. Denman, 1992, page 22
23. Lee and Orr, page 2
24. WD to HD 31/3/16, FAI

Chapter 14
1. O'Rahilly, 1925, page 382
2. WD to HD 31/3/16, FAI
3. WD to HD 31/3/16, FAI
4. Cooper-Walker, page 30
5–17. WD to HD 31/3/16, FAI
18. WO95/1976, TNA
19. WO95/1976, TNA
20–23. Cooper-Walker, pages 31–33
24–25. WD to HD 31/3/16, FAI
26–32. WD to HD 22/4/16, FAI
33. WO95/1978, TNA

34. Hans, pages 77–78
35. WD to HD 29/4/16, FAI

Chapter 15
1. Owen
2–3. WD to HD 3/5/16, FAI
4. Cooper-Walker, page 34
5. WO 95/1978, TNA
6–9. WD to HD 3/5/16, FAI
10. Barton, page 287
11. WD to HD 3/5/16, FAI
12. O'Rahilly, 1925, page 423–424
13–14. WD to HD 3/5/16, FAI
15. Cooper-Walker, page 34
16. Staniforth, IWM
17. Dunn, page 197
18. Hans, pages 77-78
19. Johnstone, pages 210-211
20. WO 95/1978, TNA
21–23. WD to HD 3/5/16, FAI
24. Cooper-Walker, page 41
25–26. WD to HD 3/5/16, FAI
27–28. WD to HD Easter 1916, FAI
29. Staniforth, IWM
30. Denman, 1992, page 70
31. WD to HD Easter 1916, FAI
32. WO 95/1978, TNI
33. O'Rahilly, 1925, footnote page 420
34. 16th (Irish) Division Parchment of Merit, FAI

Chapter 16
1. Drury, NAM
2. WD to HD 13/5/16, FAI
3. WO 95/1978, TNA
4. WO 95/1976, TNA
5. WD to HD 13/5/16, FAI
6. WO 158/269, TNA
7–9. WO 95/1976, TNA
10. Dunn, page 197
11–12. Cooper-Walker, page 35
13. WO 95/1978, TNA
14. Staniforth, IWM
15–17. Denman, 1992, Appendix, pages 69–70
18. Edmonds, footnote page 196
19. Stewart and Buchan, page 68
20–26. WO 158/269, TNA
27. Empey, 1917
28. Lucy, page 314
29–31. WO 158/269, TNA
32. WO 95/1978, TNA
33. WO 158/269, TNA
34. Stewart and Buchan, page 66
35. Edmonds, footnote page 195
36. Empey, 1917
37. Leonard, page 64
38. WO 256/10, TNA
39. Burnett-Stewart, page 43
40–41. Foulkes, pages 182, 306
42–43. Edmonds, pages 201, 193-196
44. CAB 45/289, TNA
45–46. Denman, 1992, page 69
47. Staniforth, IWM
48. Cooper-Walker, page 40
49. Dunn, page 197-198
50–52. WD to HD 13/5/16, FAI
53. *London Gazette*, 4//1/17, number 29890, page 251

Chapter 17
1–2. Yeats
3. WD to HD 13/5/16, FAI
4. Dungan, 1997, page 29
5. Laird, page 179
6. WD to HD 13/5/16, FAI
7. Coogan, page 103
8. Kearns, page 215
9. Dungan, 1997, page 29
10. Townshend, page 263
11. Ackerman et. al.: page 43
12. Jamie, page 12
13. Kearns, page 215
14. Coogan, 2001, page 103
15. Dungan, 1997, page 29
16–17. Ackerman *et. al*: pages 43, 39
18. Whitton, page 267
19. Ackerman *et. al*: Appendix page 145
20–21. Dungan, 1997, pages 33, 30
22. Denman, 1992, page 143
23–24. Dungan, 1997, pages 32-33, 31
25. Hall, page 39
26–27. Lucy, pages 352, 356
28. Hall, page 39
29–31. Dungan, 1997, pages 31, 32, 30
32. Johnstone, pages 212-213
33. Rayner, page 296

Chapter 18
1. *Disenchantment*, C.E. Montague 1867–1928
2–5. WD to HD 22/5/16, FAI
6. Cooper–Walker, pages 46 and 48
7–10. WD to HD 19/6/16, FAI
11–14. WD to HD 28/6/16, FAI
15. WD to HD 8/7/16, FAI
16–17. Cooper–Walker, pages 53, 55
18–19. WD to HD 8/7/16, FAI
20–22. WD to HD 14/7/16, FAI
23–25. WO 95/1978, TNA
26–27. WD to HD 14/7/16, FAI
28. WD to HD 31/7/16, FAI
29. Galvin to O'Rahilly, BC
30. WD to Mr Galvin, 11/7/17, Galvin Family Archive
31. WD to HD 31/7/16, FAI
32–37. WD to HD 10/8/16, FAI
38. WD to HD 21/8/16, FAI
39. Cooper–Walker, page 59
40. WD to HD 28/8/16, FAI
41. WD to HD 30/8/16, FAI

Chapter 19
1–7. WD to HD 2/9/16, FAI
8. Middlebrook, page 262 and Appendix 4 page 329
9–10. Whitton, pages 239, 310
11–12. Jünger, pages 91-92, 96-98
13. Inglefield, pages 69-70
14–17. Dungan, 1995, page 132
18. WO 95/1970, TNA
19. WO 95/2095, TNA
20. Dungan, 1995, page 136
21. Denman, 1992, page 81
22–23. Whitton, page 308, 320
24. Denman, 1992, page 81
25. Staniforth, IWM
26. Byron, page 203
27. Inglefield, pages 76-77
28. Johnstone, page 242

29. Whitton, page 311
30. Miles, page 257, note 4
31. Whitton, page 310
32. Johnstone, page 244
33–34. Dungan, 1995, page 138
35–37. Whitton, page 313
38. Feilding, page 111
39–40. WD to HD 11/9/16, FAI

Chapter 20
1. Dungan, 1995, page 138
2. WO 95/2124, TNA
3. WD to HD 11/9/16, FAI
4. Cooper Walker, page 64
5. WD to HD 11/9/16, FAI
6. WO 95/1978, TNA
7. WD to HD 11/9/16, FAI
8. Johnstone, page 247
9–10. WD to HD 11/9/16, FAI
11. Dudley Ward, page 55
12–17. WD to HD 11/9/16
18. WO 95/1978, TNA
19. WD to HD 11/9/16, FAI
20. WO 95/1978, TNA
21. WD to HD 11/9/16, FAI
22–24. WO 95/1978, TNA
25. Cooper Walker, page 68
26. WD to HD 11/9/16, FAI
27. Wyrall, page 180
28. WD to HD 11/9/16, FAI
29–30. WO 95/1978, TNA
31. WD to HD 11/9/16, FAI
32–33, Edmonds, pages 274, 275
34–35. WD to HD 20/12/16, FAI
36–38. Dungan, 1995, page 145

39–41. Lyons, pages 299, 298, 301
42–43. Feilding, pages 115, 116
44. Staniforth, IWM
45–46. Dudley Ward, pages 58, 60
47. WD to HD 11/9/16, FAI
48. WO 95/1978, TNA
49–50. WD to HD 11/9/16, FAI
51. Feilding, page 118
52. Whitton, page 318
53. Staniforth, IWM
54. Dungan, 1995, page 147
55. Johnstone, page 253 and 254
56. Denman, 1992, Appendix page 183
57. WD to HD 11/9/16, FAI

Chapter 21
1. Fr William Doyle Prayer Card, FAI
2. Johnstone, page 253
3. Dungan, 1995, page 147
4. WD to HD 23/9/16, FAI
5. Cooper Walker, page 74
6. WO 95/1978, TNA
7–8. WD to HD 23/9/16, FAI
9–13. WO 71/500, TNA
14–15. Lucy, pages 204, 296-297
16. WO 71/500, TNA
17. WD to HD 23/9/16, FAI
18. WO 95/1978, TNA
19. Newman
20–22. WD to HD 23/9/16, FAI
23. Cooper Walker, page 77
24–25. WD to HD 23/9/16, FAI
26. Cooper Walker, page 77
27. Laird, page 101
28. Feilding, page 121

29. WD to Lena 2/10/16, FAI
30. WO 95/1978, TNA
31. Laird, page 102
32–33. WD to HD 11/10/16, FAI
34. Wolff, page 81
35. Cooper Walker, page 79
36–40. WD to HD 11/10/16, FAI

Chapter 22
1. WD to HD 26/10/16, FAI
2. WD to HD 7/11/16, FAI
3. WD to HD 30/11/16, FAI
4–6. WD to HD 6/12/16, FAI
7–8. WD to HD 13/12/16, FAI
9. Laird, pages 100-101
10. WO 95/1974, TNA
11–14. O'Rahilly, 1925, pages 455-456
15. WD to HD 9/1/17, FAI
16. WD to HD 20/12/16, FAI
17. O'Rahilly, 1925, page 460
18–23. WD to HD 20/12/16, FAI
24–26. WD to HD 28/12/16, FAI
27. WD to HD 20/12/16, FAI
28. WO 95/1974, TNA
29. WD to HD 28/12/16, FAI
30. WO 95/1974, TNA
31. WD to HD 28/12/16, FAI
32. WO 95/1974, TNA
33–34. WD to HD 20/12/16, FAI
35. Laird, 1925, page 106
36–40. WD to HD 20/12/16, FAI

Chapter 23
1. O'Rahilly, 1925, page 202
2. Observation from *Remembering Father William Doyle* website, 24 January 2013
3. WD post card 4/1/17, FAI
4–5. WD to HD 16/1/17, FAI
6. Laird, page 102
7. WD to HD 27/1/17, FAI
8–14. WD to HD 1/1/17, FAI
15. Laird, page 104
16–18. WD to HD 1/1/17, FAI
19. WO 95/1974, TNA
20. WD to HD 1/1/17, FAI
21. WD to HD 6/2/17, FAI
22–29. WD to HD 16/1/17, FAI
30. WO 95/1974, TNA
31. Laird, page 114
32–33. WD to HD 30/1/17, FAI
34. WD to 16/1/17, FAI
35–36. WD to HD 16/1/17, FAI
37. Text of letter dated 7/2/17 taken from photo belonging to Irish Jesuits Photostream
38. WD to HD 12/12/17, FAI
39. Burke, pages 176-177
40–41. *Merry in God,* pages 139, 256
42–43. WD to HD 15/3/17, FAI
44. WO 95/1974, TNA
45. WD to HD 15/3/17, FAI

Chapter 24
1–4. WD to HD 20/3/17, FAI
5. WO 95/1974, TNA
6. Laird, pages 112-113
7. WD to HD 21/3/17, FAI
8–9. WD to HD 20/3/17, FAI
10. WO 95/1974, TNA
11. Laird, pages 101-102

12–14. WD to HD 20/3/17, FAI
15. Laird, page 127
16. WD to HD 20/3/17, FAI
17–18. WD to HD 29/3/17, FAI
19. WO 95/1974, TNA
20–21. Laird,1925, page 133
22. WO 95/1974, TNA
23. WD to HD 10/4/17, FAI
24. Laird, page 135
25–26. WD to HD 10/4/17, FAI
27. Laird, page 134
28–33. WD to HD 10/4/17, FAI
34. WD to HD 18/4/17, FAI
35. Laird, page 111
36. WD to HD 18/4/17, FAI
37. Laird, page 136
38. WD to HD 18/4/17, FAI
39. Laird, pages 138-139
40. WO 95/2505, TNA
41. WD to HD 29/4/17, FAI
42–43. WD to HD 10/4/17, FAI
44. O'Rahilly, 1925, footnote page 489
45–48. WD to HD 10/4/17, FAI
49. WD to HD 27/4/17, FAI

Chapter 25
1. WD to HD 7/5/17, FAI
2–3. Laird, pages 139-140, 141
4. Glanville, IWM
5. WD to HD 7/5/17, FAI
6. Chapter 7, page 12
7–11. WD to HD 7/5/17, FAI
12. Laird, pages 141-142
13. WD to HD 7/5/17, FAI
14. WD to HD 15/5/17, FAI

15. Laird, page 142
16–17. WD to HD 15/5/17, FAI
18. Cooper Walker, pages 94-95
19. WD to HD 15/5/17, FAI
20–21. Laird, pages 144, 145
22–24. WD to HD 15/5/17, FAI
25. WD postcard 25/5/17, FAI
26. WD to HD 29/5/17, FAI
27–28. WO 95/1974, TNA
29–33. WD to HD 29/5/17, FAI
34. WO 95/1974, TNA
35. IWM 21037
36. Drury, NAM
37. WO 95/1974, TNA
38. Laird, page 148
39. IWM 21037
40–46. WD to HD 3/6/17, FAI
47–48. O'Rahilly, 1925, pages 503, 504

Chapter 26
1. Laird, page 145
2. Feilding, page 193
3. Fox, page 94
4. WO 95/1972
5–6. WD to HD 11/6/17, FAI
7–9. WD to HD 12/6/16, FAI
10. Laird, pages 147-8
11. WD to HD 12/6/17, FAI
12–14. WO 95/1974, TNA
15–16. WD to HD 12/6/17, FAI
17. Laird, page 149
18. WD to HD 12/6/17, FAI
19. Johnstone, page 277
20. WD to HD 12/6/17, FAI
21. Laird, page 150

22. WO 95/1972, TNA
23. Laird, page 150
24. WD to HD 12/6/17, FAI
25. Sheldon, page 3
26. WD to HD 12/6/17, FAI
27. Laird, page 151
28. O'Rahilly, 1925, page 510
29. WD to HD 12/6/17, FAI
30. Laird, page 152
31. WD to HD 12/6/17, FAI
32. Edmonds, pages 52-53
33. Laird, page 152
34. WD to HD 12/6/17, FAI
35. Glanville, IWM
36. Feilding, pages 188-189
37–38. WD to HD 12/6/17, FAI
39. O'Rahilly,1925, page 512
40. MacDonald, pages 46-47
41–42. WD to HD 12/6/17, FAI
43. Laird, Dublin, pages 113-114
44. WD to HD 12/6/17, FAI
45. Healy to Charles Doyle, circa end of 1917
46. Laird, page 153
47. WD to HD 12/6/17, FAI
48. Feilding, page 189
49. WD to HD 12/6/17, FAI
50. WO 95/1972, TNA
51–52. WD to HD 12/6/17, FAI
53. Laird, page 154
54. WO 95/1974, TNA
55. Laird, page 154
56. Feilding, page 193
57. Glanville, IWM
58. WO 95/1972, TNA
59. WD to HD 12/6/17, FAI
60. Cooper Walker, page 106
61. Glanville, IWM
62. Feilding, page 194
63. WD to HD 12/6/17, FAI

Chapter 27

1–2. Feilding, pages 192-193, 189
3. Johnstone, page 255
4. Dungan, 1995, page 162
5. Johnstone, page 278
6. WD to HD 24/6/17, FAI
7. Cooper Walker, page 109
8–9. Staniforth, IWM
10. WO 95/1974, TNA
11. WD to HD 24/6/17, FAI
12. Feilding, page 195
13–14. WD to HD 24/6/17, FAI
15. Laird, page 154
16. WD to HD 24/6/17, FAI
17. Laird, page 154
18. Dunn, page 435
19. Lucy, page 199
20. Feilding, page 192
21. WD to HD 24/6/17, FAI
22. WD to HD 17/7/17, FAI
23. O'Rahilly, 1925, pages 519-520
24. Cooper Walker, page 110
25–27. WD to HD 21/7/17, FAI
28–29. O'Rahilly, 1925, footnote pages 522, 520-523
30–31. WD to HD 21/7/17, FAI
32. O'Rahilly, 1925, footnote page 517

REFERENCES

Chapter 28
1–15. WD to HD 25/7/17, FAI
16. Cooper Walker, private publication, page 110

Chapter 29
1. Steel and Hart, page 138
2. WD to HD 2/8/17, FAI
3–4. Steel and Hart, pages 59, 37
5. Whitton, page 367
6. Wolff, page 133
7. Lucy, pages 365-6
8. Cooper Walker, page 111
9. WD to HD 2/8/17, FAI
10. Sheldon, page 52
11–12. Coop, pages 53-54
13–14. Steel and Hart, pages 108, 109
15. WD postcard 6/8/17, FAI
16. WD to HD 31/7/17, FAI
17–21. WD to HD, 30/7/17, FAI
22. Cooper Walker, page 111
23. WD 30/7/17, FAI
24. Stewart and Buchan, page 168
25–30. WD to HD 30/7/17, FAI
31–32. Steel and Hart, pages 136, 137

Chapter 30
1. Glanville, IWM
2. Staniforth, IWM
3. Jeffreys, page 47
4. WD to HD 30/7/17, FAI
5. WO 95/2502, TNA
6. WO 95/1970, TNA
7–9. WD to HD 30/7/17, FAI
10. WO 95/1974, TNA
11. WD to HD 30/7/17, FAI
12. WO 95/1974, TNA
13. WD to HD 30/7/17, FAI
14. WD to HD 12/8/17, FAI
15–19. WD to HD 6/8/17, FAI
20. WO 95/1974, TNA
21. WD to HD 6/8/17, FAI
22. WO 95/1970, TNA
23. WD to HD 6/8/17, FAI
24. Staniforth, IWM
25–30. WD to HD 6/8/17, FAI
31. WD to HD 14/8/17

Chapter 31
1. *A Year's thoughts: collected from the writings of William Doyle,* Longmans, Green & Co., 1922
2. WO 95/1974, TNA
3. Sheldon, page 121
4. Edmonds, page 194
5–6. Steel and Hart, pages 147-148, 147
7. Drury, NAM
8. Edmonds, page 195
9. WO 95/1974, TNA
10. Steel and Hart, page 148
11. Sheldon, pages 128-129
12–14. WO 95/1974, TNA
15. Boraston and Bax, pages 147-148
16–20. WO 95/1974, TNA

Chapter 32
1. Johnstone, page 282
2. O'Rahilly, 2009, page 300
3–4. WO 95/1975, TNA
5. Boraston and Bax, page 145

6. Stewart and Buchan, page 179
7. WO 95/1974, TNA
8. Hickie to Kays 18/11/17, FAI
9–12. O'Rahilly, 1925, pages 551, 551, 552, 301
13–14. WO 95/1953, TNA
15. Healy to Charles Doyle, circa end of 1917, FAI
16. O'Rahilly, 1925, page 558
17. Van Walleghem, IFFM
18. Hickie to Kays 18/11/17, FAI
19. Denman, 1992, page 124
20. Johnstone, page 282
21. Hickie to Kays 18/11/17, FAI
22. O'Rahilly, 1925, page 552
23. Galvin to O'Rahilly, circa 1919, BC
24. Dungan, 1997, page 69

Chapter 33

1. Dungan, 1995, page 173
2. Edmonds, pages 194–195
3. Galvin to O'Rahilly, circa 1919, BC
4–6. Denman, 1992, pages 123, 123, 124
7–9. WO 339/123587, TNA
10. O'Rahilly, 1925, page XVI
11–13. WO 339/123587, TNA
14. Denman, 1992, pages 127–128
15–16. Feilding, pages 229–230, 240–241
17. Smith to Caenepeel, 19/5/70, IFFM
18. Hickie to Kays 18/11/17, FAI
19. WO 339/123587, TNA
20. WO 339/13046, FAI
21. Denman, 1992, page 123
22. Laird, page 196

Chapter 34

1. O'Rahilly, 1925, page 555
2. Browne 15/8/17
3–4. Corrigan, pages 102, 103
5. Hickie to Kays 18/11/17, FAI
6–9. T333/1 TNA
10–11. Crook, page 217
12. Hickie to Kays 18/11/17, FAI
13–15. Hosie, pages 437, 438, 436
16. WO 256/2
17. Williamson, page 323
18. WD to HD 7/8/17, FAI
19. Browne 15/8/17, FAI
20–22. WO 256/21, TNA
23. Feilding, page 202
24. Hickie to Kays 18/11/17, FAI
25. Johnstone, page 290
26. WO 256/21
27. Browne 15/8/17, FAI
28. WO 256/21
29. Clayton, page 202
30. O'Rahilly, 1925, page 555
31. The *London Gazette,* 14/9/17
32–33. Clayton, pages 210, 163
34. T331/1, TNA
35–36. Clayton, page 220
37. WD to HD 11/9/17, FAI
38. WD to HD 10/8/17, FAI
39. Hickie to Kays 18/11/17, FAI
40. Galvin to O'Rahilly, circa 1919, BC
41–44. O'Rahilly, 1925, pages 553, 556, 557
45. *The Clongownian,* CWC
46. Fletcher to O'Rahilly, 3/4/20, BC
47. Fletcher to O'Rahilly, 25/4/20, BC

REFERENCES

48. www.dnw.co.uk
49. Leonard, page 64
50. Williamson, page 317/8
51. Leonard, page 123

Chapter 35
1–2. WO 95/13046, TNA
3. Hall, page 46
4. Galvin to O'Rahilly, circa 1919, BC
5. Lena to O'Rahilly, 19/2/20, FAI
6–8. Doyle Family Archive, Ireland
9. Castles 14/9/2012
10–12. WO 339/123587, TNA
13. Lucy, page 46
14–17. *Irish Messenger*
18. Lucy, page 318
19–21. Castles 14/9/2012
22. Drury, NAM
23. McMahon, Belfast 1999
24. Smyth, The Furrow, March 1958
25. Smith to Caenepeel, 26/4/70, IFFM
26. Smith to Caenepeel, 19/5/70, IFFM
27. Caenepeel to Smith, 19/5/70, IFFM
28. McMahon, Belfast 1999
29. Dungan, article
30. *A Journey of Reconciliation Trust,* inaugural document, November 1996
31. Dungan, 1995, page 173
32. *Remembering Father William Doyle,* website, 26 February 2013
33. F.K. letter, *The Clongownian*, VOL. VIII.No2. June, 1918 page129-131, CWC

Appendix B
1. *Glasgow Evening News* 1/9/17
2. Browne, 15/8/17, FAI
3. *Catholic News* 15/9/17
4. O'Rahilly, 1925, page 556
5. *Irish News* 29/8/17
6–7. O'Rahilly, 1925, pages 559, 555
8. Healy to Charles Doyle, circa end of 1917, FAI
9. Galvin to O'Rahilly, circa 1919, BC
10–11. Smith to Caenepeel, IFFM

Appendix C
1–6. *Merry In God,* page 86–91

BIBLIOGRAPHY & SOURCES

Doyle descendants' family material and privately held papers – typed transcripts

Willie Doyle to his sister Mai, written from Limerick on Good Friday 1911

Willie Doyle to Hugh Doyle letter *ON THE ROAD TO MANDALAY OR ELSEWHERE* written from Bordon Camp England, Thursday 17 February 1916

Letter dated 15 August 1917 from Fr Francis Browne to unknown recipient (probably Hugh or Charles Doyle)

Typed transcript of Captain C.F. Healy's recollections to Charles Doyle, (undated but probably end of 1917)

WD to HD or Mai 1916–1917

N.B. The 'WD to HD' are all typed transcriptions of letters or 'budgets' i.e. diary type narratives written by Willie Doyle from the Western Front to his father Hugh Doyle

WD to HD 21/2/16, 3/3/16, 10/3/16, 17/3/16, 24/3/16, 31/3/16, 22/4/16, 29/4/16, 3/5/16, 13/5/16, 22/5/16, 19/6/16, 28/6/16

WD to Mai 8/7/16

WD to HD 14/7/16, 20/7/16, 31/7/16, 10/8/16, 21/8/16, 28/8/16, 2/9/16, 11/9/16, 23/9/16, 11/10/16, 26/10/16, 7/11/16, 30/11/16, 6/12/16, 13/12/16, 20/12/16, 28/12/16, 9/1/17, 16/1/17, 27/1/17, 30/1/17, 6/2/17, 12/2/17, 15/3/17, 20/3/17, 21/3/17, 29/3/17, 10/4/17, 18/4/17, 27/4/17, 29/4/17, 7/5/17, 15/5/17, 22/5/17, 29/5/17

WD to Mai 2/6/17

WD to HD 5/6/17, 11/6/17, 12/6/17, 24/6/17, 17/7/17, 21/7/17, 25/7/17, 2/8/17, 6/8/17 12/8/17, 14/8/17

Hand-written letters, postcards and other original documents in the Doyle descendant's family archive:

Letter from Willie Doyle to his sister Lena dated 27 August 1900

Letter written by Willie Doyle, dated 16th February 1912, from College of the Sacred Heart

Letter sent some time in 1913 from St Patrick's College, Dundalk

WD postcard sent from Witley Camp, 27 December 1915
WD postcard 2 March 1916
WD postcard 30 August 1916
WD postcard 2 October 1916
WD postcard 4 January 1917

Letter from Fr Doyle to Mr Barry St John Galvin (Snr) dated 11 July 1916

Text of WD letter dated 7 February 1917 taken from photo, Irish Jesuits Photostream

WD postcard 25 May 1917
WD postcard 6 August 1917

Letter dated 18 November 1917 from Major General W.B. Hickie to Brigadier General H. F. Kays

Irish Messenger, booklet

Fr William Doyle Prayer Card

16th (Irish) Division Parchment of Merit

The National Archives, Kew
WO 339/123587, personal file of Fr William Doyle
WO 339/13046 personal file of Barry St John Galvin
WO 339/69132 personal file of Daniel Galvin
WO 256 series Sir Douglas Haig, Commander in Chief of British Forces, Western Front: diaries
CAB 45/289 Gas attacks: original correspondence, German replies to questionnaires, etc. concerning the use of Gas at Ypres, 1915, and Hulloch and Wolverghem, 1916
WO 158/269 various First Army Reports Numbered 136 (G) dated 5 May 1916 concerning Gas at Hulloch 1916
WO 95/1953 46th Infantry Brigade War Diary
WO 95/1970 47th Infantry Brigade War Diary
WO 95/1972 48th Infantry Brigade War Diary
WO 95/1974 8th Battalion Royal Dublin Fusiliers War Diary
WO 95/1975 7th Battalion Royal Irish Rifles War Diary
WO 95/1976, 49th Infantry Brigade War Diary
WO 95/1978 8th Battalion Royal Irish Fusiliers War Diary
WO 95/1978 16th Division War Diary, Report No. D.S. 1182, Major General W.B. Hickie, Officer Commanding, 16th (Irish) Division
WO 95/2095 Headquarters Branches and Services: General Staff War Diary
WO 95/2502 107th Infantry Brigade War Diary
WO 95/2505 108th Infantry Brigade War Diary
WO95/2124 61st Infantry Brigade War Diary
WO 71/500, Court Martial File, Joseph Carey
T333/1 Victoria Cross including warrants

Imperial War Museum Department of Documents
Glanville, Arthur E., private papers, IWM reference 21037
Starrett, David *Batman,* unpublished memoir, IWM reference 6659
Staniforth, J.H.M. private papers, IWM reference 14337
O'Sullivan, J.F.B. *At Rest in Philosophe 6th The Connaught Rangers, June 1916,* IWM reference 7155

National Army Museum Templar Study Centre
Drury, Noel E., Royal Dublin Fusiliers, personal papers, NAM reference 1976–07–69

The Royal Artillery Museum
Newman, R.H., MD 1169

The London Gazette
14 December 1915 Willie Doyle's appointment, 29404
20 April 1916
20 September 1916
20 October 1916
1 January 1917 page 33 Willie Doyle's Military Cross
4 January 1917 Willie Doyle Mentioned in Dispatches, 298980
14 September 1917
17 October 1917
24 December 1917 Willie Doyle Mentioned in Dispatches, 13490
6 July 1918

Newspapers and Journals
The Hibernian 18 November 1813
Dublin Evening Post 10 March 1873
    15 March 1873
Irish Times 16 July 1870
    29 June 1914
    5 August 1914
    10 September 1916
    12 September 1916
    9 June 1917
    17 August 1917
Irish News 29 August 1917
Drogheda Independent 2 May 1916
Drogheda Independent 6 May 1916
Dundalk Independent 20 May 1916
Dundalk Democrat 23 September 1916
The Times 16 April 1917
The Times 1 August 1917
The Times 17 August 1917
Daily Chronicle 22 August 1917
Daily Telegraph 22 August 1917
Glasgow Weekly News 1 September 1917

Glasgow Evening News 1 September 1917
Catholic News 15 September 1917
Liverpool Echo 25 September 1917
The Clongownian, VOL.VIII. No2. June, 1918 page129–131.
The Furrow, The Journal of St Patrick's Church, Maynooth, March 1958, Kevin Smyth
The Guardian 12 November 1999

British Official Histories

Edmonds, Brigadier-General Sir James E., *History of the Great War, Military Operations, France and Belgium, 1916,* MacMillan and Co., Limited, 1932

Edmonds, Brigadier-General Sir James E., *History of the Great War, Military Operations, France and Belgium, 1917,* MacMillan and Co., Limited, 1948, Volume II

Miles, Captain Wilfred, *History of the Great War, Military Operations: France and Belgium,* 1916, MacMillan and Co. Ltd., 1938

British Army and German Army Unit Histories

Akerman, Bates, Bradbridge, Brazier-Creagh, Dodds, Goadby, Maconchy, Richardson, Romer, Sandbach, Stansfield, Stirling, *59th Division 1915–1918,* privately published, 1928

Boraston, Lt.-Colonel J.H. and Bax, Captain Cyril E.O., *The Eighth Division in War, 1914–1918,* The Medici Society Limited, 1926

Burnett-Stewart, Major-General J.T. *The Tenth Battalion The Cameronians (Scottish Rifles), 1914–1918,* The Edinburgh Press, 1923

Byron, Colonel R., D.S.O., Editor *The King's Royal Rifle Corps Chronicle 1916,* Warren and Son Limited, 1919

Coop, The Rev. J.O., *The Story of the 55th Division, 1916-1919,* Liverpool 'Daily Post' Printers, 1919

Cooper, Major Bryan, *The Tenth (Irish) Division in Gallipoli,* Herbert Jenkins Ltd., 1918

Cooper-Walker, G.A., *The Book of The 7th Battalion Royal Inniskilling Fusiliers,* private publication, 1920

Dudley Ward, Major C.H., DSO, MC *The 56th Division (1st London Territorial Division),* John Murray 1921

Foulkes, Major-General C.H., *'Gas!' The Story of the Special Brigade,* William Blackwood & Sons Ltd., 1934

BIBLIOGRAPHY & SOURCES

Fox, Sir Frank, *The Royal Inniskillings in the World War,* Constable & Company, 1928

Grieve, Captain W. Grant and Newman, Bernard, *Tunnellers The Story of the Tunnelling Companies, Royal Engineers, during the World War,* Captain W. Herbert Jenkins Limited, 1936

Hans, Generalmajor a.D., *Das K.B.9. Infanterie-Regiment 'Wrede',* Wurzburg 1927

Inglefield, Captain V.E., *The History of the Twentieth (Light) Division,* Nisbet & Co. Ltd., 1921

Jamie, Lieutenant-Colonel J.P.W., *The 177th Brigade 1914-1918,* privately published, 1931

Kipling, Rudyard, *The Irish Guards in the Great War, The First Battalion,* Spellmount Limited, 1997

Molony, Major C.V., *'Invicta' With the 1st Battalion The Queen's Own Royal West Kent Regiment in the Great War,* 1923, Nisbet & Co. Ltd., 1923

Rayner, Lieutenant-Colonel F., *The Sherwood Foresters in the Great War, The Robin Hoods 1/7th, 2/7th, 3/7th Battalions,* Section II, private publication, 1921

Stewart, Lieutenant-Colonel J., D.S.O., and Buchan, John, *The Fifteenth (Scottish) Division 1914-1919,* William Blackwood and Sons, 1926

Whitton, Lieutenant-Colonel F.E., *The History of the Prince of Wales Leinster Regiment (Royal Canadians),* volume II, Gale & Polden Ltd., 1924

Wyrall, Everard, *The History of the Duke of Cornwall's Light Infantry,* Methuen & Co. Ltd., London, 1932

Published Personal Memoirs or collections of letters

Blackburne, Harry, D.S.O., M.C., *This Also Happened on the Western Front, The Padre's Story,* Hodder and Stoughton Limited, 1932

Doudney, C.E., *The Best of Good Fellows, The Diaries and Memoirs of The Rev. Charles Edmund Doudney, M.A., C.F. (1871–1915),* Jonathan Horne Publications 1995

Doyle, W.J.G., *A Year's thoughts: collected from the writings of William Doyle,* Longmans, Green & Co., 1922

Dunn, Captain James Churchill, *The War the Infantry Knew 1914–1919,* Jane's Publishing Company Ltd 1987

Empey, Arthur Guy, *Over The Top,* G.P. Putnam & Sons, 1917

Feilding, Rowland *War Letters to a Wife, France and Flanders, 1915–1919,* The Medici Society Ltd., 1929

Graves, Robert, *Goodbye to All That,* Penguin Books 2000

Hitchcock, Captain F.C., M.C., *'Stand To' A Diary of the Trenches 1915–1918,* Gliddon Books, Norwich 1988

Jeffreys, Captain R.G.B., *Collected Letters 1916–1918,* Edited by Conor and Liam Dodd, Old Tough Publications, 2007

Jünger, Ernst, *Storm of Steel,* translated by Michael Hofmann, Allen Lane, 2003

Keeling, F.H., *Keeling Letters and Recollections,* Edited by E.T. with an Introduction by H.G. Wells, George Allen & Unwin Ltd 1918

Laird, Frank, *Personal Experiences of the Great War,* Dublin, private publication, Eason & Son, 1925

Leonard, John and Leonard-Johnson, Philip, *The Fighting Padre, Letters from the Trenches 1915–1918 of Pat Leonard DSO,* Pen & Sword Military, 2010

Lucy, John. F., *There's a devil in the drum,* Faber and Faber, 1938

May, Colonel H.A.R., C.B., V.D., *Memories of the Artists Rifles,* Howlett & Son, 1929

Steinhauer, G, *Steinhauer The Kaiser's Master Spy The Story As Told By Himself,* Edited by S.T. Felstead, John Lane The Bodley Head Limited, 1930

Other Publications

Bourke, Marcus, *The O'Rahilly,* Anvil Books, 1967

Burke, Tom, M.B.E., *The 16th (Irish) and 36th (Ulster) Divisions at The Battle of Wijtschate-Messines Ridge, 7 June 1917,* The Royal Dublin Fusiliers Association, 2007

Clayton, Ann, *Chavasse Double VC,* Pen & Sword Military, 2006

Coogan, Tim Pat, *1916: The Easter Rising,* Phoenix, 2001

Corrigan, Gordon, *Mud, Blood and Poppycock,* Cassell Military Paperbacks, 2003

Crook, M.J., *The Evolution of the Victoria Cross,* Midas Books in Association with the Ogilby Trusts, 1975

Cullen, Brendan, *A Short History of Clongowes Wood College*

Denman, Terence, *Ireland's Unknown Soldiers, The 16th (Irish) Division in the Great War 1914–1918,* Irish Academic Press, 1992

Denman, Terence, *A Lonely Grave, The Life and Death of William Redmond,* Irish Academic Press Ltd, 1995

Doyle, Charles (probable author) *Merry in God, A Life of Father William Doyle, S.J.,* Roman Catholic Books, Unacknowledged author.

Dungan, Myles, *Irish Voices From The Great War,* Irish Academic Press, 1995

Dungan, Myles, *They Shall Grow Not Old, Irish Soldiers and the Great War,* Four Courts Press, 1997

Foy, Michael T. and Barton, Brian, *'The Easter Rising',* The History Press, 2011

Hall, Donal, *World War 1 and nationalist politics in County Louth 1914–1920,* Four Courts Press, 2005

Harris, H.E.D., *The Irish Regiments in the First World War,* The Mercier Press, 1968

Hart, Peter, *The Great War,* Profile Books, 2013

Holmes, Richard, *Tommy, The British Soldier on the Western Front, 1914–1918,* Harper Collins, 2004

Horne John and Pennel Catriona (ed.) *Our War, Ireland and the Great War, The 2008 Thomas Davis Lecture Series,* Royal Irish Academy, 2008

Hosie, John, *A Lonely Road, Fr Ted McGrath msc,* ATF Press Ltd., 2010

Johnstone, Tom, *Orange, Green & Khaki, The Story of the Irish Regiments in the Great War, 1914–1918,* Gill and Macmillan Ltd, 1992

Johnstone, Tom and Hegarty, James, *The Cross on the Sword, Catholic Chaplains in the Forces,* Geoffrey Chapman, 1996

Kearns, Kevin C., *Dublin Tenement Life, An Oral History,* Gill & MacMillan, 2006

Keegan, John, *The First World War,* Pimlico, 1999

Lee, Joe and Orr, Philip, *Field of Bones, The Gallipoli Campaign,* The Lilliput Press, 2006

Lyons, J.B. *The Enigma of Tom Kettle, Irish Patriot, Essayist, Poet, British Soldier, 1880-1916,* The Glendale Press, Dublin, 1983

MacDonald, Lyn, *They called it Passchendaele,* Michael Joseph, 1978

Madigan, Edward, *Faith Under Fire, Anglican Army Chaplains and the Great War,* Palgrave Macmillan, 2011

Middlebrook, Martin, *The First Day on the Somme,* Allen Lane, 1971

Neillands, Robin, *The Old Contemptibles, The British Expeditionary Force 1914,* John Murray, 2004

O'Rahilly, Professor Alfred, *Father William Doyle SJ, A Spiritual Study,* Longmans, Green and Co. 1925

O'Rahilly, Alfred, *Father William Doyle SJ,* Tradibooks, 2009

Palmer, Svetlana and Wallis, Sarah, *A War in Words,* Simon and Schuster, 2003

Raw, David, *It's Only Me, A life of the Reverend Theodore Bayley Hardy, VC, D.S.O., M.C., 1863-1918,* Frank Peters Publishing Ltd., 1988

Rickard, Mrs Victor, *The Story of the Munsters at Etreux-Festubert-Rue du Bois,* Dublin: The New Ireland Publishing Co. Ltd, 1915

Sheldon, Jack, *The German Army at Passchendaele,* Pen & Sword Military, 2007

Snape, Michael, *The Royal Army Chaplains' Department, Clergy Under Fire 1796–1953,* The Boydell Press, 2008

Snelling, Stephen, *VCs of the First World War, Passchendaele 1917*, Sutton Publishing Ltd., 1998

Spurr, Frederic C., *Some Chaplains in Khaki, An Account of the Work of Chaplains of the United Navy and Army Board,* Joseph Johnson Primitive Methodist Publishing House

Staniforth, J.H.M., *At War with the 16th Irish Division 1914–1918, The Staniforth Letters*, edited by Richard S. Grayson, in association with Imperial War Museum, Pen & Sword 2012

Steel, Nigel and Hart, Peter *Passchendaele, The Sacrificial Ground,* Cassel, 2000

Townshend, Charles, *Easter 1916 The Irish Rebellion,* Penguin Books, 2006

Williamson, Howard, *The Great War Collectors Companion*, privately published by Anne Williamson, 2011

In Flanders Field Museum, Ieper
Van Walleghem, Father Achiel, Diary
Smith, Paul, letter dated 16 April 1970 to Dr Caenepeel
Smith, Paul, letter dated 19 May 1970, to Dr Caenepeel
Caenepeel, Doctor, to Paul Smith, 19 May 1970

Blackrock College, Co. Dublin, Professor Alfred O'Rahilly (burnt) Archive
Fletcher, J.S., letter dated 3 April 1920 to Professor O'Rahilly
Fletcher, J.S., letter dated 25 April 1920 to Professor O'Rahilly
Galvin, Daniel J., undated letter circa 1919, to Professor O'Rahilly
Rosario, Mother Nesbitt, letter to Professor O'Rahilly, illegible date

Other
Castles, Fay letter 14/9/2012, private possession
Wrafter, Fr J., S.J., C.F., letter 8/11/1916, Jesuit Archive

WEBSITES
www.dnw.co.uk
www.ancestry.co.uk
www.cwgc.org
www.1914-1918.net
www.westernfrontassociation.com
www.fatherdoyle.com
www.wikipedia.com
www.ewtn.com

POETRY
Owen, Wilfred, *Dulce Et Decorum Est,* Chatto and Windus, 1994
Ryan, Tracy, *Dalkey,* Hothouse, Australian Poetry Library
Yeats, William Butler, *Easter 1916*

Miscellaneous
Dungan, Myles, *Fighting Amnesia*
McMahon, Lt Gen Gerry (retired) typescript of lecture given in Belfast 1999
A Journey of Reconciliation Trust, inaugural document, November 1996

PHOTO CREDITS & PERMISSIONS

I acknowledge with thanks the following:-

The Cumisky family for photos of items in their archive

Andrew Tonge for photos from his collection, including photos of his original trench maps and for drafting the maps of the Western Front

Genevra Charsley for the photo of Albert Basilica annotated by the sender

Charlie and Jackie Hayter for the photo of Philosophe

Paul Reed for the photo of Tower Bridge (www.battlefields1418.com)

Mark Warby, of The Bairnsfather Society, for obtaining permission from Mrs Littlejohn to use a copy of *Old Moore at the Front*.

Blackrock College archives for photos of documents in their archive

Clongowes Wood College for photos of items in their archive

Michael Murtagh for the photo of the memorial window, St Finian's Church, Dromin, Co Louth

National Library of Ireland image refs: 05909, 03980, 08917

In Flanders Field Museum, Ieper for images of Wytschaete, Frezenberg and page of Smith letter

The following kind permissions are separately acknowledged

I have included a full bibliography of sources and references of quotations. Permission has been sought for those that are within copyright and I acknowledge the kind permissions to quote. Every effort was made to contact the heirs of Lt J.F.B. O'Sullivan to quote from his papers held at Imperial War Museum, reference 14337 and also those of David Starrett, IWM reference 6659. I was unable to trace copyright holders for the previously unpublished Smith and Fletcher letters, but the contents support my belief that the writers would have had no objection to the quotes being used. I sincerely apologise to any copyright holders whose copyright I have unwittingly infringed.

In addition, the following kind permissions are separately acknowledged:

The Cumisky family for permission to reproduce typed transcriptions of Fr Doyle's letters and other correspondence

National Archives Open Government Licence for War Office war diaries and copies of Haig diary

PHOTO CREDITS & PERMISSIONS

Extracts from Field Marshall Haig's diary by permission of The National Library of Scotland

In Flanders Field Museum, Ieper, for extracts from Caenepeel and Doyle archives

Blackrock College, Co Dublin for extracts from O'Rahilly archive

Clongowes Wood College, Co Kildare for extracts from Doyle archive

National Army Museum for extracts from the papers of Noel E. Drury, reference 1976-07-69

The National Trust for extracts from: Kipling, Rudyard, *The Irish Guards in the Great War, The First Battalion*

Royal Welch Fusiliers Museum for extracts from: Dunn, Captain James Churchill, *The War the Infantry Knew 1914–1919*

Louise Sutcliffe (having Lasting Power of Attorney for Rosamunde Ann Du Cane, copyright holder) for extracts from the papers of Captain J.H.M. Staniforth, IWM reference 14337

Paddy and Jane Glanville for extracts from the papers of Lt A.E. Glanville, IWM reference 21037

Barry St. John Galvin for permission to use the previously unpublished Galvin correspondence

Rachael Horne for extracts from: Doudney, C.E., *The Best of Good Fellows, The Diaries and Memoirs of The Rev. Charles Edmund Doudney, M.A., C.F. (1871-1915)*, edited by Jonathan Horne

The Lucy family for extracts from: Lucy, John F., *There's a Devil in the Drum*

Lt Gen Gerry McMahon quotes via Michael O'Rahilly

Seamus Breslin for bringing to my attention the letter written by Fr Wrafter dated 8 November 1916

Klett-Cotta for Ernst Jünger *Storm of Steel*

Jünger, Ernst, *Storm of Steel*, translated by Michael Hofmann, Allen Lane, London, 2003, see references and bibliography, reproduced by kind permission of Penguin Books Ltd.

INDEX

Page numbers in italic type refer to illustrations and maps and those with an "n" e.g. 162n3 refer to notes.

Aberdeen, 97
Addison, Rev William Robert Fontaine, 643
advanced dressing stations, 223–4
aeroplanes, 184, 198, 414–16, 442–3, 486–7, 569
Ahern, Dermot, 682
Alacoque, Marguerite Marie, 90
Albert, 368, *368*, 376
altar breads, 485–6
altar servers, 61
Amiens, 315
amusements, 47–8
Anglo-Irish Treaty, 667
Apostleship of Prayer, 80
army chaplains *see* chaplains
Arras, 456–7
Ars-sur-Formans, 90, 91–2
artillery bombardments, 193–4, 198–9, 225, 230–1, 242, 335, 338–9, 391–2, 400–2, 409–12, 425–6, 462–4, 475–6, 496–8, 561–2, 587, 605
    creeping barrage, 491, 605
At Rest in Philosophe (O'Sullivan), 198
Austria-Hungary, 133, 134
awards and medals, 231, 323, 346, 350–1, 357, 382, 541, 633, 650
    Distinguished Service Order (DSO), 641, 661–2n4
    Military Cross, 387–8, 413, 641–2
    see also Victoria Cross (VC)

Bailleul, 371
Bairnsfather, Bruce, 292–4, *293*
balloons, 415–16, 569
Barr, Glen, 680–1
Barry, Tom, 208–9, 281, 665
baths, 187
Belgium, 132, 135–6, 138
Bellingham, Lt Col Edward, 282, 382, 396, 398–9
Bellingham, Sir Henry, 381–2
Belvedere College, Dublin, 79–80, 106–7
Berchmans, John, 104
betrayal, acts of, 604
Bismarck, Otto von, 131
Black and Tans, 666
Blackburne, Rev Harry, 170, 172–3, 187, 192–3
Boer War 1899-1902, 164, 273
Bordon Camp, 158–9, 161–2
bounties, 542
Bourke, Marcus, 68, 69
Bowen, Lt A., 263–4
box respirators, 264, 268, 272n
Bray-sur-Somme, 332
British Army
    battalion routine, 373–4
    battalion strength, 446–7
    camp chapels, 155–6, 158–9

INDEX

camp life, 145–7
conscription, 371
heavy kit, 179, 183, 528, 530, 580
new recruits, 150
reasons for enlisting, 208–9
recruitment problems in Ireland, 151–2, 153
reforms, 140–1
serving Irishmen, 148–9
structure, 147, 148
training, 152–3, 155, 156–7, 448–9, 535
see also chaplains

British Army Formations
  2nd Army, 490, 501–3, 561, 576
  5th Army, 556, 576, 603
  Artillery Brigades, 177th, Royal Field Artillery, 366
  Corps
    I Corps, 204
    II Anzac Corps, 502, 503, 561
    II Corps, 143n3, 561, 603
    IX Corps, 371, 381, 501–2, 503, 561
    X Corps, 501, 503, 561
    XIV Corps, 317, 346, 347, 561
    XIX Corps, 560, 562, 564, 571, 603
    XVIII Corps, 560–1, 603
  Divisions
    4th, 149
    5th, 322, 330, 334–5
    7th, 322, 330
    8th, 609, 618
    10th (Irish), 141, 214–15
    15th (Scottish), 185, 263, 266, 560, 569–70, 618, 621
    16th (Irish), *iv* (plate section), 141, 148, 149, 151, 154, 185, 187, 197, 203, 204, 211, 212, *217*, 260, 262, 265, 269, 285, 295, 311, 313–14, 317, 329, 330, 334–5, 346–7, 356–7, 358, 359, 360–1, 364, 365–6, 371, 381, 385, 490, 492, 501, 502, 518, 520–1, 542, 555, 560, 571, 576, 578, 601, 602, 603, 620–1, 622, 626, 627, 629, 631, 632, 634, 646–7, 648
    19th, 502
    20th, 320, 321, 322, 324, 330
    24th, 317
    30th, 331
    36th (Ulster), 141, 151, 211, 212, 317, 371, 503, 512–13, 560, 564, 579, 602, 603, 623, 626, 633–4, 646
    55th, 560, 561, 562, 564, 575, 579
    56th, 337, 353–4
    59th (North Midland), 276
  Infantry Brigades
    3rd, 196
    33rd, 492, 516
    46th, 570
    47th, 148, 247, 319–20, 321, 322, 325, 327, 330, 333–4, 347, 352–3, 511, 512, 603
    48th, 26, 148, 265, 326, 332, 347, 348, 352, 448, 483, 513, 538, 601, 603, 604–5, 617
    49th, 148, 150–1, 159, 197, 211, 218, 228, 229, 237–8, 259, 328, 332, 334–5, 347, 512, 603
    59th, 322

60th, 320, 322
61st, 322, 330
95th, 335, 343
168th, 352
177th, 276–7
178th, 276, 278

Infantry Regiments
  Black Watch, 9th Bn., 266
  Connaught Rangers, 6th Bn., 303, 320–1, 322, 328, 352, 356, 510, 579, 589, 631
  Duke of Cornwall's Light Infantry, 345
  Duke of York's Light Infantry, 6th Bn., 146–7
  East Surrey, 212
  Hampshire, 11th Bn., 324, 352
  King's (Liverpool), 10th (Scottish) Bn., 650, 651
  King's Own Scottish Borderers, 211–12, 570, 621
  King's Royal Rifle Corps, 10th Bn., 324
  Leinsters
    2nd Bn., 141–2, 317
    3rd Bn., 278
    4th Bn., 278–9
    5th Bn., 278
    7th Bn., 255, 320, 323, 326–8, 352, 356, 511, 631
  Middlesex, 2nd Bn., 618
  Royal Dublin Fusiliers
    2nd Bn., 458, 482–4, 575, 604–5, 606, 607, 610, 611–13, 619
    8th Bn., 262, 350, 381, 386, 396–7, 409–10, 418, 426–7, 432, 434–5, 436, 440, 446, 475, 478–9, 497, 505, 513–14, 516, 519, 520, 528, 529, 530–1, 534–6, 541–3, 569, 574, 578–83, 587–8, 590, 591–2, 601–2, 604–5, 608–11, 613, 617, 619, 622, 626, 627, 650–1
    9th Bn., 347, 348, 350, 351, 588, 601, 604, 606, 609, 611–12, 627
    10th Bn., 278
    cap badge, *149*
  Royal Inniskilling Fusiliers
    7th Bn., 151, 153, 178–9, 182, 190–1, 218–19, 229, 230–2, 246–7, 252, 262, 269–70, 289, 294–5, 306, 332, 344, 347, 360, 367–8, 369, 373–4, 475, 521, 537, 554–5, 559, 569, 626
    8th Bn., 190, 194, 218, 234, 289, 626
  Royal Irish
    2nd Bn., 372
    3rd Bn., 278
    6th Bn., 322, 352
  Royal Irish Fusiliers
    6th Bn., 511
    7/8th Bn., 373
    7th Bn., 150–1, 152, 218, 229–30, 350, 371
    8th Bn., 151, 153–4, 177, 189, 190, 194, 196–7, 228, 234, 238–9, 247, 248, 254, 300–1, 334–5, 341, 342, 343–4, 346, 355, 360, 361, 365–6, 369, 371
    9th Bn., 458
    cap badge, *149*
  Royal Irish Rifles

INDEX

3rd Bn., 278
7th Bn., 263, 327, 350, 601, 604, 606–7, 617
8th Bn., 218, 229–30, 626
9th Bn., 151, 626
Royal Munster Fusiliers
1st Bn., 327, 350, 511, 605
2nd Bn., 165–6
8th Bn., 182–3, 218, 283–4, 322, 352
9th Bn., 247
Royal West Kent, 1st Bn., 139
Sherwood Foresters, 284
South Staffordshire, 279
Other Units
48th Machine Gun Company, 514
250th Tunnelling Company, 456
Royal Engineers, 239, 324, 456, 472, 508, 543, 605
Special Gas Brigade, 268
British Expeditionary Force (BEF), 138–9, 141
British Official History, 139
Bromm, Leutnant Hans, 607–8
Browne, Fr Francis, 168, 389–90, 444, 505, 523, 539–41, 588, 636, 644–5, 649, 657, 686–7, 689–90
burials, 222–3, 225–6, 229, 252, 269, 294, 575
Burke, Tom, 432
Byrne, Elizabeth, 38, 49–50
Byrne, Pte M.B., *x* (plate section), 432

Calvet, Arthur, 120
camouflage, 456
cap badges, *149*

Carey, Pte Joseph, *x* (plate section), 361–5, 638
Carson, Sir Edward, 211, 213, 215
Castles, Fay, 674, 675
casualties, 188, 197, 203, 240–1, 259, 262–3, 284, 317, 346, 356–7, 518, 576, 601, 623, 626–7, 631
Catholic Herald, 164
Catholic News, 658–9, 687–8
Ceremonies of Holy Mass (pamphlet), 120
chaplains
awards and medals, 641, 642–5
camp chapels, 155–6, 158–9
contracts, 173
cooperation with other chaplains, 168
front line activities, 165–7, 307–10, 465
logistics of organising parades and services, 171–2
military titles and ranks, 172–3
noncombatant role, 164–6
numbers, 147–8
pastoral role, 169–70, 192–3
popularity with men, 173–5
training, lack of, 155, 157–8, 191–2
transport problems, 170–1
Charteris, Fr, 154
Chavasse, Capt Noel, 563, 648–56
Chinese Trench, 513–14
Christmas celebrations, 48–9, 393–8, *399*, 400
ciborium, 471, 499
Clayton, Ann, 651, 652–3
Clongowes Wood College, 66, 67–9, 71
Clongownian, The (college magazine), 73, *73*, 658–9, 687–8

commuting, 40
conscription, 371
Coogan, Tim Pat, 275, 284
Coop, Rev J.O., 561–2
Cooper, Maj Bryan, 209, 213
'corpse factory,' 532–3
Corrigan, Gordon, 637, 638
Cosgrave, W.T., 671
courts-martial, 362–3, 421, 531, 534
Cowley, Major, 601, 608, 610–12, 623
Cranbush, Fanny, 100, 697–9
creeping barrage, 491, 605
Crosse, A.E., 157
'crumps' (shells), 391, 401
Cullen, Fr James, 80–1, 547
Curragh Incident, 210

Dael, Denise, 681
Daily Chronicle, 323, 657–8
Daily Telegraph, 657–8
Dalkey, 30, 34–6, *35*, 279
    Castle Street, 36, *37*
    churches, 37
    coastline, *47*
    Dalkey Avenue, 36, 40
    poem, 44
    traders, 36, 41
Dalton, Lt Emmet, 279–80, 350–1
Daly, Fr Jimmy, 70
Davidson, Lt Col F.R., 650
Davidson, Randall (Archbishop of Canterbury), 164
Denman, Terence, 262
Derby, Lord, 654–5
Devitt, Fr Matthew, 71

Dillon, John, 214
Distinguished Service Order (DSO), 641, 661–2n4
dogfights (air battles), 184, 442–3, 486–7
Doudney, Rev Charles, 171
Doyle, Angelina (Lena), 38, 76–7, *77*, 198, 291–2, 393, 478, 533–4, 665, 675
Doyle, Charles, 31, 32–3, 38, 45, 50, 116, 379, 433, 621, 627, 629, 675, 690–1, 697, 698
    becomes Jesuit novice, 59, 62
    first Mass, 84–5
    memories of schoolteachers, 54–5
    relationship with Willie, 45
Doyle, Christina Mary, 31, 38, 51, 54, 61, 129
    anniversary of death, 201
    death, 125
    fiftieth wedding anniversary, 87, *88*
Doyle, Elizabeth (Lil), 38, 58–9, 125, 420, 675
Doyle, Frederick Timothy, 37, 38, 45, 59, 61
Doyle, Hugh, 37, 50–1, 54, 81, 129, 379, 383, 472–3, 533–4, 666
    assistance to poor, 33–4
    birthday, 565
    death, 669
    employment, 279, 454
    as a father, 38, 46
    fiftieth wedding anniversary, 87, *88*
    retirement, 667–8
    telegrams about William's death, 627
Doyle, Mary (Mai), 38, 45, 84–5, 87, 291–2, 294, 305, 379, 386–7, 430–1, 675

Doyle, Robert, 38, 39, 45, 252–3, 669–70, 674, 675, 677
Doyle, Sil, 33, 45, 46, 48, 383–4
Doyle, William, *xiii* (plate section), *11*, *53*, *88*, *96*, 202–3, *286*, 566, 591–2, 618–19
   aeroplanes, fascination with, 442–3, 486–7, 569
   and alcohol, 81
   ambition to be a martyr, 145
   appointed as army chaplain 4th class, 144
   aspirations, 114, 117, 160, 406
   awarded Military Cross, 387–8, 413, 641
   awarded Parchment of Merit 1916, *xiii* (plate section), 257
   awards and medals, *ii* (plate section), 669
   Battle of the Fosse incident, 56
   beatification, 676–7
   birth, 30–1
   blessings, 111–12
   burials, 222–3, 225–6, 229, 252, 294, 380
   challenges superiors, 83–4
   change of culture as an army chaplain, 145–6
   chased by bull, 32–3
   Christmas 1916, 394–8, 400
   Christmas parcels, 393–4
   chronology of life, 19–21
   confessions, 167, 202, 395, 414, 476–7, 578, 580
   Congo Mission, 82, 94, 96–7, 106
   conversions, 474, 566
   'corpse factory' sighting, 531–2
   cycles close to German trenches, 298–300
   death, *i* (plate section), 26, 613, 615–16
      certificate from George V, *xiv* (plate section)
      compensation, 630
      location of, 616–17, 618–19
      remains, 620–2
      reports of, 619–20, 623, 624n1
      telegrams, 627, *628*
      time and date of, 617–18, 619
   depression, 117–18
   describes destruction of Loos, 221–2
   describes sight of many battlefield dead, 340–1, 375, 425
   devoutness, 60–1, 104, 155–6, 386–7
   diary, 402–4, 408–15, 416–18, 419–21, 422–6, 427–31, 436–9
      barber anecdote, 441
      destruction of Noeux-Les-Mines church, 470–1
      guardian angel, 444–5
      name for, 388–9
      Our Lady of Victories statue, 461–2, 469, *470*
      sand-bag hut destroyed, 443–4
      shells, 390–3
      thoughts on French clergy and religion, 459, 460–1
   education, 45, 54–9
   at Enghien, Belgium, 74–6
   escapes injury from shell fragment, 430
   executions, 361, 365
   Fanny Cranbush, 100, 697–9

favours attributed to intercession of, 672–3
gas attacks, 243–4, 245, 246, 251–2, 253–5, 287, 589, 590
General Absolution, 203, 338, 438–9, 591–2
grave, location of, 670–1, 681
guardian angel, 552–3
hardships of military life, 195
health problems, 42, 59, 64, 66, 75–6, 85
helping the poor, 33–4, 41, 51, 52, 60, 81
helps young people with vocations, 120–1
humility, thoughts on, 82–3
humorous anecdotes, 207, 228, 236–7, 404, 424, 537–8
as a Jesuit missionary, 107–11
as a Jesuit novice, 60–5
joins Royal Irish Fusiliers 8th Bn., 153–4
kindness to servants, 50–1
lack of regard for own safety, 174–5, 515–16, 691
learns to swim, 46
on leave, 286–90, 380–1, 433–4
leaves Loos for the Somme, 313–16
letter to *Irish Catholic*, 488
Long Retreat, 94–6
love of Ireland, 78–9, 273
love of plants, 45–6
under machine gun fire, 416–17
marches, 179–80, 450–2, 453, 454, 460, 529–30, 571–2, 573–4, 580

memorials to, *iii* (plate section), *xv* (plate section), 27, 622, 665, 670–1
mentions in dispatches, 272, 388, 640
Messines, Battle of
 build up to, 494–6, 505–6, 507
 digging out buried men, 514
 feast of Corpus Christi, 517–18
 helps prisoners of war, 513
 mine explosions, 509–10
 zero hour, 511–12
Mikado, The, *iv* (plate section), 72–3, *72*
mortification and suffering, 112–14, 116
mother's death, 125
moves to the front line, 176–82, 183–5
musical interests, 45, 55
nightingales, 545
ordination and first Mass, 64, 85–6, *86*
pamphlets about, 672–4
personal qualities, 26–7, 69–70, 77–8
popularity with men, 174–5
postcards home, *ix* (plate section), 156, 183, 311–12, 370, 478
practical joke, 536
prayer card, 673, *678*
prayers, 65, 85–6, 95, 112–13, 500, 506
preaches at St Omer Cathedral, 538–41, 615
prefect at Clongowes, 69–70, 71–4, 79
raids, description of, 479–82
Ratcliffe College, Leicestershire, 45–6, 54–9, 81
recommended for VC, 633, 636–8, 639–40, 661n4
relationship with Charlie, 45, 84–5

relationships with schoolteachers, 54–5
relics, 677–8, *677*
retreats, 117, 122–3, 124, 125–6
roast duck incident, 57–8
saying Mass, 90, 126, 160, 161, 172,
   194, 202–3, 222, 241, 333, 375,
   428–9, 485, 566, 586, 590–1
self-denial, 115–16
shelling, descriptions of, 193–4, 225,
   243, 290–1, 338–9, 391–2, 400–2,
   409–12, 462–4, 476–7, 495–6, 499,
   519, 587, 593–4, 595
Sloper (nickname), 31, 33
Somme experiences, 328–9
   3rd-5th September 1916, 332–3, 334,
      335, 337–42
   6th-7th September 1916, 342, 345–6
   9th-10th September 1916, 346–7,
      348–9, 354–6
sporting interests, 56
at St Mary's Hall, Stoneyhurst,
   Blackburn, 76–9
stilts and policeman incident, 40–1
strain of life at the front, 233, 240,
   306–7, 437–8
sympathy letter to Lena, 76–7, *77*
teacher at Belvedere College, 80–1
temperance movement, 80–1
tending to the dying, 417–18, 518,
   588–90, 590–1, 619–20
tertianship, 87, 97–104
theological studies, 81–2
time out of the line, 449–50, 468, 468–9
travelling and pilgrimages, 88–93
trench life, descriptions of, 307–10,
   437, 552–4, 564
tributes to, 623–4, 649, 651, 656–9,
   686–96
vacation 1912, 123–4
on vocations, 551
volunteers as military chaplain, 125,
   128
will, 629–30
Ypres, Third battle of, 565–6
   desolation of Ypres, 572–3
   dressing station, description of,
      586–7
   escapes injury from a shell, 593–4
   front line conditions, 584–5
   hides in shell crater, 581
   last letter home, 595–6, *596*
   march to front line, 571–2, 573–4, 580
   religious parable, 566–8
dressing stations, 586–7
Drogheda Independent, The, 274
drunkenness, 147, 424
Drury, Capt Noel, 280, 483
Dublin, 80, 211–12, 244–5, 395, 421,
   666–7
Dublin Evening Post, 30–1, 41, 42
duds (shells), 412, 429, 553
dug-outs, 201, 218, 235, 307–8, 383, 389,
   421, 494–5
Dundalk, 664–5
Dundalk Democrat, 382
Dungan, Myles, 356, 680, 682
Dunn, Capt J.C., 247–8, 270, 532–3

Easter Rising 1916, 244–5, 253, 273,
   274–84

Edmonds, Brig Gen Sir James E., 268–9
Empey, Arthur Guy, 264, 267
Europe
　alliances, 131–2
　arms race, 132
　build-up to war, 134–5
executions, 278, 282, 284, 361–5, 638

Falkenhayn, Erich von, 316–17
Father William Doyle, S.J., A Spiritual Study (O'Rahilly), 665, 670, 682, 691–2
Field Ambulance service, 223–4
field service communion sets, 161
Feilding, Lt Col Rowland, 328, 352–3, 356, 370, 491, 510–11, 516, 520, 521–2, 524–5, 526, 530, 533, 631–2, 647
Fitzgerald, Lt Michael, 280–1
fleas, 236
Fletcher, J.S., 659–60
'Flying Pigs' (shells), 390–1, 401, 409, 412
Flynn, Sgt T., 658, 689
foot inspections, 455
Forstner, Oberstleutnant Freiherr von, 561
fox hunting, 58
France, 129, 131–2, 135, 137
Franco-Prussian War 1870, 129
Franco-Russian pact 1893, 131–2
Franz Ferdinand, Archduke, 133
Frezenberg, 590, *591*, *613*, 620–1, *666*
Friend, Maj Gen L.B., 279
friendly fire incidents, 342, 348
Furrow, The, 676

Gallipoli, 214–15

Galvin, Capt Barry, 300–1, 305, 421, 633–4, 663–4, 672
Galvin, Lt Daniel, 305, 626, 651, 657, 664, 665, 669, 691–2, *692*, *693*
gambling, 58
gas, 187, 188, 239, 241–2, 243–4, 245, 246, 247–8, 249, 250–6, 267–8, 270, 287, 589, 590
gas helmets, *258*, 260–2, 263–7, 268–9, 272n
George V, 641, 648, 649, 654, 668
German Army
　casualties, 259, 263
　Armies, Fourth Army, 558, 561
　Divisions, Bavarian 4th Infantry, 218, 247, 248
　Infantry Regiments
　　3rd (Bavarian), 508
　　5th Bavarian, 260
　　5th (Bavarian) Reserve, 247
　　9th (Bavarian), 248
　　40th (Saxon), 508
　　73rd Hanoverian Fusiliers, 319
German defences, 558
German Triple Alliance, 132
Gibbon, Monk, 275–6, 283
Gibbs, Sir Philip, 512, 620, 627, 657–8
Gill, Fr Henry, 167
Gillard, John, 67
Ginchy (Somme), 329, 330, *331*, 346–56, *349*, 358
Ginhac, Fr Paul, 120, 403, 549–50
Glanville, Capt Arthur, 467, 483, 484, 510, 520, 521, 577, 604, 607, 611–12, 623
Glasgow Weekly News, 26, 658

INDEX

Gleeson, Fr Francis, 165–6, 173
Godley, Gen Sir Alex, 214, 526–7
Gordon, Gen Hamilton, 520–1
Gough, Lt Gen Hubert, 210, 556, 602, 626, 646, 662n5
Great Yarmouth, 98–100
Green, 2/Lt Arthur Vivian, 476, 535, 612, 613, 617, 622
Gridiron (trench system), 323
Guardian, 681
guides, 319, 320, 336–8
Guillemont (Somme), 317–28, *318*, 319, 330, *331*
Guinness Brewery, 123
Gwynn, Capt Stephen, 206

Habenstein, Pte Frederick, 259–60
Haig, Gen Sir Douglas, 268, 557, 626, 641, 646–7
Haldane, Lt Gen Aylmer, 632
Hall, 2nd Lt J.H., 182–3
Hall, Donal, 664
Hampshire, HMS, 215
Hanaphy, May, 275, 277
Handley, CSM John, 576
Happy Valley (Somme), 332–3, *333*
Hardy, Rev Theodore Bayley, 174, 643–4, 661n3
Hart, Peter, 137
Harte, Paddy, 680–1
Hayes, L Cpl D., *x* (plate section), 523
Healy, Capt C.F., 515, 621, 624n1, 669, 690–1
Hell Fire Corner, 578
Hibernian Magazine, 67

Hickie, Maj Gen William Bernard, *v–ix* (plate section), *xii* (plate section), 257, 260, 321, 363, 385, 501, 619, 622, 624, 632–3, 636, 637–8, 640, 647, 656–7, 659, 666, 667, 668, 670, 675–6, 684–5, 690
Hillery, Dr Patrick, 679
Hindenberg Line, 359, 631
Hitchcock, Capt F.C., 141–2
Holland, Lt John Vincent, 323, 326
Holy Hour, 121–2
Home Rule Bill, 210, 211
horses, 170–1, 204, 306, 459–60, 531
Hughes, Pte Tom, 323
Hulluch, 204, *217*
Hunt, Capt John Patrick, 351

Ignatius of Loyola, St, 62, 65n, 568
Illustrated London News, 39
IRA, 663, 665, 667
Ireland
 food shortages, 472–3
 memorials to war dead, 664–5, 671–2, 675, 679
 political troubles, 209–13, 244–5, 663, 664, 666–7, 668–9
 remembrance services, 679–80
 see also Easter Rising 1916
Irish Catholic, 488
Irish Independent, 274
Irish Messenger, *xi* (plate section), 670, 672–3
Irish News, 658, 689
Irish Times, The, 26, 129, 134, 135, 210, 211, 212–13, 274, 347, 520

Irish Volunteers, 211–12
Island of Ireland Peace Park, 681–2

Jagger, Fr J., 77–8
Jeffreys, Lt Col R.G.B., 577–8, 597n2
Jesuits *see* Society of Jesus
Jeudwine, Maj Gen, 653–4
Johnstone, Tom, 197–8, 250, 334–5, 356–7, 647–8
Journey of Reconciliation Trust, A (commemorative organisation), 680–1
Joyce, James, 70
Jünger, Ernst, 319

Kays, Horace Frances, *v–ix* (plate section), 19, 660n1, 684–5
Kearns, Kevin C., 275
Keeling, Frederic (Ben), 146–7, 156–7
Kelly, Fr Edmund, 527
Kelly, L Cpl Christopher, 522
Kemmel Chateau, 367, 374
Kemmelberg, 373
Kennedy, Rev Geoffrey Studdert, 173–4
Kenney, Fr Peter, 67, 68
Kenny, Maj G.W., 484, 534
Kenny, Pat, 682
Kenny, Fr Timothy, 61–2, 64
Kettle, Lt Tom, 351, 378
Kiernan, Lt F.M., 516, 601, 624n1, 658–9, 661n4, 687–8
Kiggell, Lt Gen L.E., 266
Kipling, Rudyard, 185, 189
Kitchener, Horatio Herbert, Baron Kitchener of Khartoum, 140–1, 214–15
Kluck, Gen Alexander von, 140

Labré, St John Baptist, 469, 489
Laird, 2/Lt Frank, 212, 369–70, 371, 415, 444, 447–8, 457, 484, 496, 501, 503, 519–20, 593, 634
   barber anecdote, 442
   CSM Tait, 514–15
   dead Germans, 532
   desire to enlist, 208
   Easter Rising 1916, 274–5
   grenade course, 457–8
   Locre convent, 384–5
   memoirs, 597n4
   memories of Fr Doyle, 174–5
   mine explosions at Messines, 508–9
   night before Battle of Messines, 505, 507
   rum ration, 427
   shell fire, 475–6, 499–500
   sports competition, 467
   Thompson brothers, 400
   trenches, 440
   weather conditions, 407–8
   working parties, 472, 473–4
   young officers' course, 476
Langemarck, Battle of, 26, 602, 625, 626, 634, 651
   see also Ypres, Third battle of
Le Cateau, 141, 143n3
Lenox-Conyngham, Lt Col J.S.M., 326
Leonard, Rev Pat, 169, 170, 172, 267–8
Leuze Wood (Somme), 336, *336*, 340, 341–6
Leveson-Gower, Brig Gen, 360–1
lice, 294
Liverpool Echo, 623

INDEX

Locre, 369–70, 467
  convent, 383–5, *384*, 527–8, 621–2
Logue, Michael (Cardinal), 164
London Gazette, The, 144, 382, 642, 643, 645, 648–9
Long Retreat, 94–6
Loos
  Calvary of Loos, 227
  destruction of, 221–2, *234*
  Double Crassier, *186*, 189
  Tower Bridge, 206, *207*
Loos, Battle of, 187–8, 222
Lossberg, Colonel von, 558
Lucy, Denis, 139, 141, 674
Lucy, John, 137, 138, 139–40, 141, 149–50, 208, 210, 213, 265, 282, 363–4, 533, 558–9, 672, 674, 677
Lusitania, 215
Lutyens, Sir Edwin, 671, 672
Lynch, Pte D., 254
Lyon, Lt Wallace, 269, 326–7

McAleese, Mary, 681
McCormack, John Francis, 223–4
McGilchrist, Maj A.M., 651
McGrath, Fr Ted, 640–1, 643
McInespie, Pte, 615–16
Mackenzie, G.E., 604
McMahon, Gerry, 676, 679, 681
Mahoney, Pte J., 542–3
Man After God's Own Heart, A: Life of Father Paul Ginhac S.J. (Calvet), 120
marches, 179–80, 446–7, 450–2, 453, 454, 460, 528–30, 571–2, 573–4, 580
Marlow, 2/Lt Charles Dwyer, 386, 498, 583, 601, 612, 613, 617, 622
Mass cards, *86*
Mauretania, 215
Maxwell, Weldon and Co (solicitors), 629, 630
May, Col H.A.R., 192
Mazingarbe, 194, 287–8
Meagher, Thomas Francis, 68
medals *see* awards and medals
medical services, 223–4
Mellish, Rev Edward Noel, 642, 644, 660–1n2
Melrose, 30, 31, *31*, 38, *286*
Merry in God (C. Doyle), 697, 698
Messines, Battle of, 484, *517*, 557
  battle plan, 503
  bite and hold tactics, 492–3
  bombardment, 496–8, 504
  casualties, 518
  desolation after battle, 521–2
  evening before battle, 505–7
  maps, *502*
  mines, 492, 507–10, 512, 523n2
  model of German defences, 490–2
  zero hour, 511–12
Mikado, The, 72–3, *72*
Military Cross, 387–8, 413, 641–2
Milltown Park, Dublin, 81
mine warfare, 188–9, 229, 238–9, 302–3, 456, 492, 507–10, 523n2
Mons, 138, 139–40
monstrance, 121, 127n1
Moore, Sgt Louis, 166
Mud, Blood and Poppycock (Corrigan), 637

Munroe, Gen Sir Charles, 196

Newman Richard, 366
Nicholas II, Tsar, 133–4
Nicholson, Maj Gen O.H.D., 265
Noeux-les-Mines, 194, 216, 306, 461–2, 469, 470–1, *470*
nose caps (shells), 423
Nulty, Pte F., 281

Official History of the War, 262
'Old Bill,' 292–4, *293*
O'Malley, Ernie, 277, 282–3
Operation Gericht, 317
O'Rahilly, Alfred, 114, 125, 257, 305, 406, 524, 536, 539, 615, 616, 619–20, 624n1, 636, 637, 659–60, 665, 667, 670, 672, 676–7, 691–2, 694
O'Reilly, John Boyle, 546, 555n
O'Sullivan, 2nd Lt J.F.B., 198, 200, 303, 320–1, 322–3, 326
Owtram, Capt Thomas, 562, 652

Paray-le-Monial, 89–90
Pas de Calais, 524–43
map, *447*
Passchendaele, Battle of, 629, 630–1, 647
Peace Tower, Messines, 681
'Penny On' (game), 50–1
'Penny Torture,' 50
Petit, Père Adolphus, 105
Philosophe, 190–1, *190*
pill boxes, 558
Pioneer Total Abstinence Association of the Sacred Heart, 80–1

Plater, Fr Charles, 78
Plumer, Gen Sir Herbert, 490, 492, 509, 511, 629, 663
pocket money, 49, 50–1
Portrait of the Artist as a Young Man (Joyce), 70
poverty, 33–4, 41
Power, Fr Matthew, 97–8
Princip, Gavrilo, 133
prisoners of war, 259–60, 303, 325–6, 350, 482, 513, 520, 563–4, 633–4
punishments, 531, 534
   see also executions
pyx, 245–6

Quadrilateral, The (Somme), 336, 346, 352–4
Quintuple Treaty of London, 138
Quo Vadis (film), 114–15

raids, 300–1, 412, 479–83
railways, 35, 39, 42–3n1
travel to the front, 177–9
Ratcliffe College, Leicestershire, 45–6, 54–9, 81
rats, 220, 221, 225, 226, 238, 308, 310, 314, 375, 393, 437
Redmond, John, 212, 213, 215, 525
Redmond, Maj William, *xii* (plate section), 523, 524–7
regimental aid posts (RAPs), 223
Remembering Father William Doyle (website), 682
reports, 258–9, 263
Retreats for Workingmen: Why not in

Ireland, 107, 122–3
Rickard, Mrs Victor, 165
Roberts, Fr Stanislaus, 100–3
Robinson, Mary, 679–80
Rokeby, Miss, 56–7
Room, Acting L Cpl Frederick, 645–6, 647–8
Rossignol Estaminet, 495–6, 497
Royal Navy, 132
   navy, 133
Rudkin, Major, 261
rum, 424, 427
'rum jars' (shells), 391, 401, 442
Russia, 131–2, 137
Ryan, Canon Arthur, 397–8
Ryan, Tracy, 44

Sacred Heart Messenger, The, 547
Schlieffen Plan, 135, 136–7, *136*, 142–3n2
   navy, 132
   unification, 129
Serbia, 133–4
servants, 51–2
Shall I be a Priest (pamphlet), 119–20, 547
Sheffield, 58–9
Sheldon, Jack, 504
'shell scandal,' 215, 412
shell-shock, 594
shells, 390–1, 401–2
Sheridan, Thomas B., 615
signalling, 343
Sinn Féin, 274, 663
Sloper, Ally (comic paper character), 31–2
Smith, Paul, 677–9, 693–4, 693–6, *695*

Smyth, Kevin, 676
Snelling, Stephen, 648
snipers, 228, 343
Society of Jesus, 62–3, 67, 68, 80
Society of the Sacred Heart, 101
Some Chaplains in Khaki (Spurr), 145–6
Somme, Battle of the, 294, 295
   3rd-5th September 1916, 332–42
   6th-7th September 1916, 342–6
   9th-10th September 1916, 346–56
   casualties, 356–7
   first day, 317
   Ginchy, 329, 330, *331*, 346–56, *349*, 358
   Guillemont, 317–28, *318*, 330, *331*
   Happy Valley, 332–3, *333*
   Leuze Wood, 336, *336*, 340, 341–6
   maps, *331*, *336*
   plans for, 316–17
   Quadrilateral, The, 336, 346, 352–4
   sunken road, *325*
souvenirs, 520
SP13, 457, 505
Spectator, 26
Spurr, Frederic C., 145–6, 168
St Mary's Hall, Stoneyhurst, Blackburn, 76–9
St Omer, 460
   cathedral, *x* (plate section), 538–41
St Patrick's Day, 196–7, 206, 435
St Stanislaus' College, Tullabeg, 59, 60
St Vincent de Paul Society, 34, 383
Staniforth, Capt J.H.M., 200–1, 247, 255–6, 262, 269, 323–4, 353, 356, 528–9, 577, 590, 597n1

Stapleton, Michael, 80
Starret, David, 151
Stations of the Cross, 116
Steinhauer, Gustav, 130–1, 133
Stirke, Lt Col H.R., 534, 620, 624n1, 688
Süssenberger, Reserve Oberleutnant, 602–3
Synopsis of the Rubrics (pamphlet), 120

Tablet, The, 164–5
Tait, CSM, 514–15
tanks, 358, 510, 537–8, 570, *628*
telephone cables, 472
temperance movement, 80–1
Tenth Avenue (trench), 197, 218, 232
Tenth (Irish) Division in Gallipoli, The (Cooper), 213
Thompson, Lt Col A.C., 400, 484, 493, 535
Thompson, Maj F.S., 400, 484
Times, The, 26, 532, 575
traffic control, 529, 543n
transubstantiation, 127n1, 155
trenches
  conditions, 197, 201, 237, 260, 389, 437, 440, 564
  description of trench system, 235
  dug-outs, 201, 218, 235, 307–8, 383, 389, 421, 494–5
  maps, *455*, *613*
  mud, 383
  routine, 199–200, 229
  shift rotations, 196, 197–8
  training, 196
  trench boards, 238
  see also rats
Tronchiennes, Belgium, 87, 88, 93–4
Tunnel Trench, 631–2
Tyne Cot, Memorial to the Missing, *xv* (plate section), 622, 670–1

Ulster Volunteer Force (UVF), 211

Verdun, 317, 359
Versailles, Treaty of, 663
Vianney, Jean Baptiste, 90, 91, 105n3
Victoria Cross (VC), 15, 317, 323, 357, 633
  Addison, Rev William Robert Fontaine, 643
  Army Form W3121, 639–40
  chaplain VCs, 642–5
  Chavasse, Capt Noel, 648–56
  criteria for award of, 638–9
  Doyle, William
    justification for award of, 644–5, 646, 649, 650–1, 656–60
    recommendation for, 633, 636–8, 639–40
  Hardy, Rev Theodore Bayley, 643–4, 661n3
  McGrath, Fr Ted, 643
  Mellish, Rev Edward Noel, 642, 644, 660–1n2
  role of George V, 641
  Room, Acting L Cpl Frederick, 645–6
  witness testimony, 640–1, 644–5
Vocations (pamphlet), 119, 546–8

Walker, G.A. Cooper, 153, 528

INDEX

Walleghem, Fr Achiel Van, 622
Walsh, Fr J., 124
washing facilities, 431
Watkins, Capt, 324–5
Watson, Lt Col S.T., 250, 256–7, 258, 262, 300–1, 355, 371
Watt, Charles Cumming, 418–19
'Weary Willie,' 391
weather conditions, 182, 189–90, 191, 339, 407–8, 424, 426–8, 440, 446, 556, 559–60, 562, 574–5, 629
Weld, Lt Charles., 256, 327
Whelan, Frank, 58–9, 419–20
'whiz-bangs' (shells), 391, 401
Wilhelm II, Kaiser, 129–31, 132, 133–4
Williamson, Howard, 641–2
Witherow, Lt T., 512–13
Witley Camp, 153, 156–7
Wolff, Leon, 372–3
'Woodbine Willie,' 173–4
workhouses, 41–2
working parties, 472, 473–4, 521, 575, 579
Wrafter, Fr, 325, 379
Wytschaete, *517*, 522

Ypres, First Battle of, 141
Ypres Salient
　description of front line sector, 369, 370, 372–3
　peaceful nature of, 366–8, 370, 372
Ypres, Third battle of, 543
　arrangement of troops, 560–1
　artillery bombardments, 561–2
　attack of 16th August 1917, 625–6
　Composite Company, 8th Royal Dublin Fusiliers, 608–11
　dispositions of 48th Infantry Brigade, 604–5
　German testimony, 607–8
　overall picture, 602–4
　situation on left of 48th Infantry Brigade, 606
　situation on right of 48th Infantry Brigade, 606–7
　zero hour, 605–6
　attack on 31 July 1917, 559–60, 561–4, 569–71
　casualties, 576, 623, 626–7, 631
　maps, *560, 582, 613*
　objectives, 562
　Passchendaele, Battle of, 629, 647
　weather conditions, 562, 569, 574–5, 629
Ypres (town), 141–2, 370, 572–3, *573*

zeppelins, 380